ISBN 978-0-428-68643-7
PIBN 11303510

FORT WAYNE CITY

AND

ALLEN COUNTY

DIRECTORY

1891-92.

pt. 1

CONTAINING

AN ALPHABETICALLY ARRANGED LIST OF BUSINESS FIRMS AND PRIVATE
CITIZENS IN FORT WAYNE—A MISCELLANEOUS DIRECTORY OF CITY AND
COUNTY OFFICERS, PUBLIC AND PRIVATE SCHOOLS, CHURCHES,
BANKS, INCORPORATED INSTITUTIONS, SECRET AND BENEV-
OLENT SOCIETIES, ETC., ETC.—A CLASSIFIED LIST
OF ALL TRADES, PROFESSIONS AND PUR-
SUITS—A FARMERS' DIRECTORY
OF ALLEN COUNTY.

SOLD ONLY BY SUBSCRIPTION.

VOLUME XIV.

R. L. POLK & CO., PUBLISHERS,

40 TO 44 LARNED STREET WEST, DETROIT, MICH.

For List of Publications, see Page 12.

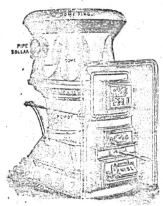

INTRODUCTORY.

THE fourteenth volume of the FORT WAYNE AND ALLEN COUNTY DIRECTORY is submitted to a discriminating public by the publishers, with a feeling of confidence that their efforts to make each succeeding volume the best have been successful. Devoting their attention exclusively to the publication of works of this class, their practical experience and facilities enable them to perform the work promptly and accurately, and a comparison with any other directory will prove that in typographical appearance the work is not inferior to similar publications in any of the large cities.

The first 58 pages are devoted to useful miscellaneous information relating to the city and county in general, comprising a street and avenue guide, ward boundaries, lists of city and county officers, fire and police departments, federal officers, courts, banks, building, loan and savings associations, cemeteries, churches, incorporated institutions, libraries, miscellaneous institutions and societies, newspapers, parks, postoffice, public buildings and halls, public schools, miscellaneous schools, secret and benevolent societies, etc. Succeeding these are 492 pages containing an alphabetically arranged directory of all the inhabitants of the city, followed by 74 pages containing a list of all persons engaged in business or the professions, classified under their respective callings. The remaining pages contain name, number of section, number of acres, assessed valuation of same, name of township and postoffice address of all farmers, etc., in Allen County. This compilation shows that there are 17,982 adult names represented in Fort Wayne, which, with the multiplier of 3 persons to each directory name — the lowest used in any city in the United States — gives a present population of 53,946.

This volume goes forth among its patrons with the appreciation and thanks of its publishers for the support and encouragement accorded the enterprise. The fifteenth volume will be issued in due time.

GENERAL INDEX.

	PAGE		PAGE
Abbreviations	59–625	Federal Officers	30
Alphabetical List of Names—		Fire Department	26
County	625–780	Incorporated Institutions	37–40
Alphabetical List of Names—		Libraries	40
Fort Wayne	59–550	Military	40
Bands of Music	31	Miscellaneous Institutions	40–45
Banks	31	Miscellaneous Schools	51
Board of Health	26	Newspapers	45–46
Board of School Trustees	32	Parks	46
Board of Police Commissioners	25	Police Department	28
Building, Loan and Savings		Postoffice	46–48
Associations	32	Public Buildings, Halls, etc.	48–50
Cemeteries	33	Public Schools	52–55
Churches	34–37	Railroads	50
City Government	25	Rates of Fare	28
City Officers	25	Secret and Benevolent Socie-	
Classified Business Directory		ties	55–58
	551–624	Street Railroads	29
Colleges	51	Streets and Avenues	13–24
Council	26	Teachers in Public Schools	52–55
County Directory	625–780	Telegraph and Telephone Com-	
County Officers	30	panies	58
Courts	30	Township Trustees	31
Farmers' Directory — Allen		Ward Boundaries	25
County	625–780	Water Works Trustees	26

INDEX TO ADVERTISEMENTS.

	PAGE		PAGE
Allen Albert S	61	Chicago, Milwaukee & St Paul	
Argo & Buck	back cover	Ry, Chicago, Ill	786
Atchison, Topeka & Santa Fe R		Chicago & Grand Trunk Ry	11
R, Topeka, Kas	782	City Carriage Works	
Banister Mrs L Webb	65		right bottom lines
Beach F J	left bottom lines	Correspondence School of Law,	
Berghoff Herman Brewing Co		Detroit, Mich	right side lines
The	back cover	Curtice J F	front cover and 63
Berndt Charles A	6	Dennison Mnfg Co, Boston,	
Binkley F C	8	Mass	backbone and 781
Bley George W	67	Diether L & Bro	right top lines
Boltz Fred C	2	Dornbush & Kirchefer	67
Bowman Charles	left top lines	Dunne K H	right bottom lines
Bowser S F & Co	right side lines	Ehle Ernest A	67
Brames L & Co	3	Everett Charles E	front cover
Carter & Son	bottom edge and 7	Fairbank C	left top lines
Centlivre C L Brewing Co		Ferguson & Palmer	backbone
	left bottom lines	and line at end of each alpha-	
Chicago, Burlington & Quincy			betical letter
R R, Chicago, Ill	785	Fleming Mnfg Co, right bottom lines

542

PAGE

Fletcher J F.................. 69
Fortriede L.........right top lines
Foster A............left top lines
Geake W & J J....left bottom lines
Geiss Louis J.................. 146
Gerding & Aumann Bros...... •
       top edge and 63
Gospel Tidings...right bottom lines
Grand Rapids & Indiana R R,
   Grand Rapids, Mich........ 787
Hail & Tower....right bottom lines
Hattersley A & Sons..line front cover
Hayden & Grier ...left bottom lines
Hull L O............right top lines
Hull S W ....right bottom lines
Jaap George..................
     left bottom lines and 569
Jenne C R.................. 65
Johnson George E...right top lines
Jones F L & Co....left bottom lines
Kaag M F ....left bottom lines
Keller & Braun.. 6
Lauer John & Peter.......... 67
Lunz John V 7
McDermut Wilson E.......... 8
Madden James .....right side lines
Mariotte Horace........63 and 351
Moellering Wm..front edge and 5
Niswonger G D.............. 69
Ogden Robert.. ....
    line back cover and 607

PAGE

Old National Bank..front cover and 4
Pape Furniture Co............
      right bottom lines
Peltier J C.................... 401
Perrin A C............... ... 73
Peters Box and Lumber Co
   The...........right bottom lines
Pfeiffer & Schlatter..right top lines
Phillips S P.................. 71
Polk R L & Co............. .. 12
Pratt & Kintz.............. 69
Pressler John.........left top lines
Riedel John M E.......front cover
Romy Robert L..back cover and · 4
Russell C M..... 69
Ryan Trucking Co.. right top lines
Scherzinger G................ 61
Schroeder A H.............. 73
Siemon & Brother.......back cover
Smith Mrs I M............... 65
Spice Robert......... left top lines
Storm J A M.......right top lines
Toledo, St Louis & Kansas City
  R R, Toledo, O............ 783
Troy Steam Laundry.........
     left bottom lines
Wah-Kee & Co............. 65
Wheeler A R....right bottom lines
Wing & Mahurin.....left top lines
Wisconsin Central Lines, Chica-
  go, Ill.................... . 784

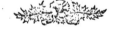

R. L. POLK, President.   A. C. DANSER, Vice-President.   J. W. WEEKS, Sec'y and Treasurer.

INCORPORATED 1885.

ESTABLISHED 1870.

R. L. POLK & CO.

GAZETTEER AND DIRECTORY

PUBLISHERS.

PUBLISHERS OF GAZETTEERS AND BUSINESS DIRECTORIES

FOR THE STATES OF

MICHIGAN,	WEST VIRGINIA,	CALIFORNIA,
ILLINOIS,	KENTUCKY,	WASHINGTON,
PENNSYLVANIA,	INDIANA,	COLORADO,
NEW JERSEY,	IOWA,	WYOMING,
MINNESOTA,	WISCONSIN,	NEW MEXICO,
MONTANA and	TEXAS,	UTAH,
THE DAKOTAS,	MARYLAND,	NEVADA,
KANSAS,	OREGON,	ARIZONA,
MISSOURI,	TENNESSEE,	ARKANSAS,
ALABAMA, and the DOMINION OF CANADA.		IDAHO.

MEDICAL AND SURGICAL REGISTER OF THE UNITED STATES,
ARCHITECTS' AND BUILDERS' DIRECTORY OF THE UNITED STATES,
MARINE DIRECTORY OF THE GREAT LAKES,

AND CITY DIRECTORIES

——— FOR ———

Baltimore, Md ; Detroit, Grand Rapids, Saginaw, Bay City, Jackson, Lansing, Muskegon, Port Huron,
Sault Ste. Marie, Ann Arbor, Ypsilanti, Kalamazoo, Flint, Alpena, Cheboygan, and Big Rapids,
Mich.; Toledo, Columbus, Findlay, Newark and Lima, Ohio; Atlanta, Columbus and
Augusta, Ga.; Birmingham and Montgomery, Ala ; Memphis, Tenn.; Indianapolis
and Fort Wayne, Ind.; St. Paul, Minneapolis and Duluth, Minn.; Ashland,
Oshkosh and Eau Claire, Wis.; Sioux City, Iowa ; Portland and
Astoria, Ore.; Helena and Butte, Mont.; Seattle, Tacoma and
Spokane Falls, Wash.; Salt Lake City and Ogden, Utah.

HOME OFFICE, 40 TO 44 LARNED STREET WEST, DETROIT, MICH.

OFFICES AT

NEW YORK, 50 Exchange Place.
PHILADELPHIA, PA., Ledger Building,
    corner Chestnut and Sixth Sts
BALTIMORE, MD., 112 North Charles St.
ST LOUIS, MO., 904 Olive St.
TOLEDO, OHIO, 306 Madison St.
COLUMBUS, OHIO, 80 North High St.
GRAND RAPIDS MICH., Widdicomb Bldg
INDIANAPOLIS, IND., Corner Circle and
    Meridian Sts.

CHICAGO, ILL., 150 Dearborn St.
ST PAUL, MINN , New Chamber of Com
    merce Building.
MINNEAPOLIS, MINN., 257 First Avenue S
SEATTLE, WASH., cor. Columbia and Front.
TACOMA, WASH., Uhlman Market Block.
PORTLAND, ORE., Marquam Building.
SALT LAKE CITY, 74 S. West Temple St.
MEMPHIS, TENN., 341 Second St.
ATLANTA, GA., Chamber of Commerce

R. L. POLK & CO.'S

FORT WAYNE DIRECTORY

1891-92.

MISCELLANEOUS INFORMATION.

STREETS AND AVENUES.

Abbott, from Pontiac south, second east of Walton ave.

Aboit, from Sherman west to Franklin ave, first south of Barthold ave.

Alexander, from Pontiac south, first east of Walton ave.

Allen, from Lafayette west to Webster, first north of Pontiac.

Alliger, from Maumee road south to Wayne Trace, second east of Walton ave.

Andrew, from Archer ave south, third east of St. Mary's ave.

Antoinette, from Walton ave east, fourth south of P, Ft W & C Ry.

Archer ave, from Wells west to city limits.

Baker, from Calhoun west to Fairfield ave, first south of Brackenridge.

Barr, from Water south to Pontiac, second east of Calhoun.

Barthold, from St Mary's river north to canal feeder, fourth west of Wells.

Bass, from Fairfield ave east to Hoagland ave, first south of Wabash R R.

Beck, see *Koch.*

Begue, from E Wayne north to N Y, C &.St L R R, first east of Harmer.

Bell ave, from Fox west to Miner, first south of Creighton ave.

Berry, from Francis east, first north of E Wayne.

Berry (East), from Calhoun east to W & E Canal, first south of Main.

Berry (West), from Calhoun west to St Mary's river, first south of Main.

Bird ave, second east of toll gate near Haven road, south to New Haven road.

Bond, from New Haven road south to Wabash R R, second east of toll gate.

Boone, from Cherry west to L S & M S Ry, first north of Main.

Bowser, from Wells west, first north of High.

Brackenridge, from Calhoun west to Broadway, second north of Penn R R.

Brandriff, from Hoagland ave east to Webster, first south of Melita.

Breck, from St Mary's river at Van Buren Street bridge, west to canal basin.

Broadway, from N Y, C & St L R R south to city limits, seventh west of Calhoun.

Brooklyn ave, west of St Mary's river, running parallel with Lavina ave.

Buchanan, from Lafayette east to Holton ave, fifth south of Wabash R R.

Burgess, from St Mary's av west, first south of Ft W, C & L R R.

Butler (East), from Calhoun east to Lafayette, first south of Williams.

Butler (West), from Calhoun west to Fairfield ave, first south of Williams.

Calhoun, from St Mary's river south to city limits, first west of Clinton.

Canal, from N Y, C & St L R R south to E Wayne.

Caroline, from Suttenfield south to Pontiac, first east of Lafayette.

Cass, from Wells north to canal feeder.

Cedar, from E Lewis north to Maumee road, first east of Ohio.

Centlivre ave, from Spy Run ave west to canal feeder, first north of Randolph.

Centre, from St. Mary's river north to canal basin, second west of Main Street bridge.

Charles, from Lafayette east to Hanna, first south of Wallace.

Cherry, from St. Mary's river north to old canal basin, first west of the river.

Chestnut, from Calhoun east to Clinton, first south of Holman.

Chestnut, from Strawberry ave west to Piqua road.

Chicago, from Calhoun west, first north of P, Ft W & C Ry.

Chute, from Maumee road south to Wabash R R, second east of Harmer.

Clark, from High north to Third, third west of Wells.

Clay, from Main south to Laselle, first east of Lafayette.

Clinton, from Superior south to Pontiac, first east of Calhoun.

Cochran, from Coombs east to Hanover, first north of N Y, C & St L R R.

Colerick, from Fairfield ave east to Hoagland ave, second south of Wabash R R.

College, from W Berry south across Jones, first west of Rockhill.

Coln, from Maumee river south to Dwenger ave.

Columbia, from Harrison east to Lafayette, first north of Main.

Columbus ave (Lakeside addition), from the bridge to city limits, first north of Edgewater ave.

Comparet, from Wayne south to Maumee road, second east of Harmer.

Coombs, from Wayne north to N Y, C & St L R R, second east of Harmer.

Cottage ave, from S Wayne ave west to Beaver ave, first south of Home ave.

Cour, from Webster east to Piqua ave, south of limits.

Court, from Main south to Berry, first east of Calhoun.

Creighton ave (East), from Calhoun east to limits, first south of DeWald.

Creighton ave (West), from Calhoun west to city limits, first south of DeWald.

Crescent ave (Lakeside addition), from Maumee river north, second east of Oneida.

Dawson, from Calhoun west to Hoagland ave, first north of Williams.

Dearborn (Lakeside addition), from Maumee river north, third east of Columbia Street bridge.

DeGroff, from Ft W, C & L R R south to Burgess, first west of St Mary's ave.

DeWald (East), from Calhoun east to Hanna, first north of Creighton ave.

DeWald (West), from Calhoun west to Broadway, first north of Creighton ave.

Diamond, from Walton ave east, second south of P, Ft W & C Ry.

Division, from Maumee road south to Wabash R R, third east of Hanna.

Dock, from Barr west to Harrison, first south of Nickel Plate track.

Dougal, from Maumee river south, second south of Glasgow ave.

Douglas ave, from Calhoun west to McClellan, second south of Jefferson.

DuBois, from Maumee road south to Wabash R R, fourth east of Walton ave.

Duck, from Calhoun east to Barr, first north of Superior.

Duryea, from Fairfield ave to Hoagland ave, first south of Butler, continuation of Poplar.

Dwenger ave, from Glasgow ave east, first north of Nickel Plate track.

Eagle, from Taylor south, second west of Broadway.

Eckart, from Hanna east to Smith, fourth south of Pontiac.

Eden Park ave (Lakeside addition), from Oneida east, first north of Elmwood ave.

Edgerton, from Winter east to Walton ave, first south of P, Ft W & C Ry.

Edgewater ave (Lakeside addition), from Columbia Street bridge east, first north of Maumee river.

Edna, from Spy Run ave to canal feeder, first north of Centlivre ave.

Edsall, *see Union.*

Eliza, from Francis east across Ohio, second south of Lewis, and from Walton ave east to Euclid.

Eliza ave, from Parnell ave east to Maysville road, first north of Romey ave.

Elizabeth, from Spy Run ave west to Spy Run, at north city limits.

Elm, from St Mary's river west to same, first south of Main.

Elmwood ave (Lakeside addition), from St Joseph river east, first north of Rivermet ave.

Emily, from Spy Run ave west to Spy Run, first south of Elizabeth.

Emily, from Thomas west to Gay, second south of E Creighton ave.

Erie, from junction of Francis and N Y, C & St L R R east, first north of Wayne.

Euclid, from Maumee road south to Mercer, second east of Walton ave.

Eva, from Huestis ave south to Maple ave, first west of Broadway.

Evans, from Hartman west to Queen, third south of Pontiac.

Ewing, from W Superior south to Brackenridge, third west of Calhoun.

Fair, from St Mary's river to same, third south of Main.

Fairfield ave, from Brackenridge to south city limits, continuation of Griffith.

Ferguson ave, from Miner west to Broadway, first south of Creighton ave.

Fifth, from Weds east to N Calhoun, fifth north of St Mary's river

Fisher, from Holton ave west, second south of Creighton ave.

Fletcher ave from Maumee road south to Wayne Trace, first east of Range road.

Force, from Herndon south to Pontiac, fourth east of Lafayette.

Fourth, crosses Wells, fourth north of St Mary's river.

Fox, crosses Creighton ave, second east of Broadway.

Francis, from N Y, C & St L R R south to Wabash R R, fourth east of Lafayette.

Franklin, from Holton ave west to Smith, fourth south of Pontiac.

Franklin ave, from Canal feeder north to Archer ave, first west of St Mary's ave.

Frederick, from Holton ave west to Smith, second south of Pontiac.

Fry, from W Main north to Boone, first west of Osage.

Fulton, from W Superior south to Jefferson, first east of Broadway.

Garden, south from M E College grounds across Jefferson, first west of Nelson.

Gay, from Hayden south to Pontiac, third east of Hanna.

George, *see Brackenridge.*

Gerke, from Holton ave west to Smith, first south of Pontiac.

Gladstone ave, from St Joseph Boulevard north, third east of Romey ave.

Glasgow, from Maumee river south to Maumee road, fourth east of Walton ave.

Grand, from Calhoun west, along south side of Wabash R R.

Grant, from Hanna east to P, Ft W & C Ry, first south of Wallace.

Grant ave, from Wayne south to Maumee road, second east of Walton ave.

Greely, from Fulton west to Jackson, first north of N Y, C & St L R R.

Greene, from John east to Holton ave, first south of Samuel.

Griffith, from W Superior south to Brackenridge, second east of Broadway.

Hamilton, from Calhoun east to Lafayette, first south of Murray.

Hanna, from N Y, C & St L R R south to city limits, third east of Lafayette.

Hanover, from Wayne north to W & E canal, first east of College.

Harmer from N Y, C & St L R R south to Hayden, second east of Hanna.

Harmony Court, from W Berry north to W Main, first west of Calhoun.

Harrison, from St Mary's river south to city limits, first west of Calhoun.

Hartman, from Pontiac south, fourth east of Walton ave.

Hayden, from Francis east, third south of Lewis.

Hendricks, from Fairfield ave west to Broadway, first north of P, Ft W & C Ry.

Henry ave, from Holton ave west to Smith, fifth south of Pontiac.

Hensch, from Archer ave south, third west of Wells.

Hermon, from St Mary's ave east to St Mary's river, first north of Nickel Plate track.

Herndon, from Hanna east to Gay, first south of Wabash R R.

High, from Wells west to St Mary's, second north of the river.

Highland, from Calhoun west to Webster, second south of
  Wabash R R.
Hillside ave, from Leo road north, second east of St Joseph
  Boulevard.
Hoagland ave, from Wabash R R shops south, third west of
  Calhoun.
Hoffman, from Wells at canal feeder, west to Tyler ave.
Holman, from Calhoun east to Hanna, second south of Lewis.
Holton ave, from P, Ft W & C Ry to south city limits, sev-
  enth east of Hanna.
Home ave, from Fairfield ave west to Broadway, fourth south
  of Creighton ave.
Horace, from John east to Holton ave, first south of Grant.
Hough, from Clay east to Hanna, first south of Holman.
Howard, from E Washington north to N Y, C & St L R R,
  first east of Hanover.
Howell, from G R & I R R east, second north of Burgess at
  canal feeder.
Huestis ave, from Broadway west, second south of Creighton
  ave.
Hugh, from Hanna east to Alliger, first south of Lewis.
Hugh, from Walton ave east to Euclid, first south of Maumee
  road.
Humphrey, from Grant east to Glasgow, first south of Wash-
  ington.
Hurd, from Holton ave east, first south of Creighton ave.
Huron, from St Mary's river west to same, second south of
  Main.
Indiana ave, from Seneca south across Home ave, second west
  of Fairfield ave.
Jackson, from N Y, C & St L R R south to P, Ft W & C Ry.
  second west of Broadway.
Jane, from Leith south, first east of Calhoun.
Jefferson (East), from Calhoun east to Division, first south of
  Washington.
Jefferson (West), from Calhoun west to Fair Grounds, first
  south of Washington.
Jenison, from Holton ave east, second south of Creighton ave.
Jesse, from G R & I R R east, third north of Burgess at canal
  feeder.
John, from P, Ft W & C Ry south of Pontiac, second east
  of Hanna.
Jones from West west to Nelson, second south of Jefferson.
Julia, from Holton ave west, first south of Creighton ave.
Kansas, from Wabash R R south to Melita, first east of Hoag-
  land ave.
Killea, from Calhoun west to Hoagland ave, first south of
  Pontiac.
King, from E Wayne south to Maumee road, first east of Harmer.

Koch, from Archer ave south, first west of Wells.

Koenig, from Meegan north, first west of Hanna.

Lafayette, from Superior south to city limits, third east of Calhoun.

Lake, from St Mary's ave at canal feeder, west to Franklin ave.

Lake ave (Lakeside addition), from St Joseph river east, third north of Maumee river.

Laselle, from Lafayette east to Hanna, first south of Charles.

Lavina, *see Pritchard.*

Leith, from Lafayette west to city limits, first south of Pontiac.

Leo road, from St Joseph Boulevard east, second east of Lakeside addition.

Lewis (East), from Calhoun east to Walton ave, first south of Jefferson.

Lewis (West), from Calhoun west to Ewing, first south of Jefferson.

Liberty, from Begue east two blocks, second north of Wayne.

Lillie, from Grant south to Pontiac, third east of Holton ave.

Lillie, from Maumee road south to Wabash R R, first west of Walton ave.

Lincoln ave, from Broadway east, third south of W Creighton ave.

Line, from Lumbard east to Bird ave, first south of New Haven road.

Locust, from Fairfield ave west, first south of Wabash R R.

Lumbard, from New Haven road south, first east of toll gate.

McClellan, from W Lewis south to Chicago, first west of Webster.

McCulloch, from Maumee road south to Wabash R R.

McDonald, from Lumbard east to Bird ave, first north of Wabash R R.

McDougall ave, from St Joseph river to Hillside ave, first north of Baker.

McLaughlin, from Leith south, second east of Calhoun.

Madison, from Barr east to Division, first south of Jefferson.

Maiden Lane, from N Y, C & St L R R south to Berry, first west of Harrison.

Main (East), from Calhoun east to N Y, C & St L R R, first north of Berry.

Main (West), from Calhoun west to city limits, first north of Berry.

Maple ave, from Broadway west, second south of Creighton ave.

Marchell, from Piqua ave west to Webster, first south of Killea.

Maria, from G R & I R R east, second south of Spring.

Marion, from High north to Third, first west of Wells.

Mary, from Runnion ave west, first north of canal feeder.

Masterson from Calhoun east to Lafayette, first south of Hamilton.

Maud, from Holton ave west, first north of Pontiac.

Maumee road, from near corner of Washington and Harmer, southeast to city limits.

Mechanic, from Fair north to canal basin, third west of Main Street bridge.

Meegan, from Hanna west, first south of Pontiac.

Melita from Harrison west to Hoagland ave, first south of Grand.

Mercer, from Walton ave east, third south of P, Ft W & C Ry.

Meridian, from Archer ave south, fourth west of Wells.

Metz, from Taylor south to Wabash R R, first west of Broadway.

Meyer, from Holton ave west to Smith, third south of Pontiac.

Milan, from Edgerton east to Walton ave, first south of Creighton ave.

Miner, from W De Wald south, first east of Broadway.

Montgomery, from Calhoun east to Hanna, first south of Lewis.

Monroe, from Berry south to Laselle, second east of Lafayette.

Muncie, from Pape east, first east of Ft W, C & L R R.

Murray, from Calhoun east to Lafayette, first south of Wabash R R.

Nelson, from W Wayne south to P, Ft W & C Ry, fourth west of Jackson.

Nirdlinger ave, from Broadway west, second south of P, Ft W & C Ry.

N Calhoun, from Superior north to canal feeder, third east of Wells.

N Cass, from Wells north to canal feeder.

N Fisher, from Maumee river south to N Y, C & St L R R, third east of Glasgow ave.

N Harrison, from Superior north to canal feeder, second east of Wells.

New Haven ave, from Pioneer ave east to city limits.

Oak, from Division east to Ohio, first south of Maumee road.

Oakland, from canal feeder north to Archer ave, first east of St Mary's ave.

Oakley, from Taylor south to W De Wald, first west of Fairfield ave.

Ohio, from Maumee road south to Wabash R R, third east of Harmer.

Old Fort (Lakeside addition), from Maumee river north, first east of Columbia Street bridge.

Oliver, from P, Ft W & C Ry south to city limits, first east of Smith.

Oneida, from Maumee river north, first east of Dearborn.

Orchard, from High north to Third, second west of Wells.

Osage, from Main north to canal basin, fourth west of Main Street bridge.

Pape, from Ft W, C & L R R south to Breck, first east of St Mary's ave.

Park, from Maumee river south to N Y, C & St L R R, fourth east of Glasgow ave.

Park ave, from Broadway west, fourth south of Creighton ave.

Park place, from Hoagland ave east to Calhoun, first south of Creighton ave.

Parnell ave, from St Joseph river north to city limits, first west of Gladstone.

Pearl, from Harrison west to Broadway, first north of Main.

Penn, from Alliger east to limits, first south of Maumee road.

Pfeiffer ave, see Archer ave.

Pine, from Taylor north, first west of Fairfield ave.

Pioneer ave, from Walton ave east to Summer.

Piqua ave, from a point on Calhoun 1½ miles from Court House, south.

Pittsburgh, from Walton ave east to Bird ave, third south of New Haven road.

Plum, see Wells.

Polk, from canal feeder east, parallel with Ft W, C & L R R.

Pontiac, from Hoagland ave east to Walton ave, fourth south of Creighton ave.

Poplar, from Fairfield ave west to Oakley, second south of Taylor.

Prince, from Bass south to Colerick, first east of Fairfield ave.

Pritchard, from Fairfield ave west to Rockhill, second north of P, Ft W & C Ry.

Prospect ave, from Spy Run ave east to St Joseph river, first north of Wagner.

Purman, from Warsaw east, first north of Pontiac.

Putnam, from Wells west to Tyler ave, first south of Pfeiffer ave.

Queen, from Pontiac south, third east of Walton ave.

Railroad, from Calhoun east to Pittsburgh shops, first north of P, Ft W & C Ry.

Randall, from Grant east to Glasgow, second south of Washington.

Randolph, from Spy Run ave to canal feeder, first north of Burgess ave.

Rebecca, from G R & I R R east, third south of Spring.

Reed, from Creighton ave south to Pontiac, first east of Holton ave.

Reynolds, from Glasgow ave east to Summer.

Richardson, from canal feeder west to G R & I R R, first north of Wheeler.

Riedmiller, from Metz west to Eagle, first south of Taylor.

Rivermet ave, from St Joseph Boulevard northeast to Crescent ave, first east of Lake.

Rockhill, from W Main south to Pritchard, second west of Jackson.

Romey ave, from St Joseph river east to Gladstone, first south of Parnell ave.

Ross, from St Mary's river south to W Superior, first west of Fulton.

Rudisill ave, from Calhoun west to Broadway, first south of Home ave.

Rumsey ave. from canal feeder north to Spring, third east of G R & I R R.

Runnion ave, from Main north to Spring, second east of G R & I R R.

Ruth, from Spy Run ave west, second north of St Mary's bridge.

St Joseph Boulevard, from Columbia ave to Sunnyside ave, on east bank of St Joseph river.

St Martin, from Lafayette east to Hanna, first south of Buchanan.

St Mary's ave, from old canal basin north to city limits, sixth west of Wells.

St Michael ave, from Ross west to Van Buren.

Savilla Place, from Broadway east to Indiana ave.

Samuel, *see Buchanan.*

Sand, from Maumee river south to N Y, C & St L R R, first west of Glasgow.

Schick, from N Y, C & St L R R south to Maumee road, fifth east of Harmer.

Scott ave, from Broadway west to Thompson ave, first south of Creighton ave.

Seneca, from Fox west to Broadway, second south of Creighton ave.

Sherman, from canal feeder north to Archer ave, second east of St Mary's ave.

Short, from Archer ave south, second west of Wells.

Siemon, from Pontiac south to Leith, east of Calhoun.

Simon, from P, Ft W & C Ry east to Walton ave, first south of Wabash R R.

Sixth, from Wells east to N Calhoun, sixth north of St Mary's river.

Smith, from P, Ft W & C Ry south to city limits, fourth east of Hanna.

South Wayne ave, from Creighton ave south across Home ave, first west of Fairfield ave.

Spring, from Sherman west to city limits, second north of canal feeder.

Spring, from canal feeder north to Mary, first west of Runnion ave.

Spy Run ave, from St Mary's river at junction of Superior and Lafayette, north to city limits.

Stophlet, from Broadway west, first south of Nirdlinger ave.

Sturgis, from Fulton west half block, first south of West Jefferson.

Summer, from Wabash R R to P, Ft W & C Ry, sixth east of Walton ave.

Summit, from Division east across McCulloch, first north of Lewis.

Sunnyside ave (Lakeside addition), from St Joseph Boulevard to Crescent ave, first north of Eden park.

Superior (East), from Calhoun east to Clay, first north of N Y, C & St L R R.

Superior (West), from Calhoun west, first north of N Y, C & St L R R.

Suttenfield, from Webster east to Hanna, second south of Creighton ave.

Swinney ave, from Nirdlinger ave west to city limits, first north of Stophlet.

Taber, from Webster east to Hanna, first south of Creighton ave.

Taylor, from Fairfield ave west to Lavina ave, fourth south of of P, Ft W & C Ry.

Tecumseh (Lakeside addition), from Maumee river north, first east of Oneida.

Third, from N Calhoun west to St Mary's ave, third north of the river.

Thomas, from P, Ft W & C Ry south to Meyer, first west of Holton ave.

Thomasetta, from Thomas west to Gay, first south of Creighton ave.

Thompson ave, from Wabash R R south, first west of Broadway.

Toledo, from Hanna to Lafayette, first south of Wabash R R.

Tons, from Maumee river south, first east of Glasgow ave.

Tyler ave, from Spring south to Howell, first west of Runnion ave.

Union, from Main south to P, Ft W & C Ry, first west of Jackson.

University, from West Wayne south to Maumee road, third east of Harmer.

Van Buren, from St Mary's river south to Pritchard, first west of Broadway.

Victoria ave, from Piqua ave south, first east of Calhoun.

Vine, from Walton ave east, first south of P, Ft W & C Ry.

Virginia, from Lafayette east to Monroe, second south of Wabash R R.

Wabash (Vordermark's addition), from city limits east, first south of Wabash R R.

Wabash ave, from East Wayne south to Maumee road, third east of Walton ave.

Wall, from Broadway west, first south of P, Ft W & C Ry.

Wallace, from Lafayette east to Smith, first south of Virginia.

Walnut, from Fairfield ave west, first south of Taylor.

Walter, from Wayne south to Maumee road, fourth east of Harmer.

Walton ave, from Maumee road south to city limits, tenth east of Hanna.

Warren, from Wabash R R south to P, Ft W & C Ry, first east of Glasgow ave.

Warsaw, from Laselle south to limits, first east of Lafayette.

Washington (East), from Calhoun east to city limits, third south of Main.

Washington (West), from Calhoun west to Fair Grounds, third south of Main.

Watkins, from W Main north to Boone.

Wayne (East), from Calhoun east to city limits, second south of Main.

Wayne (West), from Calhoun west to Schick, second south of Main.

Wayne Trace, from Walton ave south of Wabash R R, southeast to city limits.

Webster, from St. Mary's river south to city limits, second west of Calhoun.

Wefel, from High north to Third, first west of Barthold.

Wells, from W Superior north to city limits.

West, see *Rockhill.*

Wheeler, from canal feeder west to G R & I R R, first north of Mary.

Wiebke, from Lafayette east to Hanna, 1¾ miles south of Court House.

Williams (East), from Calhoun east to Lafayette, fourth south of Wabash R R.

Williams (West), from Lafayette west to Fairfield ave, fourth south of Wabash R R.

Wilt, from Broadway west to Nelson, first south of Jefferson.

Winch, from Maumee road south to Wayne Trace, third east of Walton ave.

Winter, from Lewis south to Pontiac, second east of Holton av.

Wright, from G R & I R R east, first south of Spring.

Zollars ave, from Metz west, first south of Taylor.

Zollinger, from Glasgow ave east to Coles.

WARD BOUNDARIES.

No. 1. Bounded on the north by the St Mary's river between Lafayette and Hanna streets, on the east by Hanna, on the south by the P, Ft W & C Ry, and on the west by Lafayette.

No. 2. Bounded on the north by the St Mary's river between Calhoun and Lafayette streets, on the east by Lafayette, on the south by the P, Ft W & C Ry, and on the west by Calhoun.

No. 3. Bounded on the north by the St Mary's river between Calhoun and Cass streets, on the east by Calhoun, on the south by the P, Ft W & C Ry, and on the west by Cass and Webster streets.

No. 4. Bounded on the north by the St Mary's river between Cass and the continuation of Broadway, on the east by Cass and Webster, on the south by the P, Ft W & C Ry, and on the west by Broadway.

No. 5. Bounded on the north by the St Mary's river and canal basin, on the east by Broadway, on the south by the Wabash R R, on the west by Eagle, Taylor and Cherry streets and Allen County Fair Grounds.

No. 6. Bounded on the north by the W, St L & P Ry, on the east by Calhoun, on the south by Pontiac, Webster and Creighton ave, and on the west by the Wabash R R.

No. 7. Bounded on the north by the P, Ft W & C Ry, on the east by the city limits, on the south by Pontiac and Leith, and on the west by Calhoun.

No. 8. Bounded on the north by the Maumee river, on the east by Glasgow ave, DuBois, Wayne Trace and Grange road, on the south by the P, Ft W & C Ry, and on the west by Hanna.

No. 9. Bounded on the north by Barthold, Archer ave and Spy Run creek, on the east and south by the St Mary's river, on the west by canal basin and Rumsey ave.

No. 10. Bounded on the north by the P, Ft W & C Ry, on the east by the city limits, on the south by the city limits, and on the west by Hanna street.

CITY GOVERNMENT.

Municipal Election, first Tuesday in May.

Council meets on the second and fourth Tuesday evenings of each month, and at the call of five members.

Council Chamber, City Hall Building, Barr street, between Berry and Wayne.

CITY OFFICERS.

Mayor—Charles A Zollinger.

Clerk—Rudolph C Reinewald.

Treasurer—Charles J Sosenheimer.
Attorney—Wm H Shambaugh.
Marshal—Henry C Franke.
Street Commissioner—John J Mungen.
Chief of Police—Frank Wilkinson.
Chief of Fire Department—Henry Hilbrecht.
City Engineer—Frank M Randall.
Weighmaster—Patrick Ryan.
Marketmaster—Wm Ropa.
Poundmaster—Wm Bock.
Secretary Board of Health—Samuel C Metcalf, M D.

COUNCILMEN.

First Ward—John Scheffer, Wm D Meyer.
Second Ward—Maurice Cody, H P Michael.
Third Ward—Peter Eggeman, Wm Meyer jr.
Fourth Ward—George W Ely, Anthony Kelker.
Fifth Ward—Charles Buck, Louis P Huser.
Sixth Ward—Frederick Dahman, Louis Fox.
Seventh Ward—Peter J Scheid, Philip Keinz.
Eighth Ward—John Smith, Henry P Scherer.
Ninth Ward—Fred C Boltz, Louis Hazzard.
Tenth Ward—F Charles Meyer, J E de La Grange.

BOARD OF HEALTH.

The Mayor, *ex officio* Chairman ; Dr S C Metcalf Sec.
Executive Committee—M Cody, Peter Eggeman, P J Scheid.

BOARD OF POLICE COMMISSIONERS.

The Mayor, *ex officio* Chairman.
Commissioners—Herman P Michael, Louis Hazzard, Charles
Buck, John Smith.

WATER WORKS TRUSTEES.

Christian Boseker, Pres; Wm Bittler, Charles McCulloch.

TRUSTEES OF PUBLIC SCHOOLS.

John M Moritz, O P Morgan, E A Hoffman.

CITY COMMISSIONERS.

John W Vordermark, J J Kern, Peter Certia, George Fox,
P H Kane.

FIRE DEPARTMENT.

Chief Engineer—Henry Hilbrecht, jr ; office cor Court and E
Berry.
Assistants—John McGowan, Fred Becker.
Commissioners—Mayor *ex officio*, Geo W Ely, Henry P Scherer,
Peter J Scheid, Fred C Boltz.

Hook and Ladder Company No. 1—Northwest cor Clinton and Berry. John Baker, foreman ; Peter Friebarger, driver ; Ferdinand Schroeder, tillerman ; John F Huber, John Zent, Mead Gendlesparger, laddermen ; George Brenner, Sherman Lavanway, Frank Bube, Simon Boerger, truckmen.

Hook and Ladder Company No. 2—Wallace bet Lafayette and Clay. August Tremmel, driver ; Wm Schack, tillerman.

Steamer No. 1—Northeast cor Court and Berry. John Schroeder, engineer ; Christians Rohyans, driver.

Steamer No. 2—Wallace bet Lafayette and Clay. Michael Connors, engineer ; John Stahlhout, driver.

Hose Company No. 1—Northwest cor Clinton and Berry. Charles Becker, foreman ; John D Carl, driver ; George Trautman, Gottlieb Steup, Wm Miller, Asa Lewis, hosemen.

Hose Company No. 2—Wallace bet Lafayette and Clay. George Klingman, driver ; Emanuel Hoch, Henry Aumann, Ferdinand Meier, hosemen.

Hose Company No. 3—Northeast cor Court and Berry. Charles Sheldon, foreman ; Edward Moody, driver ; Frederick Reinking, John Daly, Henry Becker, Emil Legraw, hosemen.

Chemical Engine Co—N E cor Court and Berry. Louis Steup, driver ; Fred Armack, Hugh Dix, chemicalmen.

FIRE ALARM TELEGRAPH STATIONS.

6—Corner Calhoun and Columbia streets.
7— " St Mary's ave and Spring street.
8— " Wells and Hoffman streets.
12— " Wells and Third streets.
13— " High and Clark streets.
14— " Superior and Ewing streets.
15— " Calhoun and Jefferson streets.
16— " Calhoun and Chicago streets.
17— " Calhoun and Williams streets.
18— " Calhoun and Leith streets.
23— " Washington and Clay streets.
24— " Washington and Harmer streets.
25— " Lewis and Hanna streets.
26— " Summit and Division streets.
27— " Maumee ave and Schick street.
28—White's Factory.
31—Corner Douglas ave and Webster street.
32— " Jefferson and Griffith streets.
34— " Broadway and Wilt streets.
35— " Washington and VanBuren streets.
36— " Union and Pritchard streets.
37— " Broadway and Wall streets.

38—Corner Washington and College streets.
41—Olds and Sons' Works.
42—Engine House No. 2.
43—Corner Hanna and Wallace streets.
45—   "   Grant and Smith streets.
46—   "   Hanna street and Creighton avenue.
47—   "   Lafayette and DeWald streets.
48—   "   Creighton ave and Thomas street.
51—   "   Wayne and Webster streets.
52—   "   Main and Griffith streets.
53—   "   Main and Van Buren streets.
54—   "   Main and Cherry streets.
56—   "   Boone and Osage streets.
61—Engine House No. 1.
62—Corner Harrison and Columbia streets.
63—   "   Columbia and Barr streets.
64—   "   Barr and Madison streets.
65—   "   Lafayette and Holman streets.
67—Pittsburgh Round House.
71—Corner Fairfield ave and Bass street.
72—   "   Butler street and Hoagland ave.
73—   "   Broadway and Taylor street.
74—   "   Fox and DeWald streets.
81—   "   Wayne and Walter streets.
82—   "   Lewis and Lillie streets.
83—   "   Washington street and Grant avenue.

POLICE DEPARTMENT.

Headquarters, City Hall Building, Barr street, between Berry
    and Wayne.
Chief—Frank Wilkinson.
Clerks—Wilmer Wilkinson, Andrew Schearer.
Patrolmen—Henry Lapp, Lieutenant; John O'Connell, John
    Siebold, Joseph Gushing, Stephen Fletcher, Henry Shroeder,
    George Humbrecht, John Kenelly, Edward Quinn, George
    McCrorey, John Tremmel, John Trautman, Patrick O'Ryan,
    Frank Rohle, Frederick Stahlhut, Charles M Romey, Erich
    Richter, Henry Harkenrider, Jesse Patton, Frederick
    Daseler, Henry Stohl, Frederick Limecooly, Wm Borgman,
    Joseph Loos, Patrick Murphy, Wm Knock.
Marshal—Henry C Franke.
Drivers Patrol Wagon—Henry Sanders, George Swain.

RATES OF FARE,

AS ESTABLISHED BY CITY ORDINANCES, RELATIVE TO PUBLIC
CARRIAGES.

Sec. 7. The prices to be charged by the owner or driver
of any vehicle, except an omnibus, for the conveyance of pas-

sengers for hire, within said city, shall be as follows, to be regulated and estimated by the distance on the most direct routes, namely :

For conveying a passenger not exceeding one mile . . 50c
For conveying a passenger any distance over a mile and
   less than two miles $1.00

For conveying children between five and fourteen years of age, half the above prices may be charged for like distances, but for children under five years of age no charge shall be made, unless such child is the only passenger, in which case full charge may be made.

The distance from any railroad depot or hotel to any other railroad or hotel shall, in all cases, be estimated as not exceeding one mile.

For the use of coaches drawn by two horses, with one
   or more passengers, by the day $8.00

For the use of any vehicle by the hour, with one or more passengers, with the privilege of going from place to place, and stopping when required, as follows :

For the first hour $1.50
For each succeeding hour 1.00

Every passenger shall be allowed to have conveyed upon such vehicle, without charge, his ordinary traveling baggage, not exceeding in any case one trunk.

Sec. 13. Any person who shall violate any or either of the provisions of this chapter, or any section, clause or provision of any section of this chapter, or who shall fail or neglect to comply with any or either of the requirements thereof, shall, upon conviction, pay a fine of not more than one hundred dollars.

STREET RAILROADS.

FORT WAYNE STREET RAILROAD CO.

President—John H Bass.
Vice-President—S B Bond.
Secretary—J M Barrett.
Treasurer—A S Bond.
Superintendent—L D McNutt.
  Office, corner Main and Calhoun streets.

C. L. CENTLIVRE STREET RAILWAY CO.

Capital, $30,000. Incorporated 1889.
President—L A Centlivre.
Vice-President—C L Centlivre.
Secretary—C F Centlivre.
Treasurer—John B Reuss.
  Office, north end of Spy Run ave.

4

FEDERAL OFFICERS.
GOVERNMENT BUILDING.

Postmaster—C R Higgins.
Collector of Internal Revenue—John S Cravens, Lawrence-
   burgh, Ind.
·Division Deputy Collector Internal Revenue—Wm O Butler.
Deputy Collector Internal Revenue—A C Keel.
U S Gauger—James Liggett.
U S Commissioner—Elmer Leonard.
U S District Attorney—Smiley Chambers, Indianapolis.
U S Deputy Marshal—John C Abel.
Deputy Clerk U S District Court—John Morris, Jr.

COUNTY OFFICERS.

Court House, bet Calhoun and Court, south of Main and north
   of Berry.
Judge of the Circuit Court—Hon Edward O'Rourke.
Judge of the Superior Court—Hon Charles M Dawson.
Clerk—Daniel W Souder.
Prosecuting Attorney—James M Robinson.
Sheriff—George H Viberg.
Recorder—Milton Thompson.
Treasurer—Isaac Mowrer.
Auditor—Andrew F Glutting.
Surveyor—Henry E Fischer.
Supt of Bridges—W H Goshorn.
Coroner—Abraham J Kesler.
Commissioners—Jasper W Jones, John H Brannan, and Henry
   F Bullermann.
Attorney for County Commissioners—Robert C Bell.
School Superintendent--George F Felts.

COURTS.
TIMES OF HOLDING COURT IN ALLEN COUNTY.

Circuit Court—First Monday in February, third Monday in
   April, first Monday in September, and third Monday in
   November. Hon Edward O'Rourke, Judge; James M
   Robinson, Prosecuting Attorney.
Superior Court—Second Monday in January, first Monday in
   April, second Monday in September, and second Monday
   in November. Hon C M Dawson, Judge.

U. S. COURTS.
COURT ROOMS IN GOVERNMENT BUILDING.

District Court of United States—Second Tuesdays in June and
   December. Hon W A Woods, Judge; Noble C Butler

Clerk; John Morris, Jr, Resident Deputy Clerk; Wm L
Dunlap, Marshal; John C Abel, Resident Deputy Marshal.
Circuit Court of United States—Second Tuesdays in June
and December. Hon W Q Gresham, Judge; Noble C
Butler, Clerk; John Morris, Jr, Resident Deputy Clerk;
Wm L Dunlap, Marshal; John C Abel, Resident Deputy
Marshal.

COUNTY BOARD OF TRUSTEES, WITH POSTOFFICE ADDRESS.

Aboite—Henry C Dinius, Saturn.
Adams—Barney Tibbet, New Haven.
Cedar Creek—Victor H Muller, Leo.
Eel River—John M Taylor, Churubusco.
Jefferson—Reuben B Hoops, Zulu.
Jackson—John McConnel, Monroeville.
Lafayette—Jacob F Keyser, Zanesville.
Lake—Luderic Welsheimer, Churubusco.
Madison—Wm Franke, Hoagland.
Marion—David Gibson, Root.
Maumee—Robert B Shirley, Woodburn.
Milan—Absalom Stauffer, Chamberlain.
Monroe—Christian Hoffman, Monroeville.
Perry—Florentine Roy, Fort Wayne.
Pleasant—Wm Kinerk, Sheldon.
St Joseph—Christian H Rose, Fort Wayne.
Scipio—James B Lindemuth, Hall's Corners.
Springfield—Hiram B Roller, Harlan.
Washington—Matthew A Ferguson, Fort Wayne.
Wayne—George W Brackenridge, Fort Wayne.

BANDS OF MUSIC.

First Regiment Band and Orchestra—Henry Wiegmann, Manager; Oscar Puegner, Leader; office, 199 Lafayette.
Fort Wayne City Band—Prof Philip Keinz, Leader; office, 12 W Main.
Reineke's Orchestra—Frederick J Reineke, Leader; office, 12 W Main.

BANKS AND BANKERS.

First National Bank, s e cor Court and Main. Capital and surplus, $440,000. Organized May, 1863; re-organized May, 1882. John H Bass, Pres; M W Simons, Vice-Pres; L R Hartman, Cash; W L Pettit, Asst Cash.
Hamilton National Bank, 44 Calhoun. Capital, $200,000; surplus, $200,000. Organized 1874. Charles McCulloch, Pres; John Mohr, Jr, Cash; C W Orr, Asst Cash.

Nuttman & Co (private), 32 E Main. Organized 1883. O S
Hanna, Cash.

Old National Bank The, s w cor Calhoun and Berry. Capital,
$350,000; surplus, $125,000. Organized 1885. S B Bond,
Pres; O P Morgan, Vice-Pres; J D Bond, Cash; J C
Woodworth, Asst Cash.

BUILDING, LOAN AND SAVINGS ASSOCIATIONS.

Allen County Loan and Savings Association. Organized April
7th, 1890. Capital stock, $1,000,000. Meets first and third
week each month at White's Block. Edward White, Pres;
Gottlieb Haller, Vice-Pres; Thomas C Rogers, Sec; Charles
W. Orr, Treas.

Concordia Building and Loan Association. Organized January,
1891. Meets fourth Wednesday of each month. Charles
Kaiser, Pres; Charles H Buck, Sec; Charles Stellhorn,
Treas.

Fidelity Building and Savings Bank Union. Henry P Vordermark, Pres; H L Studer, Vice-Pres; Franklin Schwartz,
Sec; Daniel Krapf, Treas. Meets Wednesday before the
20th of each month at Union Hall, 7 E Main.

Fort Wayne Building, Loan-Fund and Savings Association.
Organized April 11, 1884. Capital stock, $1,000,000.
Meets first Tuesday after the 18th of each month at Y M
C A Hall (new). Stockholders' meeting to elect officers,
etc, second Wednesday in May. F D Lasanave, Pres;
O E Bradway, Vice-Pres; C W Howey, Sec; Christopher
Hettler, Treas.

German Allen Building, Loan and Savings Association. Organ-
ized November, 1887. Capital stock $100,000. Meets first
Wednesday of each month in Custer House. Henry Zur
Muehlen, Pres; Otto Herbst, Sec; George Motz, Treas.

German Building, Loan-Fund and Savings Association, No. 1.
Organized June, 1886. Capital, $100,000. Meets last
Monday of each month at Custer House. Otto P Herbst,
Pres; Henry Zur Muehlen, Sec; George Motz, Treas.

German Building, Loan-Fund and Savings Association, No. 3.
Organized September, 1884. Capital, $100,000. Meets
fourth Friday of each month at Custer House. Stock-
holders' meeting to elect officers, etc, first Monday in
October. Wm Meyers, Pres; John H Pranger, Sec; Charles
Stellhorn, Treas.

German Building, Loan and Savings Association, No. 4.
Organized November 20, 1887. Capital, $100,000. Meets
first Wednesday of each month at Custer House. Otto
Nichter, Pres; Henry Zur Muehlen, Sec; A Fuelber, Treas.

German Building Loan-Fund and Savings Association, No. 5.
Organized January 10, 1885. Capital, $100,000. Meets

fourth Tuesday of each month at the Custer House. Peter G Holmhaus, Pres; Otto P Herbst, Sec; George Motz, Treas.

German-Jackson Building, Loan and Savings Association. Organized June, 1890. Capital stock, $100,000. Meets third Thursday of each month in Custer House. C W Jacobs, Pres; Otto Herbst, Sec; George Motz, Treas.

Germania Building and Loan Association. Organized March 1889. Meets third Thursday of each month. Peter Nussbaum. Pres; Charles H Buck, Sec.

Jefferson Building, Loan and Savings Association. Organized January, 1889. Capital stock, $300,000. Meets third Tuesday of each month in Custer House. Peter G Holmhaus, Pres; Otto Herbst, Sec; George Motz, Treas.

Summit City Building, Loan-Fund and Savings Association. Organized October 14, 1886. Capital, $100,000. Meets first Monday of each month at Custer House. J B Monning, Pres; Otto P Herbst, Sec; Geerge Motz, Treas.

Tri-State Building and Loan Association No 1. Organized July, 1889. Capital stock, $200,000. 13 and 14 Pixley & Long Building. George W Pixley, Pres; A D Cressler, Vice-Pres; C A Wilding, Sec; Joseph W Bell, Treas.

Tri-State Building and Loan Association No 2. Organized July, 1889. Capital stock, $2,000,000. 13 and 14 Pixley & Long Building. George W Pixley, Pres; A D Cressler Vice-Pres; C A Wilding, Sec; Joseph W Bell, Treas.

Washington German Building, Loan-Fund and Savings Association. Organized December, 1887. Capital, $100,000. Meets first Tuesday of each month at Custer House. Stockholders' meeting to elect officers, etc, second Tuesday in December. Otto Nichter, Pres; John H Pranger, Sec; Charles Liebenguth, Treas.

Wayne Building, Loan and Savings Association. Organized October 24, 1887. Capital, $100,000. Meets third Friday of each month at Custer House. Frank Iten, Pres; Otto P Herbst, Sec; George Motz, Treas.

CEMETERIES.

Achdnth Veshalom Congregation (Jewish), e s Broadway, bet Wabash and P, Ft W & C R R's.

German-Lutheran (St Johns), Bluffton road, 3 miles s w of city.

Concordia, n s Maumee road, e of Concordia College. Wm Meinzen, Supt.

Lindenwood, on Huntington road, half mile west of city limits. John H Doswell, Supt.

New Catholic, Hicksville State road, 2½ miles e of Columbia street bridge.

CHURCHES.

BAPTIST.

First Baptist Church, "The Tabernacle of the People," W Jefferson, near Calhoun. Rev S A Northrop, D D, Pastor. Sunday services 10:30 a m and 7:30 p m; Sunday School 2 p m; general prayer meeting Wednesday evening at 7:30.
Young People's Baptist Union meets Sunday evening at 6:30, in the Lecture room.
South Wayne Mission meets Sunday at 2 p m. E W Lewis, Supt.

CATHOLIC.

Cathedral of the Immaculate Conception, Cathedral Square, Calhoun, bet Lewis and Jefferson. Rt Rev Joseph Dwenger, D D, Bishop of the Diocese and Rector of the Cathedral; Very Rev Joseph H Brammer, V G; Rev Jno F Lang, Chancellor and Bishop's Secretary; Rev J F Delaney, Rev J R Quinlan. Sunday services 6, 7:30, 8:30 (children's services) and 10:30 a m; Sunday school 1:30 p m; Vespers 3 p m.
St Joseph's Chapel (in connection with St Joseph's Hospital). Rev Thomas Eisenring, C, P P, S, Chaplain. Sunday services 8 a m and 4 p m. Week day services 8 a m.
St Mary's Church, southeast cor Jefferson and Lafayette. Rev John H Oechtering, Pastor, Rev C M Romer, Assistant. Sunday services 8 and 10 a m and 3 p m; Sunday school 2 p m.
St Paul's Church, southeast corner Griffith and W Washington. Rev Edward Kœnig, Pastor. Sunday services 10 a m and 2:30 p m; Sunday school 2 p m.
St Peter's Church, south side St Martin's, bet Warsaw and Hanna. Rev A Messman, Pastor. Sunday services 8 and 10 a m and 2 p m; Sunday school 9 a m.

CHRISTIAN.

Central Christian Church, cor Harrison and Wayne. Rev M S Blaney, Pastor. Sunday services 10:30 a m and 7:45 p m; Sunday school 9:15 a m. Prayer meeting Wednesday 8 p m.
Christian Chapel, southeast cor W Jefferson and Griffith. Elder G H Sims, Pastor. Sunday services 10:30 a m and 7:30 p m. Sunday school 9:15 a m.

CHURCH OF GOD.

Cor Hoagland ave and DeWald. Rev Ernest H Shanks, Pastor. Sunday services 10:30 a m and 7:30 p m; Sunday school 9:15 a m.

CONGREGATIONAL.

Plymouth Congregational Church, northwest cor W Washington and Fulton. Rev James S Ainslie, Pastor. Sunday services 10:30 a m and 7:15 p m; Sunday school 12 noon. Prayer meeting Wednesday 7:30 p m.

EPISCOPAL.

Trinity Church, southwest cor Fulton and W Berry. Rev A W Seabrease, Rector. Sunday services 10:45 a m and 7:30 p m; Sunday school 9:30 a m from June to October, and 2:30 p m from October to June.

EVANGELICAL ASSOCIATION.

Church northeast cor Holman and Clinton. Rev George Schmoll, Pastor. Sunday services 10:30 a m and 7 p m; Sunday school 9:30 a m.

GERMAN REFORM.

St John's Church, southeast cor W Washington and Webster. Rev Carl Schaaf, D D, Pastor. Sunday services 10:30 a m and 7:30 p m; winter 7 p m. Sunday school 9 a m.

Salem Church, east side Clinton, bet Wayne and Berry. Rev W F Zander, Pastor. Sunday services 10:30 a m and 7:30 p m; Sunday school 2 p m in winter, and 9 a m in summer.

ENGLISH.

Grace Reformed Church, south side E Washington, bet Barr and Lafayette. Rev A K Zartman, Pastor. Sunday services 10:30 a m and 7:30 p m; Sunday school 9:30 a m. Week-day services Wednesday 7:30 p m.

HEBREW.

Achduth Veshalom Temple, s e cor Harrison and Wayne. Samuel Hirschberg, Rabbi. Services Friday 7:30 p m, and Saturday 10 a m. Children's instruction, Sunday 9 to 12 a m and Saturday 9 to 10 a m.

LUTHERAN.

Emanuel Church, south side W Jefferson, bet Union and Jackson. Revs Charles Gross and Max J F Albrecht, Pastors. Sunday services 10 a m and 2 p m.

Evangelical Lutheran Zion's Congregational Church, southwest cor E Creighton ave and Force. Rev Henry Juengel, Pastor. Services Sunday 10 a m and 2 p m.

St John's German Lutheran Church, southeast cor Washington and Van Buren. Rev Henry P Dannecker, Pastor. Sunday services 10 a m and 2:30 and 7:30 p m.

St Paul's German Lutheran Church, west side Barr bet Jeffer-

son and Lewis. Rev Henry G Sauer, Pastor. Services
Sunday 10 a m and 2:30 and 7.30 p m.
Trinity Church (English Lutheran), southeast cor Wayne and
Clinton. Rev Samuel Wagenhals, Pastor. Sunday ser-
vices 10:30 a m and 7:30 p m ; Sunday school 2 p m.

METHODIST EPISCOPAL.

Berry Street Church, northeast cor W Berry and Harrison.
Rev Wm M Van Slyke, Pastor. Sunday services 10:30
a m and 7:30 p m ; Sunday school 2:15 p m. Prayer
meeting Wednesday 7:30 p m.
St Paul's Church, west side of Walton ave south of Wabash
R R. Rev Henry Bridge, Pastor. Sunday services 10:30
a m and 7:30 p m. Sunday school 2:30 p m.
Simpson M E Church, southeast cor Dawson and Harrison.
Rev John M Driver, Pastor. Sunday services 10:45 am
and 7:30 p m ; Sunday school 9:30 a m. Prayer meeting
Wednesday 7:30 p m.
Trinity M E Church, northeast cor Cass and Fourth. Rev R
Wones, Pastor. Sunday services 10:30 a m and 7:30 p m.
Sunday school 2:30 p m.
Wayne Street Church, southwest cor Broadway and W Wayne.
Rev Geo N Eldridge, Pastor. Sunday services 10:30 a m
and 7:30 p m ; Sunday school 2:15 p m. Prayer meeting
Wednesday 7:30 p m.
Free Methodist Church, south side Creighton ave east of
Thomas. Sunday services 10:30 a m and 8 p m. Sunday
school 9:30 a m. Prayer meeting Thursday 8 p m.
African M E Church, notheast cor E Wayne and Francis.
Rev Roberson Jeffries, Pastor. Sunday services 10:30
a m and 7:30 p m ; Sunday school 3 p m.

PRESBYTERIAN.

First Presbyterian Church, northeast cor Clinton and E Washington. Rev D W Moffat, D D, Pastor. Sunday services
10:45 a m and 7:30 p m ; Sunday school 9:30 a m. Prayer
meeting Wednesday 7:30 p m.
Second Presbyterian Church, south side of Berry bet Webster
and Ewing. Rev James L Leeper, Pastor. Sunday ser-
vices 10:30 a m and 7:30 p m ; Sunday school 12 noon.
Prayer meeting Wednesday evening 7:30.
Third Presbyterian Church, northeast cor Calhoun and Holman.
Rev J M Boggs, Pastor. Sunday services 10:30 a m and
7:30 p m ; Sunday school 12 noon. Prayer meeting
Wednesday evening 7:30.
Glenwood Chapel Mission, of the Second Presbyterian Church,
S Broadway s of city limits. Sunday school 3:30 p m.

UNITED BRETHREN.

First U B Church, southeast cor E Lewis and Harmer. Rev B A Sutton, Pastor. Sunday services 10:30 a m and 7:30 p m. Prayer meeting Wednesday and Friday 8 p m.

Second U B Church, southeast cor Boone and Fry. Sunday services 10:30 a m and 7:30 p m.

INCORPORATED INSTITUTIONS.

Anthony Wayne Manufacturing Co, cor Lafayette and Wabash R R. Incorporated January 27, 1886, capital $18,000. John Rhinesmith, Pres; James H Simonson, Sec and Treas; Albert C F Wichman, Supt.

Bash S & Co. Incorporated June 4, 1890, capital $100,000. S Bash, Pres; C S Bash, Vice-Pres; W B Bash, Sec; P D Smyser, Treas.

Bass Foundry and Machine Works, Hanna s of Wabash R R. Established 1853, incorporated 1873, capital $500,000. John H Bass, Pres; J I White, Sec; R J Fisher, Treas.

Berghoff Herman Brewing Co The. Incorporated April, 1887, capital $100,000. Herman J Berghoff, Pres; Hubert Berghoff, Sec and Treas; e s Grant ave, near e Washington.

Brookside Farm Co, 1½ miles west of city. Incorporated March, 1884. John H Bass, Pres; David McKay, Sec; Frank S Lightfoot, Treas.

Dreibelbiss Abstract Co, rooms 3 and 4 Pixley & Long Bldg. Incorporated January, 1887, capital $10,000. John Dreibelbiss, Pres; R B Dreibelbiss, Sec-Treas.

First Regiment Light Artillery Band, 199 Lafayette. Organized August 8, 1888, capital $2,500. Henry Wiegman, Mngr; Oscar Buegner, Leader.

Fort Wayne Business Men's Exchange, 98 Calhoun. Incorporated January 11, 1887. A S Lauferty, Pres; D N Foster, Vice-Pres; J E Bell, Treas; Wm P Cooper, Fin and Rec Sec.

Fort Wayne City Band, 12 W Main. Organized 1874, capital $2,000. Charles Meyer, Pres; Gust Shober, Sec; F J Reineke, Treas; Philip Keinz, Leader.

Fort Wayne City Hospital. Incorporated November 2, 1878. D N Foster, Pres; W D Page, Sec; E F Yarnelle, Treas; Mrs C L Smith, Supt; s w cor Barr and Washington.

Fort Wayne Conservatory of Music. Incorporated 1871. L M Ninde, Pres; Fred J Hayden, Sec; C F W Meyer, Director. 22, 24 and 26 E Main.

Fort Wayne Electric Co. Incorporated August 12, 1889, capital $4,000,000. H G Olds, Pres; P A Randall, Vice-Pres; R T McDonald, Treas and Genl Mngr; Brainard Rorison, Sec. Broadway and Wabash R R.

Fort Wayne Electric Light Co. Organized 1882, capital
$100,000; increased to $500,000 in 1888. H G Olds, Pres;
P A Randall, Vice-Pres; M W Simons, Sec; R T McDonald,
Treas. Broadway and P F W & C R R.

Fort Wayne Furniture Co The. Incorporated November, 1887,
capital $75,000. D N Foster, Pres and Mngr; P A Randall,
Vice-Pres; W E Mossman, Sec; D B Kehler, Treas. Office
and factory e end of Columbia.

Fort Wayne Gas Light Co, s e cor Superior and Barr. Organized 1855, capital $225,000. James Cheney, Pres, Treas
and Supt; Wm J Probasco, Sec.

Fort Wayne Land Improvement Co. Incorporated February
1890, capital $250,000. D N Foster, Pres; P A Randall,
Vice-Pres; C A Wilding, Sec; George W Pixley, Treas.
12 Pixley & Long Bldg.

Fort Wayne Newspaper Union (eastern branch Chicago Newspaper Union), J F Cramer, Pres; C E Strong, Treas;
Charles D Tillo, Manager. Office 54, 55 and 57 E Columbia.

Fort Wayne Organ Co. Incorporated 1871. Office and factory,
e s Fairfield ave, s of Creighton ave. S B Bond, Pres;
C E Bond, Sec; A S Bond, Treas and Supt.

Fort Wayne Relief Union. Office 144 Pritchard. Incorporated
1882. Mrs H F Guild, Pres; Mrs J K McCracken, Vice-
Pres; Mrs G E Bursley, Sec; Miss K Hamilton, Treas.

Fort Wayne Street Railroad Co. Incorporated 1887. J H
Bass, Pres; S B Bond, Vice-Pres; J M Barrett, Sec; A S
Bond, Treas; L D McNutt, Supt. Office s w cor Main and
Calhoun.

Fort Wayne Water Power Co. J H Bass, Pres; H J Miller,
Sec; Lew R Hartman, Treas. Office w s Spy Run ave nr
Burgess ave.

Foster D N Furniture Co. Incorporated August 9, 1884, capital
$80,000. D N Foster, President; S M Foster, Sec; W J
Kettler, Treas. Office 11 Court.

Hoffman Lumber Co. Office 200 W Main. Incorporated 1887.
A E Hoffman, Pres; Wm H Hoffman, Vice-Pres; John
W Sale, Treas; M P Longacre, Sec.

Hoosier Manufacturing Co. Office and factory 28 and 30 East
Berry. Incorporated April, 1882, capital $30,000. Amos
S Evans, Pres; John P Evans, Treas; George P Evans,
Sec; Frank F Budd, Supt.

Horton Manufacturing Co, cor Main and Osage. Incorporated
1883, capital $30,000. H C Paul, Pres; W A Bohn, Sec-
Treas; J C Peters, Genl Mngr.

Indiana Installment Co, Incorporated February 1890, capital
$15,000. Office 166 Calhoun. John V Reul, Pres; E C
Graeter, Sec; W E Graeter, Treas.

Indiana Machine Works, Osage near W Main. J C Peters,

Pres; P A Randall, Vice-Pres; E H McDonald, Sec; J M Landenberger, Treas and Mngr.

Inter-State Fair Association. Incorporated 1886, capital $25,000. office 32 East Berry. Wm D Page, Pres; J W Pearse, Vice-Pres and Supt; D C Fisher, Treas; W W Rockhill, Sec.

"Jenney" Electric Light and Power Co, Spy Run ave. Office rooms 4 and 5 Bass Block. Incorporated 1883, capital $50,000. H C Graffe, Pres; G W Pixley, Vice-Pres and Treas; Emmet H McDonald, Sec; Charles G Guild, Supt.

Journal Co The, 30 E Main. Incorporated May 12, 1884, capital $10,000. W W Rockhill, Pres and Mngr; A J Moynihan, Sec and Treas.

Kerr-Murray Manufacturing Co, n e cor Calhoun and Murray. Incorporated 1881, capital $100,000. A D Cressler, Pres and Genl Mngr; G A Schust, Sec; G L Hackius, Treas.

Masonic Temple Association. Incorporated February, 1878, capital $50,000. A Hattersley, Pres; W W Rockhill, Sec; H W Mordhurst, Treas; n e cor Clinton and Wayne.

Master Builders' Association. Incorporated March 14, 1890, capital $2,000. Wm Geake, Pres; Levi Griffith, Vice-Pres; J W Wilding, Sec and Treas. Office 195 Calhoun.

Mayflower Mills The. Incorporated October 1889, capital $20,000. Charles S Bash, Pres; Joseph Hughes, Mngr; 20 W Columbia.

Old Fort Manufacturing Co. Office 419 E Wayne. Incorporated September 17, 1888, capital $20,000. James Wilding, Pres and Mngr; John M Kuhns, Sec and Treas; Joseph Potter, Supt.

Olds' Wagon Works. Incorporated 1882, capital $200,000. Henry G Olds, Pres; A H Hamilton, Vice-Pres; John Mohr, jr, Sec; W H Olds, Treas; s s Murray bet Calhoun and Lafayette.

Peters Box and Lumber Co, 79 to 105 High. Established 1870, incorporated November 26, 1873, capital $50,000. Charles Pape, Pres and Genl Mngr; W H Murtaugh, Vice-Pres; Wilson McQuiston, Sec.

Ryan Trucking Co. Incorporated 1891, capital $15,000. P A Randall, Pres; R T McDonald, Treas; T B Empie, Sec. Office 19 W Washington.

Salamonie Mining and Gas Co, 50 Clinton. Incorporated 1887, capital $600,000. Henry C Paul, Pres; Charles S Bash, Vice-Pres; Charles McCulloch, Sec; F E W Scheimann, Treas; G Max Hofmann, Supt.

Skelton B W Co The. Incorporated April 28, 1891, capital $25,000. B W Skelton, Pres; C S Bash, Vice-Pres; J B Franke, Sec and Treas; 209 Calhoun.

Standard Medical and Surgical Institute, Incorporated 1890, capital $100,000. W J Carter, A M, M D, Pres and Genl

Mngr; N B Smith, M D, Treas; W W Smith, Ph D, Sec. Office 210 Calhoun.

Star Iron Tower Co. Incorporated February, 1884, capital $25,000. J H Bass, Pres; H G Olds, Vice-Pres; R T McDonald, Sec; P A Randall, Treas; cor Plum and Nickel Plate R R.

Taylor Bros' Piano Co The. Incorporated January, 1885, capital $4,000. S R Taylor, Pres; I N Taylor, Sec. Office 138 Calhoun.

Western Gas Construction Co. Incorporated May 20, 1890, capital $50,000. Olof N Guldlin, Pres; Gordon W Lloyd, Sec and Treas, Detroit, Mich; D K Griffith, Engineer. Offices 24 to 27 Pixley & Long Bldg.

LIBRARIES.

Allen County Teachers' Library, 12 Trentman Block. George F Felts, Librarian.

Catholic Young Men's Reading Halls and Club Rooms; open every evening in Library Hall.

Fort Wayne Catholic Circulating Library and Association, 8,000 volumes, established July 1st, 1871, incorporated August 4th, 1874; Library Hall, n e cor Calhoun and E Lewis. Kilian Baker, President (*ex officio*); George A Fry, Pres; M J Houlihan, Sec; George A Litot, Treas; Rev J R Quinlan, Librarian. Association meets first Thursday in each month. Library open Sundays from 3 to 5, and 7 to 9 p m.

Emerine J Hamilton Library, 23½ W Wayne, 2,000 volumes. Margaret E Hamilton, Pres and Sec.

MILITARY.

Fort Wayne Rifles, meet every Monday evening at 166 Calhoun. C J Bulger, Capt; W H Peltier, 1st Lieut; J E Miller, 2d Lieut; Charles J Bulger, Sec; C E Reese, Company Clerk and Treas.

German Military Co. Henry Heine, Sec; 26 W Main; meets last Sunday in each month.

Zollinger Battery The, W W Munger, Capt; Wm F Ranke, 1st Lieut; Jasper E Wolf, 2d Lieut; Ford Young, Sec.

MISCELLANEOUS INSTITUTIONS AND SOCIETIES.

Academy of Medicine. Dr G W McCaskey, Pres; Dr K K Wheelock, Sec; meets every alternate Monday evening.

Allen County Asylum, n s Bluffton road, opp toll gate. John Wilkinson, Supt.

Allen County Bible Society, Dr Wm T Ferguson, Pres; W E
Griffith, Vice-Pres; H C Schrader, Sec; F D Paulus, Treas.
46 Harrison.

Allen County Licensed Liquor Dealers' Protective Association.
meets first Tuesday in each month at 2 p m, in hall 64 E
Main. Jacob Hartman, Pres; Charles Roeger, Vice-Pres;
George J Ortlieb, Cor Sec; B Weber, Fin Sec; Christ
Entemann, Treas.

Allen County Medical Society, Dr T J Dills, Pres; Dr Howard
McCullough, Sec. Meets first Tuesday evening in each
month.

Barbers' Union No 14, meets in hall in Bank Block every
second and fourth Tuesday of each month. Charles
Yeakley, Pres; Wm G Miller, Fin Sec; Joseph Burger,
Treas.

Bricklayers' Union, meets every Monday evening at 98 Calhoun. Bernard Hankens, Pres; Albert Heider, Vice-Pres;
Henry Ehle, Sec; Fred Lindenberg, Treas.

Brickmakers' Association. Office 55 Clinton. James S Field,
Agent.

Brotherhood of Locomotive Engineers, Division No 12, meets
every Sunday afternoon at 2, at hall, 140 Calhoun.

Brotherhood of Locomotive Firemen, Division No 141, meets
every Monday at 7:30 p m, at hall, 81 Calhoun.

Brotherhood of Railroad Brakemen, meets every alternate Sunday afternoon and every alternate Monday evening of each
month, at 27 Calhoun.

Brotherhood of Railroad Trainmen, meets every Tuesday at
7:30 p m, at K of P Hall, cor Harrison and Pearl.

Bruederlicher Unterstuetzungs Verein, meets third Sunday of
each month, at Trades and Labor Hall. Frederick Schmet-
zer, Pres; Charles H Buck, Sec; Wm Schmidt, Treas.

Butchers' Association, meets first Tuesday in each month, at
Nimrod Hall, 54 E Main. Gottlieb Haller, Pres; David J
Shaw, Sec; 28 Smith.

Caledonian Society, meets first and third Mondays of each
month, at 76 Calhoun. J B White, Pres; D McKay, 1st
Vice Pres; Thomas Stewart, 2d Vice-Pres; Wm Lawson,
Sec; R Dickie, Treas.

Carpenters' Union, meets every Saturday at 7:30 p m, at Trades
and Labor Hall, s e cor of Calhoun and Wayne.

Catholic Knights of America, St Bernard Branch No 103,
meets first and third Sundays of each month, at Library
Hall, n e cor Calhoun and E Lewis. Very Rev J H
Brammer, Spiritual Director; Frank H Fink, Pres; Patrick Ryan, Rec Sec.

Catholic Young Mens' Amusement Society, Library Hall,
rooms open from 8 a m to 10 p m. Rev J R Quinlan, Director.

Clerks' Union No 10 (affiliated with R C N P Association),
  organized Nov, 1890, meets every second Sunday of each
  month at 3 p m in Trades and Labor Hall. F M McLeish,
  Pres; G A Steup, Vice-Pres; G A Kramer, Sec; R P
  Sharp, Treas.

Commandery No 73, Knights of St John, under the control of
  Branch 103, C K of A. Fred Graffe jr, Capt; Louis H
  Gocke, Rec Sec.

Euphonia Double Quartette organized July 1887, meets every
  Tuesday evening in Philharmonic Hall. August Schmidt,
  Pres; W O Gross, Vice-Pres; Wm Baade, Sec; G Hor-
  mel, Mus Director.

Eureka Social Club, organized Sept, 1885. Theodore Seemeyer,
  Treas; s w cor Calhoun and Main.

Father Edward Council, No 237, C B L, meets second and
  fourth Mondays of each month in St Paul's School. Fred
  Link, Pres; Cornelius Brunner, Sec; Edward Monock,
  Treas.

Father O'Leary Council, No 327, C B L, meets second and fourth
  Sundays of each month in Library Hall. Dennis Gorman,
  Pres; E L McCamley, Sec; Joseph Sorg, Treas.

Fort Wayne Amateur Athletic Club, 14 W Berry; James B
  W White jr, Pres; Edward N Detzer, Vice-Pres; Samuel
  W Albratt, Sec; Frederick W Beach, Treas.

Fort Wayne Bicycle Club, 142 Calhoun, organized 1884.
  Membership, 60. C W Edgerton, Pres; John L Hannah,
  Sec; F M Smith, Treas.

Fort Wayne Cigarmakers' Union No 37, meets every Saturday
  evening and first and third Friday evenings of each month,
  in rooms 98 Calhoun. A J Seigfried, Pres; W T Jeffries,
  Sec; Conrad Bayer, Treas.

Fort Wayne City Hospital, cor Barr and Washington. D N
  Foster, Pres; W D Page, Sec; E F Yarnelle, Treas.

Fort Wayne Electric Club, meets first Tuesday in each
  month, in Schmitz Blk. Charles C Miller, Pres; Harry C
  McKinley, Vice-Pres; Eugene McLachlin, Sec; Lewis
  Freyer, Treas.

Fort Wayne Saenger Bund, organized Feb 10, 1869, meets
  every Tuesday for rehearsal. Regular meeting first Sunday
  after first Tuesday in each month at Nimrod Hall, 54 E
  Main. Wm Hahn, Pres; August Langhorst, Sec; Henry
  Brewer, Director.

Fort Wayne Social Club, meets in hall 195 Calhoun, second
  and fourth Sundays of each month. U G Rhodes, Pres;
  Fred Krebs, Vice-Pres; Rudolph Krull, Treas; Frank M
  Rhodes, Sec.

Fort Wayne Trades and Labor Council meets second last Friday
  evening of each month, in Carpenters' Union Hall, Bank
  Block, 30 E Main. Philip Rapp, Pres; Henry Scheuster,
  Vice-Pres; Wm P Duffy, Cor Sec; L C Kasten, Treas.

Fort Wayne Typographical Union, meets first Sunday after-
noon of every month at Trades and Labor Hall. N
Conover, Pres; Wm P Duffy, Vice-Pres; Lew H Green,
Sec.

Fort Wayne Vocal Society, meets every Monday evening at the
Conservatory of Music, 22, 24, and 26 E Main. C F W
Meyer, Director.

German Military Society, organized October 1885, meets
second and last Sundays of each month at 26 W Main.
Herman Hohnholz, Pres; Moritz Truebenbach, Sec;
Charles Roeger, Treas.

Hod Carriers' Union, meets at German Military Hall, 26 W
Main, every Monday evening.

Humane Society, organized Jan 23, 1888. Annual meetings
fourth Monday in January of each year. Charles McCulloch, Pres; Dr Edward J McOscar, Sec and Treas.

Indiana Commandery, No 172, Knights of St John, under control of No 302, C B L Jacob Hartman, Capt; Henry
Wiegand, Sec.

Journeymen Plasterers' Union, meets every Wednesday evening
at 30 E Main.

Kekionga Council National Union, meets second and fourth
Fridays of each month, in Bass Bldg. Geo D Adams Pres;
C O Essig, Sec; J H Tibbles, Treas.

Morton Club, meets n e cor Wayne and Calhoun, on first Monday of each month. W D Page, Pres; G D Adams, Rec
Sec; A T Lukens, Fin Sec; C A T Keimmel, Treas.

Northern Indiana Poultry Association, meets second Monday
in each month. J B Niezer (Monroeville), Pres; W J
Blackbird (Huntington), Sec; G Knisely, Treas.

Order of Railway Conductors, meets every Sunday afternoon
at 106 Broadway. Richard C Ross, Sec.

Philharmonic Club, organized May, 1891, meets second Monday
of each month, 103 Calhoun st. Fred Reineke, Pres;
August Schmidt, Vice-Pres; C J Scheimann, Sec.

Plumbers, Steam and Gas Fitters' Union, meets every Tuesday
at 138 Calhoun.

Q & O Club, organized December, 1886. Wm Fields, Pres;
Frank Carter, Vice-Pres; Conrad Bayer, Sec; Daniel F
Hauss, Treas; meets first Tuesday of each month at n e
cor Calhoun and Main.

Relief Union The, 144 Pritchard. Mrs A D Guilds, Pres;
Miss Emma E Eckels, Supt.

St Agnes Young Ladies' Society, meets first Sunday in each
month at 3 p m at St Peter's Church. Regina Wiegand,
Pres.

St Aloysius Society of St Mary's Catholic Church, meets the
last Sunday in each month. H Zurbruch, Pres; George
App, Sec; Henry Kramer, Treas.

St Boniface Society, meets every fourth Sunday at n e cor W
Washington and Griffith. Fred Link, Pres; Jacob Weick,
Vice-Pres; John Wunderlin, Sec; Peter Wunderlin, Fin
Sec; Michael Gruber, Treas.

St Charles Boromeo Benevolent Society, meets first Sunday in
each month at St Mary's Hall, s w cor Lafayette and
Jefferson. Harry Brink, Pres; Louis Haas, Sec.

St Charles Uniform Rank, meets second Tuesday in each month
at St Mary's Catholic School. Jos Hartman, Pres; Henry
Pranger, Sec.

St Joseph's Hospital, s w cor W Main and Broadway. Sister
Secunda, Superior; Rev Thomas Eisenring, C S S, Chaplain.

St Joseph's Catholic Benevolent Society, meets second Sunday
in each month at Library Hall, n e cor Calhoun and Jefferson. Kilian Baker, Pres; Patrick Ryan, Sec.

St Joseph's School Society, meets first Sunday in each month at
St Mary's Hall, s w cor Lafayette and Jefferson. Henry
Lauer, Pres; Frank Luley, Sec.

St Julian Council, No 89, C B L, meets first and third Tuesdays of each month in Library Hall. C J Sosenheimer,
Pres; Owen Barry, Sec; Joseph J Besson, Treas.

St Martinus Benevolent Society, meets second Sunday in each
month at St Peter's School, s w cor Hanna and St Martin.
George Jacoby, Pres.

St Mary's, No 14 (col'd), meets first Monday in each month in
hall, 254 Calhoun. Furney Turman, W M; James Smith,
Sec.

St Patrick's Catholic Benevolent Association, meets the fourth
Sunday in each month at Library Hall, n e cor Calhoun
and E Lewis. Daniel McKendry, Pres; Patrick Ryan, Sec.

St Rosa Society, meets first Sunday of each month at St Mary's
Church. Miss Lizzie Snilker, Pres; Miss Mary Zurburch,
Sec.

St Stanislaus' Society, meets last Sunday of each month at St
Mary's School. Peter Zurbruch, Pres; Clement Shuckman,
Sec and Treas.

St Stephen's Young Men's Society, meets third Sunday of each
month at St Peter's Church. J W Wiegand, Pres.

St Vincent de Paul Society, instituted for relief of the poor,
rooms Library Hall, n e cor Calhoun and E Lewis. Rev
John Quinlan, Spiritual Director; Mrs C Dinnen, Pres;
Mrs Eliza Kelley, Sec; Mrs Delia Breen, Treas.

St Vincent Orphan Asylum, e s Wells n of Putnam. Rev B T
Borg, Chaplain; Sister Eudoxia, Superior.

Standard Club, cor Berry and Harrison; Max B Fisher, Pres;
Marx Frank, Vice-Pres; Joseph Lohman, Sec; Benjamin
Lehman, Treas; Charles Falk, Louis Wolf, Henry Friend,
Board of Managers.

Stonecutters' Union, meets first and second Tuesdays of each

month at 28 W Main. James McMillan, Pres; Duncan McNaught, Vice-Pres; Michael Deuter, Sec; Christian Keeter, Treas.

Stone Masons' Union, meets every Tuesday evening at 8 E Wayne. John Smith, Pres; Clemens Bymer, Sec.

Switchman's Mutual Aid Association, meets second and fourth Mondays of each month at 7:30 p m; also fourth Sunday of each month at 2:30 p m in Odd Fellows' Hall, n e cor Calhoun and Wayne.

Three Rivers Rod and Reel Society, organized April, 1888, meets second and fourth Sundays in each month, at 54 E Main. Wm Hahn, Pres; Charles Thieme, Sec; Wm Meyer, Treas.

Tinners' Union, meets every Tuesday evening at 98 Calhoun.

Tri-State Veterans' Association, headquarters 210 Calhoun. Alvin P Hovey, Pres; Colonel J W Younge, Adjt-General.

Wayne Council, No 302, C B L, meets second and fourth Wednesdays of each month in St Mary's School. Fred Witte, Pres; Frank Wolhnker, Sec; M W Lauer, Treas.

Young Men's Christian Association, organized March 18, 1886. 105 Calhoun. E A Hackett, Pres; D F Bower, Sec.

Young Men's Christian Association (Railroad Department), cor Calhoun and Holman. C H Newton, Chairman; J W Burns, Gen Sec.

NEWSPAPERS.

Business Guide The, established September, 1887. C G Smith, mngr, 52 and 57 E Columbia. Issued monthly at 50 cents per annum.

Fort Wayne Dispatch (weekly, Ind), James Mitchel, propr and pub, 26 Clinton; issued every Thursday.

Fort Wayne Freie Presse (daily), Otto F Cummerow, propr, n e cor Calhoun and Main.

Fort Wayne Gazette (daily, weekly and Sunday, Rep), R N Leonard, propr, 41 E Berry. Daily issued every morning at 10 cents per week; weekly issued every Thursday, $1.00 per annum.

Fort Wayne Journal (daily and weekly, Dem), The Journal Co, publrs, 30 E Main. Daily issued every morning at 10 cents per week; weekly issued every Thursday, $1.00 per annum.

Fort Wayne Journal of the Medical Sciences (monthly), subscription $1.00 per annum. C B Stemen, editor; George C Stemen, assistant editor; Charles E Archer & Bro, publishers, Clinton.

Fort Wayne News (daily and weekly, Ind), Wm D Page, propr, 19 E Main. Daily issued every evening, $3.00 per annum; weekly every Friday, $1.00 per annum.

5

Fort Wayne Sentinel (daily and weekly, Dem), E A K Hackett, propr, 107 Calhoun. Daily every evening, 10 cents per week; weekly every Wednesday, $1.00 per year.

Gospel Tidings, A R Wheeler, propr, 9 Foster block; issued first day of each month.

Indiana Deutsche Presse (weekly), Otto F Cummerow, propr, n e cor Calhoun and Main.

Indiana Staats Zeitung (daily and weekly), John D Sarnighausen, propr; A Louis Greibel, business manager; Anselm Fuelber, city editor. 37 E Columbia. Daily $4.00 per year; weekly $2.00 per year.

Labor Herald (weekly), Trades and Labor Council, proprs and publrs, 36 Schmitz blk.

Local Preachers' Magazine (quarterly), C B Stemen, M D, L L D, managing editor, 25 Broadway. Terms, $1.00 per annum.

Poultry and Pets. Devoted to Poultry, Pigeons and Pet Stock. Published monthly by Wm D Page, 19 E Main. Terms, $1.00 per year.

Press The (daily and weekly), Fred J Wendell, Pres. 17 Court. Daily issued every morning.

Watchman The (monthly), Mrs H A Berry, propr and editor. P O box, No 129.

PARKS.

Allen County Fair Grounds, west end Washington, bet St Mary's river and P, F W & C Ry.

Anthony Wayne Park, on north side of Maumee river, e of Main st bridge. A summer resort for parties, picnics, etc.

Centlivre's Park, west side Spy Run ave, n of canal feeder. A summer resort for parties, picnics, etc.

City Park, cor Broadway and Taylor.

Hayden Park, e s Harmer, bet Maumee road and E Jefferson.

League Park (Base Ball), e s Calhoun n of E Superior.

McCulloch Park, Broadway opp Nirdlinger ave.

North Side Park, e s N Clinton, bet 5th and 6th.

Swinney's Park, see Fair Grounds.

Vordermark's Grove, s s Maumee road 1 e of Glasgow ave.

Williams Park, s s Creighton ave, bet Webster and Hoagland avenue.

POSTOFFICE.

Southeast cor Berry and Clinton.

Postmaster—C R Higgins.

Assistant Postmaster—Charles W Howey.

Office hours—Week days, 7:15 a m to 9 p m; Sundays, 9 to 10 a m. Corridors open until 11 p m daily.

Money Order Department—Clerk, George D Adams; office hours 8 a m to 5 p m.

Orders are issued in sums of not more than $100. Larger amounts may be transmitted to the same person by additional orders.

Rates for Orders to any part of the United States—Not exceeding $10, eight cents; over $10 and not exceeding $15, ten cents; over $15 and not exceeding $30, fifteen cents; over $30 and not exceeding $40, twenty cents; over $40 and not exceeding $50, twenty-five cents; over $50 and not exceeding $60, thirty cents; over $60 and not exceeding $70, thirty-five cents; over $70 and not exceeding $80, forty cents; over $80 and not exceeding $100, forty-five cents. Postal notes to any amount not exceeding $4.99, three cents.

Rates on all International Money Orders—On orders not exceeding $10, ten cents; over $10 and not exceeding $20, twenty cents; over $20 and not exceeding $30, thirty cents; over $30 and not exceeding $40, forty cents; over $40 and not exceeding $50, fifty cents.

Mailing Department—Chief Clerk, Thos W Blair; Assistants, J M Moderwell, George Humphrey.

General Delivery Department—Chief Clerk, F J Drake.

Registered Letter Department—Clerk, C S Swann. Office hours 8 a m to 5 p m.

Stamp Department—Clerk, P F Poirson. Office hours, 7:15 a m to 9 p m.

Distributing Clerk—F M Morgan.

Free Delivery Department—Superintendent of Letter Carriers, C F Kettler.

Carriers:
No 1—C F Kettler.
No 2—Wm Slater.
No 3—Wm H Griswold.
No 4—F W Gallmeier.
No 5—George L Ashley.
No 6—Fred Reiling.
No 7—P M Lindsley.
No 8—Charles Rau.
No 9—C D Bourie.
No 10—Norval W Wright.
No 11—C M Rouzer.
No 12—John Soliday.
No 13—H C Niedhammer.
No 14—Wm Stahl.
No 15—John B Reitze.
No 16—J K Carson.
No 17—Frank Horstman.
Substitutes—Thomas A Davis, C P Josse, E E Banks.
Special Delivery Messengers—Fred Etzold, Adam Lamar.

Five deliveries daily in the business portion of the city, viz:
at 7:15 a m, 1, 2:30, 4:30 and 10 p m.
Two deliveries daily outside the business portion of the city,
viz: 7:30 a m and 3 p m.
Factory deliveries, viz: 7:15 a m, 1 and 3 p m.
Sundays, office open from 9 to 10 a m. Three city collections
by the carriers are made at 4, 6 and 10 p m. One collection outside business portion at 6 p m.
Postage—The postage on letters to be forwarded in the mails
to any part of the United States is two cents per ounce,
prepaid by stamp. The postage for letters dropped in this
office for delivery in the city, two cents per ounce, prepaid
by stamp.
Canada and the British Provinces—Two cents per ounce; pre-
payment compulsory.
Postage to all countries included in Universal Postal Union—
For prepaid letters, five cents per half ounce; for unpaid
letters received, ten cents per half ounce; for postal cards,
two cents each; for newspapers, if not over two ounces in
weight, one cent each; for books, other printed matter,
legal and commercial documents, pamphlets, music, visit-
ing cards, photographs, prospectuses, announcements and
notices of various kinds, whether printed, engraved or
lithographed, one cent per each weight of two ounces or
fraction of two ounces; merchandise, ten cents for each
eight ounces or fraction thereof, and parcel not to exceed
that weight.
Registration—Valuable letters to any part of the United States
and Canada and the Universal Postal Union, will be
registered on application, for which a charge of ten cents
(in addition to postage) will be made.

PUBLIC BUILDINGS, HALLS, ETC.

Allen County Jail, w s Calhoun nr Superior.
Anderson's Block and Hall, n w cor Broadway and Jefferson.
Arcade Building, s s Berry w of Calhoun.
Arion Hall, cor Main and Harrison.
Anger Block, 65 E Main.
Aveline House Block, s e cor Berry and Calhoun.
Barr Street Market House, s e cor Barr and Berry.
Bank Block, s e cor Main and Court.
Bursley Block, e s Calhoun bet Washington and Jefferson.
Centennial Block, 197 and 199 Broadway.
Certia Block, w s Calhoun bet Wayne and Berry.
City Hall, w s Barr bet Berry and Wayne.
Colerick's Hall, over 49 and 53 Columbia.
Court House, e s Calhoun bet Main and Berry.
Driscoll's Hall, s e cor Calhoun and Wabash R R.

298 Calhoun.
₃ W Superior.
s Berry bet Calhoun and Clinton.
w cor W Main and Harrison.
e s Calhoun bet Washington and Jefferson.
₂ck, 34 and 36 Calhoun.
ty Hospital, 166 Barr.
e s Court bet Main and Berry.
w cor Calhoun and Main.
ıilding, s e cor Berry and Clinton.
e s Calhoun bet Wayne and Washington.
₂stead, s e cor Clinton and Lewis.
ck, e s Fairfield ave bet Williams and Bass.
176 Calhoun.
s Main bet Calhoun and Harrison.
₂, s w cor Calhoun and Columbia.
w cor Calhoun and E Lewis.
₂ck, n w cor Calhoun and Berry.
ı e cor Wayne and Clinton.
e, cor Wayne and Clinton.
s Clinton bet Berry and Main.
e cor Clinton and Wayne.
08 Fairfield ave.
s w cor Broadway and W Jefferson.
k, 5 and 7 N Harrison.
₂alhoun.
₂ E Main.
₂all, Bank Block.
all (new), n s Berry bet Calhoun and Harrison.
₂all, 108 Calhoun.
w s Calhoun n of Main.
Block, e s E Berry bet Calhoun and Clinton.
₂r Berry and Clinton.
Rink, s e cor Main and Fulton.
₂, s w cor Broadway and Washington.
Calhoun bet Washington and Jefferson.
n w cor Barr and Washington.
₂k (old), 242 Calhoun.
₂k (new), s e cor Broadway and W Washington.
Calhoun.
n s Main bet Barr and Clinton.
pital (Catholic), s w cor Broadway and E Main.
s w cor Lafayette and Jefferson.
₂0-44 W Berry.
₂8 W Main.
11, 13 and 15 E Main.
₂l, 94 Harrison.
₂r Hall, s e cor Wayne and Calhoun.
, e s Calhoun bet Berry and Wayne.

Union Block, n w cor Main and Clinton.
Verth's Hall, 267 E Wayne.
Wolke Block, s w cor Calhoun and Wayne.
Young Men's Christian Association Building, 105 Calhoun.

RAILROADS.

Cincinnati, Richmond and Ft Wayne, leased and operated by
the Grand Rapids and Indiana.
Ft Wayne, Cincinnati & Louisville. Passenger depot and
office 1st nr Wells; George L Bradbury, Genl Mngr.
Grand Rapids and Indiana, offices, freight and passenger depots
with Pittsburgh, Ft Wayne & Chicago Ry. W Odne
Hughart, Pres and Genl Manager; J H P Hughart Assist-
ant to President; W R Shelby, Vice-Pres and Treas; F A
Gorham, Auditor; E C Leavenworth Genl Freight Agent;
C L Lockwood, Genl Passenger Agent; W B Stimson,
Supt Northern Division—General Offices Grand Rapids,
Mich. P S O'Rourke, Supt Southern Division—Office, Ft
Wayne Ind. R B Rossington, Freight Agent; John E
Ross, Ticket Agent.
Lake Shore & Michigan Southern, office, freight and passenger
depots cor 1st and Railroad. John Newell, Pres and
Manager, Cleveland, O; R C Harris, Division Supt, Hills-
dale Mich; E S Philley, Freight and Ticket Agent, Ft
Wayne, Ind.
New York, Chicago & St Louis ("Nickel Plate"), general
offices Cleveland, O; passenger depot on old W & E canal,
bet Calhoun and Clinton; freight depot w s Harrison nr
Superior. D W Caldwell, Pres, Cleveland, O; Lewis
Williams, Genl Manager, Cleveland, O; C D Gorham,
Supt; H C Moderwell, Freight Agent; F W Gardener,
Ticket Agent, Ft Wayne, Ind.
Pennsylvania Company, operating the P, Ft W & C Ry, office
e s Clinton, bet Holman and Railroad; freight depot
n e cor Clinton and Railroad. Joseph Wood, Genl Man-
ager, Pittsburgh, Pa; E B Taylor, Genl Supt Transporta-
tion, Pittsburgh, Pa; Charles Watts, Genl Supt, Pitts-
burgh, Pa; C D Law, Supt Western Division; F D
Casanave, Supt Motive Power; R B Rossington, Freight
Agent, Ft Wayne, Ind; John E Ross, Ticket Agent.
Pittsburgh, Fort Wayne & Chicago, leased and operated by
Pennsylvania Company.
Wabash, general offices St Louis, Mo; Master Mechanic's office
cor Fairfield ave and Wabash R R; passenger depot s e
cor Calhoun and Wabash R R; freight depot, s w cor
Calhoun and Wabash R R. Charles M Hayes, Genl Man-
ager; H L Magee, Genl Supt; F Chandler, Genl Pass-
enger Agent; M Knight, Freight Traffic Mngr, St Louis,

Mo; E A Gould, Supt, Peru, Ind; J M Osborn, Division Freight Agent, Toledo, O; C H Newton, Local Freight Agent, office, Freight Depot; R G Thompson, Passenger Agent, Fort Wayne, Ind.

MISCELLANEOUS SCHOOLS.
CATHOLIC.

Academy of Our Lady of the Sacred Heart. Conducted by the Sisters of the Holy Cross, Mother Arserne, Superior. P O Address, Academy, Allen Co, Ind.

Cathedral Schools, in charge of the Brothers of the Holy Cross. Rev J R Quinlan, Director; Brother Engelbert, Superior. Cathedral Square, s w cor Clinton and Jefferson.

St Augustine's Academy (for girls), under the direction of the Sisters of Providence. Cathedral Square, s e cor Calhoun and E Jefferson. Sister M Cyril, Superior.

St Mary's (for boys), under direction of Sisters of Notre Dame, s w cor Jefferson and Lafayette. Rev J H Oechtering, Director.

St Mary's (for girls), under the direction of the Sisters of Notre Dame, s e cor Jefferson and Lafayette. Rev J H Oechtering, Director.

St Patrick's School, conducted by the Sisters of Providence. Rev Joseph Delaney, Director. Cor Fairfield ave and Duryea.

St Paul's (for boys), s e cor W Washington and Griffith. J Hauk, Director.

St Paul's (for girls), under the direction of the Sisters of the Poor Handmaids.

St Peter's, s s St Martin's, bet Warsaw and Hanna, conducted by the Sisters of Notre Dame. Rev A Messman, Director.

GERMAN LUTHERAN.

Emanuel's, northeast cor Union and Wilt. Rev Charles Gross, Principal.

St John's, s e cor W Washington and Van Buren. Rev Henry P Dannecker, Principal.

St Paul's, n e cor Barr and Madison. Rev Henry G Sauer, Director; John H Ungemach, Principal.

Zion German Lutheran, s w cor Creighton ave and Force. Frederick A Klein, Principal.

COLLEGES.

Concordia College (German Lutheran), e s Schick, bet Washington and Maumee road. Organized in Missouri in 1839.

Established in Fort Wayne in 1861. Rev Andrew Baepler, Director.

Fort Wayne College of Medicine, Medical Department of Taylor University, foot of Wayne. Christian B Stemen, M D, Dean; W P Whery, M D, Sec.

Indiana School for Feeble-Minded Youth, located 1¾ miles n e of Court House, opened July 10, 1890. John G Blake, Supt; Mrs Mary E Orr, Matron.

McDermut's Fort Wayne Business College, n w corner Calhoun and Berry. W E McDermut, Pres; G W Lahr, Professor Bookkeeping, Penmanship, Arithmetic, Commercial Law, etc; Miss M J Swayne, Principal Stenographic Dept. Average number of pupils, 150. Day and evening sessions. Evening sessions from September 1st to June 1st.

Taylor University of Fort Wayne, foot of Wayne. Rev T C Reade, A M, Pres; Charles McCulloch, Treas; H C Schrader, Sec.

Westminster Seminary (for young ladies), 251 W Main. Mrs D B Wells, Principal.

PUBLIC SCHOOLS.

BOARD OF SCHOOL TRUSTEES.

President—John M Moritz.
Secretary—A Ely Hoffman.
Treasurer—Oliver P Morgan.
Superintendent—John S Irwin, M D, LL D.
Office Clerk and Librarian—Miss Mary Irwin.
Janitor-in-Chief—James A Gavin.

SPECIAL TEACHERS.

Reading—Miss Blanche C Sargent.
Music—Miss Mary Belle Clark.
Writing—John L Tyler.
Stenography—Wilson E McDermut.
Book-keeping—George W Lahr.

BLOOMINGDALE SCHOOL.

N W COR MARION AND BOWSER STREETS.

Principal—Miss Margaret M McPhail.
Teachers—Miss Emma Stanley, Mrs Sarah J Stahl, Mrs Mabel E Clayton, Miss Emma H Ersig, Miss Alice L Hamil, Miss Grace C Glenn, Miss Edith Holsworth, Miss Jane E Bowman, Miss Katherine Freeman, Miss Victoria Carter, Miss Emilie S Weber.

CENTRAL GRAMMAR SCHOOL.

EAST WAYNE STREET.

Principal—Chester T Lane, A B.
Teachers—Melvin A Brannon, A B; Miss Hannah E Evry, Miss Mary L Jay, Miss Sarah A Updegraff, Miss Ellen McKeag, Miss E Louise Hamilton.

CLAY SCHOOL.

N W COR CLAY AND WASHINGTON STREETS.

Principal—Miss Mary McClure.
Teachers—Miss Sarah E McKean, Miss Emma L Armstrong, Miss Louvie E Strong, Miss Elizabeth Collins, Miss M Georgina Wadge, Miss Annette A Gaskins, Miss Georgina Boyd, Miss Della Mitchell, Miss Rose E Kohn, Miss Nellie M McKay, Miss Annie G Habecker, Mrs Jennie S Woodward.

EAST GERMAN SCHOOL.

IN HARMER SCHOOL BUILDING.

Principal—Miss Emma C Weber.
Teacher—Miss Bertha Ritter.

FRANKLIN SCHOOL.

N E CORNER FRANKLIN AVENUE AND HOFFMAN STREET.

Principal—Miss Mary E Freeman.
Teacher—Miss Jessie Robinson.

HAMILTON SCHOOL.

N E CORNER PONTIAC AND CLINTON STREETS.

Principal—Miss Anna M Fairfield.
Teacher—Mrs Delia F Wilson.

HANNA SCHOOL.

S W COR HANNA AND WALLACE STREETS.

Principal—Miss Belle R Lloyd.
Teachers—Mrs Marion H Brenton, Miss Margaret A Wade, Miss Addie H Williams, Miss Martha E Wohlfort, Miss Cecilia Foley, Miss May C Hedekin, Miss Sadie L Sturgis, Miss Kittie O'Rourke, Miss Grace M Waldo, Miss Clara F Humphrey, Mrs Elizabeth O Collins.

HARMER SCHOOL.

N W CORNER HARMER AND JEFFERSON STREETS.

Principal—Mrs Mary S Waldo.
Teachers—Miss Matilda E Knight, Miss Edith M Boseker, Miss Mary E Christie, Miss Fannie R Conover, Miss Henrietta M Winbaugh.

I

HOAGLAND SCHOOL.

N E CORNER HOAGLAND AVENUE AND BUTLER STREET.

Principal—Miss Frances Hamilton.
Teachers—Miss Mary A Abel, Miss Mary E Dick, Miss Katie
A Ross, Miss Emma F Gaskins, Miss Minnie F Homsher,
Miss Mary Ella Orff, Miss Miriam R Cohen, Miss Mary B
Lincoln, Miss Maude F Hendricks, Miss Nellie I Newell,
Miss Carrie A Snively, Miss Elizabeth B Mitchell, Miss
Lillie B Beaber.

HOLTON AVENUE SCHOOL.

S W CORNER HOLTON AND CREIGHTON AVENUES.

Principal—Miss Edith M Brewster.
Teachers—Miss Cora Doughty, Miss Martha Stumpf.

JEFFERSON SCHOOL.

S W CORNER JEFFERSON AND GRIFFITH STREETS.

Principal—Miss Harriet E Leonard.
Teachers—Miss Clara Phelps, Miss Elizabeth M Biegler, Miss
Janet A McPhail, Miss Elizabeth E Chapin, Miss Mary
Smyser, Miss Ella R Williard, Miss Helen Brenton, Miss
Anna M Trenam, Miss Mary I Smith, Miss Ruth Etta
Cothrell, Miss Marina J Geake.

McCULLOCH SCHOOL.

N W CORNER McCULLOCH AND ELIZA STREETS.

Principal—Miss Edith E Ersig.
Teachers—Miss Emma M McElfatrick, Miss Clara Greer.

MINER STREET SCHOOL.

COR MINER AND DE WALD STREETS.

Principal—Miss Alice M Habecker.
Teachers—Miss Martha M Clark, Miss Lillian Fisk, Miss C
Gertrude Clippinger, Mrs Elsie A Hall.

NEBRASKA SCHOOL.

S E CORNER OF BOONE AND FRY STREETS.

Principal—Miss Susan S Sinclair.
Teachers—Miss Lillie V Bowen, Miss Prudence L Bowman.

WASHINGTON SCHOOL.

S W CORNER WASHINGTON AND UNION STREETS.

Principal—Miss Margaret S Cochrane.

Lettie A Van Alstine, Miss Jessie L Hum-
Lizzie F Irwin, Miss Josephine Updegraff,
C Boles, Miss Effie B Richey, Miss Mabel
Miss Leola M Connett, Miss Edith M Cothrell,
,umbard.

WEST GERMAN SCHOOL.

STREET, SOUTH OF WASHINGTON STREET.

Schwarz.
;arah C Schaaf.

Γ AND BENEVOLENT SOCIETIES.

MASONIC.

northeast cor Clinton and Wayne.

Ϊo 25, F & A M. Meets first Saturday on or
noon; J C Craig, W M; D L Harding, Sec.
dge, No 170, F & A M. Meets first Friday in
; A F Brintzenhoeft, W M; Daniel W Souder,

o 342, F & A M. Meets first Tuesday in each
is C Kasten, W M; T C Warner, Sec.
odge, No 359, F & A M. Meets second Mon-
 month; C B Stemen, W M; Wm E Hood, ▾

pter, No 19, R A M. Meets first Wednesday
th; Levi Griffith, H P; G W Spencer, Sec.
ncil, No 4, R & S M. Meets second Wednes-
month; J M Henry, Ill M; G W Spencer, Sec.
nmandery, No 4, K T. Meets third Thursday
th; C E Read, E C; G W Spencer, Rec.
nd Lodge of Perfection, A & A S Rite, N M
rst and third Tuesdays of each month; Wm
 G M; C B Fitch, Sec.
Princes of Jerusalem, A & A S Rite, N M J.
d and fourth Tuesday of each month; C M
? G M; C B Fitch, Sec.

ODD FELLOWS.

Hall in Bank Block.

dge, No 14. Meets every Monday evening;
haels, N G; S B Hartman, Sec.
ayne, No 17, Patriarchs Militant. Meets first
Tuesdays of each month; H L Williamson,
Kelsey, Clerk.

ncordia Lodge, No 228. Meets every Wednesday evening in Harmony Hall; E Younghans, N G; Gottlieb Haag, Rec Sec.

ncordia Rebekah Degree Lodge, No 41 (German). Meets first and third Thursdays in each month at Harmony Hall; Mrs Susanna House, N G; Lisetta Faust, Rec Sec.

borah Rebekah Degree Lodge, No 110. Meets second and fouth Tuesdays in each month at Harmony Hall; Mrs Prudence Craig, N G; Mrs Mary Brown, Rec Sec; Mrs Jennie Johnston, Per Sec; Mrs Alice Barbier, Treas.

een Esther Rebekah Degree Lodge, No 324. Meets second and fourth Saturdays of each month in hall in Bank Block; Mrs Nanna Hammond, N G; Mrs Julia Fredericks, V G; Mrs Jennie Benoy, Rec Sec; Mrs Clara Lipes, Per Sec; Mrs G Parry, Treas.

t Wayne Encampment, No 152. Meets second and fourth Friday evenings in each month; O E Moehler, C P; Wm Beck, S W; F Frisbee, J W; A Levy, H P; John Kocher, R S; D L Harding, P S; T J Rodabaugh, Treas; E M Powers, I G; G S Carl, O G.

rmony Lodge, No 19. Meets every Thursday evening at Harmony Hall; J H Payne, N G; R W Scarlett, V G; M A Mason, R S; H H Barcus, P S; Wm Myers, Treas.

nmit City Encampment, No 16. Meets first and third Friday evenings in each month at Harmony Hall; Albert Barbier, N G; R P Sharp, C P; J N Kelsey, Rec Sec.

GRAND ARMY OF THE REPUBLIC.

hony Wayne Post, No 271. Meets in Nill's Hall, 80 Calhoun, first and third Fridays of each month; A R McCurdy, P C; W H Davis, Q M; Jos Lombard, Adjt.

rge Humphrey Post, No 530. Meets at Foster Hall, Foster Blk, first and third Saturdays of each month; Crawford Griswold, P C; Patrick Ryan, S V; Amon Sine, J V; R G Renfrew, Q M.

S Bass Post, No 40. Meets at Nill's Hall, 80 Calhoun, second and fourth Fridays of each month; Frank Gibson, P C; Enos White, Adjt; Sol Soliday, Q M.

m Veteran Legion, Encampment No 51. Meets second and fourth Mondays of each month, in Nill's Hall; A M Darroch, Col Com; S W Stirk, Q M; M M Thompson, Adjt.

A. O. U. W.

Wayne Lodge, No. 19. Meets every Tuesday evening at their hall, 138 Calhoun. Wm Birbeck, M W; D B Kehler, Recorder; T H Hibbins, Foreman; F N Hayden, Financier; W F Reitz, Receiver.

nee Lodge, No 50. G L Ashley, M W; G E Mong, Foreman; C W Inman, Overseer; Fred Gorsline, Recorder;

B A Strawn, Financier; E M Powers, Receiver; J W Kehler, Guide; J A Velvick, I W; H Plock, O W.

Summit City Lodge, No 36. Meets every Thursday evening at their hall, 138 Calhoun. C W Holverstott, P M W; Julius Koch, M W; N Conover, Recorder; M M Haines, Foreman; J B Saunders, Financier; F E Purcell, Receiver; R B Ross, Guide; J R Shafer, I W; J Racine, O W.

IMPROVED ORDER OF RED MEN.

Me-che-can-noch-qua Tribe, No 106. Meets every Tuesday night in Trentman Bldg. Isaac Prime, Sachem; H C Eckels, Senior Sagamore; S W Engle, Chief of Record.

INDEPENDENT ORDER OF B'NAI B'RITH.

B'nai B'rith Lodge, organized April 15, 1865. Meets first and third Sundays in each month in hall in Bass Block; Henry Friend, Pres; Louis Wolf, Vice-Pres; E Strass, Sec; J Lohman, Treas.

KNIGHTS OF HONOR.

Fort Wayne Lodge, No 1547. Meets second Wednesday in each month, at 30 Calhoun; C A Zollinger, Dictator; Abraham G Barnett, Reporter.

KNIGHTS OF LABOR.

No 2315, Liberty Assembly. Meets every Thursday evening at K of L Hall, Postoffice Bldg.

KNIGHTS OF PYTHIAS.

Goethe Lodge, No 99. Meets every Thursday evening in Bass Blk. Conrad Bauss, C C; B Hartmann, V C; Theodore Bruck, Prelate.

Phœnix Lodge, No 101. Meets every Monday evening in Randall Hall. L C Hunter, C C; E V Emrich, V C; C F Shaw, Prelate; D J Shaw, K of R and S.

Fort Wayne Lodge, No 116. Meets every Tuesday evening in Bass Blk. Walter Lyman, C C; B Van Sweringen, M D, V C; Theo Thorward, K of R and S.

Loyal Lodge, No 182. Meets in Bass Blk every Wednesday evening; F A Hull, C C; R P Smith, V C; C J Lose, K of R and S; Wm Geiger, Prelate.

Summit City Uniform Rank. Camp meets second and fourth Fridays of each month in Randall Blk; E L Siver, S K C; U G Lipes, S K T; A E Doswell, S K H; H L Herring, S K R.

KNIGHTS OF THE GOLDEN EAGLE.

Meets every Wednesday at 8 p m in Seidel Block, 52 Calhoun; John A Miller, Noble Chief.

ORDER OF CHOSEN FRIENDS.

John H Bass Council, No 3.   Meets second and fourth Tuesday
evenings in each month at 34 Calhoun; C C Gumper, C C;
Harry Hamill, V C;   H P Vordermark, Rec Sec and
Financier; Peter Morganthaler, Treas.

PATRIOTIC CIRCLE.

Fort Wayne Circle, 101.   Meets every Wednesday evening at
Phœnix Lodge Room, Phœnix Block; Isaac Strauss, O;
George Walke, V O; Samuel Headford, Sec.

ELKS.

B P O E, No 155.   Meets every Wednesday evening in hall,
Trentman Building; A McPherson, E R; L Heilbroner,
Sec.

ROYAL ARCANUM.

Howard Council, No 246.   Meets first and third Fridays of
each month at Bass Block; Wm Tigar, Regent; George
Reiter, Past Regent; H C Moderwell, Sec and Treas.

SONS OF ST. GEORGE.

Robin Hood Lodge.   Meets second and fourth Tuesdays of
each month in hall, 26 E Berry; Albert Tomkinson, Pres;
George Doswell, Sec; Robert Ogden, Treas.

TELEGRAPH AND TELEPHONE COMPANIES.

Edison Mutual Telegraph Co, C G Harrison, Mngr; office,
Wayne Hotel.
Western Union Telegraph Co, Oscar L Perry, Mngr; office,
Aveline House Block.
Central Union Telephone Co, W P Chapman, Mngr; office, 34
Calhoun.

R. L. POLK & CO.'S

FORT WAYNE DIRECTORY

1891-92.

ABBREVIATIONS.

adv............advertisement	n e cor......................northeast cor
agt..............................agent	nr................ ..near
assn..........................association	n s............................ north side
asst..............................assistant	n w cor ....northwest cor
ave......................avenue	opp ....opposite
bds..............................boards	pres........ ....president
bet...........................between	propr..................proprietor
bldg........................building	publr........................publisher
blksmith....... ....blacksmith	res................................resides
carp..........................carpenter	Rev............................Reverend
cash..............................cashier	rd............................. ....road
col'd........................colored	s..................south or south of
cor..............................corner	s e cor........... ......southeast cor
e..............east or east of	sec......................... ....secretary
e s............................east side	s s.............. ....south side
lab..............................laborer	supt...................... superintendent
mach..........................machinist	treas............................treasurer
mkr......... .... maker	whcl............................wholesale
mnfg....................manufacturing	w.................. ....west or west of
mnfr....... ....manufacturer	w s ....west side
mngr..............................manager	wks.............................. works
n............. ....north or north of	

ALPHABETICAL LIST OF NAMES.

A

Abbott Wm T, real estate, 1 Foster blk, res 172 E Berry.

Abdon Eva, stenogr Ft Wayne Electric Co, bds 19 W Jefferson.

Abdon George, plumber James Madden, rms 94 Calhoun.

Abel, *see also Ebel and Habel.*

Abel John C, Lawyer, 3 and 4 Bank Blk, bds 405 Calhoun.

Abel Miss Mary A, teacher Hoagland School, bds 405 Calhoun.

Abel M Kate, teacher, bds 405 Calhoun.

Abercrombia John, engineer G R & I R R, bds 38 Brackenridge.

Aborn Thomas E, printer Archer, Housh & Co, res 107 W Berry.

Academy of Our Lady of the Sacred Heart, conducted by the Sisters of the Holy Cross, Mother Arsene superior, 6 miles n of Court House.

ARCHITECTS. WING & MAHURIN, 41 and 42 Pixley & Long Bldg. Telephone 328.

60   R. L. POLK & CO.'S

Achduth Veshalom Temple, s w cor Harrison and Wayne.
Achenbach Harry, musical instruments, 210 Calhoun, res 50 E Butler.
Acker, *see also Aker, Ecker and Eicher.*
Acker Wm J, painter L O Hull, res 53 Madison.
Ackermann, *see also Eckermann.*
Ackermann Charles L, lab Penn Co, res 64 Summit.
Ackermann John, lab, res 77 Summit.
Ackermann John, lab Penn Co, bds 64 Summit.
Adams Andrew J, millwright Herman Berghoff Brewing Co, res 107 John.
Adams Charles C, engineer, res 226 E Lewis.
Adams Elizabeth, bds 48 Brackenridge.
Adams Express Company, Wm Geiger Agt, 95 Calhoun.
Adams George, reporter, bds Harmon House.
Adams George D, clerk Postoffice, res 165 Griffith.
Adams Israel, mach, res W Main nr Lindenwood Cemetery.
Adams Israel B, engineer, res 48 Brackenridge.
Adams James C, photographer, 135 Broadway, res same.
Adams John H, dentist, 102 Calhoun, res same.
Adams Louisa, bds 48 Brackenridge.
Adams Mary, bds 48 Brackenridge.
Adams Minnie, bds 165 Griffith.
Adams Oscar S, molder, res 42 Wells.
Adams Thomas H, brakeman, res 104 Hayden.
Adams Walter W, mach Bass F & M Works, bds 226 E Lewis.
Adams Wilhelmina (wid Charles), res 215 W Washington.
Adams Wm, painter Penn Co, res 7 Union.
Adamson George W, bds 106 Hanna.
Adamson Lewis R, dynamo winder Ft Wayne Electric Co, res 16 Walnut.
Aderman Christina (wid Charles), bds August Tasler.
Adkins Albert C, helper Penn Co, res 48 Laselle.
Adkins Mary E (wid Armus W), bds 353 Calhoun.
Adler Anna (wid Andrew), res 61 Wall.
Adler Frederica, seamstress Hoosier Mnfg Co, bds 61 Wall.
Aebi J R, lab Penn Co, bds cor DuBois and Maumee rd.
Aehnelt Adelbert, steward Concordia College, res same.
Aehnelt Caroline, matron Concordia College, res same.
Aelig Max, apprentice Keller & Braun, bds 2 Elm.
Affolder John, lab Bass F & M Works, bds 6 Oliver.
Affolder Ludwig, lab Bass F & M Works, res 147 Buchanan.
Affolder Wilhelmina, seamstress, bds 147 Buchanan.
African M E Church, n e cor Wayne and Francis.
Agenbroad John F, coachman 240 W Berry.
Agster Annie M (wid Gottlieb), res 42 W Jefferson.

CUSTER HOUSE

16 AND 18 W. MAIN ST.,

Fort Wayne, - Indiana.

This Hotel is located in the central part of the City, one square from the Postoffice, Telegraph Office and Court House, and is fitted up with every modern convenience, including Sample Rooms for Commercial Travelers.

THE BAR IS ALWAYS SUPPLIED WITH THE

Choicest Wines, Liquors and Cigars.

Rates $1.50 and $2.00 per Day,

According to Location of Rooms.

SPECIAL ARRANGEMENTS FOR TROUPES. G. SCHERZINGER, Propr.

Albert S. Allen

HOUSE, SIGN AND CARRIAGE

PAINTER

Also, GRINDER OF PAINTS.

43 Dock St., rear of 43 E. Columbia.

6

Agster Charles A, mach Wabash R R, res 206 Hoagland ave.
Ahearn Edward, molder Bass F & M Works, res 98 Lillie.
Ahern Dennis F, switchman N Y, C & St L R R, bds 199 Barr.
Ahern Edward E, fireman, bds 199 Barr.
Ahern Johanna (wid Eugene), res 199 Barr.
Ahern Mary, bds 199 Barr.
Ahern Patrick T, tel opr Edison Mutual Telegraph Co, bds 199 Barr.
Ahern Thomas, plasterer, res 71 Wagner.
Ahern Thomas W, rms 226 Calhoun.
Ahern Wm, lineman, res 65 E De Wald.
Ablers Frederica (wid John), dressmkr, res 117 Montgomery.
Ahlersmeyer Wm, mason, res s s Wayne Trace 1 e of Winch.
Ahner Jacob, car builder Penn Co, res 141 Walton ave.
Ahrens Edward J, finisher, bds 52 Laselle.
Ahrens Matilda (wid Anton), res 52 Laselle.
Aichele Dora, starcher Troy Steam Laundry, res 79 St Mary's avenue.
Aichele George F, polisher Brunner & Haag, res 79 St Mary's avenue.
Aiken, see also Eakin.
Aiken Charles, yardmaster, res n s 4th 1 e of Wells.
Aiken John H, Lawyer, 36 Calhoun, bds 362 W Main.
Aiken John W, conductor, res 195 W Superior.
Aiken Wm A, porter G E Bursley & Co, res 206 E Washington.
Ainsbaugh Lizzie, waiter Rich's Hotel.
Ainslie Rev James S, pastor Congregational Church, res 330 W Washington.
Ainsworth Amos M, teamster, res 217 W Superior.
Ainsworth Wm H, driver, bds 124 Union.
Ainsworth Wm M, lab S Bash & Co, res 76 Wells.
Ake Elias, lab, res 21 Savilla ave.
Ake Rosanna (wid Zedekiah), res 19 Lincoln ave.
Aker, see also Acker and Eicher.
Aker Ambrose B, lab, res 199 Sherman.
Aker Miss Aurelia, bds 199 Sherman.
Aker Charles, lab, res 11 Howell.
Aker Miss Minnie, bds 199 Sherman.
Akers Florence, bds 29 E 2d.
Akey James E, cabinetmkr Ft Wayne Furniture Co, res 283 E Washington.
Akret Martin, lab, bds Jewel House.
Albers Elizabeth (wid Herman), res 69 Force.
Albers Herman, died January 24, 1891.
Albers Herman J, molder Bass F & M Works, bds 69 Force.
Albers Mary, dressmkr, bds 69 Force.

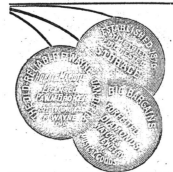

Albers Peter R, clerk, res 75 Smith.
Albers Philip E, lab Penn Co, res 324 E Jefferson.
Albersmeyer Charles, molder Bass F & M Works, bds 192 Madison.
Albersmeyer Christian H, clerk Martin Detzer, bds 192 Madison.
Albersmeyer Frederick, carp, bds 192 Madison.
Albersmeyer Louisa (wid Frederick), res 192 Madison.
Albert Anton, lab, bds 40 Pritchard.
Albert Josephine A, teacher Conservatory of Music, bds 164 E Lewis.
Albert Mary (wid Julius), res 164 E Lewis.
Alberty Adolph (F C Boltz & Co), res 209 W Jefferson.
Albrecht Anton, cigarmkr A N Ehle, res 516 E Lewis.
Albrecht Bruno, clerk, bds 334 Hanna.
Albrecht Charles F, cigarmkr John Zern, bds 516 E Lewis.
Albrecht Edward, carriage trimmer, bds 112 E Main.
Albrecht Frank A, clk Ft Wayne Electric Co, res 268 W. Washington.
Albrecht Frank L, bds 41 Harmer.
Albrecht Gustav R, mach hand Wayne Knitting Mills, bds 391 W Main.
Albrecht Martin L, res 41 Harmer.
Albrecht Rev Max J F, pastor Lutheran Emanuel Church, res 338 Broadway.
Albrecht Otto, finisher Ft Wayne Furniture Co, res 182 Smith.
Albrecht Pauline (wid John), res 12 Wilt.
Albrecht Peter, shoemkr, 117 Broadway, res 14 Elm.
Albrecht Samuel W, bkkpr, bds 41 Harmer.
Albrecht Wm F, cigarmkr Louis Bender, res 334 Hanna.
Albro Francis, driver U S Exp Co, res South Wayne, Ind.
Alden Samuel R, Lawyer, 18 Bank Block, res 135 E Washington.
Alderman Dayton (Shordon & Alderman), res 324 W Jefferson.
Alderman Frank (Louis Schmidt & Co), res 303 W Washington.
Alderman Frank jr, clk Louis Schmidt & Co, bds 303 W Washington.
Aldine Hotel The, James Humphrey Propr, n s E Berry bet Clinton and Barr.
Aldrich Bessie, domestic 587 E Washington.
Aldrich Elisha M, bds 301 Fairfield ave.
Aldrich George, lab, res 365½ E Lewis.
Alexander Frank E, car builder Penn Co, res 65 Buchanan.
Alexander Lucius F, clk H W Bond, bds 54 E Washington.
Alexander Reece H, foreman H W Bond, res 54 E Washington.
Alexander Samuel M, cutter Samuel M Foster, bds 53 Holton avenue.

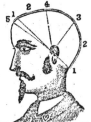

Alexander Stephen, lab, res 58 Wells.

Alfelt Emil, coremkr Bass F & M Works, res 22 W Main.

Alfelt Sophia, domestic 142 W Berry.

Allegear, *see also Allgeier.*

Allegear Charles, driver Powers & Barnett, bds 57 Barr.

Alleman May, bds 339 Harrison.

Alleman Norah, bds 339 Harrison.

Allen Albert S, House and Sign Painter and Paper Hanger, 43 Dock, res same. (*See page 61.*)

Allen County Asylum, John Wilkinson supt, w s Bluffton rd opp toll gate.

Allen County Fair Grounds, w end of W Wayne.

Allen County Jail, w s Calhoun nr Superior.

Allen County Loan and Savings Association, Edward White Pres, Gottlieb Haller Vice-Pres, T C Rogers Sec, Charles W Orr Treas, 6 and 7 White's Block.

Allen County Teachers' Library, G S Felts librarian, 12 Bass block.

Allen Cyrus W, builder, 324 W Washington, res same.

Allen Frank, driver, rms 16 Chicago.

Allen Frank F, supt, res 198 W De Wald.

Allen Jennie M, teacher, bds 324 W Washington.

Allen John F, carp Penn Co, res 373 Hanna.

Allen Louis P, cigarmkr, res 11 McClellan.

Allen Lyman P, supt Fair Grounds, res 360 W Washington.

Allen Mrs Nellie, removed to Boston, Mass.

Allen Richard, engineer Jenney Electric Light and Power Co, res 39 Wabash ave.

Allen Robert, painter Wayne Paint and Painting Co, bds Washington House.

Allen Mrs Rose M, died Oct, 1890.

Aller Isaac N, wks Ft Wayne Electric Co, res 334 W Washington.

Allgeier, *see also Allegear.*

Allgeier Anton, lab, res 162 Taber.

Allgeier Charles, tinsmith S F Bowser & Co, bds 262 E Washington.

Allgeier Frank J, tinsmith, res 36 E 4th.

Allgeier Henry, propr Allgeier Mnfg Co, 262 E Washington, res same.

Allgeier Mary, market stall 84, res Adams twp.

Allgeier Mnfg Co, Henry Allgeier propr, tinsmiths, 262 E Washington.

Alliger Frank, teamster Ft Wayne Artificial Ice Co, rms 3 N Harrison.

Alliger James, pedler Ft Wayne Artificial Ice Co, rms 3 N Harrison.

lway, *see Alway.*

ms Lloyd, brakeman G R & I R R, res 30 Lillie.

onza Wm, tailor L J Feist, bds 226 Lafayette.

t Anton, lab, res 149 Suttonfield.

tekruse Henry R, carp Penn Co, res s w cor Warren and Reynolds.

tekruse Wm E, carp, res 29 N Calhoun.

tenburger Basilius, res 161 Monroe.

ter Albert C, clk A C Katt, bds 133 E Main.

ter Anna, bds 20 Wilt.

ter Bros (Jacob A jr and Henry A), painters, 20 Wilt.

ter George, lab, res 18 Buchanan.

ter Henry A (Alter Bros), res 19 Pritchard.

ter Jacob A, res 20 Wilt.

ter Jacob A jr (Alter Bros), bds 20 Wilt.

ter John D, molder Bass F & M Works, bds 27 John.

ter Nicholas, clk P A Ofenloch, res 133 E Main.

ter Peter, carp, res 27 John.

ter Peter jr, lab Penn Co, bds 27 John.

ternau Charles H, plasterer, res 55 Madison.

tevogt Henry, clerk R Steger & Co, bds 150 Montgomery..

tevogt Herman F, res 38 Allen.

tevogt Louis, mach hand Bass F & M Works, bds 38 Allen.

tevogt Wm R, mach Bass F & M Works, res 42 Allen.

vord Frances D (wid Alvin A), res 154 W Berry.

way Edward, car repairer N Y, C & St L R R, res 89 Richardson.

ann Celia, bds 215 E Washington.

ann Charles, conductor, res 51 St Martin.

ann Frank C, molder Bass F & M Works, bds 51 St Martin.

ann John H, molder Bass F & M Works, bds 215 E Washington.

ann Joseph F, clerk Root & Co, bds 215 E Washington.

ann Louis, plasterer, res 215 E Washington.

bler Emmet E, gas inspector, res 12 W 5th.

buster, *see Armbroster.*

erican Electrical Directory, Star Iron Tower Co publrs, cor Plum and Nickel Plate R R.

merican Express Co, L P Hulburd Agent, Court opp Court House.

merican Wheel Co, cor Lafayette and Wabash R R.

es George W, res 15 Hamilton.

oss Jasper M, collector N Y Installment Co, rms 43 E Columbia.

oss Mrs Sarah, res 110 W Main.

ersen Anna, domestic 401 Lafayette.

Andersen Louis N, student, res 27 Pritchard.
Andersen Miss Matilda, bds 28 E Williams.
Andersen Peter, wagonmkr, res 28 E Williams.
Andersen Thorwald A, boxmkr Olds' Wagon Works, bds 28 E Williams.
Anderson Andrew, conductor, res 165 High.
Anderson's Block and Hall, n w cor Broadway and Jefferson.
Anderson Calvin, res 123 W Wayne.
Anderson Claes A, saw-filer Peters Box and Lumber Co, res 90 Harrison.
Anderson Columbus C, brakeman, res 222 Hugh.
Anderson Edward M, brakeman, res n w cor Rumsey ave and Howell.
Anderson Eli G, asst cash Penn Co, res 123 W Wayne.
Anderson Frederick A, compositor Ft Wayne Gazette, bds 183 W Jefferson.
Anderson George, driver, res 29 Boone.
Anderson George, fireman Penn Co, res 17 Pritchard.
Anderson George D, wks Ft Wayne Electric Co, bds 234 W Washington.
Anderson Goldie, bds 165 High.
Anderson Harry A, acting supt Standard Oil Co, res 337 W Main.
Anderson James R, engineer, res 411 Calhoun.
Anderson John N (col'd), lab Bass F & M Works, res 31 Pearl.
Anderson John R, lab, rms 37 Barr.
Anderson John W, painter Ft Wayne Electric Co, res 207 Broadway.
Anderson Joseph, driver, bds Arlington Hotel.
Anderson Joseph, lab, bds 112 E Main.
Anderson Julia (widow James), dressmkr, 90 E Main, res same.
Anderson Miss Minnie M (Anderson & Large), res 36 W Wayne.
Anderson Peter, blksmith Bass F & M Works, res 300 E Washington.
Anderson Robert E, mach E B Kunkle & Co, bds 123 W Wayne.
Anderson Sarah, cash, bds 123 W Wayne.
Anderson Wilson D (J W Darroch & Co), bds 189 Ewing.
Anderson Zora G, binder Archer, Housh & Co, bds 165 High.
Anderson & Large (Minnie M Anderson, Josephine Large), music teachers, 36 W Wayne.
Andre Amelia, clk T H McCormick, bds e s Fulton 1 n of Nickel Plate track.
Andreasen Hans, wheelmkr, bds 28 E Williams.
Andreasen Villads P, gearmkr, bds 28 E Williams.
Andrew David, boilermkr Penn Co, res 201 Barr.

Geo. E. Johnson, DENTIST, 74 Calhoun Street.
Res., 188 W. Berry St.

FORT WAYNE DIRECTORY. 71

S. P. PHILLIPS, M. D.

PHYSICIAN AND SURGEON,

Special Attention Given to Catarrhal Diseases of the Nose, Throat, Ears and Lungs,

 By a new scientific method with medicated air in treatment of diseases of the Nose, Ear, Throat, Bronchi and Lungs. On the diagram you will notice the cavities of the head and throat that by other methods are not reached. No. 3 Frontal cavity, No. 4, Lachrymal canal leading to the eye, No. 5, Ganglionic nerve, No. 1, Sphenoid cavity, or No. 2, Eustachian tube leading to drum of the ear. the stronghold of Catarrh. Many cases already have taken treatment and pronounced it superior to all others. Consultation free.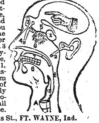

Office, 362 Calhoun St. Residence. 16 W. Williams St., FT. WAYNE, Ind.

Office Hours: 10 to 12 a. m., 2 to 4 and 6 to 8 p. m.

Andrew Jeannette, bds 201 Barr.
Andrew Lizzie, milliner, bds 201 Barr.
Andrews Charles, removed to Monroeville, Ind.
Andrews Harry, teamster M M Smick, bds 106 Chicago.
Andrews James, lab, res 106 Chicago.
Andrews James C, boilermkr, res 598 Calhoun.
Andrews Josephine, bds 339 W Main.
Andrews Pearl, opr Hoosier Mnfg Co, bds 106 Chicago.
Andrews Rebecca, domestic 151 Wells.
Andrus Cora A, bds 78 Douglas ave.
Andrus George H, engineer, res 78 Douglas ave.
Angelbeck Augusta, domestic 135 E Washington.
Angell Byron D, lumber, res 242 W Berry.
Angell John J, conductor N Y, C & St L R R, res 9 Breck.
Angell Mary C (widow Orange), res 166 W Berry.
Angevine George E, blksmith, 5 Pearl, bds 82 Force.
Angevine Wm E, trav agt, res 82 Force.
Angst Catherine, boxmkr W H Davis, bds 56 Madison.
Angst Joseph, clerk Root & Co, bds 56 Madison.
Angst Theresa (widow Leonhard), res 56 Madison.
Ankenbruck Frank, driver L Brames & Co, bds 162 E Jefferson.
Ankenbruck John, carp, bds 48 Harmer.

ROBERT SPICE, WINDMILLS AND DRIVE WELLS, LIGHTNING RODS and FIXTURES, 48 West Main and 11 Pearl Streets.

72   R. L. POLK & CO.'S

Ankenbruck Joseph, car bldr Penn Co, res 30 Erie.
Ankenbruck Louis, driver A Kalbacher & Co, bds 67 Force.
Ankenbruck Martin H, driver Beadell & Co, res 48 Harmer.
Ankney Mary, seamstress, bds 367 Force.
Anstett George, driver J P Tinkham, res 71 Huron.
Anthony Wayne Mnfg Co, John Rhinesmith pres, James H
    Simonson sec and treas, Albert C F Wichman supt, wash-
    ing machine mnfrs, cor Lafayette and Wabash R R.
Antrim Mrs Eva, bds 135 Wallace.
Antrup Frederick W, res 79 W Main.
Anweiler George W, mach hand Indiana Machine Works, bds
    168 Ewing.
Anweiler Minnie (widow Louis), housekeeper, 168 W Creighton.
App, see also Happ.
App Annie, bds 104 W Washington.
App Block, 106 Calhoun.
App Bros (Henry J and George J), shoe mnfrs, 46 W Main.
App Clement P, clerk Mathias App, bds 104 W Washington.
App George J (App Bros), bds 104 W Washington.
App Henry J (App Bros), res 362 E Washington.
App Martin, pressman Journal Co, res 360 E Washington.
App Mathias, Boots and Shoes, 106 Calhoun, res 104 W
    Washington.
Apple Emery, brakeman, rms 18 Brackenridge.
Applegate Charles W, clerk Tri-State Building and Loan Associ-
    ation, bds 106 E Main.
Arantz Emma, bds 58 E Washington.
Arantz Miss Mary, bds 58 E Washington.
Arantz Philip, res 58 E Washington.
Arantz Simon P, woodworker Olds' Wagon Works, res 447
    Lafayette.
Arantz Wm, filer, res 296 E Lewis.
Arcade Building, s s Berry w of Calhoun.
Archer Charles E (Archer, Housh & Co), res 152 Wells.
Archer David L, lab S Bash & Co, res 45 E 2d.
Archer Frederick, lab, bds 45 E 2d.
Archer Grace, student, bds 45 E 2d.
Archer, Housh & Co (Charles E Archer, John Housh,
    R S Taylor, W Sherman Archer), Printers and Publishers,
    82 Clinton.
Archer John H, res 39 E 2d.
Archer Joseph F, fireman Penn Co, res 83 Baker.
Archer Mary J, seamstress, bds 176 Hoffman.
Archer Mary L, seamstress, bds 39 E 2d.
Archer Olive E, bkkpr Archer, Housh & Co, bds 39 E 2d.
Archer Perry J (Coverdale & Archer), res 75 Wells.

Archer Wm L, clerk B W Skelton Co, res 35 E 4th.
·Archer W Sherman (Archer, Housh & Co), res 74 S Wayne av.
Archibald Abraham F, clerk Wabash R R, res 468 Harrison.
Archibald James L, helper Kerr-Murray Mnfg Co, bds 5 St
    Mary's ave.
Ardler Mary, domestic 16 Gay.
Arens Bernard, lab, res 90 John.
Arens Herman, bds 152 E Washington.
Arens Herman J, helper Kerr-Murray Mnfg Co, bds 90 John.
Arens John, grocer, 122 Madison, res 124 same.
Arens Mary, opr Hoosier Mnfg Co, bds 90 John.
Argerbright James M, clk Pape Furniture Co, res 127 N Cass.
Argo Martin E (Argo & Buck), rms 52 Calhoun.
Argo & Buck (Martin E Argo, Wilson S Buck), Genl Agts
    Equitable Life Assurance Society, 52 Calhoun. (*See back*
    cover.)
Arick John J, propr Nickel Plate Hotel, 31 W Columbia.
Arieon Lewis, mason, res 232 E Jefferson.

Arion Hall, cor Main and Harrison.
Armack J Bernard, mach Penn Co, res 169 Montgomery.
Armack Dorothea (wid Albert), bds 73 W Jefferson.
Armack Frederick, fireman Chemical Engine Co No 1, rms Engine House No 1.
Armbruster Lorenz, lab Bass F & M Works, res 136 Horace.
Armel Charles C, hostler J W Pearse, res 143 Wallace.
Armel Milton, carp, res 86 Wagner.
Armel Walter, carp, bds 85 Wagner.
Armel Wm, bds 47 Laselle.
Armel Wm jr, conductor, res 47 Laselle.
Armfield John C, trav agt Carnahan & Co, bds Aldine Hotel.
Armstrong Charles, brakeman, rms 16 Bass.
Armstrong Charles E, finisher, res 196 E Jefferson.
Armstrong Emma, waiter Indiana School for Feeble-Minded Youth.
Armstrong James A, whol millinery, 109 Calhoun, res 148 W Berry.
Arney Scott, lab, res e s Glasgow 1 s of E Washington.
Arnold Anthony A, vise hand Indiana Machine Works, bds 478 Harrison.
Arnold Anthony N, cabinetmkr Ft Wayne Organ Co, res 478 Harrison.
Arnold Amos W, driver Troy Steam Laundry, res 60 Home ave.
Arnold Charles W, clk, bds rear 56 E Main.
Arnold David A, carp, bds Windsor Hotel.
Arnold Emma A, bds 478 Harrison.
Arnold Harry A, clk Root & Co, bds 478 Harrison.
Arnold John, lab, bds 360 W Washington.
Arnold John J, lab, res rear 56 E Main.
Arnold Louisa, domestic 144 Maumee ave.
Arnold Samuel, switchman, rms 133 Holman.
Arns Edward, lab, bds 52 Laselle.
Arns Herman R, bellowsmkr Ft Wayne Organ Co, bds 52 Laselle.
Arns Matilda (wid Anthony), res 52 Laselle.
Arp Charles W A, clk Frank Ofenloch, bds 120 Clinton.
Arter Ephraim, lab David Tagtmeyer, bds 100 Superior.
Arter Joseph, lab David Tagtmeyer, res s w cor Hoffman and Wells.
Artis James (col'd), lab, res 7 Dwenger ave.
Ash Charles, trav agt, bds 16 Hamilton.
Ash Mrs Cora H, bkkpr, bds 104 E Main.
Ash Henry J, stoves, 9 E Columbia, res 104 E Main.
Ash Ida, domestic 67 E Main.
Ash Lillian G, bds 104 E Main.

?, bkkpr, bds 104 E Main.
ea A (wid Philo H), res 160 W Washington.
ndus E, bds 28 Nirdlinger ave.
ge L, carrier Postoffice, res 61 Madison.
arnabas, lab Penn Co, res 68 Force.
, carp J M Henry, res 44 Pritchard.
y, brakeman, bds Racine Hotel.
hn A, agt, bds Hedekin House.
ed J, clk J H Hartman, res 167 Hayden.
k J, lab, bds 34 Smith.
J, lab, res 132 Horace.
h, res rear Leikauf's packing house.
h J, mach hand Rhinesmith & Simonson, res 15

s, lab Penn Co, bds 17 Nirdlinger ave.
l, turner, res 17 Nirdlinger ave.
, lab, res 108 Wells.
jr, tailor John Rabus, bds 108 Wells.
, bds 17 Nirdlinger ave.
X, helper Henry Freistroffer, bds 108 Wells.
e C, conductor Penn Co, bds 17 Nirdlinger ave.
, janitor Concordia College, res same.
mach Olds' Wagon Works, res 49 E Williams.
lab, res w s Walton ave 3 s of Pontiac.
I, clk J C Figel & Bro, bds 108 Wells.
nach hd, bds 17 Nirdlinger ave.
harles, plumber C W Bruns & Co, bds 17

udolph J, lab, res 247 E Washington.
arles, saloon, 36 W Main, res same.
s Mary, bds 36 W Main.
nnie, bds 36 W Main.
Louis, Propr City Greenhouse, 16 E Washington,
th Wayne, Ind; Greenhouse, cor Creighton ave
bster, res 16 E Washington.
es, res 453 E Wayne.
s, lab C Scotton, bds same.
erica C, clk Root & Co, bds 251 E Jefferson.
niah W, car inspr Penn Co, res Dunkirk, O.
rles, lab, res 28 Orchard.
rad, helper Penn Co, res 118 Gay.
ry E W, clk Siemon & Bro, bds 16 Orchard.
ry F (Gerding & Aumann Bros), bds 118 Gay.
ie, dressmkr 28 Orchard, bds same.

ARCHITECTS. WING & MAHURIN,
41 and 42 Pixley & Long Bldg. Telephone 358.

76   R. L. POLK & CO.'S

Aumann Wilhelmina, seamstress, bds 118 Gay.
Aumann Wm, watchman Peters Box and Lumber Co, res 16 Orchard.
Aumann Wm jr, bkkpr J B White, bds 16 Orchard.
Aumann Wm H (Gerding & Aumann Bros), bds 118 Gay.
Aurentz Anna P, bds 129 W Main.
Aurentz Emma, bds 129 W Main.
Aurentz Frank, clk S A Aurentz, bds 129 W Main.
Aurentz Robert J, clk S A Aurentz, bds 129 W Main.
Aurentz Skelley P, clk S A Aurentz, bds 129 W Main.
Aurentz Solomon A, grocer, 31 W Main, res 129 same.
Austin Birdie, bds 46 Centre.
Austin Clarence R, brakeman, res 103 Gay.
Austin Daniel S, photographer, 156 Horace, res same.
Austin Emma, bds 46 Centre.
Austin Hieronymus B, patent rights, res 46 Centre.
Austin Jaline (wid Wm M), bds 156 Horace.
Austin Louise (wid John C), bds 144 Horace.
Auth Anthony P, bds 281 Hanna.
Auth Anton P, car builder Penn Co, res 65 Buchanan.
Auth Catherine (wid Peter), res 23 4th.
Auth J Henry, bartndr John Christen, res 135 W Wayne.
Aveline House, s e cor Calhoun and Berry.
Aveline House Block, s e cor Calhoun and Berry.
Avis John, driver, res 65 W 4th.
Axner Robert, lab, res n e cor Holton ave and Maud.
Axt August, lab, bds n s Hugh 1 e of Ohio.
Axt Charles W, molder Bass F and M Works, res 213 Madison.
Axt Mrs Melissa, bds 197 E Lewis.
Axt Moritz, res 129 Francis.
Axt Wm T, car builder Penn Co, bds 186 Francis.
Ayres Henry B, mnfrs' agt, rms 56 Pixley & Long bldg.
Ayers Philip G, trav agt, res 176 W Creighton ave.

B

Baade, see also Bade.
Baade Conrad H, carp Penn Co, res 10 Nirdlinger ave.
Baade Eliza, bds 263 E Jefferson.
Baade Ernst, carp, res 69 Hugh.
Baade Ernst. bds 59 Maumee ave.
Baade Frederick C, clk Salimonie Mining and Gas Co, res 261 E Jefferson.

Baade Henry, car repairer, res 17 Barthold.
Baade Henry C (Kayser & Baade), res 19 Pritchard.
Baade Henry F, clk Root & Co, bds 17 Barthold.
Baade Wm, driver, res 263 E Jefferson.
Baade Wm C, clk Penn Co, res 251 E Jefferson.
Baade Wm C F, mach hand, res 162 3d.
Baader Carrie, domestic 91 W Berry.
Baals August (Baals & Co), res 94 W Main.
Baals Barbara (wid George), res 158 Montgomery.
Baals Emma A, nurse, bds 302 W Jefferson.
Baals Miss Mina A, clerk A Goodman, bds 302 W Jefferson.
Baals Rosanna (wid John L), res 302 W Jefferson.
Baals Sadie, milliner Mrs A C Keel, bds 302 W Jefferson.
Baals & Co (August Baals), furniture, 59 E Main.
Baatz Ernst F, lab, bds rear 65 Hendricks.
Baatz Wm, lab, bds rear 65 Hendricks.
Babb Carl H, clerk Anton Kalbacher, rms 24 Baker.
Babcock Mary (wid John F), res rear 27 W Butler.
Babcock Oliver L, mach, res 181 Montgomery.
Babcock Thomas Z, engineer Ft Wayne Electric Co, res 43
    Locust.
Bach Savannah (wid Peter R), bds 594 Lafayette.
Back Peter, mason, res 1 Walnut.
Backes, see also Beckes.
Backes Anna, bds 129 Wilt.
Backes Jacob, boilermkr Penn Co, bds 30 3d.
Backes John, boilermkr Penn Co, res 30 3d.
Backes John J, boilermkr Penn Co, res 129 Wilt.
Backes Mathias, boilermkr Penn Co, res 58 Melita.
Backes Philip W, lab Penn Co, bds 58 Melita.
Backofen Julius, carp Horton Mnfg Co, res 186 St Mary's ave.
Backes Wm, lab Penn Co, bds 129 Wilt.
Backman Frederick H, lab, res 173 Gay.
Backofen Julius, mach hand Horton Mnfg Co, res 189 St
    Mary's ave.
Bacome Frank E, foreman The Press, res 107 Lafayette.
Bacon Adeline E, bds 241 W Washington.
Bade, see also Baade.
Bade Frederick, clk F P Mensch, bds 113 High.
Baepler Andrew, director Concordia College, res college grounds.
Baer, see also Baier, Bair, Bayer and Bear.
Baer Alvin E, engineer, res 329 W Washington.
Baer August, tailor J H Grimme & Sons, res 40 Oak.
Baer Essie M, opr Samuel M Foster, bds 57 E DeWald.
Baer Francis J, opr Hoosier Mnfg Co, bds 57 E DeWald.
Baer Frank E, bartender, bds 100 Madison.

Baer Joseph M, actionmkr, bds 57 E DeWald.
Baer Mary (wid George), res 57 E DeWald.
Baer Wm M, cabinetmkr Ft Wayne Organ Co, bds 57 E De-
Wald.
Bagby Albert L, constable, res 85 W Superior.
Bahde, *see Baade and Bade.*
Bahret, *see also Barrett.*
Bahret Christian, boilermkr, bds 22 Pritchard.
Bahrets Joseph, lab Bass F & M Works, bds 6 Oliver.
Baier, *see also Baer, Bair, Bayer and Bear.*
Baier Catherine S, tailoress, rms 37 Barr.
Baiers John N, mach hand Rhinesmith & Simonson, bds 178 W
Washington.
Bail Anna, seamstress, bds n w cor Reed and Pontiac.
Bail Anthony, lab, bds n w cor Reed and Pontiac.
Bail Emily, opr Samuel M Foster, bds n w cor Reed and Pontiac.
Bail Joseph, carp Rhinesmith & Simonson, res n w cor Reed
and Pontiac.
Bail Joseph F, turner Anthony Wayne Mnfg Co, bds n w cor
Reed and Pontiac.
Bailer Jacob, grocer, 38 Maumee rd, res same.
Bailer Samuel, clk J Bailer, bds 38 Maumee rd.
Bailey, *see also Baillie and Baily.*
Bailey Alexander, barber, res 6 Melita.
Bailey August, lab, res 204 Hanna.
Bailey Catherine (wid Jacob), bds 486 Hanna.
Bailey Frank, brakeman, res 146 W Main.
Bailey Frederick P, blksmith, res 238 St Mary's ave.
Bailey Harriet, bds 76 W Creighton ave.
Bailey Louis A, teamster J W Pearse, bds 6 Melita.
Bailey T Emanuel, printer The Press, res 50 Chicago.
Baillie, *see also Bailey and Baily.*
Baillie Andrew, boilermkr, bds 166 Jackson.
Baillie Ella, opr Hoosier Mnfg Co, bds 166 Jackson.
Baillie George S, butcher J C Doyle, bds 166 Jackson.
Baillie John, blksmith Kerr-Murray Mnfg Co, res 166 Jackson.
Baillie John W, blksmith Wabash R R, res 100 Wilt.
Baillie Thomas S, fireman, bds 166 Jackson.
Baily, *see also Bailey and Baillie.*
Baily Alpheus H, harnessmkr, res 86 Wagner.
Baily August, lab Penn Co, res 495 E Washington.
Baily Frank, lab Ft Wayne Gas Light Co, res 12 Wagner.
Baily Frank C, stereotyper, bds 86 Wagner.
Baily Harry B, painter F W Robinson, bds 86 Wagner.
Baily James A, printer Ft Wayne Newspaper Union, res 197
Barr.

L. DIETHER & BROTHER,
44 to 54 E. Superior street.
Factory: 100 Pearl Street.

WAYNE DIRECTORY.   79

Bower, res 86 Wagner.
obert Spice, rms 94 W Main.
er Mayflower Mills, res 198 St Mary's

lder Ft Wayne Electric Co, res 23

4 E Berry.
, Bayer and Bear.
L Johns & Co, res 301 W Main.
s 120 Boone.
e.
ne Paint and Painting Co, rms 191

fer & Schlatter, bds 120 Boone.
diana Machine Works, bds 120 Boone.
rr-Murray Mnfg Co, bds 558 Calhoun.
Co, res 558 Calhoun.
d Boecker.
Main.
Vayne.
er, bds 40 Miner.
ved to Butler, Ind.
De Wald.
fr, 31 E Main, res Baker ave 1 mile

J S Exp Co, res 33 Barr.
es, 16 Lafayette, res 139 Clinton.
d,) res 193 W Berry.
Wayne Electric Co, bds 330 Calhoun.
s 80 Buchanan.
B H Baker, bds 139 Clinton.
us), agt Metropolitan Mnfg Co, res

Baker & Co), res 18 Laselle.
ayne Street R R Co, res 3 Glasgow.
& St L R R, bds Jacob Moore.
Baker), res Van Wert, O.
es 75 W De Wald.
79 Cass.
Baker.
s 111 Taylor.
de, res 52 Miner.
ner.
Penn Co, res 102 W Butler.
Boulevard 4 n of Lakeside addition.
Calhoun, bds 46 E Jefferson.

John, res 139 Clinton.

John (John Baker & Co), res 18 Laselle.

John & Co (John and Mrs Frances Baker), roofers, rear 7 Lafayette.

John G, saw mill, res 347 E Wayne.

Jonas E, carp, rms 29 E Main.

Joseph J, clk U S Exp Co, res 128 E Main.

Joseph L, saloon, 34 E Calhoun, res same.

Josiah C M, ticket receiver Penn Co, res 16 W Creighton ꞓnue.

r Kilian, Mnfr Hardwood Lumber, cor Superior and' fayette, res 92 E Main.

Laban, painter, res 155 Hayden.

Lawrence A, cigarmkr A C Baker, bds same.

Margaret A, bds 92 E Main.

May, housekeeper 40 Wagner.

Noah A, carp, res 162 W Creighton ave.

Thomas J, clk, res 22 Park ave.

Vincent J, plumber A Hattersley & Sons, bds 193 W' rry.

Wm H, mach Penn Co, res 469 Lafayette.

b Sarah (wid Rodney), rms 70 W Wayne.

ꞓ Lydia, bds 144 Wallace.

ꞓ Wm R, foreman Daily News, res 27 Hanna.

vin D H & Co, Pianos, Organs, Music and Musical truments, 98 Calhoun.

ꞓ Elbert D, clk Union Line, bds 189 W Berry.

ꞓ Frances (wid Elbert), res 189 W Berry.

ꞓ George, brakeman, res 18 Breck.

ꞓ Lindley J, deputy treas, res 247 W Berry.

ꞓ Merchant H, tel opr N Y, C & St L R R, bds 189 W rry.

ꞓ Walter (col'd), waiter Wayne Hotel.

ꞓ also *Boll.*

ꞓma, bds 172 W Main.

ꞓma W, bds 170 W Washington.

ꞓnklin J, printer The Press, rms 94 W Superior.

ꞓd D, cook, rms 94 W Superior.

ꞓlian, bds 172 W Main.

ꞓgdalena (wid Rudolph), grocer, 172 W Main, res same.

Levi A, helper Kerr-Murray Mnfg Co, bds 151 E ferson.

ꞓn, *see also Bollmann and Bolman.*

ꞓn Carrie, bds 33 Nimllincer ave

Ballmann Rosina, winder, bds 28 Nirdlinger ave.
Ballmann Theresa, clk F W Kiesling, bds 28 Nirdlinger ave.
Ballou Harlie, switchman, bds 18 McClellan.
Balmer Alfred, lab, bds 22 E Columbia.
Balser Lizzie, domestic-s e cor Park pl and Hoagland ave.
Balsiker Albert, janitor German Reformed Orphans' Home, bds same.
Balsiker Mrs Elizabeth, cook German Reformed Orphans' Home.
Balsinger Gottfried, lab Bass F & M Works, res 381 Lafayette.
Baltes Clara A, bds 63 Harrison.
Baltes Edward M, clk M Baltes, bds 63 Harrison.
Baltes Jacob, brick mnfr, res n e cor Wagner and Spy Run ave.
Baltes John, mason, bds n e cor Wagner and Spy Run ave.
Baltes Michael, Mnfr of White Lime and Dealer in Stone, Cement, Sewer Pipe, Etc, cor Harrison and Nickel Plate Track, res 63 Harrison.
Baltes Peter, bricklayer, res 157 E Washington.
Baltzer Ferdinand, lab, res s s Wiebke 4 e of Lafayette.
Balzell Dayton, lab, bds 28 W Main.
Balzer Valentine, watchman, res 12 Force.
Bandau Frederick, lab, res 27 Pritchard.
Bandau Theodore, lab Ft Wayne Iron Works, bds 27 Pritchard.
Bandel Nellie, bds 245 E Lewis.
Bandelier August, lab, res 17 Gay.
Bandt Frederick, carp, res 87 W De Wald.
Bandtel George F, clk Pfeiffer & Schlatter, res 358 E Wayne.
Banet Alexander, bartndr George Noirot, bds 29 E Main.
Banet Louis E, saloon, 72 E Columbia, res 11 Riverside ave.
Bangert Bonifacius, grocer, 34 Fairfield ave, res same.
Banister Euretta C, bds 46 W Wayne.
Banister Mrs L Webb, Teacher of Voice Culture and Instrumental Music, Music School 46 W Wayne, res same. (*See page 65.*)
Bank Block, s e cor Main and Court.
Banks Creed T, res 219 W Washington.
Banks Elmer E, carrier Postoffice, bds 351 E Wayne.
Banks Eugene T, bds 219 W Washington.
Banks George, boilermkr, bds 155 John.
Banks Joseph V, removed to Jackson, Mich.
Banta, *see Bente.*
Banzhoff George W, Mngr The Singer Mnfg Co, rms 121 Harrison.
Barber George K, mach, res 365 Lafayette.
Barber Harlow E, fireman Penn Co, res 11 Colerick.
Barbier Alfred, painter Penn Co, res s s Maumee rd, 1 e of toll gate.

Barbour Dolly, bds 84 E Berry.
Barbour Myron F, res 90 E Berry.
Barclay Mary, domestic 35 John.
Barcus Anzella (wid Isaac), res 271 Webster.
Barcus George, candymkr H H Barcus, bds 96 Calhoun.
Barcus Henry H, Baker and Mnfg Confectioner, Café,
    Ice Cream and Oyster Parlors, 96 Calhoun, res same.
Bard Samuel, res 39½ W Berry.
Barden Wm N, engineer Penn Co, res 28 W Creighton ave.
Bardin Louis, lab Artificial Ice Co, bds Lake Shore Hotel.
Barge James, brakeman, res 144 Horace.
Bargemann Mary (wid Diedrich), bds 100 Smith.
Barker Dwight W, yardmaster, res 62 Buchanan.
Barkley Ira L, lab L S & M S Ry, bds Riverside Hotel.
Barley Stella, bds 38 E 5th.
Barlow Jennie (wid John), res n w cor Osage and Main.
Barnard Horace S, waiter J F Cline, bds 77 Lafayette.
Barnard Wm M, clk Pfeiffer & Schlatter, res 77 Lafayette.
Barner Addie H, seamstress P E Wolf, bds 155 Montgomery.
Barner Charles F, foreman Rocker Washing Machine Co, res
    155 Montgomery.
Barner Emma, dressmkr, bds 155 Montgomery.
Barner Henrietta, dressmkr, bds 155 Montgomery.
Barner Henry C, tinner H J Ash, res 153 Montgomery.
Barner Lillian, bds 155 Montgomery.
Barnes Charles, fireman, rms 337 W Main.
Barnes Charles E, boltmkr, res 6 Fox.
Barnes Frank J, collector, bds 165 E Lewis.
Barnes James W, clk, res 28 Taber.
Barnes Jessie, bds 165 E Lewis.
Barnes Joseph, lather, res 165 E Lewis.
Barnes Rev R Monroe, removed to Denver, Col.
Barnett Abraham G (Powers & Barnett), res 18 E Wayne.
Barnett Byron H, brakeman, bds 18 E Wayne.
Barnett James C, brakeman G R & I R R, bds 82 Mont-
    gomery.
Barnett James W, clk Powers & Barnett, rms 18 E Wayne.
Barnett Simon, Propr Diamond Hotel, 233-235 Calhoun.
Barnett Wm, cooper, bds 82 Montgomery.
Barnett W Wynn, physician, 434 Calhoun, rms same.
Barney Frank M, brakeman, res 33 1st.
Barnhardt, see also Bernhard.
Barnhardt Louisa, domestic 306 Maumee rd.
Barnhart Mary, domestic, bds 34 W Superior.
Barnum Lina (wid George P), livery, 91 E Columbia, res same.
Barr James (James Barr & Bro), bds 9 Rockhill.

ıes & Bro (James and Wm J), Grocers, 32 W

ι (wid Thomas), res 9 Rockhill.
, carp, res 174 Taylor.
Market House, s e cor Barr and Berry.
(James Barr & Bro), res 63 W De Wald.
gust, plasterer, res 99 Laselle.
rene, lather, bds rear 99 Laselle.
nk, lather, res rear 99 Laselle.
nk J, collector, bds 165 E Lewis.
sie, bds 165 E Lewis.
n, lather, res 505 E Washington.
n B, foreman Louis Diether & Bro, res 30 Oak.
eph L, lather, res 165 E Lewis.
ius, lather, bds rear 99 Laselle.
er J, lather, bds rear 99 Laselle.
ılso *Bahret.*
ence (Barrett & Co), bds 135 Wells.
lerick C (Barrett & Co), res 135 Wells.
es M (Morris, Bell, Barrett & Morris), res 255
l ave.
ɔ (Frederick C and Florence Barrett), grocers, 380
ι.
W, clk Root & Co, rms 25 E Washington.
ry, lab Penn Co, res 402 Calhoun.
ı, teamster, bds 402 Calhoun.
Frank R (Diether & Barrows), Photographer,
ıun, res 242 W Wayne.
thy, carp, res 22 Winch.
ɔ *Berry.*
, lab, bds 74 Melita.
lab, res 66 Burgess.
forgeman Penn Co, res 110 Hayden.
e, bds 207 E Jefferson.
a I, bds 207 E Jefferson.
aret, bds 207 E Jefferson.
ıel, physician, 207 E Jefferson, res same.
'so *Bertels.*
e, bds 5 McClellan.
(wid Wm), res 58 Hayden.
y, carp Frederick Kraft, res St Joseph twp.
y, mach hand Ft Wayne Spoke Works, res 181

, bds 58 Hayden.
lab, res 58 Hayden.
ɔ, molder Bass F and M Works, bds 58 Hayden.

Barthold Matthew, cook Wayne Hotel.

Bartholomew Eugene E, carp, bds 90 E Lewis.

Bartholomew Frank P, carp Rhinesmith & Simonson, bds 90 E Lewis.

Bartholomew Rillman, draughtsman, res 90 E Lewis.

Bartlett Laura E, seamstress, rms 205 Madison.

Barton Daniel, removed to Crestline, O.

Baschelier Christina (wid George), bds 366 W Main.

Base Christina (wid Amand), res 150 E Jefferson.

Baser Lizzie, domestic 103 Erie.

Bash Charles S, pres Mayflower Mills, res 280 W Wayne.

Bash Daniel F, with S Bash & Co, bds 240 W Berry.

Bash Harry E, cash Mayflower Mills, bds 240 W Berry.

Bash Solomon, pres S Bash & Co, res 240 W Berry.

Bash S & Co, Solomon Bash pres, Charles S Bash, vice-pres, Willis B Bash sec, P D Smyser treas, produce, 22 W Columbia.

Bash Willis B, sec S Bash & Co, bds 240 W Berry.

Bash Winfield S, with S Bash & Co, res 183 W Berry.

Bashara Salem, fruits, res 65 W Superior.

Bashelier Philip, painter, res s w cor Webster and Pearl.

Bashet John, lab, res 127 W Superior.

Bashop Elizabeth, domestic 25 W Washington.

Bassl Margaret (wid Martin), res 133 Holman.

Bass Alfred (col'd), barber, 32 E Calhoun, res 489 E Wayne.

Bass Block, 73–77 Calhoun.

Bass Foundry and Machine Works (Capital $500,-000), John H Bass Pres, John I White Sec, Robertson J Fisher Treas, Hanna south of Railroad Crossing.

Bass Henry, foreman Indiana School for Feeble-Minded Youth.

Bass John H, pres Bass F and M Works and pres First National Bank, res 113 W Berry.

Bass Madison, cook Indiana School for Feeble-Minded Youth.

Bass Mrs Ophelia, cook Indiana School for Feeble-Minded Youth.

Bassalmann Mary, domestic 328 W Washington.

Bassett Frank (Wm H Bassett & Son), bds Wm H Bassett.

Bassett Isa (col'd), cook The Randall.

Bassett John M, trav agt American Wheel Works, res 118 Jackson.

Bassett Mary (col'd), domestic 76 Lafayette.

Bassett Wm H (Wm H Bassett & Son), res n e cor Runnion ave and Rebecca.

Bassett Wm H & Son (Wm H and Frank), dairy, n e cor Runnion ave and Rebecca.

L. O. HULL, Paints, Oils, Varnishes and Glass at 90 Calhoun Street.

FORT WAYNE DIRECTORY. 85

Bassett Wm O, mach Penn Co, res 187 E Lewis.
Bastian Jacob, (Summit City Paper Co), res 205 Madison.
Bastues Christina (wid Michael), res 224 Hugh.
Bastues John M, molder Bass F & M Works, res 399 E Lewis.
Batchelder Isaac W, painter S W Hull, bds 95 Montgomery.
Batchelder Jesse S, confr B W Skelton & Co, res 206 E Lewis.
Bates Clem F, Meat Market, n w cor Indiana and Lincoln aves, res Lakeside.
Bates Daisy, student, bds 108 E Wayne.
Bates Elizabeth, clk, bds 28 Buchanan.
Bates Miss Ida, clk, bds 390 E Wayne.
Bates John F, fruits, res 139 Griffith.
Bates Lycurgus, carp Penn Co, res 28 Buchanan.
Bates Theodore, res n s St Joseph Gravel road, 1 e of river bridge.
Bates Wm G, circulator Ft Wayne Gazette, bds 390 E Wayne.
Bates Wm H, feather renovator, 390 E Wayne, res same.
Battenberg George, carp, bds Monroe House.
Battershall Jennie, attendant Indiana School for Feeble-Minded Youth.
Battershall John M, conductor N Y, C & St L R R, res 170 Greely.
Baty Wm E, sawyer Horton Mnfg Co, res 224 W Superior.
Bauch Anna H, seamstress, bds 201 Taylor.
Bauch Rose (wid Edward), res 201 Taylor.
Bauchle John, clk Frederick Eckart, bds 91 E Wayne.
Bauer, *see also Bougher and Bower.*
Bauer Frederick, helper Kerr-Murray Mnfg Co, bds Charles Miller.
Bauer Henry, shoes, 321 Lafayette, res same.
Bauer Jacob, molder Bass F & M Works, res 117 Force.
Bauer John J, ass't foreman Ft Wayne Electric Co, bds 25 W Washington.
Bauer Joseph A, bds 242 E Lewis.
Bauer Kajetan J (Glutting, Bauer & Hartnett), res 242 E Lewis.
Bauer Tracy W, mach hnd Ft Wayne Electric Co, bds 25 W Washington.
Bauer Richard, lab, bds Washington House.
Bauer Theodore, butcher Frederick Eckart, res n w cor Main and Runnion ave.
Baughmann, *see also Baumann and Bowman.*
Baughman Hattie, domestic 77 E Berry.
Baughman Jeremiah, carp Jacob Klett & Sons, res 63 W 4th.
Baughman Newton J, engineer, res 334 W Jefferson.
Baulmer, *see Balmer.*

Baum James, mngr Chicago Furniture Co, res Columbus, O.
Baum Joseph, saloon, 14 E Columbia, rms 8 Harmony blk.
Bauman, see also Baughman and Bowman.
Bauman Elizabeth, bds 154 E Creighton ave.
Bauman Maggie, domestic 362 Fairfield ave.
Baumann John, shoemkr, 376 Calhoun, res 41 W Lewis.
Baumann Mrs Minnie, laundress, res 184 Montgomery.
Baumann Paul (Baumann & Hassler), res 51 E Main.
Baumann & Hassler (Paul Baumann, Charles G Hassler), dyers, 51 E Main.
Baumgard Charles, painter, 413 E Washington, res same.
Baumgard Max, pedler F W Kiesling, res 350 Broadway.
Baumgratz Charles, lab, res e s Calhoun 4 s of Marchell.
Baumister Frederick, molder Bass F and M Works, res 376 E Lewis.
Baus Elizabeth, opr Samuel M Foster, bds 312 Lafayette.
Baus Frederick, umbrella repairer, res 89 E Lewis.
Bauss Conrad, mach Ft Wayne Electric Co, res 155 Shawnee ave.
Baxter Isabel, bds 9 Emily.
Baxter James, mach, bds 9 Emily.
Baxter Joseph, wireman Jenney Electric Light and Power Co, bds 9 Emily.
Baxter Phœbe (wid Joseph), res 9 Emily.
Baxter Thomas, chief engineer Ft Wayne Water Works, res s e cor Barr and 7th.
Bayer, see also Baer, Baier and Bair.
Bayer Frederick, lab, bds 34 Sherman.
Bayer Jacob, tollgate keeper, bds Wm E Miller.
Bayer John, carpet weaver, 34 Sherman, res same.
Bayer Kate, bds 34 Sherman.
Bayless Absalom, lab, res 207 Gay.
Bayless August E, trav agt, res 171 Van Buren.
Bayless Cora, bds 28 Taber.
Bayless Emma, milliner, bds 28 Taber.
Bayless Frank O, agt, bds 28 Taber.
Bayless Jane N, dressmkr, bds 160 W Superior.
Bayless Leah E (wid Gustavus), res 160 W Superior.
Bayless Newton, stonecutter, rms 29 E Main.
Beaber, see also Bieber.
Beaber Daniel, carp E F Liebman, res 15 W De Wald.
Beaber De Lafayette, carp F H Boester, res St Joseph twp.
Beaber Jacob, carp E F Liebman, res 342 Broadway.
Beach, see also Beuch.
Beach Edward A, clk Coombs & Co, bds 133 E Berry.
Beach Mrs Elizabeth, bds 375 Lafayette.

Johnson, DENTIST, 74 Calhoun Street.
Res., 188 W. Berry St.

FORT WAYNE DIRECTORY. 87

erick (Morgan & Beach), res 133 E Berry.
erick, bds 15 Clark.
erick E, checker L S & M S Ry, res 124 W 3d.
'rederick J, Mnfr of Awnings, Tents, Flags,
s, Horse and Wagon Covers, Etc, 171 Broadway,
ne. (*See left bottom lines.*)
erick W, stenogr Morgan & Beach, bds 133 E Berry.
ge, res 15 Clark.
ge W, harnessmkr A L Johns & Co, bds 375 Lafay-

ry, mach hand A L Johns & Co, bds 375 Lafayette.
H, lab, res 61 W 5th.
G, sawyer Paul's Pulley Works, res 2 Zollars ave.
nry (Beadell & Company), res 343 E Wayne.
thaniel, printer, bds 343 E Wayne.
& Company (Henry Beadell, John Porteous,
ald Mitchell), Proprs People's Store; Dry Goods,
s and Gents' Furnishings, 20–22 E Berry.
a M, domestic 264 E Creighton ave.
tie, domestic 264 E Creighton ave.
n E, real estate, 22 Bank Blk, res 176 Columbia.
Behrs.
sta D, teacher, bds 19 Baker.
n, watchman, res 14 Hoffman.
as C, mach Penn Co, res 19 Baker.
n, fitter Ft Wayne Furniture Co, bds 128 E Lewis.
, seamstress, bds 128 E Lewis.
cca (wid David), res 128 E Lewis.
o *Baer, Baier, Bair and Bayer.*
eth (wid George), res 74 Barr.
, painter, bds Diamond Hotel.
H, helper Wabash R R, bds 260 Clinton.
rt, removed to Detroit, Mich.
les G, teamster J J Draker, bds 42 Pearl.
George W, lab Penn Co, res 55 W De Wald.
Harry, messenger Penn Co, bds 55 W De Wald.
rry S, clk Markey & Mungovan, res 13 E Williams.
er, hostler, res rear 35 W Main.
garet, bds 595 Calhoun.
, blksmith Ft Wayne Iron Works, res 595 Calhoun.
A, helper Ft Wayne Iron Works, bds 595 Calhoun.
leophas J, foreman Kerr-Murray Mnfg Co, res 5

va E, bds 5 Monroe.
arie L, bds 5 Monroe.
ank, conductor, res 83 Wells.

ROBERT SPICE, Natural Gasfitting and Supplies, 48 WEST MAIN AND 11 PEARL STS.

88   R. L. POLK & CO.'S

Beaver Augustus C, mngr Ft Wayne Lumber Co, res 796 S Broadway.

Beaver Charles B, Agt United States and Pacific Express Cos, 79 Calhoun, res n s Columbia 2 e of Loree.

Beaver Edward L, mngr Estate M L Albrecht, res 116 Jackson.

Beaver Harry S, elevator opr Bass Blk, bds C B Beaver.

Beaver Hugh M, clk G D Niswonger, bds C B Beaver.

Beaver Minnie, bds 305 W Washington.

Beaver Montgomery G, bkkpr Fort Wayne Lumber Co, bds 110 W Main.

Beaver Wm, teamster, bds 796 Broadway.

Beberstine George W, car builder Penn Co, res s s Rudisill ave 2 e of Calhoun.

Becheles Christina (wid George), bds 366 W Main.

Bechman *see Beckman.*

Bechner Lottie, laundress Troy Steam Laundry, bds 19 Cochrane.

Bechtel Lena, domestic 299 E Washington.

Bechtol John G, engineer Penn Co, res 354 W Washington.

Bechtold Frederick J, bkkpr McDonald, Watt & Wilt, bds 120 Harrison.

Bechtold Louis, grocer, 152 Maumee rd, res same.

Beck Abraham R, watchman, bds 48 Centre.

Beck Charles, lab Bass F and M Works, res 124 Wilt.

Beck Henry, patternmkr Penn Co, res 13 Rockhill.

Beck Miss Ida, bds 301 Calhoun.

Beck James, hostler, bds Ross House.

Beck Leopold, carpet weaver, 136 Barr, res same.

Beck Sarah C (widow Wm L), res 48 Centre.

Beck Wm G, engineer Penn Co, bds 13 Rockhill.

Beck Wm P, bkkpr George DeWald & Co, bds 39 Pritchard.

Becker Abbott Z, engineer, res 169 High.

Becker Anna (wid Peter), bds 212 E Wayne.

Becker August, driver Frederick Helling, bds 83 W Washington.

Becker August E C, grocer, 160 Fairfield ave, res 107 W Williams.

Becker Charles (Fred Becker & Bro), bds 11 E Washington.

Becker Charles M, stonecutter George Jaap, bds 31 Lillie.

Becker Conrad, butcher Frederick Eckart, res 80 Buchanan.

Becker Emma L, clk M Frank & Co, bds 220 W Berry.

Becker Fred (Fred Becker & Bro), res 11 E Washington.

Becker Fred & Bro (Fred and Charles), horseshoers, 13 E Washington.

Becker George E, clk Adams Exp Co, res 15 Harrison.

Becker Henry, carp, res 3 Jones.

Henry J, photographer, bds 54 Nirdlinger ave.
Henry W (Griebel, Wyckoff & Becker), res 51 E Jefson.
Jacob, res 119 W Washington.
John, lab, bds 249 Gay.
John J, mach, res 157 Holman.
Joseph F, clk George DeWald & Co, bds 249 Gay.
Josephine, domestic 46 W Superior.
Lawrence, grocer, 91 John, res same.
Louis, res 249 Gay.
Mary, bds 11 E Washington.
Mary E (wid Charles G), res 170 W Washington.
Mary M, domestic 100 Calhoun.
Minnie A, milliner, bds 11 E Washington.
Susanna (wid Henry J), bds 54 Nirdlinger ave.
Therese, domestic August L Fox.
Wilhelmina (wid Christian), res 220 W Berry.
Wm, lab, bds 232 Harmer.
Wm F, tinsmith Penn Co, res e s Winter 1 s of Pon-.

see also Backes.
Jacob, saloon, 221 Lafayette, res same.
John, driver Chapman & Vachon, res 210 W Creighton
nue.
Mary, domestic 113 W Berry.
n Mrs Bertha, res 119 Lafayette.
n Edward H, clk County Treas, bds 135 E Lewis.
n Ellen (wid John), res 8 Hoagland ave.
n Frederick, lab, res 173 Gay.
n Frederick G, trav agt, res 160 W Wayne.
nn George, grocer, 101 Force, res 103 same.
in George J, fireman, res 50 McClellan.
t Alice, bds 498 W Main.
t Elizabeth (wid John B), res 498 W Main.
t John A, clk Falk & Lamley, bds 498 W Main.
t Lizzie, laundress Troy Steam Laundry, bds 498 W
n.
t Mary, laundress Troy Steam Laundry, bds 498 W
n.
t Theresa, bds 498 W Main.
atherine, bds 44 Brackenridge.
harles H, res 44 Brackenridge.
va, bds 44 Brackenridge.
Daniel C, fireman Penn Co, res 67 Baker.
Conrad, carp, res 19 Cochrane.
Catherine, domestic 106 E Washington.

1

John Pressler, Plumbing, Gas and Steam Fitting.
Columbia, Barr and Dock Streets. ══

Beelow Frederick, lab Bass F and M Works, res 234 Smith.
Beerman Henry, market stall No 83, res Wayne twp.
Beermann Frederick, lab, res 39 Boone.
Beers Harry C, asst chemist Ft Wayne Electric Co, bds 266 W Jefferson.
Beezley Edward J, brakeman, res 1 Dawson.
Beggs Charles A (Booth & Beggs), res 40 Lillie.
Begue Mary (wid John), res 164 E Wayne.
Behl Mary (wid Charles), res 56 3d.
Behn Charles, car builder Penn Co, res 271 E Creighton ave.
Behren Christian, molder, res n s Guthrie 2 w of Metz.
Behrens Ferdinand, carp E H Liebman, res 68 Nelson.
Behrens Herman, lab Bass F and M Works, res 84 Gay.
Behrs Emma, bds s e cor Maumee rd and Glasgow.
Behrs John, watchman, res s e cor Maumee rd and Glasgow.
Beidler Wm S, brakeman, res 20 Cass.
Beierlein George, carp Alfred Shrimpton, bds 20 Harrison.
Beierlein John G, lab, res 107 Cass.
Beigler Daniel, clk, res 78 S Wayne ave.
Beigler Miss Elizabeth M, teacher Jefferson School, bds 78 S Wayne ave.
Beinhardt John C, helper Penn Co, res 29 John.
Beitzell Wm, res 35 W 5th.
Belding Nicholas, rms 56 E Berry.
Belger Christian, lab, bds 46 E Columbia.
Belger Michael F (Belger & Lennon), res 19 W De Wald.
Belger & Lennon (Michael F Belger, Edwin J Lennon), saloon, 140 Calhoun.
Belknap Catherine (wid James), bds 41½ W Berry.
Bell A F, trav agt Carnahan & Co, res Richmond, Ind.
Bell Charles (col'd), waiter Wayne Hotel.
Bell Charles W, conductor N Y, C & St L R R, bds 80 3d.
Bell Edgar L, trav agt J W Bell, rms 56 E Wayne.
Bell Edith, bds 170 W Washington.
Bell George A, clk J W Bell, rms 56 E Wayne.
Bell George E, brakeman Nickel Plate R R, bds 80 3d.
Bell Horace L, stock buyer, res n e cor Main and Watkins.
Bell Huldah E (wid Wm H), bds 22 Fairfield ave.
Bell Joseph W, saddlery hardware, 13 Columbia, res 285 W Wayne.
Bell Julia (wid Wm M), res 80 3d.
Bell Mary, domestic Hanna Homestead.
Bell R e C (Morris, Bell, Barrett & Morris), bds Wayne Hotel.
Bell Taylor, lab, bds 28 Chicago.
Bell Thomas H, conductor N Y, C & St L R R, res 83 3d.

TURE AND PIANO MOVING. ┌R┐ YAN TRUCKING CO.
nd 21 W. WASHINGTON. └ ┘ TEL. 122.

FORT WAYNE DIRECTORY. 91

brakeman, rms 38 Baker.
ıda A, clk Root & Co, bds 135 Cass.
Hizabeth (wid Albert F), res 135 Cass.
'rank A, circulator Journal, bds 135 Cass.
ohn, lab, res 78 St Mary's ave.
Iary E, bds 135 Cass.
icholas A, cutter Hoosier **Mnfg** Co, bds 56 E Wayne.
e *Belknap.*
ık J, deputy clerk Allen County Circuit Court, res s s
ıer 5 e of Spy Run ave.
ı C, saloon, 99 Calhoun, res s s Wagner 5 e of Spy
ıve.
Frederick, miller, res 99 Cass.
rnest, bds 303 Calhoun.
anny M, bds 303 Calhoun.
ımes A, carp, res 303 Calhoun.
chard H, lab, bds 143 Holman.
m G, driver, res 435 Lafayette.
ı C, carp, res 486 Hanna.
lbert G, plumber Ft Wayne Electric Co, bds 20
r.
.roline (wid John), bds 415 E Washington.
ıarles, cigarmkr Reuben Bender, bds 27 Melita.
ıristopher, wagonmkr H A Rose, res 343 E Creighton.
·nnis, bds 88 Madison.
mer, carp, bds 10 McClellan.
ıily (wid Phillip), res 75 W Jefferson.
orge, res 206 Francis.
hn F, cabinetmkr Ft Wayne Organ Co, bds 75 W
ıon.
ura, domestic 395 E Wayne.
vi, cigarmkr F C Boltz & Co, bds 27 Grant.
ıi, plumber J M Keyser, bds 61 E Main.
ıis, cigar mnfr, 166 E Washington, res 168 same.
ry A, domestic 311 E Wayne.
ton, teamster J J Draker, bds 42 Pearl.
ınie, bds 168 E Washington.
.er, hostler J J Draker, res 55 E Superior.
ıben, cigarmkr, 27 Grand, res same.
ıuel F, switchman, res 12 Melita.
ıula (wid Adam), res 20 Poplar.
ı C, fireman Penn Co, res 83 Broadway.
ırman, cigarmkr C A Berndt, bds 69 Charles.
m H, lab Ft Wayne Furniture Co, res 217 E Wash-

mbrose H, mach, bds 15 W Butler.

Wing & Mahurin, ARCHITECTS,
41 & 42 Pixley & Long Bldg. Telephone 328

92   R. L. POLK & CO.'S

Benedict Mrs Charlotte L, res 304 E Creighton ave.
Benedict Jacob, driver C L Centlivre Brewing Co, res 24 Randolph.
Benedict Wm, carp, res 15 W Butler.
Benedict Wm L, conductor Penn Co, bds 304 E Creighton ave.
Beneke Frederick W, car bldr Penn Co, res 225 W Creighton.
Beneke Henry, mach hand, bds 225 W Creighton ave.
Beneke Louisa, bds 225 W Creighton ave.
Beneke Wm F, Druggist, 443 Broadway, res same.
Bengs Gustav, boilermkr, bds 155 John.
Bengs Herman, mason, res 155 John.
Bengs Otto F, carp, res 175 John.
Bengs Robert, carp, bds 155 John.
Beninghoff Daniel R (Beninghoff & Futter), res 37 Hugh.
Beninghoff & Futter (Daniel R Beninghoff, Charles Futter), barbers, Harmon House.
Benjamin Aaron, editor Freie Presse, res 88 W Lewis.
Benner Conrad, painter, res 94 Montgomery.
Bennett Andrew, blksmith, res 35 W Main.
Bennett Anna W (wid John), bds 377 Hanna.
Bennett Asa, car bldr Penn Co, res 95 E Hugh.
Bennett Cynthia, nurse, bds 419 W Main.
Bennett Fannie, dressmkr, bds 336 W Main.
Bennett George, cook Belger & Lennon, rms 68 W Main.
Bennett George, lab Bass F & M Works, res 104 E Wayne.
Bennett Mary E (wid Adam J), res 26 Wallace.
Bennett Melvina, domestic 44 Brackenridge.
Bennett Wm A, lab, res 47 Buchanan.
Bennett Winton, bds n e cor Oliver and Buchanan.
Bennigan Joseph A, lab, res 365 E Lewis.
Bennigen Elizabeth (wid Hugh), res 28 Huron.
Bennigen Mollie, domestic 252 W Wayne.
Bennigin Charles F, helper Kerr-Murray Mnfg Co, bds 92 Force.
Bennigin Edward P, lab, bds 92 Force.
Bennigin Henry E, mach, res 92 Force.
Bennigin Hugh, molder Bass F & M Works, res 201 E Lewis.
Bennigin Julian J, mach Penn Co, res 207 E Lewis.
Bennigen Lena, clk George DeWald & Co, bds 201 E Lewis.
Bennigin Mary, bds 201 E Lewis.
Benoy Charles W, mach Bass F & M Works, res 155 Force.
Benoy Frank T, foreman Bass F & M Works, res 179 Hanna.
Benroth Ferdinand, toolmkr Ft Wayne Electric Co, bds 28 Nirdlinger ave.
Bensman Bernard C, patternmkr Kerr-Murray Mnfg Co, bds 47 Walnut.

I

Bensman Elizabeth (wid Rudolph), bds 76 Madison.
Bensman Mary C, clk J F Gerke & Co, bds 76 Madison.
Bensman Rudolph,boilermkr Bass F & M Works, res 92 Madison.
Bensman Wm H, clk Bass F & M Works, bds 92 Madison.
Bensman Wm J, boilermkr Wabash R R, res 76 Madison.
Bente Charles W, painter Wabash R R, res 249 W Washington.
Bente George F, painter Wabash R R, bds 155 Griffith.
Bente Harry F, hostler Rippe & Sons, bds 155 Griffith.
Bente Herman F, painter Wabash R R, res 155 Griffith.
Bente Wm, driver Rippe & Sons, bds 155 Griffith.
Bentz Henry checker Penn Co, res 318 Hanna.
Benway Wm, res 31 Prince.
Benyus Mrs Mary C, dressmkr, bds 40 Laselle.
Benz Charles F, cigarmkr, res rear 123 Madison.
Benz Otto, lab Penn Co, res 169 Holman.
Bequette Mary E, domestic 113 W Berry.
Bercot Ella F, dressmkr, s s Wagner 2 e of Spy Run ave, res same.
Berdelman Ernest H, driver, res 66 Barthold.
Berdelman John H, boxmkr W H Davis, bds 66 Barthold.
Berdelman Wm, clk S P Lade, bds 66 Barthold.
Berdine Louis, teamster, bds Lake Shore Hotel.
Berens Frederick, clk, res 28 Melita.
Berg, *see also Borg and Burg.*
Berg Christina, domestic 157 W Main.
Berg Nicholas, lab Penn Co, res 594 Lafayette.
Bergel Melinda (wid Valentine), res 23 Boone.
Bergeman Anna, operator Hoosier Manufacturing Co, bds w s Calhoun s of Rudisill ave.
Berger, *see also Boerger and Burger.*
Berger Emil, baker C C Gumpper, bds 238 Calhoun.
Berger Paul, blksmith The Herman Berghoff Brewing Co, res 252 Erie.
Berger V, car builder Penn Co, res 192 Taylor.
Berghoff Gustav A, trav agt The Herman Berghoff Brewing Co, res 106 Webster.
Berghoff Henry C, res 100 E Jefferson.
Berghoff Herman Brewing Co The, Herman J Berghoff Pres, Hubert Berghoff Sec and Treas, e s Grant ave nr E Washington. (*See back cover.*)
Berghoff Herman J, Pres The Herman Berghoff Brewing Co, res 181 E Jefferson.
Berghoff Hubert, Sec and Treas The Herman Berghoff Brewing Co, res 91 Madison.
Berghorn Frederick, boilermkr Penn Co, res 169 Holman.
Berghorn Frederick, car builder Penn Co, bds 34 Hugh.

8

R. L. POLK & CO.'S

Berghorn Henry, carp Wabash R R, res 56 Maumee rd.
Berghorn Louis H F, tailor F Hardung, bds 169 Holman.
Berghorn L, market stall No 60.
Bergk Charles, physician, 52 W 4th, res same.
Bergmann, *see Borgmann.*
Berkhold Matthew, cook, res 41 E Williams.
Berlin Emilie, bds 45 Boone.
Berlin Flora, seamstress, bds 45 Boone.
Berlin Henry J, flour packer John Orff, res 45 Boone.
Berlin Minnie, seamstress, bds 45 Boone.
Berlonge Jennie, opr Hoosier Mnfg Co, bds 210 E Washington.
Berlonge Susan, opr Hoosier Mnfg Co, bds 210 E Washington.
Bernard, *see also Barnard.*
Bernard August, lab, bds 75 Lewis.
Bernard Mrs Nancy J, bds 16 Brackenridge.
Bernard Simon, farmer, res 88 W Superior.
Berndt Charles A, Cigar Mnfr, 145 John, res same. (*See page 6.*)
Bernhard, *see also Bernhardt.*
Bernhard Bertha, music teacher, bds 75 Lewis.
Bernhard Frederick, organist, res 75 Lewis.
Bernhard Newman, trav agt S M Foster, res 136 W Wayne.
Bernhardt Christian J, lab Penn Co, res 29 John.
Bernhardt Frank, lab, res 205 Gay.
Berning Charlotte (wid Conrad), res 420 E Washington.
Berning Conrad, lab, res 40 Summit.
Berning Conrad jr, wood worker Anthony Wayne Mnfg Co, bds 40 Summit.
Berning Dora M, milliner Seaney Millinery Co, bds 40 Summit.
Berning Henry, lab, res 50 Smith.
Berning Wm, lab Penn Co, res 22 Eliza.
Berns Frederick (Hauck & Berns), res 11 Grand.
Berry, *see also Barry.*
Berry Charles, collector Metropolitan Mnfg Co, bds 199 Broadway.
Berry Hannah (wid Jacob), bds w s Glasgow 3 s of E Washington.
Berry Mrs Hattie A, mngr Watchman, res 575 Fairfield ave.
Berry James H, res 575 Fairfield ave.
Berry J F, hostler, bds Hotel Waverly.
Berry Street M E Church, n e cor W Berry and Harrison.
Berry Wesley, res s e cor Putnam and Koch.
Bersch Adam, barber, res 160 Fairfield ave.
Bersch George J, foreman Alfred Shrimpton, bds 160 Fairfield avenue.
Bertels, *see also Bartels.*

n, sewer builder, res 160 Harmer.

mil, removed to Chicago, Ill.

ederick J, lab, res 156 Gay.

uis E, baker, 88 Barr, res same.

rank A, lather, res 178 Hanna.

enry, lather, res 11 Romy ave.

osephine (wid Frank), res n s Parnell ave 1 n of St rd.

n, bds 136 Monroe.

nk, stone cutter George Jaap, res 136 Monroe.

n B, res 136 Monroe.

ph J, bkkpr John Pressler, res 22 Summit.

y, bds 136 Monroe.

es E, rms 106 E Main.

(wid John), res 29 Charles.

ie, domestic Rich Hotel.

as J, brakeman, bds 29 Charles.

candymkr, bds 50 Nirdlinger ave.

, dressmkr, bds 50 Nirdlinger ave.

rick A, baker, res 52 Nirdlinger ave.

F, lab Hoffman Bros, res 50 Nirdlinger ave.

l J, carpetlayer D N Foster Furniture Co, bds 50 ger ave.

cynthia (wid George), bds 296 Broadway.

rge A, finisher, res 296 Broadway.

lso Beach.

ust, painter, bds 444 Broadway.

, clk Penn Co, res 444 Broadway.

o, carp, res 514 E Lewis.

ice M, clk County Recorder, bds 164 E Wayne.

hn C, lab, rms 18 Madison.

seph E, saloon, 65 E Main, res 73 3d.

ur, clk Meyer Bros & Co, bds 155 Harrison.

tian F, truckman, res 155 Harrison.

, bds 34 2d.

les, lab, bds 34 2d.

les A, clk Coombs & Co, bds 26 E Washington.

k, lab, bds 34 2d.

y J, with Coombs & Co, res DeWald sq.

, lab, bds 34 2d.

B, polisher, res 34 2d.

, domestic 410 Lafayette.

mina, operator S M Foster, bds 34 2d.

ster, section hand, bds 34 2d.

Daniel, carp Penn Co, res 167 W DeWald.

Edward, lab, bds 167 W DeWald.

Bevelhaimer Wm S, carp Penn Co, res 492 Harrison.
Beverforden August, brewer The Herman Berghoff Brewing Co, res 546 E Wayne.
Beverforden George, bartender Rudolph Beverforden, bds Windsor Hotel.
Beverforden Henry F, druggist, 286 Calhoun, res 284 Harrison.
Beverforden Rudolph, saloon, 294 Calhoun, res 11 Brandriff.
Beverforden Wm H D, meats, 277 Hanna, res same.
Bevins Wm, laborer, bds 25 Hough.
Bewlah George, brakeman, bds 71 Garden.
Beyer Charles A, lab, res 80 Barthold.
Beyer Jacob, gatekeeper Maysville pike, res 80 Barthold.
Beyer Paul H, student Tolan & Riedel, bds J M E Riedel.
Beyerlein, *see also Beierlein.*
Beyerlein Charles, driver F M Smaltz, res 107 Mechanic.
Beyerlein Frederick, supt, res 46 5th.
Beyerlein George, carp, bds 20 Harrison.
Beyerlein George F, car builder Penn Co, res 30 Jones.
Beyerlein John L, lab Penn Co, bds 30 Jones.
Beyerlein Julius H, clk F M Smaltz, res 59 Boone.
Beyers Dean L, lamp repairer, res 16 Hoffman.
Beyrau August F, sawyer Olds' Wagon Works, res 226 John.
Beyrau Wm, lab N Leonard.
Biber Ernest, janitor (city dept) Y M C A, bds 1 N Calhoun.
Bice Amy (wid David), res 36 Hamilton.
Bichon Alexander, bds 329 E Wayne.
Bickel Charles, removed to Chicago, Ill.
Bickford John D, saloon, 11 N Harrison, res same.
Bicknese Frederick C, saloon, 86 Barr, res 171 E Lewis.
Bicknese Frederick W, clk J B White, res 73 W Williams.
Bicknese Herbert, mach hnd Ft Wayne Electric Co, bds 171 E Lewis.
Bicknese Sophia E M, domestic 496 S Harrison.
Bickness Henry, helper Penn Co, res 18 Madison.
Biddle C I, perfume mnfr, 169 Ewing, bds same.
Biddle Edward F, trav agt C I Biddle, bds 169 Ewing.
Biddle Frank M, clk C I Biddle, bds 169 Ewing.
Biddle Mary, bds 169 Ewing.
Biddle Thomas M, trav agt C I Biddle, res 169 Ewing.
Biddlecome John A (Ft Wayne View & Copying Co), res 100 Oliver.
Bidwell Wm P, reporter Gazette, bds 26 S Wayne ave.
Bidwell Wm S, carp, res 26 S Wayne ave.
Bieber Harvey F, carp, res 17 Laselle.
Bieber Wm, lab Ft Wayne Lumber Co, bds 796 Broadway.
Bieber Wm L, teamster Kilian Baker, res 21 Boone.

rstein John, lab Ft Wayne Artificial Ice Co, bds River-
ide Hotel.

nweg Gottfried, foreman Bass F & M Works, res Adams
ownship.

l Julius T, painter, res 52 Hugh.

er George, wagonmkr Old Fort Mnfg Co, res 9 Clay.

er George A, bkkpr Ft Wayne Transfer and Storage Co,
ds 9 Clay.

er Julian, silver plater, bds 9 Clay.

lel George, lab, res 204 Smith.

aum Frederick, car inspr, res 24 Breck.

aum Fredericka (wid Herman), res 51 Taylor.

aum Henry, teamster Rhinesmith & Simonson, bds 154
N Superior.

aum Wm F, car repairer, res 184 Greely.

ıann, *see Beermann.*

end Mrs Celestine N, bds 131 E Washington.

ı Rebecca, dressmkr, 36 Wilt, res same.

r Jacob, teamster, res s w cor Maria and Tyler ave.

r John, finisher The Peters Box & Lumber Co, res s s
ipring w of Runnion ave.

rback Joseph H, special agt Union Central Life Ins Co,
es 247 E Wayne.

rback Lizzie H, bkkpr C E Everett, bds 247 E Wayne.

Anna, opr Hoosier Mnfg Co, bds 214 Madison.

acob jr, clk H G Sommers, bds 214 Madison.

acob, lab, res 214 Madison.

ouisa, opr Hoosier Mnfg Co, bds 214 Madison.

an Charles, agt Singer Mnfg Co, rms 88 Wells.

an Henry R, barber J B Fink, bds 33 Monroe.

an Jesse F, collector Singer Mnfg Co, res 129 Oliver.

an Mrs Matilda (wid Ray), res 33 Monroe.

Lucille, bkkpr, bds 46 4th.

· Charles, lab David Tagtmeyer, res 2 High.

l George, lab, res 204 Smith.

ar Frederick, gardener Charles S Knight.

ar Josephine, domestic Charles S Knight.

er Ferdinand, lab Bass F & M Works, res w s Spy Run
ve 8 n of river bridge.

ey Elmira, domestic 20 Harrison.

tley Frank C, Pres and Mngr Binkley Telegraph
chool, res 13 W Butler.

ey Olive, domestic 20 Harrison.

:ley Telegraph School, Frank C Binkley Pres and
Ingr, Foster Block. (*See page 8.*)

:k Edward, mach Wabash R R, res 6 Bass.

Birbeck Elizabeth (wid John), bds 97 W DeWald.
Birbeck Wm, mach Wabash R R, res 97 W DeWald.
Birchoff Charles, lab, bds 111 Wells.
Bird James, farmer, res n s New Haven ave 1 e of Edsall ave.
Bird Mary, domestic 92 Thomas.
Birdsall Frank M, driver Troy Steam Laundry, res 46 Monroe.
Bireley Wm W, res 177 John.
Birk, *see also Burk.*
Birk John G, carpet weaver, rear 58 Elm, res same.
Birkenbeul Henry, lab Penn Co, res 34 Charles.
Birkner Isadore, mach Fort Wayne Electric Co, res 243 W Washington.
Bischoff Charles W, res 63 Elm.
Bischoff Rudolph, tchr Concordia College, res College grounds.
Bischoff Wm, res 156 Hoffman.
Bischoff Wm, caller, bds 63 Elm.
Bishop Charles, carp, res 103 Riverside ave.
Bishop Charles B, helper J H Welsh, bds 13 Erie.
Bishop Harry, carp, bds 103 Riverside ave.
Bishop Martha (wid Martin), res 13 Erie.
Bishop Nellie D, folder Sentinel, bds 13 Erie.
Bitler Samuel D, truss hoop mnfr, 421 E Wayne, res 319 same.
Bitner Alonzo J, molder Penn Co, res 120 W Butler.
Bitner Catherine, stripper, bds 120 W Butler.
Bitner Clark A, molder Penn Co, res 67 E DeWald.
Bitner Daisy, mach hand A L Johns & Co, bds 60 E Williams.
Bitner David W, clk Markey & Mungovan, bds 39 E DeWald.
Bitner Eliza M (wid Andrew J), res 60 E Williams.
Bitner John R, mach Penn Co, 175 E Lewis.
Bitner John S, boilermkr Kerr-Murray Mnfg Co, bds 39 E DeWald.
Bitner Mattie A, mach hand A L Johns & Co, bds 60 E Williams.
Bitsberger Emanuel F, conductor, res 102 Wallace.
Bitsberger Mrs E F, dressmkr 102 Wallace, res same.
Bitsberger Grace E, seamstress, bds 102 Wallace.
Bitsberger Hallie E, mach hand Olds' Wagon Works, bds 102 Wallace.
Bitsberger Wm H, mach hand, bds 102 Wallace.
Bittenger Miss Adah T, teacher, bds 262 W Washington.
Bittenger Jacob R, lawyer, 26 Court, res 262 W Washington.
Bittenger Lawrence E, clk Penn Co, res w s Hillside ave 2 n of Leo rd.
Bittenger Miss Marcia M, teacher, bds 262 W Washington.
Bittikoffer John, mach Fort Wayne Electric Co, bds 224 Calhoun.

ger Adam H (Bittinger & Edgerton), res 44 Archer ave.
nger & Edgerton (Adam H Bittenger, Dixon
dgerton) Lawyers, 27 and 28 Bank Block.
: Wm, water works trustee, res 301 W Jefferson.
inn Carl, lab Bass F and M Works, res 150 Smith.
ger Henry, mach hand Old Fort Mnfg Co, res 438 E
Wayne.
ger John, lab, res 67 Lillie.
ger John jr, lab, bds 26 Du Bois.
r, *see Betzler.*
Wm, farmer, res n s Maumee rd 1 e of toll gate.
Wm A, lab, bds 58 Elm.
Catherine, bds 271 W Jefferson.
Edward, hostler C W Bruns & Co, bds 153 High.
John (coi'd) janitor Nickel Plate, res 300 E Wayne.
urn George W, conductor, res 25 Gay.
urn James H, flagman, res 51 E DeWald.
urn John D, brakeman, N Y, C & St L R R, bds Schele
Iouse.
e Philip, Oculist, Aurist and Physician, treats Catarrh
id all Chronic Diseases, 47 W Berry, res same.
Henry B, fireman, bds C F Schilling.
Solon K, trainmaster Nickel Plate, res 170 W Wayne.
Thomas W, clk P O, res 220 E Wayne.
g John P (Blaising & Stevens), res rear 269 E Wash-
gton.
g Phillip J, butcher Blaising & Stevens, res 277 E Wayne.
g & Stevens (John P Blaising, John K Stevens), meats,
9 E Washington.
Mrs Ermina A F, res 4 Fulton.
John, mach, bds Windsor Hotel.
John B, foreman A L Johns & Co, res 255 E Wayne.
e John G, Supt Indiana School for Feeble-Minded
uth, 1½ miles n e of Court House.
Lillian M, teacher, bds 4 Fulton.
y Homer H, clk, bds 326 Harrison.
y Mary C (wid Wm), bds 326 Harrison.
ey Harry A, brakeman, res 36 Thomas.
ey James E, conductor, res 130 Horace.
ey John H, carp, res 105 Wallace.
ey Lottie, milliner, bds 105 Wallace.
ey Lyman M, conductor, bds 36 Thomas.
Wm F, engineer Wm and J J Geake, res 84 Broadway.
Rev Milton L, pastor Central Christian Church, bds 290
Jefferson.
ohn, lab Penn Co, res 15 St Martin.

Blase Elizabeth, bds 82 E Washington.

Blase Wilhelmina (wid Louis), res 82 E Washington.

Blaugh Linnie, seamstress, rms 16 Union.

Blauser Orleva L, domestic Hotel Waverly.

Bledsoe Miss Bessie, typewriter S F Bowser & Co, bds n e cor Columbia ave and Old Fort.

Bledsoe Nathaniel H, res s e cor Columbia and Old Fort.

Bledsoe Miss Valeria, bds s e cor Columbia and Old Fort.

Blee John A, lab, res 95 Clay.

Bleeke Emma, dressmkr, bds 263 E Jefferson.

Bleeke Frederick W, clk Wm Moellering & Sons, bds 200 E Jefferson.

Bleibtreu Frederick, mach Ft Wayne Electric Co, res 157 College.

Bleich Emil, lab, res 81½ Smith.

Bleich Herman, molder Bass F & M Works, bds 8 Gay.

Bleich John, lab, res 45 Smith.

Bleke Dietrich, lab Penn Co, res 131 Madison.

Bleke Frederick L D, lab, bds 131 Madison.

Bleke Sophie, domestic 107 W Williams.

Bley George W, Carpenter, 152 Hanna, res 173 Montgomery. (*See page 67.*)

Bley Henry, switchman, bds Theodore Bley.

Bley Joseph F, switchman, bds 10 Thomas.

Bley Theodore, yardmaster, res s s Piqua road near car shops.

Bligh Caroline (wid Stephan), res 8 Gay.

Bligh Herman, lab, bds 8 Gay.

Blinn John N, tuner Ft Wayne Organ Co, res 23 W Butler.

Bliss Frederick H, pres International Business College, res Saginaw, Mich.

Blitz Max J, ticket broker, 5 Aveline House Blk, bds Aveline House.

Bloch George, boxmkr Olds' Wagon Works, res 37 Walnut.

Bloch George A, lab, bds 37 Walnut.

Bloch Lizzie, bds 37 Walnut.

Bloch Sophia, domestic 302 W Washington.

Block Annie, domestic Wayne Hotel.

Block Frederick, yard boss Bruns & McBennett, res 135 Gay.

Block Herman, finisher, bds 20 Harrison.

Block Mary (wid Frederick), res 85 Maumee rd.

Block Wm, shoemkr, res 85 Maumee rd.

Blocker Henry P, trav agt C M Comparet, res 10 Maumee rd.

Bloemker Frederick H, car inspector, res 55 Baker.

Bloemker Henry, carp, res 44 Wall.

Bloemker John, hostler, bds 44 Wall.

Bloemker Wm, teamster, bds 44 Wall.

Blombach Hugo, plasterer, bds 49 Shawnee ave.
Blombach Otto, plasterer, res 131 Gay.
Blomenberg Christian, carp, res 123 Union.
Blondell August E, mach hand Ft Wayne Organ Co, res n s Killea 1 w of Harrison.
Blondiot Felix, res s s New Haven ave 2 w of Lumbard.
Blondiot Wm H, tailor, 47 E Lewis, res same.
Blood John, mach hand Joseph Fremion, bds 610 S Calhoun.
Bloom John A, bkkpr E F Clausmeier, res Columbia, Lakeside.
Bloomfield Clemence C (wid Frederick A), res 30 E DeWald.
Bloomfield Frederick A, clk Penn Co, bds 30 E DeWald.
Bloomingdale Mills, W H Brudi & Bro proprs, cor 6th and Wells.
Bloomingdale School, n w cor Marion and Bowser.
Blotkamp Frank J, mach Penn Co, res 26 Bass.
Blount Ambrose C, stenographer, bds 9 N Calhoun.
Blount James A, transfer agt, res 9 N Calhoun.
Blue John O, conductor, bds 320 Hanna.
Blum Catherine (wid Henry), res 19 Walnut.
Blum Catherine, opr Hoosier Mnfg Co, bds 11 Erie.
Blum Charles, lab, bds 11 Erie.
Blum Henry, boilermker Bass F & M Works, bds 84 Gay.
Blum Nicholas, stone mason, res 11 Erie.
Blum Nicholas jr, molder Bass F & M Works, bds 11 Erie.
Blust Martin, bricklayer, res 12 Sturgis.
Blust Mary E, domestic 173 Ewing.
Bly Emma, domestic 24 Wagner.
Bly Wm, lab, bds 111 Taylor.
Blye Theodore, blksmith John Rupp, res 62 E Superior.
Blynn Blanche, bds 23 W Wayne.
Blynn Catherine, teacher, bds 23 W Wayne.
Blynn Harriet A (wid Wm) dressmkr, 23 W Wayne, res same.
Blystone Carl, bellboy Aldine Hotel.
Blystone Isaac, res 16 Holman.
Blystone Oliver, carp, res 53 High.
Boaeus Julian, carp, res 158 Erie.
Boag Mary L, bds 69 W Lewis.
Boag Wm G, mach Penn Co, res 69 W Lewis.
Bobay Charles, lab, bds 62 W 5th.
Bobay Frank F, teamster Peters Box and Lumber Co, res 62 W 5th.
Bobay John A, market stall No 82, res Perry twp.
Bobay Victor, market stall No 49, res St Joseph twp.
Bobilya Louis J, trav agt, rms 80 W Creighton ave.
Bobs Christopher, mach hand Horton Mnfg Co, res s e cor St Mary's ave and Aboit.

A. FOSTER, Merchant Tailor, $\overline{15}$ W. Wayne St.

102   R. L. POLK & CO.'S

Bochman John, lab, res 57 W 5th.
Bock, *see also Buck and Buuck.*
Bock Wm C, carp, res 35 Nirdlinger ave.
Bock Wm F, pound master, bds 39 Nirdlinger ave.
Bockeloh Elizabeth, bds 83 W. Washington.
Bockeloh Mrs Emma, housekeeper 78 Dawson.
Bocksberger Francis T, lab, res 36 Koch.
Bocksberger Louis, barber L Uplegger, res 36 Koch.
Bocksberger Veronica (wid Valentine), janitor Hamilton National Bank, res 36 Koch.
Bode Dora, domestic 179 Calhoun.
Bode Frank, lab, bds 56 Smith.
Bode Frank H, teamster, res 1 Monroe.
Bodenheimer James H, molder Bass F and M Works, res 186 Harmer.
Boeker Frederick W, Druggist, 108 Fairfield ave, res 102 same.
Boecker Henry, lab, res 58 Pritchard.
Boedeker August, driver Gottlieb Niemann, bds 68 Brackenridge.
Boedeker Diedrich, car bldr Penn Co, res 19 Wall.
Boedeker Wm C, packer Pottlitzer Bros, res 195 High.
Boegel Ernst, lab Hoffman Bros, res 70 Webster.
Boegel Fredrick, molder Bass F and M Works, res 61 Elm.
Boegel Henry, lab, bds 70 Webster.
Boehm Barnett, plasterer, res 12 Winch.
Boehm Christian F, plumber, res 120 Rockhill.
Boehrer Alexis, molder Bass F and M Works, res 147 Force.
Boerger Charles R (C R Boerger & Bro), bds 194 E Washington.
Boerger C R & Bro (Charles R and Wm H), house movers, 194 E Washington.
Boerger Emma, bds 194 E Washington.
Boerger Florenz J, boilermkr Penn Co, bds 183 E Washington.
Boerger Gustave W, leather 41 E Main, res 49 Maumee rd.
Boerger Rudolph, res 183 E Washington.
Boerger Miss Sarah S, bds 183 E Washington.
Boerger Simon J, clk, bds 183 E Washington.
Boerger Wm, res 194 E Washington.
Boerger Wm H (C R Boerger & Bro), res 312 Hanna.
Boerschinger Henry J, lab Penn Co, res St Joseph Boulevard 3 n of Lakeside addition.
Boerschinger Henry L, gardener, res St Joseph Boulevard 1 n of Lakeside addition.
Boes Frank A, clk Root & Co, bds 150 E Jefferson.
Boes Louis, molder Bass F & M Works, res 510 E Lewis.

Geo. E. Johnson, DENTIST, 74 Calhoun Street.
Res., 188 W. Berry St.

FORT WAYNE DIRECTORY.   103

Boese Annie, bds 150 E Jefferson.
Boese Christina (wid Amond), res 150 E Jefferson.
Boese Dora (wid Frederick), bds 333 E Washington.
Boese Frederick, clk F H Dicke, res 137 Force.
Boese Frederick W, lab Penn Co, res s e cor Penn and Du Bois.
Boese Wm, carp, rms 29 E Main.
Boese Wm C, car bldr Penn Co, res 18 Hough.
Boester Ernst, clk Henry Butke, bds 164 Griffith.
Boester Frederick H, Contractor, 164 Griffith, res same.
Boester Henry F, student, bds 164 Griffith.
Boester John G, carp F H Boester, bds 164 Griffith.
Boettcher Charles, forgeman, bds 53 Hugh.
Boffelman Diedrich, boilermkr, res 233 Madison.
Bogash Frank, driver, bds J W Langohr.
Bogenschuetz Charles, bartndr C Entemann, res 87 Madison.
Bogenschuetz Joseph, bartndr C Entemann, bds 208 Lafayette.
Bogert George, carp, res 135 Force.
Boggs Rev John M, pastor Third Presbyterian Church, res 25
    Brackenridge.
Boggs Parks W, lawyer, 23 Bank Blk, bds 25 Brackenridge.
Bohde Augusta (wid Wm), res 333 E Washington.
Bohde Augusta, bds 333 E Washington.
Bohde Charles H, lab Ft Wayne Electric Co, res 53 Wall.
Bohde Frederick, teamster, bds 333 E Washington.
Bohde John, bds 333 E Washington.
Bohde Wm, helper Bass F & M Works, bds 333 E Wash-
    ington.
Bohen, *see also Bowen.*
Bohen Cecilia (wid Michael), res 245 E Jefferson.
Bohen Michael H, bailiff Superior Court, res 245 E Jefferson.
Bohen Thomas H, slater, res 55 E Williams.
Bohen Wm C, slater J H Welch, bds 245 E Jefferson.
Bohl George, car bldr Penn Co, res 191 Hanna.
Bohler Jacob, painter, res 28 Murray.
Bohling Henry F C, bookbinder G W Winbaugh, bds 167 Force.
Bohling Wm, lab Bass F & M Works, res 167 Force.
Bohling Wm F, clk L S & M S Ry, bds 167 Force.
Bohn Adolph T, printer Archer, Housh & Co, bds 20 Allen.
Bohn August H, student, bds 20 Allen.
Bohn Charles J P, driver Zoeller & Merz, bds 20 Allen.
Bohn Christian P, printer Archer, Housh and Co, res 20 Allen.
Bohn Louisa, dressmkr, bds 20 Allen.
Bohn Wm A, sec and treas Horton Mnfg Co, res 285 W Berry.
Bohne Charles, patternmkr, res 42 W Williams.
Bohne Frederick H, clk Wm Meyer & Bro, bds 25 Boone.
Bohne Louis C, clk F M Smith & Co, res 68 W Washington.

Robert Spice, Waterworks and General Plumbing, 48 West Main and 11 Pearl Streets.

104   R. L. POLK & CO.'S

Bohner Jacob, painter, res 28 Murray.
Boivin Frank, bookkpr, bds 73 Thomas.
Bokaw, *see also Brokaw.*
Bokaw Joseph, lab, res 29 Duck.
Boland Annie E, dressmkr, bds 98 W Superior.
Boland Asa H, plasterer, res 88 Force.
Boland John, engineer, res 98 W Superior.
Boland Walter (col'd), waiter, bds 64 Chicago.
Bolei Elizabeth (wid George), bds 79 Nirdlinger ave.
Bolei George J, painter, bds 79 Nirdlinger ave.
Bolender Levi, bds 210 Calhoun.
Boles, *see also Boltz.*
Boles Luella, teacher, bds 147 W Washington.
Boles Mrs Rachael C, teacher, bds 278 W Berry.
Boley Frank M, lab Ft Wayne Furniture Co, res 247 E Wayne.
Boley John, riveter Penn Co, res s e cor Lumbard and Line.
Boling Edward, stripper A C Baker, bds 39 4th.
Boling Lemuel R, painter, res 39 4th.
Bolinger George W, car driver, res 212 Broadway.
Bolinger Jacob, helper, res 175 Wells.
Boll, *see Ball.*
Boll Victor, tuner D H Baldwin & Co, bds 26 E Wayne.
Bollerman Lizzie, tailoress C Kruse, bds 286 W Jefferson.
Bollmann August, helper Ind Mach Works, res 14 Huron.
Bollmer Emma, clk, bds 195 W Main.
Bollmer Louisa (wid Daniel), res 195 W Main.
Bollmer Wm, clk, bds 195 W Main.
Bolman Albert F, cigar mnfr, 272 Calhoun, res 104 Barr.
Bolman Christian, foreman Olds' Wagon Works, res 47 W Lewis.
Bolman Christian D, boilermkr Bass F & M Works, bds 47 W Lewis.
Bolman Frederick, carp, bds 47 W Lewis.
Bolman Frederick A, conductor, res 188 Jackson.
Bolman Minnie, domestic 104 E Main.
Bolman Nellie, bds 188 Jackson.
Bolman Otto F, brakeman N Y C, & St L R R, bds 23 Union.
Bolman Theodore, bds 23 Union.
Boltes Louisa (Boltes & Koenig), res Spy Run ave.
Boltes & Koenig (Louisa Boltes, Theresa Koenig), Catholic goods, 201 Calhoun.
Bolton Evin S, private U S Army, Recruiting Rendezvous.
Bolton Levi, mach, res 43 Michigan ave.
Bolton Richard, lathe hd Ft Wayne Electric Co, bds 154 W DeWald.
Boltz Ferdinand F, removed to Huntington, Ind.

Boltz Fred C, Wholesale Dealer in Fine Whiskies, Wines, Liquors, Tobaccos and Cigars, 27 Calhoun, Branch Store 92 Calhoun, res 87 Cass. (*See page 2.*)

Boltz Fred G, clk Boltz & Jackson, bds 87 Cass.

Boltz F C & Co (Fred C Boltz, Adolph Alberty), Mnfrs Cigars, 137–139 Calhoun.

Boltz George C, gardener, bds 87 Cass.

Boltz Mary, bds 87 Cass.

Boltz & Jackson (Fred C Boltz, Augustus B Jackson), Saloon, 92 Calhoun.

Bolyard James, lab, bds 28 W Main.

Bolyard James D, lab, res cor Fulton and Pearl.

Bolyard Lewis, apprentice M Momper, bds 28 W Main.

Bolz, *see Boles.*

Bond Albert L, photographer, res 43 W Butler.

Bond Albert S, treas and supt Ft Wayne Organ Co, res 362 Fairfield ave.

Bond Charles E, sec Ft Wayne Organ Co, res 289 Fairfield avenue.

Bond Charles Z, mach Wabash R R, bds 164 Brackenridge.

Bond Frank D, messenger Old National Bank, bds 322 Fairfield ave.

Bond Henry W, feed mill, 65 E Columbia, bds Aldine Hotel.

Bond Herbert W, clk Ft Wayne Organ Co, bds 322 Fairfield avenue.

Bond Hugh M C, clk Nickel Plate, rms 2 E Columbia.

Bond Jared D, Cashier Old National Bank, res 3 W De Wald.

Bond Jenny M (wid Alonzo), res 164 Brackenridge.

Bond John, porter Belger & Lennon, bds 140 Calhoun.

Bond John G, puncher Ft Wayne Electric Co, bds 216 Broadway.

Bond Lucelia (wid Wm J), res 216 Broadway.

Bond Stephen B, Pres Old National Bank, res 322 Fairfield ave.

Bonfield Mary (wid Kennedy), res 180 E Wayne.

Bonnet George J, molder Bass F and M Works, res 104 E Wayne.

Bonneville Earl S, clk The Wayne, bds same.

Bonter Claude S, car bldr Penn Co, bds 59 W DeWald.

Bonter George W P, conductor, res 73 W DeWald.

Bonter Wm F C, brakeman, res 59 W DeWald.

Bookwalter, *see also Buckwalter.*

Bookwalter Alice (wid Martin), furnished rooms, 40 E Jefferson, res same.

Bookwalter Charles C, painter, bds 40 E Jefferson.

John Pressler, Mantels, Grates and Tile Floor.
Columbia, Barr and Dock Streets.

106   R. L. POLK & CO.'S

Bookwalter Clyde, paper carrier, bds 15 W Williams.

Bookwalter Elias H, pressman Gazette, res 15 W Williams.

Bookwalter John A, Iron Fences, Art Stained Glass, Church and School Supplies, 134 E Lewis, res same.

Booth Fremont D (Booth & Beggs), res 393 E Washington.

Booth Miss Mattie, dressmkr, 40 Lillie, bds same.

Booth Wm N, well driller Robert Spice, bds Monroe House.

Booth & Beggs (Fremont D Booth, Charles A Beggs), shoes, 20 Calhoun.

Bopp Andrew, lab, bds 49 Lillie.

Bopp Charles H, elevatorman, bds 136 Barr.

Bopp George, painter, bds 97 Taylor.

Bopp Henry C, woodworker Olds' Wagon Works, res 136 Barr.

Bopp Miss Maggie, bds 136 Barr.

Borcherding Ferdinand H, molder Bass F & M Works, res 35 Liberty.

Borchert August F, painter, res 59 Indiana ave.

Borg, see also *Berg and Burg*.

Borg Rev Theodore, chaplain St Vincent Orphan Asylum, res same.

Borgman, see also *Bergmann*.

Borgman August (Horstmeyer & Borgman), res 35 Nirdlinger avenue.

Borgman Christian, teamster, bds 200 Ewing.

Borgman Christian W, clk Peter Pierre, bds 35 Pritchard.

Borgman Elizabeth, dressmkr, bds 35 Pritchard.

Borgman Fredericka (wid Christian), res 35 Pritchard.

Borgman Wm, contractor, res 200 Ewing.

Borgman Wm F, policeman, res 202 Ewing.

Bork, see also *Birk and Burke*.

Bork Julius, lab, res 55 Thomas.

Borkenstein Bernhardt, carp, res 152 Greely.

Bornemann Charles, tailor, res 98 Harrison.

Bornemann Frederick C, clk Pixley & Co, bds 98 Harrison.

Bornkomp Ferdinand, bricklayer, res 7 Gay.

Bort Frank B, lab, bds 127 E Washington.

Bortner Thella, opr S M Foster, bds 222 Madison.

Bortz Albert, car bldr Penn Co, rms 152 E Wayne.

Boscheg John, lab Ranke & Yergens, res 127 W Superior.

Boschet Gottlieb, lab, res 68 W Butler.

Boschett Henry, lab, bds Z Herring.

Boseker Charles H, carp, res n w cor Richardson and Runnion avenue.

Boseker Christian, contractor, res 37 Brackenridge.

Boseker Edith, teacher, bds 66 W De Wald.

Boseker Frank H, carp, res 131 Shawnee ave.

TRANSFERING. RYAN TRUCKING CO.
TEL. 122. 19 & 21 W. WASHINGTON.

FORT WAYNE DIRECTORY. 107

Boseker Harry, clk, bds 37 Brackenridge.
Boseker Henry, trav agt, res 66 W De Wald.
Boseker Lincoln, conductor, res 290 W Main.
Boseker Louisa, laundress, bds 104 Wall.
Boseker Wm G, blksmith Penn Co, res 138 Shawnee ave.
Boseker Wm G, mach hand Horton Mnfg Co, res 104 Wall.
Boseker Wm V, driver, bds 104 Wall.
Boshler Charles W, clk J A M Storm, res 70 Butler.
Boss Anna, stenogr Wayne Knitting Mills, bds 138 E Main.
Boss Mary (wid Henry), res 138 E Main.
Bosselmann Diedrich, boilermkr Ft Wayne Iron Works, res 233
    Madison.
Bossler Henry H, real estate, 34 Clinton, res w s Spy Run ave
    1 n of Bridge.
Bossler Joseph, lab Penn Co, res 22 Gay.
Bossler Joseph jr, molder Kerr-Murray Mnfg Co, bds 22 Gay.
Bossler Kittie, clk L Wolf & Co, bds w s Spy Run ave 1 n of
    bridge.
Bossler Maggie, cook Arlington Hotel.
Bossler Wm, coachman, bds Arlington Hotel.
Bostick Emanuel, mngr, res 170 E Wayne.
Bostick John W, res 130 E Wayne.
Bostick Reuben J, clk, bds 170 E Wayne.
Bostick Wm D (E B Kunkle & Co), bds 170 E Wayne.
Boston Restaurant, John C Hinton Propr; Restaurant,
    Dining and Lunch Rooms, 270-270½ Calhoun.
Boswell Andrew J, phys, 96 Barr, res 208 E Lewis.
Boswell Asa C, phys, 316 Hanna, res 327 same.
Bosworth Percy, foreman, res 402 Broadway.
Both Ottilie (wid Theodore), bds 23 E Jefferson.
Bothner John G, saloon, 136 Calhoun, res same.
Bott Edward, patternmkr Kerr-Murray Mnfg Co, bds 26 Walnut.
Bott Frank, clk Fox Branch U S Baking Co, bds 26 Walnut.
Bott Innocenz, blksmith Penn Co, res 26 Walnut.
Bott Nellie, dressmkr, 46 Taylor, bds same.
Bott Theresa M, clk Kayser & Baade, bds 46 Taylor.
Bott Urban, mach Wabash R R, res 46 Taylor.
Bottenberg Andrew J, res 13 Liberty.
Bottenberg Benjamin F, clk Nickel Plate R R, bds 13 Liberty.
Boucher Benjamin, teamster W H Brown, bds 73 Holman.
Boues Thomas T, clk Root & Co, bds Randall Hotel.
Bougher Frank E (Riegel & Bougher), res 12 Calhoun.
Boumeister Frederick, molder, res 398 E Lewis.
Bourie Adele, bds cor Louray and Edgewater ave.
Bourie A Ophelia, typewriter Olds' Wagon Works, bds cor
    Louray and Edgewater ave.

ARCHITECTS. **WING & MAHURIN,**
41 and 42 Pixley & Long Bldg. Telephone 328.

108   R. L. POLK & CO.'S

Bourie Brutus A, bkkpr Olds' Wagon Works, res 18 W De
  Wald.
Bourie Clinton D, letter carrier P O, res 117 E Wayne.
Bourie Desdemona, res 119 W Washington.
Bourie George W, clk Pixley & Co, bds L T Bourie.
Bourie Louis T, trav agt, res cor Louray and Edgewater ave.
Bouse Emma J (wid Lorenzo), res 35 1st.
Bouwier Lisette, domestic 121 W Jefferson.
Bouyuard Joseph, lab, bds 29 Duck.
Bovine David F, lab, res n s Cottage ave 2 w of Indiana ave.
Bowden John, engineer Penn Co, bds Boston Restaurant.
Bowen Alberta, bds 229 E Washington.
Bowen Daniel W, lawyer, res 229 E Washington.
Bowen George R, bookkpr, res 108 Barr.
Bowen George W, physician, 12 W Main, res 232 E Wash-
  ington.
Bowen James, hostler Wm M McKinnie.
Bowen Lillie V, teacher, bds 229 E Washington.
Bower, *see also Bauer and Bougher.*
Bower Daniel F, Gen Sec Y M C A, City Department res
  140 Walton ave.
Bower George B M, physician, 72 Harrison, res 116 W Main.
Bower Mary, domestic 35 E Williams.
Bowers Charles A, watchman, res e s Harrison 1 s of Killea.
Bowers Emma, domestic 86 W DeWald.
Bowers Jacob, car driver, bds Harmon House.
Bowers Jacob, carp, res 19 Cass.
Bowers Jacob J, lab Ft Wayne Iron Works, bds 57 Williams.
Bowers John W, painter J H Brimmer, bds 80 N Harrison.
Bowers Kate, domestic 222 W Washington.
Bowers Maggie, domestic 96 E Berry.
Bowers Maria (wid James), res 268 W Washington.
Bowersock Andrew, propr Union House, 49 W Main.
Bowman, *see also Baughmann and Bauman.*
Bowman Arthur F, grocer, 230 W Main, res same.
Bowman Charles, Saw Repairer; also Tinners' Shears,
  Lawn Mowers, Butchers' Tools, Scissors, Plow Points, and
  All Kinds of Edged Tools Ground and put in First-Class
  Order, 18 Harrison, res 141 High. (*See left top lines.*)
Bowman Clarence H, painter Penn Co, bds 226 Calhoun.
Bowman Elizabeth J, teacher, bds 160 W Superior.
Bowman Emmeline D (wid Alfred N), res 160 W Superior.
Bowman John B, agt Metropolitan Mnfg Co, res 163 E Jeffer-
  son.
Bowman Lee B, bartndr J C Belot, res 89 W Jefferson.
Bowman Prudence, teacher, bds 160 W Superior.

Bowman Vernon, coachman Dr C B Stemen.

Bowman Victor E, lab Penn Co, res 170 W Main.

Bowman Wm, finisher Peters Box and Lumber Co,bds 141 High.

Bowser Alexander, foreman S F Bowser & Co, res 264 E Creighton ave.

Bowser Allen A (S F Bowser & Co), res 264 E Creighton ave. (*See right side lines.*)

Bowser Augustus (S F Bowser & Co), res 253 E Creighton ave. (*See right side lines.*)

Bowser Charles W R, mach hand, bds 46 Force.

Bowser Clark E, lab, res 57 W Superior.

Bowser Delilah (wid Jacob C), res 86 E Washington.

Bowser Delmore, student, bds 15 Julia.

Bowser Ernst M, molder Bass F & M Works, bds 15 Julia.

Bowser George W, fireman, res 15 Julia.

Bowser Isaiah, blksmith, res 39 E De Wald.

Bowser Margaret (wid Samuel), res 95 Summit.

Bowser Nelson J, pedler, bds 15 Julia.

Bowser Sarah M, bds 86 E Washington.

Bowser Sylvanus F (S F Bowser & Co), res 252 E Creighton ave.

Bowser Sylvester, lab, res 46 Force.

Bowser S F & Co (Sylvanus F, Augustus and Allen A Bowser), Mnfrs of Oil Tanks, 254-264 E Creighton ave. Tel 374. (*See right side lines.*)

Bowsher Amos, transfer mail agt, res 42 McClellan.

Bowsher Nellie V, stenogr and assistant McDermuts' Ft Wayne Business College, bds 42 McClellan.

Boxberger Frances, domestic 242 W Berry.

Boxon Charles O, lawyer, res 38 Taylor.

Boyce Benjamin, engineer Bass F & M Works, res 29 Lillie.

Boyd Georgiana, teacher, bds 223 Lafayette.

Boyd Minnie, opr Hoosier Mnfg Co, bds 87 Ewing.

Boyd Sarah (wid Benjamin), res 223 Lafayette.

Boyd Seymour D, clk Bass F & M Works, bds 223 Lafayette.

Boyd Thomas L, brakeman, res 171 High.

Boyer, *see also Bayer.*

Boyer Ida F, nurse Ft Wayne City Hospital.

Boyer Lulu J, nurse Ft Wayne City Hospital.

Boyes Michael, lab Paul Koehler, bds same.

Boyington Mary (wid Samuel), bds 336 E Washington.

Boylan Ella L, clk Beadell & Co, bds 266 Calhoun.

Boylan John (John Boylan & Co), res 266 Calhoun.

Boylan John & Co (John Boylan), The Hotel Restaurant and Lunch Counter; Meals at all Hours; Open Day and Night; 266 Calhoun.

9

Boyle John, brakeman, res 62 Summit.
Boyle John, car repairer Penn Co, res New Haven rd.
Boyle Margaret M, trimmer A Mergentheim, bds 50 W Superior.
Boyle Sadie, clk L Dessauer & Co, bds 37 3d.
Boyles Anna, bds 35 Miner.
Boyles Grace, bds 35 Miner.
Boyles Robert D, cabtmkr Ft Wayne Organ Co, res 35 Miner.
Brabandt Ernst R, molder Bass F & M Works, res 98 Gay.
Brabandt Henry B, molder Bass F & M Works, res 228 Gay.
Bracht Ida, bds 33 W Butler.
Bracht Joseph F, engineer, res 33 W Butler.
Bracken Richard J, electrician Ft Wayne Electric Co, bds Harmon House.
Brackenridge Charles S, asst city engineer, res 144 W Wayne.
Brackenridge Eliza J (wid Joseph), res 77 W Wayne.
Brackenridge George W, Trustee Wayne Township, Office 13 Foster Blk, res 31 Douglas ave.
Brackenridge Robert E, deputy trustee Wayne Township, bds 77 W Wayne.
Brackenridge Wm T, removed to Omaha, Neb.
Brackeusi Casper H, cigarmkr L Dessauer & Co, bds 12 Harrison.
Brackett Mary, cook Windsor Hotel.
Brackett W A, removed to Peru, Ind.
Bradbury Agnes (wid Thomas), res 122 Chicago.
Bradbury May, operator, bds 122 Chicago.
Brademeyer, *see also Bredemeyer.*
Brademeyer Wm, lab, bds 100 Montgomery.
Braden David, farmer, res 270 W Jefferson.
Bradfield Lafayette, depot agt Adams Express Co, res 374 Calhoun.
Bradley Charles S, engineer Ft Wayne Electric Co, bds 103 W Berry.
Bradley Edward O, engineer Penn Co, bds 233 E Lewis.
Bradley Frank, painter, res 201 Hanna.
Bradley George, painter, res 163 Francis.
Bradley George O, patternmkr Kerr-Murray Mnfg Co, res 33 W Williams.
Bradley Henry J, draughtsman Kerr-Murray Mnfg Co, bds Grand Central Hotel.
Bradley James K, mach Penn Co, res 233 E Lewis.
Bradley Nelson L, foreman The F Wayne Furniture Co, bds 233 E Lewis.
Bradley Robert A, student Wing & Mahurin, bds 33 W Williams.
Bradley Mrs Sarah A, propr Grand Central Hotel, 101 Calhoun.

, engineer, bds Grand Central Hotel.
, (col'd), domestic 157 E Berry.
ι, domestic 131 E Main.
ιel (col'd), porter S·G Hubbard, bds 159 Erie.
harles H, horseshoer, res 172 Madison.
lizabeth (wid Henry), res 107 Summit.
·ottlieb, car bldr Penn Co, res 59 Douglas ave.
enrietta, domestic 57 Douglas ave.
enry W, clk, bds 172 Madison.
do E, foreman Penn Co, res 216 E Lewis.
d Samuel A), bds 260 W Berry.
E, pedler, res 67 W Superior.
Root & Co), res 260 W Berry.
·o Breuer.
, shoemkr, 358 Broadway, res same.
ιds 358 Broadway.
McKinnie House, res 297 Harrison.
dressmkr, 84 W Main, res same.
·les F, engineer, res 224 High.
, mach hd Ft Wayne Spoke Works, bds 34 Gay.
, carp, res 184 Maumee rd.
jr, wheelmkr, res 182 Maumee rd.
y C, lab Frederick Myers, bds 104 Barr.
is (L Brames & Co), res 162 E Jefferson.
: Co (Louis Brames), Proprs Summit City
orks, 123 Clay. (See page 3.)
r, student Carl Schilling, rms ·193 W Berry.
ιev Joseph H, vicar-general diocese Ft Wayne,
ton.
Gustave, car repairer Wabash R R, bds 58

ιosina (wid Samuel), res 58 Oakley.
, clk Stewart & Hahn, bds 34 McClellan.
ι, cigarmkr, bds 158 Harrison.
ιuyer John Orff, res 34 McClellan.
, mach Indiana Mach Works, res 15 Boone.
ι 158 Harrison.
foreman Bass F & M Works, res 142 John.
ιΑ5 W Jefferson

Robert Spice, Waterworks and General Plumbing, 48 West Main and 11 Pearl Streets.

112   R. L. POLK & CO.'S

Brandt Minnie M, clk J M Kane, bds 34 McClellan.
Brandt Mollie, clk Stewart & Hahn, bds 34 McClellan.
Brandt Theodore W, clk, bds 45 W Jefferson.
Brandt Wm J, cigarmkr C A Berndt, res 173 John.
Brandtmeyer Frederick, molder, res 168 Ewing.
Branican Beverly (col'd), coachman, res 100 Indiana ave.
Brannan, *see also Brennan.*
Brannan Bridget, domestic 141 W Berry.
Brannan Elizabeth, bds 185 Monroe.
Brannan John H, county commissioner, res 195 E Lewis.
Brannan Judith, bds 185 Monroe.
Brannan Julia (wid Thomas), res 185 Monroe.
Brannan Mary, clk, bds 195 E Lewis.
Brannan Michael L, janitor, res 171 E Washington.
Brannan Richard T V, plumber A Hattersley & Sons, bds 195 E Lewis.
Brannan Thomas L, fireman, res 160 W Main.
Branning Conrad, lab, res 89 Wall.
Branning Ernst, farmer, res w s Fairfield ave s of organ factory.
Brannon Melvin A, teacher, rms 27 E Washington.
Branstator John A, carp, res 68 Walton ave.
Branstator Walter, lab, bds 129 Franklin ave.
Brase August C, grocer, 73 W Jefferson, res same.
Brase Frederick C, teamster, res 75 W Jefferson.
Brase Theodore F, teamster, res 176 W Jefferson.
Brase Wm C, teamster Herman Berghoff Brewing Co, res 415 E Washington.
Brauer John C, shoemaker, res 184 Griffith.
Braun, *see also Brown.*
Braun Barbara (wid John), res 78 Wall.
Braun Caroline, domestic 60 Nirdlinger ave.
Braun Carrie, operator Hoosier Mnfg Co, bds 78 Wall.
Braun Charles G (Keller & Braun), res 17 Ross.
Braun Charles G, foreman C A Berndt, res 53 Holton ave.
Braun Charles M, apprentice F Hilt, bds 78 Wall.
Braun Elizabeth (wid Philip), bds 168 E Washington.
Braun Frederick, stone mason, res 233 John.
Braun Frederick J, blksmith L C Zollinger, res 78 Wall.
Braun George, bds 54 Pritchard.
Braun George, baker, 135 Fairfield ave, res same.
Braun Henry, stereotyper Ft Wayne Newspaper Union, bds 342 E Washington.
Braun Henry G, brickmkr, bds 78 Wall.
Braun John, carp, res 342 E Washington.
Braun John jr, stonecutter, bds 342 E Washington.
Braun Louis, helper Penn Co, res 163 Hayden.

J.A.M.STORM, LEATHER and RUBBER BELTING, 7 East Columbia St.

FORT WAYNE DIRECTORY. 113

Braun Martin, boilermkr Bass F & M Works, bds 342 E Washington.
Braun Mary, bds 247 W Washington.
Braun Mary E (wid John), res 247 W Washington.
Braun Michael, bds Lake Shore Hotel.
Braun Peter M, patternmkr Bass F & M Works, res 387 E Lewis.
Braun Sarah C, seamstress, bds 78 Wall.
Braun Wm, driver George Braun, bds 135 Fairfield ave.
Brauneisen Joseph, mach Ft Wayne Electric Co, s w cor Metz and Taylor.
Braungart George, mach hand Ft Wayne Furniture Co, bds 135 Fairfield ave.
Brauntmeyer Carrie, clk, bds 168 Ewing.
Brauntmyer Charles H, mach A Hattersley & Sons, res 176 Ewing.
Brauntmeyer Frederick W, molder, res 168 Ewing.
Brawley George H, removed to Waukegan, Wis.
Brayer Leah, domestic Charles Wilding.
Breaden Ida (wid James E), boarding house, 143 Holman.
Bredemeyer, see also Brademeyer.
Bredemeyer Henry E, janitor, res 38 4th.
Bredemeyer Wm, painter, res 8 Marion.
Breeaugh John E, brakeman, res 123 High.
Breen Ellen, dressmkr, bds 15 Bass.
Breen Henry, brakeman, bds 15 Bass.
Breen James J, conductor, bds 15 Bass.
Breen Kate, stenographer Kerr-Murray Mufg Co, bds 25 W Jefferson.
Breen Maria (wid Michael), res 15 Bass.
Breen Michael, clk, bds 15 Bass.
Breen Wm P, Lawyer, over 44 Calhoun, res 121 W Main.
Breer Ferdinand, carver Ft Wayne Furniture Co, res 137 E Washington.
Breese George H, mach Bass F & M Works, res 60 Wall.
Breese Samuel E, painter, res 106 Francis.
Brehn Charles, res 213 Hayden.
Breidenstein Daniel, cook J T Wagner, rms 7 E Main.
Breidenstein Mathias, carp, bds 25 W Wayne.
Breidenstein Simpson, real estate, 25 W Wayne, res same.
Breimeier Ernest, contractor, 221 W Creighton ave, res same.
Breimeier Ernest jr, contractor, res 207 W DeWald.
Breimeier Gustave, mach Ft Wayne Electric Co, bds 221 W Creighton ave.
Breimeier Henry, res 219 W Jefferson.
Breimeier Herman, stone mason, bds 221 W Creighton ave.

Penn Mutual LIFE INSURANCE CO. of PHILA.
CLARK FAIRBANK, General Agent, 19 Court Street.

114   R. L. POLK & CO.'S

Breimeier Joseph, stonecutter Keller & Braun, res 6 Huron.
Breimeier Louis C, clk, A E C Becker, res 128 W Williams.
Bremer Henry J, clk J B White, res 47 Archer ave.
Bremer Henry J jr, driver, bds 47 Archer ave.
Bremer Wm F, clk, bds 47 Archer ave.
Brendel George, caller N Y, C & St L R R, bds 12 St Mary's ave.
Brendel Jacobine (wid John), res 12 St Mary's ave.
Brendel John A, brakeman N Y, C & St L R R, bds 12 St Mary's ave.
Brendel Joseph, caller, bds 12 St Mary's ave.
Brendel Josephine, dressmkr, 12 St Mary's ave, bds same.
Brenen Michael, lab John Dimon, bds same.
Brennan, see also Brannan.
Brennan Bernhard T, cigarmkr, res 120 St Mary's ave.
Brennan Wm T, mach Ft Wayne Electric Co, res 127 Monroe.
Brenner Charles F, mach Kerr-Murray Mnfg Co, bds 78 Wilt.
Brenner Ferdinand, lumber agt, res 54 Nirdlinger ave.
Brenner George, printer Freie Presse, res 108 Madison.
Brenner Mary (wid John), res 78 Wilt.
Brenton Eliza (wid Samuel), res 220 W Wayne.
Brenton Helen, teacher, bds 220 W Wayne.
Brenton Marion H (wid Milton H), teacher, bds 19 Madison.
Bresler Albert, brakeman, res 393 W Main.
Bresler James M, brakeman, res 54 Jackson.
Bresnahan John, wiper Penn Co, res 145 Holman.
Bresnahan John J, fireman, bds 145 Holman.
Bresnahan Mary E, tailoress Gustav Scheffler, bds 145 Holman.
Bresnahan Patrick, mach hand Ind Mach Works, bds 145 Holman.
Bresnahan Thomas F, lab Penn Co, bds 145 Holman.
Bretmiller, see Bradtmueller.
Breuer, s e also Braeuer.
Breuer Wm, foreman Herman Berghoff Brewing Co, res 574 E Washington.
Brewer Wm L, trav agt, res 69 Holman.
Brewster Edith M, prin Holton Ave School, bds 139 E DeWald.
Brewster Lucy, opr Hoosier Mnfg Co, bds 285 W Wayne.
Breyman James H, lineman Ft Wayne District Tel Co, bds 22 W Main.
Briant, see Bryant.
Brice James F, conductor, res 159 W Superior.
Brick Christina L (wid Adam), bds 122 W Jefferson.
Bricker Conrad, engineer Penn Co, res 53 Thomas.
Bricker David, engineer G R & I R R, res 25 Oliver.
Bricker D Edwin, clk S M Foster, res 299 E Lewis.
Bricker Homer A, clk D M Foster Furniture Co, bds 53 Thomas.

BUILDERS' HARDWARE, PFEIFFER & SCHLATTER, 38 and 40 East Columbia St.

FORT WAYNE DIRECTORY. 115

Bricker John M, feed barn, res 37 Barr.
Bricker Lincoln J, driver B W Skelton Co, res 31 Charles.
Bricker Seward D, fireman Penn Co, res 78 E Williams.
Brickmakers' Association, James S Fields agt, 55 Clinton.
Brickner Charles, watchman, res 99 W Jefferson.
Brickner Herman, stone mason, res 141 Erie.
Brickner Oswald, molder Bass F & M Works, bds 141 Erie.
Bridge Rev Henry, pastor St Paul's M E Church, res 136 Walton ave.
Briggeman Henry, coremkr Kerr-Murray Mnfg Co, res rear 67 Hayden.
Briggeman Henry A, clk S A Karn, bds 123 Madison.
Briggeman Wm, car bldr Penn Co, res 21 Euclid ave.
Briggs Frank W, student, bds 120 Ewing.
Briggs Hattie (wid Alfred), dressmkr, res 120 Ewing.
Briggs Lillian M, clk Root & Co, bds 120 Ewing.
Briggs Martin, porter Harmon House.
Bright Benjamin W, molder Bass F & M Works, bds 229 E Wayne.
Bright Wm J, car bldr Penn Co, res 229 E Wayne.
Brill Henry F, conductor, res 150 E Creighton ave.
Brillhart Andrew J, helper Ft Wayne Electric Co, bds 328 E Jefferson.
Brillmeyer Joseph, stonecutter, res 6 Huron.
Brimmer Joseph H, Sign and House Painter, 33 W Main, res 265 W Jefferson.
Brindel Henry, mason, res 11 Shawnee ave.
Brink Henry, mach Rhinesmith & Simonson, res 298 E Washington.
Brink John J, druggist, 44 Wells, res same.
Brink Lizzie, dressmkr, 320 E Washington, bds same.
Brink Mary E, bds 320 E Washington.
Brinker Theodore, baggagemaster Nickel Plate Depot, res 312 W Jefferson.
Brinkman Charles, bds 325 W Washington.
Brinkman Frederick, harnessmkr, rms 88 Barr.
Brinkman Henry, mason, res 173 Gay.
Brinkman John H, cigarmkr George Reiter, bds 69 Grand.
Brinkman Wm, painter, res 22 Gladstone ave.
Brinkroeger Frederick, clk H P W Brinkroeger, res 50 4th.
Brinkroeger Herman P W, grocer, 48 Harrison, bds 50 4th.
Brinsley Charles M, engineer, bds 90 E Wayne.
Brinsley George C (G C Brinsley & Son), res 264 W Washington.
Brinsley George C jr, (G C Brinsley & Son), res 85 W Main.

Brinsley G C & Son (George C and George C jr), oils, cor Pearl and Maiden Lane.
Brinsley Herbert G, draughtsman, bds 90 E Wayne.
Brinsley John C, feed barn, 28 Pearl, res 90 E Wayne.
Brintzenhofe Ammon S, mach Wabash R R, res 9 Brooklyn.
Bristol A T, wheelman Ft Wayne Water Power Co, bds 16 Barthold.
Britcher Mrs Dora, domestic 221 W DeWald.
Britcher Edward M, carp, res 83 Broadway.
Brittingham Eva, bds 60 Grant ave.
Brittingham John S, wood turner, res 469 Harrison.
Brittingham Philo E, engineer, res 60 Grant ave.
Britz Jacob, lab Herman Berghoff Brewing Co, res 546 E Wayne.
Brobst Anna, opr Hoosier Mnfg Co, bds 141 Wells.
Brock George, lab Bass F & M Works, res 364 E Wayne.
Brockerman Jacob R, plasterer, res 106 Riverside ave.
Brockerman Leonard S, plasterer, res 40 Riverside ave.
Brockerman Minnie, bds 40 Riverside ave.
Brockerman Thomas, plasterer, res 75 Riverside ave.
Brockmann Henry, lab Bass F & M Works, res 25 Smith.
Brockmeier Minnie, domestic 50 Oak.
Brockmeyer Edward, helper Bass F & M Works, bds 87 Wall.
Brockway Jennie (wid Clarence), res 11 Melita.
Brodt Ida, milliner Wm Malloy, bds 51 Liberty.
Broeking Charles, agt, res 267 E Creighton ave.
Broeking Diedrich, plasterer, res 26 Wall.
Broeking Emma, opr Hoosier Mnfg Co, bds 267 E Creighton.
Broeking Mary C, clk A Goodman, bds 26 Wall.
Broeking Wm, cigarmkr, bds 267 E Creighton ave.
Brogt Frederick, canvasser, res 51 Liberty.
Brokaw, *see also Bokaw.*
Brokaw Agnes F, bds 251 Calhoun.
Brokaw Franklin, brakeman, bds 69 Lillie.
Brokaw James H, conductor, res 20 W Creighton ave.
Brokaw Leander, caller, bds 251 Calhoun.
Brokaw Leonard W, lab, bds 69 Lillie.
Brokaw Lewis T, boarding house, 251 Calhoun.
Brokaw Mary M, bds 20 W Creighton ave.
Brokaw Robert, carp, res 69 Lillie.
Brokaw Samuel L, baggagemaster, res 294 E Lewis.
Brokmeyer Minnie, domestic 240 W Berry.
Bromley O K, clk L S & M S Ry, rms 86 N Harrison.
Bronka Anna, opr Hoosier Mnfg Co, bds 558 Lafayette.
Bronenkant Dionysius, shoemkr, 14 Nirdlinger ave, res same.
Bronson Drusilla (wid Abraham), res 5 Brandriff.
Broockman Hannah, bds 65 John.

Brookens Rachel (wid Thomas), bds 17 Richardson.
Brooks Abraham B C, cabinetmkr Peters Box and Lumber Co, res 88 4th.
Brooks Bryant (col'd), barber, 220 Calhoun, rms same.
Brooks Catherine (wid Walter T), bds 137 W Superior.
Brooks Charlotte (wid Wm), bds Wm Brooks.
Brooks Dollie (wid Robert), res 10 Runnion ave.
Brooks Ernst, barber, bds 3 E Superior.
Brooks George H, carp, res 3 E Superior.
Brooks Henry, printer Indiana Staats Zeitung, res 49 W Jefferson.
Brooks Henry C, carp, 187 W DeWald, res same.
Brooks Lotta B, clk C E Everett, bds Wm Brooks.
Brooks Mary (wid Robert), saloon, 52 W Main, res same.
Brooks Oscar H, supt Olds' Wagon Works, res 369 S Calhoun.
Brooks Robert, died June 18, 1891.
Brooks Wm, carp, res n s Creighton ave 1 e of Calhoun.
Brooks Wm H, bds 107 W Berry.
Brookshire Isham (col'd), brakeman, rms 70 Chicago.
Brookside Farm Co, Columbia City rd 1½ miles west of Court House
Broom Henry E, helper Bass F & M Works, bds 31 Gay.
Broom John N, clk S F Bowser & Co, res 31 Gay.
Broom John W, porter The Randall.
Broom Theresa, opr Hoosier Mnfg Co, bds 31 Gay.
Brosius Aaron, lumber, res 15 St Michael ave.
Brosowski Edward, polisher Ft Wayne Spoke Works, bds Martin Brosowski.
Brosowski Ernest, bartender M N Webber, bds Martin Brosowski.
Brosowski Martin, lab, res n e cor Lumbard and Line.
Brossard Clara, opr S M Foster, bds 82 Wells.
Brossard Frank, clk M Frank & Co, bds 82 Wells.
Brossard George, clk John Brossard, bds 82 Wells.
Brossard George, blksmith Wm Thiele, res 18 5th.
Brossard John, grocer, 84 Wells, res 82 same.
Brossard Louisa F, bds 33 Wefel.
Brossard Thérese, dressmkr, 33 Wefel, bds same.
Brossard Wm, blksmith Penn Co, res 33 Wefel.
Brothers of the Holy Cross, s w cor Clinton and Jefferson.
Browand Catherine, bkkpr, bds 355 E Lewis.
Browand Frances, milliner Seaney Millinery Co, bds 355 E Lewis.
Browand Mrs Mary J, res 355 E Lewis.
Browand Norman C (Gloeckle & Browand), bds 355 E Lewis.
Browand Reuben M, barber J T Baker, bds 355 E Lewis.

Brower Cain, mach hand Ft Wayne Furniture Co, res South Wayne.

Brown, *see also Braun.*

Brown August C, foreman L S & M S Ry, res 40 3d.

Brown Catherine, opr Hoosier Mnfg Co, bds 25 Randolph.

Brown Charles S, barber, bds 164 Walton ave.

Brown David J, buyer, res 174 Greely.

Brown Edward D, trav agt, rms 29 E Main.

Brown Edward H, well driver, res 165 Wells.

Brown Elizabeth T (wid Wm H), bds 139 Montgomery.

Brown Flora (wid John), res 29 Prince.

Brown Frank G, cabtmkr Ft Wayne Organ Co, res 3 Walnut.

Brown Frank I, timber purchaser Nickel Plate R R, bds 113 W Wayne.

Brown Frank L, barber, 178½ Broadway, res 7 Brookside.

Brown Frederick S, printer Journal, res 142 E Wayne.

Brown George, painter, bds 105 Barr.

Brown George H (Heilbroner & Brown), res 256 Clinton.

Brown George H, fireman Penn Co, res 101 W Williams.

Brown Harry, lab, res 3 Ruth.

Brown Harvey H, molder Bass F & M Works, res 269 E Jefferson.

Brown Hattie J, bds 270 E Lewis.

Brown James, lab, res 22 Hough.

Brown James D, mngr Harmon House.

Brown James E, conductor, res 270 E Lewis.

Brown Joel H, lather, bds 3 Duryea.

Brown Joel L, lather, bds 3 Duryea.

Brown John, blksmith, res 71 Holman.

Brown John, helper Penn Co, res 192 Lafayette.

Brown John, lab, bds 29 Prince.

Brown John A, driver Powers & Barnett, bds 77 E Superior.

Brown John B, castings inspector Penn Co, res n w cor Taylor and Pine.

Brown John E, clk Penn Co, res 166 W Berry.

Brown John O, carp, 414 W Main, res same.

Brown John S, section foreman, res 164 Walton ave.

Brown John W, barber, 44 E Columbia, res same.

Brown John W (col'd), cook, res 31 Grand.

Brown Joseph (col'd), cook Harmon House.

Brown Mrs Kate, bds 283 W Berry.

Brown Leonard D, brakeman, res 8 Mechanic.

Brown Levi, driver, bds Harmon House.

Brown Lewis B, conductor, res 4 Jackson.

Brown Louis, barber L B Pegg, res Goshen rd.

Brown Margaret (wid Joseph), res 4 Kansas.

Geo. E. Johnson, DENTIST, 74 Calhoun Street. Res., 188 W. Berry St.

FORT WAYNE DIRECTORY. 119

Brown Martha E, bds 270 E Lewis.
Brown Mary, bds 56 Madison.
Brown Mrs Mattie L, Propr Harmon House, n w cor Calhoun and Chicago.
Brown Nathaniel, carp, res 73 Oakley.
Brown Nettie, laundress Indiana School for Feeble-Minded Youth.
Brown Miss Ollie (col'd), music teacher, 31 Grand, bds same.
Brown Rufus R, res 26 E Williams.
Brown Sarah, bds 22 Hough.
Brown Seneca B, dentist, 15 Bank blk, res 100 W Berry.
Brown Stephen M, engineer J Derheimer, res 15 Oak.
Brown Thomas, died August 11, 1891.
Brown Warren H, ins agt, bds Jewel House.
Brown Wm, janitor, bds 37 E DeWald.
Brown Wm E, clk. bds 174 Greely.
Brown Rev Wm H (col'd), res n w cor Ohio and Eliza.
Brown Wm H, truckman, 73 Holman, res same.
Browne Robinson, flagman, res 213 Broadway.
Browne Wm C, fitter Ft Wayne Electric Co, bds 213 Broadway.
Brownsberger Alonzo, lab, bds 71 Garden.
Brownsberger Charles, cigarmkr G F Yergens, bds 57 E Main.
Brownsberger Charles, flagman, res 55 Taylor.
Brownsberger Samuel W, lab Ft Wayne Electric Co, res 71 Garden.
Brownsberger Wm, hostler Powers & Barnett, res 57 E Main.
Brubaker Samuel J, trav agt B W Skelton Co, res 25 W Jefferson.
Brucker Charles J, feeder The Press, bds 277 W Washington.
Brucker Frank X, deputy city treas, bds 277 W Washington.
Bruder August, Watchmaker, Jeweler and Dealer in Watches, Clocks, Diamonds and Silverware, 93 Calhoun, rms 94 same.
Brudi George J (W H Brudi & Bro), res 156 Wells.
Brudi Henry E, baker W F Geller, res 148 W Jefferson.
Brudi Josephine, domestic 109 W Berry.
Brudi Martha, domestic 133 E Berry.
Brudi Mary (wid Francois), bds 91 Summit.
Brudi Ottillie, domestic 109 W Berry.
Brudi Wm H (W H Brudi & Bro), res 29 Miner.
Brudi W H & Bro (Wm H and George J), Proprs Bloomingdale Mills, cor 6th and Wells.
Bruebach Amelia E (wid George), res 258 Clinton.
Brueck Theodore J, driver Pickard Bros, bds 53 Hugh.
Bruening Frances, domestic 61 Broadway.
Bruger Michael, cooper, res 62 Nelson.
Brugh George, lab, bds 251 Calhoun.

1

Brumbaugh Harry, brakeman, res 349 W Main.
Brundige David, mason, res 75 Franklin ave.
Brune Wm, teamster, res 14 Barthold.
Bruner Alexander, cigarmkr, res 313 W Washington.
Bruner Isaiah S, carp, res 68 Maumee rd.
Bruner Martin, lab Penn Co, res 13 Union.
Brunett Andrew, carp, bds 51 4th.
Brunett Charles, engineer Jacob Klett & Sons, bds 51 4th.
Brunett Mary (wid Joseph), res 51 4th.
Brunka Wm F, lab Wabash R R, bds 558 Lafayette.
Brunkhart Henry A, lab, res 24 Wefel.
Brunner Annie M, clk G E Bursley & Co, bds 184 W Main.
Brunner Cornelius (Brunner & Haag), res 184 W Main.
Brunner John, shoemkr Isidor Lehman, res 47 Pritchard.
Brunner Joseph A, watchmkr H C Graffe, res 183 W Jefferson.
Brunner Louis J, painter, res 79 Nirdlinger ave.
Brunner Minnie M, bds 184 W Main.
Brunner Rosa, starcher Troy Steam Laundry, bds 184 W Main.
Brunner & Haag (Cornelius Brunner, Charles J Haag), Marble, Monumental and Cemetery Work, 124 W Main.
Bruns Annie F (wid Christian F), res 224 E Jefferson.
Bruns Christian, blksmith Penn Co, res 152 Wallace.
Bruns Christian E H, car bldr Penn Co, res 332 Harrison.
Bruns Christian W (C W Bruns & Co), res 158 Griffith.
Bruns C W & Co (Christian W Bruns), Plumbers, Steam and Gas Fitters; Agents for the Bolton Hot Water Heater, and Goodrich Self-Heating and Folding Bath Tubs, 135 Calhoun.
Bruns Emilie, bds 332 S Harrison.
Bruns George W, meats, 348½ Calhoun, res 332 Harrison.
Bruns Herman, engineer Bruns & McBennett, bds 130 Gay.
Bruns John W, lab, bds 224 E Jefferson.
Bruns John, real estate, 565 E Washington, res same.
Bruns Louisa, bds 332 Harrison.
Bruns Philip, roofer, bds 224 E Jefferson.
Bruns Wm (Bruns & McBennett), res 130 Gay.
Bruns Wm, lab Wm Miller, res n w cor Pontiac and Walton ave.
Bruns Wm F, boilermkr Bass F & M Works, res 224 E Jefferson.
Bruns & McBennett (Wm Bruns, Francis McBennett), sash and blind mnfrs, cor Winter and Buchanan.
Brunskill James, res n s Eckart 2 e of Hanna.
Brunskill James jr, lab Olds' Wagon Works, bds James Brunskill.
Brunskill John, barber, bds James Brunskill.

Brunson Allan, street car driver, res 53 Shawnee ave.
Brunson Lizzie, clk Seibert & Good, bds 53 Shawnee ave.
Bruse August, lab Bass F & M Works, bds 364 E Lewis.
Brush Edward, brakeman, bds 49 Baker.
Brush Mary L (wid Edward), rms 250 Clinton.
Bryan Elijah, lab W H Brown, bds 73 Holman.
Bryan Eliza P (wid Henry), res 34 Chicago.
Bryan Jane (wid Irving), res 143 Wallace.
Bryan Olive, domestic 243½ Washington.
Bryant Addie W (wid J Frank), bds 67 Brackenridge.
Bryant Alice, domestic 25 Laselle.
Bryant George W, coremkr Bass F & M Works, res Fox ave
   outside limits of city.
Bryant Harry E, molder, bds 25 Hough.
Bryant John O, helper, bds 216 E Lewis.
Bryant Joseph, mach hand Ft Wayne Electric Co, bds 111
   Fox ave.
Bryant Joseph H, driver, res 204 Lafayette.
Bryant Miss Julia M, clk Kuhne & Co, bds 228 W Creighton ave.
Bryant Wm H, res 228 W Creighton ave.
Brye Theodore, blksmith John Rupp, res 61 E Superior.
Bube Frank, porter The Randall.
Buche Anna, seamstress, bds 54 Charles.
Buche Catherine (wid Henry), res 54 Charles.
Buche Frederick J, painter, bds 54 Charles.
Buche Louisa, bds 54 Charles.
Bucher Adam F, carp, res 15 Ross.
Bucher Mollie, domestic 64 Barr.
Bucher Wm T, packer J A Armstrong, bds 320 Calhoun.
Buchert Mathias, painter, res 88 Home ave.
Buchheit Adam, carp, res 20 Union.
Buchheit John A, clk, bds 20 Union.
Buchheit Salome, bds 20 Union.
Buchman Alfred O, ins agt, res 83 Force.
Buchman Alpheus P, Physician, 94 Calhoun, res 161 W
   Washington; Office Hours, 1:30 to 4:30 and 7 to 9 P M.
Buchwalter Corwin C, painter Penn Co, bds 40 E Jefferson.
Buck, *see also Bock and Buuck.*
Buck Carrie (wid Frederick), res 10 McClellan.
Buck Charles, agt Prudential Ins Co, res 188 Hanna.
Buck Charles, foreman Indiana Staats Zeitung, res 29 Nird-
   linger ave.
Buck Charles W jr, tel opr Wabash R R, bds 188 Hanna.
Buck Edwin C, clk, bds 269 W Jefferson.
Buck Henry, clk McDonald, Watt & Wilt, bds 290 W Jeffer-
   son.

John Pressler, Galvanized Iron CORNICES and Slate ROOFING. Columbia, Barr and Dock Streets.

122   R. L. POLK & CO.'S

Buck Sophia (wid Diedrich), res 290 W Jefferson.
Buck Wm F, messenger U S Exp Co, bds 290 W Jefferson.
Buck Wilson S (Argo & Buck), res 269 W Jefferson.
Buckles George T, lab Kilian Baker, bds 230 Harmer.
Buckles Rev James P, res 42 Harmer.
Buckles Wm T, sign-writer J H Brimmer. bds 265 W Jefferson.
Buckley Charles E, printer Gazette, bds 29 Baker.
Buckley Henry S, blksmith Wabash R R, res 29 Baker.
Buckley Joseph H, heater, bds 29 Baker.
Buckley Mary Ann, bds 29 Baker.
Bucklin Rodney A, molder, res 112 W Butler.
Buckwalter, *see also Bookwalter.*
Buckwalter Louis R, mach Penn Co, res 54 W Jefferson.
Buckwalter Mary, bds 54 W Jefferson.
Budd Francis F, supt Hoosier Mnfg Co, res 406 S Broadway.
Budde John F C, helper Kerr-Murray Mnfg Co, bds 43 St Martin.
Budde Magdalena (wid Harmon), res 43 St Martin.
Buddemeyer Ernst F, laborer, res 14 Fairfield ave.
Buddemeyer Kate, wks Troy Steam Laundry, bds 14 Fairfield.
Bueche Frederick E, clerk, bds 15 Clark.
Bueche George, laborer, res 15 Clark.
Buechner Frederick G, watchman Ind Mach Wks, res n s Harmon 4 e of St Mary's ave.
Buefink Isabella (wid George), bds 67 High.
Buefink John G, mach hd Rhinesmith & Simonson, res 69 High.
Buefink Mary, bds 69 High.
Buehler John, clerk J B White, bds 22 Oak.
Buehler Samuel E, blksmith J A Spercisen, bds 56 Taylor.
Buehler Wm C, springmkr Penn Co, res 22 Oak.
Buehrle Frank, clerk A E Trentman, res 393 E Wayne.
Bueker Ernest F, plasterer, res 46 Walter.
Bueker Henry E, Propr City Carriage Works, 11-13 Clay, res 409 E Washington. (*See right bottom lines.*)
Buell Lena A, stenogr Fort Wayne Electric Co, bds 28 W Creighton ave.
Buell Raymond R, agent, bds 46 E Jefferson.
Buelow Frederick, lab Bass F and M Works, res 210 Smith.
Buelow John, dairy, 149 Wells, res same.
Buelow Mary, domestic 93 W Wayne.
Buesching Henry, saloon, 207 Lafayette, res 209 same.
Buesching Sophie, domestic 280 W Wayne.
Buesking Conrad, Boots and Shoes, 300 Hanna, res same.
Buettel A Christian, clk Chicago Furn Co, res 234 Francis.
Buettel Dora (wid George), midwife, 234 Francis.
Buettel Henry W, foreman, 1 Eliza.

I

Buffenberger Jacob, laborer, res 21 Harrison.
Buffington Jesse C, lab J A Koehler, res e s Piqua ave 3 n of Richardville ave.
Buffink Charles C, trav agent, bds 17 Hoffman.
Bufford Edward, pumps, res 200 St Mary's ave.
Bufford John C, laborer, bds 8 St Mary's ave.
Bufford Norman, mach hd Louis Rastetter, bds 8 St Mary's ave.
Bugbee John, section foreman, res s w cor Bond and Pittsburgh.
Bugert George, car bldr Penn Co res 155 E Creighton ave.
Bugert Matthew (Rear & Bugert), res 88 Home ave.
Buhr Catherine (wid Nicholas), bds 242 E Lewis.
Buhr Charles H, clk Pfeiffer & Schlatter, bds 26 Oak.
Buhr Frederick, clk Wm Doehrmann, bds 26 Oak.
Buhrkuhl Henry, res 87 Monroe.
Bulger Charles, clk A C Trentman, bds 176 Griffith.
Bulger Edward W, draughtsman Ft Wayne Electric Co, bds 146 W Berry.
Bulger Mrs Eliza J, res 146 W Berry.
Bulger Ida E, milliner, bds 176 Griffith.
Bulger John H, teamster A C Trentman, bds 176 Griffith.
Bulger Patrick J, truckman A C Trentman, res 176 Griffith.
Bull Frank, clk A J Keller, rms 97 Broadway.
Bull John, laborer, bds 290 Calhoun.
Bullerman Henry, teamster, res 286 W Jefferson.
Bullerman Henry C, bds 286 W Jefferson.
Bullerman Henry F, county comnr, res St Joseph twp.
Bullerman Louisa C, tailoress, bds 286 W Jefferson.
Bulmahn Frederick G, student Western Gas Construction Co, bds 90 Baker.
Bulmahn Henry C, painter, res 90 Baker.
Bulow, see Buelow.
Bultemeier Frederick, carp Wabash R R, res 25 Rockhill.
Bultmeyer Ernest, carp, res 90 Wall.
Bunce Almon A, mach hand, res 94 Oliver.
Bunce Anna L (wid Theodore), bds 134 Lafayette.
Bunch John, lab, res 14½ Barthold.
Bundy Joseph, carp, res e s S Calhoun 3 s of Marchell.
Bunsold Samuel B (Turner & Bunsold), bds 65 W Lewis.
Burbage John W, tinner Penn Co, bds 105 E Washington.
Burchard Charles A, car bldr Penn Co, res 64 Madison.
Burchard George J C, helper Penn Co, bds 64 Madison.
Burdell Charles H, gasfitter, res 37 W Berry.
Burdett Samuel H, tuner, res 93 W Jefferson.
Burdg Eli B, lab, res 50 Wall.
Buret Charles A, lab, res 34 2d.
Burg, see also Berg and Borg.

ARCHITECTS. **WING & MAHURIN,**
41 and 42 Pixley & Long Bldg. Telephone 328.

124   R. L. POLK & CO.'S

Burg Frederick P, paver, bds 235 Lafayette.
Burg Jacob G, apprentice A C Baker, bds 235 Lafayette.
Burg John, lab Penn Co, bds 235 Lafayette.
Burg Nicholas, res 235 Lafayette.
Burger, *see also Berger and Boerger.*
Burger Edward W, bds 146 W Berry.
Burger George, engineer Penn Co, res 331 Harrison.
Burger Gottlieb, clk M Frank & Co, bds 224 W Jefferson.
Burger Ira G, engineer Penn Co, bds 49 Baker.
Burger Joseph A, barber Gloeckle & Browand, bds 21 W Jefferson.
Burger Louis A, printer Archer, Housh & Co, bds 224 W Jefferson.
Burger Michael, helper A Vogely, bds 52 Oak.
Burgert Milton H (Renner, Cratsley & Co), bds The Randall.
Burgess Francis, mach Wabash R R, res 178 W Jefferson.
Burgett Harley, molder Bass F & M Works, res 196 Smith.
Burgett Wm H, painter Olds' Wagon Works, res 216 Francis.
Burhenn Mary (wid Edward A), res 122 W Creighton ave.
Burhenn Olive, bds 122 W Creighton ave.
Burk, *see also Birk.*
Burk Emma, opr Hoosier Mnfg Co, bds 57 Thomas.
Burk Julius, lab, res 55 Thomas.
Burk Nellie, waiter Rich Hotel.
Burkas Albert F, carriage painter, bds 216 E Wayne.
Burkas John A, res 216 E Wayne.
Burkas Louis C, molder Bass F & M Works, bds 216 E Wayne.
Burkas Minnie E, clk A Goodman, bds 216 E Wayne.
Burkas Nettie E, milliner A Mergentheim, bds 216 E Wayne.
Burke Ann (wid Edward), res 83 Buchanan.
Burke Edward T, lab, bds 83 Buchanan.
Burke Wm, clk O B Fitch, res 27 Elizabeth.
Burkhold Daniel, res 8 Force.
Burkholder Mrs Catherine A, dressmkr, 88 Dawson, res same.
Burkholder Elias P, painter, res 88 Dawson.
Burlage Henry H, soapmkr, res 161 E Washington.
Burlage John W, tinsmith Penn Co, res 165 E Washington.
Burlager Christina, mach hand, bds 210 E Washington.
Burlager Ella, tailoress L J Feist, bds 210 E Washington.
Burlager George, res 137 E Washington.
Burlager Henry H, lab, res 161 E Washington.
Burlager Herman, lab, bds 210 E Washington.
Burlager John, lab, res n w cor Hayden and Winter.
Burlager John, spoke turner, res 43 Summit.
Burlager Oliver C, cigarmkr A F Bolman, bds 68 Hayden.
Burlager Susannah, mach hand, bds 210 E Washington.

Burlager Wm, lab, res 210 E Washington.
Burnett Alfred (col'd), cook Rich Hotel, res 210 Calhoun.
Burnett Eliza S, dressmkr Elizabeth Burnett, bds 183 Fairfield.
Burnett Elizabeth, dressmkr, 183 Fairfield ave, bds same.
Burnett Frank B, clk J H Tibbles, res 64 Home ave.
Burnett George W, boilermkr Ft Wayne Iron Works, bds 183 Fairfield ave.
Burnett Samuel, truckman, res 183 Fairfield ave.
Burnie Wm R, flagman, res 222 Madison.
Burns Arthur, lab, bds 53 E Main.
Burns Edward C, helper Bass F & M Works, bds 49 Gay.
Burns Frank J, mach Penn Co, res 43 W Williams.
Burns James, helper Penn Co, res 49 Gay.
Burns James J, fireman Penn Co, res 60 W Williams.
Burns James W, sec (R R dept) Y M C A, res 62 Brackenridge.
Burns Jenny, housekeeper 251 W Main.
Burns Kate, waiter The Randall.
Burns Mary, opr Hoosier Mnfg Co, bds 84 Force.
Burns Michael E, adv agt Journal, bds 43 W Williams.
Burns Nancy, domestic The Wayne.
Burns Patrick, mach, res 43 W Williams.
Burns Virgil R, carp, res 47 Hendricks.
Burns Walter G, clk, bds 62 Brackenridge.
Burns Wm P, painter L O Hull, rms 181 Calhoun.
Burrell Duff G, mach hd, res 312 Lafayette.
Burrell John, lab, bds 43½ Columbia.
Burrell Naomi, bds 312 Lafayette.
Burrowes Stephen A, bkkpr Morgan & Beach, res 377 Fairfield.
Bursley Block, e s Calhoun between Washington and Jefferson.
Bursley Gilbert E (G E Bursley & Co), res 301 Fairfield ave.
Bursley G E & Co (Gilbert E Bursley, James M McKay, Frank L Smock, Frank K Safford), Wholesale Grocers, 129, 131 and 133 Calhoun.
Burt Alice, mach hd Louis Horstman, bds 14 Clay.
Burwell Levi, driver Ft Wayne St R R Co, res 429 E Washington.
Burwell Peter C, teamster Rhinesmith & Simonson, bds 429 E Washington.
Busch Charles, coffee essence mnfr, 126 Franklin ave, res same.
Busch John, carp, res 72 Wilt.
Busch Sophia, bds 72 Wilt.
Buscher Gottlieb, well driller Robert Spice, res 68 Butler.
Busching Henry, lab, bds 50 Smith.
Busching Henry, saloon, 272 Hanna, res 148 Wallace.

10

Busching Wilhelmina (wid Christian), bds 148 Wallace.
Busching Wm, grocer, 272 Hanna, res 122 Wallace.
Bush Emanuel K (Malcolm & Bush), res 74 Douglas ave.
Bush James L, saloon, 36 E Columbia, res same.
Bush Wm, lab, rms 96 Barr.
Bush Wm, teamster, bds 20 W Superior.
Bushing Minnie, housekeeper 37 Miner.
Bushley Theodore, lab, bds 100 Montgomery.
Bushor Fannie A, res 51 E Main.
Business Guide Co, Clarence G Smith mngr, publrs The Business Guide, 55 E Columbia.
Business Guide The (monthly), Business Guide Co publrs, 55 E Columbia.
Busking Henry, shoes, 90 Harmer, res same.
Buskirk George, cattle buyer, res s s Savilla pl 1 w of No 20.
Busse Amelia, dressmkr, bds 156 Ewing.
Busse Charles H, fireman, bds 156 Ewing.
Busse Charlotte (wid Wm), res 156 Ewing.
Busse Clara, bds 156 Ewing.
Busse Ferdinand, painter Heine & Israel, res 200 Ewing.
Busse Frederick, foreman Olds' Wagon Wks, res 161 Hanna.
Busse Frederick C, blksmith Olds' Wagon Wks, bds 156 Ewing.
Busse Lizzie, dressmkr, bds 156 Ewing.
Butke Henry, grocer, 141 Broadway, bds 143 same.
Butler Alexander W, lab, res 11 Gay.
Butler Elizabeth, bds 22 W Butler.
Butler Ira, market stall No 92, res New Haven rd.
Butler Jacob A, market stall No 98, res New Haven road.
Butler James P (Lichtenwalter & Butler), res 218 Broadway.
Butler Jenny, domestic 13 Smith.
Butler Lewis F, grocer, 7 N Calhoun, res 46 Wells.
Butler Mary, bds 22 W Butler.
Butler Samuel (col'd), waiter The Wayne.
Butler Wm O, deputy collector, U S internal revenue, bds The Wayne.
Butt Anna, domestic 138 W Wayne.
Butz Frederick, tailor, res s e cor Calhoun and Marchell.
Butz Jacob, tailor John Rabus, res 145 Wells.
Buuck, see also Bock and Buck.
Buuck Charles, painter, bds 10 Hugh.
Buuck Conrad, shoemkr, rear 136 Calhoun, bds 172 Ewing.
Buuck Frederick, car bldr Penn Co, bds 134 Force.
Buuck Wm, car bldr Penn Co, res 10 Hough.
Byall Mrs Caroline L, drugs, 52 Oliver, res 54 same.
Byall Isaac A, postal clk, bds 54 Oliver.
Byerlein Frederick, carp, bds 34 Jones.

Byerlein John, lab Penn Co, bds 34 Jones.
Byers Ada, bds 57 Barr.
Byers Charity E (wid Hiram), boarding house, 57 Barr.
Byers Ida, bds 57 Barr.
Byers George, switchman, res 159 Holman.
Byers George L, life ins agt, res 53 Huestis ave.
Bymer Charles, lab, res 2 Franklin ave.
Bymer Christian, stone mason, bds 17 Baker.
Bymer Peter H, fireman, rms 235 Barr.

C

Cadwallader Charles H, student, bds 70 Charles.
Cadwallader Thomas H, lab Penn Co, res 70 Charles.
Caffery Thomas, master mechanic, res 143 Wells.
Cahill Edward, lab, bds 14 Union.
Cahill John A, res 14 Union.
Cahill Mary, housekeeper 14 Union.
Cain Wm, lab Salimonie Mining & Gas Co, res 10 Mary.
Cairl J Frank, driver, res 84 Baker.
Cairns, see also Karns and Kern.
Cairns Frank M, mach Penn Co, res 414 Broadway.
Cairns James, mach Penn Co, res 430 Broadway.
Cairns James T, coil winder Ft Wayne Electric Co, bds 430
    Broadway.
Cairns Mary, bds 430 Broadway.
Caldwell David H, chief despatcher Nickel Plate R R, bds 154
    Harrison.
Caldwell James, real estate, res 154 Harrison.
Caldwell Laura B, stenogr Swayne & Doughman, bds 154
    Harrison.
Caldwell Sarah E, bds 154 Harrison.
Caledonian Hall, 76 Calhoun.
Calhoun David, boilermkr, bds Windsor Hotel.
Calhoun Jacob A, watchmkr August Bruder, rms 94 Calhoun.
"Caligraph" Typewriter, W E McDermut Agent,
    n w cor Calhoun and Berry.
Callaghan Daniel, lab Penn Co, res 30 Bass.
Callaghan Daniel J, lab, bds 78 Melita.
Callaghan Dennis, fireman, bds 17 Burgess.
Callaghan Elizabeth, bds 78 Melita.
Callaghan John, lab, res 18 Bass.

Robert Spice, Pumps, Pipe, Hose, Fittings and Brass Goods
48 WEST MAIN and 11 PEARL STS.

128   R. L. POLK & CO.'S

Callaghan Patrick, flagman, res 78 Melita.
Callahan, *see also O'Callahan.*
Callahan James T, despatcher Nickel Plate R R, res 114 W Washington.
Callahan T J, mach Penn Co, bds 27 Baker.
Callahan Wilda, domestic 483 Harrison.
Callahan Wm G, lab, res 83 W Williams.
Callier Mary, bds 83 Wagner.
Calloway Etta, stripper, bds 43½ E Columbia.
Calmelat Louis J, bartender Joseph Baum, res w s Spy Run ave 3 n of St Mary's river.
Calvert Burton T, lawyer, 62½ Calhoun, rms 27 E Washington.
Cammeyer Henry, lab, res 87 St Mary's ave.
Cammeyer Sophie, bds 87 St Mary's ave.
Camp, *see Kamp, Kemp and Komp.*
Campbell Abbie, domestic 87 W Wayne.
Campbell Aldon, plasterer, bds 83 Force.
Campbell Benjamin F, engineer Penn Co, res 259 W Jefferson.
Campbell Mrs Bessie, dressmkr, 259 W Jefferson, res same.
Campbell Charles H, painter, bds 179 E Washington.
Campbell Daniel, foreman Wabash R R, res 53 Brackenridge.
Campbell Daniel A, cigars, 272 Calhoun, bds 53 Brackenridge.
Campbell Ellison T, shoemkr, res 51 Force.
Campbell Elton, brakeman G R & I R R, res 367 Lafayette.
Campbell Emma, opr S M Foster, bds 51 Force.
Campbell George E, clk, bds 361 E Washington.
Campbell George W, car bldr Penn Co, res 179 E Washington.
Campbell Lydia (wid George B), res 361 E Washington.
Campbell Mary (wid Charles), domestic 55 E Main.
Campbell Mary S (wid Joseph C), rms 47 W Washington.
Campbell Vincent E, lineman C U Tel Co, rms 29 E Main.
Campion Alice B, bds 293 Harrison.
Campion John J, postal clk, res 293 Harrison.
Campion Matthew J, bds 293 Harrison.
Canning, *see Kanning.*
Cantwell Ozias R, conductor, res 22 E DeWald.
Cap, *see Kapp and Kopp.*
Caps Wm H, trav agt, bds s s Howell 1 w of Runnion ave.
Carbaugh Alonzo, changer Ft Wayne St R R Co, bds 509 E Washington.
Carbaugh Frank, watchman Ft Wayne St R R Co, bds 509 E Washington.
Carberry Grace, bds 56 Burgess.
Carberry Henry, fireman, res 56 Burgess.
Card George F, electrician Ft Wayne Electric Co, bds Hamilton House.

Carey, *see also Carray, Carry and Cary.*
Carey Charles W, flagman Penn Co, res 133 Walton ave.
Carey Edward, teamster James Wilding & Son, bds 127 Fairfield ave.
Carey George, with Coombs & Co, res 61 Broadway.
Carey John S, brakeman Penn Co, res 33 Eliza.
Carey Michael, helper Penn Co, res 117 Montgomery.
Carey Thomas J, clk The Randall.
Carey Wm, teamster James Wilding & Son, bds 127 Lafayette.
Carey Wm R, clk Wabash R R, res 277 Webster.
Carier Clemence (wid August), res 178 E Berry.
Carier Helena, bds 178 E Berry.
Carl, *see also Carll and Carroll.*
Carl George, res n s Chestnut 3 e of Lumbard.
Carl John, cigars, 259 Calhoun, res 9 Chestnut.
Carl John D, driver fire dept, rms 44 Pixley & Long bldg.
Carl Louis, grocer, 142 Maumee rd, res same.
Carles Horace W, grocer, 40 W Berry, res 287 same.
Carley Ernst, cook, rms 58 W Main.
Carll Flora, teacher, bds 433 Lafayette.
Carll George S, cabtmkr J M Miller, res 433 Lafayette.
Carll Harriett R (wid Hiram D), res 397 Lafayette.
Carman Frank, engineer Gr R & I R R, res 53 Baker.
Carman James G, engineer Penn Co, res 168 Hanna.
Carmedy Cornelius, engineer, res 54 Hendricks.
Carnahan Robert H, student, bds 11J E Wayne.
Carnahan Wm L (Carnahan & Co), res 119 E Wayne.
Carnahan & Co (Wm L Carnahan), Wholesale Boots and Shoes, 76 to 80 Clinton.
Carnrike George W, lab Wabash R R, bds 243 Webster.
Carpenter Albert L, livery, n c cor Duck and Clinton, res same.
Carpenter Charles A, cook G C Frey, rms 34 W Main.
Carpenter Dimon L, carp, res 82 Putnam.
Carpenter Homer V, clk Ft Wayne Electric Co, bds 82 Putnam.
Carpenter John, helper F Weibel, bds same.
Carpenter John D, tel opr N Y, C & St L R R, bds 82 Putnam.
Carpenters' Union Hall, White's Block.
Carpenter Warren, fireman Ft Wayne Electric Co, res 30 Baker.
Carpenter Wesley, carp, bds Union House.
Carr John W, car bldr Penn Co, res 106 Barr.
Carr Joseph, removed to Chicago, Ill.
Carray, *see also Carey, Carry and Cary.*
Carray Edward J, clk Penn Co, bds 294 E Creighton ave.
Carray Frank J, teamster Bass F & M Works, res 294 E Creighton ave.

Penn Mutual LIFE INSURANCE CO. of PHILA,
CLARK FAIRBANK, General Agent, 19 Court Street.

130 R. L. POLK & CO.'S

Carray John E, lab, bds 294 E Creighton ave.
Carret George, lab Penn Co, res n s New Haven ave.
Carroll, *see also Carl and Carll.*
Carroll Miss Belle, teacher Indiana School for Feeble-Minded
    Youth.
Carroll Denandy A, carp, res 24 Colerick.
Carroll Harry, lab, bds 94 W Superior.
Carroll John, bricklayer, res 228 E Washington.
Carroll John, engineer, res 21 Pine.
Carroll John J, mach Bass F & M Works, bds 95 Thomas.
Carroll John M, wood, 54 4th, res same.
Carroll Julia, milliner, bds 95 Thomas.
Carroll Margaret (wid Patrick), res 94 W Superior.
Carroll Margaret R, bds 94 W Superior.
Carroll Mary (wid Thomas), bds 24 Colerick.
Carroll Miss Mary A, clk Troy Laundry, bds 94 W Superior.
Carroll Maurice, removed to Bucyrus, O.
Carroll Nellie, bds 23 Walnut.
Carroll Patrick B, watchman, res 95 Thomas.
Carroll Patrick J, removed to Bucyrus, O.
Carroll Robert E, decorator Hail & Tower, bds Waverley Hotel.
Carroll Susan F, attendant Indiana School for Feeble-Minded
    Youth, bds 24 Colerick.
Carroll Wm J, pressman, bds 94 W Superior.
Carry, *see also Carey, Curray and Cary.*
Carry Adolphus, sewer bldr, res 74 Fletcher ave.
Carry Joseph A, blksmith Penn Co, res 153 E Lewis.
Carry Miss Lettie, housekeeper 74 Fletcher ave.
Carry Louis, lab, bds 74 Fletcher ave.
Carson Jane (wid Wm W), res 95 E Berry.
Carson John, clk J B White, bds 40 Wagner.
Carson John K, letter carrier P O, res 40 Wagner.
Carter Addie, bds 27 W Butler.
Carter Charles L (Carter & Son), res 5 Riverside ave.
Carter Deborah, teacher, bds 27 W Butler.
Carter Frank, tailor A F Schoch, bds Monroe House.
Carter Hollis S, optician, 135 Calhoun, bds 27 W Butler.
Carter Isaac, bds 271 Webster.
Carter James M, carp, res 187 Jackson.
Carter Josephine, stenogr Weil Bros & Co, bds 34 Miner.
Carter Martha A, bds 83 Butler.
Carter Millie, seamstress Indiana School for Feeble-Minded
    Youth.
Carter Oliver, blksmith Penn Co, bds Monroe House.
Carter Rebecca A (wid James), res 34 Miner.
Carter Rosa, clk, bds 324 E Jefferson.

Carter Samuel, driver B Gutermuth, bds 29 Columbia.
Carter Victoria, teacher, bds 34 Miner.
Carter Wm (Carter & Son), res 127 E Main.
Carter Wm H, clk Carter & Son, bds 127 E Main.
Carter Wm J, physician, 135 Calhoun, res 27 W Butler.
Carter & Son (Wm and Charles L), Hot Air Furnaces,
Ranges, Wood and Tile Mantels and Grates, 29 Clinton.
(*See bottom edge and page 7.*)
Carto James, boilermkr Penn Co, bds 112 W De Wald.
Cartwright, *see also Cortwright.*
Cartwright Ada, bds 23 Lillie.
Cartwright Alfred W, teamster C F Muhler & Son, res Duck
alley.
Cartwright Alice E, seamstress, bds 73 Baker.
Cartwright Charles, lumber, res 50 E Washington.
Cartwright Charles A, broom mnfr, rear 23 Lillie, res 529 E
Lewis.
Cartwright Ella (wid John), seamstress, res 73 Baker.
Cartwright George W, lab, res 39 Wall.
Cartwright James, teamster, res 23 Lillie.
Cartwright John F, res 69 Baker.
Cartwright Porter D, baggageman, res 22 W DeWald.
Cartwright Wm, teamster J Derheimer, bds 23 Lillie.
Carver Daisy S, bds 320 W Washington.
Carver John F, real estate, res 320 W Washington.
Cary, *see also Carey, Carray and Carry.*
Cary Alice V, bds 200 E Washington.
Cary David B, physician, 26 Court, res 200 E Washington.
Cary Ira L, lab, bds 200 E Washington.
Cary Norman E, clk J R Bittenger, bds 200 E Washington.
Cary Samuel B, carp, res 99 Summit.
Cary Thomas, lab, bds 43½ E Columbia.
Casanave Francis D, supt motive power Penn Co, res 57 W
Berry.
Case Callie (wid Reuben), bds 13 Hoffman.
Case David, bridge carp, res n s Jesse 2 e of Rumsey ave.
Case Flora, seamstress, bds 36 Colerick.
Case Isaac H, clk D H Baldwin & Co, res 275 E Creighton ave.
Case John W, lab, bds 36 Colerick.
Case Wm H, tinsmith J J Freiburger, res 36 Colerick.
Case Wm J, fireman, res 36 Colerick.
Casey Christopher, conductor, res 54 John.
Casey John, mach Penn Co, res 38 E Williams.
Casey Margaret (wid James L), bds 13 Hamilton.
Cashman John, janitor, res 41 4th.
Cassady Jacob, ins agt, res 19 E Jefferson.

Cassell Ida, seamstress Indiana School for Feeble-Minded Youth.
Cassidy Patrick, table turner Penn Co, bds 82 Montgomery.
Casso Frank A, fruits, 156 Calhoun, res 42 Laselle.
Casteel Annie E, cook, bds 66 Maumee rd.
Casteel George, engineer, res 28 Chicago.
Casteel Mrs Mary, res 28 Chicago.
Casteel Samuel W, baker, bds 28 Chicago.
Casteel Wm M, finisher, res 26 Chicago.
Castello Martha, domestic 9 E Wayne.
Castle, *see also Kassel and Kestel.*
Castle Calvin, molder Bass F & M Works, res 94 Thomas.
Castle Catherine, opr Hoosier Mnfg Co, bds 101 Leister ave.
Castle Cora B, bds 34 Oliver.
Castle Edwin, lab, bds 34 Oliver.
Castle Elizabeth, domestic, 116 Thomas.
Castle Henry, lab, bds n e cor Tons and Dwenger ave.
Castle James F, lab, bds 34 Oliver.
Castle Robert, lab, res n e cor Dwenger ave and Tons.
Castle Samuel, boxmkr Ft Wayne Organ Co, res 34 Oliver.
Caston John E, clk C J La Vanway, bds 45 E Columbia.
Caswell Frank A, trav agt G DeWald & Co, res 341 E Wayne.
Caswell John W, clk Bass F & M Works, bds 110 E Berry.
Cathedral of the Immaculate Conception, Calhoun bet Lewis
    and Jefferson.
Cathedral School (Catholic), s w cor Clinton and Jefferson.
Catholic Orphan Asylum, Wells nr city limits.
Catholic Young Men's Reading Hall and Club Rooms, n e cor
    Calhoun and Lewis.
Cattez Frank, lab, bds 139 Buchanan.
Cattez John, boilermkr, bds 139 Buchanan.
Cattez Joseph, fireman, bds 139 Buchanan.
Cattez Julia (wid Joseph), res 139 Buchanan.
Cattez Julian J, driver Francis Sallier, bds 139 Buchanan.
Cattez Peter, tel opr, bds 139 Buchanan.
Cavanaugh, *see also Kavanaugh.*
Cavanaugh Carrie M, bds 167 Harrison.
Cavanaugh Mrs Julia, ironer, bds 22 Gay.
Cavanaugh Thomas, lab, bds 167 Harrison.
Cavanaugh Thomas, pedler, res 167 Harrison.
Caves John, brakeman, bds Weber House.
Celt Theodore, carpenter, res 75 Maumee rd.
Centennial Block, 197-199 Broadway.
Center Spencer H, boilermkr Penn Co, res 100 Chicago.
Centh Michael, helper Bass F & M Works, res 36 John.
Centlivre Charles F (C L Centlivre Brewing Co), res Spy Run
    ave.

L. O. HULL, Paints, Oils, Varnishes and Glass at 90 Calhoun Street.

Centlivre Charles L, res n end of Spy Run ave.

Centlivre Brewing Co (Louis A and Charles F Centlivre, John B Reuss), Brewers, Maltsters and Bottlers, n end Spy Run ave. (*See left bottom lines.*)

Centlivre C L Street Railway Co, L A Centlivre pres, C L Centlivre vice-pres, C F Centlivre sec, J B Reuss treas, office n end Spy Run ave.

Centlivre Louis A (C L Centlivre Brewing Co), bds C L Centlivre.

Centlivre's Park, w s Spy Run ave n of canal feeder.

Central Christian Church, w s Harrison bet E Washington and E Wayne.

Central Grammar School n s Wayne bet Calhoun and Clinton.

Central Press Association, Ferd J Wendall pres and genl mngr, Joseph B Davis res mngr, proprs The Press, 17 Court.

Central Union Telephone Co, Wm P Chapman Mngr, 34 Calhoun.

Certia Block, w s Calhoun bet Wayne and Berry.

Certia Jacob B, grocer, 116 Wells, res 114 same.

Certia Peter, saloon, 70 Calhoun, res 126 W Washington.

Chabynski John, laborer Bass F & M Works, res 14 Force.

Chadwick Jerome M, toolmkr Ft Wayne Electric Co, res 147 Griffith.

Chadwick John M, molder Ft Wayne Electric Co, res 5 S Walnut.

Chalat Lettie R, dressmaking school Arcade bldg, res 250 Clinton.

Challenger D Edward, clk Penn Co, res 20 Taber.

Chamberlain Eva M, bds 20 Chicago.

Chamberlain James, helper Penn Co, res 41 Baker.

Chamberlain Porter, engineer Olds' Wagon Works, res 71 W Butler.

Chamberlain Richard C, paper hanger, res 20 Chicago.

Chamberlain Robert B, molder, bds 20 Chicago.

Chamberlain Sarah C R (wid Wm), bds 24 Brandriff.

Chambers Alice, waiter Columbia House.

Chambers John D, Physician, 16 Brackenridge, bds same.

Chambers John W, foreman Daily News, bds Harmon House.

Chambers Mrs Nancy, nurse Indiana School for Feeble-Minded Youth.

Chandler Clement V, car builder, res 104 Madison.

Chandler Wm H, carp, res 53 W 4th.

Chaney Henry, trav agt, res 370 W Main.

Chapin Angeline F, stenogr Ft Wayne Electric Co, bds 16 Douglas ave.

The Peters Box and Lumber Co. Quartered Oak and Ash FLOORING.

Chapin Artena M, bds 16 Douglas ave.
Chapin August A (Chapin & Denny), res 16 Douglas ave.
Chapin Bertha M, wks Troy Steam Laundry, bds 18 Harrison.
Chapin Catherine B, bds 16 Douglas ave.
Chapin Elizabeth E, teacher, bds 16 Douglas ave.
Chapin Henry W, engineer, res 22 Boone.
Chapin & Denny (Augustus A Chapin, Watts P Denny),
    Lawyers, 77 Calhoun.
Chapman Amanda, domestic 11 N Harrison.
Chapman Clark, carp, bds 39 W 4th.
Chapman Eliza, bds 332 W Main.
Chapman Frank M, township assessor, res 150 Fairfield ave.
Chapman George W, lab Hoffman Bros, res 204 High.
Chapman Ira, teamster, bds 30 S Wayne ave.
Chapman Jason S, feeder Ft Wayne St R R Co, res w s Glasgow 2 s of E Washington.
Chapman Mrs Maggie B, millinery, 150 Fairfield ave, res same.
Chapman Nathan E, res 30 S Wayne ave.
Chapman Nathaniel, engineer, res 322 W Main.
Chapman Preston (Chapman & Vachon), res Pleasant Township P O, Ft Wayne.
Chapman Wm J, lab Kilian Baker, res 100 E Superior.
Chapman Wm P, mngr Central Union Tel Co, res 228 Fairfield ave.
Chapman & Vachon (Preston Chapman, Thomas Vachon), Livery, Boarding and Sale Stable, 201-205 Fairfield ave. Tel 381.
Charles Isaac, coachman Thomas Jackson.
Charleswood Sheridan G, helper Penn Co, res 55 Water.
Chartier George T, fireman, bds C F Schilling.
Chase Abbie, bds 40 Garden.
Chase Emily (wid Ira), bds 40 Garden.
Chase R Carey, fireman Penn Co, res 77 Hoagland ave.
Chase Stephen W, real estate, res 176 Hoffman.
Chaska Samuel, trav agt C Falk & Co, res 78 W Jefferson.
Chauvey Bros (Charles and Francis), wagon mnfrs, 35 E Superior.
Chauvey Celeste, bds 51 E Superior.
Chauvey Charles (Chauvey Bros), res 51 E Superior.
Chauvey Charles E, blacksmith Chauvey Bros, bds 150 N Clinton.
Chauvey Francis (Chauvey Bros), res 150 N Clinton.
Chauvey Frank A, helper Chauvey Bros, bds 150 N Clinton.
Chauvey Jane, bds 51 E Superior.
Chauvey John B, blacksmith, res 223 E Wayne.
Chauvey Joseph, painter, bds 150 N Clinton.

Geo. E. Johnson, DENTIST, 74 Calhoun Street.
Res., 198 W. Berry St.

FORT WAYNE DIRECTORY.   135

Chauvey Mary A, bds 223 E Wayne.
Chavanne Joseph, foreman L Brames & Co, res 276 E Jefferson.
Cheadle Joseph B, pres Union Credit Co, res Frankfort, Ind.
Cheever George E, bartndr D H Randall, rms 36 W Main.
Cheney James, pres Ft Wayne Gas Light Co, res New York City.
Cheney Julia (wid James), bds 142 W Jefferson.
Cherry Charles P, clk Penn Co, bds 109 W DeWald.
Cherry Clifford, repairer A B White Cycle Co, bds 106 E Washington.
Cherry Frank C, painter, bds 160 E Washington.
Cherry Frank M, boilermkr Penn Co, res 160 W Washington.
Cherry Rowland T, conductor, res 38 St Mary's ave.
Cherry Wm H, boilermkr Penn Co, res 100 E Lewis.
Cherry Wm Y, mach, bds 100 E Lewis.
Cheviron Amelia, bds 190 E Wayne.
Cheviron Frank, fireman Penn Co, res 44 Force.
Cheviron Louise, bds 190 E Wayne.
Cheviron Theresa (wid Xavier), res 190 E Wayne.
Chicago Furniture Co, James Baum mngr, 27 E Columbia.
Chilcote Frances (wid Samuel), res r 138 Wells.
Chilcote Herman B, clk L S & M S Ry, bds r 138 Wells.
Chilcote Miss Minnie, bds r 138 Wells.
Chilcote Miss Myrtle, bds r 138 Wells.
Chinworth Ida, bds Jane Chinworth.
Chinworth Jane (wid Robert), res n e cor Spy Run and Prospect aves.
Choctaw Medicine Co, George W & George O Litt proprs, 15 Maple ave.
Chodynski John, lab, bds 14 Force.
Choinard P G, trav agt Carnahan & Co, res Warsaw, Ind.
Cholvin Alphonsus, lab Wabash R R, bds 28 Nirdlinger ave.
Chorpening Ida, bds 35 1st.
Chorpening Thomas R, works J O Keller, bds 35 1st.
Chorty Florence, domestic 15 Pearl.
Christ, *see also Crist.*
Christ Edward, molder Bass F and M Works, bds 206 John.
Christ Frederick, teamster, bds 44 Grant ave.
Christ Gottlieb A, teamster Herman Berghoff Brewing Co, res 44 Grant ave.
Christ Otto A, mach Bass F and M Works, bds 206 John.
Christen Anthony, lab, res w s Walton ave 2 s of Pontiac.
Christen Edward, bds w s Walton ave 2 s of Pontiac.
Christen John, saloon, 100 Calhoun, res same.
Christen John C, lab, bds w s Walton ave 2 s of Pontiac.

Christen Wm, mngr John Christen, bds same.
Christensen Christopher E, painter Olds' Wagon Works, res 317 S Harrison.
Christian Chapel, s e cor W Jefferson and Griffith.
Christian George A, packer S M Foster, bds 196 Hanna.
Christie James K, molder Ft Wayne Electric Co, res 48 Walnut.
Christie John S, engineer Penn Co, bds 223 Lafayette.
Christie Joseph, lab, res 123 E DeWald.
Christie Miss Mary E, teacher, res n w cor Creighton and Hoagland aves.
Christie Wm P, mach, res 45 Locust.
Christiensen Christian, wood worker Olds' Wagon Works, bds 28 E Williams.
Christlieb John, teamster J C Peters, res n w cor Main and Osage.
Chronister Anna, domestic s w cor Clinton and Washington.
Church of God, n e cor Hoagland ave and DeWald.
Church of the Holy Trinity, s e cor E Wayne and Clinton.
Church Perry, lab, res 377 W Main.
Churchill Charlotte (wid Samuel), bds 171 Madison.
Cilliod Frank, engineer, bds 176 Wells.
Cincerul Bernard, musician, res 80 Fairfield ave.
Cincerul Nicholas, musician, rms 36 Baker.
Cincinnati, Richmond & Ft Wayne R R, operated by G R & I R R.
Cipher Rufus, lab, bds 43½ E Columbia.
City Attorney's Office, attorney Wm H Shambaugh, city hall.
City Bookbindery, George W Winbaugh Propr, 13 E Main.
City Carriage Works (George P Dudenhoefer, Henry E Bueker, Henry P Scherer), Carriage and Sleigh Mnfrs, 11-13 Clay. (*See right bottom lines.*)
City Clerk's Office, R C Reinewald clerk, City Hall.
City Engineer's Office, Frank M Randall city engineer, office 68 Barr.
City Fire Department, Henry Hilbrecht chief, office cor Court and E Berry.
City Green House, Charles A Doswell florist, Northside Park.
City Hall, e s Barr bet Berry and Wayne.
City Hospital, D M Foster pres, s w cor Barr and Washington.
City Market, e s Barr bet E Washington and E Berry.
City Mills, C Tresselt & Sons proprs, cor Clinton and Nickel Plate R R.
City Park, e s Broadway bet Taylor and P, Ft Wayne & C Ry.

City Treasurer's Office, C J Sosenheimer treas, City Hall.
City Water Works, P J McDonald sec, 68 Barr.
City Weigh Scales, P Ryan weighmaster, s end City Hall.
Clah Henry, lab, res Walton ave, n e cor Erie.
Clapesattle George A, clk J B White, bds 31 Wagner.
Clapham Edwin, piler, res 2 Rebecca.
Clark Alanson W, foreman Jacob Klett & Son, res 40 Wells.
Clark Alonzo K, mach, bds 121 E Main.
Clark Anna, domestic Jewel House.
Clark Anna J (wid Joseph E), res 279 E Jefferson.
Clark Annie, cook J F Cline, rms 29 E Washington.
Clark Miss Belle, music teacher public schools, bds 103 W Berry.
Clark Carrie, opr S M Foster, bds 197 E Jefferson.
Clark Charles C (Wickliffe & Clark), bds 28 E Columbia.
Clark Clifford, coachman J M Barrett.
Clark C Belle, forewoman Hoosier Mnfg Co, bds 5 Brandriff.
Clark Edward, finisher, bds 208 Thomas.
Clark Edward J (Crusey & Clark), bds 250 Calhoun.
Clark Mrs Eva, dressmkr, res 237 E Wayne.
Clark Florence A, bds 279 E Jefferson.
Clark George, bds 40 Wells.
Clark Isaac G, carp, res 208 Thomas.
Clark Jacob W, trainmaster Penn Co, res 11 Holman.
Clark Jarvis M, lab, res 148 Holman.
Clark Jessie O, bds 111 W Wayne.
Clark John A, lab, res 165 Harmer.
Clark John E, tel opr, res 240 E Wayne.
Clark John H, clk R Steger & Co, bds 125 Monroe.
Clark Joseph E, painter Ind Mach Works, bds 279 E Jefferson.
Clark Joseph M & Co (est J M Clark, Perry N DeHaven), merchant tailors, 34 E Berry.
Clark Lewis N, carp, res 125 Monroe.
Clark Lydia M (wid John H), res 111 W Wayne.
Clark Martha M, teacher, bds 279 E Jefferson.
Clark Marvin, died March 1, 1891.
Clark Mary, matron Old Ladies' Home, 144 Pritchard.
Clark Mrs Mattie T, res 5 DeGroff.
Clark May L, bds 125 Monroe.
Clark Mortimer, bds 111 W Wayne.
Clark Oliver, draughtsman H E Matson, bds 111 W Wayne.
Clark Rose M, bkkpr Louis Fortriede, bds 279 E Jefferson.
Clark Samuel, propr Jewel House, 225 Calhoun.
Clark Thomas, saloon, 102 E Columbia, res 24 Wagner.
Clark Victoria (wid James H), res 5 Brandriff.
Clark Wesley, brakeman, bds Racine Hotel.

Clark Wm W, mach Wabash R R, bds 5 Crandriff.
Clarke Franklin D, notions, 5 E Main, res Chicago, Ill.
Claus J August, carpet weaver, 16 University, res same.
Claus Max G, molder Bass F and M Works, bds 21 Gay.
Clausmeier Edward F (E F Clausmeier & Co), res 157 Montgomery.
Clausmeier E F & Co (Edward F Clausmeier, Wm Kaough), farm implements, 50 E Columbia.
Clay, *see also Klee and Kley.*
Clay Miner T, mach Ind Mach Works, bds 109 Madison.
Clay School, n w cor Clay and Washington.
Claymiller Rudolph, engineer, bds 16 Madison.
Clayton George L, trav agt, res s e cor Calhoun and De Wald.
Clayton Mabel E (wid Francis H), bds 27 Prospect ave.
Claytor J Edward, boilermkr Bass F and M Works, res 153 E Lewis.
Clear Mrs Catherine, laundress, res 289 Hanna.
Clear Wm, bartender Riverside Hotel, res same.
Cleary Dennis, mach hd Fort Wayne Electric Co, bds 51 Oakley.
Cleary Edward, watchman, res 141 Shawnee ave.
Cleary John J, lab Penn Co, res 3 Eliza.
Cleary Martin J, printer Fort Wayne Newspaper Union, bds 39 W Washington.
Clem Isaiah, engineer G R & I R R, res 30 E Butler.
Clements Agnes M, bds 57 W Williams.
Clements Daisy, opr S M Foster, bds 57 W Williams.
Clements Etta, opr S M Foster, bds 57 W Williams.
Clements John, market stall No 61, res Wayne township.
Clements Wm H, checker Penn Co, res 57 W Williams.
Clemmer Benjamin R, bartender R M Cummerow, res 124 Chicago.
Cleveland Frank (col'd), laborer, res 100 Broadway.
Clifford Thomas C, laborer, bds Union House.
Cline John F, restaurant, 99 Calhoun, res 29 E Washington.
Clinton Albert B, removed to Detroit, Mich.
Clipper.Sample Room, 14 Harrison.
Clippinger Charles L, teacher Taylor University, res 275 W De Wald.
Clippinger Miss Gertrude, teacher, bds 275 W De Wald.
Clippinger Orpha (wid Alexander), res 20 Miner.
Clizbe Lemuel L, cashier Penn Co, res 221 W Wayne.
Clodzinsky Frank, helper, res 113 High.
Close Charles F, molder Bass F and M Works, res 271 E Lewis.
Close Edward C, metal engraver, 35 E Main, bds 271 E Lewis.

!lose Henry F, driver, res 27 E 1st.
!lose Ida, domestic 156 Horace.
!lose Wm, coremkr, bds 117 Hanna.
!loss Lemuel, laborer, res 88 Fairfield ave.
!loud Richard M, car builder Penn Co, res 7 Duryea.
!low Charles L, teamster, bds 64 W Wayne.
!low Mrs Mary, res 61 Grand.
!lusserath Nicholas, lab Penn Co, res 25 Euclid ave.
!lutter Adelbert F, res 160 W. Washington.
!lutter Lulu, bds 8 Cass.
!lutter Phœbe A, removed to Huntertown, Ind.
!lutter Sarah J (wid Ryan), res 8 Cass.
'oan Hattie, seamstress D S Redelsheimer & Co, bds 204 W
    Superior.
'oates Arthur (col'd), waiter, bds 65 Baker.
oates Wm (col'd), cook, bds 65 Baker.
obelence Frank, street car driver, bds 290 Calhoun.
oblentz Jacob W, physician, 41 W Berry, res 83 E Berry.
'ochran Ella, cook G H Seabold.
ochrane Miss Agnes J, bds 258 W Berry.
'ochrane Benjamin, carp, bds 70 W Jefferson.
ochrane Edward, fireman, res 49 St Mary's ave.
ochrane Margaret, prin Washington School, res 258 W Berry.
odey Wm H, printer Fort Wayne Newspaper Union, rms 59
    E Columbia.
ody John, stonecutter, bds 157 W Main.
ody John H, foreman, res 288 W Main.
ody Miss Mary R, bds 67 E Superior.
ody Maurice, res 67 E Superior.
ody Rebecca, bds 67 E Superior.
offin John B, cook Gustav Franks, rms 181 Calhoun.
ohagan Alonzo, cigarmkr, res rear 46 W Berry.
ohen, see also Koehn and Kohn.
ohen Benjamin, trav agt, bds 73 Webster.
ohen Mrs Fanny, res 73 Webster.
ohen Henry, cigarmkr, bds 73 Webster.
ohen Marian, teacher, bds 73 Webster.
ohen Simon, printer, bds 73 Webster.
lardo May, waiter, rms 258 Calhoun.
lclesser Frank P, car bldr Penn Co, res 227 Walton ave.
ldwell Nettie, waiter Riverside Hotel.
le, see also Koehl.
le Madge, res 35 W Columbia.
le Rose, cook, rms 193 Calhoun.
eman, see also Kohlmann.
eman Mary, domestic 2 E Columbia.

Wing & Mahurin, **ARCHITECTS,** 41 & 42 Pixley & Long Bldg. Telephone 328

140   R. L. POLK & CO.'S

Coleman Mary (wid Jacob), bds 147 E Jefferson.
Coleman Nellie, dressmkr, bds 124 W Butler.
Coleman Sylvanus S, market stall No 59, res s s County rd 8 miles w of city limits.
Colerick Miss Antoinette M, res 85 E Jefferson.
Colerick Charles E, clk Penn Co, bds 266 W Wayne.
Colerick's Hall, 47–53 E Columbia.
Colerick Henry (Colerick & Oppenheim), res 117 E Main.
Colerick Mrs Margaret M, res 266 W Wayne.
Colerick Maria A, res 85 E Jefferson.
Colerick Philamon B (Colerick & France), res 167 E Berry.
Colerick Ralph, clk Colerick & Oppenheim, bds 117 E Main.
Colerick Walpole G, Lawyer, 22 Court, res 88 E Berry.
Colerick Wm E, student W G Colerick, bds 117 E Main.
Colerick & France (Philamon B Colerick, James E K France), Lawyers, 17 and 18 Pixley & Long Bldg.
Colerick & Oppenheim (Henry Colerick, Wm S Oppenheim), lawyers, 5 and 6 Pixley & Long bldg.
Coling George, removed to St Louis, Mo.
Coling J Charles, butcher Gottlieb Hallier, bds 338 Harrison.
Coling Peter, finisher, res 338 Harrison.
Coll Mary (wid Edward), res 94 Chicago.
Collins Clara, domestic s w cor Monroe and Charles.
Collins Charles, helper Penn Co, bds 171 E Madison.
Collins Dennis D, lab Penn Co, res 31 Baker.
Collins Elizabeth, bds 31 Baker.
Collins Elizabeth O (wid Charles), bds 2 Monroe.
Collins Harry C, printer Journal, bds 39 W Washington.
Collins John W, lab, bds 177 Hanna.
Collins Joseph A, cooper, res 132 W Wayne.
Collins Lindley D, miller, res 5 N Calhoun.
Collins Lizzie, bds 31 Baker.
Collins Margaret, bds 177 Hanna.
Collins Mary L, cook J F Cline, bds 31 Baker.
Collins Michael, lab, bds 498 W Main.
Collins Michael J, helper Bass F & M Works, res 31 Baker.
Collins Mollie, opr S M Foster, bds 177 Hanna.
Collins Nora, bds 31 Baker.
Collins Patrick, brakeman, bds 157 Holman.
Collins Peter, brakeman, res 176 Greely.
Collis Adam, mach Penn Co, res n s Butler 1 w of Lafayette.
Collis Frank M, clk Beadell & Co, bds 51 St Martin.
Collis Michael F, messenger G R & I R R, bds n w cor Lafayette and Butler.
Collom Dennis, fireman Penn Co, res 32 Chicago.
Colmey Christopher R, engineer Penn Co, res 39 Douglas ave.

Colmey Mrs Christopher R (Colmey & Ripley), res 39 Douglas ave.
Colmey & Ripley (Mrs Christopher R Colmey, Mrs Elizabeth L Ripley), notions, 201 Calhoun.
Colson Charles, fireman, bds 329 W Main.
Colson Gustav, lab, bds 55 E Main.
Colson Nicholas, bds 329 W Main.
Columbia House, J P Ross & Sons proprs, 25 and 27 W Columbia.
Colvin Elbert, mason, 83 Franklin ave, res same.
Colvin Evangeline, artist, 92 Dawson, bds same.
Colvin Joseph, carp, res 11 Wagner.
Colvin Wm, lab, bds 12 Wagner.
Combs Abbie, bds 226 W Superior.
Combs Eugene V, flagman, res 226 W Superior.
Combs Herbert A, flagman, res n s Greely 2 w of Fulton.
Combs Sarah A (wid Wm B), bds 226 W Superior.
Comer Linneas A, trav agt, res 209 E Wayne.
Comincavish Felix, mach Ft Wayne Electric Co, res s s Bluffton rd 3 w of river bridge.
Comincavish Marshall, electrician, res 85 Baker.
Comparet Charles M (C M Comparet & Co), res 326 E Wayne.
Comparet C M & Co (Charles M Comparet), shirt mnfrs, 22 W Berry.
Comparet David F, commission, 76 E Columbia, res 59 Erie.
Comparet Thomas L, clk Empire Line, res 10 Erie.
Compton Andrew J, conductor, bds 133 Holman.
Compton Howard P, flagman Penn Co, rms 133 Holman.
Compton Jasper, rms 133 Holman.
Compton Wm, driver J D Gumpper, bds 334 Calhoun.
Conaban John, clk, res 65 Hoffman.
Concanan Wm, fireman Penn Co, rms 39 Melita.
Concordia Cemetery (St Paul's) n s Maumee rd e of Concordia College.
Concordia College (German Lutheran), e s Schick bet E Washington and Maumee rd.
Condon John, saloon, 264 Calhoun, res 70 W Williams.
Congdon Hattie E, bds 104 Ewing.
Congdon Johanna L (wid Joshua E), res 104 Ewing.
Congelton Hiram, attendant Indiana School for Feeble-Minded Youth.
Conger John T, lab, res 112 Erie.
Conklin Charles, engineer, bds 36 5th.
Conklin Elizabeth (wid Theodore), res 207 W DeWald.
Conklin Elizabeth (wid Wm H), res 11 Wall.
Conklin Ella, bds 278 W Creighton ave.

11

Conklin George W, carp, bds 278 W Creighton ave.
Conklin Guy (Jacobs & Conklin), bds 66 W Main.
Conklin John J, engineer, res 278 W Creighton ave.
Conklin Josie, teacher, bds 207 W DeWald.
Conklin Laura J bds 11 Wall.
Conklin Wm, engineer, res 11 N Calhoun.
Conley James, wheel polisher, res 131 Wallace.
Connelly, *see also Connolly*
Connelly Frank, lab, res 37 E 1st.
Connelly James, lab, res 14 Melita.
Connelly Margaret, laundress, res 84 Fairfield ave.
Conners, *see also Connors.*
Conners Anna, bds 43 Charles.
Conners Frank, helper Wabash R R, bds 43 Charles.
Conners Michael, engineer Engine Co No 2, res 43 Charles.
Conners Wm H, mach Kerr-Murray Mnfg Co, bds 43 Charles.
Connett Allen, market stall No 23, res Wayne twp.
Connett David S, teamster A C Beaver, res 812 S Broadway.
Connett John, boilermkr Wabash R R, res Wayne twp.
Connett Leota M, teacher, bds 60 Wilt.
Connett Martin V, foreman Ft Wayne Electric Co, res 171 Holman.
Connett Mary E, bds 60 Wilt.
Connett Milon T, carp J M Henry, res 60 Wilt.
Connolly, *see also Connelly.*
Connolly James T, restaurant, 14 W Berry, res same.
Connors, *see also Conners and O'Connor.*
Connors John, lab, bds 47 Barr.
Conover Alice E (wid Addison), res 130 W Jefferson.
Conover Cora A, bds 130 W Jefferson.
Conover Fannie, bds 372 E Wayne.
Conover Norton, foreman Sentinel, res 372 E Wayne.
Conover Wm A, clk M Donald, Watt & Wilt, bds 130 W Jefferson.
Conrad *see also Coonrad.*
Conrad Carrie, domestic, 146 W Berry.
Conrad John J, engineer, res 103 Lafayette.
Conrad Mrs Mary, res 103 Lafayette.
Conrad Richard K, fireman G R & I R R, bds 15 Baker.
Conrad Wm, car repairer Penn Co, res 170 E Creighton ave.
Conrady Frederick G, car bldr Penn Co, bds 43 John.
Conrady John, car oiler Penn Co, res 43 John.
Conrady Kate, opr Hoosier Mnfg Co, bds 43 John.
Conrady Rosa, tailoress A F Schoch, bds 43 John.
Conrady Sophia, tailoress, bds 43 John.
Conroy James, blksmith, res 42 Melita.

Contant August, mach Penn Co, res 72 Laselle.
Conway Anthony, brakeman, rms 29 Melita.
Conway Bryan, lab, bds 84 Fairfield ave.
Conway Catherine (wid Edward), res 84 Fairfield ave.
Conway Edward, conductor, res 21 Hamilton.
Conway Frank O, saloon, 55 E Main, res same.
Cook Albert H, res 49 E Lewis.
Cook Annie, bds 34 John.
Cook Catherine (wid Adam), res 34 John.
Cook Charles O, mach, res 231 Webster.
Cook Christian F, mach Ft Wayne Electric Co, res 48 W
   Lewis.
Cook Clarence F, city editor Sentinel, bds 49 E Lewis.
Cook Edward F, mach hand Ft Wayne Electric Co, bds 48 W
   Lewis.
Cook Ernest W, agt, res 70 Indiana ave.
Cook Ida L, confectioner W F Geller, bds 48 W Lewis.
Cook John M, wagonmkr, res 85 W Butler.
Cook John S, engineer, res 38 E.m.
Cook Mary, bds 34 John.
Cook Miss Rose L, bkkpr L O Hull, bds 49 E Lewis.
Cooke John H, engineer, res 430 W Main.
Coolican Ellen (wid Patrick), res 21 Poplar.
Coolican Ellen, stenographer, bds 21 Poplar.
Coolican John J, armature winder, bds 21 Poplar.
Coolican Margaret, bds 21 Poplar.
Coolican Mary, dressmkr, bds 21 Poplar.
Coolman George W, carp, res 13 Wagner.
Coombes Eliza (wid John F), bds 73 E Berry.
Coombs Miss Alice, bds 336 W Washington.
Coombs Edward H, trav agt Coombs & Co, bds The Wayne.
Coombs John M (Coombs & Co), 38 E Main.
Coombs Wm H, lawyer, res 336 W Washington.
Coombs & Co (John M Coombs, Frederick A Newton),
   Iron, Heavy Hardware and Carriagemakers' Goods, 38, 40
   and 42 E Main.
Coon Alonzo, driver J P Tinkham, res 116 Fulton.
Coon Hattie, seamstress, bds 204 W Superior.
Coon Henry N, gasfitter, res 140 Lafayette.
Coon Nathan, lab, res 120 Clinton.
Cooney Patrick, bds 72 Thomas.
Coonrad, *see also Conrad.*
Coonrad John C, teamster Summit City Soap Co, res 26 Du Bois.
Coonrad Matthias, res 53 Lillie.
Coonrad Wm H, rimmer, bds 53 Lillie.
Coons Mary, bds 618 E Wayne.

Cooper Cornelius G, mach, bds 6 Jones.
Cooper George J, engineer, res 284 W Jefferson.
Cooper Libbie, domestic 199 W Wayne.
Cooper Mrs L A, book agt, res 85 Barthold.
Cooper Rev Malachi C, student Taylor University, res 302 W Jefferson.
Cooper Mary (wid Cornelius), res 6 Jones.
Cooper Wm F, brakeman Penn Co, bds 270½ Calhoun.
Cooper Wm P, solicitor Glutting, Bauer & Hartnett, res 182 W Washington.
Cope Abraham, bds 51 Barr.
Cope Christian, bottle washer L Brames & Co, res 91 Smith.
Cope Clara R (wid Samuel), res 59 W Superior.
Cope Daniel C, feed yard, w s Clinton bet Superior and League Park, res 112 E Main.
Cope David F, lab, bds 51 Barr.
Cope Eva, bds 112 E Main.
Copenhaver Frederick, lab, res 403 E Washington.
Copinus Albert, trav agt Pottlitzer Bros, bds 47 W Wayne.
Copp, see Kopp.
Corbin David M, lab, res 339 Hanna.
Corcoran Alice B, clk J W Coblentz, bds 5 Oakland.
Corcoran Anthony, molder, bds 159 Harrison.
Corcoran Bridget (wid Patrick), bds 25 Grand.
Corcoran Edward J, printer, bds 159 Harrison.
Corcoran John, lab, res 41 E DeWald.
Corcoran John, molder, bds 159 Harrison.
Corcoran John J, printer The Press, bds 159 Harrison.
Corcoran Julia, bds 159 Harrison.
Corcoran Mary (wid John), res 159 Harrison.
Corcoran Mary, bds 159 Harrison.
Corcoran Owen H, clk Dreier & Bro, res 271 Harrison.
Corcoran Peter, printer, bds 159 Harrison.
Corcoran Thomas, driver, res s w cor Oakland and Aboit.
Cordeway, see Courdevey.
Cordrey Elmer E, molder Kerr-Murray Mnfg Co, bds 196 Hanna.
Cordrey Hanna, domestic 166 W Wayne.
Cork Martin, watchman, bds 59 Boone.
Corlett Joseph E (Ft Wayne View and Copying Co), bds 75 W Washington.
Corneille Amelia J, opr Hoosier Mnfg Co, bds 41 E Superior.
Corneille August, lab, res 41 E Superior.
Corneille Casimir F (C F & E P Corneille), res 51 E Superior.
Corneille Clara A, clk C F & E P Corneille, bds 41 E Superior.
Corneille C F & E P (Casimir F and Eugenie P), confectionery, 42 E Columbia.

Corneille Eugenie P (C F & E P Corneille), bds 51 E Superior.
Corneille Jennie, opr Hoosier Mnfg Co, bds 51 E Superior.
Corneille John B. notary public, res 45 E Superior.
Corneille Louis J, harnessmkr G R Wells, res 2 Erie.
Corneille Paul E, lab, bds 41 E Superior.
Cornelley Jeremiah, switchman, bds 56 Baker.
Cornelley John, policeman, bds 56 Baker.
Cornelley Margaret (wid Michael), res 56 Baker.
Corson Silas, lab, bds 360 W Washington.
Cortwright Stanley S, printer Press, rms 78 Wells.
Corwin Lydia (wid Theodore), bds 226 Fairfield ave.
Cosgrove Frank K, trav agt, res 103 W Superior.
Cosper Mary L, res 96 W Superior.
Coste lo Timothy J, despatcher Penn Co, res 161 Holman.
Costigan James V, clk Ft Wayne Electric Co, bds 121 E
  Washington.
Cote Henry, stonecutter Keller & Braun, bds Union House.
Cothrell Allen B, removed to Chicago, Ill.
Cothrell Andrew J, bds 65 Douglas ave.
Cothrell Clinton J, engineer, bds 65 Douglas ave.
Cothrell Edith M, teacher, bds 65 Douglas ave.
Cothrell Hattie, domestic 132 Chicago.
Cothrell Mrs Ready, res 132 Lafayette.
Cothrell Ruthette D (wid Jared), res 65 Douglas ave.
Cothrell R Etta, teacher, bds 65 Douglas ave.
Cothrell Sarah B (wid Wm D), res 62 W Lewis.
Cotner Edward G, painter Penn Co, res 21 Buchanan.
Cottage Restaurant (formerly The Nickel Plate Hotel),
  Louis J Geiss Propr, 31 W Columbia. (*See page 146.*)
Cotter Bartlett E, engineer, res 23 Van Buren.
Cotter Charles F, with F D Clarke, res 54 E Washington.
Cottingham Samuel Y, gasfitter A Hattersley & Sons, bds 63
  W Main.
Couch Wm, lab, bds 45 Baker.
Couderat Jacob, lab, Penn Co, bds 305 S Hanna.
Couderat John, lab Penn Co, bds 305 Hanna.
Couderat Wm, helper Indiana Mach Works, bds 305 Hanna.
Coulson Gustav, section hand, bds 15 Pearl.
Coulter Wm H, teamster J Derheimer, res 608 Hanna.
Councell Charles E. bkkpr Leikauf Bros, res 72 Barr.
Councell George, driver, rms 72 Barr.
Council Chambers, City Hall, e s Barr bet Berry and Wayne.
County Clerk's Office, Daniel W Souder clerk, Court House.
County Commissioner's Office, Court House.
County Jail, George H Viberg sheriff, n end Calhoun.
County Surveyor's Office. Court House.

Cour Celia, domestic s w cor Clinton and Washington.
Cour Claude J A, res 261 E Washington.
Cour Eugene, laborer, res 19 Buchanan.
Cour Frank, horseshoer Fort Wayne St R R Co, res 330 E
    Jefferson.
Cour George E, sheet iron worker, bds 261 E Washington.
Cour Henry W, sheet iron worker, bds 261 E Washington.
Cour John H, lab, bds 261 E Washington.
Cour Joseph P. lab Penn Co, bds 261 E Washington.
Cour Lizzie, domestic 107 W Berry.
Cour Valentine F, bartender James Summers, bds 47 Douglas.
Cour Wm H. boilermkr Penn Co, res 259 E Washington.
Cour W Alexander, clerk Fort Wayne Newspaper Union, res
    355 E Washington.
Courdevey Annie, bds 73 Cass.
Courdevey Edward, lab J & P Lauer, bds 73 Cass.
Courdevey Henry, driver C L Centlivre St Ry Co, res 75 Wag-
    ner.
Courdevey Jerome, lab, bds 73 Cass.
Courdevey John, barber, bds 73 Cass.
Courdevey John L, armature winder Fort Wayne Electric Co,
    res 132 Shawnee ave.

Courdevey Joseph, wood worker Anthony Wayne Mnfg Co, bds 73 Cass.
Courdevey Seraphin, lab, res 73 Cass.
Court House, e s Calhoun bet Main and Berry.
Cousar Charles, chemist Bass F and M Works, res 205 E Wayne.
Covault Wm M, driver Powers & Barnett, res 70 Madison.
Coverdale Asahel S (Coverdale & Archer), res 29 2d.
Coverdale & Archer (Asahel S Coverdale, Perry J Archer), grocers, 24 Harrison.
Covey Wm H, printer, bds 61 E Columbia.
Covington Thomas E, florist, market stall 87, res 188 Ewing.
Cowell Nettie, domestic 31 Calhoun.
Cowen M Robert, engineer Penn Co, res 314 Clay.
Cowles Nelson E, bds 57 W Butler.
Cox, see als · Kocks.
Cox Arthur B, lab Penn Co, bds 225 Calhoun.
Cox Bessie, stenogr Penn Co, bds 17 Suttenfield.
Cox Eliza, opr S M Foster, bds 183 Hanna.
Cox Eliza W (wid Delos A), bds 103 W Superior.
Cox Elizabeth, nurse, rms 194 E Lewis.
Cox Ellis S, porter G E Bursley & Co, res 123 Harrison.
Cox Emma, cook Aldine Hotel.
Cox Enoch, storekeeper, res 17 Suttenfield.
Cox James B, plumber P E Cox, bds 183 Hanna.
Cox John, mach Kerr-Murray Mnfg Co, res 183 Hanna.
Cox Patrick E, Plumber, 29 W Man, res 523 Calhoun.
Cox Thomas, plumber P E Cox, bds 525 Calhoun.
Cox Wm M, brakeman, res n w cor Pontiac and Holton ave.
Coy Andrew H, trav agt F E Purcell & Co, res Huntington, Ind.
Coy Commodore P, res 495 E Wayne.
Coy John A, bkkpr Summit City Soap Co, bds 495 E Wayne.
Coy J Oliver, presser Summit City Soap Co, bds 495 E Wayne.
Crabill Levi, fireman G R & I R R, res 402 Clinton.
Crable Phœbe, waiter The Randall.
Craft, see Kraft.
Cragg Charles, lab, res 141 Taber.
Cragg Henry C, mach hd Fort Wayne Electric Co, bds 141 Taber.
Cragg Robert V, clerk Kyle & Plumadore, bds 130 Wallace.
Cragg Thomas, agt S F Bowser & Co, res 130 Wallace.
Cragg Wm J, removed to Jackson, Mich.
Crah, see Krah.
Craig Andrew, car bldr Penn Co, res 27 Boone.
Craig Atch son D, brakeman, res 141 Horace.

Craig Calvin, brakeman, bds 345 W Main.
Craig Christian C, engineer Penn Co, res 149 E Jefferson.
Craig James, mach hand, bds 28 Chicago.
Craig James C, conductor, res s w cor Masterson and Clinton.
Craig John, carp, res 345 W Main.
Craig Mrs Mary, bds 140 Holman.
Craig Ralston H, fireman Penn Co, rms 149 E Jefferson.
Craig Sarah J, domestic 114 W Williams.
Craig Sidney P, engineer Penn Co, rms 94 Calhoun.
Craig Walter, caller, bds 141 Horace.
Craigh Annie, cook S W Harmon.
Craighead B Frank, brakeman, res 204 W Superior.
Craik Robert, groom Brookside Farm Co, bds same.
Crall Charles E, tel editor Sentinel, res 147 W Washington.
Crall Fred L, bkkpr Hoosier Mnfg Co, bds 214 W Berry.
Cramer, *see also Kramer*.
Cramer Charles B, removed to Wellsville, O.
Cramer David, engineer G R & I R R, res 78 Brackenridge.
Cramer Edith, domestic 130 E Wayne.
Cramer Eli, engineer Penn Co, res 128 Creighton ave.
Cramer Francis, mach hand Ft Wayne Electric Co, bds 91 Laselle.
Cramer Frederick J, teamster, res 245 W Wayne.
Cramer Henry C, street car driver, res 227 Barr.
Cramer John F, pres Ft Wayne Newspaper Union, res Milwaukee, Wis.
Cramer Mary, domestic Aldine Hotel.
Cramer Maurice M, lab, bds 91 Laselle.
Cramer Theresa (wid Solomon), res 91 Laselle.
Cramer Wm, lab, res 194 W De Wald.
Cramp Wm S, clk Beadell & Co, rms 25 E Washington.
Cran Charles, molder Bass F & M Works, res 158 Wallace.
Cran Charles W, patternmkr Ft Wayne Iron Works, bds 158 Wallace.
Cran Robert, foreman Bass F & M Works, res 398 Calhoun.
Crance, *see also Kranz*.
Crance Edward J, brakeman N Y, C & St L R R, bds 18 Huron.
Crance Frank, res 210 St Mary's ave.
Crance Frank J, lab, bds 80 Thomas.
Crance George, grocer, s w cor Smith and Creighton ave, res same.
Crance James, lab, res 506 Hanna.
Crance John J, finisher, bds 80 Thomas.
Crance Judson, brakeman, res 16 Huron.
Crance Pritchard, lab, res 80 Thomas.
Crane Mrs Bridget M, res 192 W De Wald.

ugene T, finisher Ft Wayne Organ Co, bds 192 W De
ld.

eorge D, lawyer, s w cor Clinton and Berry, res 305
Jefferson.

)hn J, finisher Ft Wayne Organ Co, bds 192 W De Wald.

heresa R, bds 192 W De Wald.

7m M, res n e cor Fox and W De Wald.

1 Alice (wid John), res 28 Marion.

1 James, engineer, res 28 Marion.

1 Lizzie A, milliner A Mergentheim, bds 28 Marion.

1 Margaret, dressmkr, 28 Marion, res same.

see Crance and Krantz.

Frank C (Renner, Cratsley & Co), res n s Edgewater
4 w of Dearborn.

Leona, waiter 25 E Main.

e also Kiah.

Iward L, real estate, res 71 W Wayne.

rs Maria R, res 71 W Wayne.

rah B, bds 71 W Wayne.

1 B Frank, plasterer, res 40 Chicago.

1 Emil E, fireman Penn Co, bds 80 Chicago.

1 George, lab, res 8 Short.

1 Henry B, mach hand Old Fort Mnfg Co, res 26
man.

1 John, lab Penn Co, bds 66 Melita.

1 John T, carp, 439 Broadway, res same.

1 Joseph, engineer, bds Grand Central Hotel.

Martin, helper Penn Co, res 66 Melita.

Nelson J, converter Ft Wayne Electric Co, res 65
let.

Noah, section hand, res 34 S Wayne ave.

Richard, painter, res 19 Nirdlinger ave.

Sadie, operator Hoosier Mnfg Co, bds 206 Broadway.

Samantha S, res 386 E Washington.

Samuel M, lab, res 68 Melita.

ennie, cook Weber House.

ngeline, bds 37 E Williams.

drew, helper Penn Co, rms 25 Baker.

chael, engineer Penn Co, res 110 Force.

ter, lab Penn Co, rms 25 Baker.

lfred D, pres and genl mngr Kerr-Murray Mnfg Co,
1 W Berry.

onzo W, helper Kerr-Murray Mnfg Co, res 295 W

I

Crighton David K, engineer The Western Gas Construction Co, res 208 W DeWald.

Crighton Jennie C, bds 49 Brackenridge.

Crighton Wm, foreman, res 49 Brackenridge.

Crighton Wm H, draugntsman Ft Wayne Electric Co, res 212 W DeWald.

Crimmans Dennis J, fireman, res 47 E Butler.

Crist, *see also* Christ.

Crist Ira B, carp F J Beach, bds 171 Broadway.

Crist John, lab Salimonie Mining and Gas Co, bds 28 Hood.

Crist John, switchman, res 105 John.

Crist Samuel D, driver, res 28 Union.

Critchfield Owen, fireman G R & I R R, bds 23 Walnut.

Crocker Charles B, brakeman N Y, C & St L R R, rms 10 Clinton.

Crombie John A, engineer, rms 38 Brackenridge.

Cromwell Clarence W, hardwood lumber, bds 224 W Berry.

Cromwell Joseph C, bkkpr Weil Bros & Co, res 261 W Wayne.

Cromwell Joseph W, lumber, res 224 W Berry.

Cromwell Wm O, stenogr Bass F and M Works, bds 224 W Berry.

Crone *see* Krohn.

Cronin Sarah, domestic 177 W Wayne.

Croninger Edward, lab, res 89 Hanna.

Cronk Cleora, carriage trimmer City Carriage Works, bds St Joseph twp.

Crosby Edwin J, mach, res 20 S Wayne ave.

Crosby Elbert W, engineer, res 102 St Mary's ave.

Crosby George T, mach, res 111 W DeWald.

Crosby Helen I, stenogr W P Breen, bds s e cor Pontiac and Calhoun.

Crosby Hiram O, clk Penn Co, res s e cor Pontiac and Calhoun.

Crosby John T, mach Wabash R R, res 111 W DeWald.

Crosby Mary (wid Nathan G), bds 111 W DeWald.

Crosby Richard A, printer Daily News, bds s e cor Calhoun and Pontiac.

Cross Charles W, asst master mechanic Penn Co, res 26 Douglas ave.

Crouse, *see also* Krauhs, Kraus and Krouse.

Crouse Charles, harness-mkr, bds 18 Mary.

Crouse Charles R, mach hd Louis Diether & Bro, res s s Killea near Hoagland ave.

Crouse Clinton, lab, res 385 W Main.

Crouse David, lab, res 18 Mary.

Crouse Edwin, lab, bds 18 Mary.

Geo. E. Johnson, DENTIST, 74 Calhoun Street.
Res., 188 W. Berry St.

FORT WAYNE DIRECTORY.   151

Crouse Frederick, teamster, res 8 Hough.
Crouse Hugh W, reporter The Press, rms 20 W Berry.
Crouse Lena, waiter The Saratoga.
Crouse Wm, teamster, bds 8 Hough.
Crout Henry, lab, bds 57 John.
Crow Charles D, lab Penn Co, bds 319 Hanna.
Crow Club Rooms, 195 Calhoun.
Crow James A, carp, res 197 Barr.
Crow John L, lab Penn Co, bds 319 Hanna.
Crow John W, removed to Dayton, O.
Crowe John M, teacher Westminster Seminary.
Crowel James B, lab Louis Deither & Bro, res s e cor Rumsey
    ave and Howell.
Crowl Mrs Hattie, attendant Indiana School for Feeble-Minded
    Youth.
Crowl Lee, lab, bds Union House.
Crowl Lewis, lab, res 52 Spy Run ave.
Crowl Wm, conductor, res 153 Wells.
Croxton Milton E, car oiler Penn Co, res 27 Euclid ave.
Croxton Philip W, carp, res 3 Edgewater ave.
Croxton Worthington A, trav auditor Ft Wayne Electric Co,
    res 215 W Wayne.
Croy Clara, domestic 56 Baker.
Croy David, electrician Indiana School for Feeble-Minded
    Youth.
Croy Wesley B, car bldr Penn Co, bds 7 Winter.
Crull August, teacher Concordia College, res same.
Cruse Charles A, tuck pointer, bds 76 Pontiac.
Cruse Demetrius A, tuck pointer, res 76 Pontiac.
Crusey John E (Crusey & Clark), res 250 Calhoun.
Crusey & Clark (John E Crusey, Edward J Clark), saloon, 250
    Calhoun.
Crutchfield Ernest, removed to Indianapolis, Ind.
Crutchfield John, lab, res 5 Breck.
Crutchfield Wm H, removed to Indianapolis, Ind.
Culbertson Frank V, Mngr R G Dun & Co, res s e cor
    Park place and Hoagland avenue.
Culbertson Harry R, clk R G Dun & Co, bds s e cor Park
    place and Hoagland avenue.
Cull, *see also Kull.*
Cull Catherine (wid Cornelius), res 20 Baker.
Cull James, fireman G R & I R R, bds 20 Baker.
Cull Patrick J, switchman Wabash R R, res 88 Chicago.
Cull Thomas, fireman, bds 20 Baker.
Cullars Clara, waiter Aldine Hotel.
Cullen Michael, lab, bds Elizabeth Becquette.

Robert Spice, Waterworks and General Plumbing, 48 West Main and 11 Pearl Streets.

152 R. L. POLK & CO.'S

Cullison Charles E, engineer G R & I R R, res 416 Clinton.
Culver Burt, removed to Columbus, O.
Culver John M, carp, res 203 W DeWald.
Culver Wm M, filler Ft Wayne Organ Co, res 147 Shawnee.
Cummerow George, collector Freie Presse, bds 121 W Superior.
Cummerow Otto F, propr Ft Wayne Daily Freie Presse and Weekly Indiana Deutsche Presse, n e cor Calhoun and Main, res 121 W Superior.
Cummerow Rudolph M, Choice Wines and Liquors, Imported and Domestic Cigars, 276 Calhoun, res 122 W Butler.
Cummings Anna (wid Rody), res 59 Charles.
Cummings Charles E, clk T J T Cummings, bds 29 Grand.
Cummings George W (Cummings & Spencer), res 286 Calhoun.
Cummings Jeremiah, brakeman, res 41 Clay.
Cummings Judith L (wid Theodore), bds 29 Grand.
Cummings Mary (wid Michael), res 22 Baker.
Cummings Mary, tailoress, bds 59 Charles.
Cummings Nellie M, clk T J T Cummings, bds 29 Grand.
Cummings Nicholas, engineer, res 55 Charles.
Cummings Rachel, cook Grand Central Hotel.
Cummings Thomas J T, installment goods, 152 Calhoun, res 29 Grand.
Cummings & Spencer (George W Cummings, Wm H Spencer), Dealers in Fresh and Salt Meats, Sausages of all Kinds, Dressed Poultry, Butter, Eggs, Fish and Oysters, 178 Calhoun.
Cummins Abner, section hand, res 54 Walnut.
Cunningham Kate, domestic 152 W Wayne.
Cunningham Louis, bds 39 W Washington.
Cunningham Max (col'd), waiter The Wayne.
Cunningham Robert R, supt construction Star Iron Tower Co, bds 31 2d.
Curdes Louis F, tuner Ft Wayne Organ Co, res 45 W Creighton avenue.
Currall John, lab Penn Co, res n s Eckart 5 e of Hanna.
Curran Forest V, gravel roofer, res 275 E Jefferson.
Curran Isabella, opr Hoosier Mnfg Co, bds 71 Charles.
Curran John, flagman, bds 196 Hanna.
Curran Timothy, lab, bds 110 Buchanan.
Current Samuel W, lab Penn Co, res n s Wayne Trace 1 e of New Haven avenue.
Current Sylvanus S, car bldr Penn Co, res n s Wayne Trace nr Penn Car Shops.
Current Wm, brakeman, bds Monroe House.
Currier Charles A, opr Associated Press, bds 332 E Wayne.

Currier Charles H, Dealer in Staple and Fancy Groceries, 72 E Main, res 332 E Wayne.

Currier John L, tel opr W U Tel Co, res 315 E Wayne.

Currier Miss Leah, bkkpr C H Currier, bds 332 E Wayne.

Curry Amanda (col'd), domestic 385 Hanna.

Curry Frank F, lab, bds 75 Dawson.

Curry James, switchman Wabash R R, res 75 Dawson.

Curtice John F, Real Estate and Loans, Rooms 1 and 2 Trentman Bldg, res 142 Montgomery. (*See front cover and page 63.*)

Curtis Daisy, bds 100 Riverside ave.

Curtis Herbert, lather, bds 100 Riverside ave.

Curtis Jennie (wid Jeremiah), res 100 Riverside ave.

Curtis Laurence, lather, bds 100 Riverside ave.

Curtis Mary, domestic 176 W Washington.

Curtis Nellie, bkkpr Ryan Bros, bds 22 W Washington.

Curtis Samuel H, lab Penn Co, res 117 W Butler.

Cushing John, mach, bds 9 Ohio.

Cushing Nellie, milliner, bds 9 Ohio.

Cushing Timothy J, engineer G R & I R R, res 76 W Butler.

Custer House, Gerson Scherzinger Propr, 16 and 18 W Main. (*See page 61.*)

Cutler Alice, bds W M Cutler.

Cutler Elmer L, lab, bds W M Cutler.

Cutler Mary E, opr Hoosier Mnfg Co, bds 72 W 4th.

Cutler Wm, lab Ft Wayne Soap Works, bds Wm M Cutler.

Cutler Wm M, foreman Ft Wayne Soap Works, res n s New Haven ave 3 e of Lumbard.

Cutshall Frank, lab Bass F & M Works, bds 2 Monroe.

Cutshall Isaac, lab, res 239 St Mary's ave.

Cutshall Joseph H, watchman Troy Steam Laundry, res 266 W Jefferson.

Cutshall Sherman, molder Bass F & M Works, bds 2 S Monroe.

Cutshall Theodore M, lab, bds 2 Monroe.

Cutshall Wm, res 2 Monroe.

Cutshall Wm S, molder, bds 2 Monroe.

Cutter Milo O, lab Penn Co, res 331 E Creighton ave.

Cypher Mary (wid Rufus), res 39 Duck.

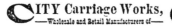
D

Dager Maggie, domestic 306 Calhoun.

Dahman Wm J, molder Bass F & M Works, res 115 John.

John Pressler, Plumbing, Gas and Steam Fitting.
Columbia, Barr and Dock Streets.

154   R. L. POLK & CO.'S

Dalh Rev John L, res 58 Division.
Dailey, *see also Daley and Daly.*
Dailey Ephraim P, bkkpr Root & Co, bds 37 Bass.
Dailey John, blksmith, bds 37 Bass.
Dailey Michael, conductor, rms 135 Holman.
Dale James M, clk Nickel Plate R R, res 323 W Jefferson.
Daler Lewis P, painter Olds' Wagon Wrks, res Maumee rd.
Daley, *see also Dailey and Daly.*
Daley John, hoseman Engine Co No 1, bds 219 Lafayette.
Daley John, mach Bass F & M Works, res 73 Charles.
Dalman Edwin F, bkkpr F M Smith & Co, bds 368 Fairfield.
Dalman Frederick, res 116 W Williams.
Dalman John, res 368 Fairfield ave.
Dalman John W, bds 368 Fairfield ave.
Dalman Robert, fish pedler, res 11 High.
Dalte Christian, mach hand, res 7 Rockhill.
Dalton Catherine, opr Hoosier Mnfg Co, bds 1 Spring.
Dalton Catherine M, clk L Dessauer & Co, bds 202 High.
Dalton Edmund, carp Louis Diether & Bro, res 32 Wilt.
Dalton Elizabeth, opr S M Foster, res Adams township.
Dalton James, lab, res 58 W Williams.
Dalton James, section hand, res 202 High.
Dalton John E, bds 32 Wilt.
Dalton Wm F, wood turner Ft Wayne Organ Co, bds 58 W
    Williams.
Daly, *see also Dailey and Daley.*
Daly Miss Alice, bds 49 E Jefferson.
Daly John, painter, rms 55 Barr.
Daly Margaret R, janitor, res 65 Melita.
Daly Mary C (wid Wm G), res 49 E Jefferson.
Dame Bertha, opr Hoosier Mnfg Co, bds 53 W 5th.
Dameier Louisa, student, bds 63 Douglas ave.
Dameier Wm, res 63 Douglas ave.
Dameier Wm jr, lab, bds 63 Douglas ave.
Dammeyer Emma, dressmkr, bds 201 Ewing.
Dammeyer Frederick, bricklayer, bds 29 Stophlet.
Dammeyer Frederick, lab, res 95 Wall.
Dammeyer Henry, blksmith Penn Co, res 201 Ewing.
Dammeyer Henry jr, cutter, bds 201 Ewing.
Dammeyer Louisa, dressmkr, bds 201 Ewing.
Danahey Cornelius, lab, res 70 Force.
Danahy Jeremiah, lab Penn Co, bds 19 Brandriff.
Danahy Philip, storekeeper, bds 19 Brandriff.
Danehy James, engineer G R & I R R, res 4 Bass.
Danehy Michael, painter, res 12 Bass.
Daniels Ferdinand, lab, bds 126 Eliza.

ALL ORDERS PROMPTLY ATTENDED TO. RYAN TRUCKING CO. 19 & 21 W. WASHINGTON. Tel. 122.

FORT WAYNE DIRECTORY. 155

Daniels Rane A C (wid Samuel S), res 68 W Jefferson.

Dannecker Rev Henry P, Pastor St John's Evangelical Lutheran Church, res 212 W Washington.

Dannenfelser George J, porter A C Trentman, res 150 Clinton.

Darker George U, timekpr Bass F & M Works, bds 77 W Butler.

Darker Martha (wid Wm), res 77 W Butler.

Darling John W, boil-rmkr, res 26 Melita.

Darling Joseph L, piano turner, res 15 E Wayne.

Darroch Austin M, res 3 Riverside ave.

Darroch John W (J W Darroch & Co), res 72 Webster.

Darroch J W & Co (John W Darroch, Wilson D Anderson), milk, 39 Harrison.

Dartnell Ernest W, clk Penn Co, bds 15 E De Wald.

Dascomb Thomas E, clk Ft Wayne Electric Co, bds 225 E. Wayne.

Daseler Charles H, painter Penn Co, bds 99 Madison.

Daseler Christian L, clk Penn Co, res 59 N rdlinger ave.

Daseler Frederick G, policeman, res 199 Lafayette.

Daseler George H, clk Hartmann & Bro, bds 99 Madison.

Daseler Henry, res 99 Madison.

Daseler Henry C, lamp trimmer, bds 99 Madison.

Daseler Henry J, boilermkr Wabash R R, res 201 John.

Daseler Louisa, bds 99 Madison.

Daseler Minnie C (wid Conrad C), res 211 Madison.

Dash Henry C, blksmith, res 72 Hamilton.

Dau August, carp Frederick Dau, bds 478 Hanna.

Dau Frederick, contractor, 478 Hanna, res same.

Dau Frederick jr, carp, bds 478 Hanna.

Daub Joseph, printer The Press, bds 105 Lafayette.

Daugharty Alfred, boots and shoes, 94 Wells, res 227 same.

Daugherty, see also Dougherty.

Daugherty Annie, bds 151 Holman.

Daugherty Charles J S, stove mounter, res 14 Cass.

Daugherty George B, engineer, res 112 3d.

Daugherty James, lab, res 151 Holman.

Daugherty James T, brakeman, bds 151 Holman.

Davenport Edward N, hostler S F Bowser & Co, res n e cor Oliver and Buchanan.

David Frederick C, coremkr, bds 108 Eliza.

David Wm H, lab N Leonard, bds Perry Shultz.

Davis Miss Addie F, teacher, bds 308 E Wayne.

Davis Alfred A, car bldr Penn Co, res 96 E Lewis.

Davis Amos, Dealer in Domestic Sewing Machines, Patterns and all Kinds of Sewing Machine Supplies, 138 Calhoun, res 137 W Superior.

Davis Benjamin, rms 103 W Main.

ARCHITECTS. WING & MAHURIN,
41 and 42 Pixley & Long Bldg. Telephone 328.

156   R. L. POLK & CO.'S

Davis Charles, fireman, bds Schele House.

Davis Charles E, Bookbinder and Blank Book Mnfr, 84 Calhoun, res 262 E Wayne.

Davis Christina, bkkpr Amos Davis, bds 137 W.Superior.

Davis Delbert C, clk Ft Wayne Electric Co, bds 176 Jackson.

Davis Edward T, foreman Penn Co, res 249 E Jefferson.

Davis Edwin G, lab Penn Co, res 44 Monroe.

Davis Eliza (wid Amos), res 137 W Superior.

Davis Eugene, lab, res s s Rebecca nr G R & I R R.

Davis E Gregg, student, bds 249 E Jefferson.

Davis Frank L, fireman, bds 176 Jackson.

Davis George H, clk, bds 55 E Lewis.

Davis Harry S, press feeder Sentinel, bds 308 E Wayne.

Davis Hezekiah M, watchman, res 76 E Columbia.

Davis John J, car inspr Penn Co, res 191 E Lewis.

Davis Joseph B, mngr The Press, res 79 W Jefferson.

Davis Laura B, domestic 278 W Berry.

Davis Mary J (wid Trueman), dressmkr, rms 34 Chicago.

Davis Oscar, lab Penn Co, res 69 Leith.

Davis P G, conductor, bds 120 Harrison.

Davis Robert B, collector, bds 467 Lafayette.

Davis Rosa, domestic 24 W Wayne.

Davis Roy, mach, bds 196 Hanna.

Davis Thomas A, letter carrier postoffice, bds 308 E Wayne.

Davis Thomas J, inspr Salimonie Mining & Gas Co, bds 55 E Lewis.

Davis Vill Roy, conductor, res 176 Jackson.

Davis Wesley T, engineer, res 308 E Wayne.

Davis Wilbur E, res 55 Brackenridge.

Davis Willard T, track layer, res 185 Lafayette.

Davis Wm, lab, bds 76 E Columbia.

Davis Wm H, Propr Empire Box Factory and Mnfr Empire Letter Files, 3d floor Bank Block, res 253 W Creighton ave.

Davis Wm T, lab Robert Ogden, res 84 Barr.

Dawkins Emma, domestic 202 W Wayne.

Dawkins Henry G, produce, market stall 97, res Jefferson twp.

Dawkins Wm, lab Penn Co, res 91 Force.

Dawsey Frederick, carp, bds 24 Oliver.

Dawsey John E, painter, bds 24 Oliver.

Dawson Amanda M (wid John W), res 140 E Berry.

Dawson And'ew, conductor, bds 46 Chicago.

Dawson Charles M, judge superior court, Court House, res 283 W Wayne.

Dawson G Wallace, musical mdse, 27 W Main, res 187 E Jefferson.

Dawson John W, brakeman, res 143 Fairfield ave.

Dawson Michael, lab, res 46 Chicago.

Dawson Ronald, student, bds 283 W Wayne.

Day, *see also Tag.*

Day Alvin M, clk F C Parham, bds 153 W DeWald.

Day Amelia, milliner, bds 147 W Superior.

Day Charles A, painter, bds 147 W Superior.

Day Henry D, painter, res 147 W Superior.

Day John, brakeman, res 39 Grand.

Dayton Louise, presser, bds 491 E Wayne.

Dayton Mrs Louisa, seamstress D S Redelsheimer & Co, bds 30 Clinton.

Deady Edwin R, molder Ft Wayne Electric Co, res 302 Harrison.

Deady Emmett A, mach S F Bowser & Co, bds 312 Harrison.

Deady Jeremiah P, painter, bds 312 Harrison.

Deagan Edward, lab, res 52 Leith.

Deagan John J, blksmith Penn Co, res 177 Hanna.

Deagan Joseph A, apprentice R S Sloat, bds 52 Leith.

Deahl, *see also Deihl and Diehl.*

Deahl Edward, carp, res 67 Barthold.

Deahl Frederick, mach hand, bds 67 Barthold.

Deahl Samuel, mach hand Peters Box & Lumber Co, bds 67 Barthold.

Deakman Mary (wid August), bds F H Seeger.

Deal Sarah (wid Peter K), res 51 Barr.

Deam Catherine, domestic 18 W Butler.

Deam Elizabeth (wid George), res 38 Ewing.

Dean Charles, lab, res 10 Barthold.

Dean Jennie domestic John Double, bds 11 High.

DeArmitt Charles J (Walton & DeArmitt), rms 13 E Wayne.

Deaucha Frank, conductor N, Y, C & St L R R, res 83 Wells.

Debelius Henry W, bds 174 W Wayne.

Debois Catherine, domestic Fritz Hotel.

De Bolt Eva, laundress Aldine Hotel.

Dechart Henry, bartndr, bds 100 W Superior.

Deck John, tailor Aaron Levy, res 578 Lafayette.

Decker Charles A, lab Bass F and M Works, bds 507 Hanna.

Decker Mary, supervisor Indiana School for Feeble-Minded Youth.

Dedolph Wm, res 237 St Mary's ave.

Dedrick Wm E, conductor, res 31 Duryea.

Deems Henry, lab J A Koehler.

De Frain Francis, carp, res n s Eckart 5 e of Hanna.

Degitz Charles, lab, res 15 Colerick.

Degitz Charles, helper Bass F and M Works, res 507 Hanna.

12

Degitz Charles A, lab, bds 507 Hanna.
Degitz Frank, lab, bds 507 Hanna.
Degitz Joseph, bottler, bds 507 Hanna.
Degitz Louis, watchman, bds 15 Colerick.
Degitz Margaret, domestic 173 W Wayne.
De Grattery Elizabeth (wid James E), res 67 Hayden.
De Guehery Louis, printer The Press, rms 226 Calhoun.
De Hart Abraham, res 43 Wall.
De Hart Wm, clk Kerr-Murray Mnfg Co, bds 182 W Superior.
De Haven Harrison D, lab Penn Co, res 107 Holman.
De Haven Mattie, opr Hoosier Mnfg Co, bds 107 Holman.
De Haven Perry N (J M Clark & Co), res n s Columbia 2 e of Oneida.
Deheny Cornelius, lab Penn Co, res 70 Force.
Dehm Frederick, lab J A Koehler, bds w s Lafayette nr Rudisill avenue.
Dehm George, lab J A Koehler, res cor Lafayette and Court.
De Hensche Wm, lab, bds Lake Shore Hotel.
Dehne Ernst, patternmkr Penn Co, res 114 Gay.
Dehne Louisa, domestic George De Wald.
Deibel Maggie, bds 133 Holman.
Deihl, see also Deahl and Diehl.
Deihl Hugh H, mach Penn Co, res 49 Harmer.
Deihl Lillie M, bds 49 Harmer.
Deister Emil, valet J H Bass.
Deitrich Wm O, driver, res 307 Calhoun.
Deitsch Rosalie M (wid Moritz), res 87 W Jefferson.
Dek Frank, res 495 Lafayette.
De La Grange Constantine C, patternmkr Fort Wayne Electric Co, bds 199 Broadway.
De La Grange Frank J, woodwkr Anthony Wayne Mnfg Co, res 68 Lasalle.
De La Grange Frank J E, Groceries, Dry Goods and Notions, 273 Hanna, res same.
De La Grange Justin, clk F J E De La Grange, bds 273 Hanna.
Delaney John, lab, bds 51 Barr.
Delaney Rev Joseph F. Rector St Patrick's Church, res n w cor Harrison and De Wald.
Delano Elizabeth D (wid Thomas), res 76 E Wayne.
Delhalber Annie, domestic G E Bursley.
Delker Caroline (wid Jacob), res 74 E Columbia.
Delker Minnie, seamstress, bds 74 E Columbia.
Delker Wm, driver, bds 74 E Columbia.
De Mass Mrs Ollie J, res 39 Duck.
De Maulpied Martin N, flagman, bds 237 Barr.
Dembyer August, lab, res s s Eckart 3 e of Hanna.

Demler Frederick, lab, bds 29 Duck.
Denehy, *see Danahey.*
Denges Herman, carp, res 23 Oliver.
Denio Cordelia (wid Wm), bds 146 Wallace.
Denner Mrs Margaret, res 409 W Main.
Dennis Albert, coremkr Kerr-Murray Mnfg Co, res 108 Butler.
Dennis Amy, domestic Harmon House.
Dennis Frederick C, lab, res 63 Buchanan.
Dennis Mrs Mary, res 268 Calhoun.
Dennis Michael, driver M Baltes, res cor Putnam and Sherman.
Dennis Wm, teamster Herman Berghoff Brewing Co, res 78 Grant.
Dennison Daisy L, teacher Binkley Telegraph School, bds 13 W Butler.
Dennison Georgia, teacher, bds 13 W Butler.
Dennison John, repairer, 119 Harrison, bds 264 Brackenridge.
Dennison Margaret, domestic 219 W Main.
Denny Watts P (Chapin & Denny), res 70 Jackson.
Denoy Charles W, mach, res 155 Force.
Dent Theresa A (wid Byron), bds 86 Wells.
Denz Joseph, watchmkr H Mariotte, res 24 E Washington.
Denzel John, framer Keil & Keil, res 398 E Lewis.
Depen Benedine (wid August), res 37 E 3d.
Depen John H, clk R G Dun & Co, bds 37 E 3d.
DePew Samuel, lab, bds 251 Calhoun.
Depler Hugh H, car bldr Penn Cq, res 27 Duryea.
Depler James A, brakeman, res 87 W Williams.
Depner George J, molder Bass F and M Works, bds 125 Cass.
Deppeller Rudolph, physician, 18 E Columbia, res same.
Deppler Anna, dressmkr, 342 W Main, bds same.
Deppler Jacob, carp, res 342 W Main.
Derheimer Catherine, bds 177 E Jefferson.
Derheimer Joseph (Wilding & Derheimer), res 177 E Jefferson.
Derheimer Joseph W, clk, bds 177 E Jefferson.
DeRome Charles, mach Kerr-Murray Mnfg Co, bds 348 Calhoun.
DeRome Solomon, res 348 Calhoun.
Desprez Victor, watchman, res 73 Laselle.
Desprez Victoria, bookbinder, bds 73 Laselle.
Dessauer Etta (wid Louis), res 90 W Main.
Dessauer Jacob, clk B Lehman, bds 90 W Main.
Dessauer Louis, clk L Wolf & Co, bds 90 W Main.
Dessauer L & Co (Isaac Trauerman), cigar mnfrs, 23 Calhoun.
Detdman Charles, lab Bass F and M Works, res 150 Smith.

Robert Spice, Waterworks and General Plumbing, 48 West Main and 11 Pearl Streets.

160 R. L. POLK & CO.'S

De Turk Lebanon, with F J E DeLa Grange, bds 273 Hanna.

Detzer August J (Klinkenberg & Detzer), res 155 W Wayne.

Detzer Edward N, bkkpr First Nat Bank, bds 155 W Wayne.

Detzer Gustave G, bkkpr Old National Bank, rms 155 W Wayne.

Detzer Martin, Druggist, 260 Calhoun, res n s Columbia ave 2 e of Old Fort.

Deuble Jennie, domestic 87 Cass.

Deutchel Andrew, car builder Penn Co, res 6 Hoffman.

Deuter Elizabeth (wid Michael J), bds 380 E Wayne.

Deuter Michael, stonecutter George Jaap, res 103 High.

Deutschman Peter, plasterer, bds 100 Montgomery.

Deutschmann Bernard, japanner Ft Wayne Electric Co, bds Weber House.

Devald Catharine (wid Nicholas), bds 175 E Wayne.

Devany Catherine C, bds 76 Baker.

Devany Edward M, wheelmkr, res 266 E Creighton ave.

Devany John I, lab, bds 76 Baker.

Devany Martin, res 76 Baker.

Devany Wm, fireman Penn Co, bds 76 Baker.

Devaux David, section hand, rms 60 E Columbia.

Devaux Edward F, bartender, res 23 Laselle.

Devendorf Alberta (wid Harry C), bds 197 Montgomery.

Devere Daniel W, driver Powers & Barnett, res 77 E Superior.

Devereaux Felicia (wid Xavier), removed to Titusville, Pa.

DeVilviss Thomas D, foreman S F Bowser & Co, res 265 E Creighton ave.

Devlin James, engineer, bds 37 Elizabeth.

Devlin Robert J, bds 24 S Wayne ave.

Devlin Wm, wiper, res 24 S Wayne ave.

DeWald Anna M, clk M Frank & Co, bds 404 Calhoun.

DeWald Anthony, clk, res 26 Clay.

DeWald Catherine, bds 141 Barr.

DeWald Miss Elizabeth M, bds DeWald sq.

DeWald George (Geo DeWald & Co), res DeWald sq.

DeWald George L, clk Geo DeWald & Co, bds DeWald sq.

DeWald Geo & Co (George DeWald, Effingham T Williams, Amelius J Lang, Robert W T DeWald,), Wholesale and Retail Dry Goods and Notions, n e cor Calhoun and Columbia.

DeWald Henry, tinsmith, 80 Barr, res 141 same.

DeWald Lucy, clk F J E De La Grange, bds 404 Calhoun.

DeWald Mary, bds 404 Calhoun.

D Wald Mary (wid Frank), res 41 Locust.

DeWald Michael, carp, res 178 W Washington.

DeWald Nicholas, helper Bass F & M Works, res 404 Calhoun.

DeWald Robert W T (Geo DeWald & Co), res 162 E Wayne.
DeWald Sophia, clk Siemon & Bro, bds 404 Calhoun.
DeWald Square, s s E DeWald, bet Hanna and Lafayette.
DeWitt Lorenzo B, lab, res 14 Lafayette.
Dexter Mrs Emma, waiter Windsor Hotel.
Dexter Wm, fireman Penn Co, res 16 Brackenridge.
Diamond Adolph, trav agt Pottlitzer Bros, res 99 E Wayne.
Diamond Harry, trav agt Pottlitzer Bros, res 170 W Jefferson.
Diamond Hotel, Simon Barnett Propr, 233-235 Calhoun.
Dick Agnes, domestic 72 W Wayne.
Dick Charles P, gasfitter, res 196 E Jefferson.
Dick David, lab Ft Wayne Electric Co, res 230 Thomas.
Dick Homer T, clk, bds 89 W Butler.
Dick Miss Mary E, teacher, bds 89 W Butler.
Dick Wm E, engineer G R & I R R, bds 89 W Butler.
Dicke Frederick H, Grocer, 29 Smith, res same.
Dicke Henry, res 192 E Lewis.
Dickerson Andrew F (col'd) porter Ft Wayne Newspaper
    Union, res 63 Baker.
Dickerson Jefferson, res 19 Lafayette.
Dickerson Samuel, well driller, res 151 Broadway.
Dickerson Sarah (col'd; wid Andrew), res 63 Baker.
Dickey Helen, bds 586 Calhoun.
Dickey Robert, res 586 Calhoun.
Dickinson Philemon, Mngr D H Baldwin & Co, res 18
    W Washington.
Dickman Henry W, pension attorney, 13 E Main, rms same.
Dickman Wm, helper, res 75 John.
Dickmeier Charles, lab Bass F & M Works, res 99 Gay.
Dickmeier Henry, lab, res 93 Gay.
Dickmeyer Ferdinand, boltmkr Penn Co, res 86 Nirdlinger ave.
Dickmeyer Wm, lab Louis Diether & Bro, res 168 Greely.
Dickson, *see also Dixon.*
Dickson James M, engineer Penn Co, res 503 Calhoun.
Didier Emeline (wid Frank), res 410 E Wayne.
Didier Frank, res 32 Oak.
Didier Frank X, clk Francis Sellier, res 78 E Columbia.
Didier James, car bldr Penn Co, res 347 E Creighton ave.
Didier Joseph C (Stace & Didier), res 66 E Columbia.
Didier Julian T, harnessmkr A L Johns & Co, bds w s Spy Run
    ave 6 w of bridge.
Didier Kate, domestic Allen County Asylum.
Didier Wm H, harnessmkr A L Johns & Co, bds w s Spy Run
    ave 6 w of bridge.
Didierjohn Joseph (Didierjohn & Hunter), res 104 Maumee rd.
Didierjohn Louis, apprentice Robert Ogden, bds 104 Maumee.

Didierjohn Rose, seamstress, bds 104 Maumee rd.
Didierjohn & Hunter (Joseph Didierjohn, John Hunter), broom-
mkrs, rear 104 Maumee rd.
Didion Amelia M, cigar box nailer Joseph Ruesewald, bds 208
Madison.
Didion Martin A, cigar boxmkr Joseph Ruesewald, res 208
Madison.
Didion Martin B, driver Peter A Moran, bds 201 E Wayne.
Didion Olivia J, cigar box nailer Joseph Ruesewald, bds 208
Madison.
Diebold Albert, stripper, bds 68 Boone.
Diebold Catherine (wid Joseph G), res 275 E Washington.
Diebold Clara, dressmkr, bds 275 E Washington.
Diebold Henry, baker B W Skelton Co, res 68 Boone.
Diebold Henry A, clk H G Sommers, bds 275 E Washington.
Diebold Mary E, opr S M Foster, bds 275 E Washington.
Diebold Wm, lab, bds 68 Boone.
Dieckman, see Dickman.
Diehl, see also Deihl and Deihl.
Diehl Michael (Diehl & Homsher), res 79 W De Wald.
Diehl & Homsher (Michael Diehl, Frank B Homsher), junk,
263-265 Calhoun.
Diek Herman H, marble cutter G W Wilson, res 17 Brandriff.
Diek John B, finisher Ft Wayne Organ Co, bds 25 Wall.
Diek Mary (wid Herman), res 25 Wall.
Diek Mary R, bds 25 Wall.
Diem Charles, musical instruments, 78 Barr, rms same.
Diener Henry G, driver, bds 260 Clinton.
Dierkes Anthony J, helper Ft Wayne Electric Co, res 77 Laselle.
Dierkes Catherine (wid Frederick), res 72 Barthold.
Dierkes Edward, lab, bds 72 Barthold.
Dierstein Frederick C, tailor John Wasserbach, bds 36 Fairfield
avenue.
Dierstein Fredericka (wid Christian), res 12 Fairfield ave.
Dierstein George C, upholsterer D N Foster Furniture Co, bds
12 Fairfield ave.
Dierstein Henry G, saloon, 24 E Berry, res same.
Dierstein Mamie, opr Hoosier Mnfg Co, bds 36 Fairfield ave.
Dierstein Samuel W, mach hand, bds 36 Fairfield ave.
Dierstein Wilhelmina (wid Samuel), res 36 Fairfield ave.
Diester Diedrich, coachman 72 W Wayne.
Diether Carl F, bds 267 W Wayne.
Diether Edward, foreman Diether & Barrows, res 128 Griffith.
Diether John H (Louis Diether & Bro), res 167 W Superior.
Diether Louis (Louis Diether & Bro and Diether & Barrows),
res 267 W Wayne.

BUILDERS' HARDWARE, PFEIFFER & SCHLATTER, 38 and 40 East Columbia St.

FORT WAYNE DIRECTORY. 163

Diether Louis & Bro (Louis and John H), Dealers in Rough and Dressed Lumber and Shingles; Mnfrs and Dealers in Sash, Doors, Blinds and Mouldings; All Kinds of Factory Work; Office and Yards bet City Mills and Gas Works on E Superior, Factory 100 Pearl. (*See right top lines.*)

Diether Thomas W A, mngr Diether & Barrows, res 296 W Jefferson.

Diether Wm A, clk Louis Diether & Bro, res 179 W Superior.

Diether & Barrows (Louis Diether, Frank R Barrows), Mnfrs Weisell Washers and Kitchen Furniture, 44 E Superior. (*See right top lines.*)

Dietrich John, teamster George Beckmann, bds 103 Force.

Diffenderfer Isabella A (wid Benjamin O), res 33 W De Wald.

Diffenderfer Mary, bkkpr, bds 33 W De Wald.

Diffenderfer Wm A, bkkpr Mossman, Yarnelle & Co, bds 33 W De Wald.

Diggins Charlotte (wid Wm G), res 76 W Creighton ave.

Dignan Ella G, bds 215 E Wayne.

Dignan Joseph L, lab, bds 215 E Wayne.

Dignan Lawrence, foreman, res 215 E Wayne.

Dildine Frank, editor Sentinel, res 88 W Jefferson.

Dill Mrs Anna, tailoress Indiana School for Feeble-Minded Youth.

Dill Charles, baker Indiana School for Feeble-Minded Youth.

Dillon James E N, printer Penn Co, bds 139 Broadway.

Dillon Julia A, dressmkr, bds 139 Broadway.

Dillon Lena L, music teacher, 139 Broadway, bds same.

Dillon Martha (wid James H), dressmkr, 139 Broadway, res same.

Dillon May, domestic Rich Hotel.

Dillman Anna, res 55 Wilt.

Dills Thomas J, Physician and Surgeon, 42 W Berry, res 40 Douglas ave. Tel 66.

Dimon Alice, stenogr D McCaskey, bds John Dimon.

Dimon Arthur, driver John Dimon, bds same.

Dimon Byron, driver John Dimon, bds same.

Dimon John, propr Fern Hill Dairy, res s s Huntingdon rd ¼ mile w of limits.

Dincher John T, bartndr T J Schuler, bds 130 W Main.

Dingman Daniel, lab, res 7 Dwenger ave.

Dingman Hiram, farmer, res 216 W Washington.

Dingman W Scott, agrl impts, res s w cor Van Buren and Main.

Dinkel Charles, carp, res 65 Wabash ave.

Dinklage Herman L, brakeman, bds 30 Gay.

Dinklage Margaret (wid Henry), bds 271 E Washington.

Dinklage Mary (wid Herman), res 30 Gay.
Dinklage Patrick O, flagman, bds 30 Gay.
Dinklager Anthony, lab A L Johns & Co, res 249 E Washington.
Dinnen James M, physician, 67 W Wayne, res 69 same.
Dirig Franz J, lab, res 68 Smith.
Dirig Henry, lab Herman Berghoff Brewing Co, bds 68 Smith.
Dirig Joseph, lab Ertel & Menefee, bds 68 Smith.
Dirks Albert, lab, res s w cor Buchanan and Holton ave.
Disbrow Frank W, clk Coverdale & Archer, res 177 Wells.
Disinger Albert, mach Indiana Machine Works, bds 80 Boone.
Disser Joseph P, harnessmkr A L Johns & Co, res 178 E
    Washington.
Distel Edward, clk Coombs & Co, bds 38 Hendricks.
Distel John, printer, res 182 E Jefferson.
Dittmann Carl, lab, res 150 Smith.
Dittman Ferdinand C, lab, bds 75 John.
Dittman Gustav H, lab, bds 75 John.
Dittman Herman, helper Bass F & M Works, bds 75 John.
Dittman Wm, lab Bass F & M Works, res 75 John.
Dittmer Jacob, removed to Columbus, O.
Dittoe Albert J (Ely & Dittoe), res 195 E Wayne.
Dittoe Charles W, clk Ely & Dittoe, bds 195 E Wayne.
Dittoe Mary C, bds 195 E Wayne.
Ditzenberger Wm N, lab, res 60 Home ave.
Dix Frank J, trimmer Jenney Electric Light and Power Co,
    bds n w cor 7th and Lafayette.
Dix Hugh, hoseman Engine Co No 1, rms same.
Dix Seth, hackman, res n w cor of N Lafayette and 7th.
Dixon, see also Dickson.
Dixon George F, lab, bds Union House.
Dixon Jennie, seamstress, res 14 Lafayette.
Dobberkau Frederick, car bldr Penn Co, res 5 Eliza.
Dobler Louis J, fireman, res 326 Hanna.
Dobler Theodore, tool inspr Penn Co, res 154 John.
Dobrick Wilhemina (wid Gottfried), bds 71 John.
Docter Wm A, driver C L Centlivre, res n s St Joseph rd 2 e
    of river.
Doctor Matthias, teamster G E Bursley & Co, res 26 Wefel.
Doctorman Mrs Carrie, waiter Indiana School for Feeble-
    Minded Youth.
Doctorman Marcellus H, brakeman L E & W R R, res 184
    Wells.
Dodane Alfred L, grocer, 92 Wells, res same.
Dodane Theodore C, clk A L Dodane, bds 92 Wells.
Dodez Edward W, student, bds 113 W Wayne.
Dodez Gustavus C, trav agt, res 113 W Wayne.

L. O. HULL, Artists' Materials, Studies, Etc. AT 90 CALHOUN STREET.

FORT WAYNE DIRECTORY. 165

Dodge Arthur, veterinary surgeon, 28 Pearl, res 143 W Berry.
Dodznski Frank, lab Bass F & M Works, res 113 High.
Doehla John, lab, res 77 Hayden.
Doehrman, *see also Doermann.*
Doehrman Charles E, car bldr Penn Co, res 165 Holman.
Doehrman Henry, lab Concordia College, res same.
Doehrmann Frederick W, carp, res 39 Nirdlinger ave.
Doehrmann Lottie, cook J M Barrett.
Doehrmann Wm, grocer, 56 Barr, res 339 E Washington.
Doelker Caroline M (wid Jacob), res cor Barr and E Columbia.
Doelker Minnie, bds cor Barr and E Columbia.
Doelker Wm J, teamster, bds cor Barr and Columbia.
Doell Wm, blksmith, res 88 Hanna.
Doelling Ernest, car repairer N Y, C & St L R R, bds 184 Greely.
Doelling Louis, mach hand Wayne Knitting Mills, bds Fritz Hotel.
Doenges, *see also Donges.*
Doenges Christian, carp, res 126 Maumee rd.
Doenges Ferdinand, lab Penn Co, bds 97 Oliver.
Doenges Frederick J, carriagemkr City Carriage Works, res 413 E Washington.
Doenges Herman, carp, bds 97 Oliver.
Doenges John, res 97 Oliver.
Doenges Louis, carp, res 59 Winter.
Doenges Peter, carp, res rear 180 Hayden.
Doenges Philip, res 11 Winch.
Doenges Philip jr, carp, bds 11 Winch.
Doenges Wm, carp, 12 Oliver, res same.
Doermann, *see also Doehrman.*
Doermann Ernest, blksmith Ft Wayne Iron Wks, res 88 Wall.
Doermann Henry, tailor J G Thieme & Son, bds 18 Rockhill.
Doermann Lizzie, domestic 399 Calhoun.
Doermer Peter, dairy, res n s New Haven ave nr Piqua rd.
Doherty, *see Daugherty and Dougherty.*
Dohner Oliver, section hand, bds 24 Huron.
Doings Ellen, seamstress, bds 52 3d.
Doings Lavina, bds 52 3d.
Doings Sarah (wid Henry), res 52 3d.
Dolan Alice, bds 8 Runnion ave.
Dolan Charles, engineer J C Peters, res 8 Runnion ave.
Dolan Charles T, carp, bds Union House.
Dolan Edward A, driver Ft Wayne St R R Co, bds 509 E Washington.
Dolan Frank J, molder, bds 8 Runnion ave.
Dolan Ina, domestic 39 W Creighton ave.
Dolan Miss Lizzie, clk F M Smaltz, bds 316 W Main.

The Peters Box and Lumber Co. } —MANUFACTURERS OF— Office Furniture

Dolan Mary (wid John), res 125 Walton ave.
Dolan Mary A, seamstress, bds 316 W Main.
Dolan Mary E, domestic 80 3d.
Dolin Sherman, musical engraver Harry Achenbach, bds n s W Superior w of Wells.
Donahoe Peter S, brakeman, res 16 Gay.
Donahoe Susan (wid John), bds 16 Gay.
Donahue Bridget E, dressmkr, bds 75 Baker.
Donahue Daniel J, molder Penn Co, bds 44 Brandriff.
Donahue Elizabeth, domestic 67 Harrison.
Donahue Ellen, bds 44 Brandriff.
Donahue Florance, section foreman N Y, C & St L R R, res 44 Brandriff.
Donahue Laura, clk A Mergentheim, bds 44 Brandriff.
Donahue Patrick W, engineer, res 12 Jackson.
Donahue Thomas, hostler Penn Co, res 39 Walnut.
Donahue Timothy P, mach Penn Co, bds 44 Brandriff.
Donald Thomas A, lab Brookside Farm Co, bds same.
Donaldson Alexander W, cabtmkr Ft Wayne Organ Co, bds 23 Poplar.
Donaldson Anna F, bkkpr Golden & Monahan, bds 23 Poplar.
Donaldson Eben R, res 23 Poplar.
Donaldson John, lab, res 199 E Washington.
Donaldson Matthew K, driver Troy Laundry, res 21½ Poplar.
Dondaro George, fruits, rms 12 E Columbia.
Dondero Philip, fruits, 28 E Main, res 45 same.
Donges Wm, engineer Bass F & M Works, res 112 Hayden.
Donges Wm, lab, res 31 Smith.
Donivan John W (Tibbles & Donivan), res 241 W DeWald.
Donnell Edward R, mach hd Ft Wayne Electric Co, bds 156 Taylor.
Donnell Wm, nickel plater, res 156 Taylor.
Donnell Wm B, lab Kerr-Murray Mnfg Co, bds 156 Taylor.
Donnelly Amelia (wid Henry), bds 131 Griffith.
Donnelly Andrew, shoemkr, res 348 Calhoun.
Donnelly Andrew H, switchman, res 18 Bass.
Donnelly Claudia, bds 131 Griffith.
Donnelly Jennie, cigar binder, bds 348 Calhoun.
Donovan John, lab, bds 47 Barr.
Donovan Peter, lab, bds 20 Harrison.
Donze Charles, lab, bds 29 Duck.
Dooley Homer, lab, bds 112 W Creighton ave.
Dooley Wm, bds Lake Shore Hotel.
Doran James, lab, bds 260 Clinton.
Doring R, car bldr Penn Co, bds 231 Barr.
Doriot Frank S, student, bds 58 Charles.

Geo. E. Johnson, DENTIST, 74 Calhoun Street.
Res., 188 W. Berry St.

FORT WAYNE DIRECTORY.   167

Doriot Harry W, brakeman Penn Co, res 58 Charles.
Doriot Julius, molder Bass F & M Works, res 58 Charles.
Dormer Deuce J, bartndr F C Boltz, rms 43 W Barry.
Dormond Jules, lab, bds 22 E Columbia.
Dornberg Wm, saloon, 91 Harmer, res same.
Dornbush Henry J (Dornbush & Kirchefer), bds Fritz Hotel.
Dornbush & Kirchefer (Henry J Dornbush, Herman A
    Kirchefer), Fresco and Scenic Artists, 22 Schmitz Blk.
    (*See page 67*.)
Dornte August, helper Penn Co, res 32 Eliza.
Dornte Carrie, bds 108 Maumee rd.
Dornte Edward, helper Penn Co, bds 108 Maumee rd.
Dornte George F, car inspr Penn Co, res 9 Ohio.
Dornte Henry, lab Penn Co, res 110 Summit.
Dornte Lena, bds 108 Maumee rd.
Dornte Wm, lab, res 108 Maumee rd.
Dorr Everett K, trav agt, res 91 E Washington.
Dorshimer Bertha M, bds 69 McCulloch.
Dorshimer Jacob A, excavator, res 69 McCulloch.
Dorwin Maggie, attendant Indiana School for Feeble-Minded
    Youth.
Doswell Alfred, florist J H Bass, bds 110 W Main.
Doswell Mrs Alfred E, cash D N Foster Furniture Co, bds
    110 W Main.
Doswell Charles A, florist City Green House, res 141 Cass.
Doswell George W, florist, 85 Calhoun, res n s W Main 1 e of
    cemetery.
Doswell Helen L, bds J H Doswell.
Doswell Henry J, asst supt Lindenwood Cemetery, bds J H
    Doswell.
Doswell John H, supt Lindenwood Cemetery, res same.
Dothage Dinah (wid Ernst), res 57 W Superior.
Dothage Sophia (wid Ernst), res 23 Wilt.
Dothage Wm, bds 57 W Superior.
Doty Amelia (wid Willis P), res 170 E Jefferson.
Doty Richard E, engineer Penn Co, res 352 Hanna.
Doty Rose, domestic 22 Ewing.
Doty Wm, engineer Penn Co, res 26 Leith.
Double John W, Propr I X L Restaurant, 29 E Main,
    res same.
Doubler Louis, res 154 John.
Doudrick Charles A, res 68 W Creighton ave.
Doudrick James S, brakeman, res 68 W Creighton ave.
Dougall Allan H (Miller & Dougall), res 323 E Wayne.
Dougall Inez, clk D H Baldwin & Co, bds 323 E Wayne.
Dougall John T, editor Journal, bds 323 E Wayne.

Dougherty, *see also Daugherty.*
Dougherty Catherine (wid Christopher), res 320 Lafayette.
Dougherty John, driver Powers & Barnett, rms 18 E Wayne.
Dougherty Samuel, trav agt, bds 39 W Washington.
Dougherty Samuel, buyer, res 12 Zollars ave.
Doughman Newton D (Swayne & Doughman), bds 320 Calhoun.
Doughty Grace D, bds 152 Force.
Doughty Wm L, clerk, res 152 Force.
Douglas Joseph H, saloon, 284 Calhoun, res 399 same.
Douglas Robert F, asst passenger and ticket agt Wabash R R, bds 399 Calhoun.
Douglass Hannah C (wid Wm B), res 262 W Jefferson.
Douglass Wm V, Real Estate, Insurance and Agent Merchants' Despatch Transportation Co, 3 Schmitz Blk, res 262 W Jefferson.
Dowie Wm A, boilermkr, res 120 Fairfield ave.
Downer George W, brakeman, res 140 High.
Downey Harry F, fireman, rms 107 Holman.
Downing Charles B, coachman 186 W Berry.
Downing Jeremiah B, bds 45 W De Wald.
Downing Myron, trav agt Fox Branch U S Baking Co, res 45 W De Wald.
Downs Charles, lab, bds 239 E Creighton ave.
Downs Mary, domestic 156 W Jefferson.
Downs Ora S, printer Gazette, rms Arlington Hotel.
Doyle Annie, opr Hoosier Mnfg Co, bds 237 Clay.
Doyle Catherine (wid Patrick), res 237 Clay.
Doyle Daniel M, trav agt G E Bursley & Co, res 47 Home ave.
Doyle James, foreman, res 198 Hanna.
Doyle James C, meats, 198 Broadway, bds same.
Doyle John H, bds 237 Madison.
Doyle John W, foreman Ft Wayne Transfer and Storage Co, res 15 Lafayette.
Doyle Joseph D, conductor, res 308 E Creighton ave.
Doyle Joseph T, mach Indiana Mach Wks, bds 237 Madison.
Doyle Mary (wid Patrick), res 300 Lafayette.
Doyle Minnie, opr Hoosier Mnfg Co, bds 237 Clay.
Doyle Thomas, engineer Penn Co, res 198 Broadway.
Doyle Thomas, patternmkr Indiana Machine Works, res 237 Madison.
Doyle Tillie, opr Hoosier Mnfg Co, bds 237 Clay.
Draeger Amelia, tailoress, bds 31 2d.
Draeger Charles, fireman, res 133 High.
Draeger Emma (wid Charles), res 31 2d.
Draeger Frank, mach hand, bds 31 2d.

Draeger Matilda, tailoress, bds 31 2d.
Drake Charles, cigarmkr G Reiter, bds 30 Calhoun.
Drake Charles A, cook J T Connolly, rms 10 Clinton.
Drake Frankie (wid George W) res 10 Clinton.
Drake Frederick J, chief clk postoffice, bds Aldine Hotel.
Drake Theodore (col'd), cook, res 35 Grand.
Drake Thomas F, engineer Penn Co, res 151 Wallace.
Draker Frank A, teamster, res 134 3d.
Draker John J, feed barn, 42 Pearl, res same.
Dratt Frederick E, tel opr, bds 36 Barr.
Dratt John A, saloon, 36 Barr, res same.
Drebert Frank, carp, res 91 W DeWald.
Dreibelbiss Abstract of Title Co The, John Dreibel-
biss Pres, Robert B Dreibelbiss Sec and Treas, Abstracts
of Title, 3 and 4 Pixley & Long Bldg.
Dreibelbiss Anna (wid John P), pgs 169 W DeWald.
Dreibelbiss Conrad W, real estate, 113 Wallace, res same.
Dreibelbiss Edward D, tel opr, res 135 W DeWald.
Dreibelbiss John, pres Dreibelbiss Abstract of Title Co, res 17
Holman.
Dreibelbiss Robert B, sec and treas Dreibelbiss Abstract of
Title Co, res 169 W DeWald.
Dreier, *see also Dreyer and Dryer.*
Dreier Lisette, domestic 240 Hoagland ave.
Dreier Wm H (Dreier & Bro), res 178 W Berry.
Dreier & Bro (Wm H Dreier), Druggists, 10 Calhoun.
Dreisbach Levi W, timekeeper, res 20 W Superior.
Drerup John, lab, 135 E Berry.
Dresch George, butcher, bds 47 Huestis ave.
Dressel Henry, car bldr, res 57 Melita.
Dressel Mary (wid George), res 158 Montgomery.
Dressel Rosina, bds 158 Montgomery.
Dressel Miss Sadie M, clk Root & Co, bds 158 Montgomery.
Dressel Valentine J, brakeman, bds 158 Montgomery.
Drew Stephen, saloon, 317 W Main, res 316 same.
Drew Wm E, carp, res 291 W Main.
Drewett George J, foreman Horton Mnfg Co, res w s Osage nr
W Main.
Drewett Wm, lab, bds s w cor Wheeler and Runnion ave.
Drewett Wm H, mach hand Horton Mnfg Co, res 371 W Main.
Dreyer, *see also Dreier and Dryer.*
Dreyer Conrad, shoemkr Charles Stellhorn, res 9 Union.
Dreyer Henry F W, helper Penn Co, res 36 Charles.
Dreyer Wm F H, helper Penn Co, res 116 Hanna.
Driftmeyer August F, watchman, res 190 W Main.
Driftmeyer Ernst, car bldr Penn Co, res 154 Madison.

John Pressler, Galvanized Iron CORNICES and Slate ROOFING, Columbia, Barr and Dock Streets.

170   R. L. POLK & CO.'S

Driftmeyer Frederick H, lab Hoffman Bros, bds 190 W Main.
Driftmeyer Henry W, electrician Ft Wayne Electric Co, bds 16 Walnut.
Driftmeyer Louisa A, bds 216 W Washington.
Drinkwitz Paul W, cigarmkr C A Berndt, res 115 Gay.
Driscoll Bridget F (wid Edward), res 70 Harrison.
Driscoll Ellen C, bds 70 Harrison.
Driscoll Edward D, bell-boy Aldine Hotel, bds 70 Harrison.
Driscoll's Hall, s e cor Calhoun and Wabash R R.
Driscoll Margaret E, dressmkr, 70 Harrison, bds same.
Driscoll Wm E, lab Ft Wayne Furniture Co, bds 70 Harrison.
Driver Carrie B, dressmkr, 101 Franklin ave, res same.
Driver George R, mach, res 101 Franklin ave.
Driver Rev John M, pastor Simpson M E Church, res 386 Calhoun.
Driver Margaret (wid Henry), bds 186 W Main.
Driver Samuel, lab Hoffman Bros, bds 164 Hoffman.
Droegemeyer Charles F, paper hanger, rms 191 Calhoun.
Droegemeyer Clara, bds 25 Nirdlinger ave.
Droegemeyer John A, clk Pixley & Co, res 25 Nirdlinger ave.
Droegemeyer Theodore F, lab, bds 25 Nirdlinger ave.
Droegemeyer Walter F, cigarmkr H W Wortmann, bds 25 Nirdlinger ave.
Droegemeyer Wm J, elevator conductor Pixley & Long bldg, bds 25 Nirdlinger ave.
Droste Christina, bds 100 W Jefferson.
Droste Diedrich, plasterer, res 100 W Jefferson.
Droste Emma, domestic 171 E Berry.
Droste Emma, bds 100 W Jefferson.
Drubenbach Henry, butcher, res 110 Van Buren.
Drubenbach Maurice, carp, res 110 Van Buren.
Drucker Elizabeth (wid Henry), res 66 W Washington.
Druhot Addie, dressmkr, bds 159 E Lewis.
Druhot Charles E, molder Bass F & M Works, bds 28 Force.
Druhot Dale, dressmkr, 159 E Lewis, res same.
Druhot Elizabeth (wid Claude), res 159 E Lewis.
Druhot Emma, opr Hoosier Mnfg Co, bds 28 Force.
Druhot Frank C, molder Bass F & M Works, res 28 Force.
Druhot John F, molder Bass F & M Works, res 140 Wallace.
Druhot Joseph C, molder Bass F & M Works, res 28 Force.
Druhot Joseph N, molder Bass F & M Works, res 3 Monroe.
Druhot May, dressmkr, bds 159 E Lewis.
Druids James, lab, res rear 382 W Main.
Drukenbrod Rufus, tinsmith S F Bowser & Co, res 118 Thomas.
Druley Louis C, confectioner, 103 Broadway, res same.
Druly Annie (wid Joseph), res 60 Chicago.

AN TRUCKING CO. **F** URNITURE and Piano
19 & 21 W. WASHINGTON. MOVING, TRANSFERING and STORAGE. TEL. 122.

FORT WAYNE DIRECTORY. 171

ond Arthur E, plumber P E Cox, bds 160 Greely.

ond Charles A, barber, bds 160 Greely.

ond Charles L, res 318 E Wayne.

ond Harry E, printer, res 314 E Wayne.

ond Sylvester, plasterer, res 160 Greely.

Michael M, calker, res 163 E Jefferson.

see also Dreier and Dreyer.

Charles R, chemist Ft Wayne Electric Co, res 150 ompson ave.

Elizabeth, domestic 517 Broadway.

Albert, lab, res 14 Lafayette.

t Charles A, bricklayer, bds Jewel House.

aefer Anna (wid Philip), bds 123 Maumee rd.

oefer Amelia, bds 336 E Wayne.

nhoefer George P (City Carriage Works), 11-13 y, res 336 E Wayne. *(See right bottom lines.)*

oefer Mary, bds 336 E Wayne.

ofer Anna, bds 11 Hough.

ng Herman, teacher Concordia College, res 441 E Wash-ton.

Jacob, clk, res 22 Ewing.

James E, collector, 1 Bank blk, bds 410 E Wayne.

Mrs Louisa, laundress Troy Laundry, bds 78 Maumee rd.

Mary M, seamstress, bds 95 W Superior.

arah J (wid James), bds 95 W Superior.

Thomas H, lab, res 102 3d.

Wm P, printer The Daily News, res 100 3d.

Mrs Savannah, res 62 Chicago.

avid M, lab, res 36 Hough.

eslle, lab Penn Co, bds 36 Hough.

n Samuel, watchman Root & Co, res 224 E Jefferson.

n A, teamster Peters Box and Lumber Co, bds 8 Clark.

& G & Co, The Mercantile Agency, F V Culbertson gr, 21 Pixley & Long Bldg.

Elizabeth E (wid John J), res 216 W Jefferson.

George L, engineer N Y, C & St L R R, bds 216 W erson.

David, carp, bds 57 Barr.

Maggie, domestic 138 W Main.

Frank, conductor, rms 40 Brackenridge.

Hugh, agt Prudential Ins Co, bds 196 Hanna,

Ernst, meats, 139 Force, res 138 same.

Alice M, bds 58 W Berry.

Charles H, removed to New York, N Y.

Emmet W, foreman Olds' Wagon Works, res s s Lake e of Old Fort.

ARCHITECTS. **WING & MAHURIN,**
41 and 42 Pixley & Long Bldg. Telephone 328.

172   R. L. POLK & CO.'S

Dunfee Harry E. cutter, bds 53 W Berry.
Dunham Charles, lab, bds 100 Montgomery.
Dunham Eugene, conductor N Y, C & St L R R, res 29 Van Buren.
Dunham Frank W, supt, res 202 E DeWald.
Dunian Thomas E, meter tester, res 28 Wilt.
Dunker Caroline, bds Hoffman House.
Dunker Wilhelmina, bds Hoffman House.
Dunlap Harvey, miller H W Bond, bds 298 E Wayne.
Dunlap Mrs J C, bds 103 Maumee rd.
Dunlap Margaret (wid Collar), res 298 E Wayne.
Dunlap Wm, teamster, res s e cor Lafayette and E Columbia.
Dunlop Andrew W, lumber inspector, res 313 Hanna.
Dunn Maggie, bds 6 Brandriff.
Dunn Robert, coachman F J Hayden.
Dunn Wm, clk, bds 121 W Main.
Dunn Wm, mach, res 6 Brandriff.
Dunne Miss Kathleen H, Propr Parlor Bath Rooms, 49 50-51 Pixley & Long Bldg, res same. (*See right bottom lines.*)
Dupont Emma, domestic 283 W Wayne.
Durbin Bertha, domestic 27 E Washington.
Durbin Robert D, brakeman, res 149 Holman.
Durbrow Charles W, teamster C F Muhler & Son, res 2 W Superior.
Durbrow Lydia (wid James), res 22 Calhoun.
Durfee Calvin, clk, bds 77 Douglas ave.
Durfee George A, trav agt The B W Skelton Co, res 39 W Butler.
Durfee Sarah A, furnishing goods, 258 Calhoun, res 77 Douglas.
Durfee Wm R, clk S A Durfee, res 77 Douglas ave.
Durnell Addie, teacher, bds 29 Duryea.
Durnell Alfred S, tinner Penn Co, res 294 E Jefferson.
Durnell Chester, engineer Penn Co, res 49 W DeWald.
Durnell Herman A, engineer Penn Co, res 177 Calhoun.
Durnell Jane (wid George), res 60 Burgess.
Durnell Louis, res 29 Duryea.
Durnell Luke, gardener, e s Spy Run ave 1 n of brewery, res same.
Durnell M Henry, fireman Penn Co, bds 29 Duryea.
Dustman George G, woodworker Anthony Wayne Mnfg Co, bds 81 Hayden.
Duval Catherine (wid Nicholas), bds 175 E Wayne.
Dwelly Charles, mach Wabash R R, res 20 McClellan.
Dwenger Rt Rev Joseph, D D, Bishop of the Roman Catholic Diocese of Ft Wayne, res 172 Clinton.

Dwyer Anna, laundress Rich Hotel.
Dyche Alvina L (wid George), bds 90 E Wayne.
Dyer Thomas F, engineer Penn Co, res 273 W Jefferson.
Dyer Thomas W, feeder Ft Wayne Newspaper Union, bds 273 W Jefferson.
Dyke Anton, lab Penn Co, res 103 John.
Dynes James F, painter Daniel Hoffman, bds 302 E Creighton.

H

Eagen Maggie, domestic 320 Calhoun.
Eagle Warren, carp, res n s Howell 2 w of Runnion ave.
Eakin, see also Aiken.
Eakin James W, lab Penn Co, res 112 E Creighton ave.
Eakin Margaret A (wid Joseph S), bds 186 W DeWald.
Eakin Rena M, bds 112 W Creighton ave.
Earl Martha, res 166 Hayden.
Early Michael, spokedriver, res 9 Ohio.
Earnest U Grant, clk Aldine Hotel.
Easley Charles P, carp J O Brown, res 12 Marion.
East End Bottling Works, The Herman Berghoff Brewing Co Proprs, cor E Washington and Wabash ave. (See back cover.)
East German School, n w cor Harmer and Jefferson.
Eastwood Harry C, removed to Logansport, Ind.
Ebel, see also Abel.
Ebel Charles, brewer, bds n w cor Edna and Spy Run ave.
Ebel Louis F, painter Olds' Wagon Works, res 151 Gay.
Eberhardt Wm, molder, res 125 Cass.
Eberle John, teamster Peters' Box and Lumber Co, res 208 St Mary's ave.
Eberlein Mrs Sophie, res 86 E Jefferson.
Eberley Anna M (wid Daniel), res 40 5th.
Eberley Edith, bds 40 5th.
Ebert, see also Hebert.
Ebert Adam, lab Horton Mnfg Co, res 127 Franklin ave.
Ebert Douglas F, brakeman, bds 219 Lafayette.
Ebert John, fireman, res 64 Boone.
Eberwein Christian, res 96 Walton ave.
Ebey Mollie (wid Oliver P), bds 225 W Main.
Ebner Caroline, bds 145 E Lewis.
Ebner Froney G, tailoress John Rabus, bds 145 E Lewis.
Ebner George, car builder Penn Co, res 39 Force.

13

Ebner Jacob J, lab Penn Co, res 145 E Lewis.
Ebner Kate, opr Hoosier Mnfg Co, bds 39 Force.
Ebner Lorenz, oiler Penn Co, res 145 E Lewis.
Ebner Verona, dressmkr Pauline Schiemer, bds 145 E Lewis.
Echelberry George, lab J C Peters, res 10 Short.
Echelberry Wm, lab, res 85 Barthold.
Echinger John, market stall No 94, res Adams twp.
Echrich Peter, helper Bass F and M Works, bds 7 Smith.
Eckard Ernest, lab J A Koehler, res w s Lafayette s of city limits.
Eckard Matilda, domestic 167 Clinton.
Eckart Anna, bds 91 E Wayne.
Eckart Block, s e cor Main and Harrison.
Eckart Carrie, bds 91 E Wayne.
Eckart David S, clk, bds 19 W Williams.
Eckart Frederick, Meat Market and Pork Packer, 35 W Main, res 91 E Wayne.
Eckart Frederick jr, mngr Eckart's packing house, res 442 W Main.
Eckart Henry, meats, 100 W Main, bds 91 E Wayne.
Eckart Jesse H, bartndr Heilbroner & Brown, bds 19 W Williams.
Eckart John C (Eckart & O'Connor), res 19 W Williams.
Eckart John C jr, trav agt F E Purcell & Co, bds 19 W Williams.
Eckart Matilda, bds 91 E Wayne.
Eckart's Packing House, Frederick Eckart Jr Mngr, 474 W Main.
Eckart Wm E, cigarmkr, res 163 E Washington.
Eckart & O'Connor (John C Eckart, Bernard O'Connor), skating rink, s e cor Main and Fulton.
Eckelburger Samuel, lab, res 143 Taber.
Eckels Elizabeth E, bds 57 Riverside ave.
Eckels Harry C, inspr C U Tel Co, res 55 Riverside ave.
Eckels James M, carp Rhinesmith & Simonson, res 57 Riverside ave.
Eckels Samuel, lab, res 16 Zollars ave.
Eckels Willis J, bkkpr Hoffman Bros, res 115 Cass.
Eckenrod David N, foreman, res 136 Wells.
Eckenrod Myra, bds 136 Wells.
Ecker, see also Acker, Aker and Eicher.
Ecker Louisa, domestic 84 E Berry.
Eckerle Albert, lab C L Centlivre Brewing Co, res n w cor Edna and Spy Run ave.
Eckermann, see also Ackermann.
Eckermann Martin, lab, res rear 88 Madison.

Eckhart Anton, lab, res rear 19 Walnut.
Eckhart Gustav, lab Olds' Wagon Works, res s e cor Fisher and Thomas.
Eckler Charles, hostler, bds 15 Pearl.
Eckley Eliza A (wid Peter), bds 24 W Jefferson.
Eckrich Peter, lab Bass F and M Works, res 7 Smith.
Edelman John J, lab Penn Co, res 431 Lafayette.
Edgerton Alfred P, res 154 W Berry.
Edgerton Clara, bds 87 W Wayne.
Edgerton Clement W, bicycles, 57 W Main, bds 87 W Wayne.
Edgerton Dixon (Bettinger & Edgerton), res 44 Archer ave.
Edgerton Edward C, bds 87 W Wayne.
Edgerton Joseph K, Real Estate and Agricultural Implements, 57 W Main, res 87 W Wayne.
Edgerton Josephine, bds 87 W Wayne.
Edington Calvin, lab, bds C Scotton.
Edington Dee, agt Singer Mnfg Co, rms 88 Wells.
Edison Mutual Telegraph Co, Charles G Harris Mngr, Wayne Hotel.
Edmunds Frank W (Edmunds & Co), bds 131 Jackson.
Edmunds Harry M (Edmunds & Co) bds 131 Jackson.
Edmunds Mary (wid James), res 131 Jackson.
Edmunds Minnie, clk A Goodman, bds 21 Cass.
Edmunds Wm, clk S Bash & Co, res 21 Cass.
Edmunds & Co (Frank W and Harry M Edmunds), electrical supplies, 18 Schmitz Block.
Edsall Clarence W, lawyer, res s s Maumee rd 1 w of Walton ave.
Edsall Jasper N, lab Rhinesmith & Simonson, res 61 Oliver.
Edsall Samuel G, wood worker Anthony Wayne Mnfg Co, res 81 Hayden.
Edsall Simon, farmer, res s s New Haven ave nr Edsall ave.
Edsall Tecumseh, brakeman, bds 61 Oliver.
Edsall Wm, clk Root & Co, bds Maumee rd nr Walton ave.
Edwards Charles W, removed to Cincinnati, O.
Edwards Daniel, foreman Penn Co, res 229 W Creighton ave.
Edwards Emery, cabtmkr Ft Wayne Organ Co, bds 28 Chicago.
Edwards Frank, painter L O Hull, res 70 Pontiac.
Edwards Jennie, bds 229 W Creighton ave.
Edwards John, blksmith, bds Riverside Hotel.
Effert Rose, domestic 89 W Berry.
Eggemann Conrad, checker Penn Co, res 52 John.
Eggemann Frederick, lab, res 73 Oakley.
Eggemann John W, messenger, bds 20 W Jefferson.
Eggemann Peter J, shoemkr, 17 E Main, res 20 W Jefferson.
Eggeman Tillie, bds 20 W Jefferson.

Robert Spice, Pumps, Pipe, Hose, Fittings and Brass Goods
48 WEST MAIN and 11 PEARL STS.

176   R. L. POLK & CO.'S

Eggimann Charles F, molder Ft Wayne Electric Co, bds 74 Pontiac.

Eggimann Peter J, clk Nickel Plate R R, res 209 High.

Egle Warren, carp, res n s Howell 1 west of Runnion ave.

Ehinger Adolph, plasterer, res 73 Riverside ave.

Ehinger Amelia, bds 176 E Lewis.

Ehinger Charles, lab, res 148 High.

Ehinger Charles C, lab, bds 148 High.

Ehinger Ella, domestic 173 Madison.

Ehinger Emma M, bds 112 Clay.

Ehinger Frank O, bkkpr Kerr-Murray Mnfg Co, bds 112 Clay.

Ehinger John, gardener, res e s Edsall ave 1 n of New Haven.

Ehinger Joseph, helper Wabash R R, res 137 3d.

Ehinger Louisa (wid Roman), res 176 E Lewis.

Ehinger Mary, bds 176 E Lewis.

Ehinger Othmar, car bldr Penn Co, res 112 Clay.

Ehinger Urban, polisher, bds 61 Laselle.

Ehle August N, Cigar Mnfr, 178 Broadway, res 180 same.

Ehle Edward T, bricklayer, res 306 West Washington.

Ehle Ernest A, Brick and Stone Contractor, 529 S Broadway, res same. (See page 67.)

Ehle Frank, cigarmkr A N Ehle, bds 180 Broadway.

Ehle Frederick E, lab Penn Co, res 27 Rockhill.

Ehle Henry C, bricklayer, res 73 Stophlet.

Ehle Michael, res 224 W Creighton ave.

Ehle Sophie M, bds 27 Rockhill.

Ehrhardt Leonard, butcher F Eckart, res 49 Archer ave.

Ehrman Charles F (Ehrman & Geller), res 175 Van Buren.

Ehrman Coleman (Ehrman & Son), res 64 E Main.

Ehrman Edward J (Ehrman & Son), bds 64 E Main.

Ehrman John W M, car bldr Penn Co, res cor New Haven and Bird aves.

Ehrman Michael, lab Penn Co, res 24 Hoffman.

Ehrman Wm H, stereotyper, bds 64 E Main.

Ehrman & Geller (Charles F Ehrman, Charles C Geller), barbers, 12 W Main.

Ehrman & Son (Coleman and Edward J), saloon, 64 E Main.

Ehrmann Alvina, bds 153 Taylor.

Ehrmann Amelia, opr S M Foster, bds 132 Greely.

Ehrmann Caroline (wid Mattice), res 132 Greely.

Ehrmann Caroline, laundress Troy Steam Laundry, bds 153 Taylor.

Ehrmann Charles, blksmith, 149 W Main, res 339 W Jefferson.

Ehrmann Charles W, blksmith Charles Ehrmann, bds 339 W Jefferson.

Ehrmann C Frederick, collarmkr A Racine, res 36 4th.

Ehrmann Frederick, lab, bds 42 Elm.
Ehrmann George J, helper City Carriage Works, bds 42 Elm.
Ehrmann John H, teamster, res 153 Taylor.
Ehrmann Michael, mach Penn Co, res 17 Taylor.
Ehrmann Minnie, bds 132 Greely.
Ehrmann Wm C, lab Ft Wayne Furniture Co, bds 153 Taylor.
Eichel Andrew, brewer C L Centlivre Brewing Co, res 50 Randolph.
Eichel Charles, butcher Edwin Rich, res 497 E Wayne.
Eichel John, cook, res 497 E Wayne.
Eichelberger Samuel, sweeper Penn Co, bds 123 Taber.
Eicher, see also Acker, Aker and Ecker.
Eicher Gottlieb, res 108 Hoffman.
Eicher Gustave. driver, bds 121 Calhoun.
Eicher Ida, starcher Troy Steam Laundry, bds 108 Hoffman.
Eicher Mary, starcher Troy Steam Laundry, bds 108 Hoffman.
Eichmeyer Charles L, carp Penn Co, res 33 Duryea.
Eickhoff Bernard H, fitter Ft Wayne Electric Co, res 72 4th.
Eickhoff Charles A, foreman Ft Wayne Electric Co, res 270 Webster.
Eifel John, lab, res n e cor Gay and Creighton ave.
Eikenbary Mary, cook 93 W Wayne.
Einsiedel Andrew, blacksmith Olds' Wagon Works, res 69 Stophlet.
Einsiedel Frederick, lab Kerr-Murray Mnfg Co, bds 69 Stophlet.
Einsiedel Michael, lab Kerr-Murray Mnfg Co, res 194 Taylor.
Eisenhut Emma, nurse 280 W Wayne.
Eisennacher Frederick, carp, res 197 Taylor.
Eisenring Rev Thomas, chaplain St Joseph's Hospital, res same.
Eising Henry, molder Bass F & M Works, bds 73 Force.
Eising John, carp Penn Co. res 73 Force.
Eising John jr, lab, bds 73 Force.
Eising Maggie, opr Hoosier Mnfg Co, bds 73 Force.
Eisler Catherine, domestic Wayne Hotel.
Eiter August, coremkr Indiana Machine Works, bds 22 Force.
Eiter Frank, molder Kerr-Murray Mnfg Co, bds 22 Force.
Eiter Henry, molder, res 103 Fairfield ave.
Eiter Joseph, molder, bds 22 Force.
Eiter Peter, lab, res 22 Force.
Eitsinger Andrew, molder, bds n s Winter 2 s of Pontiac.
Eitsinger George, molder Bass F & M Works, res 53 Gay.
Eitsinger Rosa (wid George), res n s Winter 2 s of Pontiac.
Eix August, city scavenger, res 53 Madison.
Eix August F, blksmith, res 197 Hanna.
Eix Dora C, domestic 99 E Main.
Eix Ernst, helper, res 159 Hayden.

Eix Frederick, sexton Trinity Episcopal Church, bds 60 W Washington.

Eix Henry, helper, bds 197 Hanna.

Eix John, lab Penn Co, bds 119 Hanna.

Eix Minnie, bds 197 Hanna.

Eix Sophia (wid August), res 60 W Washington.

Elbert Anthony, boilermkr, bds 40 Pritchard.

Elder Cynthia, seamstress, bds 138 Jackson.

Eldred Danford P, engineer Penn Co, res 24 Baker.

Eldridge Anna, clk Troy Steam Laundry, bds 22 Harrison.

Eldridge Rev George N, pastor Wayne Street M E Church, res 195 W Wayne.

Eldridge Lottie, clk Troy Steam Laundry, rms 55 W Main.

Eldridge Nettie, clk Troy Steam Laundry, rms 55 W Main.

Electric Club, 14 Bass blk.

Elion Charles J, molder Bass F & M Works, res 55 Oliver.

Ell Adam J, lab, bds 22 Hough.

Ell George F, lab, res 22 Hough.

Ellenwood Bertie A, bds 230 Francis.

Ellenwood Clifton A, conductor, res 134 E Lewis.

Ellenwood Cloyd C, blksmith Ft Wayne Electric Co, res 71½ Laselle.

Ellenwood George W, lab Penn Co, res 127 Madison.

Ellenwood Horace D, engineer, res 228 Francis.

Ellenwood O Rodney, engineer Penn Co, bds 228 Francis.

Ellenwood Warren, brakeman, bds 228 Francis.

Ellerman Frederick H, mach Penn Co, res 55 E DeWald.

Ellert Benoit (Walter & Ellert), res 135 Lafayette.

Ellert Louis A, apprentice Walter & Ellert, bds 135 Lafayette.

Elligsen Henry J, bds 19 Clark.

Elliott Benjamin H, conductor, res 300 E Creighton ave.

Elliott Enoch W (col'd), engineer Peters Box and Lumber Co, res 153 High.

Elliott Miss Leota M, bds 57 W Butler.

Elliott L Dell, conductor N Y, C & St L R R, res 66 Boone.

Elliott Margaret J (wid George W), bds 66 Boone.

Elliott Mary E, cook Jewel House.

Elliott Nelson, bds 57 W Butler.

Elliott Samuel B, carp, res 57 W Butler.

Ellis Robert H, carp, res 110 Gay.

Ellison George R, driver R Steger & Co, bds 13 Monroe.

Ellison Jacob L, carp, res w s Park ave 1 s of canal feeder.

Ellison James, farmer, res n s Bluffton rd nr Poor farm.

Ellison John, carp, bds J L Ellison.

Ellison John T, lab, bds 13 Monroe.

Ellison Richard E, engineer, res 13 Monroe.

ı Thomas E, Lawyer, 23–24 Bank Blk, res 167 W
yne.
ı Stock Farm, Rockhill Bros & Fleming proprs, nr
lenwood Cemetery, ¼ mile w of city limits.
ld Frederick A, clk Penn Co, bds 30 E DeWald.
ılbert, vegetables, market stall 68, res n s St Joseph
of city limits.
·ge W (Ely & Dittoe), res 81 Griffith.
Dittoe (George W Ely, Albert J Dittoe), Grocers,
Calhoun.
ıse, domestic 46 W Wayne.
German Lutheran School, n e cor Wilt and Union.
Lutheran Church, s s Jefferson nr Union.
Ann (wid Lewis), res 336 Broadway.
dward J, painter, res 193 Calhoun.
ıde F (Eme & Son), res 175 E Wayne.
ıstant J, fireman, res 40 St Mary's ave.
ius, carp, bds 57 Barr.
ius J (Eme & Son), res 93 Montgomery.
ıis J, carp, res s e cor Jesse and Runnion ave.
Son (Claude F and Julius J), real estate, 1 Foster blk.
August, watchman, res 74 Walton ave.
Emma, opr Hoosier Mnfg Co, bds 74 Walton ave.
Frederick, caller, bds 74 Walton ave.
Jacob, lab, res 38 Smith.
John, bartndr M S Wickliffe, bds 28 Columbia.
Kate, opr Hoosier Mnfg Co, bds 74 Walton ave.
Peter, gluer, bds 28 Chicago.
Preston, plasterer, res n s Prospect ave nr St Joseph

Almeron, driver, res 35 Elizabeth.
lward, paper hanger, rms 191 Calhoun.
ım, car bldr Penn Co, res 141 Montgomery.
rederick, carp, res 20 Ohio.
ına E, bds 73 E Berry.
omas B, propr Ft Wayne Transfer & Storage Co, 17
yette, res 73 E Berry.
lour Mills, John Orff, propr, nr W Main Street bridge.
Line (Fast Freight), Angus McPherson, Agt,
ıurt.
enry, lab, res 183 Madison.
mmett V, deputy prosecuting attorney, Court House,
) W Washington.
ım, filer, bds 150 Suttenfield.
ı, candymkr, bds 150 Suttenfield.
ı, lab, res 9 Caroline.

Ench Mathias, res 150 Suttenfield.
Ench Mathias jr, lab, bds 150 Suttenfield.
Engelbeck Louisa, domestic 103 E Washington.
Engelbrecht Henry B, carp Frederick Kraft, res 32 Union.
Engelking Charles H, clk Gross & Pellens, bds 172 Ewing.
Engelking Eliza A (wid Henry D), res 172 Ewing.
Engelking Frederick, lab Pottlitzer Bros, bds 148 Broadway.
Engelking F Diedrich, lab, res 148 Broadway.
Engelking Henry, saw-filer, res s e cor Spring and St Mary's ave
Engelking Louise (wid Henry), res 125 High.
Engelking Sophia, domestic cor Montgomery and Hamilton.
Engelking Wm H, lab, bds 172 Ewing.
Engels George, cooper, bds 46 Columbia.
Engine House No 1, n e cor Court and Berry.
Engine House No 2, s s Wallace 6 e of Lafayette.
Englart Catherine, domestic 143 W Wayne.
Engle Alexander, conductor, res 11 Harmer.
Engle Edward J, mach, bds 35 Taylor.
Engle Emma M, opr Hoosier Mnfg Co, bds 35 Taylor.
Engle Gertrude, opr S M Foster, bds 35 Taylor.
Engle John F, lab Wm Moellering & Co, res w s Piqua ave nr
    Rudisill ave.
Engle Seldon D, photographer, res 166 Madison.
Engle Wm, cabinetmkr, res 229 W De Wald.
Engle Wm, engineer, res 35 Taylor.
Englemeyer Samuel, carp, bds 15 Pearl.
Englert Carrie, opr Hoosier Mnfg Co, bds 49 Taylor.
Englert Lena, opr Hoosier Mnfg Co, bds 49 Taylor.
Englert Louisa (wid George), bds 49 Taylor.
Englert Wm, lab Penn Co, bds 49 Taylor.
English Maggie, dressmkr, bds 223 W Superior.
English Wm H, brakeman, res 119 Force.
English Wm J, brakeman, res 223 W Superior.
Enright Mary E, clk J B White, bds 102 Webster.
Enslen Frank M, fireman Penn Co, bds 493 Calhoun.
Enslen Wm M, physician, 286 Calhoun, rms 493 same.
Ensley Mrs Ella, domestic Indiana School for Feeble-Minded
    Youth.
Entemann Christian, Saloon, 13 E Main, res 149 W
    Berry.
Entemann Ernest E, cashr Mergel & Frey, bds 149 W Berry.
Entradacker Sebastian, car builder Penn Co, res 72 Hayden.
Enz J Frederick, lab Bass F and M Works, bds n e cor Win-
    ter and Pontiac.
Enz Wm, lab Bass F and M Works, bds n e cor Winter and
    Pontiac.

L. O. HULL, Paints, Oils, Varnishes and Glass at 90 Calhoun Street.

FORT WAYNE DIRECTORY. 181

Epple Christian, mach hd Ft Wayne Electric Co, res 40 Taylor.
Epple David, lab Peters Box and Lumber Co, bds 40 Taylor.
Epple Gottlieb, grocer, 184 Fairfield ave, res 188 same.
Epple Gottlieb jr, lab, bds 188 Fairfield ave.
Epple Rose (wid John), res 40 Allen.
Epple Wm, cabinetmkr Ft Wayne Organ Co, bds 40 Taylor.
Eppstein Babette (wid Maier), bds 54 W Berry.
Equitable Life Assurance Society, of New York City, Argo & Buck Genl Agents, 52 Calhoun. (*See back cover.*)
Equitable Life Insurance Company, of Iowa, C M Russell District Agt, rm 2 Bass Blk. (*See page 69.*)
Erhardt Leonard, butcher, res 49 Archer ave.
Erickson C J Emil, carver Peters' Box and Lumber Co, bds 43 Miner.
Erickson James E, conductor, res 335 Harrison.
Erickson John, foreman Peters' Box and Lumber Co, res 43 Miner.
Erion Jacob, coremkr Bass F and M Works, res 228 John.
Ernest Andrew, lab, res 61 Grand.
Ernest George, bds James B Crowel.
Ernest Peter, lab, res 26 Gladstone ave.
Erni Louis, sawyer George Jaap, res 108 Clinton.
Ernsting Charles, res 16 Clark.
Ernsting Charles H jr, grocer, 121 Wells, res same.
Ernsting Christian, helper Kerr-Murray Mnfg Co, res 62 Williams.
Ernsting Wm, lineman Jenney Electric L and P Co, bds 16 Clark.
Erping Henry, lab Bass F and M Works, res 354 E Lewis.
Ersig Dorothy (wid Wm), res 129 Monroe.
Ersig Edith E, teacher, bds 129 Monroe.
Ersig Emma H, teacher, bds 129 Monroe.
Ersig Wm A, horseshoer Wm Geary, res 123 Wilt.
Ertel Bernard, res 39 Laselle.
Ertel Elizabeth (wid George), bds 38 John.
Ertel George (Ertel & Menefee), res 53 John.
Ertel Henry, switchman, bds w s Lillie 1 e of Milan.
Ertel Valentine, lab, bds 85 Putnam.
Ertel Walter, lab, res 85 Putnam.
Ertel & Menefee (George Ertel, Charles M Menefee), Founders, Mnfrs and Inventors of the Duplex Cistern Top and Automatic Sewer Trap, 135-137 Oliver.
Ertle John H, barber, 377 E Washington, bds 325 E Wayne.
Ertle Lizzie, domestic 325 E Wayne.
Ertle Louis, watchman Old Fort Mnfg Co, bds 163 Erie.

Ertle Louis B, lab Old Fort Mnfg Co, bds 163 Erie.
Ervin Joseph F, bus mngr The Sentinel, res 202 W Wayne.
Erwin Belle, seamstress, rms 72 Douglas ave.
Erwin Maria (wid Joseph T), res 211 Fairfield ave.
Erwin Mary C, stenographer, bds 211 Fairfield ave.
Erwin Richard, carp, res s s Rebecca 1 e of G R & I R R.
Esmond Z Titus, removed to Denver, Col.
Esselstein Mrs Anna, laundress Troy Steam Laundry, res 14
    Cass.
Esselstein Minerva (wid Levi), bds 14 Cass.
Essig Adam P, res 39 E Superior.
Essig Charles O, mngr Ft Wayne District Tel Co, res 83 E
    Berry.
Essig George A, barber J B Fink, res 558 Calhoun.
Essig George P, clk Indiana Installment Co, bds 25 W Wash-
    ington.
Estelauer Mary, domestic 57 Maple ave.
Estep Robert, lab Artificial Ice Co, bds Riverside Hotel.
Estry Albert G, conductor, res 432 Broadway.
Estry Elwood T, conductor, res 60 Thomas.
Etchey Francis H, clk John F Curtice, bds 37 Wefel.
Etchey Frank, carp, res 37 Wefel.
Etchey Lizzie, domestic 493 Calhoun.
Etchey Michael, clk F M Smith & Co, res 39 Wefel.
Ethun Egbert, lab Bass F & M Works, res 263 Smith.
Etsell Minnie (col'd), bds 253 St Mary's ave.
Etzel Mary, dressmkr, bds 173 W Jefferson.
Etzold Anna M, tailoress, bds 110 Webster.
Etzold Clara A, tailoress John Rabus, bds 110 Webster.
Etzold Emma M, tailoress John Rabus, bds 110 Webster.
Etzold Frederick, messenger Postoffice, bds 110 Webster.
Etzold Gustav, mach hand Indiana Machine Works, bds 46
    Douglas ave.
Etzold Henry, shoemkr, 110 Webster, res same.
Etzold Minnie, seamstress, bds 46 Douglas ave.
Etzold Wm, grinder, res 46 Douglas ave.
Etzold Wm C, bkkpr Horton Mnfg Co, bds 110 Webster.
Eureka Club, 142 Calhoun.
Eureka Hall, 43 W Superior.
Evangelical Association Church, n e cor Clinton and Holman.
Evangelical Lutheran Zion's Church, s w cor Creighton ave
    and Force.
Evangelical Lutheran Zion's School, s e cor Hanna and Creigh-
    ton ave.
Evans Amos S, pres Hoosier Mnfg Co, res San Jose, Cal.
Evans Anna C (wid Josiah), res 241 Webster.

Geo. E. Johnson, DENTIST, 74 Calhoun Street.
Res., 188 W. Berry St.

FORT WAYNE DIRECTORY. 183

Evans Barbara B (wid John K), res 110 W Superior.
Evans Bertrand W, clk, bds 241 Webster.
Evans Block, s s Berry bet Calhoun and Clinton.
Evans Burnett B, res 66 W Main.
Evans Edward M, printer, bds 29 Hanna.
Evans Edwin, res 174 W Wayne.
Evans Frank D, clk Meyer & Nieman, bds 29 Hanna.
Evans George P, sec Hoosier Mnfg Co, bds 126 E Main.
Evans Gordon M, clk, bds 241 Webster.
Evans Henry J, millwright, res 107 Wilt.
Evans Ira P, clk, res 109 W Washington.
Evans Irving D, draughtsman Kerr-Murray Mnfg Co, bds 241
    Webster.
Evans Jenkin S, train despatcher Nickel Plate R R, bds 164
    W Berry.
Evans John M, bkkpr, bds 241 Webster.
Evans John P, treas Hoosier Mnfg Co, res 126 E Main.
Evans Nathan, bds 200 W Berry.
Evans Oliver F, with Hoosier Mnfg Co, res 95 E Berry.
Evans Regina C (wid Joseph A), res 29 Hanna.
Evans Riley B, conductor, res 40 E Williams.
Evans Wm A, packer Carnahan & Co, bds 174 W Wayne.
Evarts Sarah M (wid Gilbert), tailor, 140 High, res same.
Evarts Charles E, photogr F R Barrows, bds 104 Wells.
Evarts George C, candymkr, bds 104 Wells.
Evarts Nancy (wid Gilbert C), res 104 Wells.
Everett Charles E, General Agt Union Central Life
    Insurance Co of Cincinnati, O, 2d floor Old National
    Bank Bldg, res 93 W Main. (*See front cover.*)
Everett Wm, brakeman, res 65 Wells.
Everetts Perry, street car driver, bds 290 Calhoun.
Evers Henry, mason, res 199 John.
Evers Herman J, bds 323 Hanna.
Evers John, mason, res 323 Hanna.
Evers Louise, domestic 205 W Jefferson.
Every Helen E, teacher, bds 50 W Washington.
Ewald Albert P, clk, bds 63 Charles.
Ewing Aaron, lab, res 19 Charles.
Ewing Block, s w cor Harrison and Main.
Ewing Eliza (wid James), bds 17 Brackenridge.
Ewing Mary C (wid George W), res 115 W Main.
Exener Robert, lab Penn Co, bds e s Holton ave 4 s of Creigh-
    ton ave.
Eysen Catherine (wid Anthony), res 281 Hanna.

F

Fackler Caroline, domestic 441 E Washington.

Fackler Mary, domestic 75 W Berry.

Fahling, *see also Fehling.*

Fabling Frederick, teamster Peters Box & Lumber Co, bds 8 Clark.

Fahling Frederick, watchman Summit City Soap Co, res 45 Maumee rd.

Fahling Henry C, woodwkr Anthony Wayne Mnfg Co, bds 42 Harmer.

Fahlsing Augustus K, boilermkr Ft Wayne Iron Works, res 87 Barthold.

Fahlsing Charles W, clk D C Fisher, bds 47 Harmer.

Fahlsing Charles W, clk L Wolf & Co, bds 362 E Wayne.

Fahlsing Christina (wid Frederick), bds 87 Barthold.

Fahlsing Frederick, helper Olds' Wagon Works, res 9 Sturgis.

Fahlsing Frederick G, messenger G R & I R R, bds 9 Sturgis.

Fahlsing John W, clk M L Frankenstein, bds 9 Sturgis.

Fahlsing Minnie, opr C U Tel Co, bds 47 Harmer.

Fahlsing Otto, clk, bds 47 Harmer.

Fahlsing Wm C F, bailiff Circuit Court, res 47 Harmer.

Fahnestock James W, bkkpr The Wayne, bds 169 W Jefferson.

Fair Joseph, lab, res n s Wagner 7 w of St Joseph River.

Fairbank Clark, Genl Agt Penn Mutual Life Insurance Co, 19 Court, res 115 E Berry. (*See left top lines.*)

Fairchild Fannie (wid George), shirtmkr P G Kuttner, res e s Barr bet Holman and Montgomery.

Fairfield Cyrus K, real estate, 7 Bell ave, res same.

Fairfield George, mach, bds 311 W Jefferson.

Falconer John, blksmith Ft Wayne Iron Works, res 71 Williams.

Falconer Richard, mach Wabash R R, bds 71 W Williams.

Falk Charles (Charles Falk & Co), res 181 W Berry.

Falk Charles & Co (Charles Falk), whol notions, 23 W Main.

Falk Leopold (Falk & Lamley), res 181 W Berry.

Falk & Lamley (Leopold Falk, Moses Lamley), Distillers' Agents and Wholesale Dealers in Wines, Liquors, Etc, 17 E Columbia.

Falkaeng Wm, lab, bds 20 Jones.

Fallon J Frank, switchman N Y, C & St L R R, bds 20 N Cass.

Fallon Peter J, clk N Y, C & St L R R, res 23 W Lewis.

Falls David M, tallow renderer, e end Dwenger ave 1 mile e of city limits, res 163 W Wayne.
Falls Jennie, retoucher H A Jarrard, bds 86 Calhoun.
Fally Wm W, engineer, res 66 Elm.
Falvey Daniel, boilermkr, res 42 Boone.
Fanz August J, lab Penn Co, res 128 Madison.
Fark Edward, lab Penn Co, res 74 John.
Farland Albert C, conductor, bds 40 E 5th.
Farnan Miss Mary, dancing teacher Foster's Blk, bds 305 Lafayette.
Farnan Owen, flagman N Y, C & St L R R, res 305 Lafayette.
Farnan Owen, heater Bass F and M Works, res 367 Force.
Farra Joseph, lab Louis Diether & Bro, res 21 Wagner.
Farra Julius V, carp, res 63 E Superior.
Farrall John, insurance agt, res 19 St Michael ave.
Farrell Thomas, engineer, bds Lake Shore Hotel.
Farrington David A, removed to Nashville, Tenn.
Farrita Joseph (Manocchio, Farrita & Co), bds 228 Calhoun.
Faulks Norve P, foreman, res e s Barr 2 s of Williams.
Faust Adam, res 5 Union.
Faust Albert E, driver, bds 121 Calhoun.
Faust Henry, bartndr A M Mosshammer, bds 54 E Main.
Faust John, lab, bds Jacob Baker.
Faust Joseph, driver, bds 121 Calhoun.
Favery Catherine M, dressmkr Mrs G J Stier, bds 92 Madison.
Fay, *see also Fey.*
Fay Benjamin, lab C Scotton, bds same.
Fay Benjamin J, engineer South Wayne Brick Co, bds n s Scott ave 4 w of Broadway.
Fay Catherina, waiter Hoffman House.
Fay John, switchman, bds 18 McClellan.
Fay Levi, foreman, bds 105 Barr.
Fay Montford W, broker, 138 Calhoun, rms same.
Fayler George, propr Riverside Hotel, 2 Cass.
Fears Henry B (col'd), lab, res 31 Pearl.
Feasor Amos, teamster, res 60 Riverside ave.
Federspiel John B, mach hand, res 145 Shawnee ave.
Fee Frank F, Hardwood Lumber, 181 W Wayne, res same.
Fee Thomas W, res 57 Cass.
Feeny John H, tinner, res 81 W Washington.
Feeny Miranda, dressmaker, 81 W Washington, bds same.
Fehling, *see also Fahling.*
Fehling August, driver, res 103 Cass.
Fehling Frederick, clk Roembke & Hahnhaus, res s w cor Shawnee and Grace aves.
Feichter Jacob H, carp, bds 2 Zollars ave.

Feipel Frank, lab, res 164 Harmer.
Feist Louis J, tailor, 226 Lafayette, res same.
Feistkorn Charles, clk D N Foster Furniture Co, res 117 Taylor.
Felger Delia, opr Samuel M Foster, bds 44 W 3d.
Felger Elizabeth (wid Peter), res 173 W Jefferson.
Felger Emma, domestic 31 Wagner.
Felger Etta, opr Samuel M Foster, bds 299 E Washington.
Felger Rosanna (wid Jacob), bds 299 E Washington.
Felker Edward, driver, bds 94 W Main.
Felker Elizabeth J, bds 313 W Jefferson.
Felker Forest J, mason, res 12 Clark.
Fellows Jennie, dressmkr, bds 35 W Main.
Felon Peter J, bkkpr, rms 23 W Lewis.
Felt Adolph, carp Wm Doenges, bds 206 Francis.
Felt Franklin H, teamster, res n e cor Lafayette and 7th.
Felt John, painter, bds 206 Francis.
Felt Warren D, teamster, res 68 Putnam.
Felts Charles A, brakeman, res 23 Erie.
Felts George F, county supt of schools, 11 Bass blk, res 30 Lake
    avenue.
Felts H Wm, fireman Penn Co, res 60 Pontiac.
Felts Mrs Lillian, res 39 Grand.
Fenker Herman, car bldr Penn Co, res s s Chestnut 4 w of
    Lumbard.
Fenker Rudolph G, car bldr Penn Co, res w s Lumbard 2 n of
    Chestnut.
Fenson Walter, removed to Huntington, Ind.
Fenton Katharine S, opr W U Tel Co, bds 40 Brackenridge.
Ferber Henry, carp Frederick Kraft, res 269 E Lewis.
Ferch Henry, res 205 Broadway.
Ferckel Adam, molder Bass F & M Works, res 224 John.
Ferckel John, bds 224 John.
Ferckel Martin, saloon, 31 Clinton, res same.
Ferckel Martin J, harnessmkr A L Johns & Co, bds 31 Clinton.
Ferckel Tillie, bkkpr Troy Steam Laundry, bds 31 Clinton.
Ferckel Wm, clk M Frank & Co, bds 31 Clinton.
Ferguson Charles D, teamster Bass F & M Works, res 15 Smith.
Ferguson Miss Cora M, bds 203 W Berry.
Ferguson George W, driver Ft Wayne Steam Laundry, res 59
    Wagner.
Ferguson George W, mach, bds 105 Fairfield ave.
Ferguson John (Ferguson & Palmer), res 203 W Berry.
Ferguson John, plasterer, bds Union House.
Ferguson John K, lumber, bds 203 W Berry.
Ferguson John T, compositor The Sentinel, res 297 E Lewis.
Ferguson Joseph E, solicitor Labor Herald, res 312 Lafayette.

Ferguson Miss Lida K, bds 203 W Berry.

Ferguson Matthew A, trustee Washington Township, 22 Bank blk, res Lima rd 2 miles n of city limits.

Ferguson Miss Minnie E, bds 203 W Berry.

Ferguson Samuel T, brakeman N Y, C & St L R R, res 350 W Washington.

Ferguson Wm G, physician, 72 Harrison, bds 82 W Berry.

Ferguson Wm T, Physician; Diseases of Women and Diseases of the Kidneys a Specialty; Office Hours 9 to 10 a m and 1 to 2 p m, 82 W Berry, res same.

Ferguson & Palmer (John Ferguson, Earl Palmer), Wholesale Hardwood Lumber; Railroads Supplied; Room 54 Pixley & Long Bldg. (*See backbone and line at end of each alphabetical letter.*)

Ferks Albert, lab, res 152 Greely.

Ferris Anna (wid Ezekiel M), res 106 W Superior.

Ferris Frank C, brakeman, res 111 John.

Ferry Caroline P (wid Lucian P), res 119 W Washington.

Fessenden Charles, clk B W Skelton Co, res 614 Calhoun.

Fessenden Frederick, printer The Sentinel, bds 214 Calhoun.

Fessenden Jennie G, dressmkr, 214 Calhoun, bds same.

Fessenden Sylvanus C (Fessenden & Trier), res 214 Calhoun.

Fessenden & Trier (Sylvanus C Fessenden, Wm Trier), 214 Calhoun.

Fetters Andrew, driver, bds 60 Nirdlinger ave.

Fetters Arcania D, waiter Diamond Hotel.

Fetters Emma J (wid Freelen F), bds Diamond Hotel.

Fetters Martin, sawfiler, res 37 Maumee rd.

Fetters Sophronia (wid Franklin F), bds Diamond Hotel.

Fetters Wm, helper Penn Co, bds 12 Oak.

Feulner Anthony, lab, bds 33 Laselle.

Feulner Margaret (wid Frank), res 33 Laselle.

Feustel August, gardener, res e s Spy Run av 3 n of Riverside av.

Feustel Edward, bds August Feustel.

Feustel Henry, gardener, bds August Feustel.

Feustel Mathias, helper Keller & Braun, bds Washington House.

Fey, *see also Fuy.*

Fey Conrad, lab, bds 55 W Wayne.

Fey J, lab Penn Co, res 108 Erie.

Fickel George W, clk Penn Co, res 151 Harrison.

Fickes Mary E (wid Eugene B), res 97 Pearl.

Fiedler Charles E, lab Olds' Wagon Works, res 318 E Creighton avenue.

Fiedler Emil, janitor Concordia College, bds A Aehnelt.

Fiedler Emil, painter Olds' Wagon Works, bds 363 E Creighton avenue.

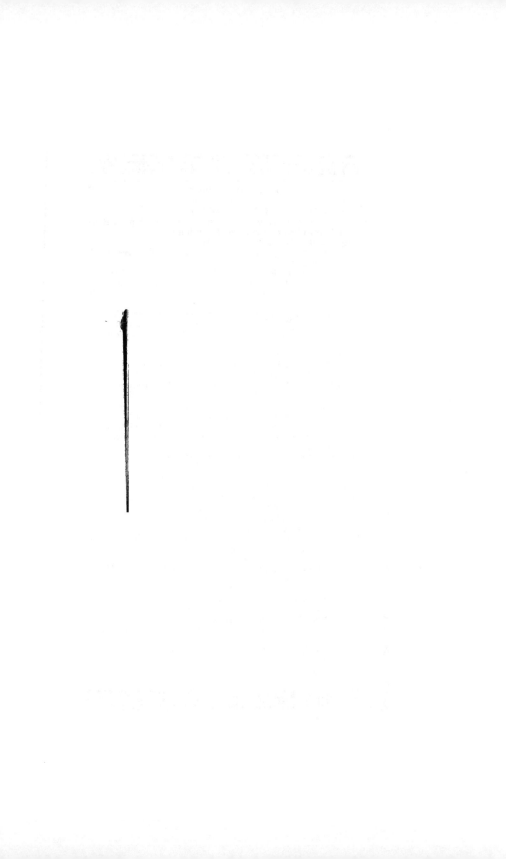

Fiedler Ida, domestic 119 W Washington.
Fiedler Oswald E, painter Olds' Wagon Works, bds 318 E Creighton ave.
Fiedler Wm, lab res 379 E Lewis.
Fiegel Carolina (wid Charles), rms s s Edna 1 n of Spy Run avenue.
Fiegel Wm, res w s Spy Run ave 1 n of Centlivre's park.
Field Wm, engineer, bds Hotel Waverly.
Fields James S, agt Brickmkrs' Association, 55 Clinton, res 180 Griffith.
Fields Wm J, cigarmkr H W Ortmann, bds 180 Griffith.
Figel Charles, res 8 Aboit.
Figel Edward, lab, res 20 4th.
Figel Frederick C, clk, bds 121 Wells.
Figel Henry, teamster, res w s Wabash ave 1 s of E Washington.
Figel John C (J C Figel & Bro), res 54 Wells.
Figel J C & Bro (John C and Robert), grocers, 54 Wells.
Figel Robert (J C Figel & Bro), res 54 Wells.
Figel Wm, tailor, res 89 Maumee rd.
Fike Cyrus, agt Powers & Barnett, res 57 Huestis ave.
Filley Emily, seamstress, rms 50 W Superior.
Filley Julia (wid Robert M), bds 251 E Washington.
Filley Nettie, music teacher, 251 E Washington, bds same.
Filley Wm S, lab, res 251 E Washington.
Fillmore Almon H, conductor L S & M S Ry, res 127 Cass.
Fillmore Bert, student, bds 127 Cass.
Fink Caroline, bds 176 E Jefferson.
Fink Cordelia, dressmkr, bds 127 Holman.
Fink Edward, fireman Penn Co, res 109 Madison.
Fink Elenora T, clk Seibert & Good, bds 176 E Jefferson.
Fink Frank H, foreman Bass F & M Works, res 176 E Jefferson.
Fink Frederick, lab Penn Co, res 138 Fairfield ave.
Fink Frederick H, mach, bds 138 Fairfield ave.
Fink George B, flagman Penn Co, res 212 Walton ave.
Fink John B, barber, 56 E Main, res same.
Fink John H, tinner Seavey Hardware Co, bds 138 Fairfield avenue.
Fink Joseph E, fireman, res 109 Madison.
Fink Mary E, clk Seibert & Good, bds 176 E Jefferson.
Fink Wm, mach hand, res 198 E Lewis.
Finke Wm F, mason, res e s Winch 1 n of Wayne Trace.
Finkhouse Frederick, brakeman, rms 258 Calhoun.
Finlayson John L, lab Penn Co, bds cor Wayne and Barr.
Finn Mary, bds 39 W Washington.
Finnell James, conductor, res 51 W Butler.

Finney Austin M, printer Journal, bds 18 Melita.
Finney John, tinner J H Welch, res 81 W Washington.
Finney Michael, watchman, res 18 Melita.
Finze Christian, bartndr F W A Hollenbeck, res 86 Gay.
Firche Joseph, carp, bds Washington House.
Firgusson, *see also Ferguson*.
Firgusson Elmer E, lab Penn Co, bds 140 Holman.
Firgusson James, blksmith, res 140 Holman.
Firgusson John, lab, res 212 Broadway.
Firgusson Walter O, lab Penn Co, bds 140 Holman.
Firks Frederick, lab Hoffman Bros, res 208 Broadway.
First Baptist Church, n s Jefferson nr Harrison.
First National Bank, John H Bass Pres, M W Simons
    Vice-Pres, Lem R Hartman Cash, Wm L Pettit Asst
    Cash, s e cor Main and Court.
First Presbyterian Church, n e cor Clinton and Washington.
First United Brethren Church, s e cor Harmer and Lewis.
Firth Frederick, agent R L Polk & Co, res 38 Lillie.
Fischer Adolph, bds C F W Meyer.
Fischer Anna C (wid Michael), res 85 E Berry.
Fischer Anna M (wid John), res 42 John.
Fischer Christopher, helper, res 49 Hugh.
Fischer Frank, lab Ft Wayne Electric Co, bds 51 Home ave.
Fischer Henry E, county surveyor, Court House, rms 96 Barr.
Fischer Herman E, clk Beadell & Co, res 182 W Creighton ave.
Fischer Jacob, tinsmith, 40 Schick, res same.
Fischer John, lab, bds 42 John.
Fischer Lizzie D, opr Samuel M Foster, bds 85 E Berry.
Fischer Miss Ned, draughtsman Kerr-Murray Mnfg Co, bds
    182 W Creighton ave.
Fischer Otto H, lab, res w s Winter 3 n of Pontiac.
Fischer Stanislaus, lab Bass F and M Works, bds 14 Force.
Fischer Virginia, seamstress, bds 282 E Washington.
Fisher Abel, foreman Penn Co, res s s New Haven rd nr toll gate
Fisher Alonzo W, lab, bds 282 Webster.
Fisher Anthony jr, blksmith Penn Co, bds 15 W Butler.
Fisher Benjamin, painter, bds 131 W Washington.
Fisher Benjamin F, trav agt, res 409 Calhoun.
Fisher Bros (Samuel S and Max B), whol paper, 125 Calhoun.
Fisher Charles, driver Gottlieb Haller, bds 366 Calhoun.
Fisher David C, Real Estate, Loans, Insurance and
    Notary Public, 32 E Berry, res 24 W Wayne.
Fisher Edwin J, trav agt Fisher Bros, bds 24 W Washington.
Fisher Ellen C, tailoress, bds 131 W Washington.
Fisher Frederick, mach Ft Wayne Organ Co, res 126 Hoag-
    land ave.

14

Fisher George, carp, res 131 W Washington.
Fisher George H, stage mngr Masonic Temple Theater, bds 131 W Washington.
Fisher Henrietta, bds 131 W Washington.
Fisher Hugh F, student, bds 409 Calhoun.
Fisher John, lab Bass F and M Works, bds 224 John.
Fisher John, lab, res 419 W Main.
Fisher John B, trav agt, bds 266 W Jefferson.
Fisher Jonathan H, mach Penn Co, res 163 Montgomery.
Fisher Leon, trav agt, rms 32 Brackenridge.
Fisher Max B (Fisher Bros), res 169 W Wayne.
Fisher Milton W, gunsmith, res 282 Webster.
Fisher Moses P, bkkpr Fisher Bros, bds 24 W Washington.
Fisher Robertson J, treas Bass F and M Works, res 151 W Berry.
Fisher Samuel S (Fisher Bros), res 24 W Washington.
Fisher Wm A, hostler J W Pearce, rms 18 Holman.
Fisher Wm F, caller Penn Co, bds 163 Montgomery,
Fishering George Wm, mngr Ft Wayne Furniture Co, res 52 Lake ave.
Fisk Wm W, clk J M Millen, res 217 W DeWald.
Fissel Charles, tel opr, bds 61 Archer ave.
Fissel George, student, bds 61 Archer ave.
Fissel Philip, driver J M Miller, res 61 Archer ave.
Fitch Charles B, purchasing agt Ft Wayne Electric Co, res 52 Brackenridge.
Fitch Clarence M, lab, bds 75 Douglas.
Fitch Delmer C, clk O B Fitch, bds 407 Calhoun.
Fitch Herbert O, conductor, res 178 Wells.
Fitch Mary E (wid Nathaniel H), res 69 Buchanan.
Fitch Nathaniel, watchman, res 75 Douglas ave.
Fitch Otis B, Boots and Shoes, 52 Calhoun, res 407 same.
Fitch Steward E, fireman, bds 178 Wells.
Fitzgerald Clara, winder Ft Wayne Electric Co, bds 42 Melita.
Fitzgerald Mrs Ellen, boarding house, 39 W Washington.
Fitzgerald Frank, lab, res 71 W 3d.
Fitzgerald Frank, painter, bds 125 Walton ave.
Fitzgerald Laura E, wks Ft Wayne Electric Co, bds 142 Melita.
Fitzgerald Lillie, opr Hoosier Mnfg Co, bds 57 Barr.
Fitzgerald Margaret, opr Hoosier Mnfg Co, bds 71 3d.
Fitzgerald Wm, printer The Press, bds 71 3d.
Fitzgibbon Margaret (wid Michael), res 94 Baker.
Fitzhugh George, lab Penn Co, res cor Du Bois and Maumee rd.
Fitzpatrick Bartley, bds 12 Chicago.
Fitzpatrick James, clk Beadell & Co, bds 46 Cass.
Fitzpatrick John, watchman N Y, C & St L R R, res 46 Bass.

ik Maggie, clk Beadell & Co, bds 46 Bass.
ik Mary E (wid Michael), res 12 Chicago.
ik Thomas, helper James Madden, bds 12 Chicago.
is Arthur, bkkpr Fleming Mnfg Co, res 138 Wells.
i Miss Anna, bds 152 Ewing.
arles R, watchman Ft Wayne St R R Co, res 332 W
i.
yrus I, carriagemkr Olds' Wagon Works, res 315
ison.
ilton G, engineer, res 41 3d.
gelbert, teamster Bruns & McBennett, res w s Walton
i s of P, F W & C Ry.
orge J, lab Penn Co, res 36 Miner.
hristopher, trav agt E F Clausmeier, bds 25 E Main.
nry, lab Bass F & M Works, res St Joseph Boulevard.
.ein Elizabeth (wid Henry), res 74 Barr.
ein Henry E, molder, res 7 Riverside ave.
.an Elizabeth M (wid John G), res 185 E Jefferson.
inn C Frederick, molder, res 2 Holton ave.
inn Eva D (wid Henry), res 30 Hoffman.
inn John B, helper Ft Wayne Iron Works, res 113
iold.
inn John M, helper Fleming Mnfg Co, res 3 Short.
inn & Co, Fox Branch U S Baking Co agts, com-
ed yeast, 145 Calhoun.
Block, e s Calhoun bet Washington and Jefferson.
[Erin, teacher Indiana School for Feeble-Minded
h.
Helen F (wid Wm), res 261 W Berry.
James W, res 61 Cass.
ohn, mach hand Paul's Pulley Works, bds n w cor
id Harrison.
g Mnfg Co, Charles Pape Propr, Mnfrs Road
ers and Graders, 78 High.   (*See right bottom lines.*)
)llie, clk Warren Sweet, bds 61 Cass.
tephen B, student, bds 261 W Berry.
homas, brakeman, res 163 E Jefferson.
Vm H (Rockhill Bros & Fleming), res 106 W Berry.
Vm J, fireman, res 67 Rockhill.
harles P, res 124 E Berry.
ohn, lab, res e s Pittsburgh 2 s of Bond.
ohn, lab Penn Co, res n e cor Lumbard and Chestnut.
r Josiah F, Livery, 32 Barr, res 48 same.   (*See
9.*)
Thomas (col'd), brakeman Penn Co, rms 72 Murray.
argaret A, dressmkr, 48 Barr, res same.

ROBERT SPICE, WINDMILLS AND DRIVE WELLS, LIGHTNING RODS and FIXTURES, 48 West Main and 11 Pearl Streets.

192　　　　　　　R. L. POLK & CO.'S

Fletcher Stephen G, policeman, res 89 Erie.
Fletter Charles, conductor, res 228 Hugh.
Fletter Henry A, lab, res 101 Taylor.
Fletter Ida, bds 101 Taylor.
Fletter Nancy M, bds 166 Hanna.
Flick Clara B, bds 132 Thompson ave.
Flick George W, florist, 132 Thompson ave, res same.
Flickinger John W, painter, 400 W Main, res same.
Flinn Charles M, blksmith, 83 E Columbia, res 11 Cass.
Flinn Theodore C, blksmith C M Flinn, bds 116 W Williams.
Flochmann Anna, bds 152 Ewing.
Florant Charles, mach Bass F & M Works, res 3 Pine.
Florence Thomas, driver, res 21 Miner.
Floyd Clara, bd 270 W Washington.
Flynn Anthony, trav agt, res 164 Hayden.
Flynn Peter, conductor, res 153 Ewing.
Foellinger Adolph G, shoes, 15 W Main, bds 441 Fairfield ave.
Foellinger Augusta, bds 126 Harrison.
Foellinger's Block, 34-36 Calhoun.
Foellinger Jacob, res 441 Fairfield ave.
Foellinger Jacob jr, shoe mnfr, 36 Calhoun, res same.
Foellinger Lizzie, dressmkr, bds 126 Harrison.
Foellinger Louis F, clk, res 126 Harrison.
Foellinger Martin C, clk A G Foellinger, res 126 Harrison.
Foerster Conrad, lab Penn Co, res 581 E Washington.
Foerster Henry, mach hand Old Fort Mnfg Co, res 579 E Washington.
Foley Miss Cecilia, teacher Hanna School, bds 236 W Jefferson.
Foley Charles, bds Lake Shore Hotel.
Foley Honora (wid Patrick), bds 37 Colerick.
Foley Miss Jane, dressmkr, bds 236 W Jefferson.
Foley Jeremiah, driver Powers & Barnett, bds Monroe House.
Foley Jeremiah, lab, res 48 Chicago.
Foley Jeremiah J, finisher Ft Wayne Furniture Co, bds 48 Chicago.
Foley John, watchman, res 236 W Jefferson.
Foley John W, carp, res 101 Barr.
Foley Thomas J, train despatcher Penn Co, bds 236 W Jefferson.
Foley Timothy, boilermkr Bass F & M Works, bds 224 Calhoun.
Foley Timothy, lab Penn Co, res 11 Walnut.
Foley Timothy jr, caller Penn Co, bds 11 Walnut.
Foley Wm, lab, bds 48 Chicago.
Folger Edward, clk Baals & Co, bds 49 W Main.
Folkeling Wm, helper, res 20 Jones.

Foltz James, lab, res rear 10 Short.

Folz John, lab Bass F & M Works, bds Adams twp.

Foncannon Oliver, carp, res w s Glasgow 4 s of Washington.

Foncannon Oliver P, paper hanger Renner, Cratsley & Co, res n s Spy Run ave 3 n of Bridge.

Fonner John B, stenogr Morris, Bell, Barrett & Morris, bds 67 W Main.

Foote Mrs Helen, res 226 W Washington.

Forbing Frank, coachman, bds 181 Montgomery.

Forbing Gertrude (wid Michael), bds 366 Hanna.

Forbing John, real estate, res 385 Hanna.

Forbing Mrs Martha, nurse, res 181 Montgomery.

Forche August, carp, rms 51 E Main.

Forche Joseph, mach, bds Lake Shore Hotel.

Ford Andrew J, engineer Penn Co, res 109 Wallace.

Ford Charles N, carp, res 18 Winch.

Ford James E, clk J B White, bds 201 E Jefferson.

Ford Jesse, lab, bds 18 Winch.

Ford John M, lab Penn Co, bds 109 Wallace.

Ford Wm O, foreman Samuel M Foster, res 201 E Jefferson.

Fordham Mrs Carrie, housekpr 45 Locust.

Fordmeier Frederick, bds w s Calhoun s of Rudisell ave.

Fordney Alberta, tailoress, bds 197 Montgomery.

Fordney George M, molder, res 197 Montgomery.

Foreman Charles E, butcher Frederick Eckart, res 35 W Main.

Foreman Clara, domestic 340 W Washington.

Forester J, lab Penn Co, res 537 E Wayne.

Forks Caroline, domestic 287 Hanna.

Forks Edward, mach hand, bds 74 John.

Forman Annie, domestic 254 W Jefferson.

Forndrin Casper, lab, res n s New Haven ave 1 w of Lumbard.

Forrest Joseph E, brakeman, res 83 Cass.

Forster Gustav, mach hand Wayne Knitting Mills, bds 38 Watkins.

Forsyth Wm, instructor Ft Wayne Art School, res Indianapolis, Ind.

Fortmeyer Ernst, tailor W H Blondoit, bds 33 Madison.

Fortmeyer Frank, lab Penn Co, bds 138 Calhoun.

Fortriede Louis, Boots and Shoes, 19 Calhoun, res 212 E Wayne. (*See right top lines.*)

Fort Wayne Advertising Co, Clarence G Smith mngr, 57 E Columbia.

Fort Wayne Art School, Wm Forsyth instructor, s w cor Lewis and Barr.

Fort Wayne Base Ball Association, Louis Heilbroner sec, 34 Calhoun.

Fort Wayne Beef Co, Sanford Rich mngr, 6 Calhoun.

Fort Wayne Board of Underwriters, Charles E Graves sec, 5 Trentman bldg.

Fort Wayne Brass Works, A Hattersley & Sons Proprs, 48 E Main. *(See embossed line front cover.)*

Fort Wayne Butchers' Association, Gottlieb Haller pres, 54 E Main.

Fort Wayne Carpet Beating Works, Paul E Wolf Propr, 33–35 Clinton.

Fort Wayne Catholic Circulating Library and Association, n e cor Calhoun and Lewis.

Fort Wayne, Cincinnati & Louisville R R, office and depot 1st near Wells.

Fort Wayne City Band, Philip Keinz leader, 70 Calhoun.

Fort Wayne City Bill Posting Co (C B Woodworth, H J Seibold), 1 Aveline House blk.

Fort Wayne City Directory, R L Polk & Co Publrs, 50 Calhoun.

Fort Wayne City Hospital, Mrs C L Smith Supt, s w cor Washington and Barr.

Fort Wayne College of Medicine, medical department of Taylor University, C B Stemen, M D, dean, W P Whery, M D, sec, foot of W Wayne.

Fort Wayne Conservatory of Music, C F W Meyer Director, Bank Block, 22, 24 and 26 E Main.

Fort Wayne Dispatch (Weekly), James Mitchel Propr, 24 Clinton.

Fort Wayne District Telegraph Co, R T McDonald Pres, W P Breen Vice-Pres, George W Beers Sec, Edward Gilmartin Treas, C O Essig Mngr, 15 W Columbia.

Fort Wayne Driving Club, Howell C Rockhill sec, 30 E Main.

Fort Wayne Electric Co, H G Olds Pres, R T McDonald Treas and Genl Mngr, Brainard Rorison Sec, Mnfrs of Dynamo Electric Machines, Lamps and Motors, Broadway and P, Ft W & C Ry.

Fort Wayne Electric Light Co, H G Olds pres, P A Randall vice-pres, M W Simons sec, R T McDonald treas, electrical apparatus mnfrs, cor Broadway and P, Ft W & C Ry.

Fort Wayne Freie Presse (Daily), Otto F Cummerow Propr, n e cor Calhoun and Main.

Fort Wayne Furniture Co, D N Foster pres, P A Randall vice-pres, W E Mossman sec, D B Kehler treas, G W Fishering mngr, folding bed mnfrs, e end of Columbia.

Fort Wayne Gas Light Co, James Cheney Pres and Treas, Wm J Probasco Sec, cor Superior and Barr.

Fort Wayne Gazette (Daily and Weekly), N R Leonard Propr, 41 E Berry.

Fort Wayne Iron Works, Mnfrs of Engines, Boilers and Band Saw Mills, Office and Works s e cor Superior and Harrison.

Fort Wayne Journal (Daily and Weekly), The Journal Co Proprs, 30 E Main.

Fort Wayne Journal of the Medical Sciences, C B and G C Stemen editors, 2 White's blk.

Fort Wayne Land Improvement Co, D N Foster Pres, P A Randall Vice Pres, C A Wilding Sec, G W Pixley Treas, Room 12 Pixley & Long Block.

Fort Wayne Lumber Co, Augustus C Beaver genl mngr, 106 W Main and 796 Broadway.

Fort Wayne Music Co, Harry Achenbach propr, 210 Calhoun.

Fort Wayne News (Daily and Weekly), Wm D Page Propr, 19 E Main.

Fort Wayne Newspaper Union (Eastern Branch Chicago Newspaper Union), John F Cramer Pres, Charles E Strong Treas, Charles D Tillo Resident Mngr, Ready Print Publishers and Paper Dealers, Printers' Supplies, Etc, 55–57 E Columbia.

Fort Wayne Organ Co, S B Bond Pres, Charles E Bond Sec, A L Bond Treas and Supt, Office and Factory e s Fairfield ave ½ mile s of city limits.

Fort Wayne Portrait Co, Milton L Blaney mngr, 153 Broadway.

Fort Wayne Rifles' Armory, 166 Calhoun.

Fort Wayne Saengerbund Hall, 54 E Main.

Fort Wayne Safety Valve Works, E B Kunkle & Co Proprs, 87 Barr.

Fort Wayne Sentinel (Daily and Weekly), E A K Hackett Propr, 107 Calhoun.

Fort Wayne Spoke Works, Homer D Winch mngr, s w cor Wabash R R and Winch.

Fort Wayne Steam Laundry, W B Phillips Propr, 46 W Main.

Fort Wayne Steam Stone Works, Keller & Braun Proprs, 86–98 Pearl. (*See p 8.*)

Fort Wayne Street Railroad Co, J H Bass Pres, S B Bond Vice-Pres, J M Barrett Sec, A S Bond Treas, L D McNutt Supt, Office s w cor Main and Calhoun.

Fort Wayne Transfer and Baggage Line, Powers & Barnett Proprs, 16–24 E Wayne.

Fort Wayne Transfer and Storage Co, Thomas B Empie propr, 17 Lafayette.

Fort Wayne Artificial Ice Co, Ronald T McDonald pres, Aaron Rothschild vice-pres and treas, Henry J Miller sec, cor Wells and Cass.

Charles Bowman Keeps in Stock E. C. Atkins' Celebrated SAWS, 18 Harrison St.

196   R. L. POLK & CO.'S

Fort Wayne View and Copying Co (J E Corlett, J A Biddlecome), photographers, 19 W Berry.

Fort Wayne Water Power Co, Jacob S Goshorn supt, w s Spy Run ave 2 n of Burgess.

Fort Wayne Water Works, P J McDonald Sec, 68 Barr.

Fosler Christian, foreman, res 69 Melita.

Foster Almond, carp, res 15 Hamilton.

Foster Andrew, Merchant Tailor, 15 W Wayne, res 150 Griffith. (*See left top lines.*)

Foster Asa, car builder Penn Co, res 15 Hamilton.

Foster Block, 15 Court.

Foster Catherine P, clk S W Hull, bds 292 E Lewis.

Foster Charlotte (wid James), res 443 Lafayette.

Foster David N, pres D N Foster Furniture Co and Fort Wayne Furniture Co, res 98 E Berry.

Foster D N Furniture Co, David N Foster Pres, S M Foster Sec, Wm J Kettler Treas, Furniture and Carpets, 11–13 Court.

Foster Frank R, student, bds 443 Lafayette.

Foster Frederick W, bds 292 E Lewis.

Foster George, removed to Warsaw, Ind.

Foster Hall, 3d floor Foster blk.

Foster Henry A, train despatcher Penn Co, bds 443 Lafayette.

Foster James A, mach, bds 443 Lafayette.

Foster Lydia T (wid Wm T), res 292 E Lewis.

Foster Nathaniel H, clk Penn Co, bds 292 E Lewis.

Foster Samuel M, shirt mnfr, n end Lafayette, res 96 E Berry.

Fouekel Moritz E, painter Olds' Wagon Works, res 226 Gay.

Fought Anna, bds 23 W Lewis.

Foulks Albert G, driver Ft Wayne Street R R Co, bds 509 E Washington.

Foulks George H, res 260 Clinton.

Foulks Morgan, driver Ft Wayne Street R R Co, bds 509 E Washington.

Foulks Nancy, domestic Harmon House.

Foulks Norve P, foreman B W Skelton Co, res e s Barr 2 s of Williams.

Fournier Frank A, lab, res 13 Purman.

Fournier Frank E, molder Bass F & M Works, bds 13 Purman.

Fournier Joseph, molder Bass F & M Works, bds 13 Purman.

Fournier Louis J, lab, bds 13 Purman.

Foust Henry, trav agt, res n e cor Oneida and Columbia.

Fowler Manufacturing Co, T J T Cumings mngr, 152 Calhoun.

Fowler Wm, lab, res 66 W 3d.

Fowles John W, tailor, 64 Barr, res same.

Fox Albert, teamster, bds 224 W Main.
Fox Albert L, car bldr Penn Co, res 209 Harrison.
Fox August L, res s w cor Fox and Walnut.
Fox Branch U S Baking Co, Louis Fox Mngr, Confectionery and Cracker Mnfrs, 145, 147 and 149 Calhoun.
Fox Catherine, opr Samuel M Foster, bds 494 E Washington.
Fox Catharine J, clk M Frank & Co, bds 58 McClellan.
Fox Celia, domestic County Jail.
Fox Charles, lab, bds 29 1st.
Fox Charlotte, bds 417 Broadway.
Fox Christian, barber, res 71 Ohio.
Fox Edward, market stall No 56, res Wayne twp.
Fox Edward S, plumber, bds 58 McClellan.
Fox Ellsworth V, electrician Ft Wayne Electric Co, bds 417 Broadway.
Fox Frank E, mach Indiana Machine Works, res 282 W Main.
Fox Frederick, lab Weil Bros & Co, res 192 Taylor.
Fox George, city commissioner, res 25 E Main.
Fox George T, clk Fox Branch U S Baking Co, bds s w cor Fox and Walnut.
Fox Gilbert L, butcher Daniel Markley, res 13 Highland.
Fox Henry, wagonmkr, bds 69 Stophlet.
Fox Henry A, meats, 319 W Main, res 315 same.
Fox James J, contractor, res 58 McClellan.
Fox Jehiel, conductor, res 514 Broadway.
Fox John, lab, res 29 E 1st.
Fox John R, mach Penn Co, res 417 Broadway.
Fox Joseph V, confectioner, 25 E Main, res 46 W Superior.
Fox Lena, bds 224 W Main.
Fox Louis, mngr Fox Branch U S Baking Co, res s e cor Walnut and Fox.
Fox Martin L, truckman, res 43 Elm.
Fox Mrs Mary, bds 71 Ohio.
Fox Mary, clk, bds 58 McClellan.
Fox Mary A (wid Francis), bds 189 Madison.
Fox Mrs Mary E, res 103 E Main.
Fox Nellie, dressmkr, bds 58 McClellan.
Fox Phœbe A (wid Henry C), boarding house, 9 E Wayne.
Fox Valentine, market stall No 32, res Wayne twp.
Fox Walter, mach Ft Wayne Electric Co, bds 417 Broadway.
Fox Wm R, bds 127 W Wayne.
Fox Wm W, grocer, 325 W Main, res 327 same.
Foxhuber John L, watchman Penn Co, res 100 W Williams.
Foy John, stonecutter Keller & Braun, bds Waverly House.
Fraikin John J, mach Bass F & M Works, bds 317 Hanna.
Fraikin Oscar J, mach, res 317 Hanna.

Fralich, *see Froelich.*

Frame John, lab, bds rear 178 Hanna.

Frame Prosper, plasterer, res rear 178 Hanna.

France, *see also Franz.*

France Abraham, lab, res 23 Thompson ave.

France Amasa, teamster, res s s New Haven ave 4 e of Lumbard.

France Frank F, bartndr The Randall.

France George, lumberman, res 73 High.

France Harry F, Justice of Peace, 13 E Main, res 600 Calhoun.

France James E K (Colerick & France), res 496 Harrison.

France Joseph S, carp, res 486 Hanna.

France Philip L, mach, res 83 Home ave.

France Rachel (wid Joseph), res 133 Fairfield ave.

France Wm O, driver Ft Wayne Street R R Co, res 620 E Wayne.

Francke Henry jr, cabinetmkr Peters Box & Lumber Co, bds 19 Barthold.

Frane Joseph, woodworker Anthony Wayne Mnfg Co, res 66 Maumee rd.

Frane Margaret (wid Xavier), res 371 Lafayette.

Frank Bessie, bds 206 Hanna.

Frank Elizabeth E, clk Weil Bros & Co, bds 142 E Wayne.

Frank Ellen (wid Francis J), res 142 E Wayne.

Frank George A, tel opr Penn Co, res 60 W DeWald.

Frank George W, carp Louis Diether & Bro, res 124 E Lewis.

Frank Henry, coachman, res 107 W Berry.

Frank John T, fireman, bds 429 W Main.

Frank Josephine, tailoress Gottlieb Stauffer, bds 60 DeWald.

Frank Marx (M Frank & Co), res 82 W Washington.

Frank M & Co (Marx and Theodore Frank), Dry Goods, 60 Calhoun.

Frank Mendel, grocer, 208 Hanna, res 206 same.

Frank Theodore (M Frank & Co), bds 82 W Washington.

Frank Wm C, compositor The Sentinel, bds 328 E Wayne.

Frank Wm T, painter, bds 142 E Wayne.

Franke August H, asst engineer City Water Works, res 154 Clinton.

Franke Charles (Wiegmann & Franke), res 129 Taylor.

Franke Charles H, shoemkr J Foellinger jr, res 237 Broadway.

Franke Christian, carp, res 364 E Lewis.

Franke Edward G, bkkpr C L Centlivre Brewing Co, bds C L Centlivre.

Franke Elizabeth, opr Hoosier Mnfg Co, bds n s Wiebke 2 e of Lafayette.

Franke Frederick, lab Bass F & M Works, bds 81 Smith.

Franke Henry, carp, res 362 E Lewis.

Franke Henry, lab, res 19 Barthold.

Franke Henry jr, cabinetmkr, Peters Box and Lumber Co, bds 19 Barthold.

Franke Henry C, city marshal, res 408 E Washington.

Franke Henry F, plumber C W Bruns & Co, bds 408 E Washington.

Franke John B, sec and treas The B W Skelton Co, bds 274 W Washington.

Franke John H, mach Penn Co, res 336 Hanna.

Franke Julian F, clk Dreibelbiss Abstract of Title Co, bds 366 S Hanna.

Franke Martin G, bds 237 Broadway.

Franke Ricka, domestic 148 W Berry.

Franke Sophia, domestic 122 Wallace.

Franke Wm, carp, res 162 Eliza.

Frankel Louis (Heller & Frankel), rms 22 W Washington.

Frankenstein Max L, Druggist, n w cor Barr and Washington, res same.

Franklin Alice M, bds George Shivers.

Frankling Anthony, lab, bds 134 Madison.

Frankling Margaret (wid Bernard), res 143 Madison.

Franks Gustav, restaurant, 31 Calhoun, res 67 Maumee rd.

Franks Joseph F, removed to Lafayette, Ind.

Franz, *see also France.*

Franz August, lab Penn Co. bds 128 Madison.

Franz Charles W, bds Windsor Hotel.

Franz George, cigarmkr F J Gruber, res 110 W DeWald.

Franz Mrs Mary A, propr Windsor Hotel, 302 Calhoun.

Franz Wm, clk Windsor Hotel.

Franzmeier Louise, domestic 119 W Wayne.

Franzmeyer Augusta, domestic 211 W Berry.

Frary Frank, mach Wabash R R, res 19 Brooklyn ave.

Frary Julian, carp, res 63 E Superior.

Frase B Franklin, lineman Jenney Electric L and P Co, bds 63 Barthold.

Frase H Washington, fireman, bds 63 Barthold.

Frase Mary (wid Charles), res 63 Barthold.

Frasia Deab, fruits, bds 65 Superior.

Fratenburg John M, lab, bds 140 Lafayette.

Frauenfelder Jacob, sawyer, bds n e cor Hanna and Eckart.

Freas Charles, blksmith Fleming Mnfg Co, res 22 Wefel.

Frech Emma, opr Hoosier Mnfg Co, bds 205 Broadway.

Frech Henry, res 205 Broadway.

Frech Henry, lab, res 3 Romey ave.

Robert Spice, Waterworks and General Plumbing, 48 West Main and 11 Pearl Streets.

00   R. L. POLK & CO.'S

'rech Sophia (wid Henry), res 289 W Jefferson.
'rech Wm, lab Louis Rastetter, bds 205 Broadway.
'rechtnicht Wm, molder, bds 65 Hugh.
'recke Auguste (wid Henry), res 175 Lafayette.
'redenburg George V, brakeman, res 216 W Superior.
'rederick Christiana (wid Jacob), res 415 Lafayette.
'rederick Edward, lab Olds' Wagon Works, res 72 Oliver.
'rederick George H, helper Robert Hood, res 17 W Lewis.
'rederick Henry, lab Bass F and M Works.
'rederick John W, mach Ft Wayne Iron Wks, res 43 Laselle.
'rederick Lena, domestic Aldine Hotel.
'rederick Maud, milliner, bds 17 W Lewis.
'rederick Samuel, mach Fleming Mnfg Co, res 13 Breck.
'rederick Wm R (Schulte & Frederick), bds 415 Lafayette.
'redericks Adolph, lab, res 67 Oliver.
'redericks Emma, opr Hoosier Mnfg Co, bds 67 Oliver.
'redrickson Catherine (wid Jacob), res 301 Calhoun.
'redrickson John, porter H G Dierstein, rms 24 E Berry.
'redrickson Wm, milk pedler, res e s Spy Run ave 3 n of
    brewery.
'ree Methodist Church, s s Creighton ave e of Thomas.
'reece Anna, laundress Troy Steam Laundry, bds 396 Broad-
    way.
'reece John J, teamster, bds 20 Harrison.
'reece Rosa, laundress Troy Steam Laundry, bds 396 Broad-
    way.
'reecel John, lab, bds 20 Harrison.
'reeman Albert, driver Ft Wayne Street R R Co, bds 509 E
    Washington.
reeman Frederick N, student, bds w s Spy Run ave 1 n of
    Elizabeth.
reeman Henry R, teller First National Bank, res w s Spy Run
    ave 1 n of Elizabeth.
reeman Julia (wid Newton B), res w s Spy Run ave 1 n of
    Elizabeth.
reeman Miss Katherine, teacher bds w s Spy Run ave 1 n of
    Elizabeth.
reeman Miss Mary E, teacher, bds w s Spy Run ave 1 n of
    Elizabeth.
'eeman Newton B, died December 30, 1890.
'eer Jennie (wid John W), res 19 Cass.
'eer Laura A, dressmkr, bds 19 Cass.
eese August, trav agt, res 178 W Creighton ave.
eese Charles, mach hd, bds 218 Fairfield ave.
eese Charles F, clerk Meyer Bros & Co, bds 177 W Wash-
    ington.

Freese Charles W, blksmith Fleming Mnfg Co, res 32 Wefel.
Freese Frederick, grocer, 379 E Washington, res 381 same.
Freese Sophia (wid Wm), res 177 W Washington.
Freese Wm, teamster Kerr-Murray Mnfg Co, res 200 Fairfield ave.
Freese Wm A, city agt Mayflower Mills, bds 177 W Washington.
Freiburger Anthony C, mach, bds 92 Smith.
Freiburger Bernard, clk J B White, res 28 Charles.
Freiburger Herman, bkkpr S Freiburger & Bro, bds 91 W Berry.
Freiburger Ignatz, res 92 Smith.
Freiburger Ignatz jr, foreman J B White, res 152 W Jefferson.
Freiburger Joseph, clk S Freiburger & Bro, bds 91 W Berry.
Freiburger Joseph J, tinsmith, 187 Broadway, bds 92 Smith.
Freiburger Leopold (S Freiburger & Bro), res 91 W Berry.
Freiburger Louis, clk J B White, bds 28 Charles.
Freiburger Mary, bds 92 Smith.
Freiburger Peter F, driver Hook and Ladder Co No 1, rms Engine House No 1.
Freiburger Simon (S Freiburger & Bro), res 95 W Berry.
Freiburger S & Bro (Simon and Leopold) leather, 24 E Main.
Freienstein Moritz, tailor J W Fowles, bds 105 Barr.
Freimel Albert, driver Ft Wayne Street R R Co, bds 509 E Washington.
Freinstein George, clk J B White, bds 227 E Washington.
Freinstroffer's Block, 41 W Main.
Freistroffer Henry, horseshoer, 41 W Main, res same.
Freistroffer Simon (Freistroffer & Jasper), res 261 E Main.
Freistroffer & Jasper (Simon Freistroffer, George W Jasper), livery, n e cor Clinton and Nickel Plate R R.
Freitag, see also Friday.
Freitag August, lab, res 142 S Wayne ave.
Freitag Lottie, seamstress D S Redelsheimer & Co, bds 142 S Wayne ave.
Freitag Wm H, lab, bds 142 S Wayne ave.
Fremion Frank (Fremion & Vollmer), res s w cor High and Wells.
Fremion Gustav, lab Joseph Fremion, bds w s Hanna 10 s of Pontiac.
Fremion John, teamster Joseph Fremion, res w s Lafayette ½ mile s of city limits.
Fremion Joseph, brick mnfr, w s Hanna ½ mile s of city limits, res same.
Fremion Joseph jr, brickmkr Joseph Fremion, res e s Hanna ¼ s of Eckart.

John Pressler, Mantels, Grates and Tile Floor.
Columbia, Barr and Dock Streets.

202   R. L. POLK & CO.'S

Fremion & Vollmer (Frank Fremion, Frederick C Vollmer),
  bottlers, 9 N Harrison.
French Blufton, lab, bds 43½ E Columbia.
French Charles G, res 442 Hanna.
French Edgar A, stopmkr Ft Wayne Organ Co, res 92 W
  Creighton ave.
French George E, printer The Press, bds 254 Clinton.
French Jeremiah, plasterer, bds 43½ Columbia.
French Maria C (wid Rufus M), res 148 E Washington.
French Mary J (wid Samuel), res 254 Clinton.
French Mrs Mattie J, bkkpr H W Bond, bds 254 Clinton.
French Nellie B, asst S B Brown, bds 254 Clinton.
French Samuel, blksmith, rms 10 W Main.
Frentzel John A N, picture frames, 227 Calhoun, res 14
  Chicago.
Frentzel Rudolph W N, bds 14 Chicago.
Freund Wm H, janitor Masonic Temple, res 33 3d.
Frey George (Mergel & Frey), res 91 Maumee rd.
Frey John, fireman, rms 37 Baker.
Frick Henry, lab Bass F & M Works.
Fricke Frederick W, carp Louis Diether & Bro, res 91 Huestis.
Fricke Joseph, gardener, res n s St Joseph rd 4 e of bridge.
Fricke Margaret, domestic 224 W Wayne.
Fricke Mary, domestic 474 Broadway.
Fricke Minnie, domestic 71 Huestis ave.
Friday, *see also Freitag.*
Friday August L, lab, bds 1 Brandriff.
Friday Henry, mach, bds 1 Brandriff.
Friday Henry A, lab, res 1 Brandriff.
Friday Louis, lab, bds 1 Brandriff.
Friday Mary, laundress Diamond Hotel.
Fridley Lewis F, lab Penn Co, res 37 Buchanan.
Friedlich Isaac (Mautner & Friedlich), bds Wayne Hotel.
Friedmann Frank, helper Bass F & M Works, bds s e cor
  Thomas and Maud.
Friedmann Mathias, lab, res s e cor Thomas and Maud.
Friedmann Wendolin, lab, res s w cor Fisher and Holton ave.
Friemuth Charles, boilermkr, res 199 W Washington.
Friend Alfred I, (A I & H Friend), res 35 W Washington.
Friend A I & H (Alfred I and Henry), clothing, 62 Calhoun.
Friend Henry (A I & H Friend), res 172 W Wayne.
Friend Jacob, res 35 W Washington.
Friend Wm, actor, bds 35 W Washington.
Frisby Frank C, brakeman, res 16 Chicago.
Frisby Frank H, car bldr Penn Co, res 402 E Wayne.
Frisby Frederick, lab, res 1 Spring.

Frisinger Simon P, driver Ft Wayne St R R Co, res 587 E Washington.

Fritcha Henry, lab, res w s Calhoun s of Rudisill ave.

Fritschler John P, trav agt, res 7 Fulton.

Fritz Hotel, Frederick Schmueckle propr, 10 E Berry.

Fritz Louisa, domestic 138 Force.

Froelich Charles, res 66 Nelson.

Frohmuth Gustave H, mach Bass F and M Works, res 93 Buchanan.

Frohmuth John, lab, res 33 N Calhoun.

Frohmuth John F M, res 95 Buchanan.

Frohmuth Theodore, appr C A Berndt, bds 95 Buchanan.

Frohnapfel George C, carp, res 285 Webster.

Fronefield Reuben, cutter Rhinesmith & Simonson, res 28 W Superior.

Frost Benjamin, res 313 Calhoun.

Frost Charles C, brakeman, bds 313 Calhoun.

Frost James S, painter, res s s New Haven ave 1 e of Lumbard.

Frost John H, agt Singer Mnfg Co, bds 250 Clinton.

Frost Mrs Josephine, market stall No 40, res Adams twp.

Fruth Henry, lab Peters Box and Lumber Co, res 50 3d.

Fry Charles F, mach hand Ft Wayne Spoke Works, res 250 Maumee rd.

Fry Charles J, stenogr Hoffman Bros, bds 61 Maud.

Fry Clara, bds 41 E 3d.

Fry Frank, brakeman N Y, C & St L R R, bds Schele House.

Fry Frank J, printer The Sentinel, bds 219 E Wayne.

Fry George, res 91 Maumee rd.

Fry Harry, brakeman Penn Co, rms 131 Holman.

Fry Hattie, dressmkr, bds 321 Harrison.

Fry Henry W, clk, res 219 E Wayne.

Fry Jacob, lab, res 52 John.

Fry James H, clk, rms 32 E Berry.

Fry James R, brakeman N Y, C & St L R R, bds Schele House.

Fry John, lab Wabash R R, bds 52 John.

Fry Maggie (wid Joseph), bds 55 Barr.

Fry Mary M (wid Jacob), bds 321 Harrison.

Fry Wm M, butcher, bds 219 E Wayne.

Fryback C D, car bldr Penn Co, bds 113 Hanna.

Fryback Oliver D, lab Jacob Klett & Sons, res 113 Hanna.

Frye Jerome B, conductor, res w s Harrison 1 s of Killea.

Fryer David L, winder Ft Wayne Electric Co, res 234 Fairfield.

Fryer Lewis E, foreman Ft Wayne Electric Co, res 52 Hendricks.

Fuchs Anna (wid Henry H), bds 163 Francis.

Fuchs Christian, barber, 76 Barr, res 71 Ohio.

ARCHITECTS, WING & MAHURIN,
11 and 42 Pixley & Long Bldg. Telephone 328.

204   R. L. POLK & CO.'S

Fuchs Francis J, bds 13 Force.
Fuchs George, res 167 E Jefferson.
Fuchs Henry, woodwkr Olds' Wagon Works, bds 69 Stophlet.
Fuchs Mary, bds 293 Hanna.
Fuchshuber August, cook J T Connolly, bds 100 W Williams.
Fuchshuber George, lab, bds n w cor Osage and Main.
Fuchshuber Jeannette, tailoress, bds 100 W Williams.
Fuchshuber John L, detective, res 100 W Williams.
Fuelber Anselm, city editor Indiana Staats Zeitung, res 23 E
    Creighton ave.
Fuelling Frederick H, helper Bass F and M Works, res 138
    Eliza.
Fuhrman Henry C, mach hand Olds' Wagon Works, bds 218
    Fairfield ave.
Fuhrman Wm, carp, bds 218 Fairfield ave.
Fulford James, lab, res Walton ave n e cor Erie.
Fulk Albert, lab, res 109 Mechanic.
Fulker Elizabeth (wid Peter), res 173 W Jefferson.
Fulker Mary E, dressmkr, bds 173 W Jefferson.
Fuller Louise (wid Job R), bds n w cor Calhoun and Superior.
Fullmer Charles L, molder Bass F & M Works, res 106 Gay.
Fullmer Ella, domestic 1 Indiana ave.
Fult George W, lab, res 83 Wagner.
Fulton Ansel M, lab, res 74 Barthold.
Fulton Charles W (Lee & Fulton), res 34 W Washington.
Fulton Florence M, bds 138 E Lewis.
Fulton James N, ins agt, bds 121 E Main.
Fulz Robert B, lab Bass F & M Works, res 558 Hanna.
Funk Jacob, dairyman, res s s Maysville rd 1½ miles e of Court
    House.
Funk Michael, brewer C L Centlivre Brewing Co, res n s
    Centlivre ave 1 w of Spy Run ave.
Funkhouser Sarah (wid Andreas), res s s Wayne Trace 2 e of
    Walton ave.
Furian Wm, candymkr, bds 5 Summit.
Furien Frederick, teamster, bds 326 Hanna.
Furlong John, hostler, bds Waverly Hotel.
Furlong John W, blksmith Bass F & M Works, bds 20 Harrison.
Furste Miss Alice M C, news, 56 Calhoun, bds 209 E Wayne.
Furste Elizabeth B (wid Francis L), res 209 E Wayne.
Furste George A, clk, bds 209 E Wayne.
Furthmiller Albert (McIlvaine & Co), res 176 Hanna.
Furthmiller Freeman, lab Penn Co, bds 190 Taber.
Furthmiller Henry, market stall No 80, res Adams twp.
Futter Charles (Beninghoff & Futter), res 72 Brackenridge.
Futter Helena, bds 93 W Superior.

tter Joseph O, barber George Thain, bds 93 W Superior.
tter Martin, finisher Peters Box and Lumber Co, res 93 W Superior.

G

ble, *see also Goebel.*
ble George F, mach Bass F & M Works, bds 74 Lillie.
ble Mary (wid Christian), res 40 Madison.
ble Peter F, stonecutter Keller & Braun, bds n s Lakeside 6 e of toll gate.
ble Philip, foreman Bass F & M Works, res 74 Lillie.
ddis Margaret A (wid James), res 231 Calhoun.
tetje John, Choice Ales, Wines, Liquors, Beer, Cigars and Tobacco, 179 Calhoun, res 92 Montgomery.
ff Perry O, removed to Dunfee, Ind.
ffney Edward F, lab Penn Co, bds 33 Bass.
ffney Margaret E, clk Root & Co, bds 33 Bass.
ffney Mary (wid Edward), res 33 Bass.
ffney Tillie, clk L Wolf & Co, bds 397 Calhoun.
ffney Wm, res 397 Calhoun.
ge Fannie (wid George), boarding house, 235 Barr.
ge Robert, broom mnfr, 318 W Main, res 320 same.
de Carl J W, clk Trenkley & Scherzinger, bds 113 W Wayne.
e George, res 40 Madison.
es Simon (col'd), lab Bass F & M Works, res Mercer nr Walton ave.
lagher Charles A, molder Kerr-Murray Mnfg Co, bds 25 Hough.
lagher Mary E, bds 26 E Williams.
land Edward, helper A Hattersley & Sons, bds 18 Brandriff.
land Henry, helper Fleming Mnfg Co, res 18 Brandriff.
ant James W, driver, bds 121 Calhoun.
meier Ernest, carp, res 69 Maumee rd.
meier Frederick W, carrier P O, res 61 Maumee rd.
meier Louisa, domestic s w cor Clinton and Lewis.
meier Wm, carp, res 136 Francis.
meyer Conrad, brickmkr, res 72 Organ.
meyer Lizzie, domestic 149 E Berry.
meyer Minnie, domestic 166 E Berry.
rath Anna, mittenmkr, bds 374 W Main.
rath Charles, mach Ind Machine Works, bds 374 W Main.
rath Wm, lab, res 374 W Main.

15

Gannon George H, carp, rms 58 Chicago.
Gans Carrie, opr Samuel M Foster, bds 3 Marion.
Gans Elizabeth, opr Samuel M Foster, bds 3 Marion.
Gans Joseph, lab Penn Co, bds 3 Marion.
Gans Louis, lab Penn Co, res 3 Marion.
Gans Michael, clk, bds 3 Marion.
Gans Paul, lab Penn Co, res 45 High.
Ganser Jacob, baker The Wayne, res 66 W 5th.
Ganser Joseph F, mach, bds 66 W 5th.
Ganser Louis J, driver F P Marsch, bds 66 W 5th.
Ganzer Stephen, clk J B White, res 400 E Lewis.
Garard Manasseh G, carp, res 31 Wagner.
Gard Brookfield, Physician and Mngr Guardian Medical
    and Surgical Institute, 13 W Wayne, res same.
Gard Margaret (wid Brookfield) res 27 Lillie.
Gardiner Frederick W, ticket agt N Y, C & St L R R, bds
    The Randall.
Gardiner James (col'd), barber Alfred Bass, rms 32 E Columbia.
Gardner DeMotte C, printer The News, res 309 Harrison.
Gardner Frank S, electrician Ft Wayne Electric Co, res 332 W
    Washington.
Gardner Fred W, painter Penn Co, bds 353 Calhoun.
Gardner George W, watchman, res 120 Chicago.
Gardner Harry W, removed to Chicago, Ill.
Gardner Henry J, brakeman, res 155 Clay.
Gardner John C, mach hand, bds 293 W Main.
Gardner Maud, clk August Bruder, bds 155 Clay.
Gardner Melvin R, wireman Jenney Electric Light and Power
    Co, res 206 W Superior.
Gardner Ross J, switchman, bds 155 Clay.
Gardot Alphonse, clk, bds 22 E Columbia.
Gardt Henry, barber, 271 Hanna, res same.
Gardt Henry jr, mach hand, bds 271 Hanna.
Gardt Kate, opr Hoosier Mnfg Co, bds 271 Hanna.
Gardt Stephen J, molder Bass F & M Works, bds 271 Hanna.
Garman Adam, painter, res 63 Pontiac.
Garman Catherine (wid Wm), res 74 Melita.
Garman Howard, painter, bds 63 Pontiac.
Garman John W, jeweler, 207 Calhoun, res same.
Garrigus Lillian M, teacher Conservatory of Music, bds 108 E
    Wayne.
Garrison Anna, domestic 131 Horace.
Garrison Anna, opr Hoosier Mnfg Co, bds 41 Force.
Garrison John H, painter, res n s New Haven ave 3 w of Lum-
    bard.
Garrison Mary (wid Albert), res 18 Colerick.

Garrison Mitchell F, fireman G R & I R R, rms 17 W Lewis.
Garrity Mary (wid Owen), bds 15 W Butler.
Garta Emma (wid James), res 150 Maumee rd.
Garta John, cigarmkr F J Gruber, bds 150 Maumee rd.
Gartee Flora, domestic 144 W Berry.
Gartz Lena, domestic The Randall.
Garver Melvin, removed to Chicago, Ill.
Garvey John A, student, rms 26 Douglas ave.
Garvey Patrick H, watchman Penn Co, rms 26 Douglas ave.
Gary Peter, vegetables, market stall No 95, res w of County
    Poor House.
Gaskill Charles, apprentice, bds 67 Franklin ave.
Gaskill Edward H, lab, bds 57 Barr.
Gaskill Harry J, lab, bds 68 Chicago.
Gaskill Harrison, lab Louis Diether & Bro, res 10 Short.
Gaskill Ida, domestic 172 W Wayne.
Gaskill J M, trimmer Jenney Electric Light and Power Co, bds
    67 Franklin ave.
Gaskill Kyle, veterinary surgeon, 159 Hoffman, res same.
Gaskill Leonard M, lab, res n w cor Hayden and Winter.
Gaskill Nehemiah O, trimmer Jenney Electric Light and Power
    Co, bds 67 Franklin ave.
Gaskill Wm, lab, res 67 Franklin ave.
Gaskill Wm, watchman, bds 15 Pearl.
Gaskins Annette A, teacher, bds 188 W Creighton ave.
Gaskins Catherine (wid Joseph), res 188 W Creighton ave.
Gaskins Emma F, teacher, bds 188 W Creighton ave.
Gaskins Harry M, finisher Ft Wayne Organ Co, bds 188 W
    Creighton ave.
Gaskins Joseph E, mach, bds 188 W Creighton ave.
Gaskins Mary E, bds 188 W Creighton ave.
Gaskins Wm B, removed to Ft Worth, Tex.
Gaspar Peter, market stall No 42, res Washington twp.
Gassart Frederick, brakeman, res 499 Lafayette.
Gaston Albert P, clk Seavey Hardware Co, bds 70 Harrison.
Gaszner John P, removed to Milwaukee, Wis.
Gates Abraham, conductor, res 326 Harrison.
Gates Benjamin F, foreman, res 51 N Calhoun.
Gates George, cigarmkr F J Gruber, rms 84 Barr.
Gates Horatio S, clk Penn Co, res 57 W DeWald.
Gates Wm H, engineer Penn Co, res 412 Clinton.
Gauff Eveline M (wid Henry D), bds 100 E Washington.
Gauspohl Henry, helper Penn Co, res 5 Oak.
Gavehn August F, tailor J G Thieme & Son, res 142 Erie.
Gavin Frank W, bds 311 E Wayne.
Gavin James A, janitor, res 311 E Wayne.

n Robert, miller C Tresselt & Sons, res 8 Harmer.

Millard F, storekpr Penn Co, res n s Chestnut 1 e of Warren.

Monroe W, carp Ft Wayne Spoke Works, res 79 Winch.

ord John M, lab, bds 231 Lafayette.

ord Julia A, res 231 Lafayette.

ord J Eben, lab, res 62 Hamilton.

ord Mary, res 24 Fulton.

ord Orville O, bds 231 Lafayette.

ord Sylvester, sawyer, bds 135 Wallace.

e Edward, stonecutter Wm & J J Geake, bds s e cor Ewing and Pearl.

e John J (Wm & J J Geake), res s e cor Ewing and Pearl.

e Mariana J, teacher, bds s e cor Ewing and Pearl.

e Walter H, stonecutter Wm & J J Geake, bds s e cor Ewing and Pearl.

e Wm (Wm & J J Geake), res 18 Union.

e Wm C, student F B Kendrick, bds 18 Union.

ke Wm & J J (Wm and John J), Steam Stone Works and Dealers in Cut and Ornamental Stone, 76-82 Pearl. *See left bottom lines.*)

hart Wm S, mach, res 353 E Lewis.

y Annie, bds 287 E Washington.

y Charles, sewer contractor, res 287 E Washington.

y Charles T, driver Ft Wayne St R R Co, res s e cor Grant ave and Humphrey.

y James P, lessee World's Museum, n s Berry bet Clinton and Barr, res 55 E Wayne.

y Leona, seamstress, bds s e cor Grant ave and Humphrey.

y Oliver, lab, bds 287 E Washington.

ry Wm, Practical Horseshoer, 5 Harrison, res 230 High.

e Hannah, dressmkr, res 65 Harrison.

e Mary, dressmkr, bds 65 Harrison.

t Alfred, bartndr Wickliff & Clark, res 100 Columbia.

t Frank (Ryan & Gebert), bds 60 Columbia.

t John L, lab C Tresselt & Sons, res 24 E Washington.

rd Casper, lab Kerr-Murray Mnfg Co, res 66 Charles.

rd Charles, molder Bass F and M Works, bds 25 Liberty.

rd David, lab, res n s Pontiac 2 w of Hanna.

rd George, harnessmkr G H Kuntz, res 25 Liberty.

rd Henry F, lab Penn Co, bds 172 Maumee rd.

rd Theodore, clk, bds 172 Maumee rd.

rd Wm, mason, res 172 Maumee rd.

rd Wm F, mach, bds 172 Maumee rd.

rt Charles, market stall No 16, res Green twp.

rt Charles jr, market stall No 86, res Wayne twp.

Gebhart Valentine, market stall No 41, res Lakeside.
Geerken Augustus, painter, bds Grand Central Hotel.
Geerken Charles F, driver H B Monning, res 135 E Lewis.
Geerken Frederick, mach Penn Co, res 36 Eliza.
Geerken George jr, boilermkr Penn Co, res 37 Eliza.
Geerken George, clk H Wiegman & Sons, res 80 Montgomery.
Geerken Henry, boilermkr Penn Co, res 170 Montgomery.
Gehring Andrew, foreman, res 206 W Creighton ave.
Gehring Paul, mach Bass F and M Works, res 73 Huestis ave.
Gehring Samuel, lab, bds 206 W Creighton ave.
Gehring Wm F, cigarmkr Christian Wonninghoff, bds 206 W
    Creighton ave.
Gehrke, see also Gerke.
Gehrke Louis G, lab Pottlitzer Bros, res 49 W Williams.
Geiger Charles H, bkkpr Herman Berghoff Brewing Co, 125
    E Jefferson.
Geiger Charles J, bookbinder, res 125 E Jefferson.
Geiger Ernest, engineer The Wayne.
Geiger Frank J (Scheffer & Geiger), res 292 Calhoun.
Geiger Joseph, lab, bds 100 Putnam.
Geiger Joseph, lab, res 88 4th.
Geiger Louis F, bkkpr, bds 125 E Jefferson.
Geiger Louisa, bds 125 E Jefferson.
Geiger Wm, agt Adams Express Co, res 57 Maumee rd.
Geiger Wm, lab Louis A Fox, bds 100 Putnam.
Geise Henry, car inspr Penn Co, res 179 John.
Geisel Peter P, barber C B Schmuck, bds 23 Grand.
Geisman Charles, lab, res 3 Bass.
Geisman Elizabeth (wid Jacob), res 40 Locust.
Geisman George, helper Kerr-Murray Mnfg Co, bds 40 Locust.
Geisman John, lab, bds 40 Locust.
Geisman Julius, brakeman, bds 40 Locust.
Geismar Adolph, trav agt, res 101 E Berry.
Geiss Emma, domestic Hotel Rich.
Geiss Julia (wid Jacob), res 58 Smith.
Geiss Louis J, Propr Cottage Restaurant (Formerly The
    Nickel Plate Hotel), 31 W Columbia. (See page 146.)
Geistdoefer Ferdinand, market stall No 48, res Washington
    township.
Geller Charles C (Ehrman & Geller), res 186 Griffith.
Geller George, lab Penn Co, res 2 Union.
Geller George G, foreman W F Geller, res 83 Nirdlinger ave.
Geller Gottlieb, saloon, 96 Broadway, res 53 Stophlet.
Geller Henry W, mach hd Ft Wayne Electric Co, bds 348
    Broadway.
Geller Lizzie, domestic 305 W Jefferson.

Penn Mutual LIFE INSURANCE CO. of PHILA.
CLARK FAIRBANK, General Agent, 19 Court Street.

210   R. L. POLK & CO.'S

Geller Theodore, market stall No 39, res 90 Hoffman.
Geller Theodore H, confr W F Geller, bds 90 Hoffman.
Geller Wm, finisher Ft Wayne Organ Co, res 348 Broadway.
Geller Wm F, Baker and Manufacturing Confectioner, 98 Broadway, res same.
Gellert Max E, tinner J L Gruber, res 34 Allen.
Gent Mary, domestic 9 E Wayne.
Genth Michael, lab Bass F and M Works, res 36 John.
Genthner Lizzie C, waiter 25 E Main.
George Ellwood H, trav agt, res 89 W DeWald.
George Ensign, painter Chauvey Bros, bds 28 W Main.
George John F, student A P Buckman, rms 238 W Wayne.
George Russell, saloon, 28 W Main, res same.
Georget Charles, cigarmkr S G Throckmorton, bds 132 Monroe.
Gepfert Louis H, butcher Rousseau & Pfeiffer, res 24 Van Buren.
Gerard, *see also Girard.*
Gerard Antoine, helper Penn Co, res 92 Lillie.
Gerard Antoine jr, yardmaster Penn Co, bds 92 Lillie.
Gerard Benoit, brakeman, res 91 Lillie.
Gerard Mary, opr C U Tel Co, bds 92 Lillie.
Gerard Nicholas, car repairer Penn Co, res 518 E Lewis.
Gerard Wm E, st car driver, res 618 E Wayne.
Gerardin Hippolyte, saloon, 70 Barr, res same.
Gerber Conrad, driver Geo DeWald & Co, res 114 Erie.
Gerber Mary A, domestic 169 W Wayne.
Gerber Peter, timber buyer, bds 22 Columbia.
Gerberding Alma, bds 201 E Lewis.
Gerberding August, teamster, res 103 Erie.
Gerberding Edward, teacher St Paul's German Lutheran School, res 69 E Jefferson.
Gerberding Henry, bds 103 Erie.
Gerberding Rudolph, teamster, bds 103 Erie.
Gerberding Rudolph E, clk M L Frankenstein, bds 69 E Jefferson.
Gerberding Walter R, clk Coombs & Co, bds 69 E Jefferson.
Gerdes Herman, lab, res 6 Oak.
Gerdes John, bricklayer, bds 88 Home ave.
Gerding Bros (Herman C and John P), livery, 66 Harrison.
Gerding Herman C (Gerding Bros), res 22 Union.
Gerding John P (Gerding Bros), res 122 John.
Gerding Wm E (Gerding & Aumann Bros), res 373 Hanna.
Gerding & Aumann Bros (Wm E Gerding, Wm H and Henry F Aumann), Hardware, Stoves, Furnaces and Tinware; Tin, Copper and Sheet Iron Workers, also Slate Roofers, 115 Wallace. (*See top edge and page 63.*)

Gerdom Ernst H, foreman Bass F & M Works, res 160 Smith.
Gerdom Herman W, molder Bass F & M Works, res 46 John
Gerdom Henry, foreman Bass F & M Works, res 160 Smith.
Gerhard Wm, mach, res 353 E Lewis.
Gerhart Charles R, saw filer, bds 95 Putnam.
Gerhart Edward L, filer Hoffman Bros, bds 95. Putnam.
Gerhart Jefferson, brakeman, bds Schele House.
Gerhart Wm, engineer, res 95 Putnam.
Gerke, *see also Gehrke.*
Gerke Charles W, bkkpr Ft Wayne St R R Co, bds 161 Gay
Gerke Christina (wid Henry), res 161 Gay.
Gerke Frederick C, clk A E C Becker, bds 107 W Williams.
Gerke Frederick J, appr Indiana Machine Works, bds 5 Mc
    Clellan.
Gerke Henry, res 25 Summit.
Gerke Henry C, bkkpr Wm Moellering & Sons, bds 81 Mont
    gomery.
Gerke Henry W, with J F Gerke & Co, res 3 McClellan.
Gerke John, carp, bds 25 Summit.
Gerke John F (J F Gerke & Co), res Goeglein, Ind.
Gerke Julia, domestic 40 E Washington.
Gerke J F & Co (John F Gerke), dry goods, 191 Lafayette.
Gerke Kate, domestic 40 E Washington.
Gerke Louis, changer Ft Wayne Street R R Co, bds 161 Gay
Gerke Louis H, clk, res 5 McClellan.
Gerke Louise, domestic 290 Fairfield ave.
Gerlach Gustave, painter Olds' Wagon Works, bds cor Pontia
    and Holton ave.
Germain Roswell M, engineer, res 97 W Main.
German Lutheran Cemetery, n s Maumee rd nr Concordi
    College.
German Lutheran Cemetery (St John's), Bluffton rd 3 miles
    w of city limits.
German Lutheran School, n e cor Union and Wilt.
German Reformed Orphan Asylum, Rev John Rettig supt, n
    Maysville rd 2 miles e of Court House.
Gerow John, butcher Frederick Eckart.
Gerow Teles D, grocer, 120 Fairfield ave, res 23 Grand.
Gerry Edward, cutter C W Weller, bds 92 W Jefferson.
Gerwig Mary (wid Louis), res 18 Liberty.
Geschwent Joseph, bartender Charles Liebenguth, rms cor Cal
    houn and R R.
Gessler Albert F, butcher, res 78 Montgomery.
Gessler Jennie C, tailoress Baumann & Hassler, bds 51 E Main
Gessler Victoria (wid Frederick), res 51 E Main.
Gessner Jesse, saloon, 108 Broadway, res same.

Getty Christopher, res 73 Buchanan.
Getty Frank, dairy, res 75 Buchanan.
Getty George, trunkmkr Fisher Bros, res 27 Buchanan.
Getz Frank E, mach Wabash R R, bds 86 Dawson.
Getz Hubert, lab Ft Wayne Iron Works, res 55 Maumee rd.
Getz John C, shoemkr, 174 Fairfield ave, res 86 Dawson.
Getz Joseph G (Notestine & Getz), res 17 Harrison.
Geves Augusta, domestic 336 W Main.
Geye Francisca (wid Henry), bds 332 E Washington.
Geye Henry, shoemkr, 424 E Wayne, res same.
Geye Herman F W, shoemkr, res 428 E Wayne.
Geyer Clara, domestic 95 E Berry.
Giannasi Pietro, lab, bds 87 W Superior.
Gibford Mrs Angela, seamstress Indiana School for Feeble-
  Minded Youth.
Gibford Harry W, clk O B Fitch, bds 90 Columbia.
Gibford Isaiah Z, hostler F M Johnson, rms 13 Pearl.
Gibford James, watchman Powers & Barnett, bds Hedekin
  House.
Gibson Eliza, dressmkr, bds 38 Oak.
Gibson Frank, trav agt, res 13 Hamilton.
Gibson Frank P, flagman, bds 13 Hamilton.
Gibson Grace, domestic 92 W Jefferson.
Gibson Jennie, clk Mrs S B Hall, bds 34 W Main.
Gibson Lena (wid Charles), res 57 W Williams.
Gibson Mary J (wid Frank), res 38 Oak.
Gibson Matilda (wid James), res 11 High.
Gibson Rose, wrapper Summit City Soap Co, bds 38 Oak.
Gibson Sherman, brakeman, res 69 Huron.
Gick Amelia C, bds 292 E Washington.
Gick Frederick H C, lab, bds 292 E Washington.
Gick George, clk Pickard Bros, res 292 E Washington.
Gick Louis, clk H J Ash, res 66 Erie.
Gidley John A, mach, bds 20 Pine.
Gidley Rebecca (wid Wm), res 20 Pine.
Gidley Richard A, boilermkr, res 24 Pine.
Gieger Frederick, lab, bds 3 Edgerton.
Gieger George, lab, res 3 Edgerton.
Gieger Jacob, lab, bds 3 Edgerton.
Gieger Wm, tailor, res 3 Edgerton.
Gieseking Henry, woodworker Henry Meier, bds 23 Ewing.
Giffin Clarence, elevator conductor Aldine Hotel.
Giffin Robert E, fireman Penn Co, res 53 Taylor.
Gilb Nicholas, cigarmkr George Reiter, res 354 Broadway.
Gilbert Charles E, fireman, bds J B Gilbert.
Gilbert Elmer H, mach hand, bds 20 Murray.

Gilbert Grace G, bds s s New Haven rd 2 w of toll gate.
Gilbert Harry, Imported Wines, Liquors and Cigars, 226 Calhoun, res 61 Brackenridge.
Gilbert I May, bds s s New Haven rd 2 w of toll gate.
Gilbert James B, blksmith Bass F & M Works, res s e cor Miner and De Wald.
Gilbert James E, printer Ft Wayne Newspaper Union, bds J B Gilbert.
Gilbert John, mngr Standard Oil Co, res 246 W Washington.
Gilbert John V, fruit grower, res s s New Haven rd 2 w of toll gate.
Gilbert Walter S, clk J B White, bds Maumee rd nr toll gate.
Gilby John, engineer Star Iron Tower Co, res 69 Garden.
Gilchrist Mrs Catherine, res 60 W Berry.
Gilchrist Elizabeth H (wid Wm L), bds 11 Monroe.
Gill Lawrence, hostler H W Tapp, bds 227 E Lewis.
Gillaume Georgia, opr Hoosier Mnfg Co, bds 179 E Washington.
Gillaume Julia, opr Hoosier Mnfg Co, bds 57 Wells.
Gillen Bernard, removed to Jackson, Mich.
Gillen Michael, horseshoer Wm Geary, bds 42 Columbia.
Gillespie Asa C, student, bds 81 Wells.
Gillespie Hattie (wid James P), bds 216 W Superior.
Gillespie Rufus R, bds 47 N Calhoun.
Gillespie Mrs Susanna L, res 63 W Superior.
Gillespie Wm R, mason, rms 22 Foster's blk.
Gillett Hollis F, bartender, res 53 E Main.
Gillette Edwin A, mach, res 43 Pritchard.
Gillham Lewis O, mngr New York Installment Co, res 15 Elizabeth.
Gilliam August, street car driver, res w s Spy Run ave 2 s of canal feeder.
Gilliom Emma S (wid Henry), res 192 E Wayne.
Gilliom Lenore D, clk F D Clarke, bds 192 E Wayne.
Gilliom Zella M, assistant H C Sites, bds 192 E Wayne.
Gillock Edward G, car bldr Penn Co, bds 208 Madison.
Gilman Charles A, mach hd Ft Wayne Electric Co, bds 3 Fisher.
Gilman Cora, boxmkr, bds 3 Fisher.
Gilman Huldah (wid Jerome), res 3 Fisher.
Gilmartin Edward, Lumber, poles and Cedar Posts, 262 Clinton, res 31 W Williams.
Gilmartin Mary, bds 31 W Williams.
Gilmartin Michael, lineman Ft Wayne District Tel Co, bds 224 Calhoun.
Gilmartin Michael J, clk Ft Wayne Electric Co, bds 31 W Williams.
Gimpel Clara, opr Hoosier Mnfg Co, bds 119 Taylor.

Gimpel Henry, coremkr Bass F & M Works, res 119 Taylor.
Gimpel Minnie, opr Hoosier Mnfg Co, bds 119 Taylor.
Gindelsparger Ida, dressmkr, s w cor Pearl and Maiden lane, res same.
Gindelsparger Mead, hoseman Engine Co No 1, rms same.
Ginder John A, brakeman, res 50 Chicago.
Ginther Mary (wid Wm M), domestic 131 E Wayne.
Girard, *see also Gerard.*
Girard Frank, helper Penn Co, res 91 Summit.
Girardot Alphonse, porter Morgan & Beach, bds 22 Columbia.
Girkle Charles, lab, res 146 High.
Givens Harry, brakeman, bds 84 W Main.
Gladbach Joseph, carp, res 169 Force.
Glanowitch John, car builder Penn Co, res 3 Lumbard.
Glaser Edward F, baker, 195 Hanna, res same.
Glaser Edward K, lab Penn Co, bds 195 Hanna.
Glaser Frank E, driver, bds 195 Hanna.
Glaser John E, baker, bds 195 Hanna.
Glass Chester C, bkkpr Root & Co, res 193 E Washington.
Glass Eliza J (wid Randall S), res 193 E Washington.
Glass John, molder Bass F and M Works, bds 506 E Wayne.
Glass Lena, clk A Mergentheim, bds 407 Clinton.
Glaze Mrs Lilly, bds 260 Clinton.
Gleitburg Wm, driver, bds 121 Calhoun.
Glenn Grace C, teacher, bds 67 W DeWald.
Glenn Robert, clk Martin Detzer, bds 266 Hoagland ave.
Glenn Thomas M, Real Estate and Fire Insurance; Agt Masonic Mutual Benefit Society of Indiana; South Side Investments a Specialty; also Passenger Conductor Penn Co, Office 352½ Calhoun, res 266 Hoagland ave.
Glenn Wm M, engineer Penn Co, res 67 W DeWald.
Glenwood Chapel, cor Broadway and Bluffton rd.
Glessman Minnie, domestic 289 W Washington.
Glessner Bros (Charles A and Samuel A), grocers, 192 Griffith.
Glessner Charles A (Glessner Bros), res 192 Griffith.
Glessner Charles H, paper hanger, bds 192 Griffith.
Glessner Cora B, clk Glessner Bros, bds 192 Griffith.
Glessner Samuel A (Glessner Bros), bds 192 Griffith.
Glissmann Christian, mach hd Ranke & Yergens, res 23 Jones.
Gloeckle John (Gloeckle & Browand), res 7 Monroe.
Gloeckle & Browand (John Gloeckle, Norman C Browand), barbers, 130 Calhoun.
Gloenowich John, carp, res n s New Haven ave 2 w of Lumbard.
Gloyd Louis L, checker Penn Co, res 410 Clinton.
Gloyd Miss Mary A, bds 410 Clinton.

.E. Johnson, DENTIST, 74 Calhoun Street.
Res., 188 W. Berry St.

FORT WAYNE DIRECTORY. 215

nkamp Frederick, foreman Lake Erie & Western R R, es 51 5th.

nkamp Frederick H, clk Indiana Machine Wks, bds 397 V Main.

nkamp Henry W, inspr Lake Erie & Western R R, res 97 W Main.

nkamp Louisa, mittenmkr, bds 397 W Main.

ting **Andrew F** (Glutting, Bauer & Hartnett), County uditor, res 114 W Main.

ting, Bauer & Hartnett (Andrew F Glutting, ajetan J Bauer, Murray Hartnett), Real Estate and Inrance, 55 Clinton.

ng Elizabeth F, res 15 W Washington.

Miss Kate, dressmkr, res s e cor Columbia and Barr.

ier Anna, bds 50 4th.

ier Bertha M, boxmkr W H Davis, bds 148 Wells.

ier Charles, engineer, res 148 Wells.

ier Michael, lab Lake Erie & Western R R, res 50 4th.

e Anthony J, umbrellamkr Emanuel Gnacke, rms 86 linton.

e Emanuel, umbrella mnfr, 86 Clinton, rms same.

John, lab Penn Co, res 15 Wabash ave.

Martin, lab, bds 15 Wabash ave.

Minnie, domestic 23 E Main.

Peter, grinder Bass F and M Works, res 13 Force.

e August A, porter G E Bursley & Co, res 91 Grant ave.

e August C, clk B R Noll, bds 162 Griffith.

Frank A, trav agt A C Trentman, res 325 E Wayne.

Henry J, clk L Wolfe & Co, res 154 Griffith.

Louis, lab, res 232 Harmer.

Louis H, bkkpr A C Trentman, res 80 Brackenridge.

y Frank A, trav agt A C Trentman, res Dayton, O.

ey James P, engineer, res Wayne twp.

l, *see also Gable.*

l Christina (wid Peter), res 219 Lafayette.

l Frank A, clk J B White, bds 219 Lafayette.

l Frederick, musician, res 32 W Main.

l Siebert, fireman Penn Co, res 52 Force.

ein Abraham, teamster, res 83 Smith.

ein Andrew J, boilermkr, res s w cor Eagle and Taylor.

ein George, lab Louis Rastetter, bds 28 Jones.

ein Jacob, teamster, res 28 Jones.

ein Margaret, domestic 33 Brackenridge.

en Joseph, tailor, res 320 E Washington.

inger John, lab, res 73 Canal.

inger Sarah, domestic 216 E Jefferson.

Dora (wid Frederick), bds 107 Force.
'm, lab Penn Co, bds 89 Shawnee ave.
Theodore, harnessmkr F Hilt, res 68 Pontiac.
Frederick coremkr Bass F & M Works, res 113 Gay.
Charles M, engineer Penn Co, bds 223 Lafayette.
Ada, dressmkr, 77 E Williams, bds same.
Wm H, checker Penn Co, res 52 Buchanan.
Minnie, teacher Indiana School for Feeble-Minded
ıth.
ner Charles W, cigarmkr Louis Bender, res 336 Hanna.
Anthony W, clk Golden & Monahan, res 200 Lafayette.
Bridget (wid Patrick), res 32 Smith.
Bridget, res 29 Melita.
Catherine, winder Ft Wayne Electric Co, bds 38
ita.
Edward J (Golden & Monahan), res 177 W Wayne.
Frank, teamster J J Draker, bds 42 Pearl.
John, brakeman, res 30 John.
John, brakeman, res 357 E Washington.
Joseph J, helper Wabash R R, bds 38 Melita.
Margaret (wid Thomas), res 38 Melita.
Mary (wid Patrick), bds 195 W DeWald.
Mary, bds 177 W Wayne.
Michael, teamster J Derheimer, bds 245 Webster.
Michael, teamster James Wilding & Son, bds 127
ayette.
Nancy, waiter Harmon House.
Patrick E, brakeman, bds 32 Smith.
Thomas F, clk Penn Co, bds 38 Melita.
ı & Monahan (Edward J Golden, Dennis Monahan),
s, Caps and Men's Furnishings, 56 Calhoun.
e Henry, canvasser, res w s Canal 1 n of E Wayne.
ι Himan, grocer, 401 E Wayne, res same.
e Samuel, agt Metropolitan Mnfg Co, bds 401 E
yne.
t Henry H, res 41 St Martin.
erman, brewer Herman Berghoff Brewing Co, bds 313
yette.
Emil, lab, res 197 Jackson.
Frederick (Gombert & Piepenbrink), res 421 E Wash-
m.
John, bds 421 E Washington.
& Pipenbrink (Frederick Gombert, Henry Pipen-
:), meats, 100 Maumee rd.
Anthony, baker H H Barcus, bds 96 Calhoun.
ulius, sawyer Olds' Wagon Works, res 23 Julia.

eibert & Good), res 102 E Washington.
k Seibert & Good, bds 102 E Washington.
ds 102 E Washington.
eorge, lab Indiana Machine Works, res 215 W

ressmkr, bds 77 Brackenridge.
s (James F and Wm), saloon, 274 Calhoun.
1es F (Goodfellow Bros), rms 274 Calhoun.
1 (Goodfellow Bros), rms 274 Calhoun.
inder, dry goods, 38 Calhoun, res 49 W Berry.
1a, clk A Mergentheim, bds 121 Ewing.
:is X, cigars, 139 E Jefferson, res same.
10n, res 121 Ewing.
1e A, helper, res 29 Buchanan.
engineer, res 70 Riverside ave.
D, stereotyper Ft Wayne Newspaper Union,
houn.
B, printer The Sentinel, res 388 E Wayne.
P, porter Adams Exp Co, res 16 Leith.
C, baggage agt Penn Co, res 375 E Washington.
3, stenogr A C Trentman, bds 16 Leith.
, clk Coombs & Co, bds 16 Leith.
E, fitter Ft Wayne Electric Co, bds 50 Taylor.
, clk Coombs & Co, bds 16 Leith.
watchman H C Graffe, res 375 E Washington.
arles D, Supt N Y, C & St L R R, bds The

1b George Jaap, bds 160 Greely.
ab, res 224 W Superior.
ine, domestic The Wayne.
, clk county auditor, rms 67 Harrison.
bds 74 Melita.
s, boilermkr Wabash R R, bds 74 Melita.
H, brakeman, res 8 Burgess.
clk Morgan & Beach, bds 176 Metz.
(wid Jesse O G), res 176 Metz.
k Morgan & Beach, bds 176 Metz.
ick, brakeman, res 312 Clay.
A, clk Heller & Frenkel, res 76 Harmer.
watchman Wabash R R, rms 288 Calhoun.
aria B, bds 76 Harmer.
cklayer, bds 24 Winch.
ab Bass F & M Works, res 44 Smith.
nin F, carp, res 8 Barthold.
A, barber O P Wilkins, bds 14 Bass.

John Pressler, Plumbing, Gas and Steam Fitting.
Columbia, Barr and Dock Streets. ═

218   R. L. POLK & CO.'s

Goshorn Jacob S, Civil Engineer and Superintendent of
  Water Power Co, 386 E Washington, res same.
Goshorn Miss Maggie L, teacher, bds 386 E Washington.
Goshorn Wm H, surveyor, rms 33 E Main.
Gospel Tidings Publishing Co, Augustina R Wheeler
  Propr, rms 24-25 Foster Blk. (*See right bottom lines.*)
Gospel Tidings, Gospel Tidings Publishing Co Publrs,
  rms 24-25 Foster Blk. (*See right bottom lines.*)
Gossow August, market stall No 58, res Washington twp.
Gotsch Christian C, tuner Ft Wayne Organ Co, bds 9 W
  DeWald.
Gotsch Lenora (wid Julius), bds 9 W DeWald.
Gotsch Theodore, clk Morgan & Beach, bds 9 W DeWald.
Gotta Anna, domestic 231 Barr.
Gotta John, bds 7 Oak.
Gotta Michael, mason, res 7 Oak.
Gould C Carroll, stenogr Penn Co, bds 86 W DeWald.
Gould Eliza E (wid Solomon), res 177 Griffith.
Gould Mrs Jennie M, dressmkr, 47 W Main, res same.
Gould Theodore H, engineer Penn Co, res 86 W DeWald.
Gould Wm A, mach Bass F and M Works, bds 86 W DeWald.
Goura Anton, gardener J H Bass.
Gouty Benjamin F, foreman, res s s Howell 2 e of Rumsey.
Gouty Emily S, clk T A Gouty, bds 252 Calhoun.
Gouty James M, res 227 W Superior.
Gouty Laura B, clerk, bds 179 W Superior.
Gouty Louis E, lab Hoffman Bros, bds 227 W Superior.
Gouty Mary, dressmkr, 179 W Superior, bds same.
Gouty Thomas A, grocer, 252 Calhoun, res same.
Gouty Walter O, driver Hoffman Bros, bds 155 Archer ave.
Gouty Wm, solicitor Archer, Housh & Co, bds 252 Calhoun.
Gouty Wm H, teamster Jacob Klett & Sons, res 155 Archer.
Government Building, s e cor Berry and Clinton.
Gowen Henry, carp Louis Diether & Bro, res High nr canal
  feeder.
Grable John, engineer Penn Co, res 111 Fairfield ave.
Grable John jr, engineer, bds 111 Fairfield ave.
Grable Samuel A, yardmaster N Y, C & St L R R, res 152 W
  Wayne.
Grace German Lutheran Church and School, s e cor Pontiac
  and Gay.
Grace Reformed Church, s s Washington bet Barr and
  Lafayette.
Grady John, bds 96 Oliver.
Grady Mary (wid Henry), res 96 Oliver.
Grady Thomas J, brakeman, bds 96 Oliver.

FURNITURE AND PIANO MOVING. RYAN TRUCKING CO.
19 and 21 W. WASHINGTON. TEL. 122.

FORT WAYNE DIRECTORY. 219

Graener Charles, brickmkr, res e s Hoagland ave in rear of Organ
factory.
Graeter Ernest C, sec Indiana Installment Co, res St Louis, Mo.
Graeter Wm F, treas Indiana Installment Co, res Indianapolis,
Ind.
Graf John, lab Penn Co, res 18 Buchanan.
Graf Philip, Dry Goods, Grocery and Saloon, 335–337
Lafayette, res 401 same.
Graffe Carrie M, res 98 Union.
Graffe Charles F (Charles F Graffe & Co), res 24 W Jefferson.
Graffe Charles F & Co (Charles F Graffe), sheet iron workers,
132 Calhoun.
Graffe Edward J, clk C F Graffe & Co, bds 24 W Jefferson.
Graffe Frederick, jeweler H C Graffe, res 138 W Wayne.
Graffe George W, engraver H C Graffe, bds 24 W Jefferson.
Graffe Henry C, Watches, Diamonds and Jewelry—Pres
Jenney Electric Light and Power Co, s e cor Calhoun and
Columbia, res 156 W Jefferson.
Graffe Julian B, bds 471 Lafayette.
Graffe Mary E (wid George W), res 471 Lafayette.
Graffe May, bds 156 W Jefferson.
Graffe Virginia C, bds 98 Union.
Graffe Wm H, clk H C Graffe, bds 24 W Jefferson.
Grage Emma L, forewoman Hoosier Mnfg Co, bds 133 Wallace.
Grage Frederick, truckman, res 185 W Jefferson.
Grage Henry F, trav salesman, res 99 E Berry.
Grage Sophia C, insp, bds 133 Wallace.
Grage Wm A, clk Seavey Hardware Co, bds 185 W Jefferson.
Grage Wm H, lab, res 133 Wallace.
Graham Belle, saleslady Root & Co, bds 212 Calhoun.
Graham Charles A, barber L Uplegger, bds 224 W Superior.
Graham Elizabeth, dressmkr, 593 S Calhoun, bds same.
Graham Elizabeth C (wid Wm), res 126 E Berry.
Graham Frederick V (James E Graham & Son), res 25 Clay.
Graham George E, painter Penn Co, res 178 E Lewis.
Graham George W, lab, res 313 E Washington.
Graham Howard M, printer, bds 313 E Washington.
Graham Jacob, market stall 10, res w s Bluffton s of city limits.
Graham James A, foreman car shops Penn Co, res 230 E Lewis.
Graham James E (James E Graham & Son), law and pension
claim attorney, 26 Bank Block, res 405 Hanna.
Graham James E & Son (James E and Frederick V),
Abstracts of Title, Real Estate, Loans, Insurance and
Steamship Agents, 26 Bank Block.
Graham John W, shoemkr, 174 Calhoun, rms same.
Graham L Maude, milliner, bds 405 Hanna.

RCHITECTS. **WING & MAHURIN,**
41 and 42 Pixley & Long Bldg. Telephone 328.

0   R. L. POLK & CO.'S

aham Mattie, domestic 25 E Main.

aham Robert L, removed to Columbia City, Ind.

aham Samuel D, carp, res 21 Huestis ave.

aham Wm F, fuel clerk Penn Co, res 74 E Williams.

ahl Clemens, teacher St Paul's Ger Luth School, res 6 Summit.

amlich John, lab, bds 197 Broadway.

A R Hall, 3d floor, 80 Calhoun.

and Central Hotel, Mrs Sarah A Bradley propr, 101 Calhoun.

rand Rapids & Indiana Railroad, Operating Cincinnati, Richmond & Ft Wayne R R, P S O'Rourke Supt, R B Rossington Freight Agt, John E Ross Ticket Agt; Offices and Depots with Pennsylvania Co, cor Clinton and Railroad. (*See adv.*)

aney Cornelius, helper Bass F and M Works, res 139 E DeWald.

aney Dennis S, actionmkr Ft Wayne Organ Co, bds 107 Fairfield ave.

aney Michael, molder Bass F and M Works, bds 107 Fairfield ave.

aney Wm, lab, res 107 Fairfield ave.

anger Claude E, removed to Andrews, Ind.

anger Frank T, brakeman, bds 271 Webster.

anger Horace G, chief clk mech dept Wabash R R, bds 202 W Washington.

anger Priscilla (wid Charles), bds 271 Webster.

annemann Anna, bds 235 Webster.

annemann Charles, carp, res 235 Webster.

annemann Emma, forewoman Hoosier Mnfg Co, bds 235 Webster.

anneman Henry C, druggist C B Woodworth & Co, res 237 Webster.

ant Daniel D, blksmith B H Baker, res 20 Lafayette.

nt Ernest, clk Aldine Hotel.

nt John H, trav freight agt N Y, C & St L R R, bds 96 E Wayne.

ssan Isaac (col'd), waiter Wayne Hotel.

ue Frederick H, bricklayer, res 86 Home ave.

ue Mary (wid George), bds 86 Home ave.

ater Gottlieb, coremkr, res 224 Gay.

ves Charles E, sec Ft Wayne Board of Underwriters, 5 Trentman bldg, res 79 Griffith.

r Cornelius, engineer, res 38 Ewing.

r James P, res 90 W Williams.

r Jane M, bds 230 E Wayne.

r John, sewing machine repairer, bds Union House.

Gray John W, R R conductor, res 230 E Wayne.
Gray Justina E, bds 230 E Wayne.
Gray Neil, engineer, bds 230 E Wayne.
Gray Wm J, conductor, bds 230 E Wayne.
Greek Charles W, teamster, res 64 W Wayne.
Greek Frederick, carp, res 39 Huestis ave.
Green Arthur, hostler, bds 533 E Wayne.
Green Charles, market stall No 96, res New Haven rd.
Green Emily L, dressmkr, 179 Jackson, bds same.
Green Flora (col'd), bds 281 E Washington.
Green Frank R, clk Diamond Hotel.
Green George W, brakeman, bds 62 Madison.
Green Hugh, res 179 Jackson.
Green John (col'd), whitewasher, res 35 Grand.
Green Joseph, helper Bass F & M Works, bds 145 E Lewis.
Green Letta M, dressmkr 179 Jackson.
Green Lewis H, compositor Ft Wayne Gazette, res 276 W
    Washington.
Green Louis (col'd), res 533 E Wayne.
Green Margaret (wid Johnston), res 62 Madison.
Green Mary A (wid Wm H), res 114 W Berry.
Green M Frances (wid Seth R), physician, 139 W Main, res
    same.
Green Gertrude, bds 139 W Main.
Green Noah (col'd), res 533 E Wayne.
Green Sarah (col'd), laundress, bds 533 E Wayne.
Green Seth F, shpg clk G E Bursley & Co, bds 139 W Main.
Green Wm H, agt, res 109 Lafayette.
Greenawalt George L, Physician and Surgeon, 151 E
    Wayne, res same.
Greene Electa, tailoress, res 63 W Superior.
Greene Mrs Ella, res 137 High.
Greene Frank, teamster, bds 140 High.
Greene Richard B, mach hand Ft Wayne Organ Co, bds 32
    Home ave.
Greene Richard E, stopmkr, bds 32 Home ave.
Greene Thomas C, engineer Hoffman Bros, res 95 W 4th.
Greene Walter A, lab, res 140 High.
Greener John, lab Bass F & M Works, res 119 Eliza.
Greenewald David D, clk C B Woodworth & Co, bds 103
    Lafayette.
Greenick Abraham A, fireman Penn Co, res 139 E DeWald.
Greenlun Helsel J, flagman, bds 57 Oliver.
Greenlun Herbert, hostler, bds 57 Oliver.
Greenlun Marion F, pdlr, res 57 Oliver.
Greensfelder Aaron, clk J B White, bds 95 Ewing.

16

Greensfelder Gustave, real estate, res 95 Ewing.
Greensfelder Josias, cashier J B White, bds 95 Ewing.
Greensfelder Mollie, bds 95 Ewing.
Greenwaldt Cora, dressmkr, bds 106 W Superior.
Greenwood Myrtle, saleswoman Singer Mnfg Co, bds 121 Harrison.
Greer Charles E, lab A L Johns & Co, bds 20 Erie.
Greer Clara, teacher, bds 20 Erie.
Greer Frank J, clk Penn Co, res 74 Calhoun.
Greer Mrs Frank J, artist, studio 74 Calhoun, res same.
Greer James L, harnessmkr A L Johns & Co, bds 20 Erie.
Greer John, res 36 Walnut.
Greer John jr, clk Ft Wayne Electric Co, res 49 Walnut.
Greer John W, carp, res 20 Erie.
Greer Thomas jr, clk county auditor, res 204 E Wayne.
Gregg Anna E (wid James S), res 176 E Wayne.
Greibel, see Griebel.
Greim Mrs Margaretta, res 92 Fairfield ave.
Grennell Melinda W (wid Hiram W), bds 392 Fairfield ave.
Grenouillet Margaret (wid Jacob), res 305 Hanna.
Grenzenbach Henry F, lab, res 22 Jane.
Grenzenbach John, painter Miller & Haller, bds Frederick Butz.
Gresham Frederick H (col'd), janitor Pixley & Long bldg, res 27 Clinton.
Gretzinger Jacob J, mach, res 230 Fairfield ave.
Greve Frederick C, cigarmkr Christian Wenninghoff, res 147 Broadway.
Greve Joseph, bridge carp, res n s Cochran 2 w of Coombs.
Greve Wm, carp, res 28 Erie.
Grey, see Gray.
Gribben Charles O, helper Penn Co, bds 24 Douglas ave.
Gribben James, fireman G R & I R R, bds 24 Douglas ave.
Gribben John F, mach Ft Wayne Electric Co, bds 24 Douglas avenue.
Gribben Mary J (wid James M), res 24 Douglas ave.
Grieb Andrew, lather, bds n s Cochran 2 e of Coombs.
Grieb John, tailor, 182 E Lewis, bds same.
Grieb John N, switchman, res 182 E Lewis.
Griebe Henrietta (wid John), bds 106 W Washington.
Griebel Annie, bds 141 W 3d.
Griebel A Louis, business mngr Indiana Staats Zeitung, res 211 W Wayne.
Griebel Charles (Griebel, Wyckoff & Becker), res 346 E Washington.
Griebel Christian, teamster, res w s Eagle 2 s of Taylor.

COUNTERS, SHELVING, Office and Store Fixtures Made on Short —Notice by—
L. DIETHER & BRO., 44 to 54 East Superior St. Factory at 100 Pearl St.

FORT WAYNE DIRECTORY. 223

Griebel Edward R, clk Andrew Jacobs, bds w s Eagle 2 s of Taylor.
Griebel George, teamster, bds 141 W 3d.
Griebel Lizzie, laundress Ft Wayne Steam Laundry, bds 141 3d.
Griebel Louis (Griebel & Son), res 58 E Jefferson.
Griebel Louis, teamster, res 141 W 3d.
Griebel Wm J (Griebel & Son), res 168 Madison.
Griebel Wm T, collarmkr F L Racine, res 36 Cass.
Griebel, Wyckoff & Becker (Charles Griebel, O C Wyckoff, H W Becker), marble and granite, 74 and 76 W Main.
Griebel & Son (Louis and Wm J), furniture, 44 E Main.
Griener Christian C, porter, res 22 Allen.
Grier Edna E, bds s w cor Pontiac and Oliver.
Grier Joseph H (Hayden & Grier), res s w cor Pontiac and Oliver.
Grier Viola L, bds s w cor Pontiac and Oliver.
Griest Albert B, painter B H Baker, rms 34 W Main.
Griffin Nora, attendant Indiana School for Feeble-Minded Youth.
Griffin Thomas T, silversmith Ft Wayne Electric Co, res 14 Walnut.
Griffith Chauncey M, draughtsman H E Matson, bds 77 W Williams.
Griffith David S, clk Stewart & Hahn, res 135 Holman.
Griffith James M (Griffith and Son), res 15 Suttenfield.
Griffith Levi (Griffith & Son), res 77 W Williams.
Griffith Maurice E, clk Stewart & Hahn, res 128 W Main.
Griffith & Son (Levi and James M), carps, 77 W Williams.
Griffiths Lewis, carp, bds 298 Hoagland ave.
Griffiths May, bds 348 W Washington.
Griffiths Wm E, hardware, 120 Broadway, res 348 W Washington.
Griftmeyer Frederick, lab Hoffman Bros, bds 190 W Main.
Griftmeyer Wm, trav agt, res 16 Walnut.
Griley Michael, fireman, res 197 High.
Grill Peter, lab, res e s Spy Run ave 1 s of river bridge.
Grim Carl, barber, bds Riverside Hotel.
Grime Edward, teamster, res 186 Montgomery.
Grimes Charles A, floor-walker Root & Co, res 244 E Washington.
Grimm Clara, dressmkr, 222 Broadway, bds same.
Grimm Flora (wid John), res 222 Broadway.
Grimm Theresa, dressmkr, bds 222 Broadway.
Grimme Frank, switchman, res 147 Madison.
Grimme Ferdinand, car builder Penn Co, res 229 Madison.
Grimme Gerbardt B (J H Grimme & Sons), res 162 Griffith.

Robert Spice, Pumps, Pipe, Hose, Fittings and Brass Goods
48 WEST MAIN and 11 PEARL STS.

224   R. L. POLK & CO.'S

Grimme John, plumber Robert Ogden, bds 229 Madison.
Grimme John C (J H Grimme & Sons), res 2 McClellan.
Grimme John H (J H Grimme & Sons), res 83 Brackenridge.
Grimme J H & Sons (John H, Gerhardt B and John C),
    Merchant Tailors, 108 Calhoun.
Grindle Alfred, draughtsman Wing & Mahurin, res 208 W
    Creighton ave.
Griner Henry, lab, res s s of Rudisill ave 1 w Piqua road.
Gripton Wm C, plasterer, res 29 Union.
Griswold Crawford, bridge builder Penn Co, res 165 W De
    Wald.
Griswold Wm H, letter carrier P O, bds 165 W DeWald.
Groddik Mrs Emma, tailoress Indiana School for Feeble-
    Minded Youth.
Groepler Martin, brewer The Herman Berghoff Brewing Co,
    bds 546 E Wayne.
Groepler Moritz, brewer The Herman Berghoff Brewing Co,
    res s w cor Humphrey and Wabash ave.
Grohmann August, propr Washington House, 121–123 Calhoun.
Groman Joseph E, painter, bds Jewel House.
Gronau Augusta, domestic 134 Eliza.
Gronau Frederick W, painter Olds' Wagon Wks, res n s Pitts-
    burgh 2 e of Lumbard.
Gronau Louis, lab Penn Co, res n e cor Pittsburgh and Lum-
    bard.
Gronau Wm, butcher Frederick Eckart, res 112 Hanna.
Grosh Gustave, mach Wabash R R, bds 501 Hanna.
Grosh Henry, car builder Penn Co, bds 501 Hanna.
Grosh Wilhelmina (wid John), res 501 Hanna.
Groshoff Frank, driver J B White, res 34 Summit.
Grosjean Augustus, res 86 Smith.
Grosjean Francis, carp, res n w cor Marion and canal feeder.
Gross Augusta, bds 241 W Jefferson.
Gross Rev Charles, pastor Emanuel Lutheran Church, res 241
    W Jefferson.
Gross Charles H, lab, bds 163 Van Buren.
Gross Emma, dressmkr, bds 284 Broadway.
Gross Gottlieb, mach hand, bds 163 Van Buren.
Gross Martin C, bkkpr Fort Wayne Electric Co, res 128 Rock-
    hill.
Gross Paulina (wid Frederick), res 163 Van Buren.
Gross Rika, bds 312 W Main.
Gross Wm O (Gross & Pellens), res 159 W Washington.
Gross & Pellens (Wm O Gross, Joseph B Pellens), Drug
    gists and Dealers in Barbers' Supplies, 94 Calhoun.
Grossenbacher Frederick, helper Wabash R R, res 7 Bass.

irosvenor Harry, carp Alfred Shrimpton, res 64 Burgess.
irosvenor Herbert J, lab Hoffman Bros, bds 64 Burgess.
irosvenor Mark H, lab Hoffman Bros, bds 64 Burgess.
irote Caroline (wid Charles), bds Fred Buechner.
irote Frederick, bds Frederick Buechner.
irote Herman, mach Ind Machine Works, bds 3 Breck.
irote Minnie, bds 120 Harrison.
irothaus Frances, bds 194 E Wayne.
irothaus George H, apprentice Seavey Hardware Co, bds 194
   E Wayne.
irothaus Henry F, res 194 E Wayne.
rothaus Joseph H, blksmith Penn Co, bds 194 E Wayne.
rothaus Lizzie M, tailoress C Kruse, bds 194 E Wayne.
rotholtman Henry A (H A Grotholtman & Co), res 28 E 4th.
rotholtman H A & Co (Henry A Grotholtman, J Henry
   Meyers), contractors, 48 W Jefferson.
rotrian Mary, domestic 261 W Berry.
rout Wm H, conductor, res 37 Huestis ave.
rove Maxwell J, boilermkr Penn Co, res 23 W Butler.
roves Oscar, conductor, res 11 Force.
rubbe Daniel, engineer, rms 49 Elm.
ruber Andrew, clerk, bds 108 Jackson.
ruber August C, coppersmith, res 64 Walnut.
ruber Charles J, lab, bds 108 Jackson.
ruber Miss Clementine, dressmkr E A Waltemath, bds 108
   Jackson.
ruber Edward J, band sawyer Ft Wayne Organ Co, res 13
   Nirdlinger ave.
ruber Edward J jr, cigarmkr F J Gruber, bds 18 Wilt.
ruber Frank J, boilermkr Bass F & M Works, res 48 E
   DeWald.
ruber Frank J, Cigar Manufacturer, 110 Calhoun, res
   60 Brackenridge.
ruber John M, res 18 Wilt.
ruber John V, sheet iron wkr, res 80 Taylor.
ruber Joseph A, mach Ft Wayne Electric Co, res 108 Jackson.
ruber Joseph L, Dealer in Hardware, Stoves and
   Furnaces, 140 Fairfield ave, res 21 Brackenridge.
uber Josephine (wid Valentine), bds 13 Nirdlinger ave.
uber Michael J jr, cigarmkr F J Gruber, bds 18 Wilt.
ueb George, baker J H Schwieters.
ueb George J, helper Wabash R R, bds 84 Nirdlinger ave.
uesbeck Wm W, tel opr Penn Co Depot, bds 46 E Jefferson.
ueter Wm, laborer, bds 100 Montgomery.
uhler Mary (wid Andrew), removed to Toledo, O.
hlka Wm, lab Bass F and M Works, res 64 Walton ave.

Penn Mutual LIFE INSURANCE CO. of PHILA,
CLARK FAIRBANK, General Agent, 19 Court Street.

226   R. L. POLK & CO.'S

Grummon Fowler, tree agt, res 170 Brackenridge.
Grummon Frederick M, stenogr, bds 170 Brackenridge.
Grund Edna L, bkkpr D N Foster Furniture Co, bds 176 W
    DeWald.
Grund John H, hoop shaver S D Bisler, res 24 Scheck.
Grund Mrs Mary, bds 57 Melita.
Grund Philip R, blksmith, res 176 W DeWald.
Grusankamp Frederick, blksmith, res 51 W 5th.
Guardian Medical and Surgical Institute, Brookfield Gard
    mngr, 13 W Wayne.
Guenther Anna, domestic Indiana School for Feeble-Minded
    Youth.
Guenther Clara, domestic 127 Harrison.
Guenther Henry, barber, 318 E Washington, res 11 Maumee
    avenue.
Guerin John, lab, bds Peter Guerin.
Guerin Mary B, domestic 14 Jackson.
Guerin Peter, farmer, res nr Allen County Asylum.
Guetner Herman H, car builder Penn Co, res 154 Smith.
Guffin Elmer H, barber Christian Fuchs, bds 45 E Main.
Gulfe Sylvester, stoker Ft Wayne Gas Light Co, res e s Spy
    Run ave 2 n of Prospect ave.
Guiff Fannie, cook 25 E Main.
Guiff Paul, market stall No 76, res w s Coldwater rd 7 miles.
Guild Albert D, accountant, res 372 Fairfield ave.
Guild Charles G (Ohnhaus & Co), res South Wayne, Ind.
Guild Charles G, supt Jenney Electric L and P Co, res 372
    Fairfield ave.
Guillaume James, carp, res 57 Wells.
Guinon Mitchell F, engineer G R & I R R, res 49 Baker.
Guise Joseph, gardener J A Shoaff.
Guldlin Olaf N, pres Western Gas Construction Co, res 67–70
    Pixley & Long bldg.
Gulke Wm, watchman, bds 64 Walton ave.
Gumbert Henry, watchman, res 192 Jackson.
Gumpper Charles H, supply agt Nickel Plate R R, bds 238 Cal-
    houn.
Gumpper Christopher C, baker, 238 Calhoun, res same.
Gumpper Jacob D, grocer, 240 Calhoun, res 16 E DeWald.
Gumpper John F, brick mason, res 46 Home ave.
Gunder Emanuel, collarmkr A Racine, res 223 Wells.
Gunkel Otto, warehouseman M Baltes, res 40 Nirdlinger ave.
Gunkel Otto F, tinsmith J J Freiburger, bds 40 Nirdlinger ave.
Gunkler John P, cabtmkr Ft Wayne Organ Co, res 140 Force.
Gunn Lucian A, fireman, res 187 Hayden.
Gunn Thomas W, sergeant, U S army recruiting rendezvous.

Gunther, *see Guenther.*
Gurnett Charles O, molder Bass F & M Works, res 108 Gay.
Gurry Alice, bds s w cor Wheeler and Runnion ave.
Gusching Jacob, truckmkr L S & M S Ry, res 137 Wells.
Gusching Joseph, policeman, res 150 Holman.
Gust August, lab, res 44 Smith.
Gust John, blksmith, res 65 Oliver.
Gust Matilda, domestic 262 E Washington.
Gutermuth Benjamin, baker, 29 W Columbia, res 155 Broadway.
Gutermuth Casper J, turner Jacob Klett & Sons, res 39 W Jefferson.
Gutermuth George, mach hd Hoffman Bros, bds 50 Archer.
Gutermuth Jeanette, bds 155 Broadway.
Gutermuth John, bds 50 Archer ave.
Gutermuth John, fireman C L Centlivre Brewing Co, res w s Hench 2 n of Hoffman.
Gutermuth John G, bds 51 Maple ave.
Gutermuth Valentine, mngr Root & Co, res 51 Maple ave.
Guth Henry P, molder Bass F & M Works, res 104 John.
Guthe Joseph, cabinetmkr Peters Box and Lumber Co, res 88 W 4th.
Guy John F, brakeman, res 206 High.
Guy Lena, domestic 137 W Wayne.
Guye Francisca (wid Henry), bds 332 E Washington.
Guyer Rudolph, market stall No 18, res St Joseph twp.
Guyer Ettie, cook 25 E Main.

H

Haag Adam, carp, bds 10 McClellan.
Haag Charles J (Brunner & Haag), res 155 Van Buren.
Haag Eliza (wid John), bds 329 W Washington.
Haag Gottlieb L, stonecutter Keller & Braun, res 23 Rockhill.
Haag John G, asst supt Prudential Ins Co, res 323 W Washington.
Haag Louisa, tailoress Gustav Scheffler, bds 155 Van Buren.
Haag Wm, wks Electric Light Works, res 329 W Washington.
Haak Theodore, market stall No 64, res Washington twp.
Haas, *see also Hass and Hess.*
Haas Louis H, lab Penn Co, res 51 Hugh.
Haas Simon, lab, res 358 E Washington.

Haas Wm J, freight clk, res 16 S Wayne ave.
Haase Frank L, lab Penn Co, res 54 Liberty.
Habbert J Henry, lab Wabash Co, res 5 Jones.
Habecker Alice M, principal, bds 64 McClellan.
Habecker Annie G, teacher, bds 64 McClellan.
Habecker Charles W, painter, bds 180 Hayden.
Habecker Charles W, printer Ft Wayne Newspaper Un'
  bds 64 McClellan.
Habecker Elias, carp, res 64 McClellan.
Habecker Frank E, printer Daily News, res 134 Lafayette.
Habecker John F, clk J B White, bds 180 Hayden.
Habecker Wm H, carp, res 180 Hayden.
Habel, *see also Abel.*
Habel Charles C, mach Wabash R R, res 164 Taylor.
Habel John G, mach Kerr-Murray Mnfg Co, res 172 Taylor
Habel Pauline, seamstress, bds 172 Taylor.
Haberkorn Emil F, mach Penn Co, res 130 Harrison.
Haberkorn Henry, mach Ft Wayne Electric Co, res 236 Hoa
  land ave.
Haberkorn Huldah, tailoress, bds 130 Harrison.
Haberkorn Theodore, mach, res 69 Douglas ave.
Habersack Christian, painter, bds Windsor Hotel.
Habig Hubert, blksmith Kerr-Murray Mnfg Co, res 34 Leitl
Hache, *see Heche.*
Hachman Frederick, stonecutter, res s s Summer 1 e of Warr
Hachmeier Henry, bricklayer, res 66 Stophlet.
Hachmeier Wm, car builder Penn Co, res 46 Stophlet.
Hackett Block, e s Calhoun bet Wayne and Washington.
Hackett Edward A K, Propr Fort Wayne Sentin
  res 207 W Berry.
Hackius F Wm, clk Root & Co, bds 71 Brackenridge.
Hackius Gustave L, treas Kerr-Murray Mnfg Co, bds
  Brackenridge.
Hackius Lena M, bds 71 Brackenridge.
Hackius Mary A (wid Andrew), res 71 Brackenridge.
Hacklander Alwill, carpet weaver, 57 W Superior, res same.
Haddon Alfred H, mach Ft Wayne Electric Co, bds 25
  Creighton ave.
Hadley Arthur L, wks Electric Light Works, bds 322 W Wa:
  ington.
Hadsell Cyrus M, teamster G C Miller, bds same.
Haegerman, *see Hagerman.*
Haenel August, driver, bds 252 Clinton.
Haenel Wm, engineer, res 244 W Main.
Haertig Ernst, mach hd Wayne Knitting Mills, bds 371 Calho
Haffner Christian, baker, 105 E Lewis, res 30 Madison.

Haffner Edward, lab M Baltes, bds 30 Madison.
Haffner Frederick C, driver, bds 30 Madison.
Haffner George M, driver, bds 30 Madison.
Haffner Lawrence, saloon, 202 Broadway, res same.
Hagan, *see also Hagen.*
Hagan Edward, barber Ehrman & Geller, bds 46 Harrison.
Hagan Mary C (wid Frank), dressmkr, res 46 Harrison.
Hagan Milton, printer, bds 122 Wilt.
Hagan Minnie R, shirtmkr P G Kuttner, bds 122 Wilt.
Hagan Robert W, lab, res 122 Wilt.
Hagan Thomas W, deputy clerk Superior Court, res 108 N Harrison.
Hagan Mrs Wm, bds 247 Webster.
Hagedorn Ernest H, lab, bds Herman Hagedorn.
Hagedorn Herman, lab Penn Co, res n e cor Pine and Locust.
Hagedorn Hulda C, tailoress Gottlieb Stauffer, bds 130 Harmer.
Hagedorn Jessie, domestic 29 W Lewis.
Hagemann Elizabeth, tailoress, bds 188 Broadway.
Hagemann Frederick W, cigarmkr L Dessauer & Co, res 70 Wilt.
Hagemann Henry W, clk Root & Co, bds 188 Broadway.
Hagemann Henry W, molder Bass F & M Works, bds 92 Oliver.
Hagemann Joseph, gardener, res s w cor Edsall ave and Wabash R R.
Hagemann Louis E, clk Root & Co, res 165 Jackson.
Hagemann Wm F, lab, res 188 Broadway.
Hagen, *see also Hagan.*
Hagen Wm, helper Ft Wayne Iron Works, res 105 W Butler.
Hager Edith E M, dressmkr, bds 391 E Washington.
Hager Emma, labeler, bds 391 E Washington.
Hager Ernst M, lab, bds 391 E Washington.
Hager George M, clk J B White, res 391 E Washington.
Hager George W F, mach hand, bds 391 E Washington.
Hagerman Henry, lab, bds 41 Gay.
Hagerman Henry, molder Bass F & M Works, bds 92 Oliver.
Hagerman John, market stall No 84, res Adams twp.
Haggerty Ella, domestic Wayne Hotel.
Haggerty John, lab, res 309 Hanna.
Haggerty Thomas P, watchman, res 59 Laselle.
Hagist Adolph, mattressmkr P E Wolf, res 4 University.
Hagist Henry, cigarmkr Louis Bender, bds 433 E Washington.
Hagist John G, sewer contractor, 433 E Washington, res same.
Hahn Albert G, clk Charles Sauer, bds 157 W Main.
Hahn John, car repairer Penn Co, res w s Abbott 2 s of Pontiac.
Hahn Frederick A, lab Hoffman Bros, bds 157 W Main.
Hahn Henry, coremkr Bass F & M Works, res 215 John.
Hahn Wm (Stewart & Hahn), res 208 W Berry.

Hahn Wm, saloon, 148 W Main, res 157 same.
Hahnet Anton, mach hand Wayne Knitting Mills, bds Washington House.
Haiber Charles F, grocer, 122–124 Wells, res same.
Haiber Frederick, Notary Public and Collection Agt, 64 Wells, res same.
Haiber George W, grocer, 378 Hanna, res same.
Haiber John, lab George Jaap, res 17 Hoffman.
Haiber Lorenz, meats, 15 High, bds 64 Wells.
Haiber Wm B, clk, bds 64 Wells.
Hail George S (Hail & Tower), res 71 Huestis ave.
Hail Martha A (wid John D), bds 20 Savilla pl.
Hail & Tower (George S Hail, Francis M Tower), Decorators and Sign Painters, 16 E Columbia. (*See right bottom lines.*)
Haines, *see also Haynes.*
Haines Ada E, bds 256 E Washington.
Haines Henry H, medicine mnfr, 256 E Washington, res same.
Haines Mary, domestic 90 E Wayne.
Haines Morris M, cabinetmkr, res 30 Buchanan.
Hake, *see also Hecke.*
Hake Frank, saloon, 26 N Wells, res 28 same.
Hakemeyer Minnie, domestic 254 W Washington.
Hale Anna, domestic 18 W Washington.
Hale Emma, domestic 35 W Washington.
Hale James C, lab Salimonie Mining & Gas Co, res 10 Ewing.
Hale Martin, lab, res 194 Taylor.
Haley Daniel P, trav agt Falk & Lamley, res 197 E Jefferson.
Haley John, brakeman, bds n e cor Grant and Oliver.
Haley Joseph A, engineer, res 339 W Washington.
Haley Michael, res 224 W Creighton ave.
Hall Albert H, lab, res 81 Winch.
Hall Almira, domestic The Saratoga.
Hall Charles S, 1st Lt 13th Infantry, recruiting officer U S A, bds Wayne Hotel.
Hall Edgar M, brakeman, res 41 Holton ave.
Hall Edward W, mach hand, res s e cor Winch and Penn.
Hall Ella (wid Ernest B) bds 18 Hamilton.
Hall Elmira, res 18 Harrison.
Hall Frank C, brakeman, res 27 Taylor.
Hall Ira E, brakeman, res 112 Richardson.
Hall James E, carp, res 254 W Creighton ave.
Hall Jennie, domestic 28 E Columbia.
Hall John S, mach hd Ft Wayne Spoke Works, bds 34 Winch.
Hall John W, lawyer, 12 Bank Block, res 235 E Wayne.
Hall Lizzie, bds 34 Winch.

Geo. E. Johnson, DENTIST, 74 Calhoun Street. Res, 188 W. Berry St.

FORT WAYNE DIRECTORY. 231

Hall Mark C, brakeman, res 191 E Washington.
Hall Mrs Mary, res s w cor Elizabeth and Spy Run ave.
Hall Rinaldo, lab, res 147 E Jefferson.
Hall Samantha B, milliner, 34 W Main, res same.
Hall Thomas N, conductor Penn Co, res 167 Holman.
Hall Wm, res 34 Winch.
Hall Wm A, asst foreman Ft Wayne Newspaper Union, res 113 E Washington.
Halleck Wm H, flagman, res s w cor Milan and Lillie.
Hallderman Jacob, trav agt, res 219 W Wayne.
Haller Adolph, lab Weil Bros & Co, res 34 Elm.
Haller Miss Frida, clk Gottlieb Haller, bds 366 Calhoun.
Haller Gottlieb (Miller & Haller), meats, 366 Calhoun, res same.
Haller Wm, meats, 109 E Lewis, bds 100 Montgomery.
Hallien Nellie, domestic 227 E Lewis.
Halmer Laura, bds 92 Franklin ave.
Halstein Henry D, clk, res 188 E Washington.
Halter, see Alter.
Hamaker Henry, brakeman, bds 100 Montgomery.
Hambrock Frederick, sawyer Olds' Wagon Works, bds 20 Jane.
Hambrock Henry C, mach hand Olds' Wagon Works, bds 20 Jane.
Hambrock Wm J, bricklayer, res 598 Lafayette.
Hamilton Miss Agnes, bds A H Hamilton.
Hamilton Albert, teamster Ft Wayne Transfer and Storage Co, bds 20 Harrison.
Hamilton Miss Alice, bds Montgomery Hamilton.
Hamilton Allen, mach Penn Co, res 19 Holman.
Hamilton Allen, student, bds A H Hamilton.
Hamilton Andrew H, Vice Pres Olds' Wagon Works, res s w cor Clinton and Lewis.
Hamilton A Louise, teacher, bds R J Hamilton.
Hamilton Bridget (wid John), res 151 W Wayne.
Hamilton Catherine S, bds n s Hanna 5 s of Pontiac.
Hamilton Miss Edith, bds Montgomery Hamilton.
Hamilton Miss Eliza, bds Hamilton Homestead.
Hamilton Eliza A (wid Benjamin), res 13 Bell ave.
Hamilton Emerine J Library, Margaret V Hamilton Pres and Sec, (2,000 Volumes), 23½ W Wayne.
Hamilton Mrs Frances, principal Hoagland school, bds 151 W Wayne.
Hamilton Frederick R, mach, bds R J Hamilton.
Hamilton George, lab Penn Co, res s s New Haven rd 2 e of Glasgow.
Hamilton Homestead, s e cor Clinton and Lewis.
Hamilton House, Wm H Jones propr, 103 W Berry.

Hamilton Ina, domestic Hotel Rich.

Hamilton I Louise (wid James), bds 204 E Wayne.

Hamilton Jane A, res 235 E Wayne.

Hamilton Miss Jessie, bds A H Hamilton.

Hamilton John, lab, bds Sarah J Hamilton.

Hamilton Joseph A, teamster J B White, res 38 Summit.

Hamilton Miss Katherine, bds A H Hamilton.

Hamilton Miss Margaret V, pres and sec Emerine J Hamilton
Library, res s e cor Clinton and Lewis.

Hamilton Montgomery, res n w cor Clinton and Montgomery.

Hamilton National Bank, Charles McCulloch Pres,
John Mohr Jr Cash, Charles W Orr Asst Cash, 44 Calhoun.

Hamilton Peter, boilermkr Wabash R R, res w s Hanna 5 s of
Pontiac.

Hamilton Robert J jr, clk Nickel Plate R R, bds n s Bluffton
rd 1 w of St Mary's river.

Hamilton Robert J, gardener, res n s Bluffton rd 1 w of St
Mary's river.

Hamilton Sarah J (wid Mathias), res e s Hanover bet E Wayne
and E Washington.

Hamilton Taber, bds A H Hamilton.

Hamilton Wm G, mach, bds w s Hanna 5 s of Pontiac.

Hamilton Wm J, sawyer, res 407 S Clinton.

Hamlet Jesse, baggageman, rms 94 Calhoun.

Hamm Andrew, market stall No 11, res Adams twp.

Hamm John, lab Penn Co, res 207 Maumee rd.

Hammer Ernst, lab Bass F & M Works, bds 35 Smith.

Hammerle Otto, molder Kerr-Murray Mnfg Co, bds 301 W
Main.

Hammerle Xavier, grocery and saloon, 299 W Main, res 301
same.

Hammill Harry H, Propr The Annex Sample Room, 60½
Calhoun, res 254 W Jefferson.

Hammond Harrison, lab, bds 464 E Wayne.

Hammond James (col'd), cook, res 21 Melita.

Hammond Martin E, lab, res 30 W Butler.

Hammond Newton, lab, bds 464 E Wayne.

Hammond Robert, Propr The Home Billiard Hall and
Saloon, 20 W Berry, res 130 Lafayette.

Hammond Thomas G, caller Penn Co, res 9 Indiana ave.

Hanafeld Cord, carp, res 190 E Lewis.

Hanagan John, lab, res 11 Breck.

Handenschild John, lab Penn Co, bds 199 Broadway.

Handschiegel Anthony, potashmkr Christopher Strasburg, res
119 Lafayette.

andy Harry H, fireman, bds Hotel Waverly.
anes John, mach hand Rhinesmith & Simonson, res 14 Fairfield avenue.
aney, *see also Heany.*
aney Mary (wid Josiah), bds 16 Colerick.
ankel Christina, domestic 197 W Wayne.
ankens Bernard, brick mason, res 141 Suttenfield.
anker Huldah, opr S M Foster, bds 40 Charles.
anker Laura, opr S M Foster, bds 40 Charles.
anley Albert H, lab, res 73 Cass.
anley Ellen (wid James H), res rear 43 Baker.
anley Paul J, foreman Penn Co, res 4 Monroe.
anna C Hovey, bds Hanna Homestead.
anna Elizabeth C (wid Henry C), res 135 E Berry.
anna Henry C, lawyer, 8 and 9 Bank blk, res 135 E Berry.
anna Homestead, s s Lewis opp Division.
anna Hugh T, bds Hanna Homestead.
anna James T, real estate, 8 and 9 Bank blk, res 266 W
Wayne.
anna John L, clk, bds 288 W Berry.
anna Joseph T, trav salesman, bds 135 E Berry.
anna Miss Marguerite, artist, bds 288 W Berry.
anna Martha E (wid Samuel T), res 288 W Berry.
anna Oliver S, cashier Nuttman & Co, res 130 W Berry.
anna Robert B, lawyer, 8 and 9 Bank blk, res 135 E Berry.
anna School, s w cor Hanna and Wallace.
annink George, coachman 203 W Berry.
anrahan Timothy, res rear 20 Bass.
ans Adam, blksmith Olds' Wagon Works, res 18 Charles.
ans Bruno, tinner Gerding & Aumann Bros, bds 53 Hugh.
ans Charles A, blksmith Bass F & M Works, res 253 Broadway.
ans Hermann, carp, bds 53 Hugh.
ans Laura, domestic 16 E De Wald.
ans Minnie, bds 53 Hugh.
ans Theresa (wid Carl), res 53 Hugh.
ansen Peter C, saloon, 162 Holman, res 208 Monroe.
ansen Richard C, steam fitter A Hattersley & Sons, res 31
Summit.
ansen Wm E, mach Ft Wayne Iron Works, bds 31 Summit.
anson Albert P C, blksmith Olds' Wagon Works, res 61 Charles.
anson H Clark, lab Olds' Wagon Works, bds 10 McClellan.
anson Elizabeth (wid Thomas), bds J H Doswell.
anson Joseph, bandsawmkr Ft Wayne Iron Works, res 395
Broadway.
pp, *see also App.*
pp Elizabeth, domestic 169 W Wayne.

Happ Nicholas, stonemason, res 89 Summit.
Happ Wm, mason, bds 89 Summit.
Harbauer Peter, driver Am Ex Co, res 115 College.
Harber, *see also Harper and Herber.*
Harber August A, clk M H Wefel, bds 390 Hanna.
Harber Gerhard T, lab Bass F & M Works, bds 38 Oak.
Harber Henry J, flagman, bds 390 Hanna.
Harber Jacob, carp, bds 38 Oak.
Harber Joseph, fireman, bds 17 Burgess.
Harber Joseph W, fireman, bds 390 Hanna.
Harber Mary T, dressmkr Mrs G J Stier, bds 97 John.
Harber Peter, mach, res 390 Hanna.
Harber Peter M, messenger, bds 390 Hanna.
Harber Philip, carp, bds 38 Oak.
Harber Valentine, helper Olds' Wagon Works, res 97 John.
Harden Daniel B, washer Lee & Fulton, rms 18 W Wayne.
Hardendorf Charles, teamster Jacob Klett & Sons, res 169 Gay.
Hardendorf Eugene, trav agt, bds 113 W Wayne.
Hardendorf Myron R, blksmith Penn Co, res 22 Laselle.
Hardendorf Rosselle, helper Penn Co, bds 22 Laselle.
Hardendorf Theodore, wood turner Louis Diether & Bro, res 13 Barthold ave.
Hardesty Mrs Mary A, bds 43 W Superior.
Hardesty Wm H, lab, res 43 W Superior.
Hardigan James, engineer, rms 24 Boone.
Harding Mrs Sadie, bds 70 W Jefferson.
Harding Daniel L, real estate, 28 Bank blk, res 174 W DeWald.
Harding Frank, brakeman, rms 18 Brackenridge.
Harding Jennie, bds 467 Harrison.
Harding Joseph F, brakeman, bds Monroe House.
Harding Perry, lab, res 96 Franklin ave.
Harding Robert F, clk Ft Wayne Electric Co, bds 174 W De Wald.
Hardung Casper, painter, bds 8 Force.
Hardung Frederick, merchant tailor, 35 E Main, res 207 Madison.
Hardy Charles E, switchman N Y, C & St L R R, bds 34½ Centre.
Hargan Frederick, lab, bds 364 E Lewis.
Harges Edward, trimmer City Carriage Works, bds 329 E Washington.
Harges Theodore C, carriagemkr City Carriage Works, bds 329 E Washington.
Harges Wm F, blksmith, res 329 E Washington.
Hargon Frederick, lab, bds 364 E Lewis.
Harkemper Wm, bkkpr H C Graffe, rms 2 E Columbia.
Harkenrider, *see also Hergenrather.*
Harkenrider Henry J, policeman, res 294 Hanna.

rider John, lab, res n s Jesse 1 w of city limits.
rider John M, brakeman, res 44 Elm.
rider Joseph, car builder Penn Co, bds 501 Hanna.
rider Wm, butcher John Suelzer, res 76 Buchanan.
d Henry, coremkr Bass F and M Works, bds 225 Jones.
res Elizabeth, domestic 241 W Main.
n *see Herman.*
r School, n w cor Harmer and E Jefferson.
yer Cyrus L, lab Bass F and M Works, bds 17 Gay.
yer Frederick, yard foreman Louis Diether & Bro, res
　Maiden Lane.
yer Henry J, conductor, res 288 E Creighton ave.
yer John F, wood worker Olds' Wagon Wks, bds 17 Gay.
yer Lowell C, lab, bds 17 Gay.
yer Wm, res 17 Gay.
n Blanche, bds 70 Douglas ave.
n Daniel, res 46 Brackenridge.
n Elma, bds 70 Douglas ave.
1on House, Mrs Mattie L Brown Propr, n w cor Cal-
un and Chicago.
n Michael, res 99 Lasalle.
n Samuel W, restaurant, 278 Calhoun, res 70 Douglas
enue.
dorfer *see Hermsdorfer.*
chfeger Elizabeth (wid Martin), bds 78 Buchanan.
chfeger Joseph, mach hd, bds 78 Buchanan.
chfeger Peter, lab Penn Co, res 78 Buchanan.
h Jacob, lab, res rear of 85 Wagner.
, *see also Harber.*
Alexander J, wood carver Fort Wayne Furniture Co,
s 521 E Lewis.
Anna L (wid James), res 209 E Wayne.
Benjamin F, lawyer, 10 and 11 Pixley & Long bldg,
is 365 W Main.
Edward, brakeman, bds 6 Fulton.
George, conductor, bds 6 Fulton.
er James B, Lawyer, 12 Bank Blk, res 76 E Wash-
gton.
Mary (wid John), res 365 W Main.
Oliver, mach, bds 521 E Lewis.
Thomas E, conductor, res 6 Fulton.
Thomas H, brakeman N Y, C & St L R R, bds 323 W
ain.
Wm, brakeman, bds 60 Fulton.
Dorothy (wid Frederick), res 507 E Lewis.
l James W, clk The Wayne, rms 69 W Berry.

Wing & Mahurin, ARCHITECTS, 41 & 42 Pixley & Long Bldg. Telephone 328

236   R. L. POLK & CO.'s

Harries Miss Lydia M, bds 63 W Jefferson.
Harries Mary (wid John), res 63 W Jefferson.
Harries Wm F G, clk, res 79 Hanna.
Harrington James W, grainer Hail & Tower, bds n e cor 1st
    and Wells.
Harrington Mrs Josephine, bds 16 Gay.
Harris Annie, waiter John Boylan & Co, rms 268 Calhoun.
Harris Charles, brakeman, rms 23 Baker.
Harris Charles, teamster, bds 83 Holman.
Harris Charles G, Mngr Edison Mutual Telegraph Co,
    res 50 W Superior.
Harris Charles S, driver, bds 121 Calhoun.
Harris Ella F, phys, 148 Calhoun, res same.
Harris Elwood E, steam fitter A Hattersley & Sons, res 200 E
    Washington.
Harris Emmett, lawyer, 19 Court, res 205 Taylor.
Harris Guy, trav agt Mayflower Mills, res Lima, O.
Harris Henry E, brass molder Penn Co, res 157 Taylor.
Harris John H, res 63 W Jefferson.
Harris Joseph D, apprentice, bds 108 Wallace.
Harris Lyman P, phys, 148 Calhoun, res same.
Harris Mary, waiter, rms 268 Calhoun.
Harris Wm H, asst supt Prudential Ins Co, bds 164 S Harrison.
Harrison Agnes H, clk M M Mintch, bds 172 Calhoun.
Harrison Harry (Paulus & Harrison), res 210 Calhoun.
Harrison John, laundryman Indiana School for Feeble-Minded
    Youth.
Harrison Josephine, bkkpr S M Foster, bds 96 E Berry.
Harrison Robert H, foreman Penn Co, res 20 Charles.
Harrison Thomas (col'd), bds 145 Erie.
Harrison Wm, mach Penn Co, res 88 E Lewis.
Harrison Wm H, res 145 Fairfield ave.
Harrod Daniel V, carp, res 16 Sturgis.
Harrod Eunice, domestic 180 E Lewis.
Harrod George W, lab, bds 17 Pritchard.
Harrod H Seymour, carp, bds 17 Pritchard.
Harrod Melinda, res 17 Pritchard.
Harrod Morse, Physician and Surgeon, 87 Maumee ave,
    res same.   Tel 388.
Harsch, *see also Hersh and Hirsch.*
Harsch John, teamster, res 168 Maumee ave.
Harsh George G, conductor, bds 164 Harrison.
Harshman John H, lab Bass F and M Works, res 200 Thomas.
Hart Mrs Catherine, cook Riverside Hotel.
Hart Chauncey S, lab Penn Co, bds 150 Maumee ave.
Hart George C, lab Penn Co, res 37 Charles.

Hart James, lab, res 47 E Superior.
Hart John C, car bldr Penn Co, bds 57 Barr.
Hart John T, molder Kerr-Murray Mnfg Co, res 196 Hanna.
Hart Wm P, baggageman Penn Co, res 60 Buchanan.
Hart Wm S, brakeman, res 20 Breck.
Harter George M, lab, res 84 Van Buren.
Harter Joseph, blksmith, res 170 W Main.
Harter Joseph M, lab, res 87 Richardson.
Harter Phillip, clk Geo DeWald & Co, res 202 W Washington.
Hartford Nelson S, painter, bds F W Robinson.
Hartle Samuel C, coachman H C Sites, 15 W Lewis.
Hartley Egbert, lab Penn Co, bds 5 Bass.
Hartley Nelson L, lab, res 116 Boone.
Hartman Anna, seamstress D S Redelsheimer & Co, bds 53 W Jefferson.
Hartman Apollonia (wid Valentine B), res St Joseph's Hospital.
Hartman Bert, carp, bds s w cor Putnam and St Mary's ave.
Hartman Rev Charles, asst supt the German Reformed Orphans' Home, res same.
Hartman Charles A, tel opr Ft Wayne Electric Co, bds 611 S Broadway.
Hartman Eliza, waitress Monro House.
Hartman George B, postal clk, res 611 S Broadway.
Hartman George O, lab, res 19 Richardson.
Hartman Gottfried, baker J P Ross & Sons, res 54 Force.
Hartman Herman, res 130 E Washington.
Hartman Homer C, lawyer, 80 Calhoun, res 65 Maple ave.
Hartman Jacob, saloon, 277 E Washington, res 414 E Wayne.
Hartman John, lab, res s w cor Putnam and St Mary's ave.
Hartman John F, molder Kerr-Murray Mnfg Co, res 14 Brandriff.
Hartman John H, Staple and Fancy Groceries, Flour, Feed and County Produce, also Wines and Liquors, 126 E Washington, res same. Tel 106.
Hartman Joseph R, fireman, res 44 Burgess.
Hartman Josephine, music teacher, 65 Maple ave, res same.
Hartman Lem R, cashier First National Bank, res 241 W Wayne.
Hartman Lena, domestic Aldine Hotel.
Hartman Lida, domestic Monroe House.
Hartman Margaret (wid Amos), res 15 Caroline.
Hartman Margaret, domestic Wayne Hotel.
Hartman Nancy A (wid George), bds 139 E DeWald.
Hartman Stevenson, lab, res s s Maria 1 e of G R & I R R.
Hartman S Brenton, dentist, 1 Schmitz Block, res 536 S Broadway.

17

Hartman Theresa (wid Adolph), res 344 E Wayne.
Hartman Valentine, coremkr Bass F & M Works, res 34 Hanna.
Hartman Wilton W, removed to Chicago, Ill.
Hartmann Annie, bds 130 E Washington.
Hartmann Charlotte (wid Christian), res 53 W Jefferson.
Hartmann Frederick, lab, res 62 Wall.
Hartmann Henry (Hartmann & Bro), bds 344 E Wayne.
Hartmann Henry F, helper Penn Co, res 162 John.
Hartmann Henry V, carp, bds 175 John.
Hartmann John, cigarmkr, bds 344 E Wayne.
Hartmann John F, lab, bds 62 Wall.
Hartmann Joseph H (Hartmann & Bro), res 63 E Wayne.
Hartmann Wm, lab, bds 53 W Jefferson.
Hartmann & Bro (Joseph H and Henry), grocers, 63 E Wayn
Hartnett James, yard foreman Wabash R R, res 14 Melita.
Hartnett James F, plumber, bds 25 Baker.
Hartnett Margaret (wid James), res 25 Baker.
Hartnett Morris W, painter, bds 25 Baker.
Hartnett Murray (Glutting, Bauer & Hartnett), res 140 E Mair
Hartnett Peter R, clk, bds 68 Baker.
Hartnett Peter R, lab Penn Co, bds 68 Baker.
Hartnett Richard, mach Penn Co, res 68 Baker.
Hartnett Wm, painter Wayne Paint and Painting Co, bds 2 Baker.
Hartshorn Alice M, tel operator, bds 114 W Butler.
Hartshorn Alzina (wid Luther), res 35 W Main.
Hartshorn Clarence E, clk Frederick Eckart, bds 35 W Mair
Hartshorn Cora A, dressmkr L Hartshorn, bds 114 W Butler
Hartshorn Mrs Louise, dressmkr, 114 W Butler, res same.
Hartshorn Salem J, res 114 W Butler.
Hartsuff Wm D, clk Penn Co, res 235 W Jefferson.
Hartstein Andrew, actionmkr Ft Wayne Organ Co, res Cottage ave.
Hartstein Louis, helper Keller & Braun, res 6 Cottage ave.
Hartstein Paul, coachman G E Bursley.
Hartup Alonzo C, brickmason, res 116 Fairfield ave.
Hartwig, *see also Hertwig.*
Hartwig Herman H (C Schiefer & Son), res 99 E Main.
Hartzell James D, plasterer, res 34 W Butler.
Hartzell Lulu, waiter 28 E Columbia.
Hartzler Arthur, clk, bds 74 W Main.
Hartzler Elizabeth (wid Adam), res 74 W Main.
Hartzler Leroy, despatcher Nickel Plate R R, bds 74 W Mair
Harvey John W, painter, res 35 Buchanan.
Harvey Thomas, lab Salimonie Mining & Gas Co, rms 55 Bar

od Stella,teacher Indiana School for Feeble-Minded Youth
ck Peter, horse trader, res 6 Oliver.
Miss Hannah B, teacher Westminster Seminary, bds
l W Main.
Julius J, lab Hoffman Bros, res 38 Watkins.
uss John, saloon, 31 Calhoun, res same.
uss Otto A, apprentice Hail & Tower, bds 31 Calhoun.
uss Walter D, bartndr John Hasenfuss, bds 31 Calhoun.
l George W, brakeman, res 16 Breck.
l George W, painter, res 36 Leith.
l James, bds 126 W Williams.
l James M, clk, res 126 W Williams.
James A, helper Penn Co, res 163 Hanna.
ee also Haas and Hess.
acob, helper Bass F & M Works, res 253 E Jefferson.
acob N, mach Ft Wayne Iron Works, rms 181 Calhoun.
d George, res cor Fletcher ave and Wayne Trace.
d Henry, bds cor Fletcher ave and Wayne Trace.
George, cabinetmkr Ft Wayne Organ Co, res 47 Huestis
enue.
:, *see Hazzard and Hessert.*
ger Wm H, conductor, res 63 St Martin.
Bessie H, stenogr Ft Wayne Organ Co, bds 249 E
fferson.
Charles G (Baumann & Hassler), bds 72 Brackenridge.
Kossitt D, driver Troy Steam Laundry, res 72 Pearl.
Rebecca, stenogr, bds 249 E Jefferson.
Sarah J (wid Joseph B), res 72 Brackenridge.
ιs George, student, bds Weber House.
John, expressman, bds 65 W 4th.
ß Webster, plasterer, res s s High 1 e of Custer av.
l Burton S, student, bds 50 Oliver.
l Emma A, opr Samuel M Foster, bds 50 Oliver.
l George I, cabinetmkr Ft Wayne Organ Co, res 50
ver.
Lizzie, dressmkr, bds 45 Indiana ave.
Wm, bartender W J Riethmiller, bds 186 Fairfield ave.
y Mazzerit F, clk Beadell & Co, bds 86 E Main.
f Albert A, mach hd Hoffman Bros, res 15 Elm.
Jacob, lab Jacob Klett & Sons, res 107 Taylor.
l Jennie, stenogr and asst tchr McDermut's Ft Wayne
siness College, bds 91 W Superior.
l Lucy, domestic 368 Fairfield ave.
ay Sarah A (wid John), res 419 W Main.
ie Edward J, genl auditor Ft Wayne Electric Co, bds
yne Hotel.

Hattendorf Anton, bottler C L Centlivre, bds 37 Elizabeth.

Hattendorf Caroline (wid Wm), res 30 St Mary's ave.

Hattendorf Henry, cabtmkr Peters Box and Lumber Co, bds 110 High.

Hattendorf Henry J, fireman Peters Box and Lumber Co, res 9 Herman.

Hattendorf Wm H, driver Peters Box and Lumber Co, bds 30 St Mary's ave.

Hattersley Alfred (A Hattersley & Sons), res 33 Elizabeth.

Hattersley A & Sons (Alfred, Willis and Byron E), Plumbers, Steam and Gas Fitters, 48 E Main. (*See embossed line :front cover.*)

Hattersley Byron E (A Hattersley & Sons), res 131 E Main.

Hattersley Willis (A Hattersley & Sons), res 60 E Washington.

Hatton Alfred, mach, bds 25 W Creighton ave.

Hauck, *see also Hawk.*

Hauck John J (Hauck & Berns), res 111 Griffith.

Hauck & Berns (John Hauck and Frederick Berns), catholic books, 288½ Calhoun.

Haudenschild Jacob, lab, res 72 Franklin ave.

Haudenschild John, lab, res 80 St Mary's ave.

Hauenstein Charles, printer Archer, Housh & Co, bds 224 W Main.

Hauerstein Julius, teamster, bds 157 W Main.

Haugk August, carp, bds 66 Erie.

Hauke Frederick, boilermkr Lake Erie and Western, res 104 Summit.

Hausbach Jacob, boilermkr, res 547 Lafayette.

Hausbach Michael, mach Wabash R R, res 181 W DeWald.

Hause Christopher C, lab, bds 35 E DeWald.

Hauser, *see also Houser.*

Hauser Elizabeth, laundress, bds 278 E Jefferson.

Hauser Henry, lab, res w s Hanna 8 s of Pontiac.

Hausmann Charles, market stall No 31, res Wayne twp.

Hauss Daniel F, tank inspr Nickel Plate R R, bds 8 McClellan.

Hauss David H, printer Ft Wayne Newspaper Union, bds 8 McClellan.

Hauss Frederick, lab, bds 8 McClellan.

Hauss Louis E, tailoress, bds 8 McClellan.

Hauss Susan (wid David), res 8 McClellan.

Hautch George A, helper Ft Wayne Furniture Co, bds 371 W Main.

Hautch Peter, lab, bds 371 W Main.

Hautch Simon, lab, res 371 W Main.

Havens Frank E, coilwinder Ft Wayne Electric Co, bds 398 E Washington.

onald, Watt & Wilt, res 73 Maumee

kr Wm Scheele, res 53 Maumee ave.
Tel Co, bds 53 Maumee ave.
r Penn Co, res 138 Lafayette.
mith, bds 138 Lafayette.
, bds 138 Lafayette.
Beadell & Co, bds 86 E Main.
146 Holman.
a, bds 119 Holman.
odore), res 119 Holman.

64 E Berry.
Indiana School for Feeble-Minded

uis Diether & Bro, bds 110 W Main.
8 Barthold.
kr, bds 94 Wells.
el), res 8 Barthold.

lressmkr, res 110 Calhoun.
ector, res 55 Huestis ave.
lus), res 236 W Main.
bds 236 W Main.
E Hayden, res 182 Calhoun.
est, 68 Barr, res Hanna Homestead.
& Grier), lawyer, 2 Bass blk, res 68

bet Maumee ave and E Jefferson.
e, 184 Calhoun, res 162 same.
ohn W Hayden, Joseph H Grier),
s, 2 Bass Blk. (See left bottom lines.)

is), res 79 W Lewis.
to Chicago, Ill.
master Wabash R R, res 31 Colerick.
ass F and M Works, bds Windsor

, res 354 Hanna.
enn Co, res 136 Fulton.
Co, res 298 Hanna.
9 Elm.
V Lewis.
es 155 High.
d to Portland, Ore.
rick.

Hayes Thomas D, lab, rms 10 Ewing.
Hayes Thomas J, molder, bds 79 W Lewis.
Haynes, *see also Haines*.
Haynes Edith, bds 36 W Williams.
Haynes Frank, engineer Penn Co, res 36 W Williams.
Hays, *see also Hayes*.
Hays Benjamin F, conductor, res 20 W Williams.
Hays Charles A, Lawyer, Justice, Propr Crystal Springs
  Celery Gardens, 13 E Main, res Rockhill Heirs' Addition.
Hays Wm H, brakeman, res 10 Jackson.
Hazer Laura M, bds 134 E Main.
Hazer Lillian E, bds 134 E Main.
Hazzard, *see also Hessert*.
Hazzard Albert W, cigarmkr L Dessauer & Co, bds 39 Marion.
Hazzard Henry, grinder American Wheel Co, bds 37 Maumee
  road.
Hazzard John, mach, bds 37 Maumee rd.
Hazzard Louis N, oil inspector, res 39 Marion.
Healy James, barber E C Hagen, res 103 Barr.
Healy Mrs Lauretta, dressmkr, 103 Barr, res same.
Heany, *see also Haney*.
Heany Anna M (wid Antoine), res 22 W 4th.
Heany Frank, barber C Hoemig, bds 22 W 4th.
Heany Isaac, mach hd Hoffman Bros, bds 22 W 4th.
Hearlihie Ellen (wid Thomas), res 48 Baker.
Heath Benjamin F, painter, res 94 Barr.
Heath Curtis, bds 102 N Harrison.
Heath Edward, res 102 N Harrison.
Heath Fronie E, dressmkr, 94 Barr, res same.
Heath Stephen, county assessor, bds 3 E Superior.
Heathman David, lab, res 233 Wells.
Heathman Edward L, painter J H Brimmer, bds 233 Wells.
Heathman Frank, lab Ranke & Yergens, bds 233 Wells.
Heaton, *see also Eaton*.
Heaton Charles E, Physician and Druggist, 36 E Berry,
  res 90 same.
Heaton Ellis J, stenogr Vesey & Heaton, bds 260 Hoagland
  avenue.
Heaton Owen N (Vesey & Heaton), res 260 Hoagland ave.
Heaton Samantha (wid Jesse), res 260 Hoagland ave.
Hebberson George M, foreman, res 28 W Williams.
Heber Peter, res 308 W Jefferson.
Hebert, *see also Ebert*.
Hebert Josephine J, clk Union Credit Co, bds 73 Thomas.
Hebert Oliver, engineer Penn Co, res 73 Thomas.
Hebrew Cemetery, w of Lindenwood Cemetery.

Heche Cecilia S, res 10 Erie.
Hechler Frederick, lab Bass F & M Works, res 6 Lillie.
Heck Christian, mach hand Peters Box and Lumber Co, bds 191 Oakland.
Heck Ernest, mach hand Peters Box and Lumber Co, bds 191 Oakland.
Heck Louis C, cigar mnfr, 79 E Washington, res 49 W same.
Hecke Kate, opr Hoosier Mnfg Co, bds 152 E Washington.
Hecke Mary, opr Hoosier Mnfg Co, bds 152 E Washington.
Hecke, see also Hake.
Hecke Rosa (wid Herman), res 152 E Washington.
Hecker Katherine C (wid Philip J), res 134 E Main.
Hecker Minnie, domestic Lake Shore Hotel.
Heckert Clara F, stenogr J A Armstrong, bds 105 Wallace.
Heckey Daniel, conductor, bds Lake Shore Hotel.
Heckler Morris, engineer, bds Lake Shore Hotel.
Heckler Charles W, hostler, bds 15 Pearl.
Heckler Elmer, helper Robert Spice, bds 15 Pearl.
Heckler George, boarding house, 15 Pearl, res same.
Heckman George E, lab, bds 118 Franklin ave.
Heckman Wm C, res 168 W Jefferson.
Hedden George E, brakeman N Y, C & St L R R, bds 64 W Main.
Heddens James, cook, bds 71 Butler.
Hedekin House, J W Swaidner propr, 25 Barr.
Hedekin Mary M, bds 156 W Wayne.
Hedekin Thomas B, res 94 W Wayne.
Hedges Bailey S, fireman Penn Co, res 19 Colerick.
Hedges John P, trav agt, res 16 W 3d.
Hedges Thomas J, gate-keeper Penn Co, res 323 W Main.
Heersche Herman, mach Bass F & M Works, bds 91 John.
Heffelfinger John M, clk Pixley & Co, res 150 Greely.
Heffelfinger Wm J, brakeman, bds 150 Greely.
Heffert John, mason, res 100 Montgomery.
Hefter Wilhelmina (wid Adolph), dressmkr, 19 Pritchard, res same.
Hegerfeld Charles, teamster Olds' Wagon Works, res 33 Smith.
Hegerhorst Christian J, carp Frederick Kraft, res 180 W Jefferson.
Hegley Joseph, lab Kerr-Murray Mnfg Co, res 30 W DeWald.
Heibler Emma L (wid Franklin), res n w cor Superior and Wells.
Heibler Jane P (wid George W), bds 116 Butler.
Heid, see Heit and Hite.
Heidenierth Minnie, seamstress, bds 42 E 3d.
Heidenreich Amand J, lab, res 110 W DeWald.

nreich Henry, barnman James Wilding & Son, res 134 'airfield ave.

nreich Jacob, fireman G R & I R R, bds 110 W DeWald.

nreich Joseph E, molder Bass F & M Works, bds 110 W)eWald.

r Albert, bricklayer, res 87 Wall.

r Wm, bricklayer, res 250 E Wayne.

ich Mary, domestic 213 W Berry.

Wm F, carp, res 326 Hanna.

wfsky Augusta, domestic 93 W Main.

wski Augusta, clk, bds 211 John.

wski Florentina (wid Ferdinand), res 211 John.

roner Abraham, res 62 W Main.

roner Louis (Heilbroner & Brown), res 56 W Wayne.

roner Lewis, clk Isidor Lehman, bds 62 W Main.

roner Samuel, res 56 W Wayne.

roner Samuel A, shoemkr, 27 Pearl, bds 62 W Main.

broner & Brown (Louis Heilbroner, George H 3rown), Saloon, 18 W Berry.

ruth Andrew, mach Penn Co, res 60 E Washington.

John H, cigarmkr H W Ortmann, bds 183 Calhoun.

, see also *Heiny.*

Anna C, domestic 110 W Main.

Christina (wid Frederick), midwife, bds 96 Madison.

Conrad, blksmith H Winte, bds 218 Fairfield ave.

Ernest F, clk S W Harmon, bds 52 Douglas ave.

Frederick C (Heine & Israel), res 139 Wallace.

Frederick C, clk Tri-State Bldg and Loan Assn, bds 52 'ouglas ave.

Frederick W, carp Penn Co, res 52 Douglas ave.

Gottlieb W, boilermkr Bass F and M Works, res 291 anna.

Henry, engineer, res 87 Grant ave.

Henry W, lab Penn Co, res 14 Wallace.

John, lab Penn Co, res Abbott's add ¼ mile e of yards.

John C, mach Bass F and M Works, res 98 Madison.

Minnie, bkkpr, bds 167 Hanna.

Wm, hostler Concordia College.

Wm, lab, res 167 Hanna.

Wm C, boilermkr, res 96 Madison.

Wm C D, hoopmkr S D Bitler, bds 167 Hanna.

Wm F, tinner Gerding & Aumann Bros, bds 139 Wal- e.

Vm G, hoopmkr S D Bitler, bds 167 Hanna.

& Israel (Frederick C Heine, Charles Israel), painters, Wallace.

L. O. HULL, PAINTING and PAPER HANGING AT 90 CALHOUN STREET.

FORT WAYNE DIRECTORY. 245

Heineman Matilda, domestic 61 Brackenridge.
Heiney *see Heiny*.
Heingartner Emma, tailoress J W Fowles, bds 155 W Main.
Heingartner Frederick, molder J H Lauer, bds 155 W Main.
Heingartner Sibila (wid Martin), res 155 W Main.
Heinlen Arthur, mach Wabash R R, bds 128 W Butler.
Heinlen Eugenie M, bds 128 W Butler.
Heinlen Wm J, mach Wabash R R, res 128 W Butler.
Heinrich Elizabeth, bds 85 Monroe.
Heinrich Louis A (Stahn & Heinrich), res 85 Monroe.
Heinrich Rudolph J, clk H F Beverforden, bds 85 Monroe.
Heiny Nicholas, clk A C Trentman, res 122 E Wayne.
Heiskel Amandus, lab, res 46 S Wayne ave.
Heisner, *see also Hisner*.
Heisner Annie, domestic 40 Douglas ave.
Heist Frederick, removed to Altoona, Pa.
Heit, *see also Hite*.
Heit Alexander, butcher, res 74 Wells.
Heit Amos, warehouseman C F Muhler & Son, res 129 W De Wald.
Heit Anthony W, trav agt Fox Branch U S Baking Co, res 39 W Creighton ave.
Heit Charles F J, clk Zoeller & Merz, bds 129 W De Wald.
Heit Christopher, trav agt Fox Branch U S Baking Co, res 188 Griffith.
Heit Elizabeth, bds 74 Wells.
Heit Frank, cutter, bds 21 Nirdlinger ave.
Heit George H, tinner J L Gruber, bds 129 W De Wald.
Heit Joseph J, trav agt Fox Branch U S Baking Co, bds 190 Griffith.
Heit Josephine (wid Anthony), res 190 Griffith.
Heit Lena, opr Hoosier Mnfg Co, bds 74 Wells.
Heit Matilda, tailoress A F Schoch, bds 74 Wells.
Heit Samuel, billiard marker, rms 55 W Main.
Heit Wm, cabinetmkr Fort Wayne Organ Co, bds 21 Nirdlinger ave.
Heitkam Charles P, mach, bds 505 Lafayette.
Heitkam Eliza (wid Charles), res 505 Lafayette.
Heitkam Martin, mach, bds 505 Lafayette.
Heitwinkel Henry, bds 43 Charles.
Heitzler Mrs Margaret M, res 48 Walter.
Heitzler Joseph, coachman 151 W Berry.
Heitzman, *see Hitzemann*.
Helbig Charles E, tinner Pickard Bros, bds 53 Hugh.
Helden Bertha, seamstress D S Redelsheimer & Co, bds 227 Gay.
Heldt Barbara (wid John M), res 182 E Wayne.

Heldt John, barber Charles Shidel, bds 182 E Wayn
Heley Arthur, driver C H Currier, bds 340 E Wayne
Heley George Wm, lab, res 158 Harmer.
Helker, *see also Hilker and Hilleka.*
Helker Frederick, res 175 W Washington.
Helker Wm, res 175 W Washington.
Hellberg Frederick, lab, bds 160 Gay.
Helle Andrew, lab, res 74 Murray.
Heller, *see also Hille.*
Heller Miss Adah M, stenogr Ft Wayne Newspap
   bds 32 W Washington.
Heller Dora, bds 72 Cass.
Heller George W (Heller & Frankel), rms 22 W Wa
Heller John C, bkkpr McDonald, Watt & Wilt, b
   Washington.
Heller John W, trav agt Seavey Hardware Co, re
   Jefferson.
Heller Mahlon, deputy sheriff, res 72 N Cass.
Heller Peter, lab, res 167 Force.
Heller Phillip A, clk C Falk & Co, bds s e cor 3d and
Heller Samuel, hostler T L Lintz, rms Schmitz blk.
Heller Thomas S, farm implements, 58 E Columbia, r
   Washington.
Heller Wm E, clk U P Tea and Coffee Store, bds 32 V
   ington.
Heller Wm L, mach Peters Box and Lumber Co, r
   Mary's ave.
Heller & Frankel (George W Heller, Louis Frankel),
   40 Calhoun.
Helley Charles F, mach hand Rhinesmith & Simonson
   Jackson.
Helling Frederick W, ice dealer, res 83 W Washingto
Helling John F W, driver Frederick W Helling, res 189
Hellinger Minnie, domestic Nickel Plate Hotel.
Helmer Fannie (wid Harry), housekeeper 7 Duryea.
Helmkamp Henry, carp Wiegmann & Franke, res 51
Helmke Edward F jr, cabinetmkr Peters Box and Lu
   bds 13 Douglas ave.
Helmke Frederick W E, shoes, 212½ Calhoun, res 13 Dou
Helmke Herman, shoes, 45 W Main, res same.
Hellwig Bertha, mach opr, bds 227 Gay.
Hellwig Juliana (wid Emil), carpet weaver, 227 Gay,
Hemmann Benjamin M, teacher St Paul's German
   School, res 166 Barr.
Hemmings George, section hand, bds 4 Rebecca.
Hemmings Wm, cook, bds 4 Rebecca.

Geo. E. Johnson, DENTIST, 74 Calhoun Street.
Res., 188 W. Berry St.

FORT WAYNE DIRECTORY. 247

Hench, *see also Hensch.*
Hench George R, printer, res 383 E Wayne.
Hench Robert H, printer, res 383 E Wayne.
Hench Samuel M, lawyer, 31 E Main, bds 9 E Wayne.
Henderson Alexander, engineer Wabash R R, res 407 Broadway.
Henderson Andrew R, res 115 E Wayne.
Henderson Angeline M (wid Wm D), res 86 E Main.
Henderson Arthur G, clk Penn Co, bds 62 McClellan.
Henderson Charles, trimmer est M L Albrecht, bds Arlington Hotel.
Henderson Charles W, clk Penn Co, bds 115 E Wayne.
Henderson David, dyer, res 62 McClellan.
Henderson David S, lab, bds 102 W Superior.
Henderson Harry C, mach, res 149 Barr.
Henderson James, car driver, bds Harmon House.
Henderson Melton J, driver Powers & Barnett, bds 62 McClellan.
Henderson Samuel C, foreman copper shop Penn Co, rms 29 W Wayne.
Henderson Thomas J, clk Wabash R R, bds 31 Colerick.
Henderson Wm (col'd), porter Hotel Rich.
Henderson Wm D, feed, 69 E Columbia, res 86 E Main.
Hendler Joseph, mach Olds' Wagon Works, bds 20 Murray.
Hendricks Maud, bds 113 W Wayne.
Hendrix George A, conductor Penn Co, res 279 E Creighton.
Hendrix Thaddeus F, tel opr Penn Co, bds 279 E Creighton.
Heneline, *see Henline.*
Hengerer Christian, bds 338½ Force.
Hengerer Christopher, bds 29 W Washington.
Hengsteler Charles F, shoemkr L P Huser, bds 197 Broadway.
Hengsteler Martin, blksmith Bass F & M Works, res 222 Gay.
Henkel Ferdinand, wagonmkr Charles Ehrmann, res 83 Shawnee ave.
Henkenius Clemens, lab, res 128 Chicago.
Henkenius Frank, carp Penn Co, res 92 E Jefferson.
Henkenius George, grocer, 227 St Mary's ave, res same.
Henkenius Peter, confectioner, res 12 Columbia ave.
Henker Clara, bds 40 Charles.
Henler John, brakeman, rms 16 Chicago.
Henler Joseph, mach, bds 20 Murray.
Henley Albert, lab, bds 73 Cass.
Henline John H, carp, res 18 Wefel.
Henline Samuel, carp, res 65 Barthold.
Henline Wm D, carp, res 36 Pritchard.
Henneger Annie, domestic 126 E Main.
Henueger Gottfried, lab, res 99 Riverside ave.
Hennessey Alexander, car inspr, res 1 Breck.

R. L. POLK & CO.'S

Wm, actor, bds 1 Breck.
Wm, stonecutter, bds 72 Gay.
rederick J, lab, res 4 Rebecca.
a A, bds 20 Harrison.
ust, shoemkr, 24 Barr, res same.
ol B, brakeman, bds 325 W Jefferson.
rge A, pdlr, bds s e cor Creighton ave and Oliver.
b, pictures etc, 379 Lafayette, res same.
es M, contractor, 161 W Jefferson, res 41 Grace ave.
a A, boarding house, 20 Harrison.
a A, carp, bds 93 Shawnee ave.
a G (Livenspargar & Henry), bds 20 Harrison.
a M, carp, res 325 W Jefferson.
W, shoemkr, s e cor Creighton ave and Oliver, res

as A, riveter Penn Co, res 15 Oak.
s G, carp, bds 93 Shawnee ave.
s G, pdlr, bds s e cor Creighton ave and Oliver.
y A, bds 93 Shawnee ave.
, bds 20 Harrison.
H, lab Penn Co, res 93 Shawnee ave.
also Hench.
gust, lab, res s s Echart 2 e of Hanna.
dward E, fireman, bds 164 Ewing.
rnst H, coremkr Bass F & M Works, res 242 E
n.
enry F, brakeman, res 28 Holton ave.
fenry G, car repairer, res n s Chestnut 2 w of

enry J, clk Coombs & Co, res 164 Ewing.
m R, lab Penn Co, res 222 Francis.
rt G, harnessmkr F Hilt, bds 37 Gay.
L, dressmkr, bds 37 Gay.
, contractor, 37 Miner, res same.
F, mach Ft Wayne Iron Works, res 37 Gay.
F H, helper Olds' Wagon Works, bds 37 Gay.
ard, fireman Penn Co, bds 164 Ewing.
T, assembler Ft Wayne Electric Co, bds 152

as (col'd), waiter, bds 65 Baker.
tin, blksmith, res 222 Gay.
milliner, bds 102 Wells.
hoemkr, res 102 Wells.
, molder Ft Wayne Iron Works, bds 102 Wells.
, gas fitter, rms 29 E Main.
so *Harber.*

Herber Frederick E, car bldr Penn Co, res 495 E Washington.
Herber Frederick I, truck repairer Penn Co, res 144 Force.
Herber John F, carp, res 86 Walton ave.
Herbst Dora (wid Frederick), res 507 E Lewis.
Herbst Otto P, bkkpr Hamilton Nat Bank, res 319 Lafayette.
Herchenbach R Hugo, clk The Herman Berghoff Brewing Co, bds 183 Calhoun.
Herderhorst Ernest, carp Wm Gallmeier, bds 136 Francis.
Herer Wm, lab Ft Wayne Iron Works, bds 107 Force.
Hergenrader Michael, plasterer, res 43 Wall.
Hergenrather, *see also Harkenrider.*
Hergenrather Joseph, bricklayer, res 389 E Washington.
Hergenrather Joseph jr, mach Rhinesmith & Simonson, bds 43 Nirdlinger ave.
Hergenrather Margaret (wid Joseph), res 43 Nirdlinger.
Hergenrother Henry, cooper, res 299 Hanna.
Hering, *see also Herring.*
Hering Wm F, printer The Press, bds 34 W Superior.
Herman, *see also Harmon and Herrmann.*
Herman Carrie, bds 175 Van Buren.
Herman David, brakeman, bds 157 Holman.
Herman Frank, res s s Wheeler 2 w of Runnion ave.
Herman John, engineer John Orff, res 40 Boone.
Herman John jr, painter, bds 40 Boone.
Herman John A, carp, res 339 Hanna.
Hermann Gustave, clk G H Wilson & Son, bds 176 Gay.
Hermans Henry H, boots and shoes, 406 Calhoun, res same.
Hermas, *see Hermes.*
Hermeler Henry F, mach Hoffman Bros, res 28 Huron.
Hermen Nicholas, lab Penn Co, res 54 Thomas.
Hermes August, patternmkr Kerr-Murray Mnfg Co, res 54 Smith.
Hermes John, lab Penn Co, bds 54 Smith.
Hermsdorfer Frederick C, bartndr, res 222 W Washington.
Hermsdorfer George A, grocer, 281 W Jefferson, res same.
Hermsdorfer John D, bds 120 Rockhill.
Heron Margaret (wid James), bds 119 Fairfield ave.
Herr Minnie, bds Vordermark Homestead.
Herr Sarah (wid George), res 9 Hoffman.
Herrick Ruth (wid Wm), res 1 Ruth.
Herring, *see also Hering.*
Herring George, lab, bds 72 Baker.
Herring Howard L, collector Indiana Installment Co, rms. 17 W Lewis.
Herring Isaac, lab, bds Z Herring.
Herring John P, conductor, res 267 E Creighton ave.

Herring Oliver, lab, bds Z Herring.
Herring Thomas A, bds Monroe House.
Herring Zachariah, lab, res n s Romey ave.
Herrington Block, e s Fairfield ave bet Williams and Bass.
Herrington Elizabeth, domestic 149 W Washington.
Herrmann, *see also Harmon and Herman.*
Herrmann D Alexander, Physician, 176 Gay, res same.
Herrmann George, lab, res 82 Walton ave.
Herrmann George jr (Raab & Herrmann), bds 82 Walton ave.
Herrmann Michael J, carp, 99½ Laselle, res same.
Herrold Daniel J, painter, bds e s Spy Run ave 2 n of Wagner.
Herron Frank, printer, bds 34 W Superior.
Herschfelder, *see Hirschfelder.*
Hersh, *see also Harsch and Hirsch.*
Hersh Joseph W, clerk, res 3 Monroe.
Hershey Christian, tanner, res 329 W Main.
Hershman John N, lab, res 200 Thomas.
Herst Lena, bds 298 E Wayne.
Hertwig, *see also Hartwig.*
Hertwig Paul E, carpet weaver, 40 Eliza, res same.
Hesemeier Henry, bricklayer, res 15 Pritchard.
Hess, *see also Haas and Hass.*
Hess Charles F, mach hand Ft Wayne Electric Co, bds 28 Nirdlinger ave.
Hess Charlotte (wid Jacob), res s w cor Lafayette and Leith.
Hess Frank J, painter City Carriage Works, bds 51 Elizabeth.
Hess George F, mach Penn Co, bds 132 E Creighton ave.
Hess John, expressman, res 38 Wefel.
Hess John R, tinner C A Scharf, bds 38 Wefel.
Hess Mary, bds 38 Wefel.
Hess Nicholas W, carriagemkr B H Baker, res 51 Elizabeth.
Hess Philip J, mach Penn Co, res 132 E Creighton ave.
Hess Wm E, mach hd Peters Box and Lumber Co, bds 38 Wefel.
Hess Wm H, finisher Paul's Pulley Works, bds 51 Elizabeth.
Hess Wm J, asst stamp clerk P O, bds 132 E Creighton ave.
Hesser Jennie F, waiter The Randall.
Hessert, *see also Hazzard.*
Hessert Barnett, teamster, res 162 W Superior.
Hessert George, teamster, res 218 W Superior.
Hessert John, lab, bds 162 W Superior.
Heston Watson, cartoonist, res s s Maumee ave 2 e of toll gate.
Heth Emma, clk bds 206 Lafayette.
Heth Tillie, stenogr, bds 206 Lafayette.
Hetrick Jacob (J Hetrick & Co), physician, res 160 E Wayne.

Hetrick Jacob A, clk Beadell & Co, res 203 E Washington.
Hetrick J & Co (Jacob Hetrick, John M Neufer), druggists, 303 E Washington.
Hettler Albert, lab, bds 61 Laselle.
Hettler Christopher F, agent, res 99 E Lewis.
Hettler Clara, dressmkr, bds 61 Laselle.
Hettler Ehinger, polisher, bds 61 Laselle.
Hettler Gottlieb, sewer builder, 84 Charles, res same.
Hettler Mrs Harriet, res 61 Laselle.
Hetzel Matthew, lab Penn Co, res 208 Lafayette.
Heubner Jacob, carp, res e s Webster 1 s of Killea.
Heuer Christian, watchman, res 107 Force.
Heuer Elizabeth W, domestic 50 Smith.
Heuer Ernst, boilermkr, res 59 Maumee ave.
Heuer Fredericka (wid Herman), res 55 W Wayne.
Heuer Martin, lab, bds 55 W Wayne.
Heuer Wm F, lab, bds 107 Force.
Heugnard, see Huguenard.
Hewes, see also Hughes.
Hewes James C, boilermkr, res 142 E Lewis.
Hewitt Etta, opr Sam'l M Foster, bds 204 Walton ave.
Heyman Jenny, dressmkr Frances Julliard, bds 133 Barr.
Hibbens Thomas H, slater, res 74 Baker.
Hibernia Hall, 176 Calhoun.
Hibinger John D, brakeman, bds 228 W Superior.
Hibler Anthony, lab J A Koehler, res e s Lafayette 5 s of Pontiac.
Hibler Bernard, teamster, res e s Lafayette 4 s of Pontiac.
Hibler Bernhardt A, blksmith, bds 46 Miner.
Hibler Henry, helper Wabash R R, res e s Lafayette 4 s of Leith.
Hibner John, lab, res 66 Baker.
Hickman Cora B, forelady, bds 216 W Washington.
Hickman Daniel, teamster, res 195 Sherman.
Hickman Edward, lab, bds 195 Sherman.
Hickman Edward, teamster, bds 118 Franklin ave.
Hickman Eugene, sawyer Hoffman Bros, res 43 Putnam.
Hickman George, lab, bds 118 Franklin ave.
Hickman James, fruit, res 216 W Washington.
Hickman John C, mach Penn Co, res 49 Indiana ave.
Hickman John W, carpet weaver, 157 Wells, res same.
Hickman Laura E, opr Samuel M Foster, bds 216 W Washington.
Hickman Rosa D, opr Samuel M Foster, bds 195 Sherman.
Hickman Samuel, bds 157 Wells.
Hickman Wm, lab, res 118 Franklin ave.

ARCHITECTS. WING & MAHURIN,
41 and 42 Pixley & Long Bldg. Telephone 328.

252   R. L. POLK & CO.'s

Hickox James E, clk John Langard, res 68 E Columbia.

Hicks Wm, lab P Koehler, bds same.

Hicks Wm H, laundryman Indiana School for Feeble-Minded Youth.

Hie Allie, waitress Riverside Hotel.

Hische, see Heche.

Hiel Frederick, driver Fred Eckart, bds 91 E Wayne.

Hierholzer Mary M (wid Kolmanus), bds 50 W Main.

Higginbotham John, mach Ft Wayne Electric Co, bds 147 Griffith.

Higgins Cecilius R, Postmaster, Government Building, res 166 E Berry.

Higgins Frank P, engineer Penn Co, res 143 E Jefferson.

Higgins George W, bds 29 W Butler.

Higgins Miss Maggie, bds 143 E Jefferson.

High Charles F, carp, res 104 Hanna.

Highland Henry, lab, bds 221 John.

Higley Joseph E, lab, 35 E DeWald.

Higley Martha J (wid Edward), res 35 E DeWald.

Hilbrecht Henry, res 230 W Jefferson.

Hilbrecht Henry jr, chief fire dept, engine house No 1, res 61 Clinton.

Hilbrecht Miss Louisa S, bds 230 W Jefferson.

Hild Albert D, mach hand Ft Wayne Electric Co, bds 159 Van Buren.

Hild Henry, painter, 140 W Main, res 159 Van Buren.

Hild Otto G, clk H F C Rust, bds 159 Van Buren.

Hildebrand Charles H, painter S W Hull, bds 215 Madison.

Hildebrand Frederick, carp, res 215 Madison.

Hildebrand Frederick W, hostler C Rippe & Son, bds 234 W Washington.

Hildebrand Louisa, res 92 Wilt.

Hildebrand Wm H, res 234 W Washington.

Hildinger John J, lab Penn Co, res 15 Erie.

Hile Frederick, driver Frederick Eckart, bds 91 E Wayne.

Hiler Frank E, bkkpr, bds n s Killea 2 e of Hoagland ave.

Hiler John V, carp, res n s Killea 1 e of Hoagland ave.

Hilgemann Alvina, opr, bds 66 Smith.

Hilgemann August, switchman, res 241 Barr.

Hilgemann Emma, opr Hoosier Mnfg Co, bds E H Hilgemann.

Hilgemann Ernst H (Ernst H Hilgemann & Son), res s s Baker 2 e of Fairfield ave.

Hilgemann Ernst H & Son (Ernst H and Louis), carps, s e cor Baker and Fairfield ave.

Hilgemann Ernest R, car repairer Wabash R R, res 559 Broadway.

emann Florence W, mach, bds 24 Walnut.

emann Franklin H, clk H F Hilgemann, bds 121 W Jefferson.

emann Frederick G, lab Fort Wayne Electric Co, res 24 Walnut.

emann Frederick H, lab Bass F and M Wks, res 66 Smith.

emann Frederick H jr, lab Penn Co, bds 66 Smith.

emann Frederick W, carp, res 399 E Washington.

emann F Wm, mach hand Fort Wayne Electric Co, bds 24 Walnut.

emann Gustave F, carp, bds 216 E Washington.

emann Henry, bds 399 E Washington.

emann Henry, carp, res 379 E Lewis.

emann Henry, lab, bds 216 E Washington.

emann Henry, lab, res 91 W Jefferson.

emann Henry F, grocer, 121 W Jefferson, res same.

emann Henry F, wood worker Anthony Wayne Mnfg Co, bds 66 Smith.

emann Henry W, carp, res 184 Ewing.

emann Jacob, helper, bds 109 Wall.

emann Jacob W, carp, 216 E Washington, res same.

emann Lena, opr Samuel M Foster, bds 109 Wall.

emann Louis (Ernst H Hilgemann & Son), res s s Baker 3 e of Fairfield ave.

emann Louise, domestic 16 Douglas ave.

emann Louise, opr Samuel M Foster, bds 66 Smith.

emann Mary, opr Hoosier Mnfg Co, bds cor Baker and Fairfield ave.

emann Matilda, opr Hoosier Mnfg Co, bds 66 Smith.

emann Minnie, opr Samuel M Foster, bds 66 Smith.

emann Wm, carp, res 109 Wall.

ter, see also Helker and Hilleka.

ter Anthony, carp, bds 180 E Washington.

ter Carl D W, carp Penn Co, res 137 Francis.

ter Charles A, lab, res 231 John.

ter Charles C, lab, bds 231 John.

ter Charles F J, mach hand Jacob Klett & Sons, res 166 Harmer.

ter Diedrich F W, mach hand Olds' Wagon Works, res 63 Buchanan.

ter Frank, lab Jacob Klett & Sons, bds 180 E Washington.

ter Herman, lab Weil Bros & Co, res 118 Eliza.

ter Herman H, clk J Certia, res 4 Hoffman.

ter Mrs Margaret, res 181 Madison.

ter Wm, lab, res 227 John.

Alice M, bds 27 Prospect ave.

18

Hill Andrew, engineer Louis Rastetter, res 65 Hendricks.
Hill Arthur L, bkkpr Robert Ogden, bds 27 Prospect ave.
Hill Barbara (wid Valentine), res 158 W Main.
Hill Benjamin W, lab Frederick Myers, bds 104 Barr.
Hill Charles A, clk D H Baldwin & Co, res 74 Calhoun.
Hill Charles E, removed to Bucyrus, O.
Hill Charles L, pianos and organs, 38 Clinton, res 27 Prospect avenue.
Hill David, lab, res 64 3d.
Hill Edward C, mach Penn Co, bds 8 Locust.
Hill Frank H, clk L Wolf & Co, bds 90 W 4th.
Hill Frank W, fireman, bds 295 W Jefferson.
Hill George, mach Penn Co, res 206 Lafayette.
Hill Henrietta, opr, bds 65 Hendricks.
Hill Henry, lab Louis Rastetter, bds 65 Hendricks.
Hill Ida, seamstress, bds 65 Hendricks.
Hill John C, nurse 152 E Berry.
Hill John D, mach hand Louis Diether & Bro, bds 64 W 3d.
Hill Kittie, trimmer A Mergentheim, bds 22 Lavina.
Hill Louis H, mach hd Louis Diether & Bro, res 81 Rockhill.
Hill Louisa K, wks Troy Steam Laundry, bds 64 W 3d.
Hill Mandeville E, stopmkr Ft Wayne Organ Co, res 18 W Creighton ave.
Hill Maria A (wid Edward), res 18 W Creighton ave.
Hill Martha (wid John), res 174 Hayden.
Hill Minnie M, works J O Keller, bds 90 W 4th.
Hill Nettie (wid Edward R), res 18 W Creighton ave.
Hill Onslow G, res 316 W Jefferson.
Hill Paulina T, clk J O Keller, bds 90 W 4th.
Hill Richard S, asst designer Ft Wayne Organ Co, bds 445 S Calhoun.
Hill Thomas, foreman Ft Wayne Organ Co, res 445 S Calhoun.
Hill Wm, plasterer, res 78 Barr.
Hill Wm W, weighmaster N Y, C & St L R R, res 295 W Jefferson.
Hillabrand Frederick, trav agt A C Trentman, res Perrysburg, Ohio.
Hille, see also Heller.
Hille Henry, carp Penn Co, res 106 Wall.
Hille Henry, helper Wabash R R, res 256 W Jefferson.
Hille Jacob, helper Bass F & M Works, bds 16 Gay.
Hille Wm, carp E F Liebman, res 72 Baker.
Hille Wm, lab, bds 106 Wall.
Hilleka Anthony J, boilermkr, res 78 W Williams.
Hilleka Henry, lab Penn Co, res 44 Hendricks.
Hilleke August, porter A C Trentman, bds 114 Fairfield ave.

Hilleke Catherine, bds 114 Fairfield ave.
Hilleke Henry, porter A C Trentman, res 114 Fairfield ave.
Hilliard Etta, teacher Indiana School for Feeble-Minded Youth.
Hilliard May, teacher Indiana School for Feeble-Minded Youth.
Hilliker Wm H, engineer Penn Co, res 46 McClellan.
Hills Anna R (wid Frank), notions, 15 E Main, res 17½ same.
Hills Mrs Frances, bds 39 W Washington.
Hills Leslie W, clk A R Hills, bds 17½ E Main.
Hills Sarah E (wid Ambrose A), res 123 Fairfield ave.
Hilt Frederick, harnessmkr, 18¼ E Columbia, res 26 Baker.
Hilt Fredericka, bds 26 Baker.
Hilton Charles S, supt Ft Wayne Electric Co, res 227 W De
    Wald.
Hilton Hattie, stenographer Ft Wayne Electric Co, bds 415
    Lafayette.
Hilyard Frank, lab Jacob Funk, bds same.
Himbert John A, teamster, bds 14 Pritchard.
Himbert John M, foreman bottling dept The Herman Berg-
    hoff Brewing Co, res 578 E Washington.
Himbert Michael, agt, res 14 Pritchard.
Himbert Wm, coachman R T McDonald, bds 215 W Main.
Himes Lucian M, painter, res 97 Taylor.
Hinds Richard, fireman, bds Schele House.
Hine, *see Heine.*
Hines Adolphus J, carp Griffith & Son, bds 20 N Harrison.
Hines Emanuel, blacksmith Charles Ehrmann, bds 248 Calhoun.
Hines John, plumber C W Bruns & Co, res n s Spy Run ave
    5 n of Wagner.
Hines Phillip, carp, res 6 Short.
Hines Rudolph, carp, bds 20 N Harrison.
Hinkel Ernst, mach hand Wayne Knitting Mills, bds 375 W
    Main.
Hinkel Kate (wid Henry), res 9 Elm.
Hinton Alice, waiter Boston Restaurant, bds 270 Calhoun.
Hinton John C, Propr Boston Restaurant, 270–270½ Cal-
    houn, rms 39 Brackenridge.
Hinton Samuel, bds 30 Baker.
Hinz Charles, lab Bass F & M Works, res 344 Force.
Hinz Frederick W, molder Bass F & M Works, bds 344 Force.
Hipp Edward F, car builder Penn Co, res 57 John.
Hippard George R, removed to Columbus, O.
Hippenhammer John W, clk, res 381 E Wayne.
Hire Elias, clk C H Currier, res n s Prospect ave nr St Joseph
    river.
Hire Elma D, bds Elias Hire.
Hireland Henry, lab, bds 227 John.

Robert Spice, Waterworks and General Plumbing, 48 West Main and 11 Pearl Streets.

256　　　　　　　　R. L. POLK & CO.'S

Hirsch, *see also Harsch and Hersh.*
Hirsch Bertha, cashr Louis Wolf & Co, bds 75 Webster.
Hirsch Caroline S (wid John G), res 65 Stophlet.
Hirsch David, bkkpr A Goodman, bds 49 W Berry.
Hirsch Frederick, helper, res 208 John.
Hirsch Hannah (wid Leopold), res 75 Webster.
Hirsch Henrietta (wid Moses), bds 87 W. Jefferson.
Hirsch Herman, salesman, bds 75 Webster.
Hirsch Louis, cigars, The Randall, bds 75 Webster.
Hirsch Martin, student, bds 65 Stophlet.
Hirsch Samuel C, lab, res 35 Walnut.
Hirsch Seymour, clk, bds 75 Webster.
Hirschfelder Caroline (wid Michael), res 240 E Wayne.
Hirschfelder Henry, stone mason, res 118 Maumee ave.
Hirschfelder Louis, mason, res 360 E Wayne.
Hirschmann John, cabinetmkr Ft Wayne Organ Co, res 601 S Calhoun.
Hirschmann Louisa, waiter Custer House.
Hirt Jacob, lab, bds 20 Harrison.
Hirtz Daniel, hostler Powers & Barnett, rms 29 E Wayne.
Hiser Samuel A, engineer Penn Co, res 23 W Lewis.
Hiser Wm H, lab, res 69 Taylor.
Hisner Charles, teamster, res 170 Gay.
Hisner Charles H, clk Golden & Monahan, bds 186 Gay.
Hisner John, lab, res 186 Gay.
Hisner Lizzie, dressmkr, bds 68 Wilt.
Hisner Wm F, carp J O Brown, res 68 Wilt.
Hisner Wm F jr, carp, bds 68 Wilt.
Hitchins Henry F, engineer G R & I R R, res 44 Baker.
Hite, *see also Heit.*
Hite Andrew K (Hite & Son), res 192 Oakland.
Hite Frederick (Hite & Son), bds 192 Oakland.
Hite Samuel H, elevatorman Ft Wayne Organ Co, res 611 S Calhoun.
Hite & Son (Andrew K and Frederick), carpenters and contractors, 192 Oakland.
Hitz Oscar, lab, res 71 Hoffman.
Hitzeman Charles, feeder, bds 36 Pritchard.
Hitzeman Charles F, clk Ft Wayne Street R R Co, bds 24 Summit.
Hitzeman Christian, clk Geo DeWald & Co, res 290 W Washington.
Hitzeman Frederick, stone mason, res 36 Pritchard.
Hitzeman Frederick H D, lab, bds 36 Pritchard.
Hitzeman George, grocer, 47 Maumee ave, res 24 Summit.
Hitzeman Kate, clk G Hitzeman, bds 24 Summit.

itzeman Louise (wid Henry C), res 244 E Washington.

itzeman Sophia E (wid Wm), bds 219 W Jefferson.

itzeman Sophie, domestic 150 Montgomery.

itzeman Sophie, seamstress, bds 24 Summit.

itzemann Elizabeth, domestic 96 W Wayne.

itzemann Ernest F, finisher Ft Wayne Organ Co, res 111 Wall.

itzemann Frederick J (G H Hitzemann & Son), bds 49 Wilt.

itzemann Gottlieb H (G H Hitzemann & Son), res 49 Wilt.

itzemann Gottlieb H jr, clk Henry Butke, bds 49 Wilt.

itzemann G H & Son (Gottlieb H and Frederick J), tailors, 133 Broadway.

itzemann Henry C, clk Pfeiffer & Schlatter, res 164 W Creighton ave.

itzemann Lizzie C, domestic 96 W Wayne.

itzemann Mary, domestic 155 W Wayne.

itzemann Sophia, bds 49 Wilt.

ively Adam H, blksmith Bass F & M Works, res 205 Hanna.

oadley Miss Anna C, artist, 128 Calhoun, bds 68 W Jefferson.

oadley Miss Jennie B, hairdresser I M Smith, res 68 W Jefferson.

oadley May, dressmkr, bds 68 W Jefferson.

oagland Miss Merica, bds 106 W Berry.

oagland School, n e cor Hoagland ave and Butler.

oagland Susan C (wid Americus), bds n e cor Fox and W DeWald.

obbs Eva, seamstress, bds 113 Barr.

obbs John, teamster, bds 168 Maumee ave.

obbs Julia (wid Reuben), res 113 Barr.

obbs Oscar L, conductor, res 298 Hoagland ave.

obrock Albert A, painter Olds' Wagon Works, bds 298 Harrison.

obrock Anna, bds 94 Fairfield ave.

obrock Annie, bds 94 Fairfield ave.

obrock August C, mach, bds 94 Fairfield ave.

obrock Caroline, clk, bds 94 Fairfield ave.

obrock Cora, opr Hoosier Mnfg Co, bds 50 Buchanan.

obrock Edward L, car bldr Penn Co, bds 94 Fairfield ave.

obrock Eva (wid Wm), res 298 Harrison.

obrock Henry, rubber Olds' Wagon Works, bds 298 Harrison.

obrock John H, carp Penn Co, res 94 Fairfield ave.

obrock J Herman, clk Penn Co, bds 94 Fairfield ave.

obrock Martin H, lab, bds 168 Ewing.

obrock Wm H, helper Penn Co, res 134 E DeWald.

och Emanuel, pipeman Engine Co No 2, res 103 Wallace.

och Henry C, mach, res s s Eliza 2 w of Harmer.

och Wm jr, meats, 121 Wallace, bds 313 Lafayette.

och Wm, saloon, 313 Lafayette, res same.

Penn Mutual LIFE INSURANCE CO. of PHILA.
CLARK FAIRBANK, General Agent, 19 Court Street.

258 R. L. POLK & CO.'S

Hochstetter Wm, painter Penn Co, res Romey ave.
Hochstrasser John, teamster, res Centlivre's Park.
Hochstrasser John jr, bottler, res Centlivre's Park.
Hock, *see Hawk.*
Hockaday Deborah (wid Samuel L), res 73 Grand.
Hockaday James M, cooper F X Brucker, bds 73 Grand.
Hockemeyer Charles F, printer Ft Wayne Newspaper Union,
  bds 317 W Washington.
Hockemeyer Henry, bricklayer, res 115 Madison.
Hockemeyer Lizzie, domestic 310 E Wayne.
Hockemeyer Lizzie S, clk, bds 317 W Washington.
Hockemeyer Mary (wid Charles), res 317 W Washington.
Hockemeyer Sophia (wid Christian), bds 51 Holton ave.
Hockley Mrs Kate, bds 305 Harrison.
Hockley Wm H, teacher, res 299 Harrison.
Hodges H Frank, fireman G R & I R R, res 58 Oliver.
Hoelle Martin, lab Bass F & M Works, res 194 Taylor.
Hoeltje Hannah, domestic 97 W Main.
Hoeltje Henry C, cigarmkr F J Gruber, res 46 Elm.
Hoemig Charles, barber, 61 Wells, res same.
Hoemeyer, *see Homeyer.*
Hoeneisen Bertha, domestic 171 Clinton.
Hoeneisen Jacob, lab, res 2 Madison.
Hoenel Rose, domestic 98 Broadway.
Hoeppner Charles, helper Wm L Logan, bds 160 Gay.
Hoeppner Fred, lab Penn Co, res s s Pontiac 1 e of Smith.
Hoeppner Herman, boilermkr Penn Co, bds 160 Gay.
Hoeppner John C, lab, res 160 Gay.
Hoeppner Wm, lab, bds 160 Gay.
Hoerner Peter, helper, res 167 Force.
Hoevey Frank I, clk, res 322 E Jefferson.
Hoewischer Frederick A, cabtmkr, res 92 Chicago.
Hofaker George, mach hd Horton Mnfg Co, res 391 W Main.
Hofer Charles, clk A R Hills, bds 49 Lake ave.
Hofer John, lab, res 1 Van Buren.
Hofer Theodore, janitor, res 140 Cass.
Hoff Mary (wid Anthony), res 17 Wefel.
Hoffer Andrew, butcher, res 49 Lake ave.
Hoffer Celia L, clk Stewart & Hahn, bds 37 Cass.
Hoffer Edward A, clk Frank Parrot, bds 49 Lake ave.
Hoffer Frederick, molder Ft Wayne Iron Works, bds 224 W
  Main.
Hoffer John, lab, res n s W Main 2 w of Runnion ave.
Hoffer John, mach Star Iron Tower Co, bds 37 Cass.
Hoffer John G, carp, res 37 Cass.
Hoffer Lena, domestic 25 W Lewis.

**UILDERS'
HARDWARE,** **P**FEIFFER & SCHLATTER,
38 and 40 East Columbia St.

FORT WAYNE DIRECTORY. 259

er Robert, carriagemkr City Carriage Works, bds 49 Lake ave.

man, *see also Hoffmann, Hofman and Huffmann.*

man Adam J, molder Bass F & M Works, res 142 Wallace.

man A Ely (Hoffman Bros and J R Hoffman & Co), res 188 W Wayne.

man Barbara, opr Hoosier Mnfg Co, bds 31 Force.

ffman Bros (A Ely and Wm H), Lumber Mnfrs, 200 W Main.

man Charles, car bldr Penn Co, res 515 E Washington.

man Cynthia A, saleslady Root & Co, bds 2 Riverside ave.

ffman Daniel, Painter, s w cor Reed and Jenison, res same.

man George, teamster, res w s Begue nr Liberty.

man George, wagonmkr L C Zollinger, res 2 Riverside.

man Henry, butcher Frederick Eckart, res 32 Runnion ave.

man Henry A, carp, 52 W Creighton ave, res same.

man Jacob R (J R Hoffman & Co), res Charleston, W Virginia.

ffman J R & Co (Jacob R, A Ely and Wm H Hoffman), Patent Band Saw Mills, 200 W Main.

ffman Lumber Co, A Ely Hoffman Pres, Wm H Hoffman Vice-Pres, John W Sale Treas, Milton P Longacre Sec, Hardwood Lumber and Logs, 200 W Main.

man Margaret (wid Adam), bds 31 Force.

man Martin C, carbldr Penn Co, res 6 Zollars ave.

man Mary, domestic 152 W Jefferson.

man Mary E, clk, bds 2 Riverside ave.

man Nicholas, clk J B White, res 31 Force.

man Peter E G, painter Daniel Hoffman, bds s w cor Reed and Jenison.

man Susan C (wid Frank), bds C H Worden.

man Urban S, clk Root & Co, res 8 Riverside ave.

man Wm H (Hoffman Bros and J R Hoffman & Co), res 200 W Berry.

mann, *see also Hoffman, Hofmann and Huffmann.*

mann Adolph, lab Bass F & M Works, res 165 Hayden.

mann Alois, stonemason, res 417 E Lewis.

ffmann Charles A, Wholesale and Retail Dealer in Cider, Apple Wine and Cider Vinegar, and Propr Hoffmann House, 183-185-187 Calhoun, res same.

ffmann House, C A Hoffmann Propr, 183 Calhoun.

mann Mary, domestic 204 W Berry.

mann Peter, lab Penn Co, res rear 167 Clinton.

meister Henry, cooper, 12 W 3d, res same.

ner, *see Haffner.*

R. L. POLK & CO.'S

Hofmann, *see also Hoffman, Hoffmann and Huffmann.*

Hofmann G Max, supt Salimonie Mining & Gas Co, res 429 Broadway.

Hogan Catherine (wid Michael), res 58 Prince.

Hogan Dennis, lab, res 22 Murray.

Hogan Eliza, bds 176 Fairfield ave.

Hogan Frank, wks Indiana Machine Works, bds 176 Fairfield av.

Hogan Hugh P, messenger Penn Co, bds 94 Baker.

Hogan Hugh T, foreman Penn Co, res 94 Baker.

Hogan Jane (wid Samuel), res 93 Ewing.

Hogan John P, plumber A Hattersley & Sons, bds 176 Fairfield ave.

Hogan John W, slater, bds Hoffmann House.

Hogan Mary T (wid Timothy), res 11 Grand.

Hogan Michael, lab Penn Co, bds 58 Prince.

Hogan Patrick, lab, res 176 Fairfield ave.

Hogan Stephen A, bartndr J A Dratt, bds 36 Barr.

Hogston James M, cabinetmkr Ft Wayne Furniture Co, res n s Prospect ave 3 e of Spy Run ave.

Hogue Lee A, lab, bds 31 Prince.

Hoham Frederick D, druggist, 298 Calhoun, res 484 Harrison.

Hoham Wm H, driver Covendale & Archer, res 102 W Superior.

Hohmann Emily, dressmkr, 175 High, bds same.

Hohmann Frank, tailor, res 175 High.

Hohmann Henry, barber O Wobrock, bds 175 High.

Hohmann Lizzie, clk Siemon & Bro, bds 175 High.

Hohnhaus Charles W, messenger, bds 63 Wall.

Hohnhaus Emma, bkkpr W H Brudi & Bro, bds 63 Wall.

Hohnhaus George J, awningmkr P E Wolf, bds 63 Wall.

Hohnhaus George (Roembke & Hohnhaus), res 212 Fairfield.

Hohnhaus George P, carp, res 63 Wall.

Hohnhausen George P, mason Bass F & M Works, res 33 Taylor.

Hohnhausen Magdalena (wid Nicholas), bds 33 Taylor.

Hohnholz Herman, res 29 Wagner.

Hoke Anna, candymkr, bds 52 Pontiac.

Hoke George S, baker, bds 52 Pontiac.

Hoke Mary, opr Hoosier Mnfg Co, bds 52 Pontiac.

Hoke Nicholas, laborer, res e s Hanna 3 s of Eckart.

Hoke Rosanna (wid Jacob), res 52 Pontiac.

Hokemeyer Henry, lab J H Wilder, bds 256 Fairfield ave.

Holbrook Minnie, domestic Wayne Hotel.

Holcomb Luther W, painter J H Brimmer, res 70 Harrison.

Holland Mary A, domestic 341 W Washington.

Holland Thomas M, brakeman N Y, C & St L R R, bds Schele House.
Hollenbacher Arthur J, cutter, bds 141 Francis.
Hollenbacher Louis C, shipping clerk, res 141 Francis.
Hollenbeck Amelia E G, bds 137 E Jefferson.
Hollenbeck Frederick W A, saloon, 144 Calhoun, res 137 E Jefferson.
Hollenbeck Gerhard F, res 273 Webster.
Hollenkamp John, fireman, bds 72 W 3d.
Holley John, conductor, res 41 Boone.
Holley Wm H, tel opr N Y, C & St L R R, bds 41 Boone.
Hollinger Alfred, brakeman, bds 76 E Columbia.
Hollinger Anna, stenogr, bds 16 W Williams.
Hollinger Elizabeth (wid Daniel), res 76 E Columbia.
Hollinger Harry M, driver F E Purcell & Co, bds 76 E Columbia.
Hollinger Wm, bartender, bds 76 E Columbia.
Hollingworth Minnie, opr Hoosier Mnfg Co, bds cor Hugh and Harmer.
Hollister A Judson (Hollister & Son), res 104 W Williams.
Hollister Clara J, cash Stewart & Hahn, bds 104 W Williams.
Hollister Edwin J (Hollister & Son), res 82 W Williams.
Hollister & Son (A Judson and Edwin J), cigar mnfrs, 104 W Williams.
Hollmann August, carp, res 394 E Washington.
Hollmann Charles E F, mach hand Olds' Wagon Works, bds 46 Wall.
Hollmann Frederick, carp, res 48 Wall.
Hollmann Wm, lab Wm Miller, bds same.
Holloway C Peter, brakeman N Y, C & St L R R, bds Waverly Hotel.
Holman Christina (wid John), bds 41 Miner.
Holman Henry, carp J W Hilgemann, bds 216 E Washington.
Holmes Abiram T, engineer Penn Co, res 189 Barr.
Holmes Fountain, mach, bds 108 Wallace.
Holmes Frank L, barber, bds 18 Gay.
Holmes George W, landscape gardener, res 18 Gay.
Holmes Joanna (wid Wm J), res 108 Wallace.
Holmes Joshua, bds 18 Gay.
Holmes Lillian K, clk A Mergentheim, bds 108 Wallace.
Holmes Simon, carp, res 616 S Calhoun.
Holmes Wm A, clk H W Carles, bds 616 S Calhoun.
Holstein Mary, bds 568 E Washington.
Holsworth, see also Holzwarth and Holzworth.
Holsworth Addie M, saleslady Root & Co, bds 158 W Wayne.
Holsworth Addison, res 158 W Wayne.

h, teacher Bloomingdale School, bds 158 W

ik P, clk Klinkenberg & Detzer, bds 158 W

nestic 328 E Wayne.

t genl agt Union Central Life Ins Co, res 245

derick J, lab, res 169 Gay.
School, s w cor Holton and Creighton aves.
3 (wid Thomas J), bds 151 W Berry.
foreman, bds 105 Barr.
el M, engineer Standard Oil Co, res 9 Wheeler.
e, bds 21 Duryea.
rles H, bander Ft Wayne Electric Co, res 13

ton W, clk McDonald, Watt & Wilt, res 319
;ton.
i Z, mach, res 21 Duryea.
rd, teamster, res 127 W Superior.
emoved to New Orleans, La.
h O, keeper Station D, res 28 Scott ave.
i, domestic 215 W Berry.
beth, domestic 89 W DeWald.
y, helper Kerr-Murray Mnfg Co, res 143 Oliver.
lso Holsworth.
itian E, brakeman, res 11 Bass.
tte, domestic 122 W Wayne.
erine, opr Hoosier Mnfg Co, bds 99 E Wash-

;e A, actionmkr Ft Wayne Organ Co, bds 6

A, lab, res s s Richardson nr canal feeder.
all, Harmony Court bet Berry and Main.
D, lab, res 202 Fairfield ave.
ick C, truckman Ft Wayne Organ Co, res 164

C D, mach Bass F & M Works, res 160 W

rimmer E C Smith, bds 57 W High.
C, clk A E C Becker, bds 164 W DeWald.
nina, domestic 179 W Berry.
atchman, res 57 High.
eke.
na (wid John), bds 161 Gay.
in F, engineer Penn Co, res 255 Webster.
rtic A, teacher, bds 255 Webster.

.E. Johnson, DENTIST, 74 Calhoun Street.
Res., 188 W. Berry St.

FORT WAYNE DIRECTORY. 263

her Frank B (Diehl & Homsher), res 79 W DeWald.

ner Miss Minnie F, teacher, bds 255 Webster.

neim. *see also Hontheim.*

heim Jacob, carp, res 31 Pine.

heim Jacoh jr, wheel finisher, bds 31 Pine.

heim Maggie A, shoes, 156½ Fairfield ave, res 31 Pine.

heim Michael, gasfitter, res s s Taylor 2 w of No 51.

heim Michael, plumber, res 51 Hendricks.

:k, *see also Ohneck.*

:k Emma, bds 151 Montgomery.

:k Fredericka L, tailoress Frederick Kayser, bds 2 Elm.

:k Henry, lab, res 2 Elm.

:k Louisa (wid Henry), bds 115 Madison.

ck Herman, carp Wm Ruchel, res 165 Madison.

ick John, painter, res 58 W Williams.

ck Wm, mach hand Bass F & M Works, bds 39 Hough.

neim, *see also Hondheim.*

neim John J, mach Wabash R R, res 12 McClellan.

neim Peter T, blacksmith, bds 12 McClellan.

Florence, bds 21 W Jefferson.

George, bill clk, bds rear 138 Wells.

James W, student, bds 21 W Jefferson.

John O, car cleaner Penn Co, bds 130 W 3d.

Julia E (wid James), res 21 W Jefferson.

Martha (wid George), res 130 W 3d.

Mollie, clk, bds 130 W 3d.

Robert, meats, 98 Barr, res 25 W Lewis.

Wm E, bkkpr Carnahan & Co, res 34 Garden.

Wm E jr, clk Salimonie Mining & Gas Co, bds 34 Garden.

and Ladder Co No 2, s s Wallace 4 e of Lafayette.

er John G, clk, rms 143 W Berry.

er Samuel T, engineer, res 117 Boone.

ngarner George C, lab Penn Co, res 210 Fairfield ave.

ngarner Levi, car driver, bds Harmon House.

ngarner Millard F, lab Penn Co, res 37 Bass.

ngarner Wm H, painter, 152 Griffith, res same.

nann Diedrich C, coremkr Bass F and M Works, res 112 Eliza.

nann Henry, carp, bds 216 E Washington.

nann Henry F C, coremkr Bass F and M Works, res 115 Eliza.

er C, lab Penn Co, res 495 E Washington.

sier Mnfg Co, Amos S Evans Pres, John P Evans Treas, George P Evans Sec, F F Budd Supt, Mnfrs of Diamond Staid Overalls, Sack Coats, Jumpers, Jeans Pants and Lined Duck Clothing, 28 and 30 E Berry.

raham, car builder Penn Co, res 91 E Lewis.
roline, domestic 21 W Jefferson.
hn, lab Penn Co, bds Jewel House.
homas (col'd), cook Riverside Hotel, res same.
alous, farmer, res 30 Huron.
lenry, laundry, 180 Calhoun, res same.
n, clk H C Hoppe, bds 140 Force.
a A (wid Henry W), res 20 Wall.
vin G, clk G B Irwin, bds 20 Wall.
ry C, car builder Penn Co, res 397 Hanna.
man, res 10 Franklin ave.
man C, grocer, s w cor Hanna and Creighton ave,
me.
l O, asst stamp clk P O, bds 20 Wall.
na, bds 20 Wall.
hie, domestic 30 Lake ave.
artin V B, teamster G E Bursley & Co, res 131 W

mas A, foreman est M L Albrecht, bds Arlington

remiah, switchman N Y, C & St L R R, bds 20 Cass.
orge, teacher, res 16 McClellan.
inand, lab, res 482 Hanna.
L, deputy county clerk, res w s Hillside ave 1 s of
ve.
carp, bds 482 Hanna.
F, lab Bass F & M Works, res 35 Smith.
F jr, cigarmkr C A Berndt, bds 35 Smith.
mma (wid Wm), res 166 Holman.
ax, engineer Penn Co, res 312 Harrison.
Amelia, bds 266 S Wayne.
Carrie, clk Theodore Nieman, bds 272 E Washing-

Frank W B, driver, bds 203 Hanna.
George H, student, bds 203 Hanna.
lenry C, car builder Penn Co, res 203 Hanna.
lenry G, apprentice P E Cox, bds 203 Hanna.
ouis, buggy top mnfr, 9 Superior, rms 48 Barr.
lichard F, letter carrier P O, res 14 Clay.
Annie, binder G W Winbaugh, bds 90 Force.
Charles, lab, res 227½ John.
Frederick H, tailor, 376 Calhoun, res 266 S Wayne.
Gustav, contractor, 110 Grant ave, res same.
lohn B, lab, res 90 Force.
August C, printer Journal, bds 197 Ewing.
Charles H, clk Kape & Baade, res 197 Ewing.

Horstmeyer Frederick, car builder Penn Co, res 83 Nirdlinger avenue.
Horstmeyer Henry (Horstmeyer & Borgmann), res 30 Saville avenue.
Horstmeyer Henry C, teamster, bds 216 Indiana ave.
Horstmeyer Louis, mach hand Fort Wayne Furniture Co, res 244 Beaver ave.
Horstmeyer Wilhelmina (wid Frederick), res 80 Nirdlinger avenue.
Horstmeyer Wm, carp Wabash R R, res 197 Ewing.
Horstmeyer Wm F, boilermkr, bds 197 Ewing.
Horstmeyer & Borgmann (Henry Horstmeyer, August Borgmann), saloon, 276 Broadway.
Horton Alvina, chambermaid The Randall.
Horton Elijah, brakeman, bds 84 W Main.
Horton John C, detective, res 368 W Main.
Horton Mnfg Co, Henry C Paul pres, Wm A Bohn sec and treas, John C Peters genl mngr, wooden novelties, cor Main and Osage.
Hose Charles jr, bds s e cor Sherman and Aboit.
Hose Charles, baker, res n w cor Sherman and Aboit.
Hose Co No 2, s s Wallace 4 e of Lafayette.
Hosenfeldt Barbara, domestic 50 W Washington.
Hosenfeldt Bertha, domestic 67 W DeWald.
Hosey Wm, mach Penn Co, rms 131 E Washington.
Hosier Charles, mach hand, res 412 E Washington.
Hosier Joseph H, helper, res 8 Erie.
Hoskins Wm A, brakeman, res 42 Walnut.
Hosler Abraham, carp, bds 71 Melita.
Hosler Calvin, teamster, res 71 Melita.
Hosler J Wm, fireman, rms 337 W Main.
Hossfield Charlotte (wid Frederick), domestic 52 Charles.
Hossfield Frederick, lab, bds 46 Hoagland ave.
Hostetter Minnie, domestic J H Bass.
Hostman Charles W, clk, bds 86 W Jefferson.
Hostman Christian, res 86 W Jefferson.
Hostman Frederick J, driver C F Myers, bds 86 W Jefferson.
Hostman Mary (wid Christian), res 88 W Jefferson.
Hotel Randall, Dick Townsend & Co proprs, Harrison head W Columbia.
Hotel Rich, Paulus & Harrison Proprs, n w cor Calhoun and Douglas ave.
Hotel Waverly, J C Short Propr, 12 Harrison.
Houck John, teacher St Paul's Catholic School, res 111 Griffith.
Houck Robert C, bkkpr F M Smaltz, bds 353 W Main.
Hough, see also Huff.

n Pressler, Plumbing, Gas and Steam Fitting.
Columbia, Barr and Dock Streets.

R. L. POLK & CO.'S

h Frank L, shipping clk Ft Wayne Electric Co, res 84 W
DeWald.

k **Frank E,** Upholsterer and Furniture Dealer, 36
Clinton, res same.

han Bridget A, milliner Wm Malloy, bds 93 W Williams.

han James J, bkkpr Morgan & Beach, bds 93 W Williams.

han John, lab, res 93 W Williams.

han John J, mach, res 119 W Williams.

han Michael J, clk county auditor, bds 93 W Williams.

han Thomas W, bkkpr H B Monning, bds 93 W Williams.

rigan John, carp, res 53 Home ave.

e John S, trav agt Coombs & Co, res 45 Home ave.

e Morton E, carp, res 71 Oakley.

e Wm F, painter J W Muldoon, res 172 Montgomery.

er, *see also Hauser.*

er Charles, fireman, res 101 Franklin ave.

er David E, mach Ft Wayne Electric Co, res 212 Metz.

er John A, foreman Fleming Mnfg Co, res 88 Wells.

er Lizzie, wks Troy Steam Laundry, bds 278 W Jefferson.

er Minnie E, clk Seibert & Good, bds 88 Wells.

h Miss Ella, clk Archer, Housh & Co, bds 40 Home ave.

h John E (Archer, Housh & Co), res 40 Home ave.

h Laura, bds 72 Nelson.

ter Wm H, harnessmkr A L Johns & Co, bds Arlington
Iouse.

harter Maniel, lab, bds Jewel House.

rd George F, removed to Cleveland, O.

rd Jane (wid Charles), bds 149 Wallace.

rd Jennie, domestic 16 W DeWald.

Horatio A, confectionery, 85 Calhoun, rms 84 same.

Nelson, mach Ft Wayne Electric Co, bds Diamond Hotel.

ll Charles A, mach Penn Co, res 39 Miner.

ll Etta, bds Hotel Waverly.

l Grace C, bds 39 Miner.

stein Franklin, photographer, 44 Calhoun, res 160 Ewing.

stein Mrs Helen, bds 171 E Wayne.

stein John C, photographer, bds 160 Ewing.

r Aaron B, bkkpr, res 67 Wilt.

Alice (wid Charles W), res 87 W Berry.

Frank I, clk Penn Co, res 398 E Jefferson.

Wm T, saloon, 354 Calhoun, res same.

nd Wm, tinner G W Staub, bds Harmon House.

r Bernard C, lab Penn Co, bds 47 Barr.

r Catherine (wid Thomas), boarding house, 47 Barr.

r Kate A, opr Hoosier Mnfg Co, bds 47 Barr.

r Martin A, helper Bass F & M Works, res 187 E Jefferson.

ALL ORDERS PROMPTLY ATTENDED TO. RYAN TRUCKING CO. 19 & 21 W. WASHINGTON, Tel. 122.

FORT WAYNE DIRECTORY. 267

Howley Martin J, apprentice Wm Miller, bds 47 Barr.
Howrand Bernard, carp, res 20 Stophlet.
Hoy Frank L, cashier L S & M S Ry, res 86 E Lewis.
Hoynes Daniel J, fireman Penn Co, bds n s Holman 3 e of Calhoun.
Hoynes Wm J, trav agt Mossman, Yarnelle & Co, bds 10 W Superior.
Hoyt Clara (wid Clark), bds 43 Shawnee ave.
Hubbard Alvin L, clk L F Butler, res 9 Harrison.
Hubbard Clara, wks Troy Laundry, bds cor High and Bartlett.
Hubbard G K, Mnfr Bee Hives, 277 Harrison, res 124 Hoagland ave.
Hubbard Joel S, bds 9 Harrison.
Hubbard John H, lab Ft Wayne Spoke Works, res 48 Penn.
Hubbard Sidney G, barber, 21 W Columbia, res 48 Wells.
Huber Anthony J, mach Penn Co, res 126 E Lewis.
Huber Bertha, opr Hoosier Mnfg Co, bds 276 E Washington.
Huber Caroline (wid George), res 126 E Lewis.
Huber Catherine T, bds 126 E Lewis.
Huber Frederick, lab Jacob Klett & Sons, res 276 E Washington.
Huber George, fireman Penn Co, rms 30 Baker.
Huber John F, hoseman Engine Co No 1, rms same.
Huber Louisa, bds 276 E Washington.
Huber Martha, opr Hoosier Mnfg Co, bds 276 E Washington.
Huber Theresa M, dressmkr Mrs G J Stier, bds 276 E Washington.
Huber Ulrich, teamster, res n s Cochran 5 e of Coombs.
Hubertus Nicholas, bds Joseph Fricke.
Hudgel Rezin D, trav agt McDonald, Watt & Wilt, res 271 W Jefferson.
Hudry Louis W, mach Bass F & M Works, bds 186 Montgomery.
Hudry Nicholas, car bldr Penn Co, res 186 Montgomery.
Hudson, *see also Hutson.*
Hudson Edward, painter Keil & Keil, bds German Hotel.
Hue Francis, fireman, bds 150 Greely.
Hueber Barbara (wid Tobias), bds n s 4th 7 w of Wells.
Hueber Isadore, ice pedler Ft Wayne Artificial Ice Co, res 63 High.
Hueber John, lab, bds 325 E Lewis.
Huebner John, mach Kerr-Murray Mnfg Co, res 66 Baker.
Huebner Reinholdt, lab Bass F & M Works, res 46 Walton ave.
Huelf Johanna S, tailoress Gustav Scheffler, bds 52 W 4th.
Huer, *see Heuer.*
Huestis Alexander C, bds 205 W Berry.
Huestis Charles D C, res 205 W Berry.
Huestis Wm H, trav agt McDonald, Watt & Wilt, res 16 Monroe.

ARCHITECTS. **WING & MAHURIN,**
41 and 42 Pixley & Long Bldg. Telephone 228.

268   R. L. POLK & CO.'S

Huff, *see also Hough.*
Huff Cortland, brakeman, bds 28 W Main.
Huff Hiram, flagman Nickel Plate R R, res 5 Brandriff.
Huff Udney, brakeman, res 53 Oliver.
Huffert, *see Heffert.*
Huffman, *see also Hoffman, Hoffmann and Hofmann.*
Huffman George C, carp, res 75 W 3d.
Huffman Henry, market stall No 66, res Adams twp.
Huffman Ira, opr S M Foster, bds 57 Barr.
Huffman Jacob O, finisher P E Wolf, res 75 Lafayette.
Hughes, *see also Hewes.*
Hughes Alice, clk Beadell & Co, bds 25 Walnut.
Hughes Andrew M, comp Journal, bds cor Harrison and Lewis.
Hughes Annie A, tailoress Gottlieb Stauffer, bds 25 Walnut.
Hughes James, cabinetmkr Ft Wayne Organ Co, res 38 Walnut.
Hughes James, lab, bds 290 Calhoun.
Hughes James, lab, res 25 Walnut.
Hughes James E, fireman, bds 25 Walnut.
Hughes Joseph, mngr Mayflower Mills, res 284 W Wayne.
Hughes Margaret A, seamstress, bds 196 Hanna.
Hughes Mary (wid Edwin), res 115 Hanna.
Hughes Mary (wid James), res 25 Walnut.
Hughes Ollie, opr Hoosier Mnfg Co, bds 293 W Main.
Hughes Rose A, dressmkr Victoria Walton, bds 196 Hanna.
Hughes Sarah M, bds 196 Hanna.
Hughes Thomas E, boilermkr, bds 25 Walnut.
Hugo Bertha, domestic 52 E Jefferson.
Huguenard August C, res 152 High.
Huguenard Frances (wid Peter C), bds 63 E Superior.
Huguenard Frank, lab, bds 152 High.
Huguenard Harriet, bds 63 E Superior.
Huguenard Julia (wid Charles), boarding house, 29 Hough.
Huguenard Julius C, grocer, 107 Maumee ave, res 109 same.
Huguenard Mollie, domestic Harmon House.
Huguenard Victor A, feed stable, 62 E Superior, res 63 same.
Huhn Amand, cabtmkr Ft Wayne Organ Co, res 70 Nird-
    linger ave.
Huhn August, coremkr, res 72 Nirdlinger ave.
Huhn Edward, lab, bds 236 Smith.
Huhn Frank, lab, res w s Lillie 1 s of E Creighton ave.
Huhn Frederick, stonecutter Keller & Braun, res 51 Nird-
    linger ave.
Huhn Frederick E, lab, res 236 Smith.
Huhn Henry, stonecutter Keller & Braun, res n e cor Fox and
    Walnut.
Huhn John, wiper Penn Co, bds 236 Smith.

Pius, lab Bass F and M Works, res 70 Nirdlinger ave.

urd **Loyal P**, Agt American and National Express os, rms Gross & Pellen's Block.

'red A, stockkpr Ft Wayne Newspaper Union, res e s oy Run ave 2 n of Riverside ave.

ra, driver, res 25 W 5th.

saac P, paperhanger Siemon & Bro, res 288 W Jefferson.

oseph P, fireman, res 38 Watkins.

Lewis O, Wall Paper, Paints and Painting, Artists' aterials, 90 Calhoun, res 201 W Wayne. (*See right top nes.*)

imon P, fireman, res r 164 High.

Sylvester W, Painter and Paper Hanger, 27 Clinton d 134 Broadway, res 247 E Lewis. Tel 250. (*See right ottom lines.*)

Vm F, elevator conductor, bds 202 W Superior.

Vm H, carp, res 202 W Superior.

ter Frank, trav agt, rms 27 E Washington.

Elwin M, clk Ft Wayne Electric Co, bds 210 W De-Vald.

Wm L, mach Penn Co, res 210 W DeWald.

Wm S, draughtsman Ft Wayne Electric Co, bds 210 W eWald.

el John, lab, res 50 W Butler.

el Rudolph, mach Ft Wayne Organ Co, res 50 W Butler.

ert James, stableman J F Fletcher, rms 32 Barr.

recht George, policeman, res 42 W 3d.

recht Henry G, clk H G Sommers, bds 42 W 3d.

ke Diedrich, lab Penn Co, res 225 John.

James, lab, res 138 Wells.

Wm T, conductor, res 3 E Williams.

el Charles, teamster James Wilding & Son, res 127 airfield ave.

el Ella V, bds 127 Fairfield ave.

el John, lab B Thompson, res rear 474 Broadway.

el J George, teamster, res 192 E DeWald.

brey Ann (wid John M), res 38 Brackenridge.

hrey Clara F, teacher Hanna School, bds 175 W Berry.

hrey George B, asst mailing clk P O, bds 175 W Berry.

phrey James, Propr The Aldine Hotel, n s E Berry et Clinton and Barr.

hrey James A, car tracer Penn Co, res 32 Maple ave.

hrey Jane (wid James) res 171 W Berry.

hrey Jessie L, teacher, bds 175 W Berry.

hrey Louise M (wid George), res 175 W Berry.

brey Lucena W (wid Noah), res 19 Madison.

19

Humphrey Marshall, clk J D Gumpper, bds 38 Brackenridge.

Humphrey Matthew, bds 171 W Berry.

Hunsche Carrie, works Troy Laundry, bds 202 Ewing.

Hunsche Frederick, carp, res 65 Elizabeth.

Hunsche Henry J, mach hd Louis Diether & Bro, res 41 Wells.

Hunsche Mary, domestic 175 E Lewis.

Hunsche Wm, driver Centlivre Brewery, bds Lake Shore Hotel.

Hunt Charles E, brakeman, res 76 Chicago.

Hunt Edward J, fireman G R & I R R, bds 6 Smith.

Hunt Edward T, despatcher Penn Co, rms 188 Calhoun.

Hunt Hascall, brakeman, res 344 W Main.

Hunt Hoyt B, Genl Agt Northwestern Mutual Life Insurance Co, 6 and 7 Trentman Bldg, res 41 Huestis ave.

Hunt John T, horses, 14 Randolph, res same.

Hunt Leonard R, despatcher Penn Co, rms 188 Calhoun.

Hunt Patrick, teamster, res 6 Smith.

Hunt Robert, porter, rms 55 W Main.

Hunt Thomas, teamster, res 12 Randolph.

Hunt Thomas R, helper Kerr-Murray Mnfg Co, bds 6 Smith.

Hunter Charles, lab, res 339 Hanna.

Hunter James L, res 153 Hayden.

Hunter James W, master transportation G R & I R R, res 26 McClellan.

Hunter John L (Didierjohn & Hunter), bds 153 Hayden.

Hunter Lewis C, clk county treas, res 67 Cass.

Hunter Wm E, clk G R & I R R, bds 196 Calhoun.

Huntheim, see Hondheim and Hontheim.

Hunting Fred S, engineer, res 322 W Washington.

Hunting Hiram, lab, bds 14 Summit.

Hunting Wm H, lab Olds' Wagon Works, res 14 Summit.

Huntoon Loudean P, civil engineer, res 110 W Washington.

Huntsman Elizabeth A (wid Israel), res 74 Madison.

Huntsman Melvina, dressmkr, 74 Madison, bds same.

Hunziker Jacob, Saloon and Boarding House, 25-27 Force.

Huppe Herman, lab C Tresselt & Sons, res Wayne twp.

Hurd Oscar D, asst custodian P O, res 74 Calhoun.

Hurlbut Edward S, shipping clk, res 188 W DeWald.

Hurlburt Isabella, opr Hoosier Mnfg Co, bds 17 Hoffman.

Hurlburt Sidney C, pdlr, res 34 Buchanan.

Hurlbut Wm R, mach Olds' Wagon Works, bds 188 W DeWald.

Hurless James O, flagman, rms 258 Calhoun.

Hurley Daniel, boilermkr Penn Co, res 45 W Williams.

Hurley Timothy J, mach Kerr-Murray Mnfg Co, bds 171 Clinton.

RED Cedar Shingles at L. Diether & Bro.'s
Yard, 44 to 54 East Superior St. Factory at 100 Pearl St.

FORT WAYNE DIRECTORY. 271

Hursh Annie (wid Luther E), bds 118 Eliza.
Hursh Olive, domestic 29 Garden.
Hursh Samuel C, mach hd Ft Wayne Electric Co, res 35 Walnut.
Hurst James M, lab, res 9 Bass.
Hurst Lydia, cook Indiana School for Feeble-Minded Youth.
Huser Catherine, domestic 87 W Jefferson.
Huser Louis P, shoemkr, 178 Broadway, res 167 Jackson.
Hushour Clara, bds 50 Chicago.
Hushour Louis B, switchman Wabash R R, res 52 Chicago.
Huston John H, painter, res 4 Colerick.
Hutchinson Mrs Blanche, dressmkr, 130 W 3d, bds same.
Hutchinson Mahlon R, cabinetmkr, res 7 Caroline.
Hutchinson Mate M (wid David B), dressmkr, res 212 Calhoun.
Hutchinson Oliver G, tanner and mitten mnfr, cor Boone and
    Cherry, res 296 W Main.
Hutchison Alonzo M, plasterer, res 154 Clay.
Hutchison Elmer E, truck driver, bds 198 Lafayette.
Hutchison Frank M, painter, bds 198 Lafayette.
Hutchison John H, trav agt, res 185 E Jefferson.
Hutchison Van Rensselaer, agt, res 198 Lafayette.
Hutker Louisa, domestic Allen County Asylum.
Hutson, see also Hudson.
Hutson Charles, carbldr Penn Co, res 104 Gay.
Hutton D Edwin, trav agt A L Johns & Co, res 517 Broadway.
Hutton Mrs Rebecca, removed to Warsaw, Ind.
Hutzel John, res 200 W Washington.
Hutzell Daniel, saloon, 378 W Main, res 376 same.
Hutzell Joseph, clk F Barrett & Co, bds 376 W Main.
Hutzell Valentine, bartndr Daniel Hutzell, bds 376 W Main.
Huxley Frank S, engineer Nickel Plate R R, res 114 Boone.
Huxoll August, grocer, 92 Barr, res 173 Harmer.
Huxoll August W, clk August Huxoll, bds 173 Harmer.
Huxoll Frederick W, clk August Huxoll, bds 173 Harmer.
Hyde Alexander, teamster, bds 81 Grant ave.
Hyde Charles L (Nogal & Hyde), rms 252 Clinton.
Hyde George W, engineer, res 27 E 3d.
Hyer Edward A, propr Hyer House, 3 Railroad.
Hyer House, E A Hyer propr, 3 Railroad.
Hyle Louise, domestic 126 E Berry.
Hyman Edward A, clk H W Soest, bds 338 Calhoun.
Hyman Philip H jr, clk Miller & Haller, bds 338 Calhoun.
Hyman Philip H, res 338 Calhoun.
Hynes, see Hines.

I

Iba Elizabeth (wid Wm), res 129 Fairfield ave.
Iba Floretta, bds 129 Fairfield ave.
Iba George S, fireman City Water Works, res 39 W Jefferson.
Ibel Charles, maltster C L Centlivre Brewing Co, bds Albert Eckerle.
Ichel Andrew, brewer, res 50 Randolph.
Iehl Virgil, baker, res 21 Force.
Ifel John, sheet iron wkr Penn Co, bds 54 Smith.
Igmeyer Charles, carp, res 33 Duryea.
Imbody Adam, turner Ft. Wayne Organ Co, bds 83 W De-Wald.
Imbody Clara C, bds 83 W DeWald.
Imbody Daniel, molder Bass F & M Works, res 189 Ewing.
Imbody Dorothy (wid Harrison), res 83 W DeWald.
Imbody Eliza, clk W U Tel Co, bds 83 W DeWald.
Imbody Henry A, finisher Ft Wayne Organ Co, res 322 Broadway.
Immel Amelia, bds 568 E Washington.
Immel Edward A H, bds 568 E Washington.
Immel John, janitor, res 63 McClellan.
Immel John C, bottler, bds 568 E Washington.
Immel Louisa (wid Henry), res 568 E Washington.
Immel Walter H, clk Herman Berghoff Brewing Co, bds 568 E Washington.
Imswiler Wm H, foreman, res 216 Indiana ave.
Inch John, cupola tender Indiana Machine Works, res 9 Caroline.
Indiana Buggy Co, Theodore Mayer propr, 25 E Columbia.
Indiana Deutsche Presse, Otto F Cummerow Propr, n e cor Calhoun and Main.
Indiana Installment Co, John V Reul Pres, Wm F Graeter Treas, Ernest C Graeter Sec, Mnfrs' Agents and Installment Goods, 166 Calhoun.
Indiana Machine Works, John C Peters pres, Perry A Randall vice-pres, Emmet H McDonald sec, John M Landenbenger treas, n e cor Osage and Main.
Indiana School for Feeble-Minded Youth, 1½ miles n e of Court House.
Indiana Staats Zeitung (Daily and Weekly), John D Sarnighausen Propr, 37 E Columbia.
Indiana State Asylum for Feeble-Minded, St Joseph rd 1 mile n e of Court House.

Indiana State Gazetteer, R L Polk & Co Publrs, 50 Calhoun.

Ingelbeck Louisa, domestic 295 W Berry.

Inman Charles W, painter, res 63 Riverside ave.

Inman Isaac F, lab, bds John Crowl.

International Business College, F H Bliss Pres, Schmitz Blk cor Calhoun and Washington.

Inter-State Fair Association, W D Page pres, J W Pearse vice-pres, D C Fisher treas, W W Rockhill sec, grounds ½ mile w of city office, 32 E Berry.

Irey Anna E (wid Alfred K), res 147 Griffith.

Irey Frank J, clk, bds 147 Griffith.

Irey Sarah (wid Wm), bds 147 Griffith.

Irion Jacob, lab, res 228 John.

Irmscher Max, bricklayer, res 504 E Lewis.

Irvin Lee, lab, bds 43 E Superior.

Irvin Lena, bds 43 E Superior.

Irvin Michael, lab, res 43 E Superior.

Irvine Rebecca (wid Robert), res 18 Hamilton.

Irwin Anna H (wid Thomas), bds 37 Wilt.

Irwin George B, dry goods, 125 Broadway, res 240 W DeWald.

Irwin George H, brakeman Penn Co, bds 37 Wilt.

Irwin George H, clk J E Klinger, bds 67 E Columbia.

Irwin George U, bds 241 W Main.

Irwin John S, M D, L L D, Supt of City Schools, res 241 W Main.

Irwin J Wm, boilermkr Bass F and M Works, res 37 Wilt.

Irwin Lizzie F, teacher, bds 240 W DeWald.

Irwin Mary, clk, bds 241 W Main.

Irwin Rose, bds 241 W Main.

Israel Charles (Heine & Israel), res 16 Sturgis.

Israel Emil, lab George Newcomer, bds w s Smith 2 s of Pontiac.

Israel Frederick, blksmith Olds' Wagon Works, bds 215 W Main.

Israel Henry, mach hd Ft Wayne Electric Co, res 121 Broadway.

Israel Wm, teamster, res 136 Maumee rd.

Iten Catherine (wid John), bds 112 E Creighton ave.

Iten Frank, inspector City Water Works, res 51 Buchanan.

Iten John, carp, res 13 Begue.

Ivins Leon A, clk Penn Co, rms 18 Brackenridge.

Penn Mutual LIFE INSURANCE CO. of PHILA.
CLARK FAIRBANK, General Agent, 19 Court Street.

274   R. L. POLK & CO.'s

J

Jaap George, Cut and Ornamental Stone Contractor, 79–81 E Columbia, res 180 Wells. (*See left bottom lines and card in classified Cut Stone Contractors*).

Jaaqwith Wm, bds 354 E Washington.
Jabas Emil, bricklayer, res 361 E Lewis.
Jabas Louis E, bricklayer, bds 361 E Lewis.
Jackel Leonard, stonecutter, res 45 Force.
Jackson Allen P (Kime & Jackson), res 82 S Wayne ave.
Jackson Anthony A, lab, res 206 Broadway.
Jackson Augustus B (Boltz & Jackson), rms 92 Calhoun.
Jackson Brownell, bartndr H A Wiebke, bds 45 E Main.
Jackson Edward M, waiter J F Cline, res 70 Dawson.
Jackson Effie, bds 82 S Wayne ave.
Jackson Emma (wid Jacob), res 45 E Main.
Jackson Frank B, mach, res 9 Brandriff.
Jackson Grace, bds 55 Brackenridge.
Jackson Ira C, bds 82 S Wayne ave.
Jackson James. paper hanger, Kiel & Kiel, bds Diamond Hotel.
Jackson John, horse-shoer, 88 E Columbia, res 104 E Wayne.
Jackson John A, baggageman L S & M S Ry, res 35 Douglas avenue.
Jackson John C, helper John Jackson, bds 104 E Wayne.
Jackson Johnson P, conductor, res 16 W DeWald.
Jackson Kirby, engineer Penn Co, res 55 Brackenridge.
Jackson Lillian, bds 155 W Washington.
Jackson May, seamstress F J Beach, bds 35 Douglas ave.
Jackson Peter, cigarmkr F J Gruber, res 111 Jackson.
Jackson Sampson, boarding house, 35 Douglas ave.
Jackson Silas A, market stall No 9, res Wayne twp.
Jackson Thomas, engineer maintenance of ways, Penn Co, res 297 Fairfield ave.
Jackson Thomas, teamster, bds 498 W Main.
Jackson Wm, flagman, res 322 Broadway.
Jackson Wm A, finisher Ft Wayne Electric Co, bds 322 Broadway.
Jackson Wm A, trav agt, res n w cor Creighton and Hoagland avenues.
Jackson Wm H, carp, res 200 Fairfield ave.
Jackson Wm T, engineer Penn Co, res 155 W Washington.
Jacob Henry, lab Penn Co, res 115 Hayden.
Jacobs Andrew, grocer, 354 Broadway, res 42 Stophlet.
Jacobs Caroline (wid Peter), bds 116 Madison.
Jacobs Charles, meats, 197 E Washington, res 116 Madison.
Jacobs Charles W, res 297 W Washington.

Jacobs Christopher C (G H Jacobs & Bro), bds 62 E Main.
Jacobs David, teamster, bds 163 Clinton.
Jacobs Elmer E, lab, res 62 E Main.
Jacobs Miss Emma, res 171 E Wayne.
Jacobs Frances, domestic 54 E Washington.
Jacobs George (Jacobs & Conklin), res 73 Wall.
Jacobs George H (George H Jacobs & Bro), res 62 E Main.
Jacobs George H & Bro (George H and Christopher C), bakers, 62 E Main.
Jacobs Gustav, watchman, res 38 Watkins.
Jacobs Harry N, compounder Julius Nathan & Co, bds Aveline House.
Jacobs Henry, lab, res 75 W Washington.
Jacobs Henry G, removed to Richmond, Ind.
Jacobs James, foreman Ryan Bros, res 159 Harrison.
Jacobs John H, farmer, res w s Spy Run ave 1 n of canal feeder.
Jacobs John W, foreman George H Jacobs & Bro, res rear Leikauf's Packing House.
Jacobs Lizzie, bds 297 W Washington.
Jacobs Mary, opr Samuel M Foster, bds 40 Alice.
Jacobs Philanda (wid John), bds 163 Clinton.
Jacobs Shoe Store, Isidor Lehman propr, 17 Calhoun.
Jacobs Sophie, bds 297 W Washington.
Jacobs Thomas, teamster, res 163 Clinton.
Jacobs Wm F (George H Jacobs & Bro), bds 62 E Main.
Jacobs & Conklin (George Jacobs, Guy Conklin), pianos, 210 Calhoun.
Jacobson Rosalie (wid Victor), res 136 W Wayne.
Jacoby Edward, lab, res 104 E Wayne.
Jacoby Frederick, carp, res 40 Buchanan.
Jacoby George C, carp, bds 40 Buchanan.
Jacoby Mary, seamstress, bds 40 Buchanan.
Jacoby Matilda, clk, bds 40 Buchanan.
Jaebker August, lab, res 15 Summit.
Jaeger, see also Yager and Yeager.
Jaeger Christian, clk Freese & Fehling, bds 178 W Creighton av.
Jaeger Mary, opr Hoosier Mnfg Co, bds 59 Force.
Jaekel Moritz, lab, res 226 Gay.
Jager Christian, clk, bds 178 W Creighton ave.
Jahn, see also John.
Jahn Charles C, car bldr Penn Co, res Wayne Trace n of east yard.
Jahn Elizabeth (wid Herman), res 123 Union.
Jahn Herman, painter, res 84 Buchanan.
Jahn Wm, porter Ehrman & Geller, bds 1 Rockhill.
James Eliza (wid Elisha), res 83 St Mary's ave.

ı (wid Daniel), bds 157 Shawnee ave.
ા, lab, bds 83 St Mary's ave.
ın, painter, res 30 W 4th.
carp, res 157 Shawnee ave.
;ineer H W Bond, bds 63 W Superior.
ab, res 161 Shawnee ave.
gineer Penn Co, res 85 Greene.
:, lab, res s s Rebecca nr G R & I R R.
ık, cabtmkr Ft Wayne Furn Co, res 47 Wagner.
ab, res 217 John.
ar repairer, res 214 John.
iV, actionmkr Ft Wayne Organ Co, bds 167 W
n.
L, conductor, res 277 E Creighton ave.
ા, photographer, 86 Calhoun, res same.
s F, clk Scheffer & Geiger, res 24 Brandriff.
, lab, bds 24 Brandriff.
ı (wid Rudolph), bds 49 W Washington.
k, carp Penn Co, res 49 W Washington.
k, lab, bds 203 W Superior.
iV (Freistroffer & Jasper), res 51 W Washing-

:arp, res 203 W Superior.
̃autz.
ar repairer, res 113 High.
gardener, res 3 Polk.
ılper H J Ash, bds 113 High.
ver Peters Box & Lumber Co, bds 113 High.
:ander W, cutter, bds 31 Wefel.
ıhard, tailor, 83 Calhoun, res 31 Wefel.
ırp, bds 12 Winch.
:her Central Grammar School, rns 64 E Jeffer-

nk, lab, res 47 Buchanan.
ʒarmkr, bds 84 W Main.
W, propr Summit City Woolen Mill, 96 E
ı 131 E Wayne.
bertson, pastor, African M E Church, res 273 E

cigarmkr George Reiter, res 7 McClellan.
R, removed to Chicago, Ill.
I', car repairer Penn Co, res 175 Hayden.
s w cor Jefferson and Griffith.
ıer, res 19 Buchanan.
ıd Barnett), res 114 Clinton.
bds 89 W Berry.

O. HULL, Paints, Oils, Varnishes and Glass at 90 Calhoun Street.

FORT WAYNE DIRECTORY. 277

son Mrs Harriet E, removed to Richmond, Ind.

son Joseph J, lawyer 15 Pixley & Long bldg, res 89 W :rry.

son Wm E, tester, res 91 W Washington.

e Chauncey R, Agt Hercules Powder Co and Cam- ι Mnfr, 18 W Columbia, res same. (*See page 65.*)

Edward C, clk C R Jenne, bds 18 W Columbia.

Fred C, bkkpr C R Jenne, bds 18 W Columbia.

s Charles H, mach Rocker Wash Mach Co, res 293 W fferson.

ey Electric Light and Power Co, H C Graffe ·es, R T McDonald Vice-Pres, E H McDonald Sec, G ˙ Pixley Treas, Charles G Guild Supt, Office 4 and 5 Bass ock, Plant Spy Run ave.

gs Clem V, brakeman, res 509 E Lewis.

gs George, driver, bds 63 E Wayne.

Hans, blacksmith Olds' Wagon Works, res 39 John.

James O, livery, bds Lake Shore Hotel.

Abigail J (wid John), rms 3 N Harrison.

Wm A, bartndr Boltz & Jackson, res 47 W Superior.

κy Annie, helper Wm C Seidel & Bro, bds 29 Liberty.

κy Anton, lab Bass F & M Works, res 29 Liberty.

κy Mary, helper Wm C Seidel & Bro, bds 29 Liberty.

ə Solomon, res 14 Murray.

House, Samuel Clark propr, 225 Calhoun.

Mrs Elizabeth, res 58 W Berry.

Frank, clk Robert Spice, rms 94 W Main.

see also Yobst.

Anna, opr Hoosier Mnfg Co, bds 1 Oak.

Balbina (wid Alexander), res 1 Oak.

Charles, lab City Water Works, bds 1 Oak.

Frank H, lab City Water Works, res 303 Hanna.

Theresa, opr Hoosier Mnfg Co, bds 1 Oak.

ı John J, bds 168 Calhoun.

ı Louis, books, 168 Calhoun, res same.

Frank, cigarmkr Schele Bros, bds 84 W Main.

ι Andrew, lab Penn Co, res 248 E Jefferson.

ι Andrew jr, baker, bds 248 E Jefferson.

ι Catherine, opr Samuel M Foster, bds 248 E Jefferson.

ι Frank L, clk Rear & Bugert, bds 248 E Jefferson.

ι George N, mach hand Ft Wayne Furn Co, res 177 E ∶wis.

ι Theresa, bds 248 E Jefferson.

ιy George B, removed to Cleveland, O.

∶ee also Jahn.

'aulina (wid Charles), res 56 Miner.

John Robert, engineer, res 398 W Main.
Johnell Benjamin, bds s s Wheeler 2 w of Runnion ave.
Johnell Francis, bds 155 High.
Johnell Henry J, lab N Y, C & St L R R, res 137 High.
Johnell Lawrence W, lab, res 155 High.
Johns Alfred L (A L Johns & Co), res 287 W Washington.
Johns Alfred S, res 308 W Washington.
Johns A L & Co (Alfred L Johns), saddlery hardware, 51 E Columbia.
Johns Grant U, lab, res 33 W 5th.
Johns Mary, domestic Rich Hotel.
Johns Nicholas, res 1 Rockhill.
Johns Pauline (wid Charles), bds 1 Rockhill.
Johns Sophia M, confectioner W F Geller, bds 123 Union.
Johns Wm, barber, bds 1 Rockhill.
Johnson Alfred S, asst train despatcher Nickel Plate R R, res 255 W Wayne.
Johnson Andrew, res 238 St Mary's ave.
Johnson August, coremkr Bass F & M Works, bds 208 Hanna.
Johnson Augustine, engineer Penn Co, res 203 Barr.
Johnson A Lincoln, helper Ft Wayne Electric Co, res 154 W De Wald.
Johnson Belle, bds 203 Barr.
Johnson Benjamin F, lab, bds 116 Fulton.
Johnson Bernard, helper, res 87 Holman.
Johnson Byron J, mach Penn Co, res 93 Hugh.
Johnson Charles E, bartndr Russell George, res 96 Clay.
Johnson Charles E, mach Horton Mnfg Co, res 29 Elm.
Johnson Charles E, painter Chauvey Bros, bds 28 W Main.
Johnson Charles W, lab, res 110 Shawnee ave.
Johnson Charles W, oiler Penn Co, res Brookside nr Broadway.
Johnson Della L, stenographer, bds 320 Calhoun.
Johnson Elbe C, painter, res 45 Calhoun.
Johnson Emmett, helper Penn Co, res 42 St Mary's ave.
Johnson Frank, fireman Penn Co, res 4 Grant.
Johnson Frank M, boarding stable, 13 Pearl, res 320 Calhoun.
Johnson George, res 202 John.
Johnson George E, Dentist, 74 Calhoun, res 188 W Berry. *(See right top lines.)*
Johnson George W, clk, bds 20 W 3d.
Johnson Grace, domestic 243 W Washington.
Johnson Henry, bds 173 Griffith.
Johnson Henry, lab Penn Co, bds 217 John.
Johnson Jacob, helper Penn Co, res 214 John.
Johnson Jennie, domestic Nickel Plate Hotel.
Johnson John, cooper, bds 46 E Columbia.

Geo. E. Johnson, DENTIST, 74 Calhoun Street.
Res., 188 W. Berry St.

FORT WAYNE DIRECTORY. 279

Johnson John W, clk, res 136 W De Wald.
Johnson Josiah, oiler Penn Co, res 33 Walnut.
Johnson Laura J, tailoress C Kruse, rms 55 W Jefferson.
Johnson Lida, domestic 19 W Williams.
Johnson Loran H, grocer, 14 Baker, res same.
Johnson Mary, domestic The Wayne.
Johnson Marcus R, mach Ft Wayne Electric Co, res 231 W Jefferson.
Johnson Mary, bds 136 W De Wald.
Johnson Mary, seamstress D S Redelsheimer & Co, bds 202 John.
Johnson Matthew, res 14 Murray.
Johnson May E, dressmkr, bds 129 Broadway.
Johnson Myrtle, music teacher, bds 14 Baker.
Johnson Ollie (wid Albert), milliner, 109 Maumee rd, bds 509 E Washington.
Johnson Oscar B, clk, res 129 Broadway.
Johnson Oscar B jr, engraver, bds 129 Broadway.
Johnson Peter H, blksmith Ft Wayne Electric Co, res 73 Shawnee ave.
Johnson Phœbe, bds 42 St Mary's ave.
Johnson Rose, teacher Conservatory of Music, bds 108 E Wayne.
Johnson Sarah E (wid Elias), rms 69 W Berry.
Johnson Thomas, student, bds 202 John.
Johnson Wesley H, lab L S & M S Ry, res 135 W 3d.
Johnson Wm M, cooper, res 20 W 3d.
Johnston Monroe, gardener, res 71 W 3d.
Johnston Russell E, gymnast, bds 103 Lafayette.
Johnstonbaugh Emory, foreman K Hubbard, res 63 Melita.
Joho John, lab, bds 22 E Columbia.
Joly, see also Jully.
Joly Emma F, clk, bds 61 E Columbia.
Joly Frank, clk J Langard, res 29 Randolph.
Jones Ambrose F, clk, res 301 Harrison.
Jones Arthur L, mach hd Ft Wayne Electric Co, bds 112 Wells.
Jones Mrs Belle M, res 121 E Main.
Jones Benjamin F, polisher Ft Wayne Furn Co, bds 63 W Butler.
Jones Cass A, carp, res 272 W Jefferson.
Jones Catherine (wid John), bds 22 John.
Jones Catherine (wid Paul), res 51 Oliver.
Jones Charles, clk, res 145 Fairfield ave.
Jones Charles A, physician, 444 Hanna, res same.
Jones Charles M, clk Penn Co, res 116 Force.

Daisy (col'd), domestic 369 Calhoun.
David W, printer, 13 E Main, res 21 Leith.
Dora E, rms 49 E Main.
Edward, removed to St Louis, Mo.
Edward, clk J B Certia, bds 112 Wells.
Edward I (col'd), porter E C Hagen, bds 65 Baker.
Edward S, engineer G R & I R R, res 83 W Butler.
Mrs Elizabeth, res 127 Fairfield ave.
Ella, domestic 55 E Superior.
Eva J, housekpr, 63 W Butler.
Frederick (col'd), porter, bds 65 Baker.
Frederick W, horse trainer, res 289 W Washington.
Fremont L (F L Jones & Co), res 246 Hoagland ave.
's F L & Co (Fremont L Jones, Ogden Pierce), Proprs
roy Steam Laundry, 48-50 Pearl. (*See left bottom lines.*)
George A, clk Seavey Hardware Co, res s Cochrane 3 w
Coombs.
George W, real estate, 36 Calhoun, res 146 Jackson.
Griffith, brakeman N Y, C & St L R R, bds Schele
ouse.
Harry A, bkkpr M L Jones, bds 121 E Main.
Harvey P, foreman Troy Steam Laundry, res 21 Leith.
Henry, engineer Penn Co, res 47 E DeWald.
Henry P, brakeman, bds 51 Oliver.
Jasper W, county commissioner, res Jackson twp.
John, clk J B Certia, bds 112 Wells.
John, farmer, res e s Lafayette 2 s of Piqua ave.
John, mach, res 63 W Butler.
John L, painter Rocker Wash Mach Co, bds 63 W But-

Joseph H, physician, 320 W Jefferson, res same.
Levi M, res 152 E Berry.
Lloyd, clk, res 112 Wells.
Margaret, dressmkr, bds 208 W DeWald.
ary (wid David W), bds 53 W Superior.
Maurice L, photo supplies, 44 Calhoun, res 2 E Columbia.
Oliver S, finisher D N Foster Furn Co, bds 63 W Butler.
arke, lab Penn Co, bds Jewel House.
obert M, engineer Penn Co, res 146 Wallace.
homas, clk Coombs & Co, res 30 Pine.
'm, cigarmkr, bds 112 Wells.
'm, lab, bds 68 W Butler.
'm H, propr Hamilton House, 103 W Berry.
'm H, sawyer Kilian Baker, res 58 5th.
'm H, teamster, bds 260 Clinton.
e also Yoast.

Albert, piano teacher, res 132 W Jefferson.

in Annie (wid Joseph), res rear 330 Harrison.

n, *see also Jourdain.*

n Charles, helper The Randall.

n George S, engineer, res 190 W Superior.

n Joseph F, mach Bass F & M Works, res 142 Madison.

d Ernest A, woodwkr Anthony Wayne Mnfg Co, res 11 lough.

Hiram, lab, bds 1 Hoffman.

a Hiram, lab, bds 22 W 4th.

larold M, rms 110 E Wayne.

Anna, bds 138 Wells.

Charles P, letter carrier Postoffice, res 154 High.

Lizzie, bds 138 Wells.

Louisa (wid John M), res 138 Wells.

George, driver L P Scherer, bds 99 Maumee ave.

ain, *see also Jordan.*

ain Celestin J, grocer, 98 Maumee ave, res 94 same.

al Co, W W Rockhill mngr, publrs Ft Wayne Daily and Veekly Journal, 30 E Main.

Irs Fannie, res 74 Montgomery.

David L, mach Penn Co, res 35 Fairfield ave.

George H, foreman Penn Co, res 23 E Williams.

Lloyd W, mach hand Penn Co, bds 23 E Williams.

Oscar B, blksmith Penn Co, res 262 E Lewis.

ʒel Rev Henry, pastor Evangelical Lutheran Zion's Church, es e s Hanna 2 s of Creighton ave.

ʒel John H T, student, bds e s Hanna 2 s of Creighton venue.

en August H, brickmkr, res w s Lafayette rd 2 n of Piqua.

rd Frances, dressmkr, 105 Broadway, res same.

, *see also Joly.*

Clara M, domestic 126 W Jefferson.

Louis, barber, 114 St Mary's ave, res 112 same.

Sophie, domestic 123 W Williams.

Edward, lab, bds 22 Ewing.

Charles, bkkpr, res 146 W Wayne.

Clemence J, painter, 179 Taber, res same.

Paulina, bds 146 W Wayne.

ı August, market stall No 20, res Adams twp.

ıans Edwin F R, cabtmkr Bruns & McBennett, res s w or Harrison and Allen.

es Wm F, fireman Penn Co, res 113 Madison.

Beecher W (Junk & Rensberger), res 66 Monroe.

Jacob, lab Penn Co, bds 74 Leith.

Peter, helper Penn Co, bds 74 Leith.

& Rensberger (Beecher W Junk, Alpheus D Rensberger),
icture frames, 181 Calhoun.
nsen Peter K, clk Morgan & Beach, res s s St Joseph
gravel rd 1 e of river bridge.
see Yost.

K

August, helper, res 71 Nirdlinger ave.
Ferdinand, coremkr Bass F & M Works, res 166 W
reighton ave.
Herman, mach Wabash R R, bds 71 Nirdlinger ave.
John, molder Bass F & M Works, bds 71 Nirdlinger
ve.
Wm, coremkr Bass F and M Works, bds 166 W
reighton ave.
Bertha A, clk M F Kaag, bds 45 Cass.
Carrie E, clk Beadell & Co, bds 283 W Jefferson.
Charles F W, clk, bds 45 Cass.
Eliza, clk Mary Myers, bds s e cor Spring and Oakland.
Margaret (wid Jacob), res 203 W Jefferson.
Matthias F, Crockery, Glassware, Bar Goods,
amps and Chandeliers, 5 E Columbia, res 45 Cass. (*See
ft bottom lines.*)
Peter, res s s cor Spring and Oakland.
Wm, lab Hoffman Bros, bds s e cor Spring and Oakland.
h Franz (Kabisch & Son), res 182 Fairfield ave.
h Frederick C (Kabisch & Son), res 180 W DeWald.
h Jennettie, bds 182 Fairfield ave.
h John H, barber, 137 Fairfield ave, res 108 W Williams.
h Rudolph J, tinner, bds 182 Fairfield ave.
h & Son (Franz R and Frederick C), meats, 156 Fairfield
e.
cher, *see Kalbacher and Kohlbacher.*
see also Kaler, Kaylor, Kehler, Keller, Koehler and
hler.
Henry, lab, bds 30 Hoffman.
in, *see Koehnlein.*
Wm, fireman Penn Co, res 57½ Laselle.
e Kane.
see also Kayser, Keiser, Keyser and Kiser.
Anton H, clk Penn Co, res 353 E Washington.
Charles, blksmith Wabash R R, res 6 Union.

Kaiser Charles, plasterer, bds 496 W Main.
Kaiser Conrad, foreman Ranke & Yergens, res 43 Cass.
Kaiser Ernst, mach Penn Co, res 186 E Lewis.
Kaiser Frederick E, boilermkr Wabash R R, res 148 Force.
Kaiser Frederick F, boilermkr, bds 148 Force.
Kaiser Henry D, sawyer Ranke & Yergens, res 67 Wells.
Kaiser Isaac G, plasterer, res 496 W Main.
Kaiser John, lab, res n s Putnam 1 W Franklin.
Kaiser John, lab, res 42 Wallace.
Kaiser Leonora, dressmkr, bds 186 E Lewis.
Kaiser Minnie, dressmkr Victoria Walton, bds 148 Force.
Kaiser Oscar, lab, res 334 Force.
Kaiser Rudolph, lab, bds 86 Oakley.
Kaiser Sebastian, Fine Whiskies, Wines, Liquors,
    Tobaccos and Cigars, 46 E Columbia, res same.
Kaiser Wilhelmina, seamstress, bds 148 Force.
Kaiser Wm, coachman Dr McCaskey, bds 6 Union.
Kaiser Wm G, patternmkr, bds 43 N Cass.
Kalb Caroline (wid George A), res 16 Bell ave.
Kalbac John, butcher, res 127 Madison.
Kalbacher, *see also Kohlbacher.*
Kalbacher Anton (A Kalbacher & Co), grocer, 13-15 Grand,
    res 234 E Wayne.
Kalbacher A & Co (Anton Kalbacher, Wm Potthoff), flour and
    feed, 296 Calhoun.
Kalbacher Edward H, clerk, bds 234 E Wayne.
Kalbacher Kate, bkkpr A Kalbacher, bds 234 E Wayne.
Kalbacher Theresa, clerk, bds 234 E Wayne.
Kalbus John, lab, res 153 Archer ave.
Kaler, *see also Kahler, Kaylor, Kehler, Keller, Koehler and
    Kohler.*
Kaler Charles P, conductor, res 235 W Washington.
Kaliker Fredina, domestic 290 Hanna.
Kallan Kate, dressmkr J G Fessenden, bds n e cor Rumsey ave
    and Richardson.
Kallen Peter, sawyer Hoffman Bros, res n e cor Rumsey ave
    and Richardson.
Kallenbach George, helper, res 32 Charles.
Kallenbach Hattie (wid George), res 32 Charles.
Kallenbach Henrietta, domestic 243 W Creighton ave.
Kallenbach Louis, lab, bds 14 Force.
Kalpin Bertha, domestic 165 Jackson.
Kamm Julius, tinner Gerding & Aumann Bros, bds 512 E
    Lewis.
Kamm Peter, engineer, res 512 E Lewis.
Kamm Wm, engineer Mayflower Mills, res 512 E Lewis.

er, *see also Kohlmeyer.*

er Ernst C, driver Kayser & Baade, bds 57 Baker.

er Henry, lab Nickel Plate, res 87 St Mary's ave.

Henry, lab Bass F & M Works, res 133 Madison.

Louis, coremkr Bass F & M Works, res 85 Lillie.

er Ferdinand, carp, bds 300 Hanna.

er Richard, pulleymkr Paul's Pulley Works, bds 81 l.

ee also Kemp and Komp.

atherine, opr Hoosier Mnfg Co, bds 26 Nirdlinger ave.

ate, domestic 190 W Berry.

Adolph C, res 50 W Lewis.

Charles A, bds 306 W Jefferson.

Christian J, clk Penn Co, res 217 W Jefferson.

Ernest G, bkkpr S Bash & Co, bds 50 W Lewis.

Gustav, teacher, res 306 W Jefferson.

Otto F, upholsterer P E Wolf, bds 84 W Jefferson.

Ernst, cabtmkr Peters Box and Lumber Co, res 109 lison.

es Henry, butcher Leikauf Bros, res 8 Hanover.

es John, helper Kerr-Murray Mnfg Co, bds 38 Wall.

es Mary (wid Joseph), res 38 Wall.

Francis J, conductor, res 86 W Williams.

Lee H, conductor, res 88 W Williams.

W, lab Penn Co, res 310 Harrison.

lock, s s Main bet Calhoun and Harrison.

arles E, clk J M Kane, bds 88 W Berry.

niel W, clk J M Kane, bds 88 W Berry.

nnah (wid James), rms 46 W Berry.

nes M, notions, 24 Calhoun, res 88 W Berry.

n P, conductor, res 504 Hanna.

ia A, bds 50 W Berry.

tie, domestic 100 W Berry.

ry, domestic 105 W Berry.

ry, dressmkr, rms 46 W Berry.

rick H, cigars Wayne Hotel, res 50 W Berry.

n, lab Olds' Wagon Works, res 11 Wiebke.

ugust F, foreman, res 53 Charles.

roline (wid Frederick), bds 315 E Washington.

ederick H, clk Fisher Bros, res 95 Montgomery.

ohn, bricklayer, res 41 Monroe.

Henry, bricklayer, res 68 Stophlet.

Henry F, blksmith, res 135 E Lewis.

Henry W, shpg clk Frederick Eckart, res 59 E Wayne.

Louis F, molder, bds 59 E Wayne.

Sophia (wid Louis), bds 135 E Lewis.

Kanning Sophia (wid Wm), res 59 E Wayne.
Kanning Wm H, woodworker Penn Co, bds 59 E Wayne.
Kaough Elizabeth, bds 166 Montgomery.
Kaough Margaret (wid Nicholas), bds 166 Montgomery.
Kaough Richard, clk H A Rockhill, bds 166 Montgomery.
Kaough Wm (E F Clausmeier & Co), res 166 Montgomery.
Kapler, *see Kepler.*
Kappel Catherine (wid John H), res 180 E Washington.
Kappel Henry, lab Penn Co, res 349 E Lewis.
Kappel Henry, paperhanger Kiel & Kiel, bds 180 E Washington.
Kappel Herman G, clk Geo DeWald & Co, bds 180 E Washington.
Kappel John A, paperhanger Kiel & Kiel, bds 180 E Washington.
Kappel John H, clk W L Moellering, bds 349 E Lewis.
Karbasch Louis, molder, res 14 Force.
Karber Frederick, jeweler, res 203 High.
Karber George D, carp, res 75 Grant ave.
Karber James, carp, res 123 Walton ave.
Kariger Samuel, res 187 Harmer.
Karn, *see also Kern and Kirn.*
Karn Bros (Kaim and Joseph), Meat Market, 16 W Main.
Karn Joseph (Karn Bros), res 133 W Washington.
Karn Kaim (Karn Bros), bds 133 W Washington.
Karn Samuel A, pianos, 118 Calhoun, res 25 E Washington.
Karns Jesse L, mach Kerr-Murray Mnfg Co, bds Diamond Hotel.
Karns Wilson C, photographer, res 118 Fulton.
Karp Helena, bds 223 Walton ave.
Kartholl Caroline (wid Joseph), bds 112 Clay.
Kasbaum Charles, spoke driver, bds Richard Mulcahy.
Kasch Adam, boilermkr, rms 78 Wilt.
Kasten Louis C (Kasten & Kohlmeyer), res 116 W Jefferson.
Kasten & Kohlmeyer (Louis C Kasten, Edward Kohlmeyer), cigar mnfrs, 173 Broadway.
Kastner Nicholas, stone mason, res 319 Hanna.
Kathner Getto, painter, res 198 Lafayette.
Katt August C, Books and Stationery, News Stand, Bicycles, Type-Writers, Etc, 82 Calhoun, res 69 W Berry.
Katt Gustavus E, printer Indiana Staats Zeitung, bds 41 Maumee rd.
Katzenwadel Jacob, brewer The Herman Berghoff Brewing Co, res 60 Hoffman.
Kauder Bernard, lab, res 131 Taber.
Kauffman Harry St C, tel opr, bds 262 W Berry.
Kaufman Catherine (wid Christian), res 348 Hanna.
Kaufman Julia, opr Hoosier Mnfg Co, bds 348 Hanna.

20

alentine, lab Kerr-Murray Mnfg Co, res rear 40

ıa (wid Bernard), res 200 Gay.
;topher, baker G H Jacobs & Bro, bds 62 E Main.
see also Cavanaugh.
Irs Julia, wks Troy Steam Laundry, bds 22 Gay.
'homas, blksmith, res 34 Bass.
'homas, collector, res 167 N Harrison.
'homas J, lab, bds 167 N Harrison.
Key.
anda, res 37 Bass.
n, mach, res 44 Hoagland ave.
b, bds 44 Hoagland ave.
dso Kahler, Kaler, Kehler, Keller, Koehler and

h, driver, bds 43 N Calhoun.
.n, lab, bds 23 Lillie.
A (wid Peter), bds 43 N Calhoun.
, lab Salimonie Mining & Gas Co, res 525 E Lewis.
en, lab, bds 26 Orchard.
domestic 16 Hamilton.
butcher, John Raab, bds 26 Orchard.
'so Kaiser, Keiser, Keyser and Kiser.
ı, tailor, res 252 W Jefferson.
st, mach Indiana Machine Wks, bds 129 Broadway.
es H, cigarmkr F J Gruber, bds 346 E Wayne.
tian H C, painter Penn Co, res 200 Francis.
t, lab Pottlitzer Bros, res 129 Broadway.
rick, tailor, 42 Harrison, res same.
rick C, springmkr, bds 346 E Wayne.
rick D, shoemkr P J Eggemann, res 346 E Wayne.
e E, mach hand Indiana Machine Works, bds 252
son.
, domestic 234 W Berry.
J, dressmkr E A Walthemath, bds 252 W

ie L, dressmkr E A Walthemath, bds 252 W

ore S, clk Louis Fortriede, bds 252 W Jefferson.
Kayser & Baade), res s w cor Huestis and Broad-

D, printer Indiana Staats Zeitung, bds 346 E

3aade (Wm Kayser, Henry C Baade), Groceries,
ry Goods and Glassware, 129–133 and 500 Broad-
l 181 and 269.

Kearns, *see Kerns*.

Kee Wah, laundry, 203 Calhoun, res same.

Keech Arthur S, lab, bds 112 Force.

Keech J Edward, mach Bass F and M Works, res 112 Force.

Keefe John, brakeman, res 10 Marion.

Keefe Mary (wid Cornelius), bds 58 Douglas ave.

Keefer, *see also Keever, Keffer and Kiefer*.

Keefer Christian, stone-cutter Keller & Braun, res 275 W Jefferson.

Keefer Frederick, mach hd Horton Mnfg Co, res 6 Zollars ave.

Keefer John, lab Paul Koehler, res w s Lafayette 5 s of Pontiac.

Keefer Mary, bds 6 Zollars ave.

Keefer Susan, seamstress D S Redelsheimer & Co, bds 6 Zollars avenue.

Keegan Edward A, clk Coombs & Co, bds 147 W Washington.

Keegan Hugh G, clk Coombs & Co, bds 147 W Washington.

Keegan Patrick H, engineer Penn Co, res 147 W Washington.

Keehner Kate, cook Boston Restaurant.

Keel, *see also Keil, Kiel and Kyle*.

Keel Aurora C, deputy collector U S internal revenue, res 24 W Berry.

Keel Mrs Aurora C, milliner, 22 W Berry, res 24 same.

Keel Miss Minnie, bds 24 W Berry.

Keeley, *see also Kieley*.

Keeley Wm F, fireman G R & I R R, res 75 Baker.

Keener Frank L, driver Fort Wayne Street Railroad Co, bds 104 Glasgow.

Keener Lucedy, domestic 20 Van Buren.

Kees, *see also Keys and Kiess*.

Kees Christian, tailor, bds 35 Wilt.

Kees Frank, storekeeper, res 35 Wilt.

Kees John, boilermkr Wabash R R, bds 35 Wilt.

Keever, *see also Keefer, Keffer and Kiefer*.

Keever Samuel, lab, res 85 Wagner.

Keffer, *see also Keefer, Keever and Kiefer*.

Keffer Isaac P, pdlr, res 41 Force.

Kegelman Charles, upholsterer P E Wolf, bds 539 E Wayne.

Kegelman Julius, mattressmkr, res 539 E Wayne.

Kegelman Kate, bds 539 E Wayne.

Kegg Emanuel S, carp, res 116 W Butler.

Kegg Lillian (wid Wm A), bds 108 W Butler.

Kehler, *see also Kahler, Kaler, Kaylor, Keller, Koehler and Kohler*.

Kehler Daniel B, treas Fort Wayne Furniture Co, bds n e cor Spy Run and Prospect aves.

hler George A, foreman Fort Wayne Furniture Co, res 395
E Wayne.

hler Joseph W, mach hand Fort Wayne Furniture Co, res 7
Prospect ave.

il, *see also Keel, Kiel and Kyle.*

il Frederick W (Keil & Keil), bds 145 W Superior.

il Jacob H (Keil & Keil), res 139 W Superior.

il Louis D (Keil & Keil), res 145 W Superior.

il Luther H, clk Hoffman Bros, bds 139 W Superior.

eil & Keil (Jacob H, Louis D and Frederick W), Wall
Paper, 116 Calhoun.

inking Frederick, hoseman Engine Co No 1, rms same.

intz John, engineer, res 293 Hanna.

inz Philip, saloon, 307 Lafayette, res same.

iser, *see Kaiser, Kayser, Keyser and Kiser.*

ister Lottie, waiter Hotel Rich.

leker Josie, domestic 33 E Williams.

lker Anthony, engineer Penn Co, res 174 Griffith.

lker Harry O, engineer, res 61 Hayden.

lker John H, truck driver, res 71 Holman.

lker Orlo L, bartndr R Hammond, res 24 E Washington.

lker Samuel S, engineer Penn Co, res 16 W Lewis.

lker Wm, carp, res 120 Clinton.

lker Wm C, engineer, res 89 Baker.

llemeier Wm, coachman J H Bass.

ller, *see also Kahler, Kaler, Kaylor, Kehler, Koehler and
Kohler.*

ller Abraham, teamster, res 124 Union.

ller Albert J, uphlstr Pape Furniture Co, res 224 W Main.

ller Andrew J, druggist, 97 Broadway, res 83 Brackenridge.

ller Caspar, lab Bass F & M Works, res 11 Gay.

ller Charles, died April 29, 1891.

ler Edmund W, lab, bds 99 Shawnee ave.

ler Elizabeth (wid Charles), res 224 W Main.

ler Frederick J, farmer, res 99 Shawnee ave.

ler Henry (Keller & Braun), res 141 W Superior.

ler Isaac E, teamster, res 342 W Jefferson.

ler Jacob, hammerman Bass F & M Works, bds 68 Walton ave.

ler James, lab Penn Co, res 68 Walton ave.

Wm, teamster, res 162 Shawnee ave.

Wm E, teamster, res 124 Union.

W Alba, clk J C Figel & Bro, bds 56 Wells.

r & Braun (Henry Keller, Charles G Braun), Proprs Wayne Steam Stone Works, 86–98 Pearl. (*See page 6.*)

1an Frederick, lab, res s e cor Hayden and Ohio.

1eyer Christian, driver J M Riedmiller, res 312 Broad-y.

see also Kelly.

George W, clk Salimonie Mining & Gas Co, bds 171 nton.

Harry, lab Ft Wayne Electric Co, res 72 Nelson.

John B, clk W C Kelley, bds same.

John M, switchman, res 158 Horace.

Lizzie (wid Michael), res 171 Clinton.

Richard, brakeman N Y, C & St L R R, bds Schele 1use.

Mrs Sarah A, bds 116 W Main.

Wm C, hardware, 356 Calhoun, res same.

Wm F, brakeman res 98 Ewing.

ier Wm, coachman 113 W Berry.

; John H, engineer Penn Co, bds Boylan's Restaurant.

Joseph M, Medical Examiner for the Relief Dept nn Co, Office Penn Depot, res 397 Calhoun.

ee also Kelley.

1bbie, opr Hoosier Mnfg Co, bds 20 Brandriff.

1ndrew, lab, bds 20 Brandriff.

'hristopher, constable, res 82 Madison.

1iara, domestic 114 Clinton.

'aniel, lab, res 204 E Wayne.

'ennis, lab, res 60 Leith.

dmund, molder Kerr-Murray Mnfg Co, bds 25 Hough.

rank, finisher, res 41 Force.

rank, fireman, bds 17 Burgess.

larry, lab, res 94 Wilt.

ohn, helper Penn Co, res 313 Harrison.

ohn, lab, bds 204 E Wayne.

ohn H, bds 9 Walnut.

ohn T, lab, res 81 Hoagland ave.

P, clk Penn Co, res Maumee rd nr tollgate.

illie, opr Hoosier Mnfg Co, bds 41 Wallace.

largaret, bds 9 Walnut.

argaret, opr Hoosier Mnfg Co, bds 313 S Harrison.

ary, tailoress, bds 81 Hoagland ave.

atrick, lab, res 9 Walnut.

atrick J, lab, bds 9 Walnut.

Penn Mutual LIFE INSURANCE CO. of PHILA.
CLARK FAIRBANK, General Agent, 19 Court Street.

290   R. L. POLK & CO.'S

Kelly Robert E, engineer, res 108 W 3d.
Kelly Thomas, res 108 W 3d.
Kelly Thomas, brakeman, bds 313 S Harrison.
Kelly Timothy, painter Penn Co, bds 20 Brandriff.
Kelly Timothy W, lab Penn Co, res 20 Brandriff.
Kelly Wm B, brakeman, res 48 Buchanan.
Kelly Wm C, frescoer, bds 143 Holman.
Kelsey Alfred N, trav agt, res n w cor Putman and Sherman.
Kelsey Charles, lab, bds 40 Pearl.
Kelsey Charles B, farmer, res 45 Indiana ave.
Kelsey Elias M, meats, 502 Broadway, res 43 Indiana ave.
Kelsey Elva C, butcher, res s s Huestis ave 1 w of No 57.
Kelsey Henry, res rear 409 W Main.
Kelsey Jesse N, carp, bds 23 Hoffman.
Kelsey Joseph, feed barn, 40 Pearl, res same.
Kelsey Phœbe (wid James T), res 22 Harrison.
Kelsey Walter D, hostler Powers & Barnett, bds 22 Harrison.
Kelsey Wm A, barber, res 40 Bass.
Kelsey Wm A, woodworker Anthony Wayne Mnfg Co, res 42 W Jefferson.
Kelsey Wm H, res 417 W Main.
Keltsch Adam, lab Kerr-Murray Mnfg Co, res 78 Wilt.
Keltsch Nicholas, cabtmkr Peters Box and Lumber Co, res 49 Barthold.
Kemmel, see Kimmel.
Kemp, see also Kamp and Komp.
Kemp Charles M, clk, bds 169 E Wayne.
Kemp Cornelius W, carp Penn Co, res 160 Hoffman.
Kemp Edgar, trav agt Geo DeWald & Co, res 169 E Wayne.
Kemp Herbert L, shpg clk Mossman, Yarnelle & Co, bds 169 E Wayne
Kemp Jonathan, carp, bds 160 Hoffman.
Kemp Martin W, foreman Penn Co, res 301 E Lewis.
Kemp Whitley, carp, res 160 Hoffman.
Kempf Anna, opr Hoosier Mnfg Co, bds 17 High.
Kempf Charles F, wheel worker American Wheel Co, bds 17 High.
Kempf Etta, opr Hoosier Mnfg Co, bds 17 High.
Kempf John W, woodworker Anthony Wayne Mnfg Co, res 221 Madison.
Kempf Wm, lab, res 17 High.
Kempf Wm, lab, res 217 Madison.
Kendall Jedediah, lab, res 3 Dwenger ave.
Kendall Wallace E, armature winder Ft Wayne Electric Co, res 114 Jackson.

Kendrick Frank B, architect, 25 Schmitz Block, res 199 W
Wayne.
Kendrick Hattie B, clk Wabash R R, bds 21 W DeWald.
Kendrick Louisa, bds 21 W DeWald.
Kendrick Wm G, res 21 W DeWald.
Kendrick Wm H, mngr Remington-Lawton Co, res 56 W
DeWald.
Kennawell Ella, dressmkr, 108 W DeWald, bds same.
Kennawell Maggie, dressmkr Ella Kennawell, bds 108 W De-
Wald.
Kennedy John, engineer, res 80 Boone.
Kennedy Kate, domestic Hanna Homestead.
Kennedy Ransom, plasterer, res 68 Riverside ave.
Kennelly Jeremiah, lab, res 56 Baker.
Kennelly John, policeman, bds 56 Baker.
Kennelly Margaret (wid Michael), bds 56 Baker.
Kennelly Michael, grocer, s e cor Winter and E Creighton ave,
res same.
Kennerk Cecilia, opr S M Foster, bds 26 Murray.
Kennerk John, lab, bds 26 Murray.
Kennerk John, produce buyer, res 26 Murray.
Kennerk Louis F, helper Penn Co, bds 26 Murray.
Kennerk Wm, bell boy The Randall.
Kenode Edward, fireman Penn Co, bds 59 Brackenridge.
Kensill Emma, boxfitter Ft Wayne Electric Co, bds 173
Holman.
Kensill George W, engineer Penn Co, res 148 Clay.
Kensill George W jr, engineer Penn Co, res 30 Suttenfield.
Kensill John C, boilermkr Penn Co, res 173 Holman.
Kensill John C, engineer Penn Co, res 213 Hanna.
Kensill Kittie, milliner, bds 143 Clay.
Kent Charles S, lab Wabash R R, bds 243 Webster.
Kent Harry, driver, bds 121 Calhoun.
Keopf Amelia, domestic 303 W Washington.
Keopf Jacob, boilermkr, bds 309 W Washington.
Kepler John H, lab, bds 26 Gay.
Kepler Louisa (wid John G), res 26 Gay.
Keplinger Frank E D, bkkpr First Nat Bank, bds 21 W
Creighton ave.
Keplinger Henry A, clk Hamilton Nat Bank, res 21 W
Creighton ave.
Keplinger Jacob A, engineer Penn Co, res 118 Force.
Keplinger Maud, milliner, bds 118 Force.
Keplinger Minnie, domestic 77 W Wayne.
Keppler Wm, brewer, bds 546 E Wayne.
Kerbach, see Kirbach.

L. POLK & CO.'S

& M Works, res 256 Hanna.
itrait), res 341 E Wayne.
V L Kerlin, J F Strait), Undertakers
Calhoun.   Tel 362.
l Kirn.
39 E Berry.
nissioner, res 107 W Washington.
imonie Mining and Gas Co, rms 57 Barr.
res 94 Laselle.
is 107 W Washington.
Winkelmeyer Bros, bds 64 E Berry.
mas), res 2 Brandriff.
i, bds 2 Brandriff.
.erp), res 372 Calhoun.
'ress, bds 186 Jackson.
filliams.
ufacturing Co, Alfred D Cressler
ɜr, G Adolph Schust Sec, Gustave L
rs Gas Works Machinery, Gas Holders
of All Descriptions, cor Calhoun and

bds 353 E Wayne.
l Collector, Pension, Bounty and War
E Main, res 186 Jackson.
.ry Public, Conveyancer and General
i, rms same.

ician, 286 Calhoun, res 154 Wallace.
ʈm Miller, bds same.
res 55 Thomas.
Bros & Co, res 521 E Lewis.
ɜ3 E Washington.
Washington.
ɡel & Frey, bds 363 E Washington.
ɜ E Washington.
3 E Washington.

Bass F & M Works, res 359 E Lewis.
ashington House.
Bass F & M Works, res 359 E Lewis.
etmkr, bds 37 Pine.
Penn Co, bds 99 Madison.

Gruber, res 59 W Butler.
ɜss D S Redelsheimer & Co, bds 23

Ketcher John, res 23 Charles.

Ketcher Paul, mach Kerr-Murray Mnfg Co, bds 104 W Washington.

Ketchum Clement V, caller, res 21 Pritchard.

Ketchum Herman V, lab Penn Co, res 212 Broadway.

Ketker Elizabeth (wid Frederick), res 18 Pritchard.

Ketker Frederick W, brass molder Ft Wayne Electric Co, res 51 Huestis ave.

Ketker Fredericka S, tailoress, bds 18 Pritchard.

Ketker Sophia, tailoress, bds 18 Pritchard.

Kettler Conrad F, supt letter carriers P O, res 205 E Jefferson.

Kettler Eliza (wid Conrad), bds 205 E Jefferson.

Kettler Miss Mary, bds 205 E Jefferson.

Kettler Wm J, treas D N Foster Furniture Co, res 46 Erie.

Key, *see also Kay.*

Key Clayton H, spoke driver, res 239 Barr.

Key Morris B, lab South Wayne Brick Co, bds 239 Barr.

Key Sherman (col'd), porter Hotel Rich.

Keys, *see also Kees and Kiess.*

Keys Catherine (wid John), res 84 Fairfield ave.

Keyser, *see also Kaiser, Kayser, Keiser and Kiser.*

Keyser Charles H, bkkpr J M Keyser, bds 95 Glasgow.

Keyser Jacob M, Natural Gas Fitter; A Full Supply of Natural Gas Appliances, 63 E Main, res 95 Glasgow.

Keyser Rose, domestic 103 W Berry.

Keyser Wm A, painter, bds 95 Glasgow.

Keystone Block, s w cor Calhoun and Columbia.

Kibiger Edward, lab, bds 105 Barr.

Kibiger George, teamster H J Ash, bds 105 Barr.

Kibiger Henry, apprentice, bds 105 Barr.

Kibiger John F, hostler Frank J Gruber, bds 105 Barr.

Kibiger Louisa (wid George), boarding house, 105 Barr.

Kibiger Wm, lab, bds 105 Barr.

Kickley, *see also Kikley.*

Kickley Charles M, mach Wabash R R, res 38 Bass.

Kickley Ida, bds 90 Chicago.

Kickley Joseph, brass molder, res 90 Chicago.

Kickory Emil, section hand, res n s New Haven ave 4 e of Lumbard.

Kickory Paul, lab Winch & Son, bds n s Chestnut 2 w of Lumbard.

Kidd John, stonecutter Wm & J J Geake, res 3 Liberty.

Kidd Julia (wid Robert G), bds 205 W Jefferson.

Kidd Kate, dressmkr, bds 205 W Jefferson.

Kiddie Duncan, brakeman, bds 69 Wilt.

Kiddie Henry, lab Bass F & M Works, res 69 Wilt.

ddie Jennie, domestic 246 W Washington.

efer, *see also Keefer, Keever and Keffer.*

efer Adolph, driver Centlivre's brewery, res 69 Elizabeth.

efer Christian, clk P F Kiefer, bds 16 Wilt.

efer Christian F, carp, bds 490 Fairfield ave.

efer Edwin, hostler Jenney Electric Light & Power Co, bds 63 Elizabeth.

efer George A, grocer, s e cor Spy Run and Riverside aves, res same.

efer Henry, car bldr Penn Co, res 273 E Creighton ave.

efer Henry, clk Mossman, Yarnelle & Co, res 59 Elizabeth.

efer Julius, fireman, res 70 Elizabeth.

efer Kate, bds 59 Elizabeth.

efer Oscar P, lab. bds 59 Elizabeth.

iefer Philip F, Groceries and Provisions, 16 Wilt, res same.

efhaber Frederick, coil winder, res 22 Pritchard.

efhaber George, res 168 VanBuren.

el, *see also Keel, Keil and Kyle.*

el Henry F, policeman, res 264 Webster.

el Mary, bds 264 Webster.

el Wm C, helper, res s w cor Hanna and Creighton ave.

el Wm F, mach hd Ft Wayne Electric Co, bds 264 Webster.

eler Charles H, market stall No 73, res Lake twp.

eley, *see also Keeley.*

eley Dennis T, mach Ft Wayne Electric Co, bds 33 Colerick.

enzle Christian, teamster, res 105 Hoffman.

ep John, lab, bds 137 E Washington.

ep Theodore, helper Ft Wayne Iron Works, res 254 E Jefferson.

ep Wm, soapmkr, res 137 E Washington.

rmeier Michael, tailor, res 178 Gay.

rspe Charles, mach Wabash R R, res 39 Locust.

rspe Charles J, mach Wabash R R, res 30 Nirdlinger ave.

rspe Frederick W, wood carver Ft Wayne Organ Co, res 346 Broadway.

rspe George J, bkkpr Root & Co, bds 39 Locust.

sling Ferdinand W, baker, 142 Broadway, res 255 same.

ss, *see also Kees and Keys.*

ss John F, store-keeper Ft Wayne Electric Co, res 73 Wilt.

ss Joseph A, clk Ft Wayne Electric Co, bds 165 Holman.

tzmann Albert, teamster, res Huntingdon rd opp Lindenwood Cemetery.

er Perry A, relief agt Nickel Plate R R, res 114 W Washington.

ey, *see also Kickley.*

,E. Johnson, DENTIST, 74 Calhoun Street.
Res., 188 W. Berry St.

FORT WAYNE DIRECTORY. 295

Isadore P, conductor, res 53 W DeWald.
John C F, lab Penn Co, res 237 Lafayette.
y Robert, mach hand Ft Wayne Organ Co.
Bridget, seamstress, bds 33 Colerick.
Dennis T, lab, bds 33 Colerick.
John, paver, bds Jewel House.
John J, removed to Lafayette, Ind.
Margaret, seamstress, bds 33 Colerick.
Mary (wid Thomas), res 33 Colerick.
re Wm R, fireman Penn Co, res 11 W Butler.
George G, helper Penn Co, bds 365 E Creighton ave.
Wm, blacksmith Penn Co, res 331 E Crighton ave.
Harry E, electrician Penn Co, rms 71 Pixley & Long
uilding.
trick Grace L, bds 138 Cass.
trick Harry E, fireman, res 142 Cass.
trick James, clk Wabash R R, res 339 Harrison.
trick Oscar D, engineer, res 138 Cass.
all Frederick N, trav agt, res 61 Douglas ave.
all Laura A, cashier, res 29 Rockhill.
all Mary E, bds 29 Rockhill.
all Wilbur R, electrician Ft Wayne Electric Co, bds
Vayne Hotel.
Franklin C (Kime & Jackson), res 102 S Wayne ave.
Rachel A (wid Isaac M), bds 20 Bell ave.
Wesley, waiter Mergel & Frey, res 20 Bell ave.
Wm T, barber Ehrman & Geller, res 20 Bell ave.
& Jackson (Franklin C Kime, Allen P Jackson), grocers,
30 Shawnee ave.
el Christian, carbldr Penn Co, res 69 Oliver.
el Jacob C, lab Ft Wayne Organ Co, res 63 Home ave.
el John, farmer, res 266 Beaver ave.
el Mary E (wid David), bds 196 E DeWald.
el Milo, mach hand Ft Wayne Furniture Co, bds 266
eaver ave.
el Milton G, engineer Ft Wayne Organ Co, res 172 In-
iana ave.
el Nancy, dressmkr L A Worch, bds 266 Beaver ave.
ell Edward, carbldr Penn Co, res 67 Oliver.
ell Frank E, brakeman, res 64 Force.
id Frank, lab, bds Jacob Funk.
r Michael, carbldr Penn Co, res 159 Taber.
r Paul, carp, res 39 E 4th.
y Christian, lab C A Hoffman, bds Hoffmann House.
Wm P, lab Electric Light Co, res 172 W Jefferson.

r L, draughtsman The Western Gas Construction 65 Harrison.

l W, mach, res 413 Calhoun.

M, bds 52 Clinton.

, engineer Penn Co, bds 80 Chicago.

d M, brakeman Nickel Plate, res n e cor Howell nsey ave.

M (wid George E), res 125 Montgomery.

s (wid Diamond), bds 203 Berry.

E, rodman Penn Co, rms 65 Harrison.

W, cutter S M Foster, res 17 Cass.

stenogr Seavey Hardware Co, bds Maumee ave Glasgow.

h M (wid Francis), res 301 Calhoun.

J, harnessmkr A L Johns & Co, bds 271 E Wash-

E, molder Bass F and M Works, bds 271 E Wash-

an T, harnessmkr A L Johns & Co, res 262 E

, bds 43 Baker.

D, lab, res s e cor Dubois and Maumee ave.

opr S M Foster, bds 271 E Washington.

J, bds 62 Clinton.

, car inspr, res 271 E Washington.

, trav agt, rms 108 E Wayne.

innie, bds s e cor Dubois and Maumee ave.

hard, clk J P Ross & Sons, bds 25 W Columbia.

seph H, coppersmith Penn Co, bds n e cor St ave and Spring.

tto, blksmith Olds' Wagon Works, bds 53 Hugh.

O, uphlstr F E Houk, bds 96 Montgomery.

exander, mach Penn Co, bds 25 W Williams.

nis S, draughtsman Penn Co, bds 25 W Williams.

ry W, bds 25 W Williams.

bert, mach Wabash R R, res 25 W Williams.

ah (wid James), bds 232 E Jefferson.

W, molder, bds 392 Calhoun.

ha A (wid John M), res 392 Calhoun.

J, lab Penn Co, bds 123 W DeWald.

el, lab Penn Co, res 123 W DeWald.

B, printer, bds 63 Wells.

n W, brakeman, bds 63 Wells.

n L, printer Journal, bds 63 Wells.

A (wid Gideon), res 63 Wells.

Koontz and Kuntz.

Kintz Alexander, bricklayer, res 52 E 3d.
Kintz Alice, opr Samuel M Foster, bds 52 E 3d.
Kintz Ambrose W (Pratt & Kintz), res 149 Archer ave.
Kintz Charles, mason, res Centlivre's Park.
Kintz Henry, engineer C L Centlivre Brewing Co, res n s Edna 3 w of Spy Run ave.
Kintz John, car builder Penn Co, res 11 Lillie.
Kintz John, driver Centlivre's St Railway, res w s Spy Run ave 2 s of canal feeder.
Kintz Phœbe (wid Alexander), bds Thomas Knight.
Kirbach Annie domestic C E Bond.
Kirbach Emil R, mach hd Ft Wayne Electric Co, res 171 Taber.
Kirbach Ernst F, lab, res 159 John.
Kirbach Frank F, lab S F Bowser & Co, bds 159 John.
Kirbach Frederick, mason, 159 Gay.
Kirbach Paul, cigarmkr Louis Bender, bds 159 John.
Kirbach Robert, removed to Chicago, Ill.
Kirbach Wm, carp, bds 159 Gay.
Kirby James, driver, res 283 Hanna.
Kirby Michael, engineer Penn Co, res 333 Harrison.
Kirchefer Herman A (Dornbush & Kirchefer), res 114 Force.
Kirchheimer Joseph, trav agt C Falk & Co, bds 60 W Main.
Kirchner Charles, res 44 Oak.
Kirchner Elizabeth, bds 16 Nirdlinger ave.
Kirchner Elizabeth, domestic 106 Broadway.
Kirchner Ernest, lab, res 161 Eliza.
Kirchner Ferdinand, watchman Ft Wayne Spoke Works, res 40 Winch.
Kirchner Gettoe, painter James Wilding & Son, res 197 Lafayette.
Kirchner Gottlieb W, lab, res 16 Nirdlinger ave.
Kirchner Laura, opr Hoosier Mnfg Co, bds 161 Eliza.
Kirchner Mary, mach hand, bds 161 Eliza.
Kirchner Wm, clk C O Lepper, bds 16 Nirdlinger ave.
Kirk Winfield T, rms s e cor Park pl and Hoagland ave.
Kirkendaff Mrs Jennie, rms 21 Foster blk.
Kirkendall Edwin L, lab, res 76 Barr.
Kirkendall George, lab, bds John Dimon.
Kirkham Mary (wid John), bds 253 W Creighton ave.
Kirkhoff Caroline (wid Frederick), res 157 Broadway.
Kirkley James B, removed to Danville, Ill.
Kirkpatrick Charles, postal clk, res 38 Michigan ave.
Kirkup Richard, wood carver Ft Wayne Organ Co, res s e cor Wayne and Organ.
Kirn, see also Karn and Kern.
Kirn John M, cabinetmkr Ft Wayne Organ Co, res 82 Walnut.

ilia, domestic 91 W Berry.
lso Kaiser, Kayser, Keiser and Keyser.
ie L (wid Daniel), res 96 Ewing.
n A, bds 70 W Wayne.
les S, patternmkr Ft Wayne Electric Co, bd 70 W
e.
W, civil engineer, bds 70 W Wayne.
cca (wid Peter), res 70 W Wayne.
, lab, res 110 E Creighton ave.
John, res 6 Smith.
Leander, removed to Elkhart, Ind.
Wm B, conductor, res 331 W Jefferson.
i A, carpet weaver, res 16 University.
Robert (Scheumann & Klaehn), res 225 W Jeffer-

irles, bartndr George Ortlieb, res 148 Ewing.
; *Klenke.*
ry, clk A L Johns & Co, res 146 Franklin ave.
ie, domestic 144 W Wayne.
garet A, binder G W Winbaugh, bds 146 Franklin.
astian B, engineer, res 297 Hanna.
lso Clay and Kley.
e, opr Hoosier Mnfg Co, bds 378 E Washington.
painter, res 378 E Washington.
J, helper A L Johns & Co, bds 378 E Washington.
'aul A, lab Wm Miller, res n s Winter bet Eliza and
n.
Carrie, seamstress Hoosier Mnfg Co, bds 37 Wall.
Dietrich, tailor, res 37 Wall.
Dora, seamstress Hoosier Mnfg Co, bds 37 Wall.
Edward, lab, bds 37 Wall.
lso Cline and Kline.
ony, painter, bds 147 E DeWald.
ia, clk L Wolfe & Co, bds 258 Clinton.
id, painter Anthony Wayne Mnfg Co, bds 147 E
d.
rick A, teacher, res 412 Hanna.
h, res w s Walton ave 2 s of Pontiac.
h, hostler H H Schroeder, bds H J Schroeder.
, shoemkr J F Noll, bds 273 W Jefferson.
dwin S, fireman Penn Co, rms 25 E Washington.
ydia (wid Christian C), rms 25 E Washington.
Ada C, clk M Frank & Co, bds 153 Harrison.
Ienrietta (wid Adolph), res 153 Harrison.
Henry, res 55 Madison.
Frank, carp Penn Co, bds 19 Wall.

Kleinrichert John B, carp Penn Co, res 288 E Jefferson.
Kleinrichert Josephine (wid John), res 19 Wall.
Kleinschmidt Wm, hostler Peters Box & Lumber Co, res 8
Clark.
Kleinsorge Herman, res 164 High.
Kleinsorge Louise, seamstress D S Redelsheimer & Co, bds 164
High.
Kleinsorge Minnie, tailoress C Kruse, bds 164 High.
Kleinsorge Wm, clk, C J Pierre, bds 164 High.
Klenke Conrad, lab C Tresselt & Sons, res 58 W Lewis.
Klenke Frederick, carbldr Penn Co, res 241 Barr.
Klenke Henry, carbldr Penn Co, res 411 E Lewis.
Klepper Charles, carbldr Penn Co, res 92 Oliver.
Klepper Charles, mach hand S F Bowser & Co, bds 92 Oliver.
Klepper Henry A, carp, bds 92 Oliver.
Klepper Wm, lab Bass F & M Works, bds 93 John.
Klerner George, saloon, 156 E Washington, res 109 Wells.
Klett Edward, res 328 Broadway.
Klett Jacob (Jacob Klett & Sons), res 328 Broadway.
Klett Jacob & Sons (Jacob, John A and Wm B), Retail
Dealers in Lumber, and Mnfrs Moulding, Casing, Siding,
Ceiling, Flooring; Scroll Sawing; also Mnfrs Embossed
Casing; Yards cor Ewing and Pearl; Mill cor Superior and
Plum.
Klett John A (Jacob Klett & Sons), bds 328 Broadway.
Klett Wm B (Jacob Klett & Sons), bds 328 Broadway.
Kleve John H, clk A L Johns & Co, res 146 Franklin ave.
Kley, *see also Clay and Klee.*
Kley Carrie, clk L Wolf & Co, bds 336 W Main.
Kley Frederick, res 336 W Main.
Kley Frederick jr, cooper, res 97 Cass.
Kley Lizzie, clk L Wolf & Co, bds 336 W Main.
Kline, *see also Cline and Klein.*
Kline Annie, domestic Louis A Fox.
Kline Bernard, market stalls 28 and 30, res Wayne twp.
Kline Catherine (wid Christian), res 240 Smith.
Kline Charles W, lab L C Zollinger, bds 14 Riverside ave.
Kline Charles W, saloon, 242 Calhoun, res same.
Kline Edward, foreman Salimonie Mining and Gas Co, res 30
Bass.
Kline Frederick, res 11 Pritchard.
Kline George, lab, bds 240 Smith.
Kline Harry E, helper Ft Wayne Electric Co, bds 11 Pritchard.
Kline Henry, clk Jacob Kline, bds 30 E Columbia.
Kline Jacob, grocer, 30 E Columbia, res 118 E Berry.
Kline John, brakeman, bds 194 E Lewis.

Laura W, dressmkr, bds 194 E Lewis.
Louisa (wid Charles), res 133 E Lewis.
Milton F, car bldr Penn Co, res 210 Metz.
Oren, hostler Liggett Bros, rms 5 N Harrison.
Peter, res 32 5th.
Wm, bds 118 E Berry.
Wm C, lab, res 14 Riverside ave.
George, tailor, res 153 Madison.
Peter, lab Bass F & M Works, res 213 John.
el Carrie, domestic 57 W Berry.
el Eva B (wid John M), res 76 Laselle.
el John M, coremkr Ft Wayne Iron Works, bds 76 Lasel
enberger Chester, carp, res 113 Force.
enberger George, res 392 E Wayne.
enberger George, car bldr, bds 285 Hanna.
enberger John, car bldr Penn Co, res 285 Hanna.
enberger John H, car bldr Penn Co, bds 285 Hanna.
enberger Joseph M, teamster, res n s Cochrane 3 e
Coombs.
enberger Xavier, painter, bds 285 Hanna.
er Allen W, lab Kilian Baker, res 174 Hoffman.
er James E, 2d hd goods, 67 E Columbia, res same.
er John, lab, res 329 E Lewis.
er John, lab, bds 4 Rebecca.
er Joseph, lab Ft Wayne Electric Co, res 16 Guthrie.
er Wm, stone cutter, bds 67 E Columbia.
mann Albert M, molder Bass F & M Works, bds 3
afayette.
mann Edward J, lab, bds 373 Lafayette.
mann George W, driver Engine Co No 2, res 110 Wallac
mann John G, drover, res 373 Lafayette.
mann Kate M, clk C H Waltemath & Sons, bds 3
afayette.
mann Wm, molder Bass F & M Works, bds 373 Lafayett
Frederick, carp, res 241 Barr.
Henry, car bldr Penn Co, res 411 E Lewis.
l Michael, conductor, res 36 Lillie.
l Wm, clk, bds 19 E Jefferson.
nberg Otto (Klinkenberg & Detzer), res 62 Clinton.
kenberg & Detzer (Otto Klinkenberg, August
tzer), Druggists and Photo Supplies, 80 Calhoun.
Wm, clk E Vordermark & Sons, bds 19 E Jefferso
rt George, baker, 393 Lafayette, res same.
er Henry, helper Wabash R R, res 19 Wilt.
er Henry C, boilermkr Ft Wayne Iron Works, bds
ilt.

ɔpper Wm, lab, res 93 John.

ger, *see Kluger.*

mp Wm, mach hand Fort Wayne Organ Co, res cor St Joseph rd and Romey ave.

tz Daniel (Klotz & Kerp), dry goods, 372 Calhoun, res 546 same.

tz Daniel, painter Olds' Wagon Works, bds Herman Klotz.

tz Elizabeth, opr Hoosier Mnfg Co, bds Herman Klotz.

tz Frank G, clk Daniel Klotz, bds 546 Calhoun.

tz Herman, lab Penn Co, res w s Calhoun 1 s of Cour.

tz Joseph, painter Olds' Wagon Works, bds Herman Klotz.

tz Mary, opr Hoosier Mnfg Co, bds Herman Klotz.

tz & Kerp (Daniel Klotz, Wm J Kerp), binder mnfrs, 372 Calhoun.

g Charles, carp, res rear 112 Erie.

g Elizabeth C, bds 190 Hanna.

g George M, car builder Penn Co, res 112 Erie.

ɪg Gregor, Shoemaker, 194 Hanna, res 190 same.

g G Nicholas, trav agt, bds 190 Hanna.

g Henry A, bds 190 Hanna.

g Joseph G, lab, bds 293 E Wayne.

g Josephine, domestic 23 W Wayne.

g Martin, carp, res 293 E Wayne.

g Wm M, molder, bds 293 E Wayne.

ger Joseph, lab, res n s Cottage ave 1 w of Indiana ave.

ppel George J, carp, bds 77 Smith.

ppel John G, stone mason, res 77 Smith.

ppel Sophia, dressmkr Krull Sisters, bds 77 Smith.

ɪmann Frederick, lab Wm Miller, res 229 John.

ke Wm, lab Penn Co, bds 310 Harrison.

pp Charles, cabtmkr, bds 39 Elm.

pp Frederick C, lab, res 39 Elm.

pp Wm, lab Lindenwood Cemetery, bds 108 Howell.

se Charles, painter, res 49 Taylor.

spel Emil, teamster Bass F & M Works, bds 23 Julia.

ɔht Catherine, bds 260 E Jefferson.

ɔht Frank J, florist, 301 E Wayne, bds 27 Erie.

lcler Frederick, market gardener, 815 Broadway, res same.

ese, *see also Ness, Neise and Nies.*

ese August H, cabtmkr Fort Wayne Organ Co, res w s Fairfield ave.

ɪnoeller Sophie, domestic 32 W Washington.

pper Elmer, student, res 28 W Superior.

ɔper Emma, seamstress D S Redelsheimer & Co, bds 28 W Superior.

ɔper Joseph D, barber, res 110 W Superior.

21

Knepper Margaret, market stall 73, res Illinois road, Aboite township.

Knepper Wm J, truckman, res w s St Mary's ave 3 s of Hoffman.

Kneubuhler Gottfried, gardener John Orff, bds same.

Knight Charles S, trav agt, res n s Spy Run ave 5 n of Prospect ave.

Knight Cheney, bds C S Knight.

Knight Miss Eliza M, teacher, bds 15 E De Wald.

Knight Elizabeth, bds 173 W Superior.

Knight John H, fireman Penn Co, rms 37 Baker.

Knight Oras A, clk A F Bowman, bds 230 W Main.

Knight Sarah J (wid Noel), res 31 Randolph.

Knight Sarah J, res 199 W Washington.

Knight Thomas, car builder, res 35 N Calhoun.

Knight Willard, coilwinder, bds C S Knight.

Knight Wm H, foreman Penn Co, res 15 E De Wald.

Knisely Wm H, teamster, res e s Spy Run ave 5 n of Wagner.

Knispel Emil, driver Bass F & M Works, bds 23 Julia.

Knitchie Emil, lab Bass F & M Works, bds 43 Smith.

Knobel Gottlieb, shoemkr, 110 Wells, res 30 same.

Knoche August D, painter Olds' Wagon Works, res 96 Oliver.

Knoche Frederick A, carp Frederick Kraft, bds 112 Thomas.

Knoche Johanna M, dressmkr, bds 112 Thomas.

Knoche John P, lab Bass F & M Works, bds 112 Thomas.

Knoche Peter, lab Bass F & M Works, res 112 Thomas.

Knock Charles, helper Fort Wayne Furniture Co, bds 39 Elm.

Knock Frederick, lab, res 39 Elm.

Knock Wm F. policeman, res 168 Taylor.

Knode Ernest H, fireman, res 59 Brackenridge.

Knoder George W, painter Penn Co. res 29 Hugh.

Knoedler Frederick, lab, rms 86 Barr.

Knoedler Henry, lab, bds 26 W Main.

Knoll Annie L, binder G W Winbaugh, bds 15 Miner.

Knoll Emma, binder G W Winbaugh, bds 15 Miner.

Knoll Peter, painter Penn Co, res 129 E Jefferson.

Knoll Wm H, mach Wabash R R, res 15 Miner.

Knothe Charles, apprentice Robert Ogden, bds 72 Dawson.

Knothe Charles F, asst master mechanic Ft Wayne Electric Co, res 72 Dawson.

Knothe Julius, bds Paul E Wolf.

Knott Isaac, attendant Indiana School for Feeble-Minded Youth.

Knott Jenny R, nurse Ft Wayne City Hospital.

Knox Thomas E, watchman Star Iron Tower Co, res 43 Elizabeth.

RS, SHELVING, Office and Store Fixtures Made on Short
— Notice by —
ETHER & BRO., 44 to 54 East Superior St. Factory at 100 Pearl St.

·y, driver Ft Wayne Gas Light Co, res 55 Putnam.
min, teamster, bds Jewel House.
h, painter, w s Comparet 1 s of Maumee ave, res 66
ave.
so Cook.
ony, lab Olds' Wagon Works, res 57 W Lewis.
sta H, tailoress Frederick Kayser, rms 57 W Lewis.
lict, lab Kerr-Murray Mnfg Co, res 265 Hanna.
min, mach hand Ft Wayne Electric Co, bds 122 E
igton.
rine (wid Adam), res 34 John.
es, cabinetmkr, res 25 W Washington.
es, carp, res 146 E Creighton ave.
ian, wagonmkr, res 72 Brackenridge.
ian A, driver, bds 72 Brackenridge.
eth (wid Christian), res 45 W Jefferson.
eth (wid John W), res 119 Lafayette.
:, carp, bds n e cor Erie and Canal.
·, cigarmkr Hollester & Son, res 9 Duryea.
y A, lab Olds' Wagon Works, bds 72 Bracken-

clerk, bds 25 W Washington.
sheet iron worker Kerr-Murray Mnfg Co, res 97

B, grocer, 122 E Washington, res 124 same.
D C, cigarmkr F C Boltz & Co, bds 72 Bracken-

, mach, res 261 Webster.
iret (wid John), died April 17, 1891.
ret (Estate of), Mrs Carrie L Pfleager mngr, notions,

i (wid Anthony), bds 58 W Lewis.
i, dressmkr, bds 57 W Lewis.
: (wid John), res 83 E Wayne.
ore C, cigarmkr G F Yergens, bds 72 Brackenridge.
ab Penn Co, res 148 Taylor.
: F, saloon, 117 E Lewis, bds 58 W Lewis.
·ge, removed to Wabash, Ind.
i, carp, res 130 Greely.
iael, carp, res 132 Greely.
F, lab, bds 132 Greely.
so Cox.
: C, painter Penn Co, res 28 St Joseph Boulevard.
: J, mach hand Peters Box and Lumber Co, res 27

r B, shoemkr Louis Fortriede, res 28 W 3d.

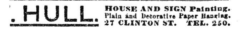

Kocks John B, sawyer Hoffman Bros, res 174 E Lewis.
Koeble Charles J, slater J H Welch, res 224 E Jefferson.
Koeble Eva (wid J George), bds 224 E Jefferson.
Koegel Emma, confr, bds 54 Pritchard.
Koegel Mary (wid Christian), res 54 Pritchard.
Koehl, *see also Cole and Kuhl.*
Koehl Adam, coremkr Penn Co, res 111 E Creighton ave.
Koehl Adam jr, coremkr Penn Co, res 111 E Creighton av(
Koehl Anna (wid Adam), bds 111 E Creighton ave.
Koehl Jacob, stonecutter Wm & J J Geake, res 125 E DeW
Koehl John, helper Penn Co, bds 111 E Creighton ave.
Koehl Michael, stonecutter Keller & Braun, res 493 Lafay(
Koehl Wendlin, molder Bass F & M Works, res 336 Force
Koehlein August, car repairer Penn Co, s e cor Calhoun
    Washington.
Koehler, *see also Kahler, Kaler, Kaylor, Kehler, Keller*
    Kohler.
Koehler Alfred, lab P Koehler, bds same.
Koehler Frederick, lab J A Koehler, bds same.
Koehler Henry, baker L P Scherer, res 150 Eliza.
Koehler John A, brick mnfr, e s S Calhoun 1 s of Cour,
    w s Lafayette 10 s of Pontiac.
Koehler John M, lab, bds J A Koehler.
Koehler Lewis, lab J A Koehler, bds same.
Koehler Paul, brick mnfr, s e cor Rudisill and Hoagland a\
    res n w cor Webster and Rudisill ave.
Koehlinger Anna L, res 64 E Berry.
Koehlinger Gustave A, clk Root & Co, res 65 Wall.
Koehlinger Peter, lab, bds 46 E Columbia.
Koehn, *see also Cohen, Kohen, Kohn and Kuhn*
Koehn Edward W, mach Indiana Machine Wks, bds 348 W M
Koehn Regina, domestic 55 Maple ave.
Koehn Wm, lab Olds' Wagon Works, res 11 Wiebke.
Koehn Wm F, shoemkr C Schiefer & Son, res 217 E Jeffers
Koehnlein Emma B, seamstress S M Foster, bds 14 Wilt.
Koehnlein Henry J, barber Ehrman & Geller, res 14 Wilt.
Koehnlein Julia, clk, bds 14 Wilt.
Koehnlein Mary F, seamstress S M Foster, bds 14 Wilt.
Koehnlein Wm, blksmith Fleming Mnfg Co, res 14 Cass.
Koeneman Anna, domestic 82 W Washington.
Koenemann John, scavenger, res 32 Colerick.
Koenemann Wm F, helper Wabash R R, bds 11 McLaugh
Koenig Anna, domestic 55 E Jefferson.
Koenig Charles, carp, res 98 Summit.
Koenig Charles F C, clk C F Koenig, res 335 E Washing'

ealer in Groceries, Provisions,
Feed, 89 Harmer, res 187 Madi-

32 E Washington.
2 W Main, res same.
R R, res 48 Oak.
W 4th.
ay.
enig), res 95 Griffith.
ington.
Wayne Iron Works, res 332 E

ashington House.
Charles Miller.
ller.
H C Graffe, res 203 High.
116 Erie.

eiburger & Bro, bds Hoffmann

n Penn Co, res 168 Harmer.
tgomery Hamilton.
M Works, res 525 Hanna.
and Kuhn.
E Jefferson.
E Jefferson.
Plate R R, bds n s Richardson 4 e

r.
Kohlbacher, res 268 E Wayne.
Dealer in Groceries, Provisions,
ayne, res same.
443 Lafayette.
cor New Haven and Edsall aves.
er, Kaylor, Kehler, Keller and

n Co, res 461 Calhoun.
61 Calhoun.
V Jefferson.
ess, bds 461 Calhoun.
Co, bds 461 Calhoun.
), res 92 Montgomery.
, bds 92 Montgomery.
or Richardson and Rumsey ave.
Marion.
rad), res 9 Marion.

Kohlmann Mary (wid Jacob W), res 147 E Jefferson.
Kohlmann Valentine, mach hand Hoffman Bros, bds 9 Marion.
Kohlmeier Christian, market stall No 91, res Washington twp.
Kohlmeyer, *see also Kammeier.*
Kohlmeyer Christian, cigarmkr Kasten & Kohlmeyer, bds 275 Webster.
Kohlmeyer Christian H, carp Alfred Shrimpton, bds n s Prospect ave 2 e of Spy Run ave.
Kohlmeyer Edward (Kasten & Kohlmeyer), res 275 Webster.
Kohlmeyer Edward C, brass molder Ft Wayne Electric Co, res 4 Zollars ave.
Kohlmeyer George E, cigarmkr Kasten & Kohlmeyer, bds 275 Webster.
Kohlmeyer Henry, helper Wabash R R, res 21 Jones.
Kohlmeyer Henry C E, clk F D Hoham, rms 298 Calhoun.
Kohlmeyer John H, cigarmkr Kasten & Kohlmeyer, bds 275 Webster.
Kohn, *see also Cohen, Kohen and Kuhn.*
Kohn Charles, meats, 42 Maumee ave, res same.
Kohn Miss Rose E, teacher Clay School, bds 42 Maumee ave.
Kohrmann Andrew, tailor, res 312 E Wayne.
Kohrmann Henry M, lab Hoffman Bros, bds 215 W Superior.
Kohrmann Henry W, porter G E Bursley & Co, res 301 Fairfield avenue.
Kohrmann John J, clk, bds 215 W Superior.
Kohrmann Mary (wid John B), res 215 W Superior.
Kohte Ernst, molder Bass F & M Works, res 192 Montgomery.
Koll Adam J, car bldr Penn Co, res 83 Montgomery.
Kolb Caroline, cash Kayser & Baade, bds 16 Bell ave.
Koldeway Carrie, domestic 153 E Berry.
Kolkmann Dora (wid Henry), res 229 John.
Kolkmann Frederick, lab Wm Miller, res Adams twp.
Kollmann Mathias, lab Salimonie Mining & Gas Co, bds 595 Lafayette.
Kollock Fred N, Agt Union Line, 79 Calhoun, res 215 W Berry.
Kollock John K, student, bds 215 W Berry.
Kolthoff Frederick, res 23 Wall.
Kolthoff Louise, bds 23 Wall.
Kolthoff Mary, bds 23 Wall.
Kolthoff Wm, wood turner, bds 23 Wall.
Komp, *see also Kamp and Kemp.*
Komp Daniel, Real Estate, 27 and 28 Bank Blk, res s e cor Hoagland ave and Pontiac.
Komp Wm, saloon, cor St Joseph Boulevard and Romey ave, res same.

BUILDERS' HARDWARE, **PFEIFFER & SCHLATTER,** 38 and 40 East Columbia St.

FORT WAYNE DIRECTORY. 307

Komp Wilson F, armature winder Ft Wayne Electric Co, bds D Komp.
Koons Andrew, engineer Penn Co, res 212 Francis.
Koons Edgar, teamster, bds Henry Koons.
Koons Ella, bds 212 Francis.
Koons Emma, cash J B White, bds Henry Koons.
Koons Henry, teamster, res n s Prospect ave 1 e of Spy Run.
Koons Ida, dressmkr, bds Henry Koons.
Koons John, res 90 Maumee rd.
Koontz, *see also Kintz and Kuntz.*
Koontz Wm F, brakeman, res 204 Thomas.
Koop Frederick, molder Bass F & M Works, res 53 Buchanan.
Koop Henry C, teamster, res 91 Smith.
Koopman Henry F, boilermkr Wabash R R, res 23 Jones.
Koorsen Adelina, seamstress, bds 80 Smith.
Koorsen George H, wood turner Penn Co, res 76 Gay.
Koorsen Henry, lab, bds 80 Smith.
Koorsen John B, foreman, res 82 Smith.
Koorsen John M, lab, res 80 Smith.
Kopp John H, mach Bass F & M Works, res s e cor Lillie and Creighton ave.
Kopp Joseph, clk, bds 177 Jackson.
Kopp Louis, mach Bass F & M Works, bds s e cor Lillie and Creighton ave.
Kopp Michael, lab Bass F & M Works, res s e cor Lillie and Creighton ave.
Kopp Wm, mach hand Bass F & M Works, bds s e cor Lillie and Creighton ave.
Koppe Jacob, brewer The Herman Berghoff Brewing Co, bds 546 E Wayne.
Koppenhofer Frederick, butcher, 205 Lafayette, res 203 same.
Korff Augusta, opr S M Foster, bds s s Baker 3 e of Fairfield.
Korn Amelia D, housekpr, 281 W Jefferson.
Korn August, grocer, 194 Broadway, res 60 Nirdlinger ave.
Korn Frederick, butcher, res 92 Summit.
Korn John, grocer, 136 Fairfield ave, res same.
Korte Frederick, carp, res 65 Maumee ave.
Korte Frederick, teamster Rhinesmith & Simonson, res 194 Gay.
Korte John, lab American Wheel Co, res w s Hanna s of city limits.
Korte Louisa, seamstress, bds 65 Maumee ave.
Korte Wm, carp, bds 65 Maumee ave.
Korte Wm, molder Bass F and M Works, res 21 Charles.
Kortrey Kunigunda (wid John), bds 104 E Wayne.
Kortum Henry, helper, res 39 Hough.

ıv (Weil Bros & Co), res cor Schick and Erie.

one mason, res 41 Maumee ave.

l W, fresco painter, bds O J Kover.

h J, fresco artist, res s w cor Howell and Rumsey.

oraham, bds 290 E Washington.

ax, real estate, rms 290 E Washington.

ock.

ıcob, boilermkr, bds 377 E Washington.

molder Bass F & M Works, bds 317 Lafayette.

F, lab Wabash R R, res 271 W Washington.

ɔk, boilermkr Penn Co, res 333 E Lewis.

ɔk jr, molder Bass F & M Works, bds 333 E

ɔk W, carp, n s Montgomery 4 e of Lafayette,

ıfayette.

lab, res 14 Cedar.

molder Bass F and M Works, bds 333 E Lewis.

ıs 271 W Washington.

L, tailoress Frederick Kayser, bds 271 W Wash-

Craw.

ı F, bricklayer, res 159 Griffith.

ı H, clk, bds 159 Griffith.

, mason, res 82 Wilt.

V, collector Indiana Staats Zeitung, rms 37 E

bundle wrapper Root & Co, bds 159 Griffith.

o Cramer.

ı lab, res 59 Greene.

ı J, painter, 163 John, res same.

opr Hoosier Mnfg Co, bds 465 Lafayette.

r A, painter, res 145 John.

ıt R, mngr notion dept L Wolf & Co, res 336 E

on.

ɹd, bkkpr Herman Berghoff Brewing Co, res 49

ɹd E, clk A C Trentman, bds 49 Madison.

bds 167 W DeWald.

ıe, domestic 322 Fairfield ave.

an, street sprinkler, res 108 W Jefferson.

an C, clk Root & Co, res 380 E Wayne.

l, painter Penn Co. res 3 Summit.

ɹ M, molder Bass F and M Works, res 155 E

ıve.

ɹth, dressmkr, bds 92 Hanna.

L.O. HULL, Artists' Materials, Studies, Etc. AT 90 CALHOUN STREET.

FORT WAYNE DIRECTORY. 309

Kramer Ernest, Sign Painter; all kinds of Gilding, Decorating, Frescoing and Fancy Painting done to order at Lowest Prices, 90 E Main, res 216 Shawnee ave.

Kramer Fred, painter Penn Co, res 126 John.

Kramer Frederick E, lab, res 115 Wall.

Kramer George (Kress & Kramer), res 173 Wells.

Kramer Gottlieb, lab, res 19 Centre.

Kramer Henry C. bkkpr A C Trentman, bds 49 Madison.

Kramer Jacob, removed to Chicago, Ill.

Kramer John, overall cutter, res s w cor Spy Run ave and Ruth.

Kramer John G, clk J B White, res 136 Jackson.

Kramer Joseph C, pressman The Journal Co, bds 49 Madison.

Kramer Louis A, clk G H Loesch, bds 49 Madison.

Kramer Louisa, housekeeper John Kramer.

Kramer Martin, foreman Penn Co, res 167 W DeWald.

Kramer Mathias, foreman, res 465 Lafayette.

Kramer Minnie, dressmkr, bds 92 Hanna.

Kramer Minnie, opr Samuel M Foster, bds 350 E Wayne.

Kramer Peter, bds John Kramer.

Kramer Rosa, clk G F Yergens, bds 465 Lafayette.

Kramer Rosina (wid Frederick), bds 59 Indiana ave.

Kramer Wm C, car bldr Penn Co, res 21 Summit.

Kramer Wm C, lab. res 92 Hanna.

Kramer Wm F, molder Bass F & M Works, res 350 E Wayne.

Krane, see Crane.

Kranichfeld Theodore F, sawyer Hoffman Bros, res 221 W Superior.

Krantz, see also Crantz.

Krantz Casper, bds 14 Force.

Krans Valentine, lab Bass F and M Works, res 14 Force.

Kranz, see also Crance.

Kranz Peter, painter, res 94 Summit.

Kranzman Wm H, bellowsmkr Ft Wayne Organ Co, res 21 Taylor.

Krapf Daniel, clk Morgan & Beach, res 238 E Jefferson.

Kratner Serepta (wid Edward), res 28 Cass.

Kratzmann Simon, shoemkr Mathias App, res 267 Hanna.

Kratzsch Charles R, clk A I & H Friend, res 93 Baker.

Kratzsch Eleanor (wid Herman), milliner, 114 Calhoun, res 15 W Wayne.

Kratzsch Emil, clk Eleanor Kratzsch, bds 15 W Wayne.

Kratzsch Frederick C, clk Root & Co, bds 168 Greely.

Kratzsch Herman, agt, res 15 W Wayne.

Krauhs, see also Crouse, Kraus and Krouse.

Krauhs Carl C, shoemkr, res 169 Jackson.

Krauhs Charles, lab, res 61 Shawnee ave.

Krauhs Henry J, shoemkr Gustav Spiegel, bds 169 Jackson.

Krauhs John C, barber J H Kabisch, bds 169 Jackson.
Krauhs Wm C, mach hand, bds 169 Jackson.
Kraus, *see also* Crouse, Krauhs *and* Krouse.
Kraus Mrs Bertha, bds 2 Madison.
Kraus Edward, teamster, bds 139 Madison.
Kraus Emily (wid Ferdinand), res n end Coombs.
Kraus George M, lab, res 139 Madison.
Kraus Jacob, lab, res 33 Charles.
Kraus Joseph, tinsmith S F Bowser & Co, bds 230 Thomas.
Kraus Wm, teamster, bds 139 Madison.
Krause Henry, lab, res 42 Oak.
Krauskopf Carl G W, art student, bds 88 W Washington.
Krauskopf Carrie, waiter The Randall.
Krauskopf Henry, lab, res 42 Oak.
Krauskopf Mary A (wid Henry), bds 114 W Main.
Kraut Henry, lab, bds 57 John.
Krauter Gottlieb, coremkr Bass F & M Works, res 224 Gay.
Krauter John, blksmith, bds 138 Force.
Krebes Edward, wagonmkr, res 46 W Butler.
Krebs Frederick G, cigarmkr C A Berndt, bds 176 Gay.
Kreckmann Jacob L, boilermkr Ft Wayne Iron Works, bds
    377 E Washington.
Kreckmann Mollie, domestic A H Hamilton.
Kreckmeyer Henry, upholsterer P E Wolf, res Washington twp.
Kreibaum Frederick, wall paper, 90 Barr, res 17 Sturgis.
Kress Amos, lab Olds' Wagon Works, bds 213 W DeWald.
Kress Catherine M, bds 10 Zollars ave.
Kress Eliza B, bds 24 Poplar.
Kress Elizabeth (wid Isaac), res 213 W DeWald.
Kress Eustachius, lab, bds 213 W DeWald.
Kress George J, boxmkr Olds' Wagon Works, res 10 Zollars.
Kress Jacob M, brakeman, bds 24 Poplar.
Kress Jacob W, lab Olds' Wagon Works, bds 10 Zollars ave.
Kress John, woodwkr, res 112 W Butler.
Kress John N, propr Racine Hotel, n e cor Cass and 1st.
Kress Michael, res 29 Pine.
Kress Philip, bds 29 Pine.
Kress Theodore (Kress & Kramer), res 5 N Harrison.
Kress Walter B, fireman, res rear 134 Fairfield ave.
Kress & Kramer (Theodore Kress, George Kramer), tinsmiths,
    96 Wells.
Kresse Charles A, carp. res 4 Fox.
Kressler Lizzie, domestic 316 E Jefferson.
Kretsinger Christian, res 35 Putnam.
Kretsinger Constantine, lab Penn Co, bds 1 Piqua ave.
Kretsinger Henry R, real estate, 13 E Main, res 1 Piqua ave.

:. Johnson, DENTIST, 74 Calhoun Street.
Res., 188 W. Berry St.

FORT WAYNE DIRECTORY. 311

er John R, foreman Penn Co, res 267 E Jefferson.
Charles, cigarmkr, res 170 Madison.
omer, painter, rms 29 E Main.
Jay, foreman J H Welch, bds 22 E Columbia.
Jesse, paper hanger, bds e s Calhoun.
lbert, wagonmkr, bds 46 E Columbia.
arney, driver J Wilding & Son, bds 13 St Mary's ave.
eorge, clk C W Spencer, res 56 Madison.
eorge, polisher G W Wilson, res 13 St Mary's ave.
ichael, saloon, 223 Calhoun, res 232 Lafayette.
'm J, plumber Robert Spice, bds 13 St Mary's ave.
rg Frederick, lab Penn Co, bds 65 Lillie.
l Carrie, bds 55 Douglas ave.
l Charles A T (Root & Company), bds 55 Douglas ave.
l Christian, carp Penn Co, res 55 Douglas ave.
l Julius, piano tuner, bds 55 Douglas ave.
nna, domestic 151 E Main.
nselm, contractor, res 325 E Lewis.
Benedict, lab Kilian Baker, res 130 Maumee rd.
Benjamin, molder Bass F & M Works, bds 416 E
yne.
Feorge, carp, bds 416 E Wayne.
Feorge, lab Bass F & M Works, res 364 E Wayne.
essie A, dressmkr, bds 416 E Wayne.
ohn, carp, res 416 E Wayne.
Mary, opr Hoosier Mnfg Co, bds 364 E Wayne.
Vm, carp, bds 416 E Wayne.
berger George, helper, bds 182 Metz.
berger Jacob, lab, res 182 Metz.
berger Jacob jr, teamster, bds 182 Metz.
berger John, mach hand, bds 182 Metz.
· Mrs Margaret, bds 53 Wagner.
· Wilhelmina (wid Charles), bds 3 Summit.
r Fredericka, bds 86 Oakley.
· Wm F, switchman Wabash R R, res 86 Oakley.
Frederick, boilermkr, res 136 John.
Henry, lab, bds 136 John.
August, car bldr Penn Co, res 200 Smith.
Bros (Charles and Wm), saloon, 582 E Washington.
Charles (Krohn Bros), res 62 Grant ave.
Frederick, plumber A Hattersley & Sons, bds 49 W 4th.
Louisa (wid Henry), res 49 W 4th.
Wm (Krohn Bros), bds 49 W 4th.
Herman, guns, 13 E Berry, res 96 E Jefferson.
berger Rosanna, cook Custer House.
John, driver Ft Wayne Spoke Works, bds 20 Winch.

loses, carp, res n s Edgarton 3 w of Lillie.

r Charles, mach hand Ft Wayne Electric Co, bds Ianna.

r Charles W, harnessmkr A L Johns & Co, bds 50 iperior.

r Edward, helper A Hattersley & Sons, bds 43 Tay-

r Elizabeth, milliner Mrs A Schulte, bds 566 Hanna.

r George, carp J M Henry, res 38 Putnam.

r George A, brakeman, bds 43 Taylor.

r George N, lab Penn Co, res 43 Taylor.

r Henry,molder Kerr-Murray Mnfg Co,bds 566 Hanna

r John, carp J M Henry.

r Louisa, opr Hoosier Mnfg Co, bds 43 Taylor.

r Peter, cook George Ortlieb, rms 88 Calhoun.

oyal C, fireman, res e s St Mary's ave 21 above feeder.

ank J, truckman L S & M S Ry, res 96 W 3d.

ee also Crouse, Krauhs and Kraus.

rederick, mach, res 49 Shawnee ave.

enry C, lab Penn Co, bds 161 Montgomery.

Vm, lab, res 139 Griffith.

rg Christian, market stall 75, res St Joseph twp.

eyer Henry, uphlr, res 6 Franklin ave.

nna F, stenogr J M Robinson, bds 29 W Jefferson.

Charles F, coal, n e cor Francis and Hayden, res n s 1 w of McCulloch.

eorge H, clk C F Krudop, bds 29 W Jefferson.

ottlieb, carp, bds 29 W Jefferson.

ohn E, wiper Penn Co, bds 2 Madison.

August C, bkkpr Siemon & Bro, res 183 Calhoun.

Charles J, lab Penn Co, res 170 Suttenfield.

ugust, trav agt, res 53 Cass.

also Crull.

nard J, harnessmkr A L Johns & Co, bds 266 E ington.

ry F, clerk, bds 266 E Washington.

A (Krull Sisters), bds 266 E Washington.

raret A (Krull Sisters), bds 266 E Washington.

olph, car inspr Penn Co, res 266 E Washington.

udolph L, Jeweler, 128 E Washington, bds 266

rs (Lena A and Margaret A), milliners, 268 E ngton.

ust, clk Wm Busching, bds 122 Wallace.

ust, driver Bass F & M Works, bds 364 E Lewis.

les, lab, bds 161 Montgomery.

e **Charles,** Merchant Tailor, 13 Harrison, res same.
Ferdinand, mach Bass F & M Works, bds 169 Gay.
Frederick, truss hoopmkr S D Betler, bds 415 E Wayne.
Gustav, clk Wm Busching, bds 122 Wallace.
Henry, carp, res 415 E Wayne.
Henry, clk C Kruse, bds 13 Harrison.
Henry C, mach, res 161 Montgomery.
Lena, domestic 142 Montgomery.
Louis F, oil pdlr, res 134 Francis.
Minnie, domestic 226 W Creighton ave.
Wm, bds 43 W Lewis.
Wm, helper Kerr-Murray Mnfg Co, bds 107 Gay.
Wm C, clk O B Fitch, bds 415 E Wayne.
Wm F, brass molder, bds 161 Montgomery.
Wm F, contractor, res 67 E Jefferson.
Henry W, fireman Penn Co, bds 226 Francis.
Wm, helper, bds 107 Gay.
nann Mary, bds 216 E Washington.
Elizabeth (wid John W), res 119 Lafayette.
r Rev John J, res 39 Savilla pl.
r Herman N, clk Penn Co, bds 39 Savilla pl.
r Paul C, driver Adams Exp Co, bds 39 Savilla pl.
r Theodore, mach Penn Co, bds 39 Savilla pl.
r Theophilus, stenogr S Bash & Co, bds 39 Savilla pl.
ck Charles A, coremkr Bass F and M Works, res 150
)hn.
Wm, lab, res s s Wiebke 2 e of Lafayette.
ert August, market stall No 21, res Washington twp.
el Francis J, mach, res 136 Wallace.
ss Julius, mach Wabash R R, res 18 Colerick.
see also Cole and Koehl.
Edward, clk A I & H Friend, bds 9 Line.
Martin, lab, res n s Line 2 e of Lumbard.
ach Elizabeth (wid Wm), res 119 Lafayette.
ach Henry, painter, bds John Kuhlbach.
ach John, cellarman, res n s Richardson 4 e of Runnion.
ach Wm, fireman, bds John Kuhlbach.
ach Wm, teamster The Herman Berghoff Brewing Co,
s 231 Harmer.
see also Cohen, Kohen and Kohn.
Wm H, car bldr, res 57 Barr.
ne **Charles W,** Lawyer, 19 Court, rms 144 E Berry.
Frederick W (Kuhne & Co), res 124 W Jefferson.
H Richard (Kuhne & Co), rms 144 E Berry.
Paul F (Kuhne & Co), rms 124 W Jefferson.

Kuhne & Co (Frederick W Kuhne), The Abstract Office; Insurance, Loan, Real Estate and Steamship Agts; Agts Remington Type Writers, 19 Court.

Kuhns John M, sec and treas The Old Fort Mnfg Co, res **364** Fairfield ave.

Kukkuck Dorothea (wid Louis), res 181 Jackson.

Kukuk Joseph, shoemkr, res 162 Madison.

Kull, *see also Cull.*

Kull Christina (wid Gottlieb), bds 105 Hoffman.

Kull Dora (wid George S), res cor Lake and St Mary's ave.

Kull John, hostler, res 147 W 3d.

Kull Mamie, bds Dora Kull.

Kumberger Christian, lab, bds 27 Force.

Kumfer Owen, res 96 Smith.

Kummer Albert R, mach Penn Co, res 114 E Creighton ave.

Kummer Catherine, bds 114 E Creighton ave.

Kummer Eliza, domestic Fritz Hotel.

Kummer Frederick, painter Olds' Wagon Works, bds 114 E Creighton ave.

Kunkle Ella A, bds 138 E Wayne.

Kunkle Erastus B (E B Kunkle & Co), res 138 E Wayne.

Kunkle E B & Co (Erastus B Kunkle, Wm D Bostick), Proprs Fort Wayne Safety Valve Works, 87 **Barr.**

Kunse August, lab, bds 364 E Lewis.

Kuntz, *see also Kintz and Koontz.*

Kuntz Adam, butcher, res 362 W Main.

Kuntz Charles, res 90 Maumee ave.

Kuntz Elizabeth (wid Peter), res 550 Calhoun.

Kuntz Eva (wid Adam), res 48 Force.

Kuntz Frank B, harness, 14 Pearl, res 208 W Superior.

Kuntz George, upholsterer Penn Co, res 156 E Jefferson.

Kuntz George H, harnessmkr, 11 Harrison, res same.

Kuntz Mary (wid Jacob), bds 32 Brandriff.

Kuntz Philip, inspr Jenney Electric Light and Power Co, bds s w cor Calhoun and Allen.

Kuntz Philip H (Kuntz & Bro), res 550 Calhoun.

Kuntz Samuel (Kuntz & Bro), bds 550 Calhoun.

Kuntz & Bro (Philip H and Samuel), saloon, 548 Calhoun.

Kurtom Henry, lab, res 39 Hough.

Kuse Henry W, fireman, res 278 E Lewis.

Kutsch August, brakeman, res 42 Brandriff.

Kutswiller Louis, bds Riverside Hotel.

Kuttner Joseph G, car repr Penn Co, res 237 E Jefferson.

Kuttner Peter G, shirt mnfr, 144 Calhoun, bds 237 E Jefferson.

Kutz Wm F, foreman James Madden, bds 90 E Wayne.

Kyburz Wm J, ass't sec (city dept) Y M C A, rms Y M C A bldg.

!so *Keel, Keil and Kiel.*
ham P, flagman Penn Co, res 72 Chicago.
C, brakeman, res 118 Fairfield ave.
W, brakeman, res 72 Chicago.
B, bds 72 Chicago.
D (Kyle & Plumadore), res 58 W Wayne.
madore (Wm D Kyle, H A Plumadore), music
, 82 Calhoun.

L

[, lab Penn Co, bds 88 W Williams.
Leeser.
ph, lab Penn Co, res 198 Madison.
's Emma, dressmkr, bds 39 W Washington.
erald (Weekly) Trades and Labor Council Proprs
blrs, 35-36 Schmitz Block.
melia, domestic 22 Chicago.
enious, carp John Suelzer, res 414 Hanna.
lvin, carbldr Penn Co, res 28 Gay.
Madison, carp John Suelzer, res 193 Taber.
arles L (col'd), cook The Wayne, res 169 Harrison.
, brakeman, bds 17 Burgess.
G, died May 12, 1891.
phia P (wid Max G), 'Guns, Fishing Tackle and
g Goods, 58 E Main, res 98 Harrison.
r, *see also Landenberger.*
r Henry, lab Olds' Wagon Works, bds 81 Shawnee

er Peter, lab Olds' Wagon Works, res 81 Shawnee
.
)avid, kiln bldr, res 312 W Main.
eorge, helper Indiana Machine Works, bds 312 W

POLK & CO.'S

ι72 Hanna.
res 45 St Martin.
ır.
niel), res 67 Union.
F Reinkensmeier, bds 67 Union.
ıs 41 Taylor.
ı, res 64 W Williams.
ls w s Lillie 2 s of Milan.
64 W Williams.
res w s Lillie 2 s of Milan.
Bass F & M Works, bds w s Lillie

Vholesale Stationery, Notions, Etc,
wis.
ın Co, res 61 W Lewis.
Jimonie Mining and Gas Co, bds

ss F & M Works, bds w s Lillie 2

ier Mnfg Co, bds w s Lillie 2 s of

Williams.
3ass F & M Works, bds w s Lillie

ır.
commercial dept McDermut's Ft
e, bds 261 W Wayne.
es 19 Fletcher ave.
ı Co, res 96 W DeWald.
N DeWald.
ehlfeith), res 10 W Main.
ı Laible, Charles A Muehlfeith),

ır.
ı.
 E Creighton ave.
ı6 E Creighton ave.
ı Creighton ave.
'g Co, ıds 156 E Creighton ave.
ınn Co, res 459 Lafayette.
ı, bds 459 Lafayette.
river e of Columbia Street bridge.
ıssus propr, 6 Cass.
ıthern Ry, office, passenger and
l Wells.
Savilla pl.

Lallow Charles F, carp, bds 61 Pontiac.
Lallow Louis J, carp, res 61 Pontiac.
Lamar Adam, messenger Postoffice, bds 144 Wallace.
Lamar John, engineer Penn Co, res 144 Wallace.
La Master George W, clk Dreier Bros, res 33 W Washington.
Lamb David, mach, res 158 Fairfield ave.
Lamb George A, fireman Penn Co, res 215 W Jefferson.
Lamb Jacob, clk C L Hill, rms 209 Brackenridge.
Lambert Jennie (wid Walter), bds 380 E Washington.
Lambert Norris W, regulator Ft Wayne Organ Co, rms 48 Mc-
 Clellan.
Lamborn Wm B, agt, rms 168 E Jefferson.
Lamley Mary, domestic Centlivre Homestead.
Lamley Moses (Falk & Lamley), res 128 W Wayne.
Lamont Annie, opr Hoosier Mnfg Co, bds 169 N Harrison.
Lamont Frank E, clk A I & H Friend, bds 61 E Columbia.
Lamont Laura, domestic Hanna Homestead.
Lamont Mollie, domestic Mergel & Frey, bds 70 Gay.
La Mott Matilda, waiter The Randall.
Lampke Conrad J, porter Coombs & Co, res 128 Madison.
Lancaster Charles J, molder Bass F & M Works, res 67 W
 Butler.
Lancaster Lewis H, clk D N Foster Furniture Co, bds 213 W
 Main.
Lancaster Nelson W, asst yardmaster N Y, C & St L R R, res
 213 W Main.
Landenberger Frederick G, clk Horton Mnfg Co, bds 175 W
 Superior.
Landenberger John M, treas and mngr Indiana Machine Wks,
 res 185 W Berry.
Landergraff Mary, opr Hoosier Mnfg Co, bds 187 Gay.
Landford George, baker D J Shaw, bds 24 Oliver.
Lane Chester T, prin Central Grammar School, res 55 Maple ave.
Lane Frederick K, constructor Western Gas Construction Co,
 bds Aveline House.
Lane John P, mach Wabash R R, bds 112 W Creighton ave.
Lane John W, piano tuner, res 57 Garden.
Lane Perry, lab, bds 112 W Creighton ave.
Lane Wm, lab, res 57 Grand.
Lang, see also Long.
Lang Albert, clk J J Brink, bds 4 Marion.
Lang Amelius J (Geo De Wald & Co), res 304 W Wash-
 ington.
Lang Aurora L, stenogr A Hattersley & Sons, bds 25 W But-
 ler.
Lang Christian, engineer Keller & Braun, res 6 Hensch.

22

ig Ernst D, bds 124 Harrison.

ig John, clk M F Kaag, res 4 Marion.

ng Rev John F, Chancellor and Secretary Roman Catholic Diocese of Fort·Wayne, res 172 Clinton.

ig Leonard, engineer, res 75 W Butler.

g Maggie, clk Beadell & Co, bds 165 Ewing.

ig Rosa, bds 4 Marion.

ig Rose, bds 75 W Butler.

g Wm, sawyer Keller & Braun, bds 6 Hensch.

ig Wm P, hostler, bds 165 Ewing.

ngard John, Grocer, Meat Market and Dealer in Choice Wines, Liquors, Cigars and Tobaccos, 68–70 E Columbia, res w s Spy Run ave 4 n of St Mary's bridge.

igard Joseph, res 70 E Columbia.

gdon Mrs F L, trav agt, rms 15 W Washington.

ge August, pedler J H Lange & Sons, bds 327 Calhoun.

ge Christian (J H Lange & Sons), bds 327 Calhoun.

ge Herman, teamster, bds 120 Montgomery.

ge John (J H Lange & Sons), bds 327 Calhoun.

ge John H (J H Lange & Sons), res 327 Calhoun.

ge J H & Sons (John H, Christian and John), grocers, 327 Calhoun.

ge Louis, baker J H Lange & Sons, bds 327 Calhoun.

ge Wm, clk Root & Co, res 30 Pritchard.

gel Frank, brakeman L S & M S Ry, res n e cor Harrison and 5th.

genbacher Mathias, res 22 Wall.

genfeld John, clk J B White, res 67 Charles.

ger Charles, cabinetmkr, res 133 W 3d.

ghals John, tailor J H Grimme & Sons, res 8 Oak.

gheinrich Rachel F (wid Ernst), bds 13 St Martin.

ghenry Wm, fireman Penn Co, rms 235 Barr.

ghorst August W, saloon, 267 E Wayne, res same.

gle John T, music agent, res 38 E 5th.

igohr Andrew J, Ice Cream Mnfr, 144 Broadway, res same.

gohr Amelia (wid John), res 129 Wells.

gohr Anna B, tailoress, bds Christian Griebel.

gohr Charles W, pedler A J Langohr, bds 144 Broadway.

gohr Henry W, pedler A J Langohr, bds 144 Broadway.

gohr John W, driver, res w s Spy Run ave 2 n of canal feeder.

gohr Louis, lab, res 37 Elizabeth.

gohr Louis E, lab, res 59 Elizabeth.

son Miriam (wid Richard), res 72 Madison.

staff Ida, dressmkr, 19 Laselle, res same.

Langstaff Walter H, car inspr Penn Co, res 19 Laselle.
Langtry Walter, veterinary surgeon, 7 N Harrison, bds 88 same.
Lanigan James F, engineer Penn Co, bds 67 Melita.
Lanigan Patrick, flagman Penn Co, res 67 Melita.
Lanigan Thomas J, trav agt, rms 44 W Washington.
Lankenau Catherine (wid Francis), res 80 W Jefferson.
Lankenau Christian, clk M Frank & Co, bds 80 W Jefferson.
Lankenau Frederick W, bkkpr Ft Wayne Electric Co, res 83 Wilt.
Lankenau Louise, domestic 119 Wilt.
Lankenau Wm J, clk Root & Co, res 40 Wilt.
Lankenau Wm J jr, bds 83 Wilt.
Lannan Annie (wid Wm), res 103 W Washington.
Lannan Augustus J, lab, bds 103 W Washington.
Lannan Edward, lab, bds 103 W Washington.
Lannen James, saloon, 268 Calhoun, rms 226 same.
Lannert Elizabeth, domestic 27 Force.
Lansdown Job A, car bldr Penn Co, res w s Rumsey ave nr Richardson.
Lansing Harry, engineer, res 218 E Washington.
Lantcraf Elizabeth (wid John), res 187 Gay.
Lantcraf John, painter, bds 187 Gay.
Lantcraf Mary, opr, bds 187 Gay.
Lanterman Frank E, printer Labor Herald, rms 68 E Main.
Lanternier August, gardener, market stall No 36, res s e cor Walton ave and Wayne Trace.
Lanternier Joseph, gardener, bds August Lanternier.
Lanternier Louis, gardener, bds August Lanternier.
Lanx Wm, mach hand Wayne Knitting Mills, bds 38 Watkins.
Lapoint George C, brakeman, res s s Jesse nr Runnion ave.
Lapp Albert, mason, res 22 W 4th.
Lapp Charles J, molder, bds 52 W Williams.
Lapp Henry, policeman, res 52 W Williams.
Lapp Henry G, finisher A Hattersley & Sons, bds 52 W Williams.
Lapp Henry J, carp J M Henry, res 34 Stophlet.
Large Miss Josephine (Anderson & Large), res 36 W Wayne.
Larimore George W, decorator L O Hull, bds 296 W Jefferson.
Larimore James T, fireman Penn Co, res 77 E Williams.
Larimore Levi, res 111 Howell.
Larkin Anna, waiter Hotel Rich.
Larrabee Thomas J, lab Penn Co, res 74 E Lewis.
Larson Magnus, street car driver, bds 84 Baker.
Larue Charles M, train despatcher Penn Co, res 139 Fairfield av.
Larwill John L, res 93 E Berry.
Larwill Othniel H, lawyer, 19 Bank blk, bds 9 E Wayne.
Lasher Edgar H, cigarmkr, res 57 Wells.

her Ria, dressmkr, 57 Wells, res same.

sus John B, propr Lake Shore Hotel, 6 Cass.

ham Harry S (Riegel & Latham), bds 66 Wilt.

ham Zachariah, conductor N Y, C & St L R R, res 200 W
  Superior.

hrop Elias L, trav agt, res 125 E Main.

ta Charles S, watchman, res 28 Winch.

, *see also Lau and Lowe.*

  Julian, shoemkr P J Eggmann, bds 122 Calhoun.

  Miss Maggie M, milliner, 31 E Main, bds 122 Calhoun.

  Thomas, carp, res 122 Calhoun.

  Thomas J, bkkpr U S Baking Co, bds 122 Calhoun.

bach A J, physician, 127 E Washington, res same.

bschar John, lab Anthony Wayne Mnfg Co, res 25 Laselle.

derberg Charles, mach, res 60 Barthold.

er, *see also Laier and Layer.*

er Annie R, seamstress, bds 289 E Washington.

er August, baker H H Barcus, bds 113 Hanna.

er Barbara (wid Paul), res 70 E Jefferson.

er Conrad, lab, res 116 Maumee rd.

er Christina, opr Hoosier Mnfg Co, bds 150 Barr.

er Edward, lab Penn Co, bds Diamond Hotel.

er Edward M, helper John & Peter Lauer, bds 206 Gay.

er Elizabeth, milliner, bds 159 Taber.

er Ferdinand, butcher Wilkins Bros, res 126 Chicago.

er Ferdinand, lab, bds 166 Smith.

er Frank, lab, bds 116 Maumee rd.

er Frank X, car inspr, bds 159 Taber.

er Frederick, molder Bass F & M Works, bds 166 Smith.

er Frederick, molder Bass F & M Works, res 370 E Lewis.

er George, clk J A M Storm, bds 84 Maumee rd.

er George R, student, bds 151 Hanna.

er Gregory, carp, res 84 Maumee rd.

er Gustav, contractor, 159 Taber, res same.

er Henry, carbldr Penn Co, res 129 Lafayette.

er Henry, cigarmkr Louis Bender, bds 289 E Washington.

er Henry, helper John & Peter Lauer, res 206 Gay.

er Henry, lab, bds 108 Wells.

er Henry, lab, res 118 Maumee rd.

er Henry P, barber, 562 E Washington, bds 109 Barr.

er John, saloon, 150 Barr, bds 70 E Jefferson.

ter John & Peter (John H and Peter L Lauer),
Iron Founders, n end of Barr. (*See page 67.*)

er John G, res 113 Hanna.

er John H (John & Peter Lauer), bds 204 Gay.

er Joseph, carp, res 130 Erie.

auer Joseph, lab, res 119 Lafayette.
auer Justin, carp, res 151 Hanna.
auer Kate, domestic 56 Smith.
auer Miss Lizzie, dressmkr, 70 E Jefferson, res same.
auer Martha, opr Hoosier Mnfg Co, bds 159 Taber.
auer Mary C, seamstress, bds 289 E Washington.
auer Mathias W, patternmkr Ind Mach Works, res 520 E Wayne.
auer Michael, carp, res 196 Gay.
auer Michael L, carp, res 77 Erie.
auer Nicholas, mason, res 202 Gay.
auer Nicholas J, carp, bds 151 Hanna.
auer Paul, lab, res 167 Gay.
auer Paul H, molder John & Peter Lauer, bds 206 Gay.
auer Peter, finisher Ft Wayne Organ Co, bds 126 Chicago.
auer Peter, lab Bass F & M Works, res 289 E Washington.
auer Peter L (John & Peter Lauer), res 83 Summit.
auer Sarah (wid John A), res 62 E Main.
auer Wm C, lab Bass F & M Works, bds 166 Smith.
auer Wm P, lab Bass F & M Works, res 166 Smith.
auferty Alexander S, mngr M E Lauferty, bds 75 W Berry.
auferty Betty (wid Isaac), res 75 W Berry.
auferty M E, Alexander S Lauferty Mngr, Clothing, 73-75 Calhoun.
aughlin Alonzo, sawyer Ft Wayne Organ Co, bds 50 Oakley.
aughlin Catherine M, stenogr Mossman, Yarnelle & Co, bds 49 E Lewis.
aughlin James, driver C F Myers, bds Monroe House.
aughlin John, molder Penn Co, bds 224 Calhoun.
aughlin Lawrence C, foreman Kerr-Murray Mnfg Co, res 49 E Lewis.
aughlin May, dressmkr, rms 83 Baker.
aughlin Michael, engineer, res 332 Lafayette.
aughlin Wm, switchman, rms 30 Baker.
aumann, *see also Lohmann and Lohrmann.*
aumann Herman J, carp, res 127 W 3d.
aumann Minnie, dressmkr, 127 W 3d, bds same.
aumann Rudolph H, carp, bds 127 W 3d.
aurent Frank, bartndr Lake Shore Hotel.
aurents Alexander, butcher, res 241 E Washington.
aurentz, *see Lorenz.*
avack Charles, lab, bds 8 Hough.
avack Frank, lab, bds 8 Hough.
Vanway Charles J, feed, 45 E Columbia, res same.
Vanway Frank, painter, res w s Hanna 1 n of Lewis.
Vanway Luke, res n s Cochran 1 e of Coombs.

Penn Mutual LIFE INSURANCE CO. of PHILA.
CLARK FAIRBANK, General Agent, 19 Court Street.

322   R. L. POLK & CO.'S

LaVanway Sherman, driver U S Ex Co, res 66 E Columbia.
LaVanway Silas, clk F E Purcell & Co, bds 66 E Columbia.
Law, *see also Lau and Lowe.*
Law Charles D, supt Penn Co, res 151 E Berry.
Law David, bds 302 W Washington.
Law Herbert J, trav agt, bds 302 W Washington.
Lawrence, *see also Lorenz.*
Lawrence John, fireman, res 56 Williams.
Lawson Wm, foreman G E Bursley & Co, res 45 Home ave.
Lawton Daniel H (The Remington-Lawton Co), res Chicago, Ill.
Lawyer, *see also Lauer and Loyer.*
Lawyer Hester, laundress Troy Steam Laundry, bds 192 Buchanan.
Lawyer Mark, lab, res 192 Buchanan.
Laydon Michael, winder Ft Wayne Electric Co, bds Harmon House.
Layer John, painter Olds' Wagon Works, bds 156 E Creighton avenue.
Layman, *see also Lehman.*
Layman Charles, cigar mnfr, 290 Hoagland ave, bds same.
Layman George, conductor, res 114 Runnion ave.
Layman Jacob, lab, res 290 Hoagland ave.
Lazzarini Amadeo, saloon, 37 Barr, res same.
Leach Edward, helper Penn Co, res 64 Eckart.
Leach James, bds 83 Laselle.
Leach John T, boilermkr Penn Co, res 83 Laselle.
Leach Mabel, domestic 198 E DeWald.
Leach Rebecca (wid John), res 166 W DeWald.
Leach Richard, engineer Nickel Plate R R, rms 366 W Main.
Leach Walter, barber, bds Edward Leach.
Leach Wm, lab Penn Co, bds 83 Laselle.
Leader Wm J, bartndr J H Douglas, res 24 McClellan.
League Park (Base Ball), e s Calhoun n of E Superior.
Leahr Ada, waiter Rich Hotel.
Leakey Thomas, lab C Scotton, bds same.
Leammle Mrs Adeline, res 25 Poplar.
Leaner Annie, opr Hoosier Mnfg Co, bds 289 E Washington.
Leaner Lizzie, opr Hoosier Mnfg Co, bds 129 Lafayette.
Leaner Martha, opr Hoosier Mnfg Co, bds 159 Taylor.
Leapple Christian, carp, res 51 Grand.
Learmonth Robert, chief clk Penn Co, rms 15 Douglas ave.
Leary Daniel, clk, rms 32 E Berry.
Leary James T, clk Penn Co, res 32 E Berry.
Lease John B, engineer Penn Co, bds 35 Douglas ave.
Lebrecht Frederick, lab Penn Co, res 346 Force.
Lechler Henry M, bkkpr Singer Mnfg Co, res 335 W Jefferson.

er James A, clk Keller Medicine Co, bds 335 W Jefferson.

an Edward, ice cream mkr W F Geller, bds 441 Broadway.

.llison (col'd), lab, res 1 Glasgow.

harles W, carbldr Penn Co, bds 381 Hanna.

:dward L, teamster, res 241 St Mary's ave.

effery J, carbldr Penn Co, res 22 Madison.

ohn F, fireman, bds 34 W Washington.

ohn O (Lee & Fulton), res 34 W Washington.

,ouis H, lab Joseph Fremion, res cor Lafayette and Piqua venue.

[argaret, bds 154 Holman.

[orris J, mach Penn Co, res 381 Hanna.

amuel, carp, bds 172 Hoffman.

amuel S, carp, res 172 Hoffman.

)phia C (wid Israel), boarding house, 120 Harrison.

& Fulton (John O Lee, Charles W Fulton), Livery, 18 V Wayne.

r, *see also Lepper.*

r Rev James L, pastor Second Presbyterian Church, res 5 Pixley & Long Bldg.

r Joseph, engineer Penn Co, res 85 E Washington.

: Alvin H, clk Meyer Bros & Co, bds 14 Wall.

r Amelia, bds 14 Wall.

r Emma, housekpr 6 Summit.

r Mary (wid Charles H), res 14 Wall.

· Pauline A H, milliner A Mergentheim, bds 14 Wall.

r Edward, finisher App Bros, res 368 E Washington.

, John, clk A Neumeier, bds 368 E Washington.

er Calvin W, bridgebldr, res 29 Grace ave.

er Philip, carp, res 31 Walton ave.

s John, molder Bass F & M Works, res 23 Oak.

t Ida, domestic 291 Harrison.

1w August, meats, s s Spy Run ave 2 n of Wagner, res 1me.

1w Emil F, clk Ely & Dittoe, bds e s Spy Run ave 2 n of Vagner.

,w Mrs Julia, housekpr 172 Clinton.

1w Margaret (wid Louis), res e s Spy Run ave 2 n of Vagner.

1n, *see also Lahman.*

1u Ada (wid Samuel), res 67 Harrison.

1n Benjamin, clothing, 18 Calhoun, rms 13 Harmony blk.

1u Charles, molder Bass F & M Works, res 166 E reighton ave.

1n Charles L, winder Ft Wayne Electric Co, bds 290 [oagland ave.

L. POLK & CO.'s

2 Calhoun, res 608 same.
E Washington.
Jeo DeWald & Co, bds 67 Harrison.
20 E Lewis.
36.E Creighton ave.
;20 E Lewis.
man, rms 13 Harmony block.
ts and Shoes, 17 Calhoun, res 138 W

res 290 Hoagland ave.
res 222 E Washington.
ass F & M Works, res 185 Hayden.
608 Calhoun.
E Washington.
Jacob), res 54 W Williams.
kr Olds' Wagon Works, bds 290 Hoag-

148 E Washington.
cian, bds 15 W Jefferson.
152 E Berry.
c 319 Lafayette.
Bass F & M Works, res 102 Gay.
, bds 546 E Wayne.
J L Centlivre Brewing Co, res Cent-

cor Mechanic and Huron.
perhanger Miller & Haller, res 35

th, res 49 W Williams.
er Penn Co, res 324 Hanna.
mkr John Zern, bds 324 Hanna.
and Leonard.
ary), res 344 Broadway.
, bds 344 Broadway.
ds 344 Broadway.

nn Co, res 152 E Lewis.
& Co, bds 66 Cass.
ds 66 Cass.
n Co, bds 225 Lafayette.
res 66 Cass.
7ashington.
E Wayne.
81 Madison.
er Mnfg Co, res 95 Shawnee ave.
' Wagon Works, bds 28 Chicago.

JLL, Paints, Oils, Varnishes and Glass at 90 Calhoun Street.

T WAYNE DIRECTORY. 325

Bass F & M Works, res 204 Francis.
r, res 391 E Wayne.
Joseph), boarding house, 231 Barr.
iessmkr A L Johns & Co, bds 91 E Main.
smkr, bds 91 E Main.
)1 E Main.
vey Hardware Co, bds 91 E Main.
es 12 Chicago.
:auf.
John), res 86 E Wayne.
and Frank), meats, 94 Barr.
uf Bros), res 162 E Lewis.
ls 86 E Wayne.
er Leikauf Bros, res 110 Erie.
auf Bros), res 42 Hanna.
b, res 12 Orchard.
cabtmkr Peters Box and Lumber Co, res

ls 19 Marion.
pet layer Root & Co, bds 19 Marion.
9 Marion.
all No 55.
per Bass F & M Works, res 27 Force.
appr Gustav Scheffler, bds 15 Sturgis.
, res 119 Lafayette.
er N Y, C & St L R R, bds 15 Cass.
Hamilton Homestead.
, bds 11 Jones.
rper & Baade, res cor Nirdlinger ave and

enn Co, res 11 Jones.
ter, res 161 Barr.
tler L Brames & Co, res 65 Grant ave.
es 17 Custer ave.
ewer, res s s Edna 1 n of Spy Run ave.
brewer, res 17 Wabash ave.
mmle.
l John), res 295 W Main.
ician, 25 W Jefferson, res same.
chman, bds 24 Oliver.
lk Penn Co, bds 315 Hanna.
nductor, res 315 Hanna.
J B White, bds 18 Oak.

err-Murray Mnfg Co, bds 366 E Wash-

'oreman Penn Co, res 366 E Washington.
s 366 E Washington.
tenogr S C Lumbard, res 364 E Washington.
(Belger & Lennon), bds 19 W DeWald.
.b, res 194 E Lewis.
, res 41 Hough.
tz.
h hand Horton Mnfg Co, bds 20 Mary.
iolder Bass F & M Works, bds 78 Oliver.
ach Penn Co, res 212 Lafayette.
rewer, bds 70 Grant ave.
ieats, 170 Hanna, res 172 same.
Bass F & M Works, res 78 Oliver.
ber Penn Co, res 21 Gay.
wer, res 70 Grant ave.
ldr Penn Co, res 20 Mary.
Lenhart and Lennart.
V & E Leonard), bds e s Spy Run ave n of

k, res 41 Stophlet.
riet E, prin Jefferson School, bds 142 W

stenogr Penn Co, bds 61 Brackenridge.
bkkpr Indiana School for Feeble-Minded

lk Beadell & Co, bds 71 W Superior.
ienogr H C Hartman, bds 183 Montgomery.
ie, teacher, bds Nelson Leonard.
, propr Ft Wayne Gazette, 41 E Berry, res

ick mnfr, e s Leo Gravel rd 1 s of toll gate,

Geo. E. Johnson, DENTIST, 74 Calhoun Street.
Res., 188 W. Berry St.

FORT WAYNE DIRECTORY. 327

Lepper Frederick G, clk C H Waltemath & Sons, bds 95 Summit.
Lepper Frederick H W, clk M L Frankenstein, bds 324 E Washington.
Lepper Henry C, blksmith Olds' Wagon Works, res 44 Harmer.
Lepper Henry W, clk Geo DeWald & Co, bds 242 E Jefferson.
Lepper Jennie, domestic 260 W Berry.
Lepper J E, trav agt Griebel, Wyckoff & Becker, res Kendallville, Ind.
Lepper Lizzie, cook 22 E Columbia.
Lepper Louis H, driver J B White, res 65 Lillie.
Lepper Louisa (wid Henry), res 242 E Jefferson.
Lepper Maggie, waiter 22 E Columbia.
Lepper Peter, mach Penn Co, res 186 Francis.
Lepper Susan, domestic 338 Calhoun.
Lepper Wm, helper Penn Co, bds 37 Hough.
Lepper Wm D, carriagetrimmer, bds 112 E Main.
Lepper Wm H, carp, res 490 Fairfield ave.
Lepper Gottlieb, oiler Penn Co, res 17 Duryea.
Lerch Archibald, mach Kerr-Murray Mnfg Co, bds 401 Clinton.
Lerch Barbara (wid Leonard), bds 103 Force.
Lerch Casper, switchman, res 121 Force.
Lerch Frank, watchman, res 79 Force.
Lerch Henry, sheet iron worker Penn Co, res 350 Force.
Lerch Joseph, shoemkr, 127 Fairfield ave, res 401 Clinton.
Lerch Mary, clk Charles Rosenberger, bds 79 Force.
Lerch Wm M, mach Bass F & M Co, res 361 E Wayne.
Lesh Emmett, driver W F Gellers, bds 112 Broadway.
Leu John, trav agt, bds Weber House.
Leurs Charles, res s s Pontiac 1 e of Smith.
Leuthner Barbara, laundress, res 278 E Jefferson.
Leuthner Wm, meats, 544 Calhoun, res same.
Levenberger John H, car repairer Penn Co, res 43 Force.
Levi August, pedler, res 78 W Main.
Levi Belle, clk M Frank & Co, bds 78 W Main.
Levi Carl, clk Mautner & Friedlich, bds 78 W Main.
Levi Leon, stonecutter, bds 78 W Main.
Levy Aaron, clothing, 78 Barr, rms same.
Levy Abraham, huckster, res 278 E Washington.
Levy Hannah, milliner, bds 278 E Washington.
Lew Peter, bds 429 Lafayette.
Lewis Bayless, dyer, res 16 Madison.
Lewis Catherine, bds 142 Montgomery.
Lewis Cora G, bds Washington s w cor Glasgow.
Lewis David, hostler, rms 45 E Main.
Lewis Douglas, molder Kerr-Murray Mnfg Co, bds 36 Hough.

ppr Robert Ogden, bds 16 Madison.
V, mngr S B Thing & Co, res 20 Savilla pl.
dressmkr, 16 Madison, bds same.
ngineer Indiana Mach Works, res 405 W Main.
, printer Archer, Housh & Co, res s e cor Grif-
earl.
k W, clk S B Thing & Co, bds 110 W Main.
l, fireman, res 24 E Williams.
, druggist, 434 Calhoun, res 425 same.
1, washing machines, 142 W Main, res same.
lper Kerr-Murray Mnfg Co, bds 251 Calhoun.
, gasfitter Robert Ogden, bds 16 Madison.
), molder, bds 25 Hough.
(wid Levi), bds 600 Calhoun.
y, res 38 Clinton.
(wid Sylvester), res Washington s w cor Glas-

(wid David), boarding house, 25 Hough.
teamster, bds s e cor Glasgow and Washington.
dressmkr, 142 W Main, res same.
city circulator The Press, res 142 W Main.
es 228 Calhoun.
eth, clk Nicholas Leykauf, bds 23 Union.
N, plumber A Hattersley & Sons, res 25 Union.
N, brakeman, res 150 Taylor.
clk, bds 23 Union.
las, grocer, 209 Broadway, res 23 Union.
mach hand, bds 198 E Lewis.
w cor Calhoun and Lewis.
Albert L, barber Lichtenwalter & Butler, res 260

eorge, mach hd Diether & Barrows, res 43 Wilt.
)rrin J, brakeman, 185 Jackson.
olomon F, farmer, res 260 E Lewis.
Valter A (Lichtenwalter & Butler), res 39 Wilt.
V Maurice, clk Notestine & Getz, res 22 Boone.
& Butler (Walter A Lichtenwalter, James P
bers, 272 Calhoun.
ib St Joseph's Hospital.
1e, mach hand, bds Peter P Lichtle.
) Bass F & M Works, bds Peter P Lichtle.
lab Bass F & M Works, res n s Ruth 3 w of
e.
, lab, res n s Cochran 4 e of Coombs.
r W, clk George DeWald & Co, res 382 E
l.

Johanna (wid Wm), res 15 Summit.
iron, bds 551 E Washington.
ith Albert, molder Bass F & M Works, res 89 Laselle.
ith Charles, saloon, cor Calhoun and Railroad, res
'.
harles, bricklayer, res 1 Tam.
mil, lab Penn Co, bds 1 Tam.
erman, brakeman Penn Co, res 10 Simon.
.ichard, caller Penn Co, bds 1 Tam.
an Ernst F, Carpenter and Contractor, 106 W
yne, res same.
n Reinhold, shoemkr, res 109 Barr.
n Wm G, stripper H W Ortmann, bds 111 Barr.
John, porter Meyer Bros & Co, res 110 High.
Bros (James and Robert A), livery, 5 N Harrison.
James (Liggett Bros), U S gauger, res 89 W Superior.
James M, street car driver, res 67 Baker.
Phraortes C, clk M J Blitz, bds 89 W Superior.
Robert A (Liggett Bros), res 73 Wells.
it Frank S, bkkpr Bass F & M Works, res 176 W
shingtou.
it Melinda (wid George), res 158 W Berry.
ieorge, fireman, bds 2 De Groff.
tin, saloon, 150 Calhoun, res 149 E DeWald.
er, lab, res 147 E DeWald.
lerritt B, flagman, res 27 Smith.
i Herman, blksmith Wabash R R, res 79 Wall.
ily, see also Lehmculy.
ily Charles G, clk Penn Co, bds 453 Lafayette.
ily Frederick R, policeman, res 453 Lafayette.
ily Frederick W, clk L F Limecooly, res 568 Calhoun.
ily George C, clk, bds 453 Lafayette.
ily Louis F, grocer, 546 Calhoun, bds 453 Lafayette.
n Frank, harnessmkr A L Johns & Co, bds 85 Cass.
Caroline B (wid Edmund), res 22 W Butler.
Charles, lab Penn Co, res 117 Holman.
Etta, opr Samuel M Foster, bds n e cor Lillie and
an.
George W, pedler, res n e cor Lillie and Milan.
Miss Mary B, teacher Hoagland School, bds 22 W
ler.
f Oscar F, assembler Ft Wayne Electric Co, bds 25 W
shington.
an Frederick H, clk F W Boecker, bds 106 Wilt.
an George, helper Keil & Keil, bds 106 Wilt.
an Gottlieb, lab Penn Co, bds 106 Wilt.

Henry, bkkpr G E Bursley & Co, bds 106 Wilt.
John H, car builder Penn Co, res 106 Wilt.
Wm, mach Wabash R R, bds 106 Wilt.
Bernhard, lab, res 41 Fair.
Clara, dressmkr, bds 81 Wilt.
Daniel M, teacher, res 81 Wilt.
Elizabeth, removed to Decatur, Ind.
Ernst W, res 8 Rockhill.
Rev Frederick, pastor St Paul's German Lutheran
, res 178 Barr.
Frederick, wiper Penn Co, res 166 Broadway.
Gustave, carp, bds 404 E Washington.
John, helper Bass F & M Works, bds 21 Charles.
Julius, dyer, bds 8 Rockhill.
Matilda, music teacher, 81 Wilt, bds same.
Oscar, engineer Bass F and M Works, res 363 E

Robert, tinner J J Freiburger, bds 166 Broadway.
Theodore, molder Indiana Mach Wks, bds 81 Wilt.
Wm, carp, res 404 E Washington.
Wm, coachman 76 W Berry.
Christian, mach Ft Wayne Iron Works, res 24

Christian W, clk James Wilding & Son, bds 24

Frederick, lab Ft Wayne Electric Co, bds 55
t.
Frederick W, bricklayer, res 55 Stophlet.
Wm F, bkkpr James Wilding & Son, bds 24 Union.
Cemetery, Huntington rd w of city limits.
Cemetery Association, Oliver P Morgan pres,
A Wilding sec, 12 Pixley & Long bldg.
Emma, milliner, bds 313 W Washington.
ia, bds 108 W Jefferson.
ib, feed stable, 16 Pearl, res 6 Pritchard.
ip J, collector, bds 108 W Jefferson.
ward J, clk Penn Co, bds 258 Clinton.
rry J, brakeman, bds 258 Clinton.
rew, shoemkr Louis Fortriede, res 89 Putnam.
rles W, turnkey County Jail, res 3 E Superior.
es E, engineer, res 82 W 3d.
cy M, carrier Postoffice, res 86 Wells.
e.
rie, domestic 121 W Main.
inie, domestic 121 W Main.
ck B, brakeman, res 103 Wells.

FURNITURE AND PIANO MOVING. RYAN TRUCKING CO.
19 and 21 W. WASHINGTON. TEL. 122.

FORT WAYNE DIRECTORY. 331

Lingel Theodore, lab, res 191 St Mary's ave.
Lininger Frank E, conductor, res 210 Walton ave.
Lingloff Oscar, bds 25 W Washington.
Link Adam, trav agt, res 102 E Main.
Link Annie M (wid George N), res 236 E Jefferson.
Link Bernhard, boxmkr Olds' Wagon Works, bds 114 Baker.
Link Frederick, stonecutter, res 116 Chicago.
Link Henry J, cash Root & Co, bds 236 E Jefferson.
Link John, lab Lindenwood Cemetery, bds 11 Mary.
Link Kate, opr Hoosier Mnfg Co, bds 116 Chicago.
Link Maggie, laundress Troy Steam Laundry, bds 11 Mary.
Link Mary, laundress Troy Steam Laundry, bds 11 Mary.
Link Mary (wid Thomas), res 11 Mary.
Link Wm B, foreman Nickel Plate R R, res 12 Cass.
Linker Christina (wid Henry E), res 46 W Berry.
Linker Dora, domestic 147 E Berry.
Linker Henry F, bds 46 W Berry.
Linker John V, clk Herman Berghoff Brewing Co, bds 66 Grant
    avenue.
Linker Ludwig, lab, bds 66 Grant ave.
Linker Valentine, watchman, res 66 Grant ave.
Linn Frederick, carp, rms 29 E Main.
Linnamann, *see also Lindeman.*
Linnamann Bernard, cabinetmkr Peters Box & Lumber Co, res
    183 Oakland.
Linnemeier, *see also Lindermeyer.*
Linnemeier Charles, helper Bass F and M Works, bds 225½
    John.
Linnemeier Wm, clk W D Meyer, res 131 Monroe.
Linnemeier Wm, lab, bds Washington House.
Linnemeyer Dietrich, carp, bds 244 E Washington.
Linsky Thaddeus, foreman Ft Wayne Spoke Wks, res 5 Fisher.
Linton Alice, bds 108 Howell.
Linton Emma, bds 108 Howell.
Linton John, car repairer Ft Wayne St R R Co, res 96 Mont-
    gomery.
Linton Samuel, plasterer, res 108 Howell.
Lintz, *see also Lenz.*
Lintz Anthony W, foreman, res 34 Baker.
Lintz Delia (wid Anthony), res 14 E Columbia.
Lintz Frederick, lab, bds 185 Hayden.
Lintz Josephine, clk T L Lintz, bds 14 E Columbia.
Lintz Theodore L, crockery, 12 E Columbia, res 14 same.
Lipes Alexander T, printer Ft Wayne Newspaper Union, bds
    176 W DeWald.
Lipes Andrew, jeweler, bds 69 Archer ave.

& Mahurin, ARCHITECTS,
41 & 42 Pixley & Long Bldg. Telephone 328

R. L. POLK & CO.'s

arles L, driver Adams Exp Co, res 22 W DeWald.

nrad, lab Bass F & M Works, bds 20 Force.

vid D, res 303 E Lewis.

hn M, instrumentmkr, res 98 W Main.

ysses S, physician, 303 E Lewis, bds same.

nry, lab, bds 83 Washington.

Aaron, notary, 551 E Washington, bds same.

rles, brakeman, bds 17 Burgess.

pp Louis, baggageman, bds 310 Harrison.

nan, baker L P Scherer, bds 395 E Washington.

1 C, carp, res 395 E Washington.

ger George, lab, res 164 Indiana ave.

eorge, carp, res 81 Wagner.

ward L, boilermkr Ft Wayne Iron Works, bds s w cor
Run ave and Randolph.

orge A, glazier Rhinesmith & Simonson, res s w cor
Run ave and Randolph.

orge J, bds s w cor Spy Run ave and Randolph.

eph V, finisher Ft Wayne Electric Co, res 165 Clinton.

ge O (Choctaw Medicine Co), bds 15 Maple ave.

ge W (Choctaw Medicine C), res 15 Maple ave.

also Lyttle.

bert, painter Penn Co, res 164 Madison.

an, wheel inspr Olds' Wagon Works, bds 320 Calhoun.

becca (wid George J), res 34½ John.

n A, mach hd Rocker Wash Mach Co, bds 34½ John.

1 David M, mach hand Wabash R R, bds 19 Poplar.

Jane M, domestic 64 McClellan.

Wm, blksmith, res 19 Poplar.

ger Albert M, trav agt, res 47 N Calhoun.

ger Elizabeth, bds 63 W Superior.

ger James B (Livensparger & Henry), bds Diamond
l.

ger & Henry (James B Livensparger, John G Henry),
rs, 119 Fairfield ave.

also Loyd.

s Belle R, prin Hanna School, bds 141 E Berry.

don W, sec and treas The Western Gas Construction
es Detroit, Mich.

John P, res 141 E Berry.

omas M, clk Geo DeWald & Co, bds 141 E Berry.

a R (Loag & Mungen), bds 103 W Berry.

ungen (Anna R Loag, W Wallace Mungen), dentists,
olumbia.

ewis A, brakeman, res 7 Harmon.

lenry E, finisher American Wheel Co, res 218 John.

mach hand A L Johns & Co, bds 312 Lafayette.
carp E F Liebman, res 250 E Jefferson.
opr Samuel M Foster, bds 312 Lafayette.
T, toolmkr Ft Wayne Electric Co, bds 25 W
ve.
rick, butcher Frederick Eckart, res 38 Watkins.
eamfitter, res 189 E Wayne.
rge H, Druggist, 96 Barr cor Wayne, res 52
gton.
bkkpr, bds 121 Calhoun.
ı, winder Ft Wayne Electric Co, bds 42 Baker.
, mach hand Ft Wayne Electric Co, bds 42

arp, res 314 Harrison.
J, court reporter, 34 E Berry, bds 26 W Wash-

orakeman, res 314 Harrison.
ılksmith, r 192 Calhoun, res 42 Baker.
ın, lab, res 133 Franklin ave.
o *Laumann.*
, cutter, res 51 Maumee rd.
, res 98 W Berry.
y J, molder Bass F & M Works, bds 187 Taber.
, engineer Penn Co, bds 154 John.
ıstave, stonecutter, res 4 Elm.
ırman, lab, bds 300 E Wayne.
ı *Lamont.*
A, foreman Paul Bros Pulley Works, res 100

(wid Peter), res 70 Gay.
et (wid Adolphus), res 551 E Washington.
' (wid Francis T), res 169 N Harrison.
A, milliner Mrs A Schulte, bds 266 E Lewis.
ı E. binder The Sentinel, res 400 E Wayne.
C, conductor, res 197 E Lewis.
V, mach, res 266 E Lewis.
ıret (wid Thomas D), bds 197 E Lewis.
, mach Penn Co, res 168 Harmer.
er J, baggagemaster Penn Co, res 124 W

ıarp, res 211 Fairfield ave.
ang.
ı George), res 30 Wells.
ınstress, bds 63 Elizabeth.
ımstress, bds e s Spy Run ave 3 n of brewery.
lithographer, bds 77 E Berry.

Long Emma (wid Charles A), res 182 E Washington.
Long Harry M, wall paper, 15 Arcade bldg, res 77 E Berry.
Long Ida, domestic 81 Wells.
Long James B, clk Stewart & Hahn, res 77 E Berry.
Long Mrs James B, dressmkr, 77 E Berry, res same.
Long John E, engineer Penn Co, res 19 Pine.
Long Mason, lecturer, rms 33 Pixley & Long bldg.
Long Nancy D (wid John C W), res 415 Calhoun.
Long Pearl B, messenger Penn Co, bds 182 E Washington.
Long Silas, lab Jacob Funk, bds same.
Long Wm, helper, bds 91 Laselle.
Longacre Milton P, sec Hoffman Bros, res 29 Garden.
Longfield Edward J, clk D C Fisher, res 67 Charles.
Loomis Ray M, agt Singer Mnfg Co, rms 70 Harrison.
Loos Anna, bkkpr H C Loos, bds 419 Lafayette.
Loos Charles H, mach, bds 419 Lafayette.
Loos Henry C, grocer, 421 Lafayette, res 419 same.
Loos Henry C jr, boilermkr, bds 419 Lafayette.
Loos John, clk H C Loos, bds 419 Lafayette.
Loos Joseph E A, policeman, res 395 Hanna.
Loos Ulrich, clk H C Loos, bds 419 Lafayette.
Loos Wm A, apprentice Penn Co, bds 88 W Williams.
Loose Leander, mach hd Wayne Knitting Mills, bds 38 Watkins.
Lopshire Abraham L, engineer G R & I R R, res 13 St Martin.
Lopshire Mrs Abraham L, milliner, 13 St Martin, res same.
Lord Edmund P, asst engineer motive power Penn Co, bds 167 E Main.
Lordier August F, res 537 E Wayne.
Lordier Clara P, bds 37 Baker.
Lordier Francis J, depy County Surveyor, bds 537 E Wayne.
Lordier Michael J, helper James Madden, bds 37 Baker.
Lordier Philip, shoemkr, 35 Baker, res 37 same.
Lorenz Charles, wireworker, 16 E Washington, res n e cor Spring and Jesse ave.
Lorenz George W, lab G W Doswell, bds Charles Lorenz.
Lorenz Joseph, lab, res 45 Gay.
Lorenz Mary, seamstress D S Redelsheimer, bds 30 Clinton.
Lose Cyrus J, foreman Journal Co, bds 43 Douglas ave.
Lose Levi H, car builder Penn Co, res 43 Douglas ave.
Lott John C, winder Ft Wayne Electric Co, res 244 W Washington.
Lott Wm C, foreman Ft Wayne Electric Co, res 332 W Washington.
Lotz Charles A, painter Mong & Meisner, bds 23 Walnut.
Lotz George, butcher Frederick Eckart, res 37 Breck.
Lotz John H, tailor A F Schoch, res 416 E Washington.

Lotz Philip G, cook Mergel & Frey, res 222 Hugh.

Lotz Wm, bds 37 Breck.

Loucks Amos, carp, res 139 Shawnee ave.

Louis, *see also Lewis.*

Louis Dominick, fruits, res 31 Duck.

Lounsburg James B, patternmkr Kerr-Murray Mnfg Co, res 40 St Mary's ave.

Louraine Louisa, domestic 180 Wells.

Lourent, *see also Laurent.*

Lourent August, bartnder J H Schele, res 155 W Superior.

Louth Maggie, bds 115 Hayden.

Louthain George T, switchman, res 142 Holman.

Louttit Catherine (wid James J), bds 17 W Creighton ave.

Louttit George W, lawyer, 26 Court, res 188 Smith.

Lovall Harriet (wid Samuel B), res 327 Hanna.

Love Wm, lab, res 332 Force.

Lovejoy D, brakeman N Y, C & St L R R, bds 323 W Main.

Lovell John, hostler Lee & Fulton, rms 18 W Wayne.

Lowe Charles, lab N Leonard, bds cor Lafayette and Washington.

Lowe George W, mach, res 280 W Washington.

Lowe Rachel (wid John), res 140 Lafayette.

Lowe Samuel D, fireman, res 31 Boone.

Lown Allen W, cabtmkr Ft Wayne Organ Co, res 115 W De Wald.

Lowrey Lottie, clk W F Geller, bds 98 Broadway.

Lowry Anna A, stenogr Ferguson & Palmer, bds 92 W Berry.

Lowry Annie, domestic Arlington Hotel.

Lowry Fannie, bds n s Edgewater ave 4 w of Dearborn.

Lowry Maggie E (wid James W), res 6 E Columbia.

Lowry Mary, nurse Indiana School for Feeble-Minded Youth.

Lowry Robert, Lawyer, 5 and 7 Court, res 92 W Berry.

Loyd, *see also Lloyd.*

Loyd George, pedler, res 2 Hanover.

Loyd Thomas W, pedler, res 435 E Washington.

Loyer, *see also Lauer and Lawyer.*

Loyer Stephen N, lab, res 88 Laselle.

Lubenjans Anna, opr Hoosier Mnfg Co, bds 82 Smith.

Lubenjans Benjamin, lab, bds 36 Buchanan.

Lucey Daniel, lab, bds 36 Union.

Lucey Timothy, lab, res 36 Union.

Luckey Jacob, teamster Louis Diether & Bro, res n e cor Lake and Franklin ave.

Lucky Elizabeth (wid John), bds 106 Wallace.

Ludeman Frederick, driver A Kalbacher & Co, bds 290 Calhoun.

nes A, mach Penn Co, rms 74 Douglas ave.
domestic 349 W Washington.
iis, mach Wayne Knitting Mills, bds 212 John.
ohn, tailor A F Schoch, res 91 Franklin.
iony, tinner, res 16 Cedar.
ider, res 1 N Calhoun.
uis, baggageman Wabash R R, bds 310 Harrison.
ider, tailor A F Schoch, res 54 E 3d.
ie, domestic Hoffman House.
ilso Layman and Lehman.
est, carp, bds 144 Erie.
lerick, lab, res 447 E Wayne.
lerick jr, printer, bds 447 E Wayne.
ave, painter City Carriage Works, bds 59 Canal.
ry C, clk J G Thieme & Son, res 51 Maumee rd.
iie M, domestic 107 E Main.
, carp, res 71 Canal.
C D, tailor, bds 447 E Wayne.
F, tailor, res 59 Canal.
ilso Lohrmann.
Anna M, res 213 W Washington.
itian, teamster, bds 213 W Washington.
ry C, mach Ft Wayne Electric Co, bds 213 W
in.
ry (wid Wm), domestic 133 E Berry.
T, res 236 W Berry.
rtist, rms 82 Baker.
enn Co, res cor Smith and Pontiac.
B, bkkpr Pickard Bros, bds 171 E Jefferson.
, mach Indiana Machine Works, bds 279 Hanna.
foreman Bass F & M Works, res 171 E Jefferson.
', foreman Ft Wayne Iron Works, res 256 E

r, patternmkr Bass F & M Works, bds 171 E

mach, bds 171 E Jefferson.
f, molder Ft Wayne Iron Works, bds 171 E

reman Indiana Machine Works, res 279 Hanna.
iolder Indiana Machine Works, bds 279 Hanna.
Effie, teacher, bds 164 W Wayne.
A (wid Sanford), res 164 W Wayne.
idney C, Insurance, Real Estate and Loans,
Iouse Blk. res 137 W Wayne.

Ida, opr C U Tel Co, bds 172 W Creighton ave.
:e Norman, lab John Dimon, bds same.
James F, lab, res 33 W Lewis.
George, market stall No 33; res Adams twp.
z **John V**, Agt-Vermont Farm Machinery Company,
'ostoffice Box No 56, res Maysville rd 3 miles east. (*See*
age 7.)
n Lawson T, clk, bds Grand Central Hotel.
n Patrick C, engineer G R & I R R, rms 17 W Lewis.
r Margaret, janitor Indiana School for Feeble-Minded
'outh.
Miss Flora, nurse German Reformed Orphans' Home.
ell Rev John L, removed to Dunkirk, O.
John, tailor, res 416 E Washington.
Julia (wid John), res 35 1st.
nberger Bertha, domestic 32 W 4th.
ph Eliza A (wid Frederick), bds 99 E Main.
lbert E, fireman Penn Co, res 153 Madison.
John Q, blksmith Bass F & M Works, res 328 E Jefferson.
n Charles H, res 134 Harrison.
n Lottie, domestic 107 W Berry.
n Walter F, blksmith, res 1 Division.
Edward J, mach hand Ft Wayne Electric Co, bds 12
.ansas.
Johanna (wid Patrick), bds 195 Barr.
John, blksmith Kerr-Murray Mnfg Co, bds 322 Lafayette.
John, lab, res 195 Barr.
John J, coppersmith Penn Co, res 12 Kansas.
Mathias, lab Penn Co, bds 12 Kansas.
Thomas, boilermkr Bass F & M Works, bds Monroe House
Albert W, clk Root & Co, bds 60 E Washington.
Wm, bkkpr, res 111 W Jefferson.
Martha (wid Lewis), res 203 W Washington.
Charles, collector The Press, bds 146 E Washington.
Robert J, engineer Penn Co, res 146 E Washington.
Winfield G, engineer Penn Co, res 65 W Williams.
, *see also Little.*
Benjamin, teamster, res 84 Taylor.

Mc

e Charles, hostler, bds 24 Cass.
e Harry L (Ross & McAfee), res 36 1st.

Penn Mutual LIFE INSURANCE CO. of PHILA.
CLARK FAIRBANK, General Agent, 19 Court Street.

338   R. L. POLK & CO.'S

McAfee Henry J, teamster, bds 24 Cass.
McAfee James, hostler Ross & McAfee, bds 24 Cass.
McAfee Rose, ice cream parlors, 337 Hanna, res same.
McAfee Samuel R, blksmith Penn Co, res 333 Hanna.
McAfee Winfield P, fireman Penn Co, res 331 Hanna.
McArdle Thomas, conductor, res 72 Thomas.
McAssey Frank J, stenogr Penn Co, res 330 Harrison.
McBennett Francis (Bruns & McBennett), res 410 Lafayette.
McBennett Frank J, bkkpr Bruns & McBennett, bds 410 Lafayette.
McBride George, lab Penn Co, res 309 Lafayette.
McBride John C, res 152 Griffith.
McCaffrey Arminda M (wid Wm), res 4 Jenison.
McCaffrey Daniel E, lab Penn Co, bds 72 Melita.
McCaffrey John F, hostler, bds Hotel Waverly.
McCaffrey John F, brakeman, bds 72 Melita.
McCaffrey Mary (wid Cormac), res 72 Melita.
McCaffrey Thomas, boilermkr, res 263 Webster.
McCaffrey Thomas J, brakeman, bds 72 Melita.
McCain Mrs Emma J, res 378 Calhoun.
McCain Margaret (wid Wm), bds 84 E Berry.
McCall Julia, domestic 34 Douglas ave.
McCallahan Elizabeth, domestic 31 Douglas ave.
McCamley Edward L, saloon, 104 Calhoun, bds 341 W Washington.
McCann John, contractor, 65 Grand, res same.
McCann Wm, lab Ft Wayne Water Power Co, res s e cor Riverside and Spy Run aves.
McCarthy Ann J (wid Andrew) res 494 W Main.
McCarthy Dennis, clk, bds 3 Colerick.
McCarthy Dennis, engineer, res 160 W Superior.
McCarthy Dennis F, conductor, res 292 Hanna.
McCarthy Dennis S, hostler Penn Co, res 27 Bass.
McCarthy Ellen (wid John), bds 27 Baker.
McCarthy James, blksmith, bds 290 Calhoun.
McCarthy James, cleaner Penn Co, bds 27 Bass.
McCarthy Jeremiah W, engineer Penn Co, bds 219 Lafayette.
McCarthy John, helper, bds 494 W Main.
McCarthy John C, engineer Penn Co, res 42 E Butler.
McCarthy Margaret, domestic 17 Burgess.
McCarthy Michael F, engineer, res 165 W Superior.
McCarthy Patrick, res 3 Colerick.
McCarthy Patrick F, brakeman, bds 21 Hamilton.
McCarthy Timothy, fireman Penn Co, bds 27 Bass.
McCarthy Wm B, clk, bds 160 W Superior.
McCarty Daniel D, sheet iron wkr Penn Co, bds 31 Summit.

FORT WAYNE DIRECTORY.

McCaskey George W, physician, 26 W Wayne, res 3
McCausland Eva C, res 133 Barr.
McCausland John W, removed to Chicago, Ill.
McClain, *see also McLain*.
McClain Catherine, domestic 50 W Superior.
McClaren, *see McLaren*.
McClave Mrs Belle, bds Racine Hotel.
McClellan John A, brakeman, res 24 Oliver.
McClellan John Q, engineer Penn Co, res 136 E Lew
McClellan Mrs Nancy, boarding house, 24 Oliver.
McClellan Wm, teacher, bds 136 E Lewis.
McClelland Samuel W, barber, E E Hagen, bds 15 (
McClelland Wm H, clk Morgan & Beach, res 15 Cass
McClintock Elizabeth (wid John), res 98 Montgomer
McClish Adam, gardener, res 185 S Wayne ave.
McClure Andrew, res 20 Douglas ave.
McClure David B, millwright Hoffman Bros, res 225
McClure David C, fireman, bds 319 Harrison.
McClure Drug Co, Rosser McClure Pres, P
   Medicine Manufacturers, 50 Harrison.
McClure James H, lab Bruns & McBennett, res n e
   and Oliver.
McClure Jennie, clerk, bds 319 Harrison.
McClure John H, foreman, res 319 Harrison.
McClure John H, salesman Ft Wayne Beef Co, bds
McClure Martha A (wid Joseph), bds 20 Douglas av
McClure Mollie E, teacher, bds 20 Douglas ave.
McClure Rosser, pres McClure Drug Co, res 340
   ington.
McCollem Anna C, opr Samuel M Foster, bds 225 W
McColloch, *see also McCulloch*.
McColloch George E, student, bds 230 Harmer.
McColloch Kate A (wid Samuel), res 230 Harmer.
McColloch Robert A, clk J M Kane, bds 230 Harme
McCollum Charles, lab, bds 163 Webster.
McCollum Lydia (wid John), res 163 Webster.
McConaby Mrs Bertie, nurse Indiana School for Feeb
   Youth.
McConnell Charles, sealer N Y, C & St L R R,
   Michael ave.
McConnell Joseph L, conductor, res 13 St Michael a
McCool James, brakeman N Y, C & St L R R, 1
   House.
McCormick George B, conductor, res 14 Jackson.
McCormick Thomas H, Physician and Sur

McCoy John W, mach Penn Co, res 80 Chicago.
McCoy Thomas, caller, bds 137 Fairfield ave.
McCracken James K, res 271 W Wayne.
McCracken Walter H, chemist, bds 146 Jackson.
McCrea John, painter J W Muldoon, bds G Siebold.
McCrimmon Anna G (wid Samuel), boarding house, 46 E Jefferson.
McCrory Albert J, clk Ind Installment Co, res 129 Wells.
McCrory Daniel, lab Kerr-Murray Mnfg Co, bds Monroe House.
McCrory George S, policeman, res 140 Barr.
McCulloch, *see also McColloch.*
McCulloch Charles, pres Hamilton National Bank and sec Salimonie Mining and Gas Co, res 122 W Wayne.
McCulloch John R, bkkpr Hamilton National Bank, bds 122 W Wayne.
McCulloch Park, e s Broadway nr Wabash R R.
McCulloch School, n w cor McCulloch and Eliza.
McCullom Charles, lab Rockhill Bros & Fleming, res Elmwood Farm.
McCullough Frank, lab, res 59 Grand.
McCullough Gustine, dentist, bds 34 Douglas ave.
McCullough Howard, Physician and Surgeon, Office 42 W Berry, Tel 66; rms 180 Harrison, Tel 200.
McCullough Maggie, toll gate kpr, res n s Leo Gravel rd 2 miles n of Court House.
McCullough Thomas P, Physician and Surgeon, Office 180 Harrison, res 34 Douglas ave.
McCullough Wm J, messenger, res 401 E Washington.
McCamsey Ansel M, lab Penn Co, res 47 E DeWald.
McCune George H, helper Kerr-Murray Mnfg Co, res 356 Calhoun.
McCurdy Andrew R, trav agt Geo DeWald & Co, bds 45 E 3d.
McCurdy George A, clk Ohnhaus & Co, bds 45 E 3d.
McCurdy John S, Dentist, 22 W Berry, res 157 same.
McCurdy Melvin J, brakeman Nickel Plate R R, res n s Jesse 1 e of Rumsey ave.
McCurdy Ward, clk Hotel Rich.
McDaniel Alexander, justice of peace, res n w cor Ruth and Spy Run ave.
McDaniel Frank, brakeman, res 269 E Creighton ave.
McDarby Bros (Matthew C and Wm F), Sample and Pool Room, 358 S Calhoun.
McDarby Matthew C (McDarby Bros), res 278 E Jefferson.
McDarby Wm F (McDarby Bros), bds 278 E Jefferson.
McDermott James, res 317 Calhoun.

)ermott Lewis M, dress cutting school, 98 Calhoun, res same.

)ermott Mrs Lydia A, dressmkr, 98 Calhoun, res same.

Dermut's Fort Wayne Business College, W E McDermut Pres, n w cor Calhoun and Berry. (*See page 8.*)

)ermut Nancy V (wid Josiah S), res 119 W. Washington.

Dermut Wilson E, Business College, Stenographer, and Agt "Caligraph" Typewriter, n w cor Calhoun and Berry, res 29 W Lewis. (*See page 8.*)

)ole Henry G, helper Penn Co, res 317 Hanna.

)onald Alexander, lab, bds 11 Grand.

)onald Charles, helper Am Wheel Co, bds 11 Grand.

)onald Duncan D, saloon, 288 Calhoun, rms same.

)onald Emmet H (McDonald, Watt & Wilt), sec Jenney Electric Light and Power Co, res 272 W Wayne.

)onald George, lab, bds 596 Calhoun.

)onald Hannah (wid James) bds 144 W Main.

)onald John, helper Fleming Mnfg Co, res 231 Wells.

)onald John, lab Lindenwood Cemetery, bds n e cor Main and Runnion ave.

)onald John, supervisor Nickel Plate R R, rms 6 Cass.

)onald John G, gasfitter, res 17 Calhoun.

)onald Margaret H (wid Archibald J), res 321 E Wayne.

)onald Mary J (wid David), res n s Spring 1 w of Franklin ave.

)onald Nelson, lab, res 64 Elm.

)onald Patrick J, sec Ft Wayne Water Works, res 131 Griffith.

)onald Ronald T, vice-pres Jenney Electric Light and Power Co, treas and genl mngr Ft Wayne Electric Co, res 252 W Wayne.

)onald Stephen A, brakeman, rms 23 Baker.

Donald, Watt & Wilt (Emmet H McDonald, Wm H Watt, Franklin P Wilt), Wholesale Grocers, 141-143 Calhoun.

)orman John E, helper Penn Co, bds 167 Van Buren.

)orman Mary J (wid John E), res 167 Van Buren.

)ougall's Block, n w cor Calhoun and Berry:

)owell Ella, dressmkr, res 27 Baker.

)fatrick Charles L, mach Penn Co, res 5 Monroe.

)fatrick Miss Emma M, teacher McCulloch School.

)fatrick Mary A (wid John), res 103 W Main.

)voy James B, student, bds 128 Montgomery.

)voy James H, train despatcher G R & I R R, res 128 Montgomery.

)wen Andrew, hostler W W Shryock, bds 27 W Berry.

: & co.'s

De Groff.
De Groff.
roff.
21 W Jefferson.
330 W Jefferson.
ie.
ng Mnfg Co, res 45 Calhoun.
ite, bds 176 Hayden.
ald, Watt & Wilt, bds 345 W

res 345 W Jefferson.
nion House.
117 W DeWald.
Vayne Electric Co, bds 169 W

s 169 W Jefferson.
Kee.
5 Clinton.
75 Clinton.
nton, res same.
im, bds 175 Clinton.
res 18 E Williams.
ull, res 163 Clinton.
George Reiter, res 13 Marion.
verside Hotel.
Co, bds 57 Charles.
107 Wallace.
, C & St L R R, res 167 High.
perior.
perior.
earse, bds 18 Holman.
bds 41 Hough.

338 W Main.
e Organ Co, res 25 Jane.

16 Baker.
60 Clinton.
Baker.
& I R R, bds Hotel Rich.
Co), res 174 Hanna.
vaine, Albert Furthmiller),

oadway.
g Mnfg Co, bds 66 W 3d.

ison, DENTIST 74 Calhoun Street.
, Res., 188 W. Berry St.

FORT WAYNE DIRECTORY. 343

Ic Gee and McKee.
Hoosier Mnfg Co, bds 49 Grand.
: Brookside Farm Co, res Columbia City rd
Court House.
e, mach Fleming Mnfg Co, res 3 Breck.
(G E Bursley & Co), res 134 W Main.
e M, teacher Clay School, bds 134 W Main.
rid Wm), res 149 Fairfield ave.
tes T, dressmkr, 149 Fairfield ave, bds same.
:n, teacher Central Grammar School, bds 149

McKeon.
(wid Wm T), res w s Spy Run ave opp River-

S, mach Ft Wayne Iron Works, bds Eliza

mgineer C L Centlivre, bds Eliza W McKean.
t, bkkpr J C Peltier, bds Eliza W McKean.
teacher Clay School, bds Eliza W McKean.
Mc Gee and McKay.
Edwin F McKee & Co), rms 170 W Main.
t Co (Edwin F McKee), druggists, 98 W Main.
, with The Daily News, rms 14 Barthold.
F, lab, res 160 Greely.
bds 24 Harrison.
nder, lab S B Bond, rms 322 Fairfield ave.
:arp, res 124 S Wayne ave.
i F, switchman, res 153 Hanna.
s A, timekeeper, bds 282 Harrison.
deputy City Clerk, res 233 Webster.
, asst City Engineer, res 282 Harrison.
, painter, res 11 St Martin.
3, switchman N Y, C & St L R R, bds 279

mach, res 121 W Butler.
i, with F D Clarke, res 142 W Jefferson.
id Robert), bds 281 W Jefferson.

McKinley Perry, street car driver, res 141 Ca:
McKinley Reginald, teamster, bds 141 Cass.
McKinley Thomas S, collector Indiana Installr
    W Washington.
McKinney Nathaniel C, lineman, res 114 W W
McKinnie Daniel, teacher, res 47 E Superior.
McKinnie House, Wm M McKinnie Pro
McKinnie Wm M (Wm M McKinnie &
    Kinnie House, Penn Depot, res 170 W W
McKinnie Wm M & Co (Wm M McKin
    Wayne, s s W Columbia bet N Calhoun a
McLachlan, *see also McLaughlin and MacL*
McLachlan Jane (wid Neil), res 66 W Creight
McLachlan John B, mach, res 473 Lafayette.
McLachlan Mary E (wid James C), res 209 Ba:
McLachlan Wm, trav agt Ft Wayne Iron W
    Berry.
McLain, *see also McClain.*
McLain Benoni P, res n s Prospect ave 3 e of
McLain Charles C, bkkpr S C Lumbard, res 1:
    avenue.
McLain Clara E, bds 29 Prospect ave.
McLain Zeruiah E, teacher, bds B P McLain.
McLane Mary (wid Robert), res 40 Marion.
McLaren Jesse, hostler Powers & Barnett, bds
McLaughlin, *see also McLachlan and MacLa*
McLaughlin Edward, molder Bass F & M Wor
    mee rd.
McLaughlin George W, titter Ft Wayne Ele
    Taylor.
McLaughlin John, brakeman N Y, C & St L
    Groff.
McLaughlin John L, res 132 W DeWald.
McLaughlin Mary C, bds 103 W Washington.
McLaughlin Thomas J, clk Railway Mail Ser:
    DeWald.

:73 W Main.
tor, res 324 Broadway.
enn Co, bds 224 Calhoun.
seph G), res 351 E Wayne.
r Robert Spice, bds 19 Calhoun.
stall No 27, res Wayne twp.
stall No 29, res Adams twp..
r, bds 161 Webster.
n, bds 161 Webster.
C F Myers, bds 161 Webster.
siah), res 161 Webster.
yne Electric Co, res 202 Broadway.
:3 Baker.
r, res n s Richardson nr G R & I

res 36 E 5th.
or The Daily News, res 199 Oak-

Penn Co, res rear 73 Charles.
'70 Charles, bds same.
Mathias Momper, bds 34 W Supe-

Wayne.
el), bds 410 Lafayette.
rns 29 E Main.
'he Wayne.
Penn Co, res 138 W DeWald.
'es 69 Grand.
bds 48 Walter.
s s Runnion ave 2 s of canal feeder.
nd, res e s Runnion ave 2 s of canal

Runnion ave.
194 Broadway.
44 E Williams.
ter. res 63 W 5th.

McNulty Mary (wid Anthony), res 245 Webster.
McNulty Neil F, brakeman, bds 245 Webster.
McNulty Wm (McNulty & Weber), res 154 Holman.
McNulty & Weber (Wm McNulty, Adam Weber), shoemkrs,
    211 Lafayette.
McNutt Henry T, mach, bds 427 Calhoun.
McNutt Lorenzo D, supt Ft Wayne St R R Co, res 427 Cal-
    houn.
McNutt Willard C, painter Ft Wayne St R R Co, res 438
    Broadway.
McOscar Amos J, collector, bds 16 W Jefferson.
McOscar Edward J, physician, n w cor Lewis and Lafayette,
    res 16 W Jefferson.
McOscar Emory, mach Indiana Machine Works, bds 16 W
    Jefferson.
McOscar Mary S (wid John), res 16 W Jefferson.
McPhail Miss Janet A, teacher Jefferson School, bds 192 Ewing.
McPhail Miss Margaret M, prin Bloomingdale School, bds 192
    Ewing.
McPhail Wm, mach, res 192 Ewing.
McPherson Angus, Agt Empire Line, 26 Court, res same.
McPherson Lucy, domestic, bds 229 E Wayne.
McQuarrie Allan, cabtmkr Ft Wayne Organ Co, res 28 Home.
McQuarrie Samantha (wid Duncan), nurse, res 91 E Wash-
    ington.
McQuiston John, res 70 Wells.
McQuiston Wilson, sec Peters Box & Lumber Co, res 43 E 2d.
McQuown John S, poultry w s Calhoun 1 n of County Jail, res
    4 Franklin ave.
McShane John, lab, bds 47 Barr.
McTavish Angus, tailor John Rahus, bds 25 W Washington.
McTigue Mary (wid Patrick), bds 30 Melita.
McVey Mary, opr S M Foster, bds 3 DeGroff.
McVey Michael, fireman N Y, C & St L R R, res 3 DeGroff.
McWhorter Lawrence L, printer The Gazette, bds 15 W Wil-
    liams.
McWhorter Wm A, printer The Gazette, bds 15 W Williams.

M

MacDougal John, res 143 W Wayne.
MacDougal Michael C (Root & Company), res 143 W Wayne.
Mack Catherine, domestic 137 W Wayne.

ottfried, painter, bds 132 Broadway.

wagonmkr Fleming Mnfg Co, res Archer ave nr
ts.

, shoemkr R H Neuhaus, res 132 W Main.

lressmkr, 132 W Main, res same.

dressmkr Victoria Walton, bds 132 W Main.

Ic Gee, McKay and McKee.

2e McKenzie.

ohn, lab, res s s Richardson 3 e of Rumsey ave.

see also McLachlan and McLaughlin.

Andrew F, trav agt A C Trentman, bds 27 W
;ton.

b, lab Nickel Plate R R, res 94 Franklin ave.

ames, Plumber, Steam and Gas Fitter, and
 the Perfect Hot Water Heater, Gas Fixtures,
ods, Plumbers' Supplies, Etc; Sanitary Plumbing
ty, 101 Calhoun, res 39 Baker. (*See right side*

, lab, res 37 W Williams.

, watchman, res 88 E Columbia.

in G, baker, bds 88 E Columbia.

lda (wid Allen), res 104 E Wayne.

ie, opr Hoosier Mnfg Co, bds 10 Olive.

ick M, bartndr J H Douglas, rms 38 Baker.

o, watchman, res 31 Julia.

ph, lab, res n s Howell 4 e of Rumsey ave.

el D (wid John), bds 288 E Creighton ave.

A, foreman, res 28 Sherman.

J, mach Penn Co, res 13 Hough.

Maher, Maier, Mayer, Meier, Meyer, Meyers
rs.

, carp Penn Co, res 149 Ewing.

jr, driver Kayser & Baade, bds 149 Ewing.

elevator conductor, bds 149 Ewing.

irtz and Merz.

X, gardener, res 90 Maple ave.

A, carp, res w s Winter 2 n of Pontiac.

e.
it, bds 185 Ewing.
vay Mail Service, res 185 Ewing.
John Jackson, bds 176 W Jefferson.
ck), res 176 W Jefferson.

ier, Mayer, Meier, Meyer, Meyers and

r Ft Wayne Organ Co, res 121 W

)uryea.
, presiding elder Ft Wayne M E
san ave.
0 Michigan ave.

wenger ave.
enger ave.
F C Boltz & Co, bds 19 W Jeffer-

· F Hilt, res 42 Pritchard.
), res 42 Pritchard.
s & Mahurin), res s w cor Fairfield

r, Mayer, Meier, Meyer, Meyers and

√ Foster Furniture Co, res 55 Wa-

n Co, bds 310 Harrison.
bds Washington House.

Mnfg Co, bds 61 Melita.
Infg Co, bds 61 Melita.
s 61 Melita.
, res 218 Walton ave.
196 E DeWald.
ls 172 Gay.
) Baker, bds 172 Gay.
172 Gay.
E Washington.
R & I R R, res 57 Smith.
r Maple and Thompson aves.

tor, res 132 Broadway.

ess Troy Steam Laundry, bds 77 W 3d.

John), res 77 W 3d.

X, conductor, res 71 W 4th.

(Malcolm & Bush), res 44 W Williams.

h (Sherman E Malcolm, Emanuel K Bush),

urance and Loans, Room 3 Bass Blk.

ey.

Patrick), bds 13 Brandriff.

nry), res 189 E Jefferson.

ndr Aldine Hotel, bds 189 E Jefferson.

luctor, rms 14 Chicago.

ry, 16 Calhoun, res 107 E Main.

ab Bass F & M Works, res 179 Gay.

one.

ctor, res 157 Montgomery.

, 167 Broadway, res same.

iloney.

per Penn Co, bds 1 Thomas.

b, res 1 Thomas.

res 110 John.

lumber, bds 4 Riverside ave.

bldr Penn Co, res 4 Riverside ave.

lk Golden & Monahan, bds 4 Riverside.

, supt mach dept Bass F & M Works, res

y.

, mach Ft Wayne Electric Co, bds 417

l Patrick), res 3 Walnut.

ab N Y, C & St L R R, res 64 W Main.

ngels.

stic Concordia College.

teacher, res 124 John.

Penn Co, res 144 Holman.

Olds' Wagon Works, res 162 Holman.

3 Glasgow.

), bds 62 Buchanan.

s s s Columbia 3 e of Oneida.

nning.

vyer J C Peters, bds cor Runnion ave

ab, res 15 Brandriff.

Andrew), res 173 Wells.

h Penn Co, bds 10 Holman.

ity sheriff, res 10 Holman.

gt Fred C Boltz, res 19 E Washington.

Mannor Wm A, switchman, res 97 Montgomery.
Mannweiler Christian, res 23 Duryea.
Mannweiler Herman, boilermkr Penn Co, bds 23 Duryea.
Mannweiler Mary (wid Martin), bds 1 Walnut.
Manocchio Benedetto (Manocchio, Farrita & Co), bds 228 Calhoun.
Manocchio, Farrita & Co (Benedetto and Pasquale Manocchio, Joseph Farrita), fruits, 228 Calhoun.
Manocchio Pasquale (Manocchio, Farrita & Co), res 228 Calhoun.
Manok Charles, cigarmkr L Dessauer & Co, res 195 Jackson.
Manok Crescentia (wid Simon), res 21 E Williams.
Manok Edward, clk, bds 21 E Williams.
Manok Julia, packer, bds 21 E Williams.
Manon George E, clk, bds 182 E Washington.
Manon Wm A, clk Mossman, Yarnelle & Co, res 182 E Washington.
Manor Alexander P, carp Fred Weibel, res 133 E Lewis.
Manth Albert F W, clk, bds 56 Buchanan.
Manth Amanda, dressmkr, bds 56 Buchanan.
Manth Jeannette (wid Julius), res 56 Buchanan.
Manth Louisa (wid Ephraim), res 108 Maumee rd.
Manuel Frank A, plumber A Hattersley & Sons, bds 192 E Wayne.
Manuel Josephine, bds 113 Lafayette.
Manuel Julius, clk Sam, Pete & Max, res 223 W Jefferson.
Mapes George, changer Ft Wayne St R R Co, bds n w cor Superior and Wells.
Mapes Leroy, hostler Ft Wayne St R R Co, bds Racine Hotel.
Maple Benjamin F, plasterer, res 135 W 3d.
Maple Charles E, mach hand Olds' Wagon Works, res 139 Griffiths.
Maple Vadie, laundress Boston Restaurant.
Maple Wm B, lab, res 63 Grand.
Maples Mary (wid Lemuel), res 17 Baker.
Marahrens Charles F, lab Nickel Plate R R, res 36 Smith.
Marc Charles, lab, rms 29 E Main.
Marceau Delphis, harnessmkr, bds 12 Rockhill.
March Charles W, fireman Penn Co, res 219 Lafayette.
Marchal, see Marshall.
Marhenke Augusta (wid Frederick), res 145 High.
Marhenke Christian, engineer Penn Co, res 110 Madison.
Marhenke Christian H, clk Geo DeWald & Co, bds 110 Madison.
Marhenke John, sawyer Olds' Wagon Works, res 81 Force.
Marhenke Wm F, mach hand Olds' Wagon Works, bds 110 Madison.

Mariam Ann J (wid Cyrenius), res 174 E Creighton ave.
Marine George W, tel opr Wabash R R, res 15 Hamilton.
Mariotte Benjamin, clk Horace Mariotte, rms 20 E Columbia.
Mariotte George, clk Horace Mariotte, res w s Brooklyn ave 2
miles w of St Mary's river.
Mariotte Horace, Pawn Broker, 20 E Columbia, res 104
N Harrison. (*See below.*)
Marketmaster's Office, Wm Ropa marketmaster, City Hall.
Markey Andrew J, solicitor F X Schuhler, res 286 Broadway.
Markey Bros (Edward J and Willis J), florists, 117 W Jefferson.
Markey Edward J (Markey Bros), res 109 W Jefferson.
Markey Frank L, student, bds 109 W Jefferson.
Markey Frederick, fireman, res 4 Fulton.
Markey Lawrence, res 344 Calhoun.
Markey Mary E, teacher, bds 286 Broadway.
Markey Richard F (Markey & Mungovan), clk A C Trentman,
res 414 Calhoun.
Markey Willis J (Markey Bros), bds 109 W Jefferson.
Markey & Mungovan (Richard F Markey, Franklin
Mungovan), Grocers and Bakers, 256 Calhoun. Tel 81.
Markley Daniel, meats, 13 Highland, res 108 S Wayne ave.
Marks Charles Q, brakeman, res 26 Fisher.
Marks Margaret, domestic 29 W Lewis.
Marks Simon L, barber, bds 264 E Washington.
Marks Simon P, inspr Penn Co, res 264 E Washington.
Marks Wilbert T, mach Penn Co, res 284 Broadway.
Marquardt Catherine (wid John), bds 59 W Washington.
Marsh Thomas J, carp, res 79 Putnam.
Marshall Clement (col'd), waiter The Wayne.

Marshall Kate, cook Hotel Rich.

Marshall Peter, gardener, res n e cor Lumbard and New Haven ave.

Marshall Rachel M (wid Thomas), bds 84 W Main.

Marshall Wesley, fireman, res 227 E Jefferson.

Martin, *see also Mertens.*

Martin Alexander A, saloon, 74 E Columbia, res same.

Martin Alice (wid Bernard), res 52 Baker.

Martin Allen, clk Geo DeWald & Co, bds 339 Hanna.

Martin Alonzo, painter Mong & Meisner, res 59 Hugh.

Martin Anna M (wid Lambert), res 206 W Washington.

Martin Anthony D, clk Penn Co, bds 206 W Washington.

Martin August, lab, res 169 N Harrison.

Martin Bernard, fireman G R & I R R, bds 355 Calhoun.

Martin Charles, helper T S Tuttle, bds 3 St Mary's ave.

Martin Charles, inspr Salimonie Mining & Gas Co, bds 112 E Main.

Martin Christian, foreman, res n w cor St Mary's river and N Y, C & St L R R.

Martin Christian F, lab, res 73 John.

Martin Christopher, teamster, bds 225 Broadway.

Martin Daniel, res 355 Calhoun.

Martin Daniel C, asst bkkpr C L Centlivre Brewing Co, bds 355 Calhoun.

Martin Diedrich, janitor, res 57 Wilt.

Martin Edward, mach hand Penn Co, res 235 E Washington.

Martin Emmett, gas fitter, 359 Hanna, bds same.

Martin Eugene, lab, bds 359 Hanna.

Martin Frank A J, finisher Peters Box and Lumber Co, bds 169 N Harrison.

Martin George, gas fitter, bds 359 Hanna.

Martin Henry W, car bldr Penn Co, res 126 Smith.

Martin Jacob, lab, res 163 E Jefferson.

Martin Jane (wid Francis H), janitor Old National Bank, res 115 W Superior.

Martin John, stripper H W Ortmann, bds 79 Harrison.

Martin John, lab, bds 52 Baker.

Martin Joseph L, carp, res 214 St Mary's ave.

Martin Joseph P, fitter P E Cox, bds 359 Hanna.

Martin Leonard, mach hand Ft Wayne Electric Co, bds 157 College.

Martin Mrs Lottie, laundress, res 60 Chicago.

Martin Louis E, clk, res 110 Chicago.

Martin Nancy, laundress Troy Steam Laundry, bds 3 E Superior.

Martin Paul, lab Penn Co, res n s Chestnut 3 e of Lumbard.

Martin Terrence, blksmith Penn Co, res 359 Hanna.

Martin Victor, lab, res s s Chestnut 1 e of Warren.

Martin Wm, lab, res 37 Marion.

Martin Wm, press feeder Ft Wayne Newspaper Union, bds 73 John.

Martin Wm, mach hand, bds 112 E Main.

Martin Wm H, sheet iron worker Kerr-Murray Mnfg Co, res 110 Chicago.

Martin Wm W, engineer Penn Co, res 28 John.

Martins Wm, house mover, 225 Broadway, res same.

Martz, *see also Merz*.

Martz Christian, physician, 15 W Jefferson, res same.

Masbaum Anthony, carp Penn Co, res 177 Madison.

Masbaum George G, bkkpr M Baltes, res 221 E Washington.

Masel Martin, fireman, res 162 Hoffman.

Mason David L, fireman, res 270 Harrison.

Mason Eugene J, clk U S Baking Co, bds 21 W Jefferson.

Mason Henry M, clk Penn Co, res 203 W Washington.

Mason James, bkkpr, bds 21 W Jefferson.

Mason Joseph, market stall No 72, res Pleasant twp.

Mason Melville A, dentist, 26 W Wayne, bds 203 W Washington.

Mason Nancy (wid John F), res s e cor Clinton and Williams.

Mason Sidney, helper Penn Co, bds 298 Calhoun.

Masonic Hall, n w cor Calhoun and Berry.

Masonic Temple, n e cor Wayne and Clinton.

Massman Henry, bricklayer, rms 181 Calhoun.

Mast Augusta, seamstress, bds 198 Madison.

Mast Josephine, opr Samuel M Foster, bds 311 E Washington.

Master Builders' Association, James W Wilding sec and treas, 195 Calhoun.

Master Carpenters' Association, J Henry Meyers sec, 195 Calhoun.

Masterson Ellis H, foreman Ft Wayne St R R Co, res 38 Wells.

Match, *see Matsch*.

Mather Edward, book agt, res 29 W Jefferson.

Mathews, *see also Matthews*.

Mathews George W, hostler Stapleford & Co, bds E Columbia bet Lafayette and Clay.

Mathews Wm C, lab, res 48 Oliver.

Mathews Wm H, lab, bds Union House.

Mathis T Eugene, mach hd Ft Wayne Electric Co, bds 391 Hanna.

Mathis Julia (wid John), res 391 Hanna.

Matott Charles T, conductor, res 131 Buchanan.

Matsch Catherine (wid Wm), res 82 Montgomery.

Matsch J Christopher, clk Bass F & M Works, res 165 E Creighton ave.

R. L. POLK & CO.'S

Penn Co, bds 35 Hugh.
·chitect, Ninde bldg, res 59 Erie.
·mestic 177 Madison.
, mason, res 192 Taylor.
ardmaster Hoffman Bros, res 26 Frederick.
nith City Carriage Works, bds 59 Greene.
fathews.
noved to Grand Rapids, Mich.
·, res 30 S Wayne ave.
d), lab, res 37 Grand.
d), lab, res 33 W Lewis.
·sterer, bds 130 Maumee rd.
·b, bds Joseph Matthiew.
·, res n s New Haven ave 4 w of Lumbard.
·man, res 3 Julia.
·gineer, res 115 Boone.
·nductor, res 61 Maud.
·b, res 78 Pritchard.
·orer.
Kerr-Murray Mnfg Co, res 179 Oakland.
·offman Bros, res 621 E Washington.
·ler, rms 33 Brackenridge.
·id Ferdinand), res 621 E Washington.

·ter, res n s E Washington 1 e of Walton.
·ster, res s e cor Spring and Sherman.
·utner & Friedlich), res 171 W Wayne.
·(Isadore Mautner, Isaac Friedlich), cloth-

·tor The Western Gas Construction Co, res

·ier, bds Hedekin House.
, bds Hedekin House.
·ver, bds 20 Harrison.
·ch hand Ft Wayne Organ Co, res 271 W

·l'd), barber J H Roberts, bds 205 Calhoun.
·iller, res 99 Summit.
·, bds 99 Summit.
·Aldine Hotel.
·ls 60 E Butler.
·*Maher, Maier, Meier, Meyer, Meyers and*

·mach Ft Wayne Electric Co, bds 148

·terer Henry Schwartz, bds 61 Stophlet.

B UILDERS' P FEIFFER & SCHLATTER,
HARDWARE, 38 and 40 East Columbia St.

FORT WAYNE DIRECTORY. 355

Mayer Eugene, clk J G Mayer, bds 6 Force.
Mayer Jacob G, saloon, 6 Force, res same.
Mayer Julia (wid Andrew), res 29 W Wayne.
Mayer Lawrence, res 47 E Jefferson.
Mayer Louis, student, bds 149 Griffith.
Mayer Moses, bkkpr Theodore Mayer, bds 149 Griffith.
Mayer Theodore, Carriage Dealer, Propr Indiana Buggy Co, 25 E Columbia, res 149 Griffith.
Mayer Theodore W H, plasterer Henry Schwartz, res 61 Stophlet.
Mayers Eleanor M (wid Louis), res cor Clinton and Lewis.
Mayers Henry, teamster, bds 57 Barr.
Mayfield James B, lab, res 105 Gay.
Mayflower Mills, Charles S Bash pres, Joseph Hughes mngr, 20 W Columbia.
Mayhew Allen, apprentice Penn Co, res 282 W Main.
Mayhew Mrs Mary E, clk Penn Co, bds 271 W Wayne.
Mayhue Lizzie, attendant Indiana School for Feeble-Minded Youth.
Mayland, see also Mailand.
Mayland August F, mach hand Ft Wayne Electric Co, bds 236 W Washington.
Mayland Henry F, driver Rippe & Sons, res 236 W Washington.
Mayland Mary (wid Frederick), res 236 W Washington.
Mayland Paulina, dressmkr, bds 236 W Washington.
Meckley Charles, brakeman, rms 20 Breck.
Medsker Isaac N, trav agt, res 473 Lafayette.
Medsker James R, mach Penn Co, res 70 Baker.
Medsker John H, trav agt, rms 25 W Lewis.
Meegan Thomas, clk Penn Co, res 24 Creighton ave.
Meehan Charles, lab, bds 36 Brandriff.
Meehan Frances, tailoress L J Feist, bds 260 E Jefferson.
Meehan James, lab, bds 36 Brandriff.
Meehan James P, lab, bds 260 E Jefferson.
Meehan John M, molder Bass F & M Works, res 395 E Lewis.
Meehan Joseph N, molder Kerr-Murray Mnfg Co, bds 260 E Jefferson.
Meehan Margaret (wid James), res 36 Brandriff.
Meehan Mary E, tailoress, bds 180 E Wayne.
Meehan Michael, res 260 E Jefferson.
Meehan Wm, lab, bds 36 Brandriff.
Meek Wm H, packer F E Purcell & Co, res 75 W Washington.
Meeks U S Grant, winder Ft Wayne Electric Co, bds 90 Dawson.
Megert John, lab, bds 22 E Columbia.
Mehl, see also Mahl.

ror, res 21 Elizabeth.
M Frank & Co, bds 95 W Superior.
, bds 95 W Superior.
1), res 90 W Superior.
ir, res 123 Harrison.
Maher, Maier, Mayer, Meyer, Meyers and

Bernard), bds 20 W Jefferson.
builder Penn Co, res 310 Harrison.
cksmith, 123 Wallace, res 120 same.
res 86 Gay.
s 28 Stophlet.
r Fritz Hotel.
res 39 Franklin ave.
s 121 Calhoun.
ederick), bds 46 John.
100 E Washington.
o St Louis, Mo.
seamstress P E Wolf, bds 418 E Wash-

stic 167 Broadway.
ilper, bds 3 E Superior.
lor, 213 Calhoun, res 25 Maumee rd.
clk F J Miller, bds 25 Maumee rd.
iyer, res 241 Madison.
bds 25 Maumee rd.
F J Miller, bds 327 Lafayette.
icordia Cemetery, res same.
7m Meinzen.
1 Wagner.
her F Howenstein, bds 21 Wagner.

y), res 195 W Superior.
nefee), res 202 Thomas.
& Menefee, bds 202 Thomas.
Washington.
E Washington.
ashington.

3 Maumee rd.
n Co, res 20 Hough.
Penn Co, res 168 Francis.
, res 37 Hough.
F & M Works, res 289 Hanna.
s 65 Oliver.
ming.
, bds 164 Wells.
Columbia, res 164 Wells.
Club, res 43 W DeWald.
v cor Mary and Runnion ave.
S Redelsheimer & Son, bds

s Mensing.
ldoon, res 88 Montgomery.
s F & M Works, res 106 Eliza.
Rabus, bds 338 E Washington.
s, res 338 E Washington.
, bds 30 Douglas ave.
House.
ouse.
tion Co, W V Douglass agt, 3

, res 33 Grace ave.
Main, res 324 Calhoun.
rey), res n w cor Calhoun and

rgel, George Frey), restaurant,

ery, 38 Calhoun, res 84 W

Merica Rosa, bds 43½ E Columbia.
Merillat Joseph P, clk Coverdale & Archer, res 48 McClellan.
Merillet Emily, dressmkr, 63 Boone, bds same.
Merillet John, lab, res 63 Boone.
Meriwether James R, clk Penn Co, res 76 Lafayette.
Merklaen Frederick, molder, res 192 Taylor.
Merlet Matthew, lab Penn Co, bds 307 E Washington.
Merrell Ellen D (wid Ephraim), music teacher, 26 Chute, res same.
Merrell Frank R, printer, bds 26 Chute.
Merriam Ann J (wid Cyrenius), res 174 E Creighton ave.
Merriett Charles F, engineer, res 72 W 3d.
Merriett John T, bds 72 W 3d.
Merry Ida, res cor Barr and E Columbia.
Mertens, see also Martin.
Mertens Frederick, tailor J G Thieme & Son, res 77 Liberty.
Mertens Minnie, domestic 52 W Washington.
Merz Albert, slater J H Welch, res 41 Pine.
Merz Elizabeth, housekpr 155 Hanna.
Merz Joseph, policeman, res 25 Pine.
Merz Lena, domestic 137 E Berry.
Merz Louis (Zoeller & Merz), res 25 W DeWald.
Merz Nicholas, carbldr Penn Co, res 125 W DeWald.
Merz Peter, car bldr Penn Co, res 196 E Lewis.
Merz Theodore, bartndr Zoeller & Merz, res 37 Pine.
Mesing Emma, domestic 285 W Berry.
Messerschmidt John M, helper Bass F & M Works, res 117 Eliza.
Messerschmidt Wm, baker L P Scherer, bds 89 Erie.
Messman Emma, domestic 20 Summit.
Messmann Rev Anthony, pastor St Peter's German Catholic Church, res s e cor Warsaw and DeWald.
Messmer Gustave, driver, bds 121 Calhoun.
Metcalf Samuel C, physician, 10 Calhoun, res 109 W Superior.
Metcalf Samuel S, brakeman, res 38 Buchanan.
Metcalfe John, engineer, res 55 Force.
Metcalfe Wm E, clk F D Clarke, bds 55 Force.
Methley Charles, clk C A Hays, bds 29 E Main.
Metker Bernard, mason, res 197 E Jefferson.
Metker Emma, opr Hoosier Mnfg Co, bds 359 E Washington.
Metker John, painter estate M L Albrecht, bds cor Coombs and Cochran.
Metker Joseph, plasterer, res e s Comparet 2 s of E Wayne.
Metker Margaret, waiter, bds 121 Calhoun.
Metropolitan Mnfg Co, Harry B Ridgley Mngr, Installment Goods, 28 Clinton.

Geo. E. Johnson, DENTIST, 74 Calhoun Street.
Res., 188 W. Berry St.

FORT WAYNE DIRECTORY. 359

Metsker Allen, checker, res 243 Webster.

Mettey Elizabeth (wid Frederick), res s s Wagner 2 e of Spy Run ave.

Mettey Frederick, molder, bds s s Wagner 2 e of Spy Run ave.

Metting Wm C, clk J B White, res Allen twp.

Mettler Bernhard, cigarmkr A C Baker, bds Catherine Mettler.

Mettler Catherine (wid Peter), res w s Spy Run ave opp Riverside ave.

Mettler Kate, opr Samuel M Foster, bds 261 E Wayne.

Mettler John, clk M Frank & Co, bds Catherine Mettler.

Mettler John A, barber F L Brown, bds 613 Calhoun.

Mettler Joseph, rimmer, bds 609 Calhoun.

Mettler Matthew, cutter, bds Catherine Mettler.

Mettler Mathias, patternmkr, res 127 Francis.

Mettler Peter, lab C L Centlivre Brewing Co, res w s Spy Run ave 9 n of bridge.

Mettler Peter J, bartndr M N Webber, res 146 E Jefferson.

Metty Mrs Elizabeth, laundress Troy Steam Laundry, res 37 Barr.

Metty Frederick G, molder Bass F & M Works, bds 6 Wagner.

Metzger Elizabeth (wid Andrew), bds 40 Brackenridge.

Metzger Harry H, deputy clk Allen County Circuit Court, res 18 Monroe.

Metzger John, lab, bds 130 Maumee rd.

Metzler Charles, baker, bds 30 Madison.

Metzler Leopold, tailor, res 257 Hanna.

Metzner Jasper, conductor, res 358 Hanna.

Meuroth Louis, foreman Wabash R R, res 160 Taylor.

Meyer, *see also Maer, Maher, Maier, Mayer, Meier, Meyers and Myers.*

Meyer Ada, domestic 181 E Jefferson.

Meyer Adolph, tailor, res 54 W Wayne.

Meyer Anna M (wid John), bds 443 E Wayne.

Meyer Annie (wid Nicholas), bds 236 E Jefferson.

Meyer Anthony G, woodworker Anthony Wayne Mnf'g Co, bds 94 Buchanan.

Meyer August, mason, bds 56 Smith.

Meyer Bernhard, lab, res 100 Mechanic.

Meyer Bros & Co (Christian F G and John F W Meyer), Wholesale and Retail Druggists, 2 Keystone Blk and 9 W Columbia.

Meyer Bruno, molder Bass F & M Works, res 127 Gay.

Meyer Charles, lab, res 71 Wilt.

Meyer Charles C, lab Horton Mnfg Co, res 90 Wilt.

Meyer Charles F W, director Ft Wayne Conservatory of Music, res s s Pontiac 3 e of Hoagland ave.

Meyer Charles H, painter Heine & Israel, bds 127 Gay.

Meyer Charles W, grocer, n e cor Miner and Creighton ave, res same.

Meyer Christian F G (Meyer Bros & Co), res St Louis, Mo.

Meyer Christina, domestic 66 Douglas ave.

Meyer Miss Clara E, tailoress W H Blondoit, bds 33 Madison.

Meyer Conrad, lab, res 84 Wall.

Meyer Diedrich, res 22 W Wayne.

Meyer Diedrich H, lab Bass F & M Works, res 41 Gay.

Meyer Dorothy (wid Frederick), res 99 Wilt.

Meyer Emma, dressmkr Mrs G J Stier, bds 127 Gay.

Meyer Ernest C, res 91 Force.

Meyer Ernest D, clk, res 34 Union.

Meyer Frank H, res 76 W Washington.

Mayer Frank J, gunsmith S P Lade, res 142 Erie.

Meyer Frederick, boilermkr, res 5 Summit.

Meyer Frederick, mach hand Penn Co, res 62 Hugh.

Meyer Frederick, molder Bass F & M Works, bds 34 Union.

Meyer Frederick, teacher, bds 131 Monroe.

Meyer Frederick C, foreman Bass F & M Works, res 198 E DeWald.

Meyer Frederick H, saloon, 104 Calhoun, res 44 W Washington.

Meyer F Charles, mach Penn Co, res 338 Force.

Meyer George L, turner Horton Mnfg Co, bds 165 Ewing.

Meyer George M, molder Bass F & M Works, res 254 E Washington.

Meyer Gottlieb, lab, res 59 W 5th.

Meyer Gustav, gardener Hamilton Homestead, res 15 Poplar.

Meyer Hannah, stenogr, bds 54 W Wayne.

Meyer Henrietta, milliner A Mergentheim, bds 100 Harrison.

Meyer Henry, res 183 E Lewis.

Meyer Henry, whitewasher, res 200 E Lewis.

Meyer Henry C, tailor, 44 Harrison, res 281 W Washington.

Meyer Henry D, helper Bass F & M Works, res 41 Gay.

Meyer Henry J jr (Wm Meyer & Bro), res 37 Madison.

Meyer Henry W, draughtsman Penn Co, res 220 W Jefferson.

Meyer Henry W, foreman Bass F & M Works, res 26 Oak.

Meyer Jacob, clk Pottlitzer Bros, bds 54 W Wayne.

Meyer John, driver C L Centlivre, res w s Leo rd 3 n of canal feeder.

Meyer John F W (Meyer Bros & Co), res 290 Fairfield ave.

Meyer John H, foreman, res 519 E Lewis.

Meyer John H, packer Meyer Bros & Co, res 100 Harrison.

Meyer Lizzie, bds 76 W Washington.

Meyer Louis, tailor, bds 99 Wilt.

Meyer Louis G, sawyer David Tagtmeyer, res 76 Harrison.

lwkr Anthony Wayne Mnfg Co, bds 94

itic 216 E Lewis.
ess J G Motz, bds 99 Wilt.
stic 47 W Wayne.
inis), bds 51 Maumee rd.
ic 21 W Creighton ave.
ic n s Edgewater ave 4 w of Dearborn.
ic n s Edgewater ave 3 e of Loree.
ir, bds 91 Ewing.
rms 86 Barr.
Arndt), bds 36 Union.
stic 298 E Jefferson.
ssmkr Mrs G J Stier, bds 83 Montgomery.
ic 105 W Berry.
G W Winbaugh, bds 127 Gay.
W Miller, bds 254 E Washington.
er Ft Wayne Furn Co, bds 519 E Lewis.
rank & Co, bds 54 W Wayne.
G Thieme & Son, bds 53 E Wayne.
ess, bds 99 Wilt.
itic 76 E Washington.
23 Hanna.
vid Henry), bds 41 Gay.
Meyer & Bro), res 40 W Washington.
entmkr Ft Wayne Electric Co, bds 338

99 Wilt.
6 E Wayne, res same.
Indiana Mach Wks, bds 396 E Wayne.
roceries, Provisions, Wines and Liquors,
s 129 E Lewis.
r & Niemann), res 405 Webster.
ass F & M Works, bds 65 Hugh.
S & M S Ry, bds 127 Gay.
ro (Wm Jr and Henry J Jr), Hats, Caps
shings, 34 Calhoun.
Vm F Meyer, Gottlieb F Niemann), gents'
Calhoun.
vyer, res 180 Greely.
er, *Maher, Maier, Mayer, Meier, Meyer*

George Klippert, bds 393 Lafayette.
d Frederick C), res 24 McClellan.
bartndr H A Wiebke, bds 43 W Wash-

John Pressler, Galvanized Iron CORNICES and Slate ROOFING, Columbia, Barr and Dock Streets.

362   R. L. POLK & CO.'S

Meyers Charles C, res 128 W Main.
Meyers Charles F F, clk Root & Co, res 43 W Washington.
Meyers Christina, domestic 115 E Berry.
Meyers Dietrich, carp, bds Jewel House.
Meyers Ernest C, helper Olds' Wagon Works, bds 58 Charles.
Meyers Fred G, clk Rose Bros, res 63 Hugh.
Meyers Frederick N, finisher Horton Mnfg Co, res 74 Cherry.
Meyers George, lab, res 39 Wells.
Meyers Henrietta, domestic 50 W Superior.
Meyers Henry, lab, bds 40 Tons.
Meyers Henry, tailor John Rabus, bds 49 Hugh.
Meyers Henry, teamster, res 65 Boone.
Meyers Henry F, lab, res 132 Force.
Meyers Jane (wid Wm), res 40 Tons.
Meyers John, lab, res w s Spy Run ave 3 n of Burgess.
Meyers John H, confectioner W F Geller, bds 49 Hugh.
Meyers J Henry (H A Grotholtman & Co), res 138 Harrison.
Meyers Leander H, foreman C L Centlivre's St Ry Co, res 22 Randolph.
Meyers Margaret (wid Ferdinand), res 165 Ewing.
Meyers Parnella (wid Christian), res 47 W Washington.
Meyers Sophia, domestic 177 Jackson.
Meyers Wm, bds 122 Force.
Meyers Wm C, molder Bass F & M Works, bds 63 Hugh.
Meyers Wm C, wagonmkr, res 58 Charles.
Meyers Wm H, woodworker Anthony Wayne Mnfg Co, bds 221 Madison.
Michael Frederick H, student, bds 20 Clinton.
Michael Herman jr, clk, bds 41 E Berry.
Michael Jonathan, teamster, res 129 Wells.
Michael J Frederick, saloon, 20 Clinton, res same.
Michael Otto, student, bds 20 Clinton.
Michael Wm, lab N Y, C & St L R R, res 10 Elm.
Michaelis Charles D, cigarmkr F C Boltz & Co, bds 297 W Jefferson.
Michaelis Charles J, upholsterer P E Wolf, res 297 W Jefferson.
Michaelis Herman F, cigarmkr F C Boltz & Co, bds 297 W Jefferson.
Michaels J Christopher, farmer, bds 5 Victoria ave.
Michaels George, lab, res s w cor Eagle and Taylor.
Michel, *see also Mitchel.*
Michel Adam, lab, res 48 Taylor.
Michel Andrew J, pressman Indiana Staats Zeitung, res 404 E Wayne.
Michel Charles, clk, bds 130 Cass.
Michel Frank J, cooper, res 130 Cass.

Michel Frederick, mach hand Indiana Machine Works, bds 130 Cass.

Michel George, wagonmkr A Vogely, res 517 E Lewis.

Michel George jr, mach hand, bds 517 E Lewis.

Michel John, bds 130 Cass.

Michel Joseph, mach hd Indiana Machine Wks, bds 130 Cass.

Michel Louis, lab, bds 517 E Lewis.

Michel Minnie, domestic 383 E Wayne.

Mick Abraham C, grocer, 283 E Creighton ave, res 62 Greene.

Middaugh Wm D, turner Paul's Pulley Works, rms 35 1st.

Middendorf, see also Mittendorf.

Middendorf Bernard, contractor, res 276 E Wayne.

Middendorf Herman, mason, bds 276 E Wayne.

Middleton George W, removed to Decatur, Ind.

Mienzen, see Meinzen.

Miles Arthur A, lab, res 71 Huron.

Miles Charles, engineer, res 221 W Washington.

Miles David, lab, res 105 Wells.

Miles Helen, milliner Seaney Millinery Co, bds 267 W Washington.

Miles Mary H, milliner, bds 221 W Washington.

Miles Stella, dressmkr M C Patterson, bds 162 Montgomery.

Miles Wm, lab, bds 105 Wells.

Miles Wm, teacher Conservatory of Music, rms Taylor University.

Millard Robert, mdse broker, 20 Schmitz blk, bds 229 W Berry.

Millenbruck Henry, res 148 Greely.

Miller, see also Moeller, Mueller and Muller.

Miller Adolph, wks F J Beach, bds 28 Brandriff.

Miller Albert, brakeman N Y, C & St L R R, res 14 Huron.

Miller Albert F, carp Penn Co, res n s Suttenfield 2 w of Hanna.

Miller Albert T, mach Bass F & M Works, bds 169 E Washington.

Miller Albert W, conductor, res 31 Bass.

Miller Alvina (wid Charles T), res 96 Wilt.

Miller Amelia, tailoress L J Feist, bds 174 Wells.

Miller Andrew, fireman Penn Co, res 40 Clay.

Miller Andrew W, drugs, 363 Lafayette, res same.

Miller Anna, domestic 416 Clinton.

Miller Anthony, finisher Ft Wayne Electric Co, res 96 Wall.

Miller Asenath (wid Wm), bds 23 Miner.

Miller August, gunsmith C H Miller, res 37 Maiden lane.

Miller Barbara, domestic 495 E Washington.

Miller Bernhard F, locksmith C H Miller, bds 50 W Main.

Miller Block, w s Clinton bet Berry and Main.

Miller Carl L, clk Robert Lowry, bds 125 Cass.

r, trav agt G E Bursley & Co, res 161 Harmer.
us A, clk J M Miller, res 295 W Berry.
rine (wid Clement), res 38 Hendricks.
rine (wid John J), res 81 E Washington.
es, carp Penn Co, res 35 Force.
es, fireman Penn Co, res 86 Laselle.
es, lab Olds' Wagon Works, bds 28 Brandriff.
es, patternmkr Bass F & M Works, res 65 Charles.
es, pedler, res 85 Summit.
es, tailor, bds 35 Douglas ave.
es A, teamster, res 34 Scott ave.
es C, asst sec Ft Wayne Electric Co, bds 169 E
gton.
es H, guns, 20 W Main, res 50 same.
es J, tailor A F Schoch, bds 53 Harrison.
es L, engineer, res 126 Cass.
es O, lab Diether & Barrows, bds 513 Broadway.
otte A, mach hd, bds s w cor Lewis and Walton ave.
otte H, grocer, s w cor Lewis and Walton ave, res

cey O, painter estate M L Albrecht, res 23 Miner.
ian, carp, res 239 Madison.
ian, grocer, 61 Wells, res same.
ian C H, foreman Bass F & M Works, res 9 Force.
hristina, cook Ft Wayne City Hospital.
opher H, car repairer Penn Co, res 55 W Williams.
(wid Jacob), artist, 100 W Main, res same.
C, draughtsman, 4 Foster blk, res 101 Lafayette.
at E, clk J B White, bds 38 Hendricks.
l, butcher Frederick Eckart, res 419 W Main.
l, lab, res rear 31 Smith.
E, carp, res 25 Lincoln ave.
S, timekpr Wabash R R, bds 222 W Creighton

W, dairy, res s s Killea nr Webster.
B, carp, bds Joseph A Miller.
M, bds Aldine Hotel.
farmer, res s s Howell nr G R & I R R.
stonecutter Keller & Braun, bds Union House.
E, blksmith Fleming Mnfg Co, res 37 Duck.
, mngr Labor Herald, bds Windsor Hotel.
D, bkkpr The Press, bds s w cor Begue and Erie.
W, brakeman N Y, C & St L R R, bds Schele

V, grocer, 2 Lincoln ave, res 16 same.

Miller Emil A, reporter, bds 169 E Washington.

Miller Emma, seamstress, bds 54 Elm.

Miller Ernst, lab, res 51 W Williams.

Miller Erwin, clk McDonald, Watt & Wilt, bds 81 E Washington.

Miller Esther (wid James), bds 22 Scott ave.

Miller Ethan A, driver Markey & Mungovan, bds Cyrus W Miller.

Miller Flora E, bkkpr Strack & Baker, bds 26 W Jefferson.

Miller Frank, blksmith Kerr-Murray Mnfg Co, res 71 Charles.

Miller Frank, carp, res 69 E DeWald.

Miller Frank, helper, res 239 Barr.

Miller Frank, lab, bds 54 Elm.

Miller Frank, mach, bds Windsor Hotel.

Miller Frank, teamster Bass F & M Works, res 500 Hanna.

Miller Frank M, foreman Ft Wayne Lumber Co, res 796 Broadway.

Miller Frederica, domestic 17 Brackenridge.

Miller Frederick, brakeman, res 293 W Main.

Miller Frederick, carp, res 8 Summit.

Miller Frederick, lab Bass F & M Works, res 5 Force.

Miller Frederick, patternmkr Ft Wayne Electric Co, res 107 Jackson.

Miller Frederick C, bricklayer, bds 8 Summit.

Miller Frederick C, engineer Herman Berghoff Brewing Co, res 424 E Washington.

Miller Frederick J, drugs, 327 Lafayette, res same.

Miller Frederick M, clk Penn Co, res 28 S Wayne ave.

Miller Frederick W, bartender, res 23 Brandriff.

Miller George, res s w cor Lewis and Walton ave.

Miller George, herder Brookside Farm Co, bds same.

Miller George, roofer Gerding & Aumann Bros, bds 28 Brandriff.

Miller George A, engineer Penn Co, res 155 Wallace.

Miller George E, clk August Bruder, bds 182 E Washington.

Miller George F, clk Dreier & Bro, bds 288 E Jefferson.

Miller George F, patternmkr Bass F & M Works, res 67 Force.

Miller George F, sheet iron wkr Penn Co, res 18 Marion.

Miller George P, clk Gombert & Piepenbrink, bds s w cor Lewis and Walton ave.

Miller George S, clk S B Thing & Co, res 344 E Washington.

Miller Gilbert C, teamster, res s w cor Miner and Creighton ave.

Miller Gilbert S, trav agt F C Parham, res 105 Broadway.

Miller Gurnes E, conductor, res 40 Wells.

Miller Harry D, clk Miller & Dougall, bds 273 E Jefferson.

Miller Harvey D, carp, res 122 Fairfield ave.

25

.K & CO.'S

land ave.
yne Organ Co, res 621 Fairfield .

·es 20 Marion.
Union House.
Main.
Vayne Electric Co, res 57 Doug-

7ellman, bds 296 E Washington.
bs & Co, res 36 E DeWald.
.er), res e s Calhoun 1 s of Mar-

s 416 .Hanna.
te, bds 296 E Washington.

·ia.
ın, res same.
er, res 408 E Wayne.
nstrong, res 51 Douglas ave.
Lafayette, res same.
well nr G R & I R R.

} R & I R R.
r, bds 61 Wells.
[R R, res n s Broadway 1 w of

}.
ŭ Co, bds same.
r, bds 408 E Wayne.
hton ave.
·, res 281 E Washington.
ı ave, res same.
ave.
aven ave 2 e of Lumbard.
·ion.
ıs same.
51 W Williams.
Iain, res 52 E Jefferson.
iether & Bro, res 5 Guthrie.

ller Joseph F, trav agt U S Baking Co, bds 38 Hendricks.
ller Joseph L, engineer, res 105 Wilt.
ller Julia (wid Wm H), res 26 W Jefferson.
ller Laura J, clk Isaac Miller, bds 428 Calhoun.
ller Levi H, plasterer, res 183 Jackson.
ller Levi H jr, laborer, bds 183 Jackson.
ller Lillie M, domestic 100 E Columbia.
ller Lorenzo D, clk E F McKee & Co, bds 183 Jackson.
ller Louis, boilermkr, bds 51 W Williams.
ller Louis C, brakeman, res 46 Oliver.
ller Louis J, sheet iron wkr Kerr-Murray Mnfg Co, res 63 W Williams.
ller Louis L, mach Ft Wayne Electric Co, res 109 Fairfield avenue.
ller Louis L, oil pedler, bds 29 Hough.
ller Louisa (wid Samuel), res s w cor Begue and Erie.
ller Louisa E, domestic 186 W Berry.
ller Margaret, waiter Windsor Hotel.
ller Mrs Mary E, dressmkr, 101 Lafayette, res same.
ller Mathias A, boilermkr Wabash R R, res 274 E Lewis.
ller Michael, res 224 W Washington.
ller Minnie, domestic 267 W Wayne.
ller Nathan, fireman, res 108 Fairfield ave.
iller Nathaniel C (Miller & Dougall), Pension Attorney, 4 Foster Blk, res 273 E Jefferson.
ller Nicholas, car repairer Penn Co, res 296 E Washington.
ller Norman F, clk J B White, bds 9 Force.
ller Oscar L, florist B L Auger, bds 16 E Washington.
ller Paul, boxmkr Olds' Wagon Works, res rear 31 Smith.
ller Paul, teamster, res w s Winter 1 s of Pontiac.
ller Peter, res 28 Brandriff.
ller Philip, woodwkr, res 27 Brandriff.
ller Rachel, trimmer E C Smith, bds 58 W Main.
ller Ralph H, barber, bds 13 St Michael ave.
ller Richard, bds 20 Harrison.
ller Robert, weigher, bds Racine Hotel.
ller Robert S, conductor, res 51 Elm.
ller Rolla M, waiter Mergel & Frey, rms 19 W Jefferson.
ller Rosa, tailoress J W Fowles, bds 49 Madison.
ller Rose M, domestic 186 W Berry.
ller Samuel, brakeman, res 40 Hough.
ller Sebastian, market stall No 85, res Wayne twp.
ller Seraphine C, painter, 139 John, res same.
ller Silas E, carp, res 43 Shawnee ave.

G, mach Wabash R R, bds s s Columbia 1 w

N, tinner, res 64 Wall.
, lab, bds Elmwood farm.
, foreman N Y, C & St L R R, res 70 W Main.
ia, bds 29 Buchanan.
k mnfr, e s Hanna s of city limits, res same.
Hartmann & Bro, bds 63 E Wayne.
lener, res 70 Riverside ave.
om Brookside farm, bds same.
man Engine Co No 1, rms same.
k, 3 Dock, res Washington twp.
bds 54 Thomas.
bds 251 Calhoun.
iter, rms 12 E Columbia.
am, Real Estate, Loans, District Land and
Agent, 5 W Main, res 169 E Washington.
ib, res s s Jesse 3 w of Rumsey ave.
b, res s s Columbia 1 w of Clay.
ib Ft Wayne Electric Co, bds 23 Brandriff.
ainter Ft Wayne Organ Co, res 85 Shawnee

artndr Ulrich Stotz, bds 23 E Main.
arp Ft Wayne Electric Co, res 29 Wall.
J, Fresh and Salt Meats, Fish, Oysters, Game
, 228 W Main, res same.
I, Boilermaker, e s Barr 1 n of E Superior,

imster, bds s e cor Lafayette and Columbia.
3, dentist H C Sites, bds Harmon House.
l (Nathaniel C Miller, Allan H Dougall), law-
er blk.
(Henry M Miller, Gottlieb Haller), wall paper,

rnishmkr, bds 149 Barr.
l, carp, res 137 Force.
l C, porter G E Bursley & Co, bds 137 Force.
wid Wm), bds 320 Calhoun.
inisher Am Wheel Co, res 73 Home ave.
ganist, bds 63 Brackenridge.
attendant Indiana School for Feeble-Minded

inisher Am Wheel Co, bds 678 Broadway.
ielper A Hattersley & Sons, bds 95 Riverside

ch Ft Wayne Iron Works, bds 95 W Superior.

J.A.M.STORM, LEATHER and RUBBER BELTING 7 East Columbia St.

FORT WAYNE DIRECTORY. 369

Mills Henry, lab Am Wheel Co, bds 678 Broadway.
Mills Horatio T, mach Penn Co, res 63 Brackenridge.
Mills Lydia, attendant Indiana School for Feeble-Minded Youth.
Mills Percival E, carbldr Penn Co, res 343 W Jefferson.
Mills Theodore H, painter S W Hull, res 95 Riverside ave.
Mills Thomas, mach Wabash R R, res 35 Shawnee ave.
Mills Wm, mach Ft Wayne Electric Co, res 678 Broadway.
Mills Wm G, wheelmkr Am Wheel Co, res Walton ave near
    city limits.
Milton Louisa (col'd, wid Henry), res 35 Monroe.
Mincer Austin A, painter, res 210 W Superior.
Minder Gottfried, harnessmkr A L Johns & Co, res 249 E
    Washington.
Mine Henry, molder, bds 290 Calhoun.
Miner Block, n e cor Clinton and Wayne.
Miner Bros (Wm E and George E), real estate, 19 Schmitz blk.
Miner Charles S, bds 62 Douglas ave.
Miner Charles W, photogr F Schanz, bds 62 Douglas ave.
Miner Dana B, winder Ft Wayne Electric Co, bds 144 W De-
    Wald.
Miner Eli, teamster, res 83 Holman.
Miner George E (Miner Bros), bds 62 Douglas ave.
Miner John J, engineer Troy Steam Laundry, res 100 W
    Superior.
Miner School, s w cor Miner and DeWald.
Miner Samuel R, barber, 311½ W Main, res 313 same.
Miner Sarah (wid Byron D), res 62 Douglas ave.
Miner Silas, teamster, bds 100 W Superior.
Miner Wm E (Miner Bros), res n s High w of city limits.
Minick Frank, boilermkr Penn Co, res 389 E Lewis.
Minneker George H, blksmith Olds' Wagon Works, res 80
    Montgomery.
Minnich Harry, lab, res cor Harrison and 3d.
Minnich James W, ticket agt L S & M S Ry, res 72 Douglas
    avenue.
Minnich Orlan T, shoemkr H D Unstead, bds e s Du Bois 2 s
    of Winch.

Penn Mutual LIFE INSURANCE CO. of PHILA.
CLARK FAIRBANK, General Agent, 19 Court Street.

370   R. L. POLK & CO.'S

Minskey Samuel, junk, res 290 E Wayne.
Mintch Martin M, confectioner, 172 Calhoun, res same.
Mischo Catherine (wid Michael), res 158 Broadway.
Mischo Catherine (wid Nicholas), res 33 Pritchard.
Mischo Catherine, dressmkr, bds 33 Pritchard.
Mischo Elizabeth, dressmkr, bds 158 Broadway.
Mischo John A, mach Ft Wayne Electric Co, bds 33 Pritchard.
Mischo Julia R, domestic 246 W Berry.
Mischo Mary, dressmkr, bds 158 Broadway.
Misner, see also Meisner.
Misner Anna (wid Seymour), res 1 Julia.
Misner Christian, butcher J W Suelzer, rms 422 Lafayette.
Misner Clarence E, fireman Penn Co, bds 311 Lafayette.
Misner Harry O, bds 311 Lafayette.
Misner James A, engineer Penn Co, res 311 Lafayette.
Misner L H, lab Penn Co, res cor Julia and Holton ave.
Mitchel, see also Michel.
Mitchel James, propr Ft Wayne Despatch, 24 Clinton, rms same.
Mitchell Archibald (Beadell & Co), res Norwich, Conn.
Mitchell Miss Della, teacher Clay School.
Mitchell Miss Elizabeth B, teacher Hoagland School, bds 313 Calhoun.
Mitchell James W, hostler, res 209 W Superior.
Mitchell John C, file cutter, res 59 Gay.
Mitchell Lydia, domestic 231 W Jefferson.
Mitchell Wm, engineer, res 5 Edgewater ave.
Mittendorf, see also Middendorf.
Mittendorf Herman, brewer C L Centlivre Brewing Co, res n s St Joseph Gravel rd 1 e of bridge.
Mix Moritz, stonecutter John Jaap, res 2 Elm.
Mixell George, lab, res 3 Duryea.
Mock John A, brakeman, rms 16 Bass.
Moderwell Edward, tinner C F Graffe, res 22 W Jefferson.
Moderwell Hiram C, freight agt N Y, C & St L R R, res 93 W Wayne.
Moderwell Jay M, coal, Plum nr Wells Street bridge, res 53 W Superior.
Moderwell John, carp Paul's Pulley Works, res 73 3d.
Moehring Jennie, domestic C H Worden.
Moeller, see also Miller, Mueller and Muller.
Moeller Bina, seamstress, bds 21 Calhoun.
Moeller Christian, lab, res 66 Chicago.
Moeller Dinah, seamstress The German Reformed Orphans' Home, bds same.
Moeller Frederick, lab, bds 66 Chicago.

Moeller Frederick, teamster, res 60 Division.
Moeller Gustav F H, teamster, bds 215 W Main.
Moeller Herman, wiper, res 21 Calhoun.
Moeller Henry E, boarding house, 215 W Main.
Moellering Anna, bds 120 Montgomery.
Moellering August H F, tailor Thieme Bros, bds 33 Madison.
Moellering Charles B, clk Wm L Moellering, bds 33 Madison.
Moellering Charles E, bkkpr, bds 120 Montgomery.
Moellering Henry A, mach Penn Co, res 33 Madison.
Moellering Henry F (Wm Moellering & Sons), bds 120 Mont-
    gomery.
Moellering Minnie, bds 120 Montgomery.
Moellering Sophie, asst bkkpr, bds 120 Montgomery.
Moellering Wm (Wm Moellering & Sons and Wm Moell-
    ering & Co), Contractor, Builder, Brick Mnfr, Stone Quarry
    and Dealer in Lime, Plaster, Cement, Sewer Pipe, Etc,
    Office 53 to 59 Murray; Brick Yard, Fairfield ave; Stone
    Quarries at Wabash, Ind, res 120 Montgomery. (*See front
    edge and page 5.*)
Moellering Wm & Co (Wm and Wm H F Moellering),
    Brick Mnfrs, w s Hoagland ave s of Rudisill ave.
Moellering Wm & Sons (Wm, Wm F and Henry F),
    Wholesale and Retail Grocers, 215-217 Lafayette and 116
    Montgomery. Tel 126.
Moellering Wm F (Wm Moellering & Sons), res 118 Mont-
    gomery.
Moellering Wm H F (Wm Moellering & Co), w s Hoagland
    ave s of Rudisill ave.
Moellering Wm L, Druggist; Agent for King's German
    Heave Cure and Clipper Corn Cure, n w cor Lewis and
    Lafayette, res 100 E Washington.
Moellring Lena, domestic 241 Broadway.
Moering Henry J, lab Bass F & M Works, res 181 Monroe.
Moffat Rev David W, D D, Pastor First Presbyterian
    Church, res 126 E Berry.
Moffat Miss Helen, bds 126 E Berry.
Mogalle Julius, lab, bds 83 Shawnee ave.
Mohl George, switchman, res 150 Walton ave.
Mohl Philip, driver, res s e cor Walton ave and Erie.
Mohl Philip J, lab, bds 204 Hanna.
Mohlenbrock Henry, lab, res 148 Greely.
Mohler Alonzo D, architect, res 250 W Jefferson.
Mohler Orion E, city editor Ft Wayne Gazette, bds 120 Harri-
    son.
Mohr, *see also Moore.*
Mohr John, bds s w cor Clinton and Washington.

:, cashr Hamilton National Bank, res s w cor Clin-
Washington.
Summit City Paper Co), res 19 W Wayne.
oachman 82 W Berry.
n, lab Penn Co, res w s Hanna 4 s of Pontiac.
les, painter, bds 69 Charles.
hardt, lab, res 69 Charles.
L, carp J M Henry, bds 60 Walnut.
market stall No 69, res Wayne twp.
lso Malone.
ck E, fireman Penn Co, res 57 Laselle.
also Maloney.
les, teamster, bds 260 Clinton.
jamin H, dentist, 76 Calhoun, res 126 W Main.
vard J (Mommer & Stevenson), bds 180 E Lewis.
n, mach Ft Wayne Iron Works, res 174 E Lewis.
n W, foreman, res 6 McClellan.
ph jr, shoes, 76 Calhoun, res 133 W Main.
eph C, molder Bass F & M Works, bds 180 E

anklin, clk Joseph Mommer jr, res 99 W Wash-

s, molder Bass F & M Works, res 180 E Lewis.
J, molder Bass F & M Works, bds 174 E Lewis.
evenson (Edward J Mommer, Wm L Stevenson),
Aveline House blk.
ias, barber, 24 W Main, bds 7 Fulton.
lso Moynihan.
lis (Golden & Monahan), res 65 E Jefferson.
Ellen, carpetsewer Root & Co, res 6 Kansas.
k G, bkkpr C Falk & Co, bds 65 E Jefferson.
J, boilermkr Wabash R R, res 102 Webster.
atilda (wid Henry), res 199 W Superior.
ly, domestic 152 W Washington.
Mong & Meisner), res 76 Riverside ave.
E, paperhanger Kiel & Kiel, bds 76 Riverside ave.
er (George Mong, George Meisner), painters, 75

ULL, Paints, Oils, Varnishes and Glass at 90 Calhoun Street.

y B, Propr Fort Wayne Coffee and Spice
Flour Mills, 73-75 E Columbia, res 143 E

al estate, 61 E Berry, res 143 E Wayne.
mestic 95 E Jefferson.
dr, bds 18 McClellan.
Wm), res 92 Franklin ave.
th, propr Monroe House, 224 Calhoun.
V, electrician Ft Wayne Electric Co, bds

Elizabeth Monroe propr, 224 Calhoun.
ds Monroe House.
s F, lab L C Zollinger, bds 3 Superior.
M, brakeman, bds 71 Baker.
d (col'd), lab, res 98 Franklin ave.
. (wid Wm), res 159 Barr.
finisher, res 71 Baker.
bds 8 Short.
ver Engine Co No 1, rms cor Calhoun and

, waiter, bds 65 Baker.
res 114 Boone.
vid Wm), res 192 Lafayette.
id Enos T), res 213 Fairfield ave.
neer Penn Co, res 275 E Lewis.
r A Hattersley & Sons, bds 43 W Main.
watchman, res 24 Fulton.
, bds 24 Fulton.
b Penn Co, res n e cor Du Bois and Penn.
r.
Troy Steam Laundry, bds 48 W Main.
keman, res 226 High.
rvisor Indiana School for Feeble-Minded

bds Jewel House.
pokemkr, bds 27 St Martin.
gineer Penn Co, res 27 St Martin.
ls 48 W Main.
chman Powers & Barnett, res 48 W Main.
ector, bds Jacob Moore.
neer, res 61 Elm.
narket stall No 90, res Adams twp.
nt, bds 27 St Martin.
es n s Jesse 2 e of Runnion ave.
ds 84 Fairfield ave.
pr Hoffman Bros, res 292 W Jefferson.

W Wayne.
t Frederick Eckart, res 142 W Wayne.
F E Houk, bds 48 W Main.
ohn), res rear 84 Fairfield ave.
omas C), bds 13 Walnut.
res 168 Brackenridge.
ctor, res 23 Suttenfield.
an, res 79 Hoagland ave.
:04 W Berry.
Burgess.
Wabash R R, res 13 Walnut.
s e s Runnion ave 1 s of canal feeder.
eman, bds 407 W Main.
b, bds 164 Harmer.
rer Ft Wayne Organ Co, res 333 Hoag-

urner, bds 333 Hoagland ave.
ess, bds 201 E Wayne.
47 Barr.
er, res 201 E Wayne.
Peter), bds 201 E Wayne.
35 Hanna.
W, Drugs, Barbers' Supplies and
s, 74 Calhoun, res same.
ore.
stall No 43, res Wayne twp.
ds 196 Hanna.
iefer & Son, res 255 Broadway.
in), res 438 Fairfield ave.
bds 438 Fairfield ave.
uctor, res 51 Baker.
domestic 138 E Wayne.
ostoffice, bds 184 E Jefferson.
ealer, res 184 E Jefferson.
zemaster Penn Co, res 111 W Williams.
n), bds 28 Chicago.
an & Beach), vice-pres Old National
hington.
Oliver P Morgan, Frederick Beach),
il Hardware, 19-21 E Columbia.
k P Morganthaler, bds 141 W Wayne.
er (Original Pete), Clothing and
oods, 52½ Calhoun, res 141 W Wayne.

Bass F & M Works, res 11 Oak.

Geo. E. Johnson, DENTIST, 74 Calhoun Street. Res., 188 W. Berry St.

FORT WAYNE DIRECTORY. 375

Moring John C, messenger The News, bds 192 John.
Moritz Elizabeth (wid Peter), res 79 W Berry.
Moritz Harry L, clk Old Fort Mnfg Co, res 1 Riverside ave.
Moritz John M (Miller & Moritz), res 79 W Berry.
Moritz Vincent, fruits, 29 Calhoun, res 1 Sturgis.
Morrey, *see also Murray.*
Morrey Albert R, clerk, res 382 Lafayette.
Morris, Bell, Barrett & Morris (John Morris, Robert C Bell, James M Barrett, Samuel L Morris), Lawyers, s w cor Clinton and Main.
Morris Edward J, switchman Wabash R R, res 15 Poplar.
Morris Edwin C, wheelmkr, bds 105 Barr.
Morris James G, winder Ft Wayne Electric Co, bds 10 Bass.
Morris James J, switchman, res 10 Bass.
Morris John (Morris, Bell, Barrett & Morris), res 77 Maple ave.
Morris John jr (Worden & Morris), deputy clk U S District Court, bds 77 Maple ave.
Morris John, driver, bds 63 W Superior.
Morris Louis W, mason, res 335 Hanna.
Morris Samuel L (Morris, Bell, Barrett & Morris), res 282 W Washington.
Morris Sarah, domestic 105 Barr.
Morris Stephen jr, bkkpr Old National Bank, res 340 W Jefferson.
Morris Wm P, engineer, res 173 W Superior.
Morrison M Henry, heater Penn Co, res 41 E Butler.
Morrow Edward J, mach Kerr-Murray Mnfg Co, bds 401 Hanna.
Morsch John N, watchman, res 69 Wall.
Morse Anna E (wid John B), bds Aldine Hotel.
Morse Frank W, master mechanic Wabash R R, bds Aldine Hotel.
Morton Club, George D Adams sec, n e cor Wayne and Calhoun.
Morton Harry A, barber John Lauer, bds 274 E Wayne.
Morton Thomas, res 274 E Wayne.
Morton Wm H, lab Penn Co, res 314 E Creighton ave.
Morvilious Frank, res 104 Barr.
Mosby Jesse (col'd), waiter The Wayne.
Moser Ambrose, stonecutter Keller & Braun, bds 157 W Main.
Moser Andrew, lab, res 7 Clark.
Moser John G, teamster James Wilding & Son, res 17½ Fairfield ave.
Moser Stephen, engineer App Bros, res 310 E Wayne.
Moses John S, foreman, res 178 W DeWald.
Mosher Wm H, hostler, bds 252 Clinton.
Moshier George K, engineer G R & I R R, rms 17 W Lewis.

ROBERT SPICE, Natural, Gasfitting and Supplies, 48 WEST MAIN AND 11 PEARL STS.

376   R. L. POLK & CO.'s

Mosier Elizabeth, bds 65 Wall.

Mosiman Eliza, bds 99 E Lewis.

Moslander Asa J, baker, 441 Broadway, res same.

Moslander Wm A, clk D J Shaw, bds 24 Oliver.

Moss Frederick, flagman Wabash R R, res 40 Bass.

Moss Frederick V, tester Ft Wayne Electric Co, bds 35 Douglas avenue.

Moss Martin H, helper Bass F and M Works, res e s Lumbard 1 s of Wabash R R.

Moss Mary E (wid John), res 205 E Washington.

Mosshammer August M, Wines, Liquors and Cigars, 54 E Main, res same.

Mosshammer Jacob K, coremkr Bass F & M Works, res 359 E Washington.

Mosshammer John M, lab, res 109 Barr.

Mossman Paul B, bds 328 W Washington.

Mossman Wm E (Mossman, Yarnelle & Co), sec Ft Wayne Furniture Co, res 328 W Washington.

Mossman, Yarnelle & Co (Wm E Mossman, Edward F Yarnelle, W S Sponhauer), whol hardware, 10 W Columbia.

Mote John R, inventor, res s s Columbia, 2 e of Oneida.

Moten Moses (col'd), engineer Kerr-Murray Mnfg Co, res 70 Murray.

Motherwell Alice (Motherwell Sisters), bds 73 W 3d.

Motherwell Annie (Motherwell Sisters), bds 73 W 3d.

Motherwell Henry J, tinner A H Staub, bds 73 W 3d.

Motherwell John, carp, res 73 W 3d.

Motherwell John E, tinner, res 22 W Jefferson.

Motherwell Mary, mach hand, bds 73 W 3d.

Motherwell Michael, apprentice The Sentinel, bds 73 W 3d.

Motherwell Sisters (Alice and Annie), dressmkrs, 73 W 3d.

Motherwell Wm, plasterer, bds 73 W 3d.

Motsch Fritz, Boarding House, 518 Fairfield ave.

Motz John G, tailor and cigars, 47 W Main, res 30 E 2d.

Motz John G A, clk J G Motz, bds 30 E 2d.

Mounsir Ada, clk M Frank & Co, bds 50 Brackenridge.

Mowrer, *see also Maurer.*

Mowrer Isaac, County Treasurer; Office Court House, res 221 W Main.

Mowrer Jacob, lab, res 589 E Washington.

Mowrer Jacob jr, lab, bds 589 E Washington.

Moynihan, *see also Monahan.*

Moynihan Andrew J, editor Ft Wayne Journal, res 128 Lafayette.

Moynihan Johanna (wid Martin), bds 128 Lafayette.

Mudge Jeremiah C, carp Griffith & Son, res 108 W DeWald.

Mudge John A, carp Griffith & Son, bds 108 W DeWald.

er, bds 108 W DeWald.
A (Laible & Muehlfeith), res 42 E 3d.
ailor George Motz, bds 42 E 3d.
, maltster C S Centlivre Brewing Co, res 16

'iller, Moeller and Muller.
amstress, bds rear 186 Wells.
rp, bds 10 Pritchard.
W, engineer, res 10 Pritchard.
, tailor J G Thieme & Son, bds 49 Barthold.
mster, bds rear 186 Wells.
W, clk A C Brase, bds 73 W Jefferson.
eamster, res rear 186 Wells.
seshoer Louis Swartz, bds 84 Barr.
inisher Peters Box and Lumber Co, bds 49

domestic 216 W Wayne.
rber M Momper, rms 10 Pritchard.
lermkr, res 389 E Lewis.
les, porter Carnahan & Co, res 250 E Wash-

rles, mach hd Rhinesmith & Simonson, bds

rich C G, cabtmkr Penn Co, res 213 E Jef-

la, bds 238 E Washington.
erick, helper Penn Co, bds 213 E Jefferson.
ttreich, mngr Pape Furniture Co, res 238 E

Wm, wagonmkr Fleming Mnfg Co, bds 20

av, clk J B White, bds 238 E Washington.
sa, dressmkr, bds 238 E Washington.
ie, domestic 24 W Berry.
C, cabtmkr Peters Box and Lumber Co, bds
gton.
messenger Hamilton National Bank, bds 166

) (Charles F Muhler & Son), bds 166 W

Charles F Muhler & Son), res 166 W Wayne.
& Son (Charles F and Bernard C), lime,
nent, 1 N Calhoun.
s 129 W Main.
hlfeith.
rd, watchman The Wayne.

der, mach, s e cor Calhoun and Suttenfield.
, pedler Peter A Moran, bds 201 E Wayne.
, watchman, res w s Spy Run ave 7 n of river

blksmith est of M L Albrecht, bds Richard

J, brakeman, res 119 John.
rms 37 W Main.
, painter, 12 E Berry, bds 280 E Lewis.
et (wid Patrick), res 280 E Lewis.
s, grocer, 117 Fairfield ave, res 115 same.
er, res 67 Gay.
vid Wm), res 12 Colerick.
, printer, bds 12 Colerick.
lab, bds 12 Colerick.
b N Leonard, bds 57 Barr.
kkpr F C Boltz, rms 10 W Main.
ab N Leonard, bds 140 Barr.
Tiller, Moeller and Mueller.
iach hand Wayne Knitting Mills, bds 375 W

ister App Bros, bds 164 Harmon.
,b, res rear 31 Smith.
raughtsman Ft Wayne Iron Works, rms 123

oremkr Bass F & M Works, res 110 Eliza.
domestic 216 W Wayne.
lriver Julius Remus, bds 442 Broadway.
ear 31 Smith.
iach hd Wayne Knitting Mills, bds 212 Jones.
id Henry), res 373 Calhoun.
strumentmkr, bds 373 Calhoun.
ab, bds 47 Barr.
ggageman, bds 373 Calhoun.
strumentmkr, bds 373 Calhoun.
, brakeman, res 7 Cass.
res 52 N Harrison.
lksmith Ind Mach Wks, res 115 Barthold.
W, baker G H Jacobs & Bro, bds 62 E Main.
b Penn Co, res 96 Baker.
rician, res 98 Baker.
helper J C Peters, bds Wm Mundt.
er, res s w cor St Mary's ave and Aboit.
reet commissioner, res 214 E Wayne.
tenogr Star Iron Tower Co, bds 214 E

Mungen W Wallace (Loag & Mungen), bds 214 E Wayne.
Munger Mary (wid Claus), res 63 Maumee rd.
Mungovan Franklin (Markey & Mungovan), res 321 Harrison.
Mungovan Thomas C, steelwkr Wabash R R, res 607 Calhoun.
Mungoven Wm E, fireman G R & I R R, res 291 Harrison.
Munich John, barber, 352 Calhoun, res 37 E Williams.
Munroe, *see Monroe.*
Munson Ada, clk, bds 50 Brackenridge.
Munson Charles A, trav agt, bds 22 W Wayne.
Murphy Amos W, painter F H Treep, res 253 E Washington.
Murphy Bernard, lab, bds 47 Barr.
Murphy Daniel, lab, bds 47 Barr.
Murphy David J, mach hand, bds 138 Holman.
Murphy Dennis C, switchman N Y, C & St L R R, res 51
  Prince.
Murphy Edward, engineer G R & I R R, bds 46 E Jefferson.
Murphy Frank, engineer, res 10 St Mary's ave.
Murphy George, bell boy The Randall.
Murphy George, gardener, res 9 Colerick.
Murphy Harry, bartndr The Wayne, rms 121 Harrison.
Murphy Johanna (wid Dennis), res 7 Colerick.
Murphy John, mach Ft Wayne Electric Co, res 138 Holman.
Murphy John C, engineer, rms 34 W Main.
Murphy John H, helper, bds 53 Force.
Murphy John J, boilermkr Wabash R R, res 72 S Wayne ave.
Murphy Miss Mabel C, clk F H Treep, bds 217 E Wayne.
Murphy Michael, engineer, res 151 Fairfield ave.
Murphy Nicholas, brakeman, bds 151 Fairfield ave.
Murphy Nicholas E, mach Wabash R R, bds 151 Fairfield ave.
Murphy Patrick, brakeman, bds 138 Holman.
Murphy Patrick, policeman, res 54 Melita.
Murphy Samuel C, painter Penn Co, res 53 Force.
Murphy Thomas J, clk Nickel Plate R R, bds 12 Kansas.
Murphy Wm, brakeman Penn Co, res 138 Holman.
Murphy Wm H, lab, bds 53 Force.
Murphy Wm J, lab Ft Wayne Electric Co, res 28 Pritchard.
Murray, *see also Morrey.*
Murray Charles, teamster, res s e cor Putnam and Koch.
Murray David, blksmith Wabash R R, res 29 Pritchard.
Murray Jacob, collarmkr A Racine, bds s w cor Clark and
  Putnam.
Murray James, plumber, res 423 E Washington.
Murray John, cabinetmkr Louis Diether & Bro, res 283 E
  Washington.
Murray Mary A, tailoress A Foster, bds 39 W Washington.
Murray Newton, lineman, res 71 Smith.

y Ophelia (wid Americus), res 15 Baker.

y O B, paper hanger Keil & Keil, bds Jewel House.

gh Wm H, vice-pres Peters Box and Lumber Co, res eoria, Ill.

ı Joseph, cabinetmkr Ft Wayne Organ Co, bds 287 S roadway.

, see also Maer, Maher, Maier, Mayer, Meier, Meyer and leyers.

Alice, bds 109 Holman.

Arthur A, brakeman, res 74 Gay.

August, carp, res n s Wagner 6 w of St Joseph river. Block, 108 Fairfield ave.

Charles A, brakeman, res 140 E Washington.

Charles F, street sprinkler, res 66 Douglas ave.

Christopher, carp, res 124 Union.

Cornelius C, helper Penn Co, res 139 Francis.

Darwin S, stenogr Ft Wayne Electric Co, bds 157 W ʃayne.

Frederick H, livery, 62 E Wayne, res 49 Douglas ave.

Frederick W, finisher Horton Mnfg Co, res 393 W ain.

George, cigar mnfr, 223 Broadway, res same.

George W, helper Penn Co, bds 98 W Williams.

Hallie, bds 23 E Williams.

Harry, fireman, bds 43 Elm.

Henry, mattressmkr P E Wolf.

Henry C, lab C F Myers, bds 66 Douglas ave.

John, lab, bds 64 E Berry.

Joseph, finisher Horton Mnfg Co, bds 74 Cherry.

Josephine (wid Victor), res 200 W Superior.

Lee, brakeman, bds 43 Elm.

Martin V, carbldr Penn Co, res 409 Lafayette.

Mary (wid Christian W), grocer, s e cor St Mary's ave l Spring, res same.

Mary A (wid James D), res 109 Holman.

ɔ J Henry, chief clk Nickel Plate R R, res 171 E Berry.

Sherman H, brakeman, bds 140 Fairfield ave.

Theodore, engineer, bds 43 Elm.

Wm, blksmith Penn Co, res 98 W Williams.

Wm F, veterinary surgeon, 62 E Wagner, res 66 Doug-

N

blo Ephraim, clk Stewart & Hahn, bds 27 E Washington.
gel Frederick, storekpr Wabash R R, res 99 W Jefferson.
gel Joseph M, horseshoer Fred Becker & Bro, bds 41 Cass.
gel Kate, tailoress, bds 41 Cass.
gel Lawrence E, cigarmkr F J Gruber, bds 41 Cass.
gel Xavier, woodwkr Chauvey Bros, res 41 Cass.
hrwold, *see also Norwold.*
hrwold Charles, carp, bds 267 E Lewis.
hrwold Charles carp, res 134 Eliza.
hrwold Charles, plasterer, 265 E Lewis, res same.
hrwold Christian, boilermkr, res 147 E Lewis.
hrwold Conrad, mach Penn Co, res 267 E Lewis.
hrwold Diedrich, carp Bass F & M Works, res 164 Smith.
hrwold Diedrich jr, molder Bass F & M Works, res s w cor
  Smith and Emily.
hrwold Ernest, carp, res 415 E Lewis.
ırwold Frederick, molder Bass F & M Works, bds 122 Force.
hrwold Frederick C, lab Penn Co, res 25 Wilt.
ırwold Frederick C jr, lab Penn Co, bds 25 Wilt.
hrwold Henry, mach hand Horton Mnfg Co, bds 25 Wilt.
ırwold Louisa, domestic 248 W Wayne.
hrwold Mamie, bds 59 Wells.
ırwold Sophia, domestic 204 W Berry.
ırwold Wm, foreman Horton Mnfg Co, res 29 Wilt.
·r Katie, domestic 95 Berry.
ıby David, driver Powers & Barnett, bds 37 Barr.
ıh Frederick E, trav agt, res 173 Griffith.
ıh Henry, blksmith Olds' Wagon Works, res 72 Hamilton.
ıhan Charles, clk Julius Nathan & Co, bds 142 W Berry.
ıhan Julius (Julius Nathan & Co), res 142 W Berry.
ıhan Julius & Co (Julius Nathan, Max Rubin), wholesale
  .liquors, 137 Calhoun.
ıonal Express Co, L P Hulburd agt, Court opp Court
  House.
ıght Duncan, stonecutter George Jaap, bds 63 W 5th.
ɾe George, painter, res 11 Hoffman.
ɾe Isaac, carp, res 116 Walton ave

ase Ulysses S, lab, bds 216 W Washington.
braska School, s e cor Fry and Boone.
bur John, lab Penn Co, res 25 Lillie.
eb August J, candymkr, bds 54 Oakley.
eb Catherine (wid George J), res 54 Oakley.
eb Emma C, dressmkr, bds 54 Oakley.
eb John G, clk McDonald, Watt & Wilt, res 60 Walnut.
eb Louis, carver Ft Wayne Organ Co, bds 54 Oakley.
eb Wm G, clk, bds 54 Oakley.
edmeyer Mary, domestic Hotel Rich.
es Henry B, tinner Penn Co, res 36 Wilt.
es Henry C C, cabtmkr Penn Co, res 28 Schick.
ff August, car bldr Penn Co, res 70 Boone.
ff John H, harnessmkr A L Johns & Co, bds 224 W Main.
ff John H, farmer, res 461 W Main.
ff John S, clk U S Ex Co, bds 19 E Jefferson.
ff Mrs Martha T, bds 461 W Main.
ff Rebecca (wid Enoch), res 461 W Main.
ff Wm, driver J P Finkham, res 224 W Main.
her Catherine, domestic, bds 121 Calhoun.
her Frank, helper Bass F & M Works, bds 12 Francis.
her John V, polisher, res n s Pontiac 1 w of Warsaw.
her Joseph, shoemkr, res 12 Francis.
her Lizzie M, dressmkr Mrs G J Stier, bds 12 Francis.
dhart Joseph, cabtmkr Ft Wayne Organ Co, res 60 Madison.
dhofer Mary, bds 61 St Martin.
l John, fireman, rms 368 W Main.
man, *see Nieman.*
reiter Conrad, insurance, 269 W Washington, res same.
reiter Eva A (wid Caspar B), res 170 W Superior.
reiter Wm, mach hand Ft Wayne Electric Co, bds 269 W
  Washington.
rhood James, carp, bds 298 Hoagland ave.
ie Frederick K, clk J B White, res 151 Barr.
iwonger, *see also Niswonger.*
iwonger David H, brakeman Penn Co, res 31 Eliza.
iwonger Henry W, physician, 284 E Jefferson, res same.
iwonger Roland C, mach, bds 284 E Jefferson.
en Samuel, stonecutter, bds 157 W Main.
igan John F, mach Penn Co, res 23 W Lewis.
igan Michael, mach Penn Co, res 58 Douglas ave.
on Augustus, mach hand, bds 79 Brackenridge.
on Elizabeth (wid Elmore N), res 60 W Wayne.
on Helen E (wid DeGroff), res 262 W Berry.
on Henry, actionmkr Ft Wayne Organ Co, res 41 Miner.
on John, cabtmkr Ft Wayne Organ Co, res 116 Home ave.

Nelson Mark A, pressman Ft Wayne Newspaper Union, res 59
   Wilt.
Nelson Nels K, blksmith Olds' Wagon Works, res 49 E Williams.
Nelson Thomas N, helper Kerr-Murray Mnfg Co, bds 95 W
   Superior.
Nerhood Miss Fianna, bds 43 E Butler.
Nerhood Jacob J, carp Griffith & Sons, bds 59 W Williams.
Nerhood Lillian F, opr Hoosier Mnfg Co, bds 217 W Superior.
Nerhood Matilda, nurse Ft Wayne City Hospital.
Nern Conrad, lab, res s w cor Coombs and Cochran.
Nern Conrad jr, teamster, res 157 Erie.
Nesbit Mollie (wid Isaac), res 80 N Harrison.
Nessel Caroline P C, clk, bds 463 Lafayette.
Nessel Christina (wid Michael), res 463 Lafayette.
Nessel John G A, mach hand Penn Co, bds 463 Lafayette.
Nessel Wilhelmina I S, packer, bds 463 Lafayette.
Nessler John, lab, res w s Lumbard 1 s of Wabash R R.
Nestel Adolph G, shoes, 189 Lafayette, res 187½ same.
Nestel's Block, s w cor Broadway and W Jefferson.
Nestel Charles W, actor, bds 243 W Creighton ave.
Nestel Daniel, nurseryman, w s Broadway opp Creighton ave,
   res 243 W Creighton ave.
Nestel Daniel jr, well driver, res 114 Home ave.
Nestel Miss Eliza, actress, bds 243 W Creighton ave.
Nestel Oscar W, trav agt, res 223 W DeWald.
Nestel Philip E, painter, res 189 Lafayette.
Neu Joseph, helper Wabash R R, res 501 Lafayette.
Neubert Karl A, mach hd Wayne Knitting Mills, bds 391 W
   Main.
Neuenschwander Isaac M, res 25 Randolph.
Neufer John M (J Hetrick & Co), res 160 E Wayne.
Neufer Leonard, hostler Wabash R R, res 419 Calhoun.
Neuhaus Frank, gardener, res 61 Hoffman.
Neubaus Frank A, gardener, bds 61 Hoffman.
Neuhaus Louisa, bds 61 Hoffman.
Neuhaus Reinhard H, shoemkr, 40 Harrison, res same.
Neukamm George, dairy, res s e cor Pontiac and Smith.
Neukamm John, lab George Neukamm, bds same.
Neumann, *see also Newman.*
Neumann Albert, tinner, bds 158 Taylor.
Neumann August A, miller Mayflower Mills, res 158 Taylor.
Neumann Clara, opr Hoosier Mnfg Co, bds 158 Taylor.
Neumann Elizabeth, domestic 132 Wallace.
Neumann John, lab, res 480 Hanna.
Neumann Louis D, carp, res 57 Force.
Neumann Martha, opr Hoosier Mnfg Co, bds 119 Force.

 t & co.'s

E Creighton ave.
,ewis.
·ay Mnfg Co, res 62 Lillie.
Lewis, res same.
aylor.
37 Stophlet.
sville State rd 2½ miles ·e of

Oppelt, res 24 Chicago.
, res 145 Griffith.
wcomer, bds same.
n Co, res 79 Douglas ave.
'ark ave.
1d School, bds 79 Douglas ave.
V Main.
Tayne Electric Co, bds 174 W

res 174 W Creighton ave.
74 W Creighton ave.
eford, res 64 W Wayne.
>, res 220 E Lewis.

dancing, rms 303 Calhoun.
Sentinel, res 134 Wells.
na.
Chicago.
190 W Berry.
agt Wabash R R, res 130 W

Co), res 190 W Berry.
Winter and Creighton ave.
inter and Creighton ave.
& Co, bds 190 W Berry.
R (Nickel Plate), passenger
in and Clinton; freight depot

) Gillham mngr, installment

ime.

John J, carp, res 62 Walnut.
Joseph, mach Wabash R R, res 34 Hendricks.
Otto, molder Bass F & M Works, res 48 Hendricks.
Peter P, mach Wabash R R, res 22 Nirdlinger ave.
rman C, removed to Peoria, Ill.
late Depot, see N Y, C & St L R R Depot.
Plate Restaurant, Wm C Seidel & Bro Proprs,
cel Plate Depot.
Andrew J, engineer G R & I R R, res s e cor Simon
Winter.
James M, Fireman G R & I R R, res 78 John.
John F, engineer G R & I R R, res 130 W Washington.
Alexander, lab, bds 47 Baker.
James, receiver Ft Wayne Electric Co, bds 47 Baker.
Wm, shoemkr Joseph Lerch, res 47 Baker.
Wm C, cabtmkr Fort Wayne Organ Co, bds 47 Baker.
n Christian, lab, res 308 Harrison.
n Ezra, lab, res 81 Home ave.
n Lorenzo H, lab, res 55 W 5th.
Addison B, lumber, res s w cor Webster and Park pl.
Jay T, engineer County Jail, rms 18 E Columbia.
us Charles, carp, res 52 Grace ave.
us Oscar, lab, res 180 Metz.
Lola, domestic 24 Boone.
rederick, car builder Penn Co, res n s Chestnut 2 e of
bard.
ames, bds n s Chestnut 2 e of Lumbard.
ohn, mach Penn Co, res 32 W Butler.
ohn M, mach, res 82 W Creighton ave.
ll F Wm, student, bds 201 E Washington.
ll Henry, baker, 201 E Washington, res same.
erger Lena, domestic J H Bass.
eyer Frederick, molder, bds 24 Laselle.
eyer Joseph J, helper Bass F & M Works, res 30 La-
.
eyer Paul, res 24 Laselle.
eyer Peter, molder Bass F & M Works, bds 24 Laselle.
mer George, bill poster City Bill Posting Co, res 35
ita.
mer George H, mach, bds 35 Melita.
mer Hervey C, carrier Postoffice, bds 35 Melita.
mer Sybil A, clk, bds 35 Melita.
Gustav, lab, bds 58 Hayden.
Benjamin, pedler, res 320 E Jefferson.
Bernard, clk Theodore Nieman, bds 272 E Washington.
Clara, clk Theodore Nieman, bds 272 E Washington.

ab, bds 326 E Washington.
chman Salimonie Mining & Gas Co, res 326
n.
ainter Olds' Wagon Works, bds 326 E Wash-

onductor, res 276 W Jefferson.
ruits, res 41 Smith.
  grocer, 274 E Washington, res 272 same.
pr Hoosier Mnfg Co, bds 326 E Washington.
  grocer, 148 Calhoun, res 68 Brackenridge.
F (Meyer & Niemann), bds 68 Brackenridge.
, bkkpr Gottlieb Niemann, bds 68 Bracken-

dent, bds 68 Brackenridge.
  tailoress, bds 155 Madison.
n, res n s New Haven ave 6 w of Lumbard.
', clk Geo DeWald & Co, bds 155 Madison.
res 155 Madison.
) jr, clk Isidor Lehman, bds 155 Madison.
, clk, res 157 Madison.
teamster, bds 155 Madison.
C, lab Penn Co, res 210 W Creighton ave.
, foreman, res 385 E Wayne.
H, cigarmkr F C Boltz & Co, res 110 Rich-

rid Martin A), bds 210 W Creighton ave.
C F, physician, 298 Calhoun, res same.
s 90 Harmer.
ab Penn Co, res 118 Madison.
rp, res 51 Holton ave.
udent, bds 20 W Jefferson.
er Penn Co, bds 20 W Jefferson.
omestic Lake Shore Hotel.
mkr, bds 77½ Hoagland ave.
elper, bds 77½ Hoagland ave.
s 13 Clark.

Ninde L M & H W (Lindley M and Henry W), lawyers, 42 W Berry.

Niswonger George D, Fish, Oysters and Poultry; Game in Season, 16 Arcade Bldg, res 170 W Washington. (*See page 69.*)

Nitche Emil, helper Bass F & M Works, res 43 Smith.

Nix Charles, molder Bass F & M Works, bds 80 E Jefferson.

Nix Henry, shoemkr P J Eggemann, res 531 E Wayne.

Nix John, brakeman, bds 80 E Jefferson.

Nix John, carp, bds Weber House.

Nix Joseph, shoemkr P J Eggemann, res 142 Barr.

Nix Lizzie, dressmkr, bds 80 E Jefferson.

Nix Matilda, domestic 88 W Berry.

Nix Salina L, milliner A Mergentheim, bds 80 E Jefferson.

Nix Valentine, shoemkr, 80 E Jefferson, res same.

Nixon Roger S, butcher Ft Wayne Beef Co, res 105 High.

Noazk Augusta, domestic 127 W Wayne.

Noazk Henry, waiter Wm C Seidel & Bro, bds 52½ Calhoun.

Noble Charles, mach hand Ft Wayne Spoke Works, res s e cor Pittsburgh and Bond.

Noble Charles E, lumber, bds 33 Brackenridge.

Noble Edward D, woodworker Anthony Wayne Mnfg Co, res 80 Walton ave.

Noble Hubert E, clk Nickel Plate R R, bds 84 Brackenridge.

Noble James, driver, bds 121 Calhoun.

Noble James E, trav agt Bass F & M Works, res 33 Brackenridge.

Noble Jane (wid Wm L), bds 232 Fairfield ave.

Noble John E, electrician, 28 John, res same.

Noble Lyman, market stall No 76, res Adams twp.

Noble Nettie E, stenogr F E Ellison, bds 138 Jackson.

Noble Sarah (wid Lester), res 138 Jackson.

Noble Wm H, mach, res 84 Brackenridge.

Noble Wm K, lumber, bds 33 Brackenridge.

Noeck Christian, coremkr, res 12 Pine.

Noecker James L, bds 49 Baker.

Noecker Mary (wid Ferdinand), res 49 Baker.

Noesler John, lab Penn Co, res 1 Lumbard.

Noftzger Charles E, trav agt Mossman, Yarnelle & Co, res 382 Fairfield ave.

Nogal Leslie H (Nogal & Hyde), res 246 Calhoun.

Nogal & Hyde (Leslie H Nogal, Charles L Hyde), second-hand goods, 246 Calhoun.

Nohe Edward G, tailor Andrew Foster, res 26 Nirdlinger ave.

Nohe John, mach Ft Wayne Iron Works, res 19 Nirdlinger avenue.

vid Joseph), res 40 Hendricks.
emkr, res 21 Nirdlinger ave.
saloon, 64 E Columbia, rms same.
saloon, 49 E Main, bds 29 same.
ib, res 54 Chicago.
mach Penn Co, bds 328 Lafayette.
engineer Penn Co, res 24 Charles.
milliner, bds 328 Lafayette.
:lk B R Noll, bds 97 W Wayne.
clk J A Armstrong, bds 239 E Jefferson.
A, clk Golden & Monahan, res 63 E Jefferson.
ison, res 150 W Jefferson.
vid Martin), bds 129 E Jefferson.
ict R, Druggist, 10 E Columbia and 128
res 97 W Wayne.
H, bds 97 W Wayne.
eats, 109 Barthold, res same.
clk, bds 109 Barthold.
trav agt J A Armstrong, bds 22 Brackenridge.
ller Ft Wayne Organ Co, bds 150 W Jefferson.
, teacher Conservatory of Music, res 68 Clay.
lab Wabash R R, res 49 Nirdlinger ave.
av agt J A Armstrong, res 239 E Washington.
, Boots and Shoes, 22 Clinton, res same.
kpr Julius Nathan & Co, res 7 Harmer.
rav agt J A Armstrong, res 22 Brackenridge.
lumber Robert Ogden, bds 129 E Jefferson.
ter Penn Co, res 129 E Jefferson.
er, 11 Simon, res same.
r, res s s Main w of G R & I R R.
ch, bds 11 Simon.
B R Noll, bds 97 W Wayne.
iecutter George Jaap, bds 7 Harmer.
Penn Co, res 178 Gay.
ena M (wid Frank), res w s Spy Run ave 6 n

vid Jefferson B), res 131 E Washington.
drew, grocer, 130 Broadway, res 205 W Jef-

ie, music teacher, 205 W Jefferson, bds same.
ert G, removed to Hartford City, Ind.
Agnes Hamilton pres, Miss Helen Moffatt
r blk.
erine, res 137 Fairfield ave.
b, res 30 E Superior.
e (wid David), res 39 Duck.

L. O. HULL, PAINTING <u>and</u> PAPER HANGING
AT 90 CALHOUN STREET.

FORT WAYNE DIRECTORY. 389

Noonan Mary (wid Joseph), res 79 E Columbia.
Nordeen August, actionmkr Ft Wayne Organ Co, bds 229 Indiana ave.
Norris Calvin J, driver, bds 30 E Columbia.
Norris Jeremiah, brakeman, bds 47 W Superior.
Norris Mary (wid Calvin), res 30 E Columbia.
North David V, fireman Penn Co, res 16 Murray.
North George, bartndr, rms 29 E Main.
Northrop James L, pumper, res n e cor St Mary's ave and Spring.
Northrop Rev Stephen A, pastor First Baptist Church, res 36 Montgomery.
Norton Susan B (wid John T), res 77½ Hoagland ave.
Norwald, *see also Nahrwold.*
Norwald John E, mach hand Olds' Wagon Works, bds 383 Lafayette.
Norwald Wm C, lab, res 383 Lafayette.
Notestine Joseph H (Notestine & Getz), res 48 W 3d.
Notestine Wm M, fireman G R & I R R, res 118 W Williams.
Notestine & Getz (Joseph H Notestine, Joseph G Getz), Grocery and Saloon, 15-17 Harrison.
Nowak Edward, carp, res 234 John.
Noz Christian F, coremkr Bass F & M Works, res 12 Pine.
Nugent Edward, molder, bds 25 Hough.
Nulf Clarence M, brakeman, bds 69 Smith.
Nulf Edward L, conductor, res 139 E DeWald.
Nulf Philip H, fireman Penn Co, res 69 Oliver.
Null Wm T, carp, res 334 E Washington.
Nunemaker Cyrillus A, baggageman, res 50 John.
Nusbaum Peter, foreman, res s s Emily 1 w of Spy Run ave.
Nuse John, molder, res 490 Hanna.
Nussmann Anthony E, harnessmkr G R Wells, bds 231 E Wayne.
Nussmann Catherine (wid John), res 231 E Wayne.
Nussmann Josephine B, clk H H G Upmeyer, bds 231 E Wayne.
Nuttman Caroline L (wid Joseph D), res 130 W Berry.
Nuttman Joseph D, died Sept 6, 1890.
Nuttman & Co, Oliver S Hanna Cash, Bankers, 32 E Main.
Nyboer John H, car bldr Penn Co, res 94 Force.
Nye Lewis S, conductor Nickel Plate R R, res 189 W Superior.
Nyland Frances, seamstress, bds 95 Smith.
Nyland Henry, blksmith Bass F & M Works, res 95 Smith.
Nysewander Abraham, carp, res 458 Calhoun.

O

Oakley Chauncey B, bkkpr J C Peters, res 240 W Main.
Oaks Sumner, conductor, res 374 Lafayette.
Oberlin Lydia (wid Wm), bds 114 Runnion ave.
Oberlin Otto H, clk, bds 114 Runnion ave.
Oberly Joseph, lab, bds 27 Force.
O'Brien, *see also Bryan.*
O'Brien Catherine A, clk A Goodman, bds 134 Fulton.
O'Brien Dennis, res 225 W Washington.
O'Brien Frank, fireman, bds 84 W Main.
O'Brien Jane (wid Thomas), res 134 Fulton.
O'Brien John D, clk C E Everett, bds 225 W Washington.
O'Brien John H, plumber James Madden, bds 134 Fulton.
O'Brien Martin W, engineer, Nickel Plate R R, bds 134 Fulton.
O'Brien Mary (wid Michael), res 22 Charles.
O'Brien Michael, fireman Penn Co, bds 415 Lafayette.
O'Brien Thomas J, porter Hotel Rich, bds 134 Fulton.
O'Brien Wm P, driller Ft Wayne Electric Co, bds 225 W Washington.
O'Callahan, *see Callahan.*
O'Connell Catherine (wid Daniel), res 259 Webster.
O'Connell Edward J, clk Penn Co, res 147 Fairfield ave.
O'Connell George C, mach hand Horton Mnfg Co, bds 259 Webster.
O'Connell James, foreman Ft Wayne Furniture Co, res 420 E Wayne.
O'Connell John, policeman, res 99 W Main.
O'Connell John H, plumber A Hattersley & Sons, bds 99 W Main.
O'Connell Miss Josephine, bds 44 E Butler.
O'Connell Thomas, bds 259 Webster.
O'Connell Thomas, messenger, bds 41 Hugh.
O'Connell Wm, fireman G R & I R R, bds 99 W Main.
O'Connor, *see also Conners and Connors.*
O'Connor Bernard, res 156 W Wayne.
O'Connor Bernard S (Eckart & O'Connor), res 127 W Wayne.
O'Connor Bridget (wid Jeremiah), res 184 Madison.
O'Connor Charles, painter, bds 163 Hanna.
O'Connor Dennis, lab, res 20 Custer ave.
O'Connor Dennis, mach hand Penn Co, res 16 Poplar.
O'Connor Emma, domestic 92 W Main.
O'Connor Frederick B, train despatcher Penn Co, rms 188' Calhoun.
O'Connor Jeremiah, blksmith Penn Co, res 46 Baker.
O'Connor John, helper Penn Co, res 251 Webster.

Geo. E. Johnson, DENTIST, 74 Calhoun Street. Res., 188 W. Berry St.

FORT WAYNE DIRECTORY. 391

O'Connor Joseph M, res 167 W Washington.
O'Connor Mrs Joseph M, boarding house, 167 W Washington.
O'Connor Julia, seamstress, bds 184 Madison.
O'Connor Louise (wid Stephen), boarding house, 19 W Jefferson.
O'Connor Mary, clk Beadell & Co, bds 251 Webster.
O'Connor Nellie, dressmkr, bds 46 Baker.
O'Connor Wm F, mach hand, bds 251 Webster.
Odd Fellows' Block, n e cor Wayne and Calhoun.
Odd Fellows' Hall, 20 W Berry.
Oddou Amelia, opr Hoosier Mnfg Co, bds 74 W 5th.
Oddou Frank E, clk Joseph F Oddou, bds 48 E Columbia.
Oddou Joseph F, grocer, 48 E Columbia, res same.
Oddou Peter, carp, res 34 W 5th.
Oechtering Miss Antoinette, bds 142 E Jefferson.
Oechtering Rev John H, pastor St Mary's German Catholic
    Church, res 142 E Jefferson.
Oehler Louis G, lab J Derheimer, res 217 W Superior.
Oelschlaeger Frederick, tailor, res 66 Baker.
Oertel Herman, lab Bass F & M Works, res 101 Smith.
Oesterheld Frederick, tailor, res 126 Gay.
Oestermann, *see also Ostermann.*
Oestermann George, tinner, res 307 E Washington.
Oestermann Henry, watchman, res 320 E Washington.
Oestermeier Frederick, lab Bass F & M Works, res 99 Smith.
Oestermeyer Charles, tailor John Rabus, res 48 Leith.
Oetting Ferdinand D, saloon, 214 Fairfield ave, res 63 Shawnee
    avenue.
Oetting Frederick, contractor, 126 Eliza, res same.
Oetting Henry, mason, res 374 E Lewis.
Oetting Wm, baker B Gutermuth, bds 29 W Columbia.
Oetting Wm H, Sewer Contractor, 37 Hough, res same.
Ofenloch Catherine, clk, bds 32 Force.
Ofenloch Frank, meats, 100 Barr, bds 104 same.
Ofenloch Mary M, book sewer C E Davis, bds 130 Francis.
Ofenloch Michael, mach, res 130 Francis.
Ofenloch Peter A, grocer, 365 Lafayette, bds 32 Force.
Ofenloch Valentine, grocer, 30 Force, res 32 same.
Offerle Joseph, lab Bass F & M Works, res 27 Force.
Offerle Lawrence, brewer C L Centlivre Brewing Co, res Centlivre's addition nr brewery.
Offner John, mach, res 46 Miner.
Ogden Robert, Plumber, Steam and Gas Fitter, and Natural Gas; Dealer in Iron and Lead Pipe, Sheet Lead, Hydrants, Bath Tubs, Pumps, Brass Goods, Etc, 26 E Berry, res 64 Barr. (*See embossed line back cover.*)

POLK & CO.'S

s 429 W Main.
hysician, n w cor Creighton and Hol-
n ave.
r Bass F & M Works, bds Monroe

tel Rich.
'enn Co, res 23 Colerick.
ie.
in), res 430 E Wayne.
Sass F & M Works, res 430 E Wayne.
E Wayne.
kin House.

nd Peters Box and Lumber Co, res 39

s 58 W Williams.
Winter.
, bds 29 Hanna.
s Co), bds 29 Hanna.
Iohn E), res 29 Hanna.
iaus, Charles G Guild), men's furn-

& M Works, res Ebert nr limits.
Kief.
0 E Washington.
wis.
es W Wilding pres and mngr, John
pulley mnfrs, Pixley & Long bldg.
chard.
S B Bond Pres, O P Morgan Vice-
C Woodworth Asst Cash, s w cor
See front cover and page 4.)
31 E De Wald.
tar Iron Tower Co, res 213 Barr.
s 198 W Wayne.
n Wheel Co, bds 198 W Wayne.
. C & St. L R R. bds Schele House

Olds Wm H, treas Olds' Wagon Works, res 83 W Main.
O'Leary Bartholomew jr, baggageman, bds 202 Francis.
O'Leary Elizabeth (wid Timothy), bds 171 W Berry.
O'Leary James, foreman, res 32 Hugh.
O'Leary John, lab, bds 202 Francis.
O'Leary Mary (wid Bartholomew), res 202 Francis.
Olens Christian, res 49 Smith.
Olinger John B, car builder Penn Co, res n s New Haven ave
   1 w of Lumbard.
Olive James, mach Wabash R R, res 35 Bass.
Olive James jr, bds 35 Bass.
Olkson John, molder Kerr-Murray Mnfg Co, bds 25 Hough.
Olmsted Leslie, stableman, res n w cor Edna and Spy Run ave.
Olsen Olof, steamfitter, bds 95 W Superior.
O'Meara Patrick, brakeman, res 62 N Harrison.
O'Neil Daniel J, engineer, res 341 W Washington.
O'Neill John, lab, bds 29 Colerick.
O'Neill Margaret (wid Michael), bds 29 Colerick.
O'Neill Mary, clk McKinnie House, bds 29 Colerick.
O'Neill Patrick, clk Penn Co, res 29 Colerick.
O'Neill Patrick W, brakeman, res 17 Bass.
Opatz Frank A, blksmith, res 187 Montgomery.
Opitz Bruno, student, bds 1 Tons.
Oppelt George C, barber, 170 Calhoun, bds 26 W Superior.
Oppelt Joseph, polisher Griebel, Wyckoff & Becker, res 26 W
   Superior.
Oppenheim Wm S (Colerick & Oppenheim), bds 9 E Wayne.
Oppenheimer Abraham, res 54 W Berry.
Oppenheimer Frederick, bds 54 W Berry.
Oppenheimer Jacob, lab Weil Bros & Co, bds 46 E Columbia.
Oppenheimer Mrs Maggie, res 105 Lafayette.
Orff Charles E, cash John Orff, bds same.
Orff George E, clk Stewart & Hahn, bds 78 W Creighton ave.
Orff Henry, music teacher, 78 W Creighton ave, res same.
Orff John, flour mills, nr W Main Street bridge, res Junction
   Columbia City and Huntington rds.
Orff John R, miller John Orff, res 232 W Washington.
Orff Mary (wid Gottlieb), res 148 Clinton.
Orff Miss Mary E, teacher Hoagland School, bds 78 W Creigh-
   ton avenue.
Orff Montgomery C, bkkpr John Orff, bds same.
Ormiston Alexander, brick mnfr, w s Piqua ave 4 s of Rudisill
   ave, res same.
Ormiston Christina (wid James), res w s Lafayette 8 s of
   Pontiac.
Ormiston James, lab, res w s Lafayette s of city limits.

John Pressler, Plumbing, Gas and Steam Fitting. Columbia, Barr and Dock Streets.

394   R. L. POLK & CO.'S

Ormiston Lewis, lab, res w s Calhoun s of city limits.
Ormiston Mark, lab, bds Alexander Ormiston.
Ormiston Rufus, lab, bds Lewis Ormiston.
Ormsby Cora, waiter, rms 23 Melita.
Ormsby Henry, lab, res 23 Melita.
O'Rourk Jeremiah, conductor, res 331 Lafayette.
O'Rourke Edward, judge Circuit Court, res 134 E Washington.
O'Rourke Ellen, waiter McKinnie House.
O'Rourke John, brakeman, bds 196 Hanna.
O'Rourke John, conductor, res 235 E Lewis.
O'Rourke John B, plumber Robert Ogden, bds 225 E Lewis.
O'Rourke John C, trav agt, res 268 E Lewis.
O'Rourke Miss Kittie, teacher Hanna School, bds 235 E Lewis.
O'Rourke Margaret, waiter McKinnie House.
O'Rourke Mary (wid Michael), res 185 Montgomery.
O'Rourke Patrick S, supt G R & I R R, res 30 McClellan.
Orr Charles W, asst cash Hamilton National Bank, res 312 W
    Washington.
Orr Edwin, teamster M Orr, bds 112 Mechanic.
Orr Elmer C, mach Ft Wayne Electric Co, bds 377 Lafayette.
Orr James A, stenogr Penn Co, bds 28 W Butler.
Orr John W, bkkpr Mayflower Mills, res 28 W Butler.
Orr Joseph, lab, res 113 Mechanic.
Orr Joseph H, bkkpr First National Bank, res 21 W Butler.
Orr Mary E, matron Indiana School for Feeble-Minded Youth.
Orr Michael, sand, 112 Mechanic, res same.
Orr Michael jr, painter, bds 112 Mechanic.
Orr Minnie (wid Chester), res 21 W 4th.
Orr Reazin, street car driver, res 71 College.
Orr Robert W, butcher, res s s New Haven ave 1 w of toll-gate.
Orr Wm, stock buyer, res 377 Lafayette.
Orrock Wm W, res 145 W Berry.
Orth Christian, painter, res 124 E DeWald.
Ortlieb George, saloon, 88 Calhoun, res 125 W Jefferson.
Ortman Henry R, foreman L Dessauer & Co, res 158 Madison.
Ortman Wm H, student, bds 158 Madison.
Ortmann Henry W, Cigar Mnfr, 26 Clinton, res 22 W
    Superior.
Ortmann Henry W jr, cigarmkr Henry W Ortmann, bds 22 W
    Superior.
O'Ryan, *see also Ryan.*
O'Ryan James, mach hand, bds 50 Baker.
O'Ryan John, fireman Penn Co, bds 50 Baker.
O'Ryan Patrick, policeman, res 50 Baker.
Osborn John C, harnessmkr, 9 Poplar, res 7 Walnut.
Osborn Murlin C, lightning rod agt, res 2 W Butler.

'RUCKING CO. **F**URNITURE and Piano
W. WASHINGTON. MOVING, TRANSFERING and
STORAGE. TEL. 122.

FORT WAYNE DIRECTORY. 3U5

)rge, brakeman G R & I R R, res w s C 1 s of
ace.
.c, upholsterer Penn Co, res s s Wayne Trace 3
n ave.
n K, brakeman, res 58 John.
, domestic 142 E Jefferson.
, *see also Shaughnessy.*
Mary (wid John), res 17 Colerick.
Michael, lab, bds 17 Colerick.
Nora, housekeeper 143 W Wayne.
ne, domestic The Wayne.
B, lab Chester Scotton, bds same.
ard, lab, res 68 Force.
;aret, opr Hoosier Mnfg Co, bds 80 Olive.
erick, turner, rms 262 E Jefferson.
lso Oestermann.
, fireman, res 212 St Mary's ave.
)bert, res 239 E Washington.
nry, helper, bds 99 Smith.
an, cigarmkr G F Yergens, bds Weber Hotel.
(wid Charles), bds 328 Harrison.
painter Olds' Wagon Works.
teamster, res 56 Smith.
lomestic 235 Barr.
ond J, mach hand Ft Wayne Organ Co, bds
[otel.
)er Kiel & Kiel, res St Joseph Gravel rd.
)lder Bass F & M Works, res St Joseph Gravel

ARCHITECTS. **WING & MAHURIN,** 41 and 42 Pixley & Long Bldg. Telephone 228.

896   R. L. POLK & CO.'S

Overly Daniel, well digger, res 252 E Wayne.
Overly Harry, lab, bds 252 E Wayne.
Overly Lawrence, brewer, res n s Edna 2 w of Spy Run ave.
Owens Alice (wid Peter), res 51 Oakley.
Owens Henrietta, domestic Hotel Rich.
Owens John, lab, res 89 Force.
Owens Michael J, barber, 211 Lafayette, res 122 Maumee.rd.
Owens Owen, Meat Market, 281 E Creighton ave, res same.
Owens Wm, cabtmkr, res 56 Wells.
Owner Charles, carp, res 61 Winter.

P

Paak Henry, lab, res 20 Jones.
Paak Henry jr, mach, bds 20 Jones.
Pacific Express Co, C B Beaver Agt, 79 Calhoun.
Paff Andrew, lab, res 14 Randolph.
Page Wm, brakeman Penn Co, res 82 W DeWald.
Page Wm D, propr Ft Wayne News and propr Poultry and Pets, 19 E Main, res 316 E Jefferson.
Page Wm G, lab Penn Co, rms 73 Grand.
Pageler Frederick H, clk Am Wheel Co, bds 177 Montgomery.
Pageler Frederick J, wagonmkr, res 177 Montgomery.
Pageler Henry H, lab Ft Wayne Electric Co, bds 177 Montgomery.
Pahl, *see also Paul and Pohl.*
Pahl Sophia, dressmkr, 106 Force, bds same.
Pahl Wm J, mach Bass F & M Works, res 106 Force.
Pailliotet Josephine, domestic Lake Shore Hotel.
Paintte Laura, domestic 31 Cass.
Palleten Louis, lab, res n s New Haven ave 4 e of Lumbard.
Palmer Albert, horseshoer Frank Veith, res 20 Francis.
Palmer Albert, plasterer, res s s Pontiac 2 w of Webster.
Palmer Charles V, carp, bds 76 Buchanan.
Palmer Earl (Ferguson & Palmer), res 31 Cass.
Palmer George, lab, bds 109 Van Buren.
Palmer Henry, lab, bds 46 E Columbia.
Palmer Hiram, bricklayer, res 109 Van Buren.
Palmer Jennie, rms 57 E Main.
Palmer John W, engineer, res 8 Pritchard.
Palmer Milford S, lab, bds 109 Van Buren.
Palmer R Dilworth, clk Am Exp Co, rms 9 Foster blk.
Palmer Wm W, hammersmith Bass F & M Wks, res 180 Taber.

Panne Minnie, domestic 260 Calhoun.
Pantlind Henry D, driver J C Peltier, res 12 Wagner.
Pantlind Mrs Martha, bds 12 Wagner.
Panyard John J, mach hd Old Fort Mnfg Co, bds 65 Grant ave.
Panyard Joseph, painter, res 65 Grant ave.
Panyard Joseph, pedler, bds 41 Force.
Pape, *see also Pepe and Pope.*
Pape Miss Amelia, bds 56 St Mary's ave.
Pape Charles (Fleming Mnfg Co), propr The Pape Furniture
    Co and pres The Peters Box and Lumber Co, res 56 St
    Mary's ave.
Pape Charles G, bds 56 St Mary's ave.
Pape Furniture Co The, Charles Pape Propr, 28–30 E
    Berry. (*See right bottom lines.*)
Pape Miss Lizzie, bds 56 St Mary's ave.
Pape Miss Sophie, bds 56 St Mary's ave.
Pape Wm, res 151 High.
Pape Wm C, foreman Rhinesmith & Simonson, res 185 Taber.
Pappert Amand, cooper, res 252 E Wayne.
Pappert Amand J, cigarmkr G F Yergens, bds 252 E Wayne.
Pappert Wm F, molder Bass F & M Works, res 37 John.
Paramore Herschel H, city editor The Press, bds Aldine Hotel.
Pardee W McKay, division engineer Nickel Plate R R, res
    281 W Wayne.
Pardoe Samuel J, clk, res s e cor 9th and John.
Parham Frederick C, farm impts, 29 Barr, res 155 W DeWald.
Parisot Alexander J, clk Wabash R R, res 74 Buchanan.
Parisot Angeline (wid Frank), res 35 Duck.
Parisot Edward, lab, bds 322 Hanna.
Parisot Frank S, rimmer, bds 322 Hanna.
Parisot Joseph, foreman Wabash R R, res 322 Hanna.
Park Wesley, brakeman, bds 79 Cass.
Parker Alice, bds 537 Broadway.
Parker Charles, lab, bds 489 E Wayne.
Parker Edward H, clk County Auditor, res 77 Cass.
Parker James, lab Lindenwood Cemetery, res 6 Wheeler.
Parker John, hostler J W Pearse, res 61 Wall.
Parker John F, restaurant, 94½ Barr, res same.
Parker Samuel, mach, res 237 Indiana ave.
Parker Wm C, mach hand Hoffman Bros, bds 32 W Main.
Parkison Johnson S, clk, res 529 E Wayne.
Parks Emanuel, brakeman, rms 23 Baker.
Parks Volney, bds Union House.
Parlor Bath Rooms, Miss Kathleen H Dunne Propr;
    Turkish, Electric, Mineral, Sea Salt and Plain Baths,
    Rooms 49, 50 and 51 Pixley & Long Bldg. (*See right
    bottom lines.*)

cley & Co), res Bloomington, Ill.
ey Hardware Co, bds John Langard.
oosier Mnfg Co, bds 223 E Wayne.
ce Shore Hotel.
res 90 W 4th.
ohn Pressler, bds 90 W 4th.
M S Ry, res 90 W 4th.
mkr, bds F E Parrant.
t stall No 35, res e s Walton ave 1 n
y.
C J Jourdain, bds F E Parrant.
, bds F E Parrant.
tor Hanna School, res 290½ Hanna.
Penn Co, bds 290 Harrison.
res 290 Harrison.
man Penn Co, bds 290 Harrison.
Harrison.
Wabash R R, bds 322 Hanna.

E Main, res same.
J A Shoaff, bds 27 Oak.
Barcus, bds 96 Calhoun.
Oak.
)ak.
d Perry.
Carnahan & Co, bds 337 W Washing-

kr, res 75 W Williams.
r, rms 28 Douglas ave.
rnahan & Co, res 337 W Washington.
, rms 368 W Main.
Paul's Pulley Works, res w s Spy Run

aul Koehler.
nl Koehler.

Patterson Eva, trimmer, bds 162 Montgomery.
Patterson Frank, harnessmkr, bds 179 W Washington.
Patterson George M, engineer, res 304 Harrison.
Patterson Mrs Helen, bds 30 Douglas ave.
Patterson James W, harnessmkr F Hilt, res 179 W Washington.
Patterson Jesse F, despatcher Penn Co, bds 232 W DeWald.
Patterson John F, foreman, res 41 N Calhoun.
Patterson Mary (wid Byron), res 232 W DeWald.
Patterson Mary C (wid Benjamin), dressmkr, 162 Montgomery, res same.
Patterson Minnie M, clk A Mergentheim, bds 304 Harrison.
Patterson Robert B, lab, res 32 Baker.
Patterson T Austin, trav agt, res 50 Brackenridge.
Patterson Virgil, mach hd American Wheel Co, bds 105 John.
Patterson Warren C, brakeman, bds 162 Montgomery.
Patton, *see also Patten.*
Patton George D, trav agt, res e s Coombs 1 n of E Wayne.
Patton Wm S, carp, 58 Brackenridge, res same.
Paul, *see also Pahl and Pohl.*
Paul Augusta, clk Louis Wolf & Co, bds 38 W Jefferson.
Paul Benjamin, carp, bds 26 Harrison.
Paul Benjamin F, lab, bds 19 Laselle.
Paul Charles, watchman, res 45 High.
Paul Charles A (Paul Pulley Works), bds 38 W Jefferson.
Paul Christian, mach hd Old Fort Mnfg Co, bds 296 Harrison.
Paul Emil, lab, bds 45 High.
Paul Ernest, engineer, res 29 W 3d.
Paul Florence, domestic Grand Central Hotel.
Paul Ferdinand, lab Ft Wayne Electric Co, bds 296 Harrison.
Paul Frederick, clk C Schiefer & Son, res 178 Ewing.
Paul Frederick, helper Keller & Braun, bds 48 Archer ave.
Paul Frederick, mach Penn Co, res 296 Harrison.
Paul Henry C, pres Horton Mnfg Co and Salimonie Mining and Gas Co, res 119 W Wayne.
Paul Lena, housekpr 296 Harrison.
Paul Pulley Works (Wm jr and Charles A Paul), n w cor 6th and Calhoun.
Paul Wm, res 38 W Jefferson.
Paul Wm jr (Paul Pulley Works), bds 38 W Jefferson.
Pauley Edward J, bartndr John Condon, res 113 W Williams.
Pauley Eugene J, mach, bds 76 W Williams.
Pauley James, lab, bds 76 W Williams.
Pauley John J, clk The Randall, res 108 E Wayne.
Pauley Mary, dressmkr, bds 76 W Williams.
Pauley Thomas, watchman Penn Co, res 76 W Williams.

Lightning Source UK Ltd.
Milton Keynes UK
UKHW011324260119
336227UK00004B/114/P